XML Developer's Handbook

XML Developer's Handbook™

Kurt Cagle

SYBEX®

San Francisco • Paris • Düsseldorf • Soest • London

Associate Publisher: Richard Mills
Contracts and Licensing Manager: Kristine O'Callaghan
Acquisitions & Developmental Editor: Denise Santoro Lincoln
Editors: Jeff Gammon, James A. Compton, Emily K. Wolman
Production Editor: Leslie E. H. Light
Technical Editor: Piroz Mohseni
Book Designer: Robin Kibby
Graphic Illustrator: Tony Jonick
Electronic Publishing Specialist: Franz Baumhackl
Proofreaders: Laurie O'Connell, Nancy Riddiough
Indexer: Nancy Guenther
CD Coordinator: Kara Eve Schwartz
CD Technician: Keith McNeil
Cover Designer: Design Site
Cover Illustrator: Jack D. Meyers

Library of Congress Card Number: 00-102849

ISBN: 0-7821-2704-5

Manufactured in the United States of America

10 9 8 7 6 5 4 3 2 1

Software License Agreement: Terms and Conditions

The media and/or any online materials accompanying this book that are available now or in the future contain programs and/or text files (the "Software") to be used in connection with the book. SYBEX hereby grants to you a license to use the Software, subject to the terms that follow. Your purchase, acceptance, or use of the Software will constitute your acceptance of such terms.

The Software compilation is the property of SYBEX unless otherwise indicated and is protected by copyright to SYBEX or other copyright owner(s) as indicated in the media files (the "Owner(s)"). You are hereby granted a single-user license to use the Software for your personal, noncommercial use only. You may not reproduce, sell, distribute, publish, circulate, or commercially exploit the Software, or any portion thereof, without the written consent of SYBEX and the specific copyright owner(s) of any component software included on this media.

In the event that the Software or components include specific license requirements or end-user agreements, statements of condition, disclaimers, limitations, or warranties ("End-User License"), those End-User Licenses supersede the terms and conditions herein as to that particular Software component. Your purchase, acceptance, or use of the Software will constitute your acceptance of such End-User Licenses.

By purchase, use, or acceptance of the Software, you further agree to comply with all export laws and regulations of the United States as such laws and regulations may exist from time to time.

Reusable Code in This Book

The author created reusable code in this publication expressly for reuse for readers. Sybex grants readers permission to reuse for any purpose the code found in this publication or its accompanying CD-ROM so long as the author is attributed in any application containing the reusable code, and the code itself is never sold or commercially exploited as a stand-alone product.

Software Support

Components of the supplemental Software and any offers associated with them may be supported by the specific Owner(s) of that material, but they are not supported by SYBEX. Information regarding any available support may be obtained from the Owner(s) using the information provided in the appropriate `read.me` files or listed elsewhere on the media.

Should the manufacturer(s) or other Owner(s) cease to offer support or decline to honor any offer, SYBEX bears no responsibility. This notice concerning support for the Software is provided for your information only. SYBEX is not the agent or principal of the Owner(s), and SYBEX is in no way responsible for providing any support for the Software, nor is it liable or responsible for any support provided, or not provided, by the Owner(s).

Warranty

SYBEX warrants the enclosed media to be free of physical defects for a period of ninety (90) days after purchase. The Software is not available from SYBEX in any other form or media than that enclosed herein or posted to `www.sybex.com`. If you discover a defect in the media during this warranty period, you may obtain a replacement of identical format at no charge by sending the defective media, postage prepaid, with proof of purchase to:

SYBEX Inc.
Customer Service Department
1151 Marina Village Parkway
Alameda, CA 94501
(510) 523-8233
Fax: (510) 523-2373
e-mail: `info@sybex.com`
WEB: `HTTP://WWW.SYBEX.COM`

After the 90-day period, you can obtain replacement media of identical format by sending us the defective disk, proof of purchase, and a check or money order for $10, payable to SYBEX.

Disclaimer

SYBEX makes no warranty or representation, either expressed or implied, with respect to the Software or its contents, quality, performance, merchantability, or fitness for a particular purpose. In no event will SYBEX, its distributors, or dealers be liable to you or any other party for direct, indirect, special, incidental, consequential, or other damages arising out of the use of or inability to use the Software or its contents even if advised of the possibility of such damage. In the event that the Software includes an online update feature, SYBEX further disclaims any obligation to provide this feature for any specific duration other than the initial posting.

The exclusion of implied warranties is not permitted by some states. Therefore, the preceding exclusion may not apply to you. This warranty provides you with specific legal rights; there may be other rights that you may have that vary from state to state. The pricing of the book with the Software by SYBEX reflects the allocation of risk and limitations on liability contained in this agreement of Terms and Conditions.

Shareware Distribution

This Software may contain various programs that are distributed as shareware. Copyright laws apply to both shareware and ordinary commercial software, and the copyright Owner(s) retains all rights. If you try a shareware program and continue using it, you are expected to register it. Individual programs differ on details of trial periods, registration, and payment. Please observe the requirements stated in appropriate files.

Copy Protection

The Software in whole or in part may or may not be copy-protected or encrypted. However, in all cases, reselling or redistributing these files without authorization is expressly forbidden except as specifically provided for by the Owner(s) therein.

I dedicate this book to my two daughters, Katie and Jennifer. The technology that I am writing about today will be the plumbing for the world they live in tomorrow, and it heartens me to know that I will have had a material impact on their lives for years to come.

ACKNOWLEDGMENTS

This is a big book; writing such a book is much like scaling a mountain of Jello: Your chances of seeing the summit are pretty slim, and it becomes all too easy to find yourself buried within the thing that you were attempting to climb.

With the hugeness of this endeavor in mind, I thank Denise Santoro Lincoln, the Acquisition and Developmental Editor on this book, especially for recognizing when I needed to pull out for a bit after the birth of my second daughter. Likewise, I acknowledge the efforts of the editors, technical editor, production editors, proofreaders, and layout artists at Sybex who helped move this to a point of completion.

Much of this book is focused on the Microsoft MSXML3 parser, and I thank Chris Lovett, Charlie Heinemann, and Peter Krebs at Microsoft for letting me work with an early release of this parser and for providing a great deal of technical support afterwards.

Mark and Tracey Wilson, authors themselves of the superb *XML Programming with VB and ASP* by Manning Press, run the VBXML Web site and have been both good friends and receptive audiences for some of my travails. Visit their site (`http://www.vbxml.com`); you'll be glad you did.

Finally, I thank my wife Anne, who has put up (sometimes with only the greatest of restraint) with being married to a computer book writer.

CONTENTS AT A GLANCE

CONTENTS

INTRODUCTION

I first encountered XML in late 1997, coming to it from a background of developing and writing DHTML projects for publication and private clients. At the time, I was working on a project for Microsoft, a program that generated Web sites for small business that would help determine the benefits of purchasing certain software configurations. The program, written in the Internet client using far too much JavaScript code, was essentially designed as a way to manage hierarchical information in a clean and reasonable fashion. However, I ended up spending far too much time trying to load the data into the system, and pretty much despaired before coming across a mention of a beta piece of technology that Microsoft had (quietly) dropped into the Internet Explorer 4 browser: an XML parser.

I'd heard people talking about XML, of course; the prevailing wisdom at the time was that it would eventually end up replacing HTML as a client language, once all the browsers were enabled for working with it. Still, as I began working with the language, I found it to be something that was both crude and cryptic, that required a pretty deep understanding of mysterious things like DTDs and external entities.

The few books that were out were written by SGML experts and talked condescendingly about XML as if it was SGML-lite, something that everyone should understand was just a baby language compared to the true mother tongue. Even worse, there were no books about how to program with the language. This was perhaps understandable in that very few people were even thinking about using XML to pass data around, although it is (as I hope to show in this book) an absolutely wonderful mechanism for expressing complex data structures.

When I talked with the SGML gurus in the field who were beginning to push XML, most of them just clicked their tongues and said, "Poor neophyte, you don't program with XML; it's just a markup language." There is a certain satisfaction in being able to prove them wrong.

The first Microsoft XML parser (the first parser I had direct experience with) was a crude tool, useful for navigating around a hierarchical tree node by node but not for much else. While it can still be found in certain older Internet Explorer 4 browsers, this parser has largely been relegated to the trash heap (thankfully).

As is the case with Microsoft's efforts in general, the XML parser that exists now is a considerably more powerful engine, capable of doing some truly incredible things, and will prove to be the engine that powers much of Microsoft's newly announced .NET strategy. It is arguably one of the best such parsers on the planet.

Writing a book of this length takes time, which can prove problematic when the technology is in transition. This is the case here. I am writing this introduction shortly before the book goes to press. In a few cases, what is written elsewhere in the book will likely fall out of date even before these pages hit the presses; the XML Schema Definition Language, for instance, is likely to see at least one more round of revision before the summer is over. This is the nature of book publishing, though even that is likely to change.

What I hope to be able to do with this book is to help you make the shift in thinking that is necessary in order to go from the procedural paradigm of traditional languages to the declarative paradigm of XML and its associated standards. XML can take some getting used to: You find yourself thinking in sets and trees and paths and transformations rather than in properties and methods and events. After playing with it for a while, you get irritated with complex SQL statements that give you largely flat database results, you find yourself wondering why you can't get your Java and VB programmers to use the same interfaces, and you tend to start out all of your Word documents with the tag `<document>`.

We are in the early stages of a revolution that will completely remake the computer landscape, especially when you recognize that the power in a computer lies less in its ability to "compute" and more in its ability to communicate. XML is a way to communicate information in a completely machine-neutral manner. Your server and my client can be written in totally different programming languages by two different companies working off of competing operating systems, but with XML in place, this doesn't matter.

Moreover, XML is an invasive technology: When you introduce XML into your system, even in a very minor role, the potential places where it can be deployed become obvious. After a while, the snippet of XML code that you used for writing a temporary INI file has mutated into an entire architecture. As a student of chaos theory, I like to say that XML is thus an emergent technology, evolving to replace other architectures around it. Indeed, what you're seeing is a major paradigm shift that will likely have repercussions throughout society for several decades to come.

In part, this is due to the likely shift on the Internet from HTML to XML—a shift that is already underway. XML can be transformed via XSLT, which means that you can create documents (such as those using the OpenDoc specification) that represent the logical structure of large and complex documents and then transform them into representations on different browsers. In some cases, those browsers are the ones we are most familiar with—Internet Explorer, Netscape Navigator, and so forth—but, increasingly, the browser is a small window on your cell phone or is a credit-card-sized strip on your Palm Pilot. These devices are already strongly placed in the XML world, using the Wireless Application Protocol (WAP); soon, they may also be taking advantage of voice-enabled XML languages, such as VoxML.

These new forms show the advantages of separating your message from the medium, and are only the first of many.

So start out by playing with the code contained herein. You'll find the filename of each code listing either within the body of its listing heading or within parentheses at the end of its listing heading; then you can locate each listing's corresponding file (whether a complete, executable file or a code snippet) on the accompanying CD-ROM. And take a look at Sybex's companion volume, *Mastering XML*, which contains a much more in-depth look at the XML specification itself. Look for patterns, ways of thinking that can help you put your own work together; once you get comfortable with the language, such patterns will jump out at you. It's a cool technology—it will be a pervasive one—and it opens up all kinds of possibilities for development.

Where to Go for More Information

Staying up to date with XML is not always easy, but, in general, I strongly recommend that you keep an eye on the W3C Web site (`http://www.w3.org`) and specifically on the collection of Recommendations, Working Drafts, and Notes that the organization maintains (`http://www.w3.org/TR`). The Microsoft XML Web site on MSDN (`http://msdn.Microsoft.com/xml`) contains up-to-date information concerning the new parser and XML technologies in general (I'm currently writing the MSDN XSLT user's guide for this site, so I can say this with some certainty) and should be a primary bookmark on your browser. Also, you can keep up with the current developments in the industry at XML.com (`http://www.xml.com`), which is edited by Edd Dumbill, and with more technical programming issues associated with XML at the VBXML Web site (`http://www.vbxml.com`), which is edited by Mark Wilson and is where I also maintain articles and resources for XML and XSLT.

Finally, feel free to contact me at `cagle@olywa.net`. I can't guarantee I'll be able to answer all of your questions, but I enjoy the feedback.

CHAPTER 1

Why XML?

- Understanding the need for context
- Reviewing the emergence of XML
- Detailing the roles of XML
- Understanding how you can use XML

Mastering the Extensible Markup Language, or XML, will likely end up changing the way that you think about programming, communications, and even the notion of meaning and context. Even though the language itself is simple—indeed, that's one of its strengths—XML is likely to completely rearrange the computer landscape. In this chapter, you'll learn why XML will likely be the data language of tomorrow and why it's so important that you learn how to work with it now.

The Need for Context

What is meaning? This is one of those questions that first-year philosophy students inevitably trip up on. Until recently, meaning hasn't impacted computer programming significantly, but the answer to this question will ultimately prove to be the cornerstone of computing for the next several decades. The reason for this is simple: We have too much data and too little meaning.

We live in an age when data is everywhere. From the moment when you crawl out of bed, you are blasted with data—the alarm clock kicking on and broadcasting news happening in Washington, DC, and weather forecasts for the next five days. We open our papers and scan dozens of stories written less than 24 hours beforehand, get the RBIs of our favorite baseball players, and examine near-microscopic print to find out how many fractions of a dollar our mutual funds have risen or fallen since the last time we checked.

At work, we increasingly spend our lives juggling data, trying to make sense of a dip in sales figures in the western region, attempting to understand why the compiler is generating error `-43225`, and making sure that the hours billed are properly categorized. The *knowledge worker*, an appellation that covers everyone from a data entry clerk to the CEO of a large company, has replaced the blue-collar laborer as the typical wage earner. The computer revolution has rebuilt our entire society around knowledge, information, *meaning*.

Ironically, while too little data can lead to a false understanding of an issue, if you have too much data you usually have to expend a significant amount of energy and/or time to extract information from that data. For the vast period of human history, perhaps up to 1950 or so, data was expensive and relatively scarce, and the idea that one could have too much data was almost laughable.

This situation has completely reversed itself in the last 50 years as the means of creating, processing, and displaying data has leapt forward at an exponential pace. The famous prediction called *Moore's Law*, first observed by IBM chairman Gordon Moore, has proven reliable witness to this: Roughly every 18 months, processing power (and, consequently, the ability to both acquire and display data) has doubled. Perhaps somewhat frightening, even this pace has sped up in the last decade.

Connectivity has played a big part in the dramatic advances of recent years. Networks have been a part of computing since the 1960s, but it was only when people started connecting personal computers (with their high concentration of processing power) with other such computers that structures like the Internet became possible. Unfortunately, one of the characteristics of most networks is that, as they grow, the interactions between different parts of the network can often cause feedback and other unexpected phenomena, making it more difficult to build tightly integrated systems.

Data + Context = Information

Moreover, *data is not information*. Data is the raw material, the input that forms information, but, in general, data exists in a separate context than the information it generates. For example, consider a small weather station that keeps track of such pieces of data as humidity, temperature, wind speed, and barometric pressure for a particular location, an airport. It transmits this data to a central system at regular intervals, adding the newly captured data (such as a location and a timestamp) to this basic record.

The air traffic controller at the airport will transmit this information to aircraft to help them anticipate dangerous weather conditions. A news-station weather person will collect this data as well as similar data from other locations in the region to display on a regional weather map. A meteorologist will take this data, plus others from a much wider region, to prepare a short-range forecast of how the weather will change in a given area in the next few days. A climatologist will pull the data as a sample to combine with other data in order to perform a long-term modeling of weather patterns spanning years or decades.

Each of these individuals uses the same data, either alone or in conjunction with other data, but they manipulate this data within different contexts. Even if all systems technically could communicate transparently, they would still require some way of shifting the data context easily. To date, most of this shifting is performed through the use of expensive, programmer-intensive solutions. (If the number of want ads for Web developers is any indication, this demand for programmers is far outstripping the supply.)

This weather example provides a good rule of thumb: Data without any underlying framework, without context, is essentially just white noise. Information can only be retrieved from data if that data is placed into some form of context. You can think of context in this light as a function: Working with the raw data, it filters out unnecessary data and returns what's relevant. To the air traffic controller, the present wind speed is a highly important value, so the amount of processing, the context, is fairly minimal. On the other hand, to the climatologist, the wind speed at 2:00 P.M. on March 3, 2000, at the Olympia airport is largely irrelevant, except as it provides one point in a large and complex data sample.

The Birth of the Internet

As networks increase in size and number, the amount of data that these networks produce grows as well, and has long since surpassed the point where it can be effectively managed by human beings. Sometime around the summer of 1997, the amount of data being held in electronic form surpassed the total number of words in all the written works ever produced. By the time this book is published (in written form, of course), it is estimated that that number will have grown to four times the total number of words in all of human literature, with it effectively doubling every 18 months thereafter.

The Internet is obviously the world's largest network, so it's not surprising that many of the problems dealing with information overload first surfaced there. The most apparent (though by no means the only) part of the Internet is the World Wide Web, the system of interconnected HTML pages, server pages, and similar resources that has ended up consuming so many otherwise-productive office hours. While historians can point to any number of possible events that culminated in today's Internet, the World Wide Web was essentially the invention of one man, Tim Berners-Lee, at the time (1990) a programmer working for the CERN High-Energy Research Lab in Geneva, Switzerland and currently one of the principal members of the World Wide Web Consortium.

NOTE The World Wide Web Consortium, also known as the W3C, is the final arbiter for most of the information standards currently in use on the Internet. The latest XML and HTML standards can be found at the W3C Web site: `http://www.w3.org`. The W3C features prominently throughout this book.

Berners-Lee's objective when he created the basic protocols of the Web—the Hypertext Transfer Protocol (HTTP) and the HyperText Markup Language (HTML)—was hardly world domination. Instead, several scientists at CERN needed to store and transmit documents in a way that would allow easy reference by other scientists within the organization and would let scientists reference each other's pages via hypertext; Berners-Lee set out to address this need.

While hypertext systems had been around for several years before that time, they were principally proprietary in nature. The primary difference in Berners-Lee's design was that he distributed the document viewer (the first browser) as a low-bandwidth application and made both the protocols and the software freely available. Needless to say, word about the applications (and the applications themselves) spread quickly, especially once the combination of HTML and HTTP made its way to educational institutions.

The Historical Relationship between HTML and XML

The history of HTML is well known, but one facet that relates to XML is worth stressing: *HTML was originally designed to be used as a way to transmit and display physics abstracts.* Most of the abstracts at CERN made use of the Standard Generalized Markup Language, or SGML, a description language used primarily to store theses, reports, product help information, and other related documentation.

SGML can trace its roots back to the 1960s, when its precursor, the Generalized Markup Language (GML), was developed by Charles Goldfarb, Edward Mosher, and Raymond Lorie at IBM in order to help organize the vast amount of documentation that the company was beginning to produce. By 1978, the American National Standards Institute (ANSI) took the basics of GML and fashioned a nationwide standard called GCA 101-1983. Six years later, after GCA had proven so demonstratively successful at document management, the International Standards Organization (ISO) began work on a global version, which became *Information Processing—Text and Office Systems—Standard Generalized Markup Language (SGML)*, ISO 8879:1986, in 1986.

Berners-Lee created HTML as an instance of SGML; he used the rules laid down by SGML to set up the tags that the abstracts would be written in. The heading structure and similar elements that formed the earliest versions of HTML worked well in a number of circumstances, but the appearance of tags such as CITE at least hint that the structure Berners-Lee set up was never intended to go beyond creating abstracts.

Go beyond it the language did, however. By the early 1990s, HTML pages output by HTTP servers took research facilities and universities by storm. The language began to get stretched this way and that as young programmers began playing around with HTTP servers and HTML viewers (also known as browsers). One of the most successful HTTP browsers by far was Mosaic, created by Marc Andreesen and others at the newly opened National Center for Supercomputing Applications(NCSA) at the University of Illinois at Champaign.

NOTE A Personal Note: I was a student at the University of Illinois when the NCSA opened, although I missed working with Andreesen (and, no doubt, becoming a multi-billionaire) by about six months.

Mosaic put a graphical face on the Web. In the original HTML spec, an image reference was a hypertext link to a graphics document, which was then opened up in a separate viewer application. With the advent of Mosaic, you could embed graphic images directly into a document, in essence turning what had been a very dry tool for navigating physics documents into a medium for mass communication. Mosaic became *the* killer application for the World Wide Web, and Silicon Graphics founder James Clark joined forces with Andreesen to launch Netscape, Inc.

Did the Browser Wars Kill HTML?

Back to context for a moment. As previously indicated, HTML's initial purpose was to describe scientific abstracts. It had a very definite structure, with the principal headers (such as `<h1>`, `<h2>`, and `<h3>`) echoing primary and subordinate header information, the paragraph tag (`<p>`) containing paragraphs of information, the citation tags indicating document citations, and so forth. If you set up such a document, then you could reasonably expect that a program could load the document, parse it, and produce a very credible abstract based upon the tag types. In other words, the earliest HTML had a fairly well-defined context.

The allure of incorporating graphics into presentations, coupled with the extremely rapid growth of the Netscape browser market, introduced a problem. The vast majority of people are not SGML experts (thankfully). Those who started playing with Web pages designed by the seats of their pants, initially with little to no documentation about why the language had the structure it had. Graphical elements began creeping into documents not simply as informational elements (the reason they were there originally) but more and more often as navigation buttons, image maps, and related components. Netscape then lowered the bar on entry, making the HTML parser extremely tolerant of sloppy code—an open paragraph mark became implicit, image tags and rules didn't need to be closed, and emphasis (`<EM>`) and strong (`<S>`) tags became bold (`<B>`) and italic (`<I>`), respectively.

In other words, HTML began to shift from being a context-based markup language to being a typographic markup language. This is not totally surprising. Typographic languages emphasize visual presentation, and the reason that people were creating Web pages was to make visual displays, not to reference scholastic abstracts. A Web builder for an ad agency wanting to make a strong display for a client, for example, didn't need abstraction; she needed a way to translate the precise layout control that she was used to with programs like QuarkXPress and Aldus (now Adobe) PageMaker.

The browser wars of the mid-1990s contributed to this problem. Stung by critics for being late to embrace the Internet, Bill Gates chose December 7, 1995, to sound a battle cry against the dominant Internet browser company, Netscape, and he stated his determination to make Microsoft an Internet-centric company. (Whether they've managed to pull it off is still subject to some debate.) In the ensuing four years, Microsoft and Netscape battled for both mind-share of the browser market and greater control of the HTTP server market. In the end, Netscape folded. In 1999, America Online and Sun Microsystems jointly acquired the company, changing the name on the letterhead (and in the "About Box") to iPlanet, and effectively finishing off the spoils.

However, one of the major casualties in the war was context. Proposals for new tags were submitted to the W3C almost every other day, with such notorious ideas as the `blink` tag

(Netscape) and the marquee tag (Microsoft) both superlative examples of truly useless (and semantically bankrupt) elements that were included to attract users.

Yet if the blink tag was egregious, other tags rendered what little context that had been in the original document language largely moot. The TABLE, for example, is a semantically empty container for tabular data. The ability to span multiple columns or rows with a single cell meant that even basic table header information could no longer be relied upon to determine the meaning of a column programmatically. Furthermore, differences between tables in the Netscape-versus-Microsoft model meant that it was almost impossible to impart some type of context into a table even if you wanted to.

The FRAME is another example of an HTML element with dubious consequences for context. With frames, trying to understand the meaning of a given Web page became practically impossible. It also made navigation in Web pages much more complex, and differing degrees of support for the HTML version 3 standard made programming uniformly against frames a nightmare for the Web developer.

However, perhaps the low point for making contextually rich HTML documents came with the font tag. The font tag lets you specify a span's size, font name, and color. If you wanted to, you could create a font tag that made paragraph text appear identical to h1 text (or vice versa). While the original intention was fairly noble (separating the presentation layer from the context layer), most people and many applications used the font tag as a lazy way of formatting a Web page without putting any thought into the structure of the program.

Of course, all of these elements were exacerbated by the dueling standards that both Microsoft and Netscape engaged in. Both companies attempted to create features that would given them an advantage in the burgeoning browser market, and these enhancements to HTML meant that designing for the two primary browsers typically involved writing two sets of code (or more as newer versions broke older standards). The best solutions for writing dual code ultimately came down to relying on such proprietary solutions as Macromedia's Shockwave, applications that made sure that the Web experience was the same on both systems but were also essentially invisible to search engines and indexers.

The Presentation Layer Breaks Loose

By 1996, it was becoming obvious to most Web developers that HTML was badly broken. Incompatibilities between browsers, tags that stressed presentation over content, and the rise in third-party "solutions" had all weakened the standard to such an extent that the technique of simply adding more tags no longer seemed quite so viable.

About this time, the W3C convened a working group to study the viability of implementing a style sheet language into the Web standard. Style sheets have been a part of the publishing landscape for some time. In essence, with a style sheet you can map a set of attributes to a named style and then apply the style to a selection of text (or some other element on the page).

A couple of different approaches were considered. One of the first involved adapting SGML's Document Style Semantics and Specification Language (DSSSL), a transformation language that essentially processes tags and creates a formalized output from them. DSSSL is a very rich and robust language, capable of actually manipulating the order and other essential characteristics of a document, but it has the disadvantage of also being a fairly complex language, sufficiently so as to make DSSSL difficult to write for novice Web builders.

Over time, the consensus of the W3C members shifted to Cascading Style Sheets (CSS). In CSS, each style was represented by a rule, which consisted of zero or more attributes grouped together into a single unit. The rule could be applied to a single HTML element, or it could be applied as a class to specific tags. While not as robust as DSSSL, CSS was considerably simpler to use, and it more readily fit the document object model that Microsoft was beginning to push.

In December, 1996, the CSS1 model was approved, marking the beginning of Dynamic HTML, HTML code that could be changed on the fly by altering CSS attributes. A second draft of CSS (CSS2) was ratified in May, 1998, covering media specifications and internationalization. The third draft of CSS (CSS3) is currently under consideration and will likely examine behavioral extensions, Scalable Vector Graphics (SVG) integration, and incorporating input item characteristics into the CSS2 model.

NOTE Cascading Style Sheets will be covered in considerably more detail in Chapter 2, "Modeling the XML Document Object."

To find out more about the current developments in CSS, check the Web site at `http://www.w3.org/Style/css`.

The Emergence of XML

Perhaps one of the most important things to come out of the search for a better style sheet language was the awareness on the part of many experts in the Web community that it was perhaps time to reexamine the reason for HTML in the first place. As mentioned previously, HTML is basically a language for dealing with abstracts, although by 1995 it had evolved into an editorial language. This worked fairly well for editorial content—stories, articles, dissertations—but seemed to be increasingly inadequate for businesses wanting to sell their wares online, for companies that saw the Internet as a way to get crucial information out to agents in the field, or for heavily multimedia-driven sites.

The tag- and attribute-based notation used in HTML had become a standard convention by 1995, and companies increasingly began to come up with their own proprietary extensions to HTML, although these were principally for server-side code creation. Allaire's ColdFusion was one of the first to build a consistent set of proprietary tags for use in building Web pages, and Microsoft used a tag and percent notation to implement the foundation language for their MSN system, which in time because Active Server Pages.

However, such systems pretty much worked exclusively on the server since the client browser had no understanding of how to interpret the tags. The SGML proponents raised the suggestion of using SGML itself on the Web, but this particular approach had a number of problems. While SGML is not itself a proprietary system, it is an incredibly complex one: The specification for the language runs several hundreds of pages, and is most notable for the bewildering varieties of rules and exceptions that the metalanguage has.

While this complexity is necessary for the sophisticated corporate applications that use it, the demands of a Web-based solution mean that the version of SGML would have to be:

- Lightweight
- Easy to use
- Unambiguous (with as few exceptions as possible)
- Extensible (easily modified)

Of these requirements, SGML only satisfied the extensibility criterion. However, given that HTML was an SGML instance, it seemed reasonable to create a new markup language that embodied the best features of SGML but demonstrated the simplicity that had been one of the most defining characteristics of HTML. In 1997, the W3C convened a working group of Web and SGML experts to try to resolve this dilemma, and on February 10, 1998, the proposal for the Extensible Markup Language (XML) version 1 was accepted as a recommendation.

TIP

The XML version 1 specification, also known as WC3 REC-xml-19980210, can be found at `http://www.w3.org/TR/REC-xml`.

A Quick Lexicon

A typical XML structure looks much like an oddly named HTML file, although, for a number of reasons, most XML documents in use today actually are fairly highly structured. A simple example might be a purchase order that could look something like Listing 1.1.

Listing 1.1: A Purchase Order for Acme Rockets, as an XML Document

```
<?xml version="1.0"?>
<purchaseOrder type="1125" processed="false">
```

```
    <header>
        <orderFrom>Wiley E. Coyote</orderFrom>
        <orderTo>ACME Rocket Company</orderTo>
        <address>
            <street>1105 N. Sonoma Way</street>
            <city>Death Valley</city>
            <state>Arizona</state>
            </country>
        </address>
    </header>
    <body>
        <!-- The last rockets exploded prematurely. Please do
        watch your quality control. - WEC -->
        <lineItem>
            <name>Mark X Rocket</name>
            <description><![CDATA[Big, powerful red rockets,
    suitable for chasing highly mobile desert birds.]]></description>
            <number>24</number>
            <filter>if &gt; 15</filter>
            <unit>Individual</unit>
            <price>3.25</price>
            <priceUnit>USD</priceUnit>
            <discount>22.15</discount>
            <priceUnit>USD</priceUnit>
        </lineItem>
    </body>
</purchaseOrder>
```

While simple, this particular example shows most of the major elements of a stand-alone XML document (stand-alone in that there are no Document Type Definitions (DTDs) or schema information, both of which are covered in much more detail in Chapter 6, "XML Schemas"). In the preceding example, seven basic types of objects make up the document: processing instructions tags, elements tags, attributes, text, CDATA sections, entities, and comments, which have the characteristics detailed in the following sections:

Processing Instructions (PIs)

A *processing instruction* is bracketed by opening and closing question tags, as shown in the following example:

```
<? This is a processing instruction ?>
```

Processing instructions provide information outside of the normal scope of the XML structure for use by either the parser or third-party utilities. For example, you could use processing instructions to specify which display set to use when outputting the XML data. Formal XML structures should always start out with the `<?xml version="1.0"?>` PI to indicate that this is an XML document, although most parsers will not generate errors if this first line is not included.

Elements

An *element* consists of an open angle bracket immediately followed by a single word tag and zero or more name/value pairs (called *attributes*) terminated by a closing angle bracket, as shown in the following example:

```
<purchaseOrder type="1125" processed="false">
```

The closing tag is similar to the format of an HTML tag, with the terminating tag starting with a </ string (instead of <), as in the following line:

```
</purchaseOrder>
```

In HTML, certain elements don't need to be explicitly terminated, such as the `<BR>` tag. In XML, on the other hand, if an element doesn't contain any text or other elements, you still need to terminate it. However, you can use an abbreviated form for such elements, in which the forward slash is moved to the end of the tag. In that case, you don't need an explicit closing tag, as demonstrated in the following line:

```
<country/>
```

Attributes

An *attribute* is a name/value pair that's associated with a given element. For example, in the `purchaseOrder` tag, both `type` and `processed` are the names of attributes, as shown in the following example:

```
<purchaseOrder type="1125" processed="false">
```

What should constitute an attribute versus an element has spawned more than a few heated debates upon list servers and newsgroups and is a subject that will be revisited in depth later in this chapter. As a general rule of thumb, elements give you added flexibility for processing, though at the possible cost of speed, while attributes are easily accessible but are not as flexible. An attribute cannot contain a line break or XML symbols, such as < or &, and many parsers place an upper limit (typically around 256 characters) on the length of such an attribute.

Comments

A *comment* in an XML structure is a note added for clarification or coding purposes and is designated with an exclamation note and two dashes, as shown in the following example:

```
<!-- This is a single line note -->
```

Comments can include white space (such as character spaces, line breaks, tabs, and related elements) but can't include embedded comments. In other words,

```
<!-- This is a <!-- single --> line note -->
```

will generate an error since the close bracket after `single` is recognized only as the termination of the outermost comment.

WARNING Avoid the temptation to place code information inside comments. Many parsers will actually strip comment information out of the XML document for the sake of efficiency. Use PIs instead.

Text

Text in XML can be any Unicode character (that is, any 16-bit character encoding that follows the ISO Unicode standard), with a few important exceptions. While you can have XML tags embedded within text, XML treats these tags as subordinate elements (however, see the following "CDATA Sections" section). Thus, while the following highlighted characters are considered to be text:

```
<name>Mark X Rocket</name>
```

only the words `Mark` and `Rocket` are considered to be text elements:

```
<name>Mark <X/>Rocket</name>
```

While different parsers handle text differently, the standard behavior (and the one that the Microsoft parser displays) is to define the text for an element to be the set of text for all of its children elements. So the text for the element `name` in the next example is made up of the text for `firstName` followed by the text for `lastName` (for example, *Joe Smith*):

```
<name>
   <firstName>Joe</firstName>
   <lastName>Smith</lastName>
</name>
```

The element text's default behavior is to strip excess white space (such as tabs, line breaks, and leading and trailing spaces) from the text when that text is retrieved. There are ways of using schemas to modify this default behavior, preserving some or all of the white space information.

CDATA Sections

There are times when you want to include markup text in an XML document but you don't want the text to be parsed as part of the document. For example, you may have descriptive text that's marked up in HTML; you don't necessarily want this text to be interpreted as part of the XML document, especially if the HTML uses tags without terminators (such as the aforementioned <BR> tag. This is the domain of *CDATA sections*, as shown in the following example:

```
<description><![CDATA[The <B>Mark X Rocket</B>
can be used for targeting highly mobile
<I>desert birds</I>]]></description>
```

A CDATA (for *c*haracter *data*) section is delimited by the somewhat unwieldy brackets, as in `<![CDATA[` and `]]>`. As with a comment, the only thing you can't put into a CDATA section is another CDATA section, since the closing brackets of `]]>` are the only way that the parser can tell where the CDATA section ends. CDATA sections retain information about line breaks and other white space, so they're actually quite useful for keeping things like JavaScript code in one piece.

Entities

Entities come from SGML and let you use a convenient short names for longer blocks of text, even text that conceivably can contain additional XML markup (or even contain entire documents). XML currently supports only a handful of inbuilt entities, including `<` (*l*ess *t*han) for the < character, `>` (*g*reater *t*han) for >, and `&` (*amp*ersand) to represent the & character . In the preceding XML structure, the filter element's text contains an entity, as shown in the following line:

```
<filter>if &gt; 15</filter>
```

When the text is later retrieved, the output will end up looking like the following line:

```
if > 15
```

You can define additional entities through Document Type Definitions, and the current draft of the XML Schema specification calls for an equivalent structure called an XML variable.

This is not the entire zoo of XML critters, but it's a fairly representative cross section. With these building blocks, you should be able to build nearly any XML structure that you need.

The Roles of XML

If you've read any other books on XML, you may wonder why I dwell so little on the DTD, the dictionary that defines an XML structure. This actually reflects a deliberate bias on my part to focus on how to work with XML as objects or as data, rather than to stick with the more traditional approach of seeing XML as documents.

There are a number of different viewpoints as to what constitutes the best way of working with XML, each of which has an appropriate place. Perhaps the best advice I can give in this regard is to say that you should use the approach to XML that best fits your own particular needs:

- A document-centric approach works well for editorial content but poorly for sending information.
- A data-centric viewpoint can prove limiting with standard markup text but can vastly simplify programming for displaying tables or other information.

I'll stress this second point over and over throughout the book because the strength of XML ultimately is its ability to conform to the need at the moment (although, as with many strengths, this can be its weakness as well).

Throughout this section, I examine the different faces of XML and then try to show why none of them should be considered the "preferred" way of structuring your XML formats or writing your code. However, most XML documents tend to fall into one of the following patterns:

- Document format
- Document management format
- Data store or transmitter
- Filter mechanism
- Object description
- Multimedia format

As a caveat, you need to remember that XML is still a new technology and, as with most new technologies, that the deep thinking about the fundamental characteristics of XML—its metacharacteristics, if you will—has a ways to go yet.

XML As a Document Format

SGML is a document metalanguage, capable of creating sophisticated vocabularies for all types of documents. It is also immensely complicated, in great part because documents seem to have this singular resistance to being categorized. Human thought processes are wildly non-linear, so its perhaps not terribly surprising that the documents we create have a linear structure simply by dint of history. (The book is essentially a linear device, even though, with some effort, it can be made non-linear.) When we have to categorize them by concept or idea, the nice, neat, logical structures we impose on them frequently have a tendency to leak around the edges.

For this reason, while XML was originally designed for use as a more sophisticated document representation language to supplant HTML on the Web, this particular aspect of XML (the creation and application of vocabularies) has been slow to take off, for a number of reasons:

- To date, only Internet Explorer 5 supports the use of XML within the browser, but it does so inconsistently with the standards.
- To create a full document description language, you need to be able to break a document, in abstract, into multiple logical units; this is often a more difficult undertaking when working with documents than when dealing with well-defined data.
- There is typically more than one mapping of a document that's appropriate for the situation, and resolving what makes up the best such mapping can typically be a time-consuming and a frequently politically perilous occupation.

- Documents are more likely to have a requirement for a consistent display, and because of the sheer scope of such documents, this can mean creating highly complex display mechanisms.

When XML itself was in development, most of the working group responsible for creating XML came from a background in SGML, a technology that is highly geared toward document creation and management. So it is neither surprising that much of the early focus on XML concentrated on XML's document aspect (especially as a replacement for HTML) nor surprising, at least in retrospect, that this usage of XML has yet to really take off.

For the record, document-based XML is usually referred to as being *loosely-structured*; elements typically can be placed in nearly any order, text can mix freely with elements within container elements, and elements can usually have fairly complex sets of attributes with many of the attribute values defaulted. In SGML, the relationship between the elements is defined in a separate document called a Document Type Definition, which XML also supports. However, in the future, DTDs will almost certainly be deprecated in favor of XML Schemas. (See the "XML As a Data Format" section later in this chapter for details.)

Perhaps the best example to demonstrate a document-centric approach is XHTML, which is an XML compliant version of HTML. With XHTML, you have the mixed benefits of being able to parse the structure as an XML document (scanning for heads and subheads, for example) while still being able to read it in a Web browser.

Taking XHTML to the Limit

In all likelihood, XHTML will become the default document markup language of the Web within a few years. While this may not necessarily completely solve the context problem, it makes it much easier for a webBot to decipher and understand a Web page, and it also means that you could ultimately retrieve a Web page at a much higher level of resolution using the XML query language, XPath.

Once you have XML Web servers in place, I anticipate that you can do such things as embed a table from one document into the body of another through the use of a reference tag and an XML query string, like in the following example:

```
<h1>Sales figures</h1>
<p>Current sales are up, as can be shown by the sales figures
 for the last three quarters:</p>
<table href="http://www.acmeRocket.com/sales/salesFigures.xmp/
table[(@id= 'salesFigures1']/tr[td(2).value() $gt$ 19991001]" />
```

Taking XHTML to the Limit ***(continued)***

Note that in addition to pulling out an explicit structure from a document, you could conceivably query this document to retrieve specific information (in this case, all rows of the `salesFigures1` table where `td(2)` is greater than October 1, 1999).

Currently, this syntax and behavior are still hypothetical, although there are a number of servers coming to market as I write this, which should provide exactly this sort of behavior.

XML As a Document Management Format

I want to make a distinction here between document formats and document management formats. Document management formats are very closely allied to the other current rage in computing circles these days, directories.

While the conventional example of a directory is something like a phone book, I personally have had more than my share of problems with this description. In computer circles, a directory is essentially a hierarchical structure that can be queried to retrieve information about a computer system, the file structure on a network drive, user information, and so forth.

If the mention of the word *hierarchical* is ringing some bells here, then you're beginning to get a feel for working with XML. In theory, you could represent a directory system through the use of an XML document. The Lightweight Directory Access Protocol (LDAP) architecture that is currently deployed in numerous servers is built around the older X.500 protocol as a way of using a directory-like notation to retrieve information about a system. Servers that convert LDAP results into XML (or that accept XML XPath syntax for retrieving LDAP information) are likely to become commonplace by the time this book is published, as the two formats are not that dissimilar.

Similarly, XML can be used to create one or more *topic maps* into a document space. A topic map can be thought of as a hierarchical table of contents for a whole Web site. The advantage of a topic map is that it can arrange documents by their content rather than their location in a directory. For example, a simple topic map for XML might look like the following:

```
<topicMap>
    <topic>
      <title>XML Basics</title>
      <author>Kurt Cagle</author>
      <href>xmlDocs/xmlPrimary.xml</href>
      <keywords>
         <keyword>XML</keyword>
```

```
            <keyword>XSL</keyword>
            <keyword>W3C</keyword>
         </keywords>
         <topic>
            <title>A Look at XML</title>
            <author>Denise Santaro</author>
         <href>xmlDocs/XMLIntro.xml</href>
            <keyword>XML</keyword>
            <keyword>W3C</keyword>
         </topic>
      </topic>
       <topic>
         <title>XSL Basics</title>
         <author>Phileus Potts</author>
         <href>xmlDocs/xslPrimary.xml</href>
         <keywords>
            <keyword>XSL</keyword>
            <keyword>W3C</keyword>
         </keywords>
      </topic>
   </topicMap>
```

While the structure here is regular (making it more of a data-centric XML document), its primary purpose is to create a relational map to documents (or, conceivably, to subdocuments, depending on the documents and the server) in what amounts to a concept space. In its simplest form, such a space would probably be expressed as a tree-view of some sort, but, more importantly, it is a way of abstracting relationships without tying them into an explicit file directory structure. It also reduces redundancy of documents since you don't need such a document in more than one place to show a relationship.

Topic maps and XML-enabled directories will change the way that we look at document management, and will ultimately even change the way we think about documents themselves. Since more than one topic map can be assigned to a document space, topic maps essentially enable the capability of shifting your perspective about the information you have available to you. As we move increasingly into a data-rich environment (even, perhaps, into one where data is considered pollution) XML's role in document management will become critical.

XML As a Data Format

A funny thing happened on the road to XML adoption as the next HTML: Several people simultaneously discovered that a table is a data structure. For example, consider a simple table of line items from a purchase order (Table 1.1).

TABLE 1.1: Purchase Order Line Items

Product Name	Product Code	Cost Per Unit	Number of Units
Acme Big Bang	BigBang	$35.59	6
Acme Little Popper	LittlePop	$10.24	12
Acme Giant Slingshot	GslingShot	$25.99	2
Acme Suction Cups	SuctCups	$10.59	24
Acme Illusionary Paint	IllPaint	$129.95	1

Anyone who has ever had to put together a Web site knows that the HTML for that site can get a little cryptic, since the language concentrates on the display of data rather than providing any real meaning to the structure, as in the following example:

```
<table>
   <tr>
      <th>Product Name</th>
      <th>Product Code</th>
      <th>Cost Per Unit</th>
      <th>Number of Units</th>
   </tr>
   <tr>
      <td>Acme Big Bang</td>
      <td>BigBang</td>
      <td>35.59</td>
      <td>6</td>
   </tr>
   <tr>
      <td>Acme Little Popper</td>
      <td>LittlePop</td>
      <td>10.24</td>
      <td>12</td>
   </tr>
      <!-- more of the same -->
</table>
```

The HTML tells you very little—the structure is a table, the table has headers and rows, there are four elements in each row. With a little work, you could probably get code to associate each header name with its given column, but this is meaning that you impose upon the table; by all rights, the columns could, in fact, have no association with the column headers in this organization.

Suppose, however, that you could create your own HTML to deal with this problem, substituting `purchaseOrder` for `table`, `lineItem` for `tr`, and then labeling each `td` element with the name of the property it contains. Please note the following example:

```
<purchaseOrder>
     <lineItem>
```

```
            <productName>Acme Big Bang</productName>
            <productCode>BigBang</productCode>
            <costperUnit>35.59</costPerUnit>
            <numberOfUnits>6</numberOfUnits>
        </lineItem>
        <lineItem>
            <productName>Acme Little Popper</productName>
            <productCode>LittlePop</productCode>
            <costperUnit>10.24</costPerUnit>
            <numberOfUnits>12</numberOfUnits>
        </lineItem>
    <!-- Additional line items -->
    </purchaseOrder>
```

Comparing the HTML with the POML (for Purchase Order Markup Language, an imaginary HTML language), the difference that such a name change makes is dramatic. Just at a glance, you can tell that a purchase order is comprised of line items, which, in turn, include names, codes, unit costs, and number of units. You can intuit the purpose of the table, and a largely anonymous table suddenly becomes a very clear object model.

The Purchase Order Markup Language is, of course, actually an instance of XML, and therein lies the irony. SGML has always had the data structuring capability, but given the complexity of both the tools and the language itself, using SGML as a data description language was simply not cost effective. However, by cutting out a significant part of the overhead that SGML represents, the whole notion that a document is simply one form of a data structure quickly emerges.

This realization didn't bypass programmers. Most programming languages have basic data structures that are built into the language—linked lists, vectors, collections—but these are, for the most part, linear structures. One structure in particular, the associative array, does let you associate a label with a given entity in a list, and if that entity itself is an associative array, then you can build a structure similar to what XML offers. (And, in some languages, XML parsers are built in precisely this manner.)

The problem with such tree structures, however, comes from the fact that there is no consistent methodology for creating such trees; in essence, to build a logical tree, you need to write your own techniques for populating the tree, for navigating it, for querying elements within it, and so on. This problem is only made worse because such tree structures occur all the time in programming. Perhaps this is because programmers tend to organize things in hierarchical chunks, or maybe it is an intrinsic characteristic of information (one consequence of the Data + Context = Information aphorism previously related).

Describing the Data

With XML, programmers ended up with two things for free: a mechanism for creating and navigating a hierarchical data tree (the XML parser) and a way of representing hierarchy in a consistent and easily controllable fashion. Thus, even as the SGML contingent of the XML community figures out ways of adding more document-centric features, Web and application developers start incorporating XML into their application to handle the smaller, more immediate hierarchies that they face every day.

One of the characteristics of most databases is that they retain more than just the actual data of the elements in their tables; they also contain information about the data type of the element, constraints upon an element's possible value, whether a given field can be blank, and so forth. In short, a good database should also contain *metadata* about its information.

SGML has some serious shortcomings with respect to metadata. Because the language intrinsically treats its documents at all times as collections of text characters, the need to specify whether a given element has the characteristics of a date, or a real number, or an integer doesn't exist. SGML can specify that an element or attribute have data that comes from a specific set of tokens, but, even then, the capability is considerably less useful from a data standpoint because the tokens have significant limitations on how they can be formed (no spaces, no punctuation, no line breaks; just alphanumeric characters).

A *data schema language* would let developers set characteristics in their XML document that make them more database-like. For example, while the preceding version of the POML language lets you work with each entity as text, a schema expands the capabilities of POML extensively, as presented in the following example:

```
<element name="lineItem">
   <element name="productName" type="string"/>
   <element name="productCode" type="string" />
   <element name="costPerUnit" type="currency">
      <minInclusive>0.00</minInclusive</minInclusive>
   </element>
   <element name="numberOfUnits" type="integer">
      <minInclusive>1</minInclusive>
   </element>
</element>
```

This description indicates that an element with the tag name of `lineItem` contains the four elements `productName`, `productCode`, `costPerUnit`, and `numberOfUnits`, as you would expect from the initial markup. However, while the product name and product code elements are strings, the `costPerUnit` is presented as a currency (which is a unit that was defined elsewhere) and `numberOfUnits` is always an integer. Furthermore, you can never have a negative unit cost (`<minInlusive>0.00</minInclusive>`), nor can you have less than one unit of the indicated item on the purchase order.

The preceding fragment shows a small piece of the XML Schema language that is being proposed by the W3C to define XML documents. While XML Schema offers a number of benefits over the older SGML DTDs, one of the most significant is that it is itself written in XML and can thus be manipulated with the same tools as the XML it describes. Additionally, XML Schema lays the foundation for treating XML as an object-oriented data language, complete with such features as inheritance and polymorphism.

NOTE In Chapter 6, "XML Schema," these issues are examined in considerably greater detail.

XML As a Transformation Language

In the preceding section, I introduced the notion of converting a table into an XML representation. While this makes the meaning of the table somewhat more tractable, it does raise the obvious question "Well, yes, but how does the HTML browser know to display it as a table now?"

It doesn't. HTML has no contingencies for recognizing such tags as `productCode`, nor should it; the plethora of unnecessary tags was what made HTML unstable in the first place. However, in order to make XML viewable outside of anything beyond a text editor, you need some mechanism to convert the XML into a different format, such as HTML.

The Extensible Style Language fits the bill. The name can be a little deceptive, especially if you come from the Web world and are used to HTML 4 Cascading Style Sheets. When the W3C was still looking at XML as principally being a document format, CSS made perfect sense; you could create a style sheet and associate one style rule with an XML element in a similar manner to the way that you worked with HTML tags.

NOTE This technique, in fact, works perfectly well in Internet Explorer 5, which is illustrated in Chapter 7, "XML and the Browser."

The problem with CSS arises when you start treating XML as data. To format the invoice list in a table, you'd have to be able to map the XML nodes back to their HTML equivalents. However, CSS doesn't have an option to format an element as a table or a row. You could get away with it by using overlapping DIV elements, but you would have to manipulate this through Internet Explorer's object model, which loses your portability.

Furthermore, with CSS, there's no way to reorder the data, nor to filter it. Since a significant proportion of data operations are built around those two operations, this meant that you would need to programmatically manipulate the XML using some other language (such as the XML Document Object Model, covered in the next section) for even the simplest of operations.

SGML's DSSSL language, considered once for CSS and rejected, was brought back under consideration as a possible tool to allow more complex transformations. While the capabilities that it offered were attractive—the ability to reorder or filter out entities, limited search capabilities, a programmatic syntax—DSSSL suffered the same basic limitation that DTDs suffered: It wasn't written in XML.

Keeping in mind the characteristics of DSSSL, however, the XML Style Group of the W3C decided to use some of the programmatic abilities of DSSSL to create a new language, called the Extensible Style Language, or XSL. This language is written in XML and is meant to be applied either as a style sheet (a la CSS) or through a programmatic call from the Document Object Model.

XSL's primary purpose is simple, albeit very powerful: It transforms one XML document into another document. That other document could be in HTML format. It could be an XML document. It could be an XSL document, or a SQL Script, or a text file, or a Rich Text Format (RTF) file. While there are a few classes of documents that would be hard to write XSL filters for, in theory XSL should still be able to produce them. That's the goal, anyway.

However, wrapping your brain around XSL can take a little bit of work. XSL is built around the notion of templates. Each template provides a pattern to match, and when an XML element matches the pattern, the template is run, generating text that is added to a growing string of text. The XSL parser travels down the original XML document an element at a time, opening up child elements before going to the next sibling element. Put another way, XSL works recursively so that an XSL document can be remarkably compact compared to the more linear forms of procedural languages. Of course, XSL can also get considerably more cryptic for precisely the same reason.

A simple XSL script can convert the `purchaseOrder` into a table for output, as demonstrated by the following example:

NOTE This and any subsequent style sheets will probably have to be transformed to the `http://www.w3.org/1999/XSL/Transform` namespace instead.

```
<xsl:stylesheet xmlns:xsl=" http://www.w3.org/1999/XSL/Transform">
   <xsl:template match="/">
      <xsl:apply-templates select="purchaseOrder"/>
   </xsl:template>

   <xsl:template match="purchaseOrder">
      <table>
      <tr>
      <xsl:for-each select="lineItem/*">
         <th><xsl:nodeName></th>
```

```
      </xsl:for-each>
      <xsl:apply-templates select="lineItem"/>
      </table>
   </xsl:template>

   <xsl:template match="lineItem">
      <tr>
      <xsl:apply-templates select="*"/>
      </tr>
   </xsl:template>

   <xsl:template match="*">
      <td><xsl:value-of/></td>
   </xsl:template>
</xsl:stylesheet>
```

While the details will be covered in much greater detail in Chapter 4, "XSL Transform," the gist of the preceding code can be seen by realizing that there are four templates:

- The first matching the top-most element in the XML structure
- The second matching the purchase order
- The third designed to trap line items
- The fourth writing out each of the line item properties

The `apply-templates` statement essentially instructs the XSL parser to run any applicable templates against the children or other descendents of the current element.

XSL can be considerably more complex than this and, honestly, is one of the most difficult aspects of XML to comprehend. However, once you have mastered XSL, you will find that it opens up entirely new vistas for XML applications.

Consider the following sequence: A query against a database generates an XML object, but that object may not be in quite the form that you need. So you transform that object with an XSL transform, send the resultant data across the wire to another process, which reads the relevant data (possibly using another XSL script) and transforms that XML into HTML output for possible display.

One of the most exciting aspects of XSL transforms is that (at least with the Microsoft implementation) you can apply logic code to the nodes within an XSL script. This means that you can perform such things as computations on specific elements or the validation of an XML structure strictly through XSL means. Coupled with a suitable server, this has the potential to transform XML itself from a simple data language into a processing (or even event-driven) programming language.

XML As a Programming Language

When I originally had proposed this section, we scrutinized it closely. After all, the notion that XML is not a programming language has become a truism in the short time that XML has been around. I just don't feel it's true.

XML works surprisingly well within the context of object-oriented languages as a data structure. In a way, I would argue that up until now there has been a serious disconnect between the need to express objects as discrete entities and the fundamentally linear way that most procedural languages, such as Visual Basic, Java or C++, handle such objects.

Within XML, you can create objects implicitly by organization, or you can use some of the more recent additions to XML Schema, such as Archetypes, to explicitly define objects, data types, collections, and all of the other OOP (object-oriented programming) entities that have appeared in recent years. As mentioned in the previous section, with the aid of XSL the XML language is essentially geared toward transforming data from one form to another. Oddly enough, if you count mapping an object to a graphical interface or to a device driver, this is precisely the same thing that happens with more traditional programs.

The one principle difference between XML and procedural languages is that XML isn't really event driven. However, even in this context, it's worth thinking about what happens when people program in more traditional languages, such as VB. For a given data class or component, the programmer sets up a map, as in the following example, that associates the event with a routine:

```
Sub Form_OnLoad()
   'Initialize the form
   me.title="My Title"
   me.width=400
   me.height=300
End Form_OnLoad()

Sub Form_OnResize()
   'Resize the form's components
   me.textbox.width=me.width-10
   me.textbox.height=me.height-5
End Form_OnLoad()
```

It's not that much of a stretch to see an XML-based language that's built around the same notion, as demonstrated by the following example:

```
<xll:component name="Form1" type="VBA.Form">
   <xll:event name="onload">
      <!-- Initialize the form -->
      <xll:object ref="me">
            <width>400</width>
```

```
            <height>300</height>
            <title>My Title</title>
    </xll:event>
    <xll:event name="onresize">
       <!-- Resize the form's components -->
       <xll:object ref="me.textbox">
            <width>me.width-10</width>
            <height>me.height-5</height/>
    </xll:event>
 </xll:component>
```

While you would still need some mechanism that actually takes into account the association between an event map and the actual event that calls it, the structure here effectively means that you could write a script as a series of object definitions and references that are essentially built around an XML structure. You technically make the jump between XML as an object definition and XML as a programming language.

Note that while, at the moment, the `xll` namespace described above is a fiction, there are a number of different programming initiatives taking place to create a conceptually similar language in the near future. The benefits of using such an encoding are significant, as outlined in the following list:

- Languages become considerably easier to document because the tags for various actions are more explicitly spelled out than they are in normal parsed form.
- Different machines can parse the same document with different tools and still be able to reconstruct the primary actions of the code.
- Such code can be encoded with the objects upon which they act, reinforcing the notion of encapsulation, while the ability to refer to (and import or export) schemas means that an object's functionality can be changed simply by switching the namespace of the entity.
- Reflection, or the ability to read an object's property set at run time, becomes trivial because all you would need to do to get the property list of an object is query the XML structure.
- Internationalization and localization also become fairly easy since both text content and property specifications for different cultures can be contained within separate documents.

Couple the preceding benefits with the ability to refer to code from any location and the very nature of what we mean by programming begins to shift from a number of procedures run on disparate machines to a pool of intelligent objects.

In the last chapter of this book, I explore this topic further, covering the latest developments of XML within the programming sphere as well as showing how you can promote object-oriented principles within your own code.

XML As a Multimedia Format

Multimedia seems a strange place to find XML. After all, what could be farther from a simple text representation of data than video, graphics, and sound? Ironically, XML promises to play a large part in the future of media, especially as it moves in force onto the Web.

One of the characteristics that seems to repeatedly define XML is *management.* Topic maps are crucial to document management, middleware applications equally key for data management. If you look upon multimedia not as graphics and video and sound but the time or spatial management of resources, then the association between XML and multimedia should become clear.

Programs like Macromedia Director are effective because they provide a convenient mechanism for indicating when specific events occur—when graphics change position, when sounds are played, when videos are started or stopped. The Synchronized Multimedia Integration Language (SMIL) performs this same function using an XML format. This format isn't specifically Web-based, by the way; it is simply a way of providing one or more timelines that a SMIL-compatible viewer can use to animate elements.

Microsoft raised the valid issue that the SMIL format isn't terribly well optimized for use within a browser and chose to release an extension written in XML called HTML+TIME. This format provides a mechanism for animating Web elements and is built into the Internet Explorer 5 browser.

However, looking at multimedia from the standpoint of pictures appearing within a browser, XML again will play a role. One of the major problems that the Web faces is the download time of images. Most graphics on the Web are bitmaps; every pixel in an image is represented internally as one or more bytes. While, for photographic images, such resolution is necessary, many of the graphics that do exist on the Web are relatively flat images—logos, lines, arcs, and so forth. This problem becomes even more critical when animated GIFs come into play, as even simple graphics can drag a Web page down to the point where there are 200 frames of the animation.

Macromedia's Flash (under the original name Future Splash) was one of the first products to use vector graphics on the Web, in which the shapes that make up the images are given as equations rather than pixel values. This approach, coupled with a superb graphics editor, has made Flash viewer (one of a couple of flavors of Macromedia Shockwave) one of the most popular third-party extensions on the Web today.

Because vector graphics have proven so popular (and because they are vital if the Web is to ever have the capability to reproduce well as a print medium), Macromedia and Microsoft teamed up to produce a non-proprietary vector graphic solution called Vector Markup Language (VML). Adobe, Netscape, and Sun simultaneously proposed a different vector graphic format based upon the popular postscript form that Adobe uses, under the name Precision Graphics Markup Language (PGML).

The W3C took both formats under consideration in a working committee and split the difference, coming up with a hybrid format called Scalable Vector Graphics (SVG). SVG encodes each of the graphical elements as an XML element and provides sophisticated capabilities, such as clipping paths, text kerning, bitmap integration, and the ability to animate these elements using script or SMIL.

Ironically, the initial releases of Internet Explorer 5 contains the older VML implementation, although Microsoft will be releasing an SVG plug-in in its 5.1 release, and it should become a standard feature in any subsequent browser.

NOTE The most recent SVG specification can be found at `http://www.w3.org/TR/1999/WD-SVG-19991203/`.

How Can I Use XML?

Given the evolving nature of XML, it's natural to wonder where, exactly, XML can be used. Sure, it's interesting technology, but the level of hype about XML tends to obscure what it's really for.

XML actually does have a wide variety of uses, and as more companies develop for it, the scope of the language will widen at a rate comparable to the spread of Java. To best get an idea about where you can start leveraging XML technology, however, it's worth recapping both its strengths and its weaknesses.

The following are XML's pluses:

- Works especially well as a data transfer format.
- Is intrinsically flexible. You can quickly add or delete elements on the fly and can create XML subtrees automatically.
- Echoes the hierarchical structure that people are familiar with from using file directories.
- Is a transformational language: You can filter it, change it into other formats (such as HTML), and order it by multiple criteria crossing several layers.
- Is a standard, which means that even two disparate machines running different operating systems half a world apart can still communicate with it.
- Supports (with XML Schema) data typing and lends itself readily to object-oriented programming.

The following are XML's minuses:

- Isn't a large-scale database. It's not suited for searching or retrieving tens of thousands of records (at once).
- Is much more complex than HTML since it is a metalanguage rather than a language.
- Isn't a procedural language.
- Is still evolving, and, like any evolving technology, there is a certain intrinsic risk in using it.

These attributes point to applications where XML really shines: customizing Web sites, component development, document/directory management, state management, database intermediation, and multimedia management. It also works reasonably well in support roles with initialization and localization files and performs credibly as a way to communicate between applications.

Customizing Web Sites

XML was originally designed to customize Web sites, and while there have been a few bumps on the road to making this viable, the ability to change your Web sites depending upon any number of conditions is one of the real power-applications for XML.

Consider the fundamental problems that most Web pages face at the start of the 21st century:

- The browser market is split between Internet Explorer and iPlanet (née Netscape) Navigator, although Navigator's share is shrinking quickly. Additionally, several million people use America Online or WebTV to browse the Net, and these implement only a subset of the full features of either browser.
- There are several different versions of each of the browsers currently in use, and the browsers are frequently not completely backward compatible.
- The support for scripting languages is inconsistent, and advanced script features frequently generate errors in older browsers (assuming that scripting is available at all).
- Increasingly, people are using PDAs, cellular phones, and other hand-held devices to interact with the Web. These devices often don't have the processing power to handle complex scripting and frequently support fairly basic HTML only.

The Internet is facing profound balkanization, and adding another browser (or another browser version) only exacerbates rather than helps the problem. One consequence of this is that while the latest browsers have features such as the ability to display formatted XML on the client side, Web site developers are rightly leery of coding XML to the client in this fashion because the vast majority of all browsers out there do not support XML.

Therefore, developers have been moving to server-side scripting solutions for a while. Technologies such as Active Server Pages (ASP), Java Server Pages (JSP), and ColdFusion let developers write script pages that process information or data on the server and then format the results in an HTML format that can be sent to the client. Any of these can determine what type of client they are writing to and then adjust their output accordingly.

There are problems with this approach. Concentrating on Active Server Pages, the traditional architecture of a server page lets developers intermingle formatting code (HTML) with data manipulation code (server side VBScript or JavaScript), often resulting in a difficult-to-follow and computational mess, especially when client-side scripting exists as well (as demonstrated by the following example):

```
<%@Language="VBScript"%>
<html><head>
<%dim title
title=request.queryString("title")
%>
<title><%=title%></title>
</head>
<%dim bgImage
bgImage=request.queryString("bgimage")
%>
<body background="<%=bgImage%>">
<h1><%=title></h1>
<%
dim bc
set browserObj=createObject("XMLUtils.Browser")
if bc.browserName="Internet Explorer" then
%>
<script language="JavaScript">
    window.status='<%=request.queryString("windowStatus")%>';
</script>
<% end if %>
<p>This is perfectly legible, right?</p>
..
</body></html>
```

While it is possible to follow what's going on in this example, the combination of bracketed tags within tags, multiple intermixed script languages, and the lack of any programmatic flow makes such an ASP difficult to use and completely impossible to migrate to different systems. The irony here is that the preceding code is typical of how ASP pages are written on the Web, although the language itself is capable of producing far cleaner results.

Without getting into details about what's inside the XML or XSL files, the same script could effectively be reproduced using ASP in conjunction with XML, as demonstrated in the following example:

```
<%@Language="VBScript"%>
<%
```

```
Sub Main()
   ' Dimension and create the objects to be used
   ' in the script
   dim pageName
   dim xmlDoc
   dim xslDoc
   dim bc
   dim paramObj

   set xmlDoc=createObject("Microsoft.XMLDOM")
   set xslDoc=createObject("Microsoft.XMLDOM")
   set browserObj=createObject("XMLUtils.Browser")
   set paramObj=createObject("XSLUtils.Parameters")

   pageName=request("pageName")
   ' set the right source for the transformation
   ' document, based upon the browser
   select case browserObject.browserName
       case "Internet Explorer"
            xslDoc.load pageName+"_IE.xsl"
       case "Netscape Navigator"
            xslDoc.load pageName+"_NS.xsl"
   end select

   ' set the parameters that come from the HTML query
   ' string into the XSL filter
   paramObj.QueryString=Request.QueryString
   ' load the xml source document
   xmlDoc.load pageName+".xml"
   ' then transform the output
   response.write xmlDoc.transformNode(xslDoc)
End Sub

Main
%>
```

This sample includes two objects: `XMLUtils.Browser`, which gets browser capabilities information, and `XSLUtils.Parameters`, which sets parametric information within XSL documents. Notice here that the actual names of the files to be retrieved are passed as query string parameters. As a consequence, you can use the same ASP script for any page that has both an Internet Explorer and a Netscape XSL filter.

While the code is perhaps a little denser in the preceding example, it's only because there isn't much actual output text in the first ASP page. XML can significantly reduce the overhead of ASP files and speed up their execution because the bulk of the actual processing takes place within optimized DLLs rather than in slower, interpreted code. Moreover, it becomes easier to separate the data preparation layers from the presentation layer; the preceding script could be rewritten to take an XML object as a parameter, and you could then substitute the XML retrieved from a database query or passed as an object from a post command rather than load an explicit XML file from the server.

XML has become an integral part of Microsoft's future development efforts, from data access to document storage and retrieval to messaging systems and distributed computing. This is very much in keeping with their efforts to make data access a seamless part of the operating environment, with that data increasingly expressed as XML.

Creating Components and Scripts

If you are fortunate enough to be able to limit your browser as Internet Explorer 5 (IE5), you can also take advantage of several features that this browser supports. IE5 was essentially the first Internet browser to support XML features implicitly, although Internet Explorer 4 did have a crude XML parser that was available as an ActiveX control.

Behaviors easily rank as the most useful of these features. A behavior can be thought of as a way of extending HTML tags through scripting. Indeed, Microsoft's implementation of such features as Vector Markup Language (VML) is accomplished through precisely this mechanism. Moreover, you can create behaviors, such as animated clocks, that you can then insert into your code through a simple HTML declaration, like the following:

```
<DIV style="behavior:url(clock.htc);"
timezone="-8" format="hh:mm:ss.dd AM"/>
```

Or you can declare an XML namespace (covered in Chapter 2, "Modeling the XML Document Object") and create a style sheet reference, as in the following example:

```
<html xmlns:a="http://www.xmldevhandbook.com/clockspace">
<style>
   a/:clock {behavior:url(clock.htc);}
</style>
<body>
This is a clock:
<a:clock timezone="-8" format="hh:mm:ss.dd AM"/>
</body>
</html>
```

Behaviors are especially useful in creating components for use within your Web page without the complications of building ActiveX controls. On a recent project, for example, I built a component for converting a SQL server call into a formatted table. The component talked to an ASP page on the server for processing the SQL query and returning it as an XML document, and then it called a parameterized XSL file to output the data as a table. Behaviors maintain state and event information so that the table could respond to mouse-over and click events.

However, it is possible to build similar components without resorting to IE; as long as you have access to the object model, you can use the same principles for any Web browser that supports a scripting language and can capture events. These components are built on the server with the client-side scripting code included as part of the page, and XML is a remarkably powerful way to both organize and customize these server-side components.

An example of where this could be useful is a help system in which a roll-over on an item identified beforehand brings up a floating help balloon that contains more extensive information about an element's function.

As languages such as Visual Basic and Java start to become more XML-centric, many of the standard components will have options for using XML as the data source. For example, the TreeView control in Visual Basic version 6 seems almost ideally suited for use by XML, but you must have a fairly good knowledge of XML to actually take advantage of this. Over time, even standard controls will provide options for both importing or exporting data and for saving or loading in visual state information.

One of the lesser-known but more-useful additions that IE5 brought with it was the Windows Scripting Host, which lets you apply scripting behavior to the operating system itself. As an indication of Microsoft's future programming goals, the Scripting Host is written around an XML shell and gives you a way of using XML to set various applications' configurations.

Managing Documents and Data Spaces

The task of managing documents has moved from being a fairly simple operation of maintaining a decent naming convention on your 20MB hard drive to keeping track of tens of thousands of documents produced by thousands of people over a network that could extend all across the world. Without the ability to keep track of documents, a company's primary asset—its information—slowly melts away in a sea of undocumented electrons. This is already happening on the Internet, where significant portions of the Web are simply inaccessible unless you happen to know exactly where something is located. However, information entropy is likely to become a significant factor in the corporate workspace before too long, even restricting the domain to corporate intranets.

In the near term, XML's use in managing documents is likely to be oriented toward simple indexing schemes that work by mirroring file structures in XML. However, as XML concept editors and document filters become more prevalent, it's likely that many documents will be archived in an XML format (even if they're not originally written in such a format).

Directory structures, as mentioned before, currently are most frequently represented using the LDAP protocol. However, the hierarchical structure of LDAP could be fairly easily modified into an XML format (and vice versa), which means that the same system for representing document information could also work with computer state information (usernames, resource locations, business data, and so forth).

In a similar fashion, as databases become more integrated with XML standards, applications that can translate between SQL and the XPath language will become more common. SQL is not a language that lends itself to use on the Internet; its structure is verbose, the level of information that you need in order to perform a basic query can run several lines or pages, and the data that is contained within fields is often of a sensitive or protected nature that you don't necessarily want exposed. Typically, ASP acts as a buffer between the data and the outside world, but because each ASP essentially has to be generated from scratch, this can make for expensive Web interfaces.

Increasingly, XML is replacing complex ASP in this middle tier. The XML information can be easily changed from one format to another, it can provide both simple and complex validation of data, and it can determine through the use of an XSL transform whether a given record is valid before attempting an expensive write to the database. Moreover, with the ability to integrate with messaging, an XML solution can take the data that is created from a SQL query and export it to the client as a single unit, without necessarily forcing the entire client to refresh itself.

E-commerce

The ability to handle transactions easily without a lot of ASP preprocessing makes XML an ideal mechanism for handling the emerging frontier of e-commerce. Indeed, much of the drive to handle data types has come from the nascent e-commerce sector.

Electronic transactions in commerce are not new. Approximately 20 years ago, the increasingly connected business sector in the United States realized that commerce data could be sent between large companies through the new 1200bps modems. The problem, of course, came in the language used; no two companies had precisely the same set of information for accounting purposes. A secondary problem was that the slow bit speed in the modems effectively meant that any language that was used had a need to be as compact and efficient as possible.

A coalition of companies started focusing on the problem in the late 1970s, trying to find a standard that would have both the flexibility to accommodate multiple accounting systems and the efficiency to work with the slow modems of the time. The result of this effort—first in the United States and then in the United Nations—was a format called Electronic Data Interchange (EDI).

EDI has been a very effective standard, but it has some profound limitations. For example, in order to accommodate the ways that different companies performed business transactions, it exposed a large number of properties—so large a number, in fact, that one company would often choose one property while another would choose a different one for the same piece of information. The solution to this was the rise of the Value Added Networks (VANs), which, for a significant fee, kept the mappings of different companies and wrote translation routines for converting one to another.

A quarter century later, the Internet is pervasive and allows connections that are thousands of times faster than those early modems. Moreover, the number of companies that need to perform transactions has exploded, and many of them are small companies that find the EDI VAN fees prohibitively expensive.

The pressure from small companies to perform business-to-business transactions has coupled with the rise of XML to provide an incentive to change the EDI architecture to a common format. Initially, the larger EDI companies and the VANs pushed for an EDI/XML format in which the XML Schema essentially matched the field definitions of the older EDI architecture. However, as the capabilities of XML became more evident, this early EDI/XML approach was abandoned in favor of a new schema.

Microsoft, which has been one of the leading companies to push for the adoption of XML Schema, also has set up an XML standard called BizTalk, which is meant to be an XML Schema–compliant framework for performing transactions in which companies register prospective XML architectures. Trade organizations, most notably the Organization for the Advancement of Structured Information Standards (OASIS), have also proposed XML standards for various e-commerce transactions (such as invoicing, purchasing, and account queries). In all likelihood, there will be a plethora of different standards for several years to come, although XSL minimizes the possible fracturing effects of these competing schemas. (BizTalk is covered extensively in Chapter 10, "E-commerce with Microsoft BizTalk.")

However, e-commerce extends beyond business-to-business transactions. Business-to-consumer e-commerce has seen the more visible development over the last five years as the World Wide Web has become the World Wide Shopping Mall. XML will probably be slower to move into this realm since most business-to-consumer transactions take place through Internet browsers, so the XML transactions that are likely to occur will more likely happen on the server side. However, even given that XML has a role to play in presenting the information and maintaining intermediate state information before a purchase is finalized, we'll see more of XML on the browser side in the context of e-commerce.

Integrating Applications

As with most contemporary technologies, XML exposes an object model (usually called a Document Object Model, or DOM, in the case of XML) that allows programmers to write applications using specific methods of XML. These methods let developers walk an XML tree, retrieve individual elements or attributes, determine schema information, transform subtrees, and perform validation, among a number of other options.

While much has been made of XSL's transformational capabilities, the ability to use the XML DOM means that you, as a programmer, can integrate XML into your own applications, whether they are completely generated from scratch or they use the object model of other applications, such as Microsoft Office.

Microsoft Office 2000 does not have much built-in XML support (save for a few XML constructs called data islands that are used to retain information in HTML pages created by Office), but you can use XML to persist data that may exist in an Excel spreadsheet and then transform it through the use of DOM (or by the clever application of XSL) to create a table in Word or a chart in PowerPoint.

One advantage to this approach over traditional OLE (which also lets you transfer data among applications) is that OLE requires that both applications be run simultaneously. (For resource-intensive applications, like Word or Excel, running several such applications could easily leave you short of memory.) An XML stream uses the relatively lightweight MSXML component instead and doesn't even require that the data come from Excel. (For example, you may want it to come from a persisted XML file on the Web instead, or perhaps from a SQL Server database.)

This integration becomes even more important when the source of the data is located on a machine different than the consumer of the data. With XML, it is possible to use Excel as a remote server, generating data to a PowerPoint presentation, or perhaps to a Visio document, or maybe even—heavens forefend—to a Java applet running in a Netscape browser. It is this ability to facilitate remote transactions in an inexpensive, platform-independent manner that points to one of the principle uses of XML in the future.

A related venue to this is the area of messaging. Web connections aren't always possible, especially if you are in a travel-intensive occupation, such as sales. Messaging lets a salesperson write relevant information through a Web browser or other client application into a message cache if the machine isn't connected to the Internet or a private network. When they return to the office (or their cellular modem comes back within range of a transmitter), as is increasingly the case, a messaging manager sends the information that was cached on to the client. While sophisticated caching systems are needed for standard client applications, if you're simply going through a Web interface you can leverage XML's persistence capabilities and structuring to store information until the transaction can be completed.

TIP Microsoft has a sophisticated messaging system based around Microsoft Messaging Queue (MSMQ) for handling procedural messaging transactions, but a lightweight service can be set up easily in XML, as shown in Chapter 11, "XML and Programming."

The barrier here between data and programming language blurs, as I indicated earlier in this chapter, and that point serves to highlight yet another axiom that XML introduces: There really is, in the end, no difference between program and data, between actor and action; they are one and the same.

Summary

XML looks like such a trivial thing, but it will probably have more impact on the evolution of computing than any technology since the advent of HTML. XML is fundamentally a language to manage resources, whether those resources are documents, data, graphics, programs, or concepts. It has evolved out of the realization that we are becoming adrift in a sea of too much data and too little information.

Ironically, as XML has taken shape through countless hours of wrangling in conferences and newsgroups and e-mail, people have realized that the nature of information transcends the notion of a document. E-commerce systems talk money while researchers seek out context, yet the tool for both is becoming the same. Our views about programming, objects, and applications are shifting, subtly at first, but with more and more alacrity over time.

In the next chapter, I introduce the skeleton of XML, the Document Object Model. I deviate a little bit from the accepted way of writing about XML, not focusing on Document Type Definitions and not concentrating on schemas until much later (Chapter 6, "XML Schema," to be precise), because XML isn't about documents, nor about data; it's about meaning.

Oh, by the way, to revisit the question that started out this chapter:

What is Meaning?

Simple. Anything you want it to be. Have fun....

CHAPTER 2

Modeling the XML Document Object

- Understanding the XML Document Object Model
- Examining the XML document
- Working with nodes
- Understanding attributes
- Detailing comments and processing instructions
- Reviewing asynchronous XML and events

Programming in this day and age usually means working with objects to perform tasks, especially if you work with languages, such as Visual Basic (VB) or Java. Fortunately, XML lends itself well to such object models, in part because its structure is so reminiscent of the notion of nested objects with properties, data types, and encapsulation that make up traditional object-oriented or object-like languages.

In this chapter, I briefly introduce using object models in general. Then I focus on the meatier aspects of the XML Object Model (documents, elements, attributes, nodes, and so forth), showing how you can access them within your own programs.

Understanding Object-Oriented Programming

The Object-Oriented Programming (OOP), which has to have one of the most singularly incongruous acronyms I've ever encountered, is getting a little long in the tooth. Smalltalk, the predecessor of most of the "visual" languages in use today, has been influencing GUI designers since the late 1970s, while C++ has practically been synonymous with object-oriented programming since the mid-1980s. A quarter-century is a long time in the hyperkinetic world of programming, and in this time OOP has evolved from an interesting (if somewhat incomprehensible) way of simplifying the complicated morass of procedural programming into a central paradigm for designing complex systems.

TIP

In some ways, we have reached the upper threshold of OOP's capabilities and advantages, to the extent that computer historians are beginning to refer to present developments as the emergence of post-OOP design. XML may very well play a big part in this shift. More on this in Chapter 11, "XML and Programming."

One consequence of 25 years of experimentation, successes, and failures is that OOP seems to work best when structures are built that model the phenomenon being programmed, breaking down complex objects into interconnected, simpler objects. These object models can take a number of different forms but typically focus on the *properties* that an object has, the actions (or *methods*) that the object can perform, the *events* that the object responds to, and the *relationships* that the object has with other objects within its object space.

The object model for a given object space can get pretty complex. With complex applications such as Microsoft Office, for example, there are nearly 200 distinct objects that are defined with thousands of methods, properties, and events. Java goes one step further in that, with the exception of a few programming primitives, every entity in Java is an object with a distinct object model.

There are currently two major, distinct architectures for manipulating objects: Microsoft's Component Object Model (COM) and the Common Object Request Broker Architecture

(CORBA), which is a standard endorsed by the Object Management Group (OMG), a coalition of other software developers and vendors (including Sun, Apple, IBM, and several others). While it is possible to create CORBA objects in Windows, the vast majority of all objects in the Windows 9*x* and NT categories follow the COM specification, including the XML components described extensively in this book.

The XML Document Object Model

In comparison to something like Microsoft Office, the XML Document Object Model (frequently referred to as the XML DOM) is relatively simple, although, if you're not used to working with object models, it can still be a little daunting. There are 23 objects that make up the DOM, although, of those, only half a dozen or so will be used for nearly all of your XML development work. Table 2.1 summarizes what each object's interface does.

TABLE 2.1: The Various Interfaces Contained within the XML Document Object Model

Object Interface	Description
`DOMDocument`	The entry point interface for creating and manipulating XML DOM documents.
`DOMFreeThreadedDocument`	An apartment-model version of the `DOMDocument` interface, for use in server environments.
`IXMLDOMAttribute`	Interface for an XML attribute.
`IXMLDOMCDATASection`	Interface for a CDATA section, which lets you store tagged, formatted text without having it parsed.
`IXMLDOMCharacterData`	Base class for several of the other classes, including `Text` and `CDATA-Section.` (Seldom used directly.)
`IXMLDOMComment`	Interface for XML comments.
`IXMLDOMDocumentFragment`	Interface for document fragments, which are lightweight XML documents for intermediate processing.
`IXMLDOMDocumentType`	Interface for `<DOCType>` nodes; it is used to get access to the DTD.
`IXMLDOMElement`	Interface for an XML element. (This is heavily used.)
`IXMLDOMEntity`	Interface for an Entity object (found within schemas or DTDs).
`IXMLDOMEntityReference`	Interface for an Entity Reference object (the `&xxx;` references found within the body of the XML itself).
`IXMLDOMImplementation`	Interface that lets you determine whether the given version of the DOM document supports a specific feature.
`IXMLDOMNamedNodeMap`	An extended interface that adds functionality to the Entity and Attribute interfaces.
`IXMLDOMNode`	The base node interface that most other XML interfaces inherit.
`IXMLDOMNodeList`	A list structure that contains references to noncontiguous nodes.

TABLE 2.1: The Various Interfaces Contained within the XML Document Object Model *(continued)*

Object Interface	Description
`IXMLDOMNotation`	Interface for supporting Notations, declared within the DTD.
`IXMLDOMParseError`	Interface for querying the XML object to determine if (and where) specific errors occurred.
`IXMLDOMProcessingInstruction`	An interface for accessing the processing instructions (PIs) within the document.
`IXMLDOMText`	An interface for setting or retrieving the text contents of a node.
`IXTLRuntime`	An interface used extensively by XSL for processing nodes during transformations.
`XMLDocument`	An interface for dealing with the XML document. It is obsolete (use `DOMDocument` instead) but is included for backward compatibility.
`XMLDSOControl`	An interface for using the XML document as a data source.
`XMLHTTPRequest`	An interface that permits communication across the HTTP protocol.

It is worth defining a few terms here. I've used the expression *object* fairly loosely, but, in fact, an object is technically considered an *instance* of a *class*. That is to say that the class defines what properties, methods, and events are available, while an object holds the actual contents of the properties. An *interface*, in turn, is a description of the class; it specifies which properties are available, for example, but doesn't contain any explicit code to define the behaviors of those properties.

Another frequently used term concerning the interfaces is *node*. Nodes can be considered the most primitive objects within an XML document, and, in fact, nearly all XML objects inherit the node interface. In essence, a node consists of a node name and a connection to one or more other nodes. Thus, an element node might have as children one or more attribute nodes, might have a CDATA (for *character data*) node or a *text node*, and may also have a comment node (among others). (The `IXMLDOMNode` interface will be discussed in much greater detail in the "Working With Nodes" section later in this chapter.)

Examining the XML Document

In almost every case, one of the first things that you will do when working with XML is to create an XML document object, which, in Microsoft's XML Object Model, is called the `DOMDocument`. This object is frequently referred to as the *root*, or *top-level*, object in the object model, and it is one of the few objects within the XML DOM that can be created directly; almost everything else, from elements and attributes to node lists and entities, comes from the `DOMDocument`.

It's fairly easy to instantiate a `DOMDocument` object from within a scripting language. In the case of either Visual Basic Script (VBScript) or JavaScript, you need to know that the ProgID for the XML Document Object Model is `Microsoft.XMLDOM`, and then just instantiate the object using the following object creation command for either language:

```
VBScript:
    Dim xmlDoc
    Set xmlDoc=createObject("Microsoft.XMLDOM")
    ' Note: if you are using MTS, you may want to use
    ' the server.createObject instead:
    ' set xmlDoc=server.createObject("Microsoft.XMLDOM")

JavaScript:
    Var xmlDoc=new ActiveXObject("Microsoft.XMLDOM")
```

In order to use the `DOMDocument` from Visual Basic, you should first create a reference to the XML parser, as per the following steps:

1. From within Visual Basic, select the Project menu, and choose References from the pop-up menu.
2. From the References list, choose Microsoft XML, Version 2.0 (or select the option for version 3, if that is available).
3. Close the dialog box.

You can now see the XML library in the Object Browser (under the MSXML tab) and can use it within your project.

Once you've created a reference to the XML library, you can declare a variable in VB using the `DOMDocument` class, as in the following example:

```
Visual Basic:
    Dim xmlDoc as DOMDocument
    Set xmlDoc=New DOMDocument
    ' you can also use the createObjects form:
    Set xmlDoc=CreateObject("Microsoft.XMLDOM")
```

You can also use the `CreateObject()` function within Visual Basic, which may be preferable if you are planning on porting routines to VBScript, as in the following example:

```
Visual Basic:
    Dim xmlDoc as DOMDocument
    Set xmlDoc=CreateObject("Microsoft.XMLDOM")
```

NOTE Note that the XML document object sources events. That means that if you want to be able to capture specific XML events within your application, you can (and should) declare the document using `WithEvents`. See the "Asyncronous XML and Events" section later in this chapter for more information.

WARNING Some older XML documentation references the `MSXML.DOMDocument` ProgID rather than `Microsoft.XMLDOM`. This is an older, currently unsupported interface provided only for backward compatibility. You should not use it.

Creating a Standard XML Project Type

If you are trying to use XML in a Visual Basic project (rather than in ASP or DHTML), you will probably find yourself setting the reference attributes for a number of related classes repeatedly. One thing you can do to improve your productivity is to create a couple of new project types.

For example, I typically find that the same applications in which I use XML also tend to require references to the scripting engines, the DHTML type library, and the Active Server Pages library. As a consequence, I created two custom templates: the `XML Form Project` and the `XML_ASP ActiveX DLL Project`.

You can make a custom template yourself by setting up a Form or an ActiveX DLL as follows:

1. Open up a new project based upon the `Standard EXE` template (or whatever the project type is that you're attempting to emulate).
2. If setting up a form, resize the form to the dimensions that you ordinarily use, and add components to the toolbar by right-clicking the bar.
3. Add references by selecting Project ➢ References from the menu and then selecting the appropriate class references.
4. Save the project in the `VB98\Templates\Projects` folder and the form in the `VB98\Templates\Forms` folder.
5. In a similar fashion, you can save commonly used classes, property pages, user controls, and similar resources within the templates folder.
6. Whenever you create a new object of a given type (by selecting the File ➢ New menu for a project or choosing Add from one of the many VB submenus), Visual Basic will automatically look in the template directories and present the items you saved as alternatives to the standard objects.

Loading Documents

Once instantiated, the XML document object exists but is essentially empty: there's no data in it. Before you can do anything meaningful with the document, you need to load in XML data from somewhere—a file, a text string, a data island, or another DOM object. The DOM supports two distinct ways of loading data in:

LoadXML Lets you pass a string of text formatted as XML into the object.

Load Lets you pass a filename, URL, or another XML document as a parameter to populate the document.

LoadXML is especially handy for creating short XML documents on the fly. For example, Listing 2.1 presents two listings that demonstrate a way to create a short log message in XML, first in Visual Basic Script (as you might see in Visual InterDev) and then in Visual Basic.

Listing 2.1: Creating a Short XML Document with the *LoadXML* Method (*listing2-01.txt*)

```
VBScript:
Dim xmlDoc
Dim buf
Set xmlDoc=createObject("Microsoft.XMLDOM")
Buf=""
Buf=Buf+"<logMessage>"
Buf=Buf+"<author>Kurt Cagle</author>"
Buf=Buf+"<msg>This is a short message</msg>"
Buf=Buf+"<date>2000-01-12</date>"
Buf=Buf+"</logMessage>"
XmlDoc.LoadXML buf

Visual Basic:
Dim xmlDoc as DOMDocument
Dim buf as String
Set xmlDoc=new DOMDocument
Buf=""
Buf=Buf+"<logMessage>"
Buf=Buf+"<author>Kurt Cagle</author>"
Buf=Buf+"<msg>This is a short message</msg>"
Buf=Buf+"<date>2000-01-12</date>"
Buf=Buf+"</logMessage>"
XmlDoc.LoadXML buf
```

This code creates an XML-based log message, which may be added into an extended log. LoadXML works best in situations where the XML is generated as text. However, in most cases, you'll probably find that you want to retrieve your XML from a stream of some sort (a file from your local system, an ASP document, the result of a database query that generates XML, etc.). In these cases, you would call the load function instead, as demonstrated in Listing 2.2.

Listing 2.2: Various Ways of Loading In Documents from External Sources through the Load Method (*listing2-02.txt*)

```
Visual Basic:
Dim xmlDoc as DOMDocument
Set xmlDoc=new DOMDocument

VBScript:
Dim xmlDoc
Set xmlDoc=createObject("Microsoft.XMLDOM")
' Load from a local file:
XmlDoc.Load "c:\xmlDevHandbook\myData.xml"
' Load from a network drive:
XmlDoc.Load "\\resources\xmlDevHandbook\myData.xml"
' Load from a URL:
XmlDoc.Load "http://www.xmlDevHandbook/myData.xml"
' Load from a parameterized ASP page:
XmlDoc.Load "http://www.xmlDevHandbook/_
          getNewData.asp?file=myData"
' Load from SQL Query (SQL Server7.5)
' (This last example will be explained more in Chapter 9)
xmlDoc.Load "http://www.xmlDevHandbook/data?sql=SELECT *_
            FROM MyDataTable WHERE Author='Kurt+Cagle',_
            FOR XML AUTO"
```

Typically, when a load is successful, the parser will automatically remove all irrelevant white space from the document; more specifically, the parser throws away the following characters:

- Leading and trailing spaces in text elements
- Spaces within elements, except those required to separate items
- Tabs
- Carriage returns
- Line feeds

In many cases, this filtering process has no impact upon the content of the document, especially if the document is data-centric. However, for document-centric code, removing white space can make the code especially impenetrable to read or debug.

The `preserveWhiteSpace` property turns this filtering mechanism off. When set to true, the document will retain the formatting that it had going in, although typically at a cost of adding 20–30 percent to the size of the document. If your XML will likely be read as a text file, or if you have code (such as VBScript) that depends upon carriage returns embedded in the XML, then you may want to set this option. This should be set prior to loading the document, by the way; if set after the document has been loaded in, the white space will already have been stripped.

Another property that should possibly be set before loading the document is `async.` To understand the purpose of this property, consider that there are two different modes for loading a document: pulling it from a local hard drive, which is generally a very fast operation, or pulling it from a network or the Internet, which ranges from a moderately fast to a glacially slow process, depending upon your connection speed.

The `async` (short for *asynchronous*) property sets an internal flag telling `Load` to either load the full document at one time before returning to the next line (`async=false`) or to initiate loading and then proceed to the next command without waiting for completion (`async=true`). The parser is relatively intelligent in that it makes local file access synchronous by default while making most other access types asynchronous, but there are situations when you may want alternate behavior. For example, imagine that you need to load a file from the Internet before doing any other action and that you're willing to lock the application until the file is downloaded or it times out.

In general, programming this way isn't recommended, but, at the same time, asynchronous programming generally tends to be much more complex than is worthwhile for simpler applications. Similarly, there are situations when you pull from local data streams that may themselves be asynchronous (such as a SQL query). In either case, you should set `async` to the appropriate Boolean value prior to initiating the load.

NOTE The "Asynchronous XML and Events" section later in this chapter shows how you can build asynchronous XML programs using the `DOMDocument` methods.

Once you have loaded the XML document, you can retrieve its URL at any time via the `url` property. Note that, internally, the XML document will automatically convert local DOS and network paths to their URL equivalent, as demonstrated in the following example:

```
XmlDoc.load "c:\bin\resources.xml"
Debug.print xmlDoc.url
file:///C|/bin/resources.xml
XmlDoc.load "\\mySystem\bin\resources.xml"
Debug.print xmlDoc.url
file:///mySystem/bin/resources.xml
```

Error Handling with *ParseError*

Suppose something does go wrong with your download. The server may be down. The XML source may be corrupt. You may have mistyped the file location. A DTD may not be valid for the document in question.

A significant proportion of any software project involves handling exceptions to the rules, either as part of the program flow or through some form of error handling. Because XML files can be generated by hand, and due to the large number of things that can go wrong within a document alone (not to mention any of the connections *to* that document), the error mechanism for XML needs to be more robust than simply returning an error code.

Fortunately, the Microsoft XML parser's error handling mechanism is quite robust; indeed, it's a model that Microsoft itself is beginning to incorporate into some of their more advanced products. Any time an error occurs with the DOM, the parser invalidates the XML structure and then notifies a subordinate class called the `ParseError` object. This object has the properties outlined in Table 2.2 and implements them through the `IXMLDOMParseError` class.

TABLE 2.2: Interface for the `ParseError` Object

Property	Description
`ErrorCode`	Comprises the numeric code associated with the error. If no error has occurred, this value will be zero.
`Filepos`	Gives the character position within the incoming XML stream, establishing where the error occurred. (Zero if no error.)
`Line`	Identifies the line (carriage return delineated) where the error occurred. (Zero if no error.)
`Linepos`	Identifies the position, relative to the start of the current line, where the error occurred. (Zero if no error.)
`Reason`	Provides a description of the error and is usually pretty detailed. (Will be blank if no error occurred.)
`SrcText`	Retrieves the text of the line where the error occurred.
`URL`	Identifies the filename or URL where the error took place. (Note that if a file contains an external DTD, this will point to the DTD, not the XML file that was originally retrieved.)

The `ParseError` object can give you detailed information about the nature of any load or validation error and should be used whenever possible to get information about the state of an error. For example, consider a situation where the file being loaded is not completely valid, such as when an opening tag is not matched by a closing tag, as in the following example of the XML document `StatusLog1.xml`:

```
<?xml version="1.0" ?>
<!-- StatusLog1.xml -->
<log>
    <message>
       <author>Kurt Cagle
       <msg>This is a short message</msg>
       <date>2000-01-12</date>
    </message>"
</log>
```

If you attempt to load this document, you will end up generating an error (`<author>` has no closing tag), and you can trap the error using the code in Listing 2.3.

Listing 2.3: The *GetXMLDoc* Function Checks the Incoming XML Stream and Displays an Alert Dialog Describing the Error if One Occurs. (*listing2-03.txt*)

```
Visual Basic:
Function GetXMLDoc(srcURL as String) as DOMDocument
  Dim xmlDoc as DOMdocument
  Dim errorMsg as String
  Set xmlDoc=new DOMDocument
  xmlDoc.load srcURL
  If xmlDoc.parseError.errorCode>0 then
    ErrorMsg="An Error occurred (Error "
    ErrorMsg=ErrorMsg+cstr(xmlDoc.parseError.errorCode)
    ErrorMsg=ErrorMsg+")"+vbCRLF
    ErrorMsg=ErrorMsg+ xmlDoc.parseError.reason+vbCRLF
    ErrorMsg=ErrorMsg+" at char"
    ErrorMsg=ErrorMsg"+cstr(xmlDoc.parseError.linePos)
   ErrorMsg=ErrorMsg+" of line "+cstr(xmlDoc.parseError.line)
   ErrorMsg=ErrorMsg+" in file "+xmlDoc.parseError.url+vbCRLF
   ErrorMsg=ErrorMsg+"Text of line:"+xmlDoc.parseError.srcText
   Msgbox ErrorMsg
   Set GetXMLDoc=Nothing
   Exit Function
End  if
 Set GetXMLDoc=xmlDoc
End Function

Dim ErrorDoc as DOMDocument
Set ErrorDoc=GetXMLDoc("StatusLog1.xml")

Visual Basic Script:
Function GetXMLDoc()
  Dim xmlDoc
  Dim errorMsg
  Set xmlDoc=createObject("Microsoft.XMLDOM")
  xmlDoc.load srcURL
  If xmlDoc.parseError.errorCode>0 then
     ErrorMsg="An Error occurred (Error "
       ErrorMsg=ErrorMsg+cstr(xmlDoc.parseError.errorCode)+")"+vbCRLF
     ErrorMsg=ErrorMsg+ xmlDoc.parseError.reason+vbCRLF
     ErrorMsg=ErrorMsg+" at char "+cstr(xmlDoc.parseError.linePos)
     ErrorMsg=ErrorMsg+" of line "+cstr(xmlDoc.parseError.line)
     ErrorMsg=ErrorMsg+" in file "+xmlDoc.parseError.url+vbCRLF
     ErrorMsg=ErrorMsg+"Text of line:"+xmlDoc.parseError.srcText
     Msgbox ErrorMsg
     Set GetXMLDoc=Nothing
```

```
      Exit Function
    End  if
    Set GetXMLDoc=xmlDoc
  End Function

  Dim ErrorDoc
  Set ErrorDoc=GetXMLDoc("StatusLog1.xml")
```

When an error occurs, an alert box will pop up, displaying the details of the error, and then returns the `DOMDocument` set to the value `Nothing`. Note that in some cases you may actually want the function to retrieve the error message as an XML document itself; this especially makes sense in client/server systems with the client transmitting data and expecting an XML structure as a return type from the server. This technique will be explored in much greater detail throughout the book.

Outputting XML Files

Just as there are two modes for inputting XML, either from a string or from an external resource, the XML DOM parser supports two modes for outputting XML as well: the `xml` property and the `save()` method.

The `xml` property "walks" the XML tree and produces a string representation of the XML. The parser follows this basic set of rules for determining the order that it uses to reconstruct the tree:

- The parser proceeds to a child before it processes a sibling.
- The parser returns a list of children in the order in which they were entered.
- Attributes are parsed before children and are appended to the current node.
- If `PreserveWhiteSpace` is false (the default), then the parser removes any superfluous white space (tabs, carriage returns, etc) before outputting the result. If the property is true, these things are retained upon output.
- Unicode is supported.
- Namespace declarations are added for the top-most node.

You will use the `xml` property in a number of different circumstances, most notably for producing output for ASP pages and for debugging your code, as demonstrated in the following example:

```
XMLDoc.load "http://www.XMLDevHandbook.com/resources/summary.xml"
Debug.print XMLDoc.xml
```

While the `xml` property corresponds to the `LoadXML` method, the `save()` method is, of course, the counterpart to the `load()` method. `save()`converts the internal XML representation into a string and then saves that string to the location specified.

However, `save()` has some limitations that `load()` doesn't. For starters, `save()` is limited in where it can save information; you must have Write permission for the directory in which you're saving the file, or Save will generate an error. Furthermore, you can't use `save()` to save files to an `HTTP:` or an `FTP:` location, although it is possible to use specific HTTP-based calls to save an XML file (just not by using Save).

The `ParseError` object only handles errors specifically relating to parsing the data structure, but the `save()` method generates errors (such as permission locks or providing a nonexistent directory path) that can be trapped through the normal language mechanism. For example, in Visual Basic you can catch the error codes through an `On Error` statement, as demonstrated in Listing 2.4.

Listing 2.4: The *SaveXML* Function Demonstrates One Technique for Saving Code to a File. (*listing2-04.txt*)

```
Function SaveXML()
   On Error Goto CannotSave
   XMLDoc.save "c:/invalidDirectory/myXMLFile.xml"
   On Error Goto 0
   Exit Function
CannotSave:
    Select Case Err.Number
        Case -2147024891
            Msgbox "File exists and is read only."
        Case -2147024893
            Msgbox "The System cannot find the path specified."
        Case Else
            Err.Raise
    End Select
End Function
```

TIP Domain boundaries are another problem that you can run into with both loading and saving. Typically, from within a Web page, you will find that you can't load XML files from directories outside of the domain that the page itself comes from. This is a security sandbox issue. As you can run across domains when working with server code (or within a VB application that's not bound by a Web page's context), the easiest solution to this problem is to load the other domain's XML code onto the server before referencing it on the client.

Scratching the Surface

The `DOMDocument` interface is fairly rich: there are some 60 methods or properties associated with it, although most of them are tied up with creating or testing elements, attributes, or similar components that make up the document. In this section, I introduced the basic component, but you'll see much more about the DOMDocument interface throughout the next several chapters.

5050While the DOMDocument interface lets you do quite a bit, its primary import is acting as a container for those same elements and attributes. In the next section, I take a more detailed look at how you can navigate through an XML structure and work with the basic components: nodes.

Working with Nodes

From the standpoint of the DOM, an XML Document is nothing more than a collection of *nodes*. A node is a pretty primitive object, and, in most cases, it is something that you will work with through classes that are derived from it, rather than directly manipulating nodes themselves.

The MSXML DOM defines a node as being an instance of the IXMLDOMNode class and supports the properties and methods described in Table 2.3. However, a node can also be described in simple terms as an object that:

- Can be contained by other nodes
- Can contain other nodes
- Exists in some ordered relationship to its sibling nodes
- Can, but doesn't have to, contain a value
- Has a text node made up of its own text along with any text that its children have
- Serves as the base class for most other XML entities

TABLE 2.3: Properties and Methods of the IXMLDOMNode Class

Property or Method	Description
AppendChild	Adds a child node to the current node after all other nodes in the childNodes collection.
Attributes	A collection of nodes that retain attribute information.
BaseName	The name of the node without any namespace qualifier.
ChildNodes	The collection of all non-attribute nodes belonging to the current node.
CloneNode	Duplicates the current node and possibly its descendants and returns that node as the result.
DataType	When used with an XML Schema, contains the data type of the node's typedValue.
Definition	When used with an XML Schema, returns the node in the schema that defines the characteristics of the current node.
FirstChild	Retrieves the first child node in the current node's ChildNodes collection.
HasChildNodes	A Boolean value that returns as true if the node has children, and is false otherwise.

TABLE 2.3: Properties and Methods of the IXMLDOMNode Class *(continued)*

Property or Method	Description
InsertBefore	Lets you insert a new node before an already-existing **childNode** in the current node's **ChildNodes** collection.
LastChild	The last child node in the current node's **ChildNodes** collection.
NamespaceURI	Identifies the XML Schema or DTD that defines the node's characteristics.
NextSibling	Returns the current node's next junior sibling node, or nothing if the current node is also the last node in the collection.
NodeName	The name of the node, although the exact meaning changes depending upon where the node is used.
NodeType	A numeric value that indexes the type of node used (element, attribute, etc.). (The **NodeTypes** are contained in Table 2.4.)
NodeTypedValue	Contains the text of the node converted into the type specified in **DataType**. If no schema is specified (or if a DTD is used), then this will simply return the text of the node as a string.
NodeTypeString	Returns the data type of the node's typed value as a string.
NodeValue	Returns the value of the node, if specified within a DTD. Typically, this property is not used with Schemas.
OwnerDocument	Passes a pointer to the **DOMDocument** object that contains the current node.
ParentNode	Returns the containing node of the current node. The root node has no parent node (i.e., <**node.parentNode** is **Nothing**>).
Parsed	Indicates that the current node has already been parsed upon downloading. (See the "Asynchronous XML and Events," section later in this chapter).
Prefix	Is the namespace designation for the particular node. If no namespace has been declared, this is blank.
PreviousSibling	Is the next senior node in the current node's family or is **Nothing** if the node is the first node.
RemoveChild	Removes the indicated child from the current node's **childNode** list.
ReplaceChild	Replaces one child node with another.
SelectNodes	Lets you select a given collection of nodes by matching a specific criterion (heavily covered in Chapter 3).
SelectSingleNode	Lets you select one node from a collection of nodes by matching a specific criterion (heavily covered in Chapter 3).
Specified	Indicates whether a definition has been specified for this particular node in the DTD or schema.
Text	Contains the text (i.e., non-tagged) information associated with the current node.
TransformNode	Applies an XSL filter to an XML document to produce a text stream.
TransformNodeToObject	Applies an XSL filter to an XML document to produce another XML document.
Xml	Returns the XML representation of the current node and all its children.

Navigation 101

At the node level, navigating an XML document can be likened to tracing a family tree from some distant great-great grandparent to yourself. A node can have children, which can have children in turn. A node can also have siblings, which share the same parent but have a distinct birth order. Finally, all nodes except the root node also have a parent node.

The terminology used for node-level navigation follows this family metaphor. Consider the XML structure given (in part) in Listing 2.5.

Listing 2.5: Part of the *Resume.xml* File

```
<?xml version="1.0"?>
<!-- Found in file Code/Chapter2/Resume.xml on the CD -->
<resume>
   <header>
      <resumeOf>
         <firstName>Kurt</firstName>
         <lastName>Cagle</lastName>
         <middleInitial>A</middleInitial>
      </resumeOf>
      <address>
         <city>Olympia</city>
         <state>Washington</state>
      </address>
   </header>
   <skills>
      <programming>
         <language>
            <title>Visual Basic</title>
            <proficiency>Expert</proficiency>
            <years>8</years>
         </language>
         <architecture>
            <title>Client/Server Programming</title>
            <proficiency>Expert</proficiency>
            <years>4</years>
         </architecture>
      <language>
            <title>Java</title>
            <proficiency>Intermediate</proficiency>
            <years>3</years>
         </language>
         <application>
            <title>Macromedia Director</title>
            <proficiency>Expert</proficiency>
            <years>9</years>
```

```
            </application>
            <language>
               <title>JavaScript</title>
               <proficiency>Expert</proficiency>
               <years>5</years>
            </language>
         </programming>
         <!-- There's obviously much more -->
      </skills>
         <!-- More categories here, too -->
   </resume>
```

In the `<skills>` section, take a look at the second `<language>` node, associated with Java. This node is well placed to demonstrate all of the navigational properties and methods of the node class. From most nodes, you can navigate to the previous or next node using either the `PreviousSibling` or the `NextSibling` property, while the `parentNode` will return the parent of the current node. The `childNodes()` property, in turn, returns a collection of all of the children (both elements and other XML objects, such as text nodes, though not attributes) and is zero based. If a node doesn't have a corresponding sibling, parent, or child, then the associated properties return a value of `Nothing`.

Listing 2.6 illustrates what elements are retrieved with each of these properties, working on the second `<language>` node in the `<skills>` section of the resume document.

Listing 2.6: Sample Code that Demonstrates How You Can Navigate from One Node to the Next Using the XML DOM *(listing2-06.txt)*

```
Dim JavaNode as IXMLDOMNode
' Retrieve the 2nd <language> node, we don't care how
Set JavaNode=GetJavaLanguageNode()
Debug.Print JavaNode.parentNode.nodeName
"programming"
Debug.Print JavaNode.previousSibling.nodeName
"architecture"
Debug.Print JavaNode.nextSibling.nodeName
"application"
Debug.Print JavaNode.firstChild.nodeName
"title"
Debug.Print JavaNode.lastChild.nodeName
"years"
Debug.Print JavaNode.childNodes(1).nodeName
"proficiency"
 ' Note childNodes is a 0 based array.
Debug.Print JavaNode.hasChildNodes
True
Debug.Print JavaNode.childNodes.length
```

Most of these are self evident, although it is worth stressing that the `childNodes` array, which contains the children of the current node, is a zero-based array: `childNodes(0)` points to the first child, `childNodes(1)` to the second child, and so forth.

Technically speaking, `childNodes` is not a formal array. In fact, it is a structure exclusive to the XML DOM called a *node list*. Node lists are the workhorses of XML Navigation, and they play an especially big part when it comes to XML's integration with XSL. Each entry within a node list is a node—specifically a node of the `IXMLDOMNode` type (this distinction becomes important with elements, covered in the next section)—although you can think of a node list as being a collection of pointers to nodes. One implication of this is that a node list doesn't have to consist of nodes that are all children of the same parent.

One of the advantages of working with a node list is that you can enumerate over the list, just as you would with a collection or a variant array. For example, to enumerate over all of the programming skill types in the preceding resume, you could use the `OutputSkills` function shown in Listing 2.7.

Listing 2.7: The *OutputSkills* Function Demonstrates How DOM Can Be Used to Create Output from an XML File. (*listing2-07.txt*)

```
Function OuputSkills()\

Visual Basic:
   Dim xmlDoc as DOMDocument
   Dim progNode as IXMLDOMNode
   Dim skillNode as IXMLDOMNode
   Dim titleNode as IXMLDOMNode
   Dim nodeList as IXMLDOMNodeList
   Dim buffer as String
   Set xmlDoc=new DOMDocument

VBScript:
   Dim xmlDoc
   Dim progNode
   Dim skillNode
   Dim titleNode
   Dim nodeList
   Dim buffer
   Set xmlDoc=createObject("Microsoft.XMLDOM")

   XmlDoc.load "resume.xml"
   buffer="<ul>"+vbCRLF
   Set progNode=xmlDoc.documentElement.childNodes(1)._
   childNodes(0)
   for each skillNode in progNode.childNodes
```

```
        buffer=buffer+"<li><b>"+
          strConv(skillNode.nodeName,vbProperCase)+".</b>"
        set titleNode=skillNode.childNodes(0)
        buffer=buffer+"titleNode.text+"</li>"+vbCRLF
   next
   buffer=buffer+"</ul>"+vbCRLF
   OutputSkills=buffer
End Function

Debug.Print OutputSkills()
<ul>
<li><b>Language.</b>Visual Basic</li>
<li><b>Architecture.</b>Client/Server Programming</li>
<li><b>Language.</b>Java</li>
<li><b>Application.</b>Macromedia Director</li>
<li><b>Language.</b>JavaScript</li>
</ul>
```

The output format here is HTML, which renders as:

- **Language.**Visual Basic
- **Architecture.**Client/Server Programming
- **Language.**Java
- **Application.**Macromedia Director
- **Language.**JavaScript

A few things should become clear after studying the exampled script—perhaps most significantly that referencing nodes by their numeric position within the XML document is guaranteed to bring all sorts of headaches, is nearly unreadable, and seems tailor-made for a better solution. (Don't worry, I'll get to that.)

Beyond that, however, the one thing that stands out is how adding enumeration to the XML structure adds considerably to what can be done with the program. The statement

```
for each skillNode in progNode.childNodes
```

effectively iterates through each of the program node's children and lets you manipulate the subelements (through the `nodeName` and `text` properties). To a certain extent, almost all XML programming is based on either searching for a given node or iterating through a selection of nodes.

NOTE I've also surreptitiously dropped the `<documentElement>` node into the example. This property of the `DOMDocument` always points to the root element of the document.

Getting Nodes by Name

Using indexed numbers to retrieve a given node in an XML tree will usually lead to disaster. XML documents change, and if a node is added or removed, that will affect the order of any subsequent node adversely. As a consequence, it makes sense to be able to retrieve elements by their tag name.

Microsoft's XML parser has a very powerful engine, based upon the W3C's XPath specifications (which they co-wrote), for getting nearly any node or possible collection of nodes from an XML tree. This engine underlies all three of the commands that you can use to retrieve specific nodes: `getElementsByTagName`, `selectNodes`, and `selectSingleNode`.

`GetElementsByTagName()` is a method belonging to the `DOMDocument` interface and, as such, can only be called at the document level. It works by passing the name of the tag you want to retrieve and returning a node list of all of the tags that match that name. For example, consider the resume sample again, presented in Listing 2.8.

Listing 2.8: The *Resume.xml* file, Demonstrating the Use of *getElementsByTagName* (*listing2-08.txt*)

```
<resume>
   <header>
      <resumeOf>
         <firstName>Kurt</firstName>
         <lastName>Cagle</lastName>
         <middleInitial>A</middleInitial>
      </resumeOf>
      <homeAddress>
         <city>Olympia</city>
         <state>Washington</state>
      </address>
      <mailingAddress>
         <city>Lacey</city>
         <state>Washington</state>
      </address>
   </header>
   <skills>
      <programming>
         <language>
            <title>Visual Basic</title>
            <proficiency>Expert</proficiency>
            <years>8</years>
         </language>
         <architecture>
            <title>Client/Server Programming</title>
            <proficiency>Expert</proficiency>
            <years>4</years>
```

```
            </architecture>
            <language>
               <title>Java</title>
               <proficiency>Intermediate</proficiency>
               <years>3</years>
            </language>
            <application>
               <title>Macromedia Director</title>
               <proficiency>Expert</proficiency>
               <years>9</years>
            </application>
            <language>
               <title>JavaScript</title>
               <proficiency>Expert</proficiency>
               <years>5</years>
            </language>
         </programming>
         <!-- There's obviously much more -->
      </skills>
         <!-- More categories here, too -->
   </resume>
```

If you wanted to get the last name of the resume's owner, you would call `GetElementsBy-Tagname()` with the name `lastName` as a parameter, as demonstrated in the following example:

```
Dim resumeDoc as DOMDocument
Dim nodeList as IXMLDOMNodeList

Set resumeDoc=new DOMDocument
ResumeDoc.load "resume.xml"
Set nodeList=resumeDoc.getElementsByTagname("lastName")
```

Note that this function will always return a node list rather than a single node. This means that in order for you to access the node (if it is a singleton) you still need to reference the first element in the node list array:

```
Debug.Print_
   resumeDoc.getElementsByTagName("lastName")(0).text
"Cagle"
```

You can also qualify the element names somewhat. For example, if you wanted to get the city from the above resume, `getElementsByTagName` would actually return two nodes, one for the home address, the other for the mailing address. However, you can specify that you want the home address city by pre-pending the parent node to the existing node:

```
Debug.Print
resumeDoc.getElementsByTagName"homeAddress/city")(0).text
"Lacey"
```

Additionally, you can use the wildcard character to retrieve the collection of all nodes, which you can similarly qualify. For example,

```
Set nodelist=resumeDoc.getElementsByTagName("*")
```

retrieves all of the nodes in the document, while

```
Set nodelist=_
   resumeDoc.getElementsByTagName("programming/*")
```

retrieves all of the immediate children of the `<programming>` node (the five `<language>` `<architecture>` `<language>` `<application>` and `<language>` nodes, respectively). Similarly,

```
Set nodelist=_
resumeDoc.getElementsByTagName("programming/*/title")
```

will retrieve the title nodes of each of these children.

One problem is that the `getElementsByTagName` limits its own utility somewhat. All searches start from the top of the XML tree. Thus, if you have an existing node and you want to retrieve specific child nodes of that node, you have to have an exclusive path to that node before you can perform any query.

The `selectNodes` function is designed to solve that problem. It works at the node level, not the document level, and it designates the current node as the context for the search. In other words, `selectNodes` acts (more or less) like `getElementsByTagName`, with the assumption that the current node is the root node.

To simplify it even more, a singular version called `selectSingleNode` also exists; this returns the first node that satisfies the search criterion, both of which are more or less the same for either function.

You can see how these functions work well together by rewriting the `OutputSkills()` function to take advantage of the three functions demonstrated in Listing 2.9.

Listing 2.9: The *OutputSkills* Function, Rewritten to Use *selectNodes*, *selectSingleNode*, and *getElementsByTagname* (*listing2-09.txt*)

```
Function OuputSkills ()
   Dim xmlDoc as DOMDocument
   Dim skillNode as IXMLDOMNode
   Dim titleNode as IXMLDOMNode
   Dim buffer as String

   XmlDoc.load "resume.xml"
   buffer="<ul>"+vbCRLF
   for each skillNode in
      xmlDoc.getElementsByTagName("programming/*")
```

```
        buffer=buffer+"<li><b>"+_
          strConv(skillNode.nodeName,vbPro    perCase)+".</b>"
        set titleNode=skillNode.selectSingleNode("title")
        buffer=buffer+"titleNode.text+"</li>"+vbCRLF
    next
    buffer=buffer+"</ul>"+vbCRLF
    OutputSkills=buffer
End Function
```

The structure that the program works on becomes much more obvious, and you don't need to worry about what happens if the element positions are changed.

TIP Of the two, `selectNodes` is far more powerful than `getElementsByTagName`. With `selectNodes`, you can perform very detailed and selective searches that will cause errors in the other function. Much of Chapter 3, "Extracting Information with XSL Pattern and XPath," is devoted to working with `selectNodes`, so the material covered here is intentionally cursory.

Node Types

The list of properties associated with a node can be a little daunting. In practice, however, you will likely end up using a dozen or so of the properties, especially as certain of the inherited node classes (such as the element node type) simplify some of the more cumbersome aspects of node navigation, creation, and assignment.

Not all nodes are created equal. While most nodes have the same underlying structure, an element node, which would correspond to a standard tag element in an XML structure, can contain both text and other nodes. An attribute can have text but no children, and a text node has no `nodeName` and, technically, can't contain other elements.

The XML DOM currently defines 13 distinct node types, as displayed in Table 2.4. It also defines a set of globally available constants that begin with `NODE_` (left-hand column in the table), which can be used in arguments to test or create new nodes of various types, and which can be queried with the `NodeType` property. The current version of the MSXML parser also lets you retrieve the type as a string via the `NodeTypeString` property (right-hand column).

TABLE 2.4: NodeType Constants and Their Values

`NodeType` **Constant Name**	`NodeType` **Value**	`NodeTypeString` **Name**
NODE_ATTRIBUTE	2	Attribute
NODE_CDATA_SECTION	4	CDATASection
NODE_COMMENT	8	Comment
NODE_DOCUMENT	9	Document
NODE_DOCUMENT_FRAGMENT	11	documentfragment

TABLE 2.4: NodeType Constants and Their Values *(continued)*

NodeType **Constant Name**	NodeType **Value**	NodeTypeString **Name**
NODE_DOCUMENT_TYPE	10	documenttype
NODE_ELEMENT	1	Element
NODE_ENTITY	6	Entity
NODE_ENTITY_REFERENCE	5	entityreference
NODE_INVALID	0	Invalid
NODE_NOTATION	12	Notation
NODE_PROCESSING_INSTRUCTION	7	processinginstruction
NODE_TEXT	3	Text

NOTE Note that the NodeType and NodeTypeString properties are not related to the data type of the text; they indicate whether a node is an element or an attribute, not whether the text it contains is a string or a Boolean value. This property is the dataType, and it is covered in Chapter 6, "XML Schema."

Creating, Adding, and Deleting Nodes

So far, the examples I've given have assumed that, somewhere, a preexisting XML document exists. However, there are numerous times when you want to be able to generate XML documents on the fly (or, at the very least, to add or delete specific nodes from the XML tree). The XML parser provides a sophisticated collection of routines dedicated precisely to this purpose.

A node cannot explicitly create another node. Instead, it has to rely on the document object to create the node for it. Fortunately, one of the properties common to all nodes is ownerDocument, which returns a reference to the document that contains the node.

Once a reference to the document is at hand, the document can call createNode to instantiate a new node based upon the node type, as demonstrated in the following example:

```
xmldoc.createNode(type,name as String,_
   namespaceURI as string) as IXMLDOMNode
```

CreateNode returns a reference to the newly created node. It is especially worth noting at this point that the object just created belongs to the XML document but has not yet been placed *within* the XML document. *This distinction is important.* Essentially, you have created an object but haven't yet specified where the object is to go. If you persist the XML as a string, the newly created node will disappear.

There are two ways of attaching the node: through the `appendChild` method or the `insertBefore` method of the prospective parent node. `AppendChild` will automatically add the node to the end of the child nodes for the given parent node, while `insertBefore` will, well, insert the node before a specified child node.

For example, let's say that you have an XML document that contains a message log (with `<log>` root node) and you want to add a new message entry to the log. The log file, `StatusLog2.xml`, already has one message entry:

```
<?xml version="1.0" ?>
<!-- StatusLog2.xml -->
<log>
   <message>
      <author>Kurt Cagle</author>
      <title>First Message</title>
      <date>2000-01-12</date>
      <body>This is a short message</body>
   </message>"
</log>
```

The routine in Listing 2.10 loads the log file in, creates a new message from passed arguments, and appends it to the XML log file.

Listing 2.10: *AddMessage1* Is a First-Cut Pass at Writing a Routine to Append a Message to an XML Message Log. (*listing2-10.txt*)

```
Visual Basic:
Function AddMessage1(logXML as DOMDocument,_
   Author as string, Title as String,_
   Body as String) as IXMLDOMNode
   Dim MsgNode as IXMLDOMNode
   Dim AuthorNode as IXMLDOMNode
   Dim TitleNode as IXMLDOMNode
   Dim DateNode as IXMLDOMNode
   Dim BodyNode as IXMLDOMNode
```

Replace the preceding header with the following:

```
VBScript:
'Function AddMessage1(logXML,Author,Title)
'   Dim MsgNode
'   Dim AuthorNode
'   Dim TitleNode
'   Dim DateNode
'   Dim BodyNode
```

```
        Set msgNode=logXML.createNode(_
        NODE_ELEMENT,"message","")
        LogXML.documentElement.appendChild msgNode
        Set AuthorNode=logXML.createNode(_
           NODE_ELEMENT,"author","")
        AuthorNode.text=Author
        MsgNode.appendChild AuthorNode
        Set TitleNode=logXML.createNode(_
           NODE_ELEMENT,"title","")
        TitleNode.text=Title
        MsgNode.appendChild TitleNode
        Set DateNode=logXML.createNode(_
           NODE_ELEMENT,"date","")
        DateNode.text=Today
        MsgNode.appendChild DateNode
        Set BodyNode=logXML.createNode(_
           NODE_ELEMENT,"body","")
        BodyNode.text=Body
        MsgNode.appendChild BodyNode
        Set AddMessage1=MsgNode
     End Function
```

This is a lot of work to add a fairly simple node, and you may have noticed that there seems to be a certain basic pattern to the code that should be easy to exploit. In general, the code creates a new element node, sets the text for the newly created node, and then appends the node to the prospective parent node. (Note that its not necessary to attach the node to the tree to set any of the node's properties.)

The XML DOM includes wrapper functions, including the expected `createElement` function, for creating specific types of nodes. For `createElement`, you simply pass the tag name of the element you want to create. The process of assigning an object's text can likewise be handled mechanically, with the implicit assumption that a blank string indicates that no text is passed. Finally, it makes sense to pass the parent node as an argument so that the newly created element gets hooked up automatically, as shown in Listing 2.11.

Listing 2.11: *AddElement* Is a General Worker Function that Will Create a New Element, Assign a String Object to It, and Append It to Its Parent Element. (*listing2-11.txt*)

```
Visual Basic:
Function AddElement(parentNode as IXMLDOMElement,_
   elementName as String,
   optional elementText as String = "") as IXMLDOMNode
   Dim newNode as IXMLDOMNode

VBScript:
Function AddElement(parentNode,elementName,elementText)
   Dim newNode
```

```
    Set newNode=parentNode.ownerDocument.createElement(_elementName)
    newNode.text=elementText
    parentNode.appendChild newNode
    set AddElement=newNode
End Function
```

With this function, you can rewrite the AddMessage function in a more simplified fashion, as AddMessage2, as shown in Listing 2.12.

Listing 2.12: *AddMessage2* Encapsulates Some of the Complexity of Creating Elements for the Message Log. (*listing2-12.txt*)

```
Visual Basic:
Function AddMessage2 (logXML as DOMDocument,_
    Author as string, Title as String, Body as String)_
    as IXMLDOMNode
     Dim MsgNode as IXMLDOMNode

VBScript:
Function AddMessage2 (logXML,Author,Title,Body)_
    Dim MsgNode

    Set MsgNode=AddElement(logXML.documentElement,"message","")
    AddElement msgNode,"author",Author
    AddElement msgNode,"title",Title
    AddElement msgNode,"date",Today
    AddElement msgNode,"body",Body
    Set AddMessage2=MsgNode
End Function
```

Of course, there may be times when you don't want the item added at the end of the list. For example, you may wish to have a stack that grows from top to bottom so that the newest messages are always the first encountered. The InsertBefore method handles this particular instance. Since a message list is frequently queued in descending time order, its easy to create an AddMessageInverted function so that the message element is always inserted first, as demonstrated in Listing 2.13.

Listing 2.13: *AddMessageInverted* Enters Messages at the Start of the List as They Are Entered. (*listing2-13.txt*)

```
Visual Basic:
Function AddMessageInverted(logXML as DOMDocument,_
    Author as string, Title as String, Body as String)_
    as IXMLDOMNode
    Dim MsgNode as IXMLDOMNode
```

```
VBScript:
Function AddMessageInverted(logXML,Author,Title,Body) as Dim MsgNode

   'Create the message node
   Set msgNode=logXML.createElement("message")
   'If the log has other messages then
   If logXML.documentElement.length>0 then
      'Insert the message before the first one
   LogXML.documentElement.InsertBefore _
       MsgNode, logXML.documentElement.firstChild
   Else
      'Otherwise,place the message in the empty child set
      LogXML.documentElement.appendChild msgNode
   End If
   'This is identical to AddMessage2
   AddElement msgNode,"author",Author
   AddElement msgNode,"title",Title
   AddElement msgNode,"date",Today
   AddElement msgNode,"body",Body
   Set AddMessage2=MsgNode
End Function
```

Removing a node is simple as well. Using the `removeChild` method of the node object, you simply pass the reference of the child that you want to remove. When you remove a node, the node in question is disassociated from the tree but doesn't go away. (It's in essentially the same state as a node that has been created but not attached.) You also get a reference to that node and, by extension, all the node's children. `removeChild` is a handy way of moving a node from one place to another in the XML tree, as demonstrated with `MoveNode()` in Listing 2.14.

Listing 2.14: *MoveNode()* Removes a Node from One Point in the Tree and Attaches It to Another. (*listing2-14.txt*)

```
Function MoveNode(sourceNode,targetParentNode as _
   IXMLDOMNode,optional targetNode as IXMLDOMNode =_
      Nothing) as IXMLDOMNode
   Dim TempNode as IXMLDOMNode
   Function MoveNode(sourceNode,targetParentNode,_
   targetNode)
      Dim TempNode

      Set TempNode=sourceNode.parentNode.removeChild_
            (sourceNode)
      if targetNode is nothing then
          targetParentNode.appendChild TempNode
      else
          targetParentNode.insertBefore TempNode,targetNode
      end if
      set MoveNode=TempNode
End Function
```

Similarly, the ReplaceChild function will take a preexisting node and replace it with a different node. The ReplaceNode() function uses this capability to replace a given node with a new one, as shown in Listing 2.15.

Listing 2.15: *ReplaceNode()* Removes a Node and Replaces the Same Node with Another One. (*listing2-15.txt*)

```
Visual Basic:
Function ReplaceNode(oldNode as IXMLDOMNode, newNode as
   IXMLDOMnode) as IXMLDOMNode
   Dim tempNode as IXMLDOMNode

VBScript:
Function ReplaceNode(oldNode,newNode)
   Dim tempNode

Set tempNode=oldNode
   OldNode.parentNode.replaceChild oldNode,newNode
   Set ReplaceNode=tempNode
End function
```

Finally, to complete the suite of tools that look suspiciously like the Cut, Copy, and Paste functions of traditional editors, the XML DOM supports the ability to clone a node through the CloneNode() function. CloneNode() actually supports two modes: It includes a deep parameter that indicates whether the function clones just the node and its associated text (deep=false) or clones the node and all of its children, grandchildren, etc. (deep=true).

Examining Text in Nodes

Text in an XML document has always been somewhat problematic, because of XML's origins within SGML. To see why this is this case, it's instructive to look at a sample of XHTML, as in the following lines, which is HTML marked up using the XML grammar.

```
<body>
<h1>Examining Text</h1>
<p><span class="cap">T</span>ext in an XML document has always been somewhat
<i>problematic</i>.</p>
</body>
```

What should the text of the paragraph attribute be? If you make the call that the text should be only those characters that are in the scope of the paragraph but not of any subelements, then you end up with the following expression:

```
"ext in an XML document has always been somewhat"
```

On the other hand, if you declare that an element contains the text of all of its subelements, then the text of the body tag ends up looking like the following example:

```
"Examining Text Text in an XML document has always
been somewhat problematic"
```

Moreover, things can get a little sticky if you replace the text with a different string of text, since such an act would end up removing all of the subordinate tags as well. The solution that the MSXML parser has taken is to assume that the text of any given node is the text of all subordinate nodes, as well as any text that the node itself currently contains. This text is both read and write; if you change the text of a node, you remove not only the text in that node but also any subordinate tags. This is part of the reason that data-centric XML usually ends up with text found only at the leaf nodes of the tree, since changing the text may well wipe out any existing structure. For example, consider the following structure:

```
<programming>This section contains all of the
programming and related skills.
   <language>Visual Basic</language>
   <architecture>Client/Server Programming</architecture>
</programming>
```

Changing the text of the `<programming>` node removes the `<language>` and `<architecture>` nodes from the tree. On the other hand, by encapsulating the description in a separate tag (`<description>`, of course), you avoid the following problem:

```
<programming>
   <description>This section contains all of the
   programming and related skills.</description>
   <language>Visual Basic</language>
   <architecture>Client/Server Programming</architecture>
</programming>
```

With the following expression, you could easily change the description for the programming section of your resume:

```
Set progDescrNode=ResumeDoc.GetElementsByTagName(_
   "programming/description")(0)
buffer="This section contains programming and project "
buffer=buffer+"management skills."
progDescrNode.text=buffer
```

One mistake that new users to XML frequently make, however, is the idea that you can write XML into a text node and it will automatically convert into the appropriate XML nodes. This *doesn't* work. Instead, the parser will convert any symbol in the text that could be interpreted as being XML into its entity representation. For example, suppose you tried to add a tag into the following program description:

```
ProgDescrNode.text="This <I>section</I> contains
<b>programming</b> and <b>project management</b> skills."
```

```
Debug.Print ProgDescrNode.text
This &lt;I&gt;section&lt;/I&gt; contains
&lt;b&gt;programming&lt;/b&gt; and &lt;b&gt;
project management&lt;/b&gt; skills.
```

The left and right tag brackets are replaced by their entity representations (< and >, respectively). In some cases, this is desirable; if you are trying to display HTML code as output, for example, this implicit conversion can be a real boon to your programming. Unfortunately, when you are not looking for such a conversion, things get a little more complicated. In general, you will need to use a CDATA section (described in the next section) to store such information.

The text property for a node is actually a little deceptive. Internally, XML treats contiguous blocks of text that are not otherwise within a node as being text nodes. Such a node has the same structure as most other base node types, save that, internally, the node is assumed to have a nodeName of #text, and its value is given as the text contained within. If you look at the underlying structure of the node, you'll discover that an element node can actually contain a separate text node (of the IXMLDOMNodeText type) that holds the actual text data. Moreover, if you have a mixed text element (where text is interspersed with tags), then the node will contain one text node for each separate block of text. For example, consider the following XML structure:

```
<P>This is <I>highlighted</I> text
while this is <B>bold</B> text.</P>
```

The node structure internally can be described as:

```
Element:P
   Text:This is
   Element:I
       Text:highlighted
   EndElement:I
   Text:text while this is
   Element:B
       Text:bold
   EndElement:B
   Text
   :text.
EndElement:P
```

In other words, when you make a request for the text property of a given element, it iterates through all of the text nodes contained within the element and concatenates them into a single string, as demonstrated in the following example:

```
'pNode Contains the initial paragraph node
Debug.Print pNode.text
"This is highlighted text while this is bold text."
```

When you assign text, a similar process happens, although the parser protects itself by converting less-than, greater-than, ampersand, and other special XML symbols into their equivalent entity representation (for example, > becomes `<`). This structure makes mixed nodes possible, although retrieving the text from a node high up in the chain obviously takes considerably longer than retrieving node texts at their point of origin.

Note that because text nodes *are* nodes, they can be created with the `DOMDocument CreateNode` method as well as with the more specialized `CreateTextNode` method, as per the following example:

```
Dim textNode as IXMLDOMText
Set textNode=xmlDoc.createNode(NODE_TEXT,textStr,"")
' or
Set textNode=xmlDoc.createText(textStr)
' where textStr contains the text contents
```

TIP

The `nodeName` of a text node is the hashed name `#text`. If you are parsing the XML structure at the node level, you can test the node this way or by seeing if the `nodeType=3 (NODE_TEXT)`.

CDATA Nodes

There are times, however, when you may want to save XML like text without converting it into "safe" XML. A prime example of this is with the use of embedded HTML blocks. Unless you use the fairly strict variant XHTML, HTML from versions 4.*x* and earlier are not generally XML compliant. For example, if you wanted to save the following HTML code within an XML block, you would find that the parser complains that the `img` tag is not closed.

```
<skill>
   <name>Visual Basic</name>
   <htmlText>
   <div>
      <img src="visualBasic.jpg">
   </div>
   </htmlText>
</skill>
```

Older parsers (Netscape 3 and older, in particular), however, will actually crash if you pass a string that looks like `<img src = "visualBasic.jpg"/>`, with the terminating slash. Converting it into safe XML doesn't help, however, as it will only serve to place the contents of the HTML page up as a code listing.

The only way around this conundrum is to make use of CDATA sections. CDATA can be thought of as "escaped" text; it is explicitly protected from being parsed. CDATA sections always start with the somewhat-cumbersome `<![CDATA[` notation and terminate with the

]]> notation. Thus, the HTML could be safely protected in the preceding sample by enclosing it in a CDATA section, as the following example demonstrates:

```
<skill>
    <name>Visual Basic</name>
    <htmlText><![CDATA[
    <div>
        <img src="visualBasic.jpg">
    </div>]]>
    </htmlText>
</skill>
```

CDATA sections preserve white space as well as XML special characters, so using CDATA makes sense when you want to be able to save script text within an XML document, as in the following example:

```
<resume>
     <script language="VBScript"><![CDATA[
          Function IsNegative(text)
               IsNegative=false
               If isNumeric(text) then
                    If clng(text)<0 then
                         IsNegative=true
                    End if
               End if
          End function
     ]]></script>
</resume>
```

Here, even if line breaks weren't important (they are in VBScript, so this script would be in trouble regardless), the `cLng(text)<0` test would end up generating an error because the less-than sign (<) would automatically be interpreted as being the start of an XML tag. With the CDATA section in place, this won't happen.

Reading a CDATA section is easy; it's retrieved using the `text` property. Thus, if you wanted to get the preceding script (most likely to pass to a scripting object), all you'd need to do is code the following:

```
Dim scriptNode=resumeDoc.getElementsByName("script")(0)
     Debug.Print scriptNode.text
      Function IsNegative(text)
               IsNegative=false
               If isNumeric(text) then
                    If clng(text)<0 then
                         IsNegative=true
                    End if
               End if
          End function
```

Writing CDATA sections is a little more complicated, however. Just as there is a text node type, there is also a CDATA node type. Indeed, when the `text` property iterates through an element's descendants for text nodes, it also scoops up CDATA sections as it passes through. Creating a CDATA section is also similar, as the following example demonstrates:

```
Dim cdataNode As IXMLDOMCDATASection
Set
cdataNode=xmlDoc.createNode(NODE_CDATA_SECTION,textStr,"")
' or
Set textNode= xmlDoc.createCDATASection(textStr)
' where textStr contains the text contents
```

TIP

The `nodeName` of a `cdata section` node is the hashed name `#cdata-section`. If you are parsing the XML structure at the node level, you can test the node this way or by seeing if the `nodeType=4 (NODE_CDATA_SECTION)`.

I have found, especially with complex data such as scripts, that when I want to add an element I also frequently want to pass a CDATA section rather than text to the element. The final version of `AddElement()` gives you the option of specifying that the text passed is treated as a CDATA section rather than as normal text, as demonstrated in Listing 2.16.

Listing 2.16: Final Visual Basic Code for the *AddElement()* Function (*listing2-16.txt*)

```
Visual Basic:
Function AddElement(parentNode as IXMLDOMElement,_
   elementName as String,_
   optional elementText as String = ""_
   optional IsCDATASection as Boolean = False) as IXMLDOMNode
   Dim newNode as IXMLDOMNode

VBScript:
Function AddElement(parentNode,_
   elementName,_
   elementText
   IsCDATASection)
   Dim newNode

   Set newNode=parentNode.ownerDocument.createElement(_
          elementName)
   if IsCDATASection then
      Dim cdataNode as IXMLDOMCDATASection
      Set cdataNode=parentNode.ownerDocument._
       createElement(elementText)
                  newNode.appendChild cdataNode
     else
```

```
        newNode.text=elementText
    end if
    parentNode.appendChild newNode
    set AddElement=newNode
End Function
```

Understanding Attributes

Elements, text nodes, and CDATA sections provide one way of describing data within an XML document. However, XML supplies another way to describe information: the *attribute node*. *Attributes* are name/value pairs that describe elements in some fashion and are indicated by tokens with associated strings.

The relationship between elements and attributes is a complex, sometimes-contentious one. Most people are familiar with attributes through their appearance within HTML, where they essentially play the role of modifiers to the HTML objects. For example, the `image` tag in HTML has a complex set of attributes, as even the following simple example demonstrates:

```
<IMG src="myImage.jpg" lowsrc="myImageLowRes.jpg" width=100 height=80 align=left>
```

Here, `src`, `lowsrc`, `width`, `height`, and `align` are all attribute names, with their elements indicated by either quoted text or text surrounded by an = sign on one side and a space or close bracket on the other.

XML attributes are similar, although not quite identical. Principally, an XML attribute *will always be quoted*. Always. While this is generally not a problem (especially using the DOM), it does mean that it is a difficult process to convert an HTML document created by many commercial applications straight into XML, although this isn't necessarily a good idea anyway.

The W3C recommendation on XML also makes a few basic recommendations about attributes, namely that they:

- Cannot appear more than once in any given tag.
- Should not include explicit line breaks.
- Should not include XML-specific characters, such as < or >, unless the character is escaped as an entity (i.e., `<` or `>`).
- Should generally be limited in length.
- Should not include the ampersand character explicitly; instead, it too should be escaped as `&`.

With the exception of the first point, however, the current Microsoft XML parser *ignores* all of these recommendations. You can include line-break and carriage-return characters, you can include < and >, and you can have attributes holding text up to 64k characters in length. If you know that the XML that you're working with will only be used within the context of the current Microsoft parser, then you can ignore these recommendations; however, as general coding practice, you're better off following them.

Attributes versus Elements

If you want to start a religious war at an XML seminar, ask the simple question "When should attributes be used?" Things will get ugly quickly, I assure you. There are as many different views about where attributes should be used as there are XML practitioners.

In general, though, the prevailing views seem to fall into the following camps:

Attributes Are Unnecessary In this approach, attributes simply are not used at all. This approach works well in a data-centric setting where every element has a specific data type, but it is less well-suited for situations where the content is mixed.

Attributes Provide Document-Wide Characteristics Sometimes attributes work well in characterizing metadata about a document. For example, an invoice element may include a *title* attribute that can be used for creating a more meaningful description for a property (*Account Number* instead of *AcctNum*).

Attributes Contain Element Properties This is essentially the approach that both XHTML and Internet Explorer 5 (IE5) behaviors take, where each element tag describes an object and the attributes provide the properties to that object. The image tag described in the previous section demonstrates this model of attribute.

Attributes Provide Object Definition over Element Metadata This is the approach that schemas (or the Reduced Data Set that Microsoft employs) use to describe XML structure. In this case, the element information is extremely broad (e.g., `<Element name="info">`), while the attributes serve to make the element specific to the task at hand. This approach works best as metadata structures.

Attributes Identify Relations between Disconnected Information In this case, a given element may contain child elements as properties that describe the element, but contain one or more identifiers that either uniquely name that element or create a relationship between the element and another uniquely named element.

So which approach should you use when designing your own data structures? Easy: whatever works. All five approaches work to solve one problem or another, and once you become proficient with XSL you may find yourself transforming your data from one attribute type to a different one as the need arises. Don't get locked into thinking that only one type of XML structure works in every case; that will make you lose the incredible flexibility that is XML's greatest strength.

TIP This point will be stressed repeatedly throughout this book: *XML is malleable.* Standards are coming into existence that provide a common language for transmitting data between consumers, but, once at your machine, you should be willing to alter the incoming data into a format that works best for your own application.

TIP The last approach, where elements contain child elements but unique identifier attributes, works especially well when working with XML as an object description language, and will generally be the format that is used in this book.

Attributes and Nodes

With respect to the internal representation of an XML document, attributes have a fairly privileged status. In essence, a node actually maintains two sets of nodes: a set pointing to its attributes, and a second set pointing to everything else (other elements, text nodes, CDATA sections, comments—the works).

A node accesses its attributes through the `attributes` collection, which is an object of the `IXMLDOMNamedNodeMap` type. While this may sound a little forbidding, in fact, such a structure is pretty simple and is detailed in Table 2.5.

TABLE 2.5: Properties and Methods of the `IXMLDOMNamedNodeMap` Interface

Property or Method	Description
`GetNamedItem(name as String)`	Returns the node corresponding to the given name
`GetQualifiedItem(baseName as String,namespaceURI as String)`	Returns the node corresponding to the given name and namespace
`Item(index as Long)`	Returns the indexed node
`Length`	Returns the number of items in the map
`NextNode`	Returns the next node in an iteration
`RemoveNamedItem(name as String)`	Removes the node specified by the given name
`RemoveQualifiedItem(baseName as String,namespaceURL as String)`	Removes the node specified by the given name and namespace
`Reset()`	Sets the iterator back to the first item
`SetNamedItem(newItem as IXMLDOMNode)`	Appends a node to the current map

All right. So maybe it's not quite as simple as all that. In essence, when you create an attribute using the attributes object, you are working with node objects that are stored in the map. For example, going back to the message log discussed earlier in this chapter, the sample could be modified, as in Listing 2.17, so that each element appearing on output would contain a caption attribute. Furthermore, it would be handy to identify each message uniquely, so this particular element should have an `id` attribute.

Listing 2.17: *StatusLog3.xml,* Which Now Includes a Set of Standard Attributes

```
<?xml version="1.0" ?>
<!-StatusLog3.xml -->
<log>
   <message id="msg_1">
      <author caption="Message From">Kurt Cagle</author>
      <title caption="Title">First Message</title>
      <date caption="Date Submitted">2000-01-12</date>
      <body caption="Message Body">This is a short message</body>
   </message>
   <message id="msg_2">
      <author caption="Message From">Fred Schwartz</author>
      <title caption="Title">I need more information</title>
      <date caption="Date Submitted">2000-01-13</date>
      <body caption="Message Body">I need to find out more about XML. What can
you tell me?</body>
   </message>
</log>
```

In order to retrieve the caption from the second author field, you could use the `GetNamed-Item()` function, as in the following example:

```
Dim logXML as DOMDocument
Dim authElNode as IXMLDOMNode
Dim captionNode as IXMLDOMNode

Set logXML=new DOMDocument
LogXML.load "StatusLog3.xml"
Set authElNode=logXML.getElementsByTagName("message/author")(1)
Set captionNode=authElNode.attributes._    getNamedItem("caption")
Debug.Print captionNode.nodeName
caption
Debug.Print captionNode.text
Message From
```

`GetNamedItem()` retrieves the node that matches that attribute name. Once you have this, you can set or get its value through the `text` property or can retrieve the name of the attribute by using the `nodeName` property.

NOTE Remember here that `GetNamedItem()` doesn't retrieve a text string; it returns a node instead that you can query to retrieve or set the attribute value.

The `GetQualifiedItem()` function works in the same manner but lets you specify the namespace of the attribute in addition to the node's base name. (Namespaces are covered at the end of this chapter.)

SetNamedItem() works in a similar fashion. You create a node with the appropriate attribute name and text and then use SetNamedItem() to add this particular item to the map or attribute list. For example, to add an ID to a new message node in the messagelog XML, you could use the function by creating an attribute node (using either CreateNode() or CreateAttribute()—the latter functioning exactly as you would expect) and appending it to the newly created message node, as the following example demonstrates:

```
'Continuing from last example
dim msgNode as IXMLDOMNode
dim attrNode as IXMLDOMNode
set msgNode=logXML.createElement("message")
logXML.documentElement.appendChild msgNode
set attrNode=logXML.createAttribute("id")
attrNode.text="msg_3"
msgNode.attributes.setNamedItem attrNode
```

Similarly, you can remove the attribute using the RemoveNamedItem() method, or RemoveQualifiedItem() if you are removing an item that belongs to a different namespace:

```
MsgNode.attributes.removeNamedItem("id")
```

Perhaps the most significant method associated with the NamedNodeMap interface is the iterator, which actually lets you iterate through a set of attributes, touching each attribute node in turn. For example, to return the attributes associated with the HTML image object discussed previously, you could use the code in Listing 2.18. (Note that I've made the image object XML compliant.)

Listing 2.18: The *IterateAttributes* Function Retrieves Each Attribute from a Node and Converts It into a Name/Value Pair String. (*listing2-18.txt*)

```
' From Visual Basic
Function IterateAttributes(Node as IXMLDOMNode) as String
   Dim AttrNode as IXMLDOMNode
   Dim buffer as String

' From VBScript
Function IterateAttributes(Node)
   Dim AttrNode
   Dim buffer

   node.attributes.reset
   Set attrNode=Node.attributes.nextNode
   While not (attrNode is Nothing)
      buffer=buffer+attrNode.nodeName+"='"+_
         attrNode.text+"'"+vbCRLF
      Set attrNode=ImageNode.attributes.nextNode
```

```
    Wend
    IterateAttributes=buffer
  End Function

  ImageDoc.loadXML "<BODY><IMG src='myImage.jpg'_
     lowsrc='myImageLowRes.jpg' width='100' height='80'_ align='left'/></BODY>"
     Debug.Print IterateAttributes(_
  ImageDoc.getElementsByTagName("IMG")(0)
```

The iterator's `reset` statement moves the pointer for the `NamedNodeMap` collection to before the first node, while `nextNode` moves the pointer to the next item (or to the first item if applied immediately after `reset()`) until it runs out of items and returns the VB `Nothing` object. This notation is rather cumbersome in Visual Basic, although in Java or JavaScript it's considerably more compact, as the following example demonstrates:

```
Function IterateAttributesJS(Node){
Node.attributes.reset();
while (!(var attrNode=Node.attributes.nextNode)){
   buffer+=(attrNode.nodeName+"='"+attrNode.text+"'\n";
}
return buffer;
}
```

Because the notation is somewhat cumbersome in Visual Basic or VBScript, the iterator is usually used implicitly within a `for each` statement rather than using the enumerator format that Java employs. Use of the iterator in Visual Basic is demonstrated in the following example:

```
Visual Basic:
Function IterateAttributes (Node as IXMLDOMNode) as String
   Dim AttrNode as IXMLDOMNode
   Dim buffer as String

   For each attrNode in node.attributes
      buffer=buffer+attrNode.nodeName+"='"+_
        attrNode.text+"'"+vbCRLF
   Next
   IterateAttributes=buffer
End Function
```

TIP All of the XML collections can be iterated in this same fashion. The enumeration mechanism is typically hidden.

Using Attributes and Elements

The node mechanism is a clean, straightforward mechanism for working with attributes. Well, all right, that's a complete lie: The node mechanism for working with attributes is cumbersome, is complex, and is, in general, useless for working with attributes in most applications. It *is* worth understanding, however, to help you get a better idea of what happens under the hood within the XML object. Because of the special class that attributes employ, they are frequently faster than the equivalent elements.

Fortunately, in most cases, you don't need to work with this mechanism directly. The `IXMLDOMElement interface`, which represents elements within the object model, encapsulates the fairly complex attribute handling inside a few easy-to-use functions (see Table 2.6). Indeed, attribute handling is one of the few differences between the `IXMLDOMNode` and `IXMLDOMElement` interfaces.

TABLE 2.6: Attribute-Related Properties and Methods of the `IXMLDOMElement` Interface

Property or Method	Description
`attributes(index as long)`	Provides a reference to the attributes `NamedNodeMap`. Same as the node `attributes` collection
`getAttribute(name as string)`	Retrieves the value of the attribute as a string
`GetAttributeNode(name as String) as IXMLDOMAttribute`	Retrieves the named attribute as an attribute node
`RemoveAttribute(name as String)`	Removes the named attribute from the attribute list
`RemoveAttributeNode( DOMAttribute as IXMLDOMAttribute) as IXMLDOMAttribute`	Removes the specified node from the attribute list
`setAttribute(name as String,value)`	Sets the value of the named attribute (value is a variant)
`SetAttributeNode(DOMAttribute as IXMLDOMAttribute) as IXMLDOMAttribute`	Adds a node of the given name to the attribute list, or replaces the current node if a node of that name already exists

While you can do all of the same tasks that you can do with the node attribute properties and methods, the element's interface is considerably easier to use. For example, consider the following message log again:

```
<?xml version="1.0" ?>
<!-StatusLog3.xml -->
<log>
```

```
<message id="msg_1">
      <author caption="Message From">Kurt Cagle</author>
      <title caption="Title">First Message</title>
      <date caption="Date Submitted">2000-01-12</date>
      <body caption="Message Body">This is a short message</body>
   </message>
   <message id="msg_2">
      <author caption="Message From">Fred Schwartz</author>
      <title caption="Title">I need more information</title>
      <date caption="Date Submitted">2000-01-13</date>
      <body caption="Message Body">I need to find out more
about XML. What can you tell me?</body>
   </message>
</log>
```

In order to retrieve the caption from the second author field with the element attribute, you need to explicitly declare the node of the IXMLDOMElement type (instead of IXMLDOMNode), and then you can use getAttribute() to retrieve the text of the node, as in the following example:

```
Dim logXML as DOMDocument
Dim authElNode as IXMLDOMElement
Dim captionNode as IXMLDOMNode

Set logXML=new DOMDocument
LogXML.load "StatusLog3.xml"
Set authElNode=logXML.getElementsByTagName(_

      "message/author")(1)
Debug.Print authElNode.getAttribute("caption")
Message From
```

Setting it is just as straightforward, using the SetAttribute() method, as the following example demonstrates:

```
AuthElNode.setAttribute "caption","This is a message from "
Debug.Print authElNode.getAttribute("caption")
This is a message from
```

Removing a node works in the same way:

```
AuthElNode.removeAttribute "caption"
Debug.Print authElNode.getAttribute("caption") Is Nothing
True
```

The iterator for the element is the same as the iterator for the node since, in both cases, you query the attributes' NamedNodeMap collection. Thus, the code for iterating through an element's attribute collection is essentially the same as iterating through a node's attributes, as in the following example:

```
Visual Basic:
Function IterateAttributes (Node as IXMLDOMElement)
   as_ String
   Dim AttrNode as IXMLDOMAttribute
   Dim buffer as String

VBScript:
Function IterateAttributes (Node)
   Dim AttrNode
   Dim buffer

   For each attrNode in node.attributes
   buffer=buffer+attrNode.nodeName+"='"+_ attrNode.text+"'"+vbCRLF
   Next
   IterateAttributes=buffer
End Function
```

Changing Interfaces

If you work with attributes only sporadically, you may want to keep your variables declared as IXMLDOMNode. (This applies to Visual Basic only; in the scripting language, the specific type mappings are applied transparently.) When you need to work with attributes, you can then declare a variable of the IXMLDOMElement type and set the element variable to the node variable's value, as in the following example:

```
Visual Basic:
dim Node as IXMLDOMNode
dim Elmt as IXMLDOMElement
set Node=GetMyNode() ' This just retrieves a node from
     ' an unspecified location.
Set Elmt=Node ' This lets node use the attributes interface
Elmt.setAttribute "comment","This Rocks!"
```

This technique of mapping interfaces works because IXMLDOMElement derives from IXMLDOMNode. You can use a similar technique for getting at the other advanced XML interfaces, such as IXMLDOMComment or IXMLDOMAttribute.

Comments

There are a few other nodes that take on subordinate roles in XML, and while they generally don't have a huge impact on the way most XML gets processed, they can offer a few advantages to the programmer who knows what to do with them.

Comments exist as part of almost every computer language ever written, usually serving the dual role of identifying the purpose of specific pieces of code and removing certain pieces of code from normal execution. XML is no exception.

Unlike elements or attributes, comments aren't required to be within the body of an XML document. They can effectively be anywhere, with the sole exception being that they can't be the first line of text if the XML file contains an `xml` declaration (i.e., `<?xml version="1.0" ?>`). Beyond that, comments can go anywhere.

Comments begin with the sequence of characters `<!--` and end with the closing characters `-->`. Comments can contain anything (open or closing brackets, Unicode characters, even binary data), and, as a consequence, the only way that the parser knows that a comment has come to a close is when it encounters the `-->` characters. One of the most immediate implications of this is that you can't nest comments.

As with text nodes and CDATA sections, comments are stored internally through the use of comment nodes. As a consequence, you can actually associate a comment with a given node; it is a child of the node just as a text or a CDATA section would be. A comment node can be created using the document's `createNode` function or the more specialized `createComment` function, as the following example demonstrates:

```
Dim commentNode As IXMLDOMComment
Dim textStr
textStr="This is a comment."
Set commentNode=xmlDoc.createNode(NODE_COMMENT,textStr,"")
' or
Set commentNode= xmlDoc.createComment(textStr)
' where textStr contains the text contents
```

TIP The **nodeName** of a comment node is the hashed name **#comment**. If you are parsing the XML structure at the node level, you can test the node this way or by seeing if the **nodeType=8** (NODE_COMMENT).

Comments should generally not be used to store information that is immediately relevant to the data structure (other than documentation). One reason for this is that a number of XML parsers (though not the MSXML parser) will strip comments from the XML structure to reduce memory usage. If you do find that you need to store key information about the data (for example, code that may be specific to a given parser or application), then you should look at processing instructions (PIs) instead.

Processing Instructions

Processing instructions are an artifact of the older SGML specification, and they essentially contain information that may be exclusive to a given application or configuration. Processing instructions were originally designed for use with SGML documents, where they would typically contain information that was not really appropriate to the document but which was needed by the application hosting the document.

A number of vendors (for some reason, database vendors seem to be particularly keen on this) like to add PIs that can be used to retrieve XML data based upon SQL queries, as in the following example:

```
<?DatabaseCo-SQL SELECT * FROM MyDataBase
    WHERE sky='Blue'?>
```

When the document parses, the XML is retrieved and inserted into the place where the PI was found.

While this can certainly be useful, it also sets a troubling precedent by placing proprietary data into the structure that's not a part of the structure. Queries become more complicated, because only applications that know what to do with the PI can return results.

This is a personal opinion, but, in general, unless there isn't any way around it, avoid using processing instructions in favor of some other linking mechanism. They don't have much support in the DOM, and they tend to diminish rather than reinforce the object-oriented nature of XML. (In that context, I would liken processing instructions to global variables, which can also weaken OOP structures.)

There is, however, one important exception. While it is not strictly required for the MSXML parser, a fully well-formed XML document should always start out with an XML declaration, indicating the current version of XML in use along with such things as character set encoding, as in the following example:

```
<?xml version="1.0" encoding="UTF-8" ?>
```

The preceding declaration shows the basic structure of a processing instruction. A PI will always start with the characters `<?,` followed by the name used to reference the PI. After this, a PI can conceivably have anything, though the standard usage is to follow normal tag naming convention by having the information within the PI contained within attribute name/value pairs, as in the following line:

```
<?devbook system="Windows 2000"?>
```

Finally, a PI is terminated with a closing ?> character set, as shown in the preceding example.

WARNING The W3C explicitly reserves the right to use *xml* and *xml-* as names for processing instructions, as well as any case permutation of them (e.g, *XML, Xml,* and so forth). If you use a PI, start it with something other than these characters.

The attribute name/value pairs given here are conventional, but you should understand that the contents of a PI—essentially everything after the name—are a complete entity unto themselves. A PI is not parsed and is not considered text; in short, it's ideal for application-specific information.

For example, an XML application could store versioning information into a PI that would be ignored by the parser but would be accessible to a third-party program. If you were to build a product called `ResumeBuilder` that lets you edit résumés in XML, you could maintain the name of the application, who prepared the résumé, and when—storing this information in processing instructions, as in the following example:

```
<!-- resume.xml -->
<resume>
   <?devbook-preparedBy Kurt Cagle ?>
   <?devbook-datePrepared 3/Feb/2000?>
   <?devbook-application ResumeBuilder?>
   <resumeFor>Aleria Sherana</resumeFor>
   <!-- more resume material -->
</resume>
```

In order to retrieve these processing instructions, it turns out that you can take advantage of certain XPath properties with the `GetElementsByTagName()` or `SelectNodes()` functions, as the following example demonstrates. (The output of the `GetPI_Info` function is also included.)

```
Function GetPI_Info(xmlDoc as DOMDocument) as String
   Dim piNode as IXMLDOMProcessingInstruction
   Dim buffer as String
   buffer=""
   For each piNode in GetElementsByTagName("pi()")
      buffer=buffer+"["+piNode.nodeName+"]"+_
      piNode.text+vbCRLF
   Next
   GetPI_Info=buffer
End Function

Dim ResumeDoc as DOMDocument
ResumeDoc.load "resume.xml"
```

```
Debug.Print GetPI_Info(ResumeDoc)
   [devbook-preparedBy]Kurt Cagle
   [devbook-datePrepared]3/Feb/2000
   [devbook-application]ResumeBuilder
```

The `pi()` function returns a collection of all of the processing instructions contained within the document as processing instruction nodes, which, as you may have guessed, derive from `IXMLDOMNode`. The `nodeName` corresponds to the name of the PI, and the `text` is the text of the PI.

TIP There are similar query functions for elements (**`element()`**), attributes (**`attribute()`**), comments (**`comment()`**), and so forth. These are covered in Chapter 3, "Extracting Information with XSL Pattern and XPath."

You could use a similar arrangement to retrieve a specific processing instruction or to set the contents of one. The `pi()` function can take as a string argument the name of the node; if the element exists, then `getElementsByTagName()` will return a node list with one element. With this node, you can get or set the associated text value, as in Listing 2.19.

Listing 2.19: *GetPI* and *SetPI* Retrieve and Set Processing Instructions within the Passed XML Documents. (*listing2-19.txt*)

```
Visual Basic:
Function GetPI(xmlDoc as DOMDocument, piName as String) as String
   Dim piNode as IXMLDOMNode
   Set piNode=xmlDoc.getElementsByTagName(_
     "pi('"+piName+"')")_(0)
   GetPI=piNode.text
End Function
Function SetPI(xmlDoc as DOMDocument,_
   piName aString,piValue as Variant) as IXMLDomNode
   Dim piNode as IXMLDOMProcessingInstruction
   Set piNode=xmlDoc.getElementsByTagName(
   pi('"+piName+"')")_(0)
   if piNode is Nothing then
       set piNode=xmlDoc.documentElement._
    createProcessingInstruction(piName)
       xmlDoc.documentElement.appendChild piNode
   end if
   piNode.text=cstr(piValue)
Set SetPI=piNode
End Function
```

Asynchronous XML and Events

XML started out as a Web format, and it's still designed around the notion that data is being transferred from one machine or another through some form of Web protocol. When a computer loads in a file from a location on its hard drive, the access time can usually be measured in hundredths, or even thousandths, of a second—a period so small that it usually makes sense to retrieve the entire file at once.

However, on the Internet or a local intranet, file retrieval times (usually called *latency*) are often measured in seconds, minutes, or, in the case of some of today's mega-applications, hours. Any application that fails to take into account the basic latency of distributed systems will find that applications appear to hang while the files are downloaded. There are few things more aggravating than waiting an hour while your application pauses to download a file, only to retrieve a message at the end telling you that the file was unavailable.

Fortunately, the MSXML parser is well equipped to handle latency issues. You can tell the parser to load the file asynchronously (as mentioned in the "Loading Documents" section earlier in this chapter), by setting the document's `Async` property to true prior to downloading your document. In this section, I focus specifically on what setting that property does and how to handle asynchronous downloads.

When `async` is true, the nature of the document's `Load` method changes. Instead of halting the application until the load is complete, `load` creates a local input buffer and directs the socket to start filling the buffer in the background while the processing proceeds to the next statement in the code. The parser, in turn, raises the `onReadyStateChange` event every time a specific level of loading is accomplished and the `onDataAvailable` event when you can actually start using the data within the document. This function automatically sets another document property, the `ReadyState` property (as shown in Table 2.7), so that you, as the programmer, can perform an action when the event gets called.

TABLE 2.7: `ReadyState` Constants and Their Meanings

State	Numeric Value	Meaning
Not yet initialized	0	Document is not yet ready to load file.
Initialized	1	Document is ready to load file.
Loading	2	Document is beginning to load file.
Data available	3	The top-most levels of the document are populated and can be used for processing.
Complete	4	The document has been loaded and is ready to be accessed, or an error occurred and `parseError` has been notified.

As with any asynchronous event handling, the XML DOM's event handling works by creating an event handle to capture the `OnReadyStateChange` event whenever the parser fires it. This takes place in a couple of different ways, depending upon whether you are using Visual Basic or a scripting language.

For Visual Basic, the XML parser sources events; that is to say, when you declare an XML document, you can use the `WithEvents` tag in the declaration to indicate to VB that the XML object exposes events, as in the following example:

```
Dim WithEvents xmlDoc as DOMDocument
```

In the Visual Basic IDE, this will automatically add a new object (called `xmlDoc`) into the left-hand window of the scripting pane and expose the two events, `onReadyStateChange` and `onDataAvailable`, in the right-hand pane (see Figure 2.1).

WARNING Note that sourced declarations can only be placed at a module level (that is, declared as a variable in the General section of a form, module, or class), never within a procedure or method.

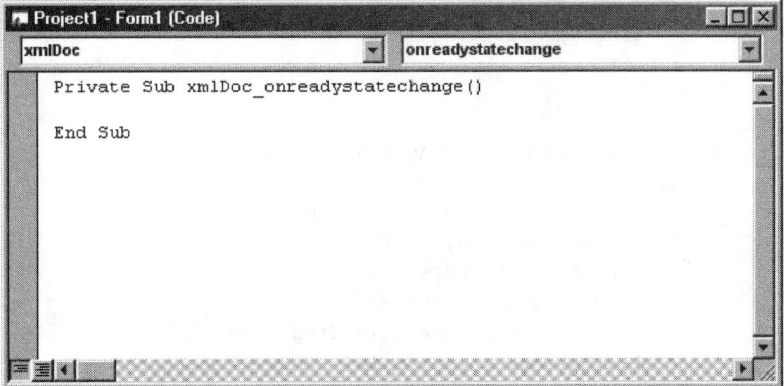

FIGURE 2.1 By sourcing your XML Document object in Visual Basic, using `WithEvents`, you can write event handlers for asynchronous transfers.

Writing asynchronous loading code requires a little more than writing synchronous code. For starters, the XML documents must be global to the project (though not necessarily public) rather than declared as a local variable. In addition to that, once you make the initial load call, you can't make any assumptions about the state of the document until either the `onDataAvailable` or the `onReadyStateChange` event occurs. For example, if you wanted to load an XML document whenever a user selects the File ➢ Open menu in a form, the code would look something like that in Listing 2.20.

Listing 2.20: The Following Code Demonstrates how an XML Document Could Be Loaded into Visual Basic through the Menu Bar. (*listing2-20.txt*)

```
Visual Basic:
Dim WithEvents XmlDoc as DOMDocument
Dim IsDocumentLoading as Boolean

Private Sub mnuFileOpen_Click()
   Dim URL as String
   URL=inputbox("Please Enter a URL","New _
     URL","http://www.xmldevhandbook.com/pointers.xml")
   If URL<>"" then
      ' Make the document asynchronous
      XmlDoc.async=True
      ' Load in the URL
      XmlDoc.Load URL
      ' Not much to do but set the cursor to a wait state
       Screen.mousePointer=vbHourglass
      ' Creating a local variable to keep track of state
      ' can help prevent actions that are dependent on the
      ' xml document.
      IsDocumentLoading=True
   End if
End Sub

Private Sub xmlDoc_onReadyStateChange()
   Dim ErrorMsg as String
   ' Check to see if operation has completed
   If xmlDoc.ReadyState=4 then
      ' restore the cursor
      Screen.mousePointer=vbDefault
      ' clear the document loading flag
      IsDocumentLoading=False
      ' If no error occurred
      If xmlDoc.ParseError.ErrorCode=0 then
         ' then use the xml for display purposes
         Display XMLDoc
      Else
         ' Display an error message in a pop-up
         Msgbox GetErrorMessage(xmlDoc)
      End if
   End if
End Sub

Function GetErrorMessage(xmlDoc as DOMDocument) as String
      Dim ErrorMsg as String
      ErrorMsg="An Error occurred (Error "
      ErrorMsg=ErrorMsg+cstr(xmlDoc.parseError.errorCode)+_
```

```
            ")"+vbCRLF
        ErrorMsg=ErrorMsg+ xmlDoc.parseError.reason+vbCRLF
        ErrorMsg=ErrorMsg+" at char"+_
            cstr(xmlDoc.parseError.linePos)
        ErrorMsg=ErrorMsg+" of line "+_
            cstr(xmlDoc.parseError.line)
        ErrorMsg=ErrorMsg+" in file"+_
            xmlDoc.parseError.url+vbCRLF
        ErrorMsg=ErrorMsg+"Text of line:"+__
            xmlDoc.parseError.srcText
        GetErrorMsg=ErrorMsg
End Function
```

In many (indeed, most) cases, you will not be concerned about the intermediate states of the load. Rather, you'll just want to know when the XML Document is available to start working with. The `onDataAvailable` event gets fired when the document is complete, and you can use it instead of the `onReadyStateChange` in most cases, as the following example demonstrates:

```
Private Sub xmlDoc_onDataAvailable()
   Dim ErrorMsg as String
   ' Check to see if operation has completed
   ' restore the cursor
   Screen.mousePointer=vbDefault
   ' If no error occurred
   If xmlDoc.ParseError.ErrorCode=0 then
      ' then use the xml for display purposes
      Display XMLDoc
   Else
      ' Display an error message in a pop-up
      Msgbox GetErrorMessage(xmlDoc)
   End if
End Sub
```

It's worth noting that the Microsoft XML parser is relatively fast and has been optimized as much as possible in the direction of speed. However, when coding, you should look at other possible opportunities to work in an asynchronous mode. In Chapters 6 and beyond, I'll explore a number of alternatives that you can consider.

Summary

Chapters on APIs are very seldom either fun to read or fun to write, but they do lay the foundation for everything to come. You may have noticed that, despite the complexity of the object model, the vast majority of activities involving the XML Document Object Model revolves around the following points:

- The `DOMDocument` object for loading documents, saving documents, and creating nodes

- The `IXMLDOMNode` (or its near-identical twin, `IXMLDOMElement`) for manipulating individual elements
- The `Attribute` methods for setting or retrieving specific attribute values
- The `ParseError` object and the two XML events, `onReadyStateChange` and `onDataAvailable`, for handling asynchronous XML calls

Manipulating the DOM programmatically is certainly important, and the requirements to do it won't go away any time soon. However, XML's strength lies in two related areas: the ability to locate a given piece of information within an XML structure and the ability to transform XML from one format into another. Direct DOM manipulation for either of these two requirements is fairly limited; manually navigating through an XML structure is slow and error prone, and transforming XML with the DOM can prove a challenge to tax the most hierarchically facile minds.

However, the Document Object Model is only one leg of the total XML picture. In Chapter 3, "Extracting Information with XSL Pattern and XPath," I will look at the other two legs: the search engine functionality of XPath and the transformative capabilities of the Extensible Stylesheet Language, otherwise known as XSL.

CHAPTER 3

Extracting Information with XSL Pattern and XPath

- Choosing one's XPath and namespace
- Retrieving elements
- Understanding predicates
- Presenting advanced XSL pattern topics

XML is only as powerful as the ability to get information from it. On its own, the XML DOM, while a useful programming tool, doesn't really have a very efficient way to get at data inside an XML tree. However, through the use of three functions that were discussed in the previous chapter (`getElementsFromTagName`, `selectNodes`, and `SelectSingleNode`), the DOM provides a gateway to a very powerful and sophisticated language for performing all kinds of searches on a document; this language is the *XML Path Language*, or *XPath*.

In this chapter, I'll show you ways that you can leverage XPath or its antecedent, XSL Pattern, to get at your data, to sort it, to filter it, and to combine it into totally unexpected forms. This will, in turn, form the foundation of XSL, which I cover in Chapter 4, "XSL Transform."

Currently, there are two parsers available from Microsoft, one released concurrently with Internet Explorer 5 in 1999 and a more recent (and more powerful) one that will likely be out around the time this book hits the stands. This chapter and Chapter 4 focus predominantly on the older parser, as it still has the largest market saturation, while Chapter 5, "The New XML Parser," looks at many of the more-advanced features of the parser being released in 2000.

The XPath Namespaces

Writing a book on emergent technology is always exciting. You're frequently dealing with standards that haven't yet been ironed out or components and applications whose underlying code may change tomorrow. XML, in particular, has been fraught with these difficulties because the metalanguages that are being developed around the XML standard are based more upon political considerations than they are upon technological innovations; gaining any kind of consensus for such things as XPath, XSL, XML Schemas, and the like has been a slow and arduous process.

When working with XPath or XSL (which heavily utilizes XPath) through the Microsoft parsers, you'll encounter parser components. `MSXML.DLL` was released with the Internet Explorer 5 browser and is based upon XML and XSL standards that were current as of December 10, 1998, conforming to a proposal that Microsoft had made to the W3C for an XML query language. (In the interim since that date, the working documents used for both XSL and XPath changed in a number of ways, largely for the better, and on November 16, 1999, the W3C released the final versions of both the XPath and XSL Transformations standards.)

The newer XPath standard provided a number of improvements to the older model, changing the focus from a DOM-based to a context-based way of thinking. Specifically, the November 1999 standards changed the parser in the following ways:

Support for Axes Axes describe one node's position relative to the current context. (See the "Context" section later in this chapter for more information on this topic.) The December 1998 implementation supported them implicitly, but you couldn't specify axes explicitly.

Redefined Node List Properties With the November 1999 implementation, you can specify the position of a node relative to the selected set of nodes, while the older parser only supports positions relative to the children of a parent node.

Simplified Predicate Expressions A predicate is a way of qualifying your search based upon element or attribute values and is perhaps one of the most powerful aspects of XPath. The November 1999 implementation cleaned up some of the more troublesome symbols and expanded the way that nodes can be referenced within predicates.

Enhanced String, Numeric, and Node Functions You can now search nodes based upon sub-string values; this is part of an overall improvement in the base set of functions that XPath provides, reducing its dependency on third-party scripting utilities.

While this is not, by any means, the entire list of improvements, it does cover the majority of those that relate to searching and retrieving node sets, the domain of XPath.

In order to differentiate between the two versions, the XML 2.6 parser (the most recent revision) makes use of two distinct namespaces, which uniquely identify the versions in question. Therefore, it's worth taking a look at the purpose and scope of namespaces before proceeding into XPath itself.

Namespaces

One of the problems with XML that appeared early on relates to the communal nature of the language. If you wanted to use XML within an HTML setting (for example, through XHTML), you conceivably could decide to create a `<div>` tag that contains information about one of your company's divisions. (If you were a novice to HTML, you probably would not realize that a `<div>` is a fundamental building block of HTML and serves to encase a block of subordinate HTML code.)

Make this example even more intriguing by saying that when you use a `<div>` in your markup it automatically renders as an organization chart. (Exactly how this automatically renders is described in much more detail in Chapter 7, "XML and the Browser.") So you have one tag called `<div>` that describes two very different actions; in the vernacular of C++, you have what is called a *namespace collision*.

A *namespace* is one of those concepts that are fairly easy to describe in theory but are somewhat more complex in practice. Think of a namespace as the set of all *unique tokens* that are defined within the domain in question.

> **NOTE** This is worth reiterating: A namespace is the set of all unique tokens that are defined within the domain in question.

In the case of the two <div> tags, the namespaces themselves are quite distinct: the organization of a company versus the conceptual elements of a document. You can think of each of these as having its own separate language (like English and French are distinct languages), where most terms don't overlap. Specific words may exist in the languages that are identical in spelling but have very different meanings; they belong to different domains.

I can define two namespaces for the domains discussed in this example—let's say `org` for the organization chart and `html` for HTML rendering. I can then differentiate between the two domains by pre-pending the namespace to the tag, achieving the results described in the following list:

- <org:div> determines the division level of the organization; its action is to display the organization chart of all subordinate positions within the division.
- <html:div> determines the division block of a document. This is used to contain other blocks within a specific bounding rectangle.

WARNING The namespace prefixes `html`, `xml`, and `xsl` are all currently reserved by the W3C, and if you are writing well-formed XML, you should avoid using these namespace names.

Of course, providing distinctions between the two different uses of the token <div> is only half the battle. In order to do anything with these namespaces, the characteristics of the elements in the namespace need to be defined. This problem is a restatement of a common question that people had when XML was first proposed. XML is a remarkably effective means for describing namespaces; after all, what is an XML document but the abstraction of an object namespace? But, obviously, if you could define your own tags, how would a browser know what to do with the tags you made?

Namespaces are one solution to this problem. You create a namespace by adding the reserved namespace attribute `xmlns:namespace` to the top-level node that starts the namespace's domain. Then you assign a URI to those attributes that uniquely identify the namespace and perhaps contain additional schema or programmatic information. For example, you could create an organization namespace, as Listing 3.1 demonstrates.

Listing 3.1: Defining an Organizational Namespace (*Listing3.01.xml*)

```
<org:company xmlns:org="http://www.vbxml.com/cagle/org">
   <org:name>Acme Rocket Company</org:name>
   <org:manager>
      <org:name>Phil Schwarts</org:name>
      <org:title>Chief Executive Officer</org:title>
      <org:domain>Administration</org:domain>
   </org:manager>
   <org:div>
```

```
            <org:name>Finance</org:name>
            <org:manager>
               <org:name>James Galway</org:name>
               <org:title>Chief Financial Officer</org:title>
            </org:manager>
         </org:div>
         <org:div>
            <org:name>Research</org:name>
            <org:manager>
               <org:name>Benny Jocum</org:name>
               <org:title>Chief Technical Officer</org:title>
            </org:manager>
         </org:div>
      </org:company>
```

The declaration `xmlns:org= "http://www.xmldevhandbook.com"` indicates that everything within the `<org:company>` tag that has an `org:` prefix (including the tag itself) belongs to the `org:` namespace.

The URI portion of the declaration, on the other hand, serves the following vital roles:

Namespace As Unique Identifier In this role, the namespace isn't actually defined, per se; it is simply associated with a unique entity such as a URL. Typically, there may be information about the schema or DTD being used at that location, but it's not used explicitly by the XML parser. An example of this role would the following namespace:

```
xmlns:org= "http://www.xmldevhandbook.com/schemas"
```

Similarly, you can user the following alternate `urn` notation:

```
xmlsn:org= "urn:xmldevhandbook:schemas"
```

Namespace As Schema Declaration In this role, the `urn` namespace explicitly points to an XML schema file. This mechanism actually imports the schema and applies it to the document within the XML parser, and will be covered more extensively in Chapter 6, "XML Schema". For example, the `org` namespace could be declared as in the following example:

```
xmlsn:org="x-schema: http://www.xmlDevHandbook.com/_
schemas/orgSchema.xml"
```

Namespace As Object Declaration In this role, the URN namespace points to an ActiveX object that defines a set of binary behaviors. (Currently, support for creating binary behaviors can only be accomplished in C++, which is beyond the scope of this book.) Microsoft's VML Web graphics language (which possibly will be superseded by SGL by the time you read this) is defined in precisely this manner, where the namespace is used in conjunction with an ActiveX control declared as an object in the Web page, as the following example demonstrates:

```
<html xmlns:v="urn:schemas-microsoft-com:vml">
```

The most important thing about a namespace is that it, effectively, is unique: it defines the namespace as belonging to a specific entity (a person or an organization). That it is used as a mechanism for linking schemas is fortuitous, but this is essentially taking advantage of a side effect of the namespace.

Typically, you will only end up dealing with one namespace in an XML document, and adding namespace prefixes is neither necessary nor desirable in such circumstances. Thus, you can typically define a *default namespace*, in which tags don't require the namespace prefix. For example, the preceding organization chart document has all of the elements within the same namespace (`org`). As such, the `org:` prefixes are essentially redundant and can be eliminated by not including a prefix in the namespace declaration, as Listing 3.2 demonstrates.

Listing 3.2: The Document from Listing 3.1 Declared Using the Default Namespace (*Listing3.02.xml*)

```
<company xmlns ="http://www.vbxml.com/cagle/org">
   <name>Acme Rocket Company</name>
   <manager>
      <name>Phil Schwarts</name>
      <title>Chief Executive Officer</title>
      <domain>Administration</domain>
   </manager>
   <div>
      <name>Finance</name>
         <manager>
            <name>James Galway</name>
            <title>Chief Financial Officer</title>
         </manager>
         </manager>
   </div>
   <div>
      <name>Research</name>
         <manager>
            <name>Benny Jocum</name>
            <title>Chief Technical Officer</title>
         </manager>
   </div>
</company>
```

You can also define more than one namespace in a document, although, obviously, only one of them can be a default namespace. If each manager includes a photograph and short descriptive text in HTML, then you can create an alternate namespace for the HTML elements, as Listing 3.3 demonstrates.

Listing 3.3: Declaring Both a Default and an Explicit Namespace in the Same Document (*Listing3.03.xml*)

```
<company xmlns ="http://www.xmldevhandbook.com"
xmlns:html="http://www.w3.org/TR/xhtml">
   <name>Acme Rocket Company</name>
   <manager>
      <name>Phil Schwarts</name>
      <title>Chief Executive Officer</title>
      <domain>Administration</domain>
      <descr>
          <html:div><html:img
             src="images/Pschwartz.jpg"
             height="125" width="85"
             align="left"/>
          <html:h2>Phil Schwartz</html:h2>
          <html:h3>CEO, Acme Rocket Company</html:h3>
         </descr>
      </manager>
      <!-- More elements -->
</company>
```

You can also change the scope of a namespace declaration if you define two namespaces with the same name, but if one appears on a subnode of the first, then the innermost namespace will apply to all descendents of that node, while the outermost namespace will apply to all other descendents of the outermost node.

Listing 3.4: Inner Namespaces Always Overrule Outer Namespaces if the Name Is the Same. (*Listing3.04.xml*)

```
<company xmlns ="http://www. www.vbxml.com/cagle/html"
xmlns:html="http://www.w3.org/TR/xhtml">
   <name>Acme Rocket Company</name>
   <html:descr><html:img src="images/companyPhoto.jpg"/></html:descr>
   <manager>
      <name>Phil Schwarts</name>
      <title>Chief Executive Officer</title>
      <domain>Administration</domain>
      <descr
         xmlns:html="http://www.vbxml.com/cagle/html">
         <html:div><html:img src="images/Pschwartz.jpg"
            height="125" width="85" align="left"/>
         <html:h2>Phil Schwartz</html:h2>
         <html:h3>CEO, Acme Rocket Company</html:h3>
      </descr>
   </manager>
   <!-- More elements -->
</company>
```

In Listing 3.4, the outer `html` namespace is given as `"http://www.w3.org/TR/xhtml">` and applies to the company's description node. However, another namespace named `html:` is applied to the CEO's description, this one pointing to `http://www.vbxml.com/cagle/html`. This means that anything within the CEO's description will use the DevHandbook HTML namespace declaration rather than the W3C's namespace.

Namespaces can extend beyond elements into attributes as well, using exactly the same *namespace:* mechanism described previously. For example, Microsoft's XML Schema defines a namespace for describing data types within SQL Server 2000:

```
<Schema xmlns="urn:schemas-microsoft-com:xml-data"
    xmlns:dt="urn:schemas-microsoft-com:datatypes">
<ElementType name="row" content="textOnly" model="closed">
   <AttributeType name="CustomerID" required="no" dt:type="string"/>
   <AttributeType name="OrderID" required="no" dt:type="i4"/>
   <AttributeType name="OrderDate" required="no" dt:type="date"/>
   <attribute type="CustomerID"/>
   <attribute type="OrderID"/>
   <attribute type="OrderDate"/>
</ElementType>
</Schema>
```

The `dt:` namespace indicates that `type` is defined within the `urn:schemas-microsoft-com:datatype` namespace. The advantage of going with such an arrangement is that you can apply a common namespace specification across a wide number of elements without having to explicitly declare them in the schema. This is discussed in much greater depth in Chapter 6, "XML Schema," and in Chapter 9, "XML and MS Databases."

Namespaces and the XML DOM

Given the extent to which Microsoft has promoted the use of namespaces, it's perhaps not surprising that the XML DOM incorporates support for namespaces within the DOM, although, for the most part, namespace usage is fairly transparent.

The `IXMLDOMNode` interface (which most other XML objects inherit) provides the following three properties for retrieving namespace properties of a node:

`BaseName` Contains the name of a node without the namespace prefix.

`NamespaceURI` Contains the namespace URI under which the node is governed.

`Prefix` Contains the namespace prefix associated with the node.

Note that if a namespace is declared for the document, then all nodes within that document will also have that same namespace URI, unless it's overridden at some point down the tree by a different URI. Likewise, all nodes will have basenames (even when a namespace isn't explicitly declared). However, only nodes that have explicit prefixes will have prefix values; otherwise, this property returns a blank string.

WARNING The three properties described here are all read-only; you cannot currently change the namespace of an already-existing node.

You can assign a namespace when you create a node. The document's `createNode` method includes a parameter for passing a namespace argument, and, with `createElement` and `createAttribute`, you can pass the namespace as part of the node name, as the following example demonstrates:

```
set node=createNode(NODE_ELEMENT,"div","org")
set node=createElement("org:div")
set attrNode=createAttribute("org:name")
```

Similarly, you can (and, in fact, generally have to) use fully-qualified names in searches, such as the following example:

```
Set node=xmlDoc.getElementsByTagName("org:div")(0)
```

NOTE A good strategy for dealing with namespace prefixes is to view them simply as part of the node name. Thus, `div` and `org:div` are two distinct elements even though they share a common base name.

Namespaces and XPath/XSL

The developers at Microsoft knew, when the XML Query Language proposal was first proposed, that the language would evolve, perhaps dramatically. The W3C is a consortium of different companies, universities, and individuals, and each of them had requirements that would likely change the standard in some way. As a consequence, they chose the (wise) path of assigning to the original XSL proposal a namespace designation:

- The December 10, 1998, XSL proposal namespace at `http://www.w3.org/TR/WD-xsl`

The `/TR/` sub-site contains all of the formal recommendations, working drafts, and public notes that the W3C has control over, and is a common element in almost all of the W3C namespace designations. The `WD-` extension is a shorthand notation for *Working Draft*, the formal name of a W3C document under development.

The newer namespace—the official one—is given as the following:

- The November 16, 1999, XSL Transformations recommendation namespace at `http://www.w3.org/TR/1999/XSLT`

When you create an XSL document, you will need to explicitly specify one or the other of these namespaces, depending upon whether you're supporting the older parser (useful for backward support with IE5) or the newer one (everywhere else).

However, when you're working with XPath alone, passing the namespaces directly is a little difficult. To get around this, the `MSXML2.DLL` `DOMDocument` provides another method, the `.setProperty` method, to tell the parser whether to use the December 1998 or the November 1999 namespace.

In order to tell the document that you want to search using the older style of XPath (called XSL Pattern in the latest Microsoft documentation), you would set the `SelectionLanguage` property to `XSLPattern`, while setting the selection language to `XPath` will work with the November 1999 XPath specification, as Listing 3.5 demonstrates.

Listing 3.5: Setting the Selection Language for an XML Document (*Listing3.05.txt*)

```
VBScript:
Dim xmlDoc
Set xmlDoc=createObject("MSXML2.DOMDocument")
xmlDoc.setProperty "SelectionLanguage","XPath"

Visual Basic:
Dim xmlDoc as DOMDocument
Set xmlDoc=new DOMDocument
xmlDoc.setProperty "SelectionLanguage","XPath"

JavaScript:
var xmlDoc=new ActiveXObject("MSXML2.DOMDocument")
xmlDoc.setProperty("SelectionLanguage","XPath")
```

NOTE The default selection-language state for any newly defined document is `XSLPattern` for backward compatibility. If you find yourself having trouble running XPath queries, it's probably because this property is set to `XSLPattern` instead.

WARNING The `SetProperty` method is part of the newer `MSXML2.DLL` parser and is not supported in the earlier parser. The newer XPath is also not supported, of course.

In the next several sections, I focus on the real power of XPath as a way to retrieve detailed, highly focused information from an XML structure. Because there is a fairly high degree of commonality, I look specifically at the newer parser and then point out differences and limitations in the older one.

Retrieving Elements

There is this curious property about many systems, especially abstract ones: They tend toward hierarchical organization. Complex systems tend to be modular and encapsulating: They can be decomposed naturally into a finite (and usually small) number of "natural" divisions, which, in turn, contain either other elements or more divisions. As just one example, molecular biologists are discovering that DNA (the molecular kind, not the Microsoft architecture, although that has a certain intrinsic organization to it too), while essentially a linear sequence of elements, tends to group functionally related genes together in specific areas within chromosomes.

One of the reasons for this is energy. If you look at DNA as being essentially a giant data structure and the mitochondria that act upon the DNA as being a parser, then structures in which the DNA molecules have to move the least (have the smallest data access times) require the least amount of energy to maintain. This is one of the reasons why most chaotic systems move to a state of higher organization, even though, in the long term, it is an antientropic configuration.

Programmatic data structures likewise tend to fit best into a small number of possible configurations, because these are the ones that provide the smallest data access time and, hence, minimize the cycle time (and consequently the "energy" of the computation). The container/contained relationship of a hierarchical tree is one of the most common of these structures, which is one of the reasons that XML is so useful in working with data.

NOTE If this sounds a little like Artificial Life (A-Life), the similarity is not accidental. Neuropsychologists are beginning to come up with a model of consciousness in humans (and conceivably in computers) that is strongly based upon the concept of self-organized systems.

What this means for XML, however, is that the mechanism for retrieving information needs to involve as little work as possible, both for the programmer and for the parser. A number of proposals have been made for the mechanism to query XML structures. One, XML Query Language (XQL), was proposed by developers from AT&T, who built a model very highly reminiscent of the `SELECT * FROM Table` notation of SQL. While initially viewed with some interest by the XML community, many developers felt that the language lacked the flexibility to handle detailed queries.

The current candidate for XML navigation is the XML Path Language, or simply XPath, which was introduced at the beginning of this chapter. At its most basic level, the XPath notation is very similar to Unix-based directory paths, with the files being the node names for elements. For example, consider a listing of the employees of a company, arranged by manager, as shown in Listing 3.6.

Listing 3.6: A Basic Organizational Document (*Listing3.06.xml*)

```
<company>
    <name>Acme Rocket Company</name>
    <manager>
        <name>Phil Schwarts</name>
        <title>Chief Executive Officer</title>
        <domain>Administration</domain>
    </manager>
    <division>
        <name>Finance</name>
            <manager>
                <name>James Galway</name>
                <title>Chief Financial Officer</title>
            </manager>
    </division>
    <division>
        <name>Research</name>
        <manager>
            <name>Benny Jocum</name>
            <title>Chief Technical Officer</title>
        </manager>
    </division>
</company>
```

To get to the node containing the name of the chief executive officer, you'd build a path that looks like the following:

```
company/manager/name
```

Note that each node name is separated by a forward slash.

However, things get a little more complicated when you want to get the node of a specific division manager. The following path, for example, is ambiguous:

```
company/division/manager/name
```

This path could point to either the manager for research or the manager for finance. XPath resolves this by actually returning both names, which introduces one of the first rules for dealing with XPath: All queries will normally return all of the possible matches to that query; even if only one item matches that query, the result set is a collection containing one item and is not a unique item itself.

NOTE This is a point worth reiterating: Regardless of whether a query returns one item, a number of items, or no items whatsoever, the XPath parser treats the result as a node set, not a single node.

The `SelectNodes()` node method, introduced in Chapter 2, "Modeling the XML Document Object," returns an `IXMLDONNodeList` with pointers to each node that satisfies that query (even if there is only one item in that list). If no nodes satisfy the query, then `selectNodes()` returns a node list with no elements.

```
Set companyDoc=new DOMDocument
CompanyDoc.load "orgChart.xml"
Set nodeList=CompanyDoc.selectNodes("company/manager/name")
Debug.Print "This has "+nodeList.length+" node(s)."
```

This produces the following result in the Visual Basic Debug window:

```
"This has 1 node(s)"
```

On the other hand, ask for the number of division manager names:

```
Set nodeList=CompanyDoc.selectNodes("company/division/manager/name")
Debug.Print "This has "+nodeList.length+" node(s)."
```

And you'll get the following response:

```
"This has 2 node(s)."
```

Finally, consider a condition where you specify a node element that doesn't exist (such as a `<phone>` node):

```
set nodeList=CompanyDoc.selectNodes("company/phone")
Debug.Print "This has "+nodeList.length+" node(s)."
```

This rightly sets the node list to an empty collection with a length of zero:

```
"This has 0 node(s)."
```

NOTE A node list with no elements in it is still an instantiated object, by the way. The test (`Nodelist is Nothing`) returns `False`, so you should test to see if the `.length` property is `0` instead (`NodeList.length=0`).

If you have multiple results from a query, you can resolve them by using indexes, as discussed in the previous chapter. For example, to retrieve the name of the second division manager, you need to use `SelectNodes` and then retrieve the second element (`index=1`, since `nodeList` is zero based), as the following example demonstrates:

```
Set nodeList=CompanyDoc.selectNodes(_
      "company/division/manager/name")
Set reasearchManNode=nodeList(1)
Debug.Print researchManNode.text
```

In this case, the research manager node retrieves the name of the second manager, Benny Jocum, although this is not a foregone conclusion.

There are a number of fundamental problems with this approach. For starters, the query forces you to rely on the external API to resolve the query. Second, you easily come up with a case where there is some ambiguity in the results. Suppose that the research department has two managers, as in the following example:

```
<division>
   <name>Research</name>
   <manager>
      <name>Allison Hart</name>
      <title>VP, Year 2000 Issues</title>
   </manager>
   <manager>
      <name>Benny Jocum</name>
      <title>Chief Technical Officer</title>
   </manager>
</division>
```

Does the second `"company/division/manager/name"` entry in the list correspond to the first manager or the second manager in the second list? In this case, `.selectNodes("company/division/manager/name") (1)` points to Allison Hart, who is the second division manager listed but the first in the Research group.

You can, however, resolve entries by taking advantage of the predicate `operator []`. The predicate lets you filter out the data set that you're dealing with and is one of the key components of XPath. You can use the scope at this point to provide a simple index, as in the following example:

```
Set node=selectSingleNodes("company/div[1]/manager[1]/name")
```

I'm specifying here that I want the query to look only at the second divisions (`div[1]`, or Research), and the second manager within that division (`manager[1]`, or Benny Jocum). Note that you can have predicate operators at any level within the query.

Now, consider a different case. In all likelihood, you're not going to be after any name; you're going to want a manager that has a specific name. In OOP terms, this is analogous to saying, "I want the manager object whose name property is Benny Jocum." The predicate operator gives you that flexibility as well:

```
Set node=selectSingleNode(_
   "company/division/manager[name='Benny Jocum']")
```

In essence, this reads as, "Return all instances of a company/division/manager node in which the name child of the manager node has the text value *Benny Jocum.*" In simplified terms, the expression `a[b='expr']` means that for node `a`, check to see if the child `b` has a text value of `expr`.

NOTE The XPath Query Language recognizes both single and double quotes as valid string delimiters. Most of the examples given in this chapter use single quotes because the query strings will be passed in the context of double-quoted VB strings.

Predicate resolution doesn't have to take place exclusively at the leaf node of a query (the right-most "directory" in the path). For example, to get a list of all of the managers' names within the research department, you'd use the following expression:

```
company/div[name='Research']/manager/name
```

WARNING XPath queries are case sensitive. The query string `company/div[name='research']/manager/name` will not find any results because the parser does not recognize `Research` as being the same as `research`.

Similarly, you can combine index and text expressions in the same query. For example, consider the following line:

```
company/div[name='Research']/manager[1]/name
```

This query will return the name of the second manager in the Research division.

Finally, consider how to write a query string that will return the titles of all division-level managers who can hire people (i.e., have `<canHire>yes</canHire>` tags), as shown in Listing 3.7.

Listing 3.7: An Organization Chart Showing Who Can Hire in the Company (*Listing3.07.xml*)

```
<!-- Code3.2.Managers.xml-->
<company>
        <name>Acme Rocket Company</name>
        <manager>
            <name>Phil Schwarts</name>
            <title>Chief Executive Officer</title>
            <canHire>yes</canHire>
        </manager>
        <division>
            <name>Finance</name>
            <manager>
                 <name>James Galway</name>
                 <title>Chief Financial Officer</title>
                 <canHire>yes</canHire>
            </manager>
        </division>
        <division>
```

```
            <name>Research</name>
            <manager>
                <name>Benny Jocum</name>
                <title>Chief Technical Officer</title>
                <canHire>yes</canHire>
            </manager>
            <manager>
                <name>Allison Hart</name>
                <title>Vice President, Year 2000 Issues</title>
                <canHire>no</canHire>
            </manager>
        </division>
</company>
```

In this case, the key is to remember again that a predicate expression can occur anywhere in the string, not just at the last path. Thus, the path `company/division/manager [canHire='yes']/title` will yield the title of all division-level managers who can hire employees.

Context

All of the preceding examples assume that you are located at the root node of the XML document. While this assumption works fine for the `getElementsFromTagName` function (which, incidentally, can use all the queries discussed previously for precisely that reason), the `selectNodes` and `selectSingleNode` functions actually work within the *context* of the node that calls them.

The idea behind context is simple: The current context of a node is where the node is located relative to the tree as a whole. If you've ever seen a directory kiosk at a mall, context should be familiar to you; the little *You Are Here* arrow on the mall map is the context for that location. Note that if the mall has multiple kiosks, then the search path would be something like `//kiosk`, which would locate all of the kiosks in the mall; however, for each of them, the location of the *You Are Here* arrow would be different. In other words, the same path can have multiple contexts. Thus, context and path are related but not always the same.

One of the nice things about working with a hierarchical tree structure is that every node in the tree is actually the root node of its own hierarchical structure. XPath notation takes advantage of this in simplifying queries. For example, consider the organization chart in Figure 3.1.

The largest of the dashed-line boxes in Figure 3.1 gives the view of the universe from the context of the document, which is essentially the world as seen from `getElementsFromTagName`. The first node in any path from here would be the `<company>` node, and a typical path would start at `company/` for both `getElementsFromTagName` and `SelectNodes`.

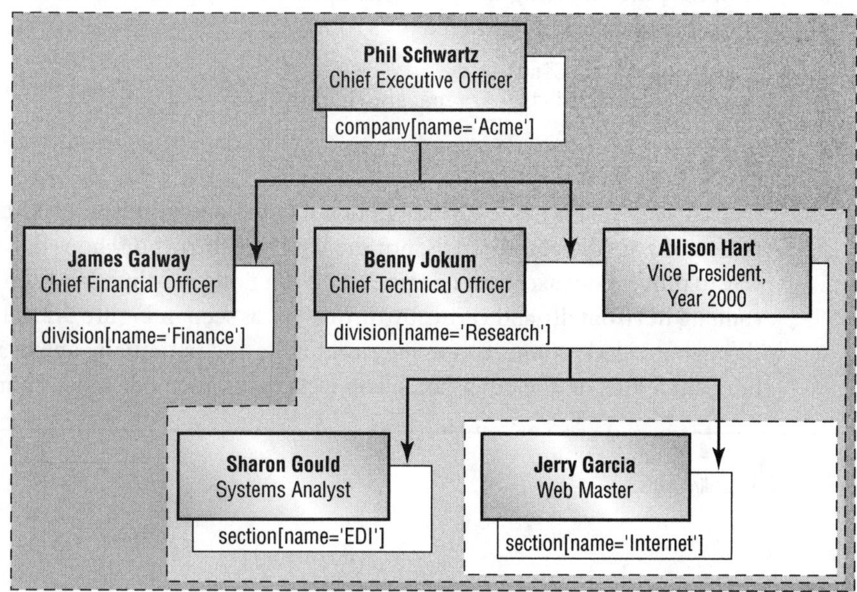

FIGURE 3.1
A hierarchical tree is made up of a series of concentric contexts.

The context of the <company> node as given is that the document is this node's parent, and the node itself has three children element types: `<name>`, `<manager>`, and `<division>`. The `selectNodes` path would thus start with one of these three—for example, `selectNodes(`*`division`*`)`—while the `getElementsTagName` for the same tag would start `company/division`.

To represent the context object, XPath actually maintains two separate tokens: the `context()` token (in the older XSL Pattern implementation) and the `.` (period) character (in both XSL Pattern and XPath). Typically, the context object is implicitly assumed to be given as the first character in an XPath query string, although there are exceptions, which are covered a bit later in this chapter. Thus, if `divNode` points to the Research division's `<div>` node, then all of the following point to the same element:

```
' In Both XSLPattern and XPath
DivNode.selectSingleNode("./manager[0]/name")
' In XSLPattern
DivNode.selectSingleNode("context()/manager[0]/name")
and
DivNode.selectSingleNode("manager[0]/name")
```

However, the following sample doesn't point to anything at all since the company node doesn't contain a child named division:

```
DivNode.selectSingleNode(_
    "company/division/manager[0]/name")
```

Axes

One concept that is new to XPath (and not contained in the older XSL Pattern syntax) is the notion of *axes* (the plural of axis, not the kind one throws or chops down trees with). The best way to think about axes is to imagine any given node as being drawn on graph paper with lines running horizontally and vertically through it, as seen in Figure 3.2. The vertical line running through the node connects it to its parent node and potentially one or more child nodes. The horizontal line, on the other hand, connects that same node to its siblings before and after.

FIGURE 3.2
Understanding axes

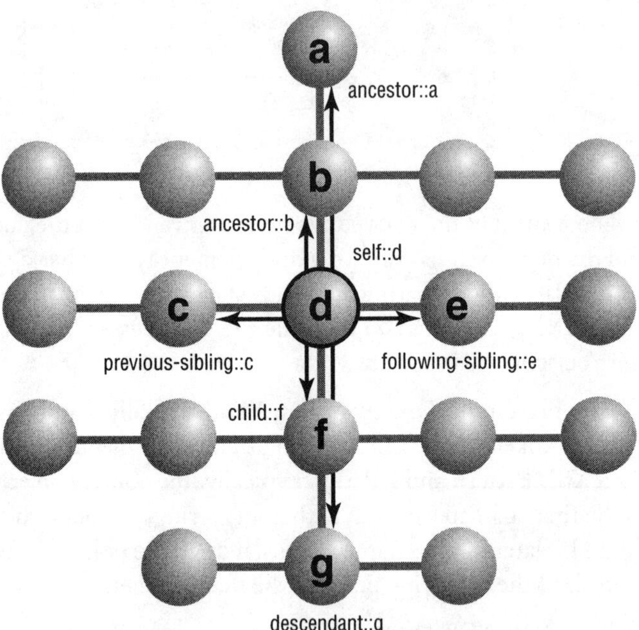

One of the most important ramifications of this division is that it is orthogonal; in other words, any node within the XML structure can be connected to the current node by any number of horizontal and vertical movements through the structure. XPath recognizes this and defines a set of axis descriptors that can actually locate a node relative to the current node; these are given in Table 3.1.

TABLE 3.1: XPath Axes

Name of Axis	Abbreviation	Description of Axis	Example
`self::`	.	References the current element	`self::*` always matches the current element node; `self::manager` only retrieves a node if the current node is a `<manager>` node.
`child::`	Default (If no axis is provided, node name is assumed to be a child node.)	References any child of the current node	`child::*` retrieves all child elements; `child::title` retrieves only those elements named `<title>`
`attribute::`	@	References any attributes of the current node	`attribute::*` retrieves all attributes, while `attribute::color` only retrieves the `color` attribute.
`descendant::`	.//	References any descendant of the current node, regardless of depth	`descendant::*` retrieves all descendants, while `descendant::salary` only retrieves `<salary>` elements that are in the subtree of the current node.
`ancestor::`	None	References any ancestor of the current node, regardless of depth	`ancestor::*` retrieves all immediate ancestors (those in a direct line between the current node and the root node), while `ancestor::company` only retrieves the ancestral `<company>` node.
`ancestor-or-self::`	None	References either the current node or any ancestor nodes	`ancestor-or-self::*` retrieves the current node and all its immediate ancestors, while `ancestor-or-self::manager` only retrieves those nodes (inclusive of the current node) that are in a direct line and are named `<manager>`.
`descendant-or-self::`	None	References either the current node or any descendants	`descendant-or-self::*` retrieves all of the nodes in the element's subtree as well as itself.
`previous-sibling::`	None	Retrieves any node that is a sibling of the current node and comes before it	`previous-sibling::*` retrieves all previous siblings of the current node, while `preceding-sibling::division` retrieves all preceding siblings with the name of `<division>`.

TABLE 3.1: XPath Axes *(continued)*

Name of Axis	Abbreviation	Description of Axis	Example
`following-sibling::`	None	Retrieves any node that is a sibling of the current node and comes after it	`following-sibling::*` retrieves all following siblings of the current node, while `following-sibling::division` retrieves all following siblings with the name of `<division>`.

One consequence of this orthogonality is that it becomes possible to express any relationship as a combination of paths and axis relationships. Thus, going back to the manager organization chart discussed previously, for example, you could find the name of James Galway's manager (starting from the current manager node) through the following path:

```
ancestor::company/child::manager/child::name
```

And you can locate the name of the next manager in the org chart with the following path:

```
following::manager/child::name
```

Axes are useful in some situations, especially when trying to find nodes that are siblings of the current node. However, they are also somewhat verbose. As a consequence, a number of axes are abbreviated, as covered in the next section.

NOTE Remember that axes are only supported for the XPath implementation, not for XSL Pattern, although the abbreviations are supported.

Breaking Context

Sometimes you need to break context. For example, consider the problem of finding the names of all of the managers in the organization, regardless of their position in the hierarchy (as shown in Listing 3.8).

Listing 3.8: An Organization Chart Showing Names within the Company (*Listing3.08.xml*)

```
<company>
     <name>Acme Rocket Company</name>
     <manager>
          <name>Phil Schwarts</name>
          <title>Chief Executive Officer</title>
          <canHire>yes</canHire>
     </manager>
     <division>
          <name>Finance</name>
```

```
        <manager>
            <name>James Galway</name>
            <title>Chief Financial Officer</title>
            <canHire>yes</canHire>
        </manager>
    </division>
    <division>
        <name>Research</name>
        <manager>
            <name>Benny Jocum</name>
            <title>Chief Technical Officer</title>
            <canHire>yes</canHire>
        </manager>
        <manager>
            <name>Allison Hart</name>
            <title>Vice President, Year 2000 Issues</title>
            <canHire>no</canHire>
        </manager>
    </division>
</company>
```

There are actually two problems to deal with in a situation like this. You can't specify an absolute path to the names, because they exist at different levels of the hierarchy. Additionally, while managers have names, divisions and the company itself also have `<name>` tags.

The descendants operator // returns not just the immediate descendents of a given node but, in fact, a search on *all* nodes within the tree (starting from the document's root, not the node). To retrieve all of the names in the tree, for example, you could use the following expression:

```
DivNode.selectNode("//name")
```

This is actually a broader search than you want here, since you only want name nodes belonging to managers, not all the name nodes of the document. You can extend the search criterion after the descendants operator, as in the following example:

```
DivNode.selectNode("//manager/name")
```

This will give you the requested set: the nodes belonging only to managers.

The default case for the descendants operator is to start at the root node; however, you can explicitly specify a context for it on the left, and then the search will start from that node. For example, to retrieve the names of managers only in the Research division, you could use the following:

```
Set researchManagersList=CompanyDoc.selectNodes(_
    "//division[name='Research']//manager/name")
```

The first descendants operator indicates to XPath that you want all <division> nodes for which the <name> node is Research as the context node, and then to retrieve all managers (at any level) within the Research division. Similarly, if you already have a node for the Research division (divNode in this example), then you can use the context operator to restrict the search to just the Research division, as the following example demonstrates:

```
Set researchManagersList=divNode.selectNodes(_
    ".//manager/name")
' or
Set researchManagersList=divNode.selectNodes(_
    "context()//manager/name")
```

Having talked about descendants, it's a good time to bring up ancestors as well. To get an immediate ancestor, you can use the ancestor operator, which can be given either as ancestor() or as .., the latter a notation that should be familiar to readers who have navigated directories in DOS or Unix. If you have a manager node and want to know the name of the division to which it corresponds, you can use either of these two forms. For Allison Hart, for example, you could use the following:

```
Set managerNode=CompanyDoc.selectSingleNode(_
      "//manager[name='Allison Hart']")
Set divNameNode=managerNode.selectSingleNode(_
      "ancestor()/name")
' or
Set divNameNode=managerNode.selectSingleNode(_
      "../name")
```

Any of the preceding lines point to the division name node corresponding to Research.

Of course, you could always combine the two queries as well, as in the following example:

```
Set divNameNode= CompanyDoc.selectSingleNode(_
      "//manager[name='Allison Hart']/../name")
```

The ancestor operator is fairly powerful, by the way. If you pass a search path as an argument into ancestor, the query will walk up the tree until it finds a name that matches that condition; thus, you could find the name of the company that Allison works for by passing company to the ancestor() operator:

```
Set divNameNode= CompanyDoc.selectSingleNode(_
      "//manager[name='Allison
       Hart']/ancestor('company')/name")
```

The *Element* and *Ancestor* Operator

Without axes, the earlier XSL Pattern parser needed to make use of other means to retrieve elements. It did so by creating special functions that could be used to retrieve specific nodes.

Many of these are no longer supported under XPath, though the ones that are have been indicated.

So far in the examples in this chapter, the assumption has been that you know which nodes you are trying to find. However, at times, you will either not know or not care about the specific name of the node, but you will want to be able to find a node that satisfies a given condition. The `element ()`operator (*) is designed for precisely this situation. When applied without an argument, the operator returns a list of all of the child elements of the current node. Its behavior in this respect is much like the behavior of the `GetElementsByTagName()` function, but it doesn't have to be called from the root node to work.

TIP The fact that you can duplicate the `getElementsByTagName` functionality with XPath queries is one of the reasons why I generally recommend using `selectNode` or `selectSingleNode` exclusively, rather than getting attached to that function.

TIP The `element()` property, like the `ancestor` property, can take a search path argument, but, as this simply duplicates the search path you'll probably want to use it primarily in its * incarnation.

In its simplest incarnation, you can use `element()` to retrieve the element children of a given node. For example, as in Listing 3.9, you could write a small program that would output to an HTML block all of a given manager's properties.

Listing 3.9: The *DescribeManager* Function Retrieves the Name of Each Manager and Presents It as an HTML String. (*Listing3.09.vbs*)

```
Visual Basic
Function DescribeManager(xmlDoc as DOMDocument,managerName as String) as String
   Dim buf as String
   Dim Node as IXMLDOMNode

VBScript
Function DescribeManager(xmlDoc,managerName)
   Dim buf
   Dim Node

   Buf="<h3>Manager</h3>"+vbCRLF
   Buf=Buf+"<ul>"+vbCRLF
   For Each Node in xmlDoc.selectNodes(_
               "//manager[name='"+managerName+"']/*")
       buf=buf+vbTab+"<li><b>"+Node.nodeName+":</b>"
       buf=buf+Node.text+"</li>"+vbCRLF
   Next
```

```
   Buf=Buf+"</ul>"
   DescribeManager=Buf
End Function
```

When the `DescribeManager` function is called, as in `Debug.Print DescribeManager("Allison Hart")`, it generates HTML code describing the details of that manager, as the following example demonstrates:

```
<h3>Manager</h3>
<ul>
   <li><b>name:</b>Allison Hart</li>
<li><b>title:</b>Vice President, Year 2000 Issues</li>
   <li><b>canHire</b>no</b></li>
</ul>
```

If this sample were output to a browser, it would look something like the following:

Manager

- **name:**Allison Hart
- **title:**Vice President, Year 2000 Issues
- **canHire:**no

Unrolling the Tree: the Power of //*

The combination of the element operator and the descendants operator can be especially potent. The query string //*will place every node in the document tree into a node list, in the "walking the tree" order that XML usually uses to traverse the tree. This is especially useful if you are writing a routine that needs to process each node in turn and you don't want to bother with complex recursive calls, or if you need to indicate the current mode of a comparison. (.//* will unravel a node in the same fashion.)

This technique is especially useful for populating TreeView controls, outlines, and list trees, which often have a linear method of entry. (I give numerous TreeView examples in Chapters 6 and 7, so I won't cover them here.)

The `element()` operator can be used in more complex queries as well. For example, suppose that you need to write a query that returns the manager to whom a given manager reports, and your management tree is considerably deeper than in the preceding sample. (Assume that Allison Hart's division includes a COBOL programming section.) Consider the following sample:

```
<division>
   <manager>
        <name>Allison Hart</name>
        <title>Vice President, Year 2000 Issues</title>
    </manager>
```

```
    <section>
        <name>COBOL Programming</name>
        <manager>
            <name>Jerry Garcia</name>
            <title>Director, COBOL Systems</title>
        </manager>
    </section>
</division>
```

Writing a generalized query for retrieving the name of a supervisor becomes more complex because the managers aren't direct ancestors; they're more like aunts or uncles. However, the organization here is clearly of the order:

```
<groupType>
    <name>Name of Group</name>
    <manager>
        <name>Manager's name</name>
        <title>Manager's Title</title>
    </manager>
    <subGroupType>
        <name>Name of Group</name>
        <manager>
            <name>Manager's name</name>
            <title>Manager's Title</title>
        </manager>
    </subGroupType>
</groupType>
```

In other words, if you know the name of a manager, you know that they have a `<manager>` node for a parent that must be bypassed, and the next node that also has a manager subnode contains the person to whom the manager reports. The specific query for Jerry looks like the following:

```
"//manager[name='Jerry Garcia']/../ancestor(*[manager])/manager/name"
```

Reading from left to right, this sample translates into the following components:

`//manager` Starting from the manager…

`[name='Jerry Garcia']` With the name Jerry Garcia…

`/..` Whose parent's…

`/ancestor(*[manager])` Ancestor has a child element of `manager`…

`/manager/name` Select that ancestor's manager's name.

You can write a function, as in the following one, that will return the node list produced using the preceding technique. (Remember that a given group can have more than one manager.)

```
Function ReportsTo(companyDoc as DOMDocument,_
    employeeName as String) as IXMLDOMNodeList
```

```
    Dim NodeList as IXMLDOMNodeList
    Dim node as IXMLDOMNode
    Dim Buf as String
    Set NodeList=companyDoc.selectNodes(_
        "//manager[name='"+employeeName+_
         "']/../ancestor(*[manager]/manager/name")
    set ReportsTo=NodeList
End Function

' To See it in action:
For each manager in ReportsTo(companyDoc,"Jerry Garcia")
    Debug.Print manager
Next
```

The preceding example sends the following to the Debug window:

```
Benny Jocum
Allison Hart

For each manager in ReportsTo(companyDoc,"Benny Jocum")
    Debug.Print manager.text
Next
```

And this example, in turn, sends the following to the Debug window:

```
Phil Schwartz
```

TIP While using Visual Basic or VBScript is one way to add parameters in search strings, you can also take advantage of the flexibility of regular expressions to do the same thing.

The *Attribute* Operator

Retrieving attributes is not much more complicated that retrieving elements. Just as the `element()` operator (*)retrieves the child elements of a given node, the `attribute()` operator (@) returns one or more attributes, although there are minor variations in usage.

Consider the following XHTML image tag:

```
<img id="myImage"
   src="http://www.xmldevhandbook.com/images/image1.jpg"
    width="100" height="200" border="0"/>
```

If `imageNode` contains a reference to the `img` element, then the XPath to retrieve the `src` attribute would be `img/@src`. The combination `/@src` indicates that all `src` attributes that belong to the given element (in this case `img`) should be retrieved. For a single node, this will, of course, return only one attribute node since an element cannot contain more than one attribute of the same name. However, the expression `//img/@src` will retrieve all of the `src` attributes of all image nodes; the expanded expression `//img/attribute('src')` will also perform this function.

Similarly, the expression `/@*` will return all of the attributes of the specific node. Thus, for the preceding example, `img/@*` will return the `src`, `width`, `height`, and `border` attributes for the `img` element. Note that this is the same as `img/attribute()`, which will likewise return all of the attributes of a given node.

In general, though, you will not want to return an attribute node from a query. Rather, you'll likely want to return a node that has that attribute as a value. You can use the `attribute()` collection within a predicate operator as well as in the path part of an expression. For example, in order to return all image nodes that include a `src` attribute, you'd use the following expression:

```
//img[@src]
```

To retrieve all elements for which a given attribute matches a specific value, you'd treat it exactly as you would an element:

```
//img[@id='myImage']
```

Similarly, you can apply attributes within more than one predicate operator throughout the path. For example, suppose that you had an XHTML document in which two different divisions had list items of varying classes, as in Listing 3.10:

Listing 3.10: A Sample XHTML Document (*ProsAndCons.htm*) Demonstrates how Attributes Can Exist at Different Levels. (*Listing3.10.html*)

```
<body>
    <div id="whyUseXPath">
        <h4>What are the advantages and disadvantages of XPath?</h4>
        <ul>
            <li class="pro">Compact</li>
            <li class="pro">Flexible</li>
            <li class="pro">Hierarchical</li>
            <li class="con">Searches only whole expressions</li>
            <li class="con">Can be cryptic</li>
        </ul>
    </div>
    <div id="Uses of XPath">
        <h4>Where can you use XPath</h4>
        <ul>
            <li class="pro">XSL</li>
            <li class="pro">XML DOM</li>
            <li class="pro">XLink</li>
            <li class="con">SQL</li>
        </ul>
    </div>
</body>
```

In order to retrieve all list items (`li`) that handle the `pro` class in the `whyUseXPath` node (the boldface items in Listing 3.10), your query string would look like the following:

```
//div[@id='whyUseXPath']//li[@class='pro']
```

Searching Other Collections

As you probably have figured, most of the major node types actually have XSL Pattern collections associated with them. Table 3.2 summarizes these collections.

TABLE 3.2: The Various XSL Pattern Collections (Applicable to the Older XML Parser)

Name	Description
`ancestor()`	Retrieves the nearest node up the tree that matches the given criterion. (See the preceding "The Element and Ancestor Operator" section.)
`attribute()`	Retrieves the specified attribute if an ancestor name is specified, or the entire set of attributes if none is given. Attributes are indicated by the `@` operator. (Refer to the attribute operator in the previous section.)
`comment()`	Retrieves the comments of a given node and its children. Comments can be enumerated, but you have to refer to a comment numerically to retrieve it otherwise. To retrieve all of the comments in a document, use the `//comment()` query expression.
`element()`	Retrieves the specified element or elements that satisfy the provided query. (See the preceding "The Element and Ancestor Operator" section.) The elements collection is also indicated by the * operator.
`node()`	Retrieves all nodes (elements, attributes, text, and so forth) that satisfy the given search criterion.
`pi()`	Retrieves all processing instructions belonging to a given node or its children, or the specified PI if a name is provided. To retrieve all processing instructions in a document, use the `//pi()` query expression.
`textnode()`	Retrieves all text and CDATA nodes of the given node and its children.

For example, if you have a processing instruction in your documents that holds versioning information (`<?version Beta Version 1.0?>`), you could retrieve that information with the `pi()` collection, as in the following example:

```
set version=xmlDoc.selectSingleNode("//pi('version')").text
```

The correspondence between these XSL Pattern functions and the axes of the XPath specification are pretty clear-cut, and, for normal associations, the XPath axes are generally the preferable way of retrieving nodes. They do have collections that, broadly, overlap the collections in XSL Pattern; however, the names differ slightly. More importantly, the emphasis shifts from collections as part of an API to collections built around the axes, or structure, of the XML document. These collections are discussed in Table 3.3.

TABLE 3.3: The Various XPath Collections (Applicable to the Newer XML Parser)

Name	Description	Example
`node()`	Retrieves any node, regardless of the node type, based upon the axis	`child::node()`retrieves all nodes immediately attached to a given element.
`text()`	Retrieves all text nodes associated with the given axis	`child::text()` retrieves all text nodes attached to the current node; `descendant::text()` retrieves all text nodes of all descendents of the node.
`comment()`	Retrieves all comment nodes associated with the given axis	`//descendant::comment()`retrieves all comments in the document.
`processing-instruction()`	Retrieves all processing instructions associated with the given axis	`//descendant::processing-instruction()` retrieves all processing instructions in the document.
`attribute()`	Retrieves all attributes associated with the given axis	`child::attribute()` retrieves all attributes of the current node.

Thus, to find (from the root node) all processing instructions associated with the division manager nodes, you could use an axis path of `descendant::manager/child::processing-instruction()`, which could also be abbreviated as `//manager/processing-instruction()`.

NOTE The principal difference between XSL Pattern and XPath collections lies in replacing `pi()` with `processing-instruction()` and `textnode()` with `text()`. At least in abbreviated form, the one usually otherwise maps easily to the other.

Predicates

When I was younger (and quite full of myself) I decided that I would read a book called *The Principia Mathematic*, by Russell Whitehead and Alfred North. This particular tome was an attempt by those two eminent philosophers late in the nineteenth century to codify all of symbolic logic within a single work. It was very impressive, although it was doomed to failure: Kurt Goedel proved conclusively 30 years later that no mathematical system can ever prove or disprove every statement that is made within its lexicon.

The relevance of the *Principia*, besides providing an object lesson in hubris, is that each of the expressions within the book was an example of a *predicate*, a logical statement that can only have the values of *true* or *false*. XPath takes this notion of predicates and embeds it deeply within its workings—a predicate looks at the indicated context specified by the XPath to that point and returns true if the expression satisfies the predicate (i.e., is true) and false if it doesn't. Each context that satisfies the predicate thus becomes part of the working set of the XPath for the next set of nodes in the path.

For example, consider the fairly simple XPath expression of `//manager[name='Allison Hart']`. In this particular case, the axis description retrieves the set of all managers. Once this set (internally known as a *node set*) is built, then the XPath processor looks at the expression within the predicate. The left-hand term *name* is retrieved and interpreted to mean a child of the current manager context with the node name of *name*. The right-hand expression is evaluated as a string. The equality operator (=) then retrieves the value of the node for each context and compares it with the string. If the strings match, the predicate is set to true, and the manager node is then added to the acting node set, where any subsequent XPath expressions are evaluated. If the strings don't match, then the node is dropped and no further evaluation is done for that context (see Figure 3.3).

FIGURE 3.3
Predicates act like gates to filter out the nodes produced by the previous path.

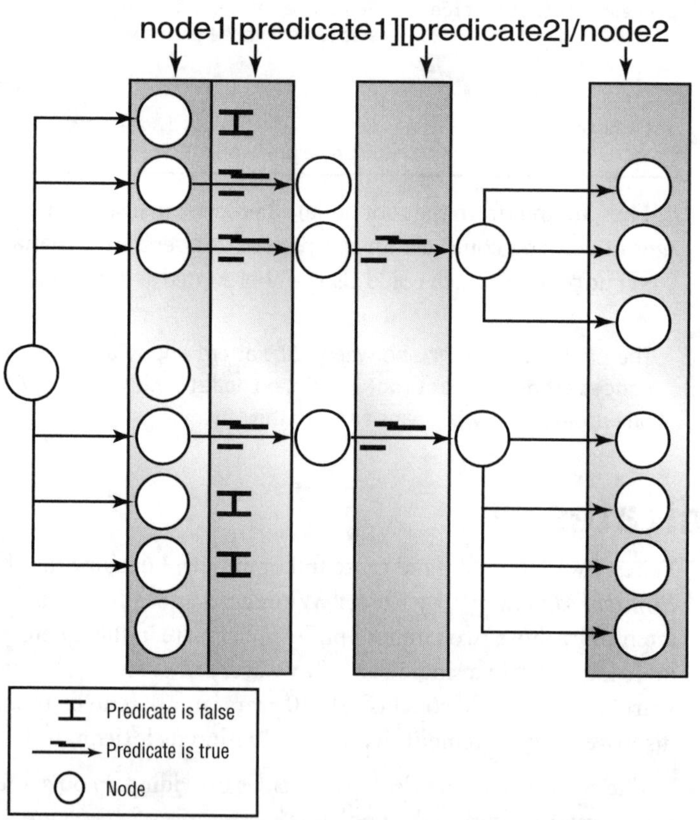

It is the use of predicates that makes XPath such a powerful tool for working with XML. The recommended version of XPath lets you search for strings within expressions, compare dates, and even evaluate expressions that are based upon variables or node information from elsewhere in the document. Procedural programming languages often incorporate complex expressions within their conditionals; XPath is no different. The core elements of such predicates thus fall into one of the following four different categories:

Existential Predicates Determine the predicate is true if a specific entity exists.

Comparison Predicates Determine whether one thing is equal, unequal, lesser, or greater than another thing.

Functional Predicates Use built-in functions to either return a set of contexts (existential predicate) or generate an expression for comparisons (comparison predicate).

Compound Predicates Combine two or more simpler predicates together using `and`, `or`, or `not`.

Existential Predicates

This is beginning to sound more like a treatise on philosophy than a book on programming, yet the basic idea behind existential predicates is simple: if an XPath expression returns a node set, then the predicate is true; if it doesn't, then the predicate is false. Note that with one exception, which is covered in the "Compound Predicates" section later in this chapter, existential tests aren't concerned with the number of nodes returned in the node set but only that the node set returns at least one member. Because of this, existential predicates are generally the fastest to evaluate. For example, consider the XML organization chart shown in Listing 3.11, which has been expanded to show vested individuals in the company.

Listing 3.11: The Company Organization Chart, Showing Vested Individuals (*Listing3.11.xml*)

```
<!-- vestedCompanyEmployees.xml -->
<company>
        <name>Acme Rocket Company</name>
        <manager>
            <name>Phil Schwarts</name>
            <title>Chief Executive Officer</title>
            <canHire>yes</canHire>
            <vested/>
        </manager>
        <division>
            <name>Finance</name>
            <manager>
                 <name>James Galway</name>
                 <title>Chief Financial Officer</title>
                 <canHire>yes</canHire>
           <vested/>
            </manager>
        </division>
        <division>
             <name>Research</name>
```

```
            <manager>
                <name>Benny Jocum</name>
                <title>Chief Technical Officer</title>
                <canHire>yes</canHire>
            </manager>
            <manager>
                <name>Allison Hart</name>
                <title>Vice President, Year 2000 Issues</title>
                <canHire>no</canHire>
                <vested/>
            </manager>
            <section>
                <name>COBOL Programming</name>
                <manager>
                    <name>Jerry Garcia</name>
                    <title>Director, COBOL Systems</title>
                </manager>
            </section>
        </division>
</company>
```

Imagine that you want to get a list of the names of all managers who have been vested within the company. As you've probably picked up from earlier sections, the expression to do this is simple:

```
//manager[vested]/name
```

This expression operates by retrieving all of the manager nodes and then checking each one in turn to see if it contains the child node `vested`. Only those nodes that satisfy the expression are added to the temporary node set. Each one of these, in turn, retrieves the associated name node. The simple VBScript program in Listing 3.12 shows how this can be utilized in practice. (The alert box that this produces is shown in Figure 3.4.)

Listing 3.12: VBScript Code to Display Vested Managers (*Listing3.12.vbs*)

```
<script language="Vbscript">
Dim xmlDoc
dim nodeList
dim buffer

Set xmlDoc=createObject("Microsoft.XMLDOM")
xmlDoc.setProperty "SelectionLanguage","XSLPattern"
xmlDoc.load "VestedCompanyEmployees"
set nodeList=xmlDoc.selectNodes("//manager[vested]/name")
buffer=""
for each node in nodelist
   buffer=buffer+node.text+vbCRLF
next
alert buffer
</script>
```

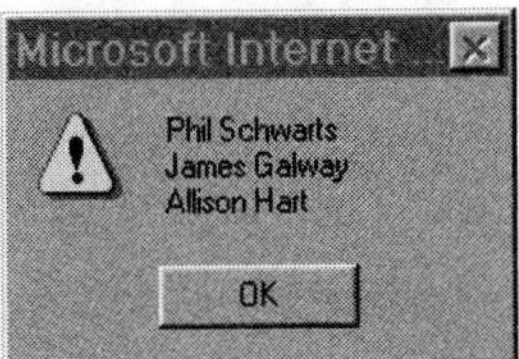

FIGURE 3.4
An alert box showing the vested managers, based upon Listing 3.12

You can also perform the logical inverse of the existential search: returning true if a given path is not found. To do this, you need to use the `not()` function, where `not()` can take any non-predicated XPath expression, as Listing 3.13 demonstrates. (Note that the usage is identical for both XPath and XSL Pattern.) The alert box in Figure 3.5 displays the names of unvested managers.

Listing 3.13: VBScript Code to Display Managers Who Aren't Vested (*Listing3.13.vbs*)

```
<script language="Vbscript">
Dim xmlDoc
dim nodeList
dim buffer

Set xmlDoc=createObject("Microsoft.XMLDOM")
xmlDoc.setProperty "SelectionLanguage","XPath"
xmlDoc.load "VestedCompanyEmployees.xml"
buffer=""
set nodeList=xmlDoc.selectNodes(_
     "//manager[not(vested)]/name")
for each node in nodelist
   buffer=buffer+node.text+vbCRLF
next
alert buffer
</script>
```

FIGURE 3.5
Listing 3.13 produces the inverse of Listing 3.12.

A similar example illustrates the use of the `$all$` operator, which is part of the older XSL Pattern syntax. Suppose that you have an XML document that represents a weekly project status report for various projects. For each project, one or more managers can indicate whether the given project has been approved (`<status>Approved</status>`), been disapproved

(<status>Rejected</status>), or is still pending (<status>Pending</status>), as shown in Listing 3.14.

Listing 3.14: A Project Report Written in XML, with Various Managers Approving, Rejecting, and Pending Given Projects (*Listing3.14.xml*)

```
<!-- projects.xml -->
<projects>
    <project>
       <name>Super Duper Rocket</name>
      <manager>
         <name>John Locke</name>
         <status>Approved</status>
       </manager>
      <manager>
         <name>James Horner</name>
         <status>Approved</status>
       </manager>
    </project>
    <project>
       <name>The Big Red Button</name>
      <manager>
         <name>John Locke</name>
         <status>Rejected</status>
       </manager>
      <manager>
         <name>James Horner</name>
         <status>Approved</status>
       </manager>
    </project>
    <project>
       <name>Pyrotechnics</name>
      <manager>
         <name>John Locke</name>
         <status>Approved</status>
       </manager>
      <manager>
         <name>James Horner</name>
         <status>Pending</status>
       </manager>
      <manager>
         <name>Karen Fowler</name>
         <status>Pending</status>
       </manager>
    </project>
</projects>
```

In order to retrieve all projects that have been approved, you can't just check to see whether or not an approved status is found within given projects, since other managers may still be reviewing the projects or may have rejected them. However, you can use the `$all$` operator, which returns a Boolean value for a given collection only if all elements within the predicate satisfy the expression, as Listing 3.15 demonstrates. (Figure 3.6 shows a screen capture of the program output.)

Listing 3.15: The *getApprovedProjects* and *DisplayApprovedProjects* Routines Show how the *all* Keyword Is Used to Filter Output. (*Listing3.15.vbs*)

```
Visual Basic:
Function getApprovedProjects(projectFileName As String) as IXMLDOMNodeList
   dim approvedProjects as IXMLDOMNodeList
   dim buffer as String
   dim projectXML as DOMDocument

VBScript:
Function getApprovedProjects(projectFileName)
   dim projectXML
   dim approvedProjects
   dim buffer

   set projectXML=createObject("Microsoft.XMLDOM")
   projectXML.load projectFileNameFigure [FILENAME]

   set getApprovedProjects=projectXML.selectNodes(_
      "//project[$all$ manager/status='Approved']")
End Function

Sub DisplayApprovedProjects()
   dim approvedProjects ' as IXMLDOMNodeList
   set approvedProjects=getApprovedProjects("projects.xml")
   buffer="Approved Projects:"+vbCRLF
   for each project in approvedProjects
      buffer=buffer+project.selectSingleNode("name").text+_
         vbCRLF
   next
   alert buffer
End Sub

DisplayApprovedProjects
```

FIGURE 3.6
Approved projects

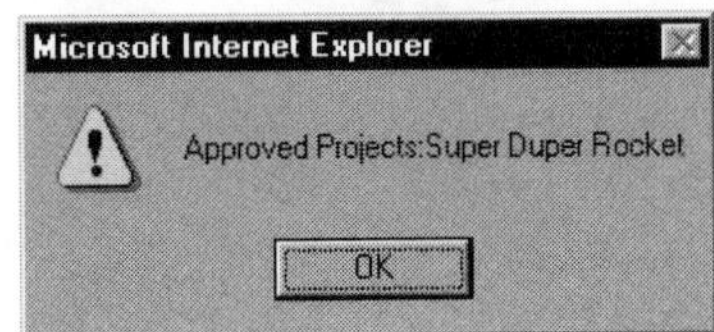

Because only the first project (the Super Duper Rocket, in Listing 3.14) has all of the `manager/status` nodes set to `Approved`, it is the only node that is retrieved.

While all of the managers must approve a project, it only takes one manager to kill a project. The `$any$` operator handles this situation: It returns a true value once the condition is found to be true for a given query. Thus, to determine all of the projects that didn't make a particular cut, for example, your code would look similar to the previous query, as Listing 3.16 demonstrates.

Listing 3.16: The *getRejectedProjects* and *DisplayRejectedProjects* Routines Show how the *any* Keyword Is Used to Filter Output. (*Listing3.16.vbs*)

```
Visual Basic:
Function getRejectedProjects(projectFileName As String) as IXMLDOMNodeList
   dim projectXML as DOMDocument
   dim rejectedProjects as IXMLDOMNodeList
   dim buffer as String

VBScript:
Function getRejectedProjects(projectFileName)
   dim projectXML
   dim rejectedProjects
   dim buffer

   set projectXML=createObject("Microsoft.XMLDOM")
   projectXML.load projectFileName

   set getRejectedProjects=projectXML.selectNodes(_
      "//project[$any$ manager/status='Rejected']")
End Function

Sub DisplayRejectedProjects()
   dim rejectedProjects ' as IXMLDOMNodeList
   set rejectedProjects=getRejectedProjects("projects.xml")
   buffer="Rejected Projects:"+vbCRLF
   for each project in rejectedProjects
      buffer=buffer+project.selectSingleNode("name").text+_
         vbCRLF
   next
   alert buffer
End Sub

DisplayRejectedProjects
```

TIP You may be wondering whether there is any difference between `$any$` and the default mode for retrieving nodes. There is, and it is one that you can take advantage of to make your code more efficient. A query that contains an `$any$` flag will automatically terminate once it finds a successful match, while the default query will continue through all matches even after a match has been found. Thus, if your code is likely to be searching through a number of different subnodes, you may want to limit its predicate with the `$any$` operator.

NOTE Neither `$any$` or `$all$` are implemented in the XPath implementation. The reason for this has to do with the fact that both of these are `implementation-dependant:` they indicate parser optimizations but don't do anything that can't be done just as easily with XPath functions. This is especially true of `$any$`, which is quite redundant.

Compound Predicates

Back to the *Principia* for a moment: most predicates are not simply existential. They typically are combinations of two or more Boolean variables, each with a possible value of true or false, that interact through the two logical operators `and` and `or`. The `and` operator returns true only if both (or all) of the individual predicates are also true and false otherwise, while the `or` operator returns true if any of the predicates are true and false only if none are. The combination of `and`, `or`, and `not` together can be used to express any statement that can be made in the field of symbolic logic.

NOTE `Exclusive OR`, for example, is a common computer operator wherein the expression is true only if one predicate or the other is true, but not both. `Exclusive OR` can be represented as `not((p and q)` or `(not(p) and not(q)))`, where `p` and `q` are predicates.

Both XSL Pattern and XPath let you create compound expressions with the tokens `and` and `or`. In the case of XSL Pattern, you must encase these operators in $ signs (i.e., `$and$` and `$or$`,) or the parser will generate an error; these aren't required in XPath.

WARNING This is a point worth reiterating: XSL Pattern searches require that you use `$and$` and `$or$` in your compound predicates; XPath uses the friendlier `and` and `or`.

Looking back to the projects scope, determining those projects that are pending likewise requires more than a simple search for "pending" projects. If a project is to be considered still pending, a manager must not have rejected it, although some of the managers (but not all) may have approved it. Since you won't have complete approval if at least one manager's decision is still pending, you can effectively ignore the state of the accepted decisions. As with the preceding example concerning existential predicates, you can use the `not()` function, in conjunction with the and operator, to determine the pending status, as Listing 3.17 demonstrates. (Figure 3.7 shows the alert box resulting from this code.)

Listing 3.17: The *getPendingProjects* and *DisplayPendingProjects* Routines Show how the *any* Keyword Is Used to Filter Output. (*Listing3.17.vbs*)

```
Visual Basic:
Function getPendingProjects(projectFileName As String) as IXMLDOMNodeList
   dim projectXML as DOMDocument
   dim buffer as String
   dim pendingProjects as IXMLDOMNodeList

VBScript:
Function getPendingProjects(projectFileName)
   dim projectXML
   dim pendingProjects
   dim buffer

   set projectXML=createObject("Microsoft.XMLDOM")
   projectXML.load projectFileName

set pendingProjects=projectXML.selectNodes(_
     "//project[($any$ manager/status='Pending')_
     $and$ ($not$ manager/status='Rejected')]") manager/status='Pending']")
End Function

Sub DisplayPendingProjects()
   dim pendingProjects ' as IXMLDOMNodeList
   set pendingProjects=getPendingProjects("projects.xml")
   buffer="Pending Projects:"+vbCRLF
   for each project in pendingProjects
      buffer=buffer+project.selectSingleNode("name").text+_
        vbCRLF
   next
   alert buffer
End Sub

DisplayPendingProjects
```

FIGURE 3.7
Pending project

You can group expressions within an XPath query string using parentheses. Parenthetic expressions evaluate before outer expressions do, giving you better control over what specifically gets evaluated when.

Thus, for example, to retrieve either approved or pending projects for which John Horner is manager, your query string would look like the following sample:

```
project[(manager/name='John Horner')_
    $and$ ((manager/status='Approved') $or$_
    (manager/status='Pending'))]
```

Other than indicating project go-ahead and that James Horner is project manager, this example demonstrates some of the power of XPath. It gives you a remarkably flexible tool for performing analyses on the XML data structure, in a way that combines the flexibility of a programmatic language with the set operation capabilities of a language like SQL. Incidentally, because most logical operators can be readily transformed, you can actually render the logical query in a number of different ways. The preceding statement, for example, is functionally equivalent to the following statement:

```
//project[(manager/name='John Horner')_
    $and$ ($not (manager/status='Rejected'))]
```

The logical and set comparison operators are summarized in Table 3.4. Note that these operators work only within the context of the predicate operator, letting you limit nodes to ones that satisfy the predicate.

TABLE 3.4: The Logical and Set Comparison Operators

XSL Pattern Operator	XPath Operator	Description
`$and$`	and	True only if both expressions are simultaneously satisfied
`$or$`	or	True if either expression is satisfied
`not()`	`not()`	True if the expression is not satisfied
`$all$`	No immediate analogy	True only if all nodes in the given predicate satisfy the expression
`$any$`	The default expression	True if any node in the given predicate satisfies the expression

Multiple Predicates

Given both the notation and the usage, it may be tempting to think of a predicate as a function. However, this can obscure the real nature of predicates in XPath: Predicates filter the possibilities that the outer paths provide. Thus, in this way a predicate is more like a gate: It either lets a particular node be added to the possible paths or it doesn't.

This gate metaphor can help to better explain the use of multiple predicates. The XPath parser (invoked anytime a `selectNodes` or a `selectSingleNode` command is called) reads a path expression until it encounters either a predicate, another path operator (the / character), or the end of the string. It then attempts to match the path at that point with existing nodes, and adds them to an internal list of valid nodes; this is essentially an expansive operation in that it grabs all possible nodes that match the particular path.

When a predicate operator (`[`) is encountered, the parser iterates through the list and removes the nodes for which the predicate is false. This ends up creating a subset (potentially empty) of the nodes to choose from. If, at this point, another predicate is encountered, it is applied to the remaining subset, filtering out the set even more. Then the nodes left standing are the subset that is used to determine the next path, or are the ones returned if the string has been completed.

This means that you can use multiple successive predicates to gate, or control, the output. While, functionally, this is equivalent to using the `and` operator discussed in the previous section, one critical difference between the two is that compound predicates evaluate each node in the set and filter the results based upon the computed "`and-ed`" value, while compound predicates filter out the items that fail the first predicate test and pass only these to the second test. For a small set of nodes, the distinction is fairly unimportant, but for a large number, the ability to filter out most of them with one check can cut down the time to do more complex filters down the road. This becomes especially important when dealing with such expensive tests as substring comparisons.

Consider the preceding test, which is repeated here for this example, for finding John Horner's projects that are either pending or approved:

```
project[(manager/name='John Horner')_
       $and$ ((manager/status='Approved') $or$_
       (manager/status='Pending'))]
```

The same expression can be rewritten to employ multiple predicates:

```
project[(manager/name='John Horner')]
       [((manager/status='Approved') $or$_
       (manager/status='Pending'))]
```

With the small number of projects listed previously, this isn't that much of an improvement, but if you had 50 projects and John Horner handled six of them, then those status expressions are evaluated only six times (rather than 50 times).

NOTE

Is there really that much of an improvement using multiple predicates? No, not really. In practice, most parsers do optimize **and** expressions, automatically truncating them if their initial predicates evaluate to false. However, multiple predicates are easier to read and work better in the paradigm of filtering than the more procedural **and** operator does.

Joining Expressions With *union*

On occasion, you'll find yourself in the situation of having to combine two different types of nodes, ones that have similar, but not identical, purposes. The `union` operator (|) serves this task; it lets you combine the results of two or more paths into a single node set and is a critical component in XSLT.

For example, suppose that you want to retrieve all of the managers in a company that are at the division level or above. (Company stock prices have fallen and the shareholders are getting restless, so you need to call a meeting.) The company manager list is shown in Listing 3.18.

Listing 3.18: The Acme Manager List of Managers Down to the Section Level (*Listing3.18.xml*)

```
<company>
        <name>Acme Rocket Company</name>
        <manager>
            <name>Phil Schwarts</name>
            <title>Chief Executive Officer</title>
            <canHire>yes</canHire>
            <vested/>
        </manager>
        <division>
            <name>Finance</name>
            <manager>
                 <name>James Galway</name>
                 <title>Chief Financial Officer</title>
                 <canHire>yes</canHire>
                 <vested/>
            </manager>
        </division>
        <division>
            <name>Marketing</name>
            <manager>
                 <name>Cynthia Dresler</name>
                 <title>VP, Marketing</title>
                 <canHire>yes</canHire>
            </manager>
        </division>
        <division>
             <name>Research</name>
             <manager>
                 <name>Benny Jocum</name>
                 <title>Chief Technical Officer</title>
                 <canHire>yes</canHire>
             </manager>
```

```
            <manager>
                <name>Allison Hart</name>
                <title>Vice President, Year 2000 Issues</title>
                <canHire>no</canHire>
                <vested/>
            </manager>
            <section>
                <name>COBOL Programming</name>
                <manager>
                    <name>Jerry Garcia</name>
                    <title>Director, COBOL Systems</title>
                </manager>
            </section>
        </division>
</company>
```

With only the operators we've discussed up until now, this is an ugly, complicated task. (It can be done, but it's not worth the headstanding to pull it off.) However, if you break the problem into two distinct sets (those managers at the company level and those at the division level), then you can use the union operator to join the two, as in the following example:

```
//company/manager/name | //division/manager/name
```

This combines two distinct paths. However, you can also use parentheses to provide a choice at any given node. The same expression could also be rendered in the following manner:

```
//(company|division)/manager/name
```

The XPath parser uses the union in the preceding statement to say that either the company node or the division node is acceptable as a valid node to add to the working node set. This also means that you can even qualify nodes with predicates within such union operators, as the following example demonstrates:

```
//(company|division[name='Finance'])/manager/name
```

This statement selects both the company and the division manager and then passes these nodes on as the gates for retrieving the respective manager names.

Note that the following two expressions are not the same:

```
//(company|division[name='Finance'])/manager/name
//(company|division)[name='Finance']/manager/name
```

The first retrieves either the company or the division with the name of `Finance`, while the latter retrieves either the company named `Finance` or the division named `Finance`. These won't be the same unless the company's name is `Finance`.

Comparison Predicates

The majority of expressions that have been given thus far have concentrated on set operations: excluding or including a node on the basis of its location or its equality to a string. However, a significant amount of work when dealing with paths involves comparing entities—is the value of this node greater than the value of that node, are two nodes not equal, is this node's value in a specific range, did this date take place before or after that date (and so forth)?

As with the existential predicates, there are some incompatibilities between XSL Pattern and XPath that make working with comparisons awkward. In general, the XPath specification provides a cleaner, easier-to-use means of working with any kind of comparisons, especially when combined with the power of variables.

The XSL Pattern operators are similar in form to those used in languages such as VBScript and JavaScript. The primary difference is that XSL Pattern recognizes both case-sensitive and case-insensitive operators and provides both standard symbols, such as the less-than (<) and greater-than (>) symbols, and text equivalents. Table 3.5 lists available operators.

TABLE 3.5: XSL Pattern Comparison Operators

Comparison Operator	Alternate Form	Description
`$eq$`	=	Equality
`$ne$`	!=	Inequality
`$lt$`	<	Less than
`$gt$`	>	Greater than
`$lte$`	<=	Less than or equal to
`$gte$`	>=	Greater than or equal to
`$ieq$`	None	Case-insensitive equality
`$ine$`	None	Case-insensitive inequality
`$ilt$`	None	Case-insensitive less-than
`$igt$`	None	Case-insensitive greater-than
`$ile$`	None	Case-insensitive less-than-or-equal-to
`$ige$`	None	Case-insensitive greater-than-or-equal-to

NOTE Note that XPath does not support tokenized operators (`$lt$`,`$gt$`, etc.) at all, even without the `$` characters. It also has different mechanisms for handling case insensitivity, as covered in Chapter 4, "XSL Transform."

A simple, stock-market-type XML structure gives some idea of both the use and the power of the XSL Pattern operators. The XML structure in Listing 3.19 contains stock price information from five fictional stocks.

Listing 3.19: Stock Price Information from Five Fictional Stocks (*Listing3.19.xml*)

```
<!-- stocks.xml -->
<stockReport>
    <stock>
        <symbol>ACME</symbol>
        <name>Acme Rocket Company</name>
        <openPrice>22.30</openPrice>
        <currentPrice>21.92</currentPrice>
        <sharesTraded>210</sharesTraded>
        <dateFirstTraded>1956-03-01</dateFirstTraded>
    </stock>
    <stock>
        <symbol>MER</symbol>
        <name>Mermaid Tails, Inc.</name>
        <openPrice>17.24</openPrice>
        <currentPrice>18.39</currentPrice>
        <sharesTraded>912</sharesTraded>
        <dateFirstTraded>2000-03-01</dateFirstTraded>
    </stock>
    <stock>
        <symbol>MIC</symbol>
        <name>Micronaut, Consolidated</name>
        <openPrice>5.25</openPrice>
        <currentPrice>9.32</currentPrice>
        <sharesTraded>87</sharesTraded>
        <dateFirstTraded>2000-02-03</dateFirstTraded>
    </stock>
    <stock>
        <symbol>LOG</symbol>
        <name>Logarhythmics, Inc.</name>
        <openPrice>93.12</openPrice>
        <currentPrice>85.12</currentPrice>
        <sharesTraded>2140</sharesTraded>
        <dateFirstTraded>1998-02-01</dateFirstTraded>
    </stock>
    <stock>
        <symbol>SYM</symbol>
        <name>Sym-Shares, LLC.</name>
        <openPrice>124.92</openPrice>
        <currentPrice>89.50</currentPrice>
        <sharesTraded>92</sharesTraded>
        <dateFirstTraded>2000-04-12</dateFirstTraded>
```

```
    </stock>
    <stock>
        <symbol>PAR</symbol>
        <name>Parallel Solutions, Inc.</name>
        <openPrice>49.95</openPrice>
        <currentPrice>47.50</currentPrice>
        <sharesTraded>42</sharesTraded>
        <dateFirstTraded>2000-01-01</dateFirstTraded>
    </stock>
</stockReport>
```

For example, assume that you want to purchase shares in a company but feel uncomfortable investing more than $50 a share. A simple query path string like the one in Listing 3.20 can give you a list of the stocks that are in your price range.

Listing 3.20: Displaying Stocks within a Given Price Range (*Listing3.20.vbs*)

```
Function getAffordableStocks(stockFileName,amount)
   dim stockDoc as DOMDocument
   dim stocks as IXMLDOMNodeList
   dim stock as IXMLDOMNode
   dim buf as String
   dim queryStr as String

   set stockDoc=new DOMDocument
   stockDoc.load stockFileName
   queryStr ="//stock[currentPrice $lt$ "+cstr(amount)+"]"
   set getAffordableStocks=stockDoc.selectNodes(queryStr)
End Function

Function displayStocks()
   Set stocks=getAffordableStocks("stocks.xml",50)
   buf=""
   for each stock in stocks
      buf=buf+stock.selectSingleNode("name").text
      buf=buf+"["+
      buf=buf+stock.selectSingleNode("symbol").text+"] "
      buf=buf+"$"+
      buf=buf+stock.selectSingleNode("currentPrice").text
      buf=buf+vbCRLF
   next
   alert buf
End Function

DisplayStocks
```

The primary difference between the query path string `//stock[currentPrice $lt$ 50.0]` and previous query strings is that the value being compared is not enclosed within quotation marks. This implicitly converts a specified value into a numeric value. You can also make the comparison explicit by using the `number()` function, as in the following example:

```
//stock[number(currentPrice) $lt$ number('50.0')]
```

Imagine that you only want to purchase stocks that have gained value in the last day. You can change the query string so that nodes are found on both sides of the comparison, as in the following example:

```
Querystr="//stock[openPrice $lt$_
    currentPrice]"
```

You can also use Boolean operators in conjunction with comparison operators. For example, if you want to find stocks that both showed an increase in stock price and were valued under $50 per share, you'd just use the `$and$` operator to combine the two expressions:

```
Querystr="//(stock[openPrice $lt$_
    currentPrice) $and$ (currentPrice $lt$ 50.0)]"
```

Advanced XSL Pattern Topics

The vast majority of all XPath expressions are relatively simple, since you typically will be dealing with information at known levels of context. However, XPath has some versatility in dealing with more complex expressions, as well as a few, very frustrating limitations.

Retrieving Exclusive Nodes

One of the few, rather curious holes in Microsoft's XPath implementation is the lack of any ability to eliminate duplicates within a selection. For example, in the company organization document discussed in Listing 3.11, the `//manager/name` query string will return seven items, one for each node. However, there are only three managers in the list (James Horner, John Locke, and Karen Fowler), with Horner and Locke repeated three times and Fowler given once.

A frequent requirement when working with data is a need to get a list of items such that any given item appears only once. It turns out, though, that the current Microsoft implementation of XPath doesn't support such a uniqueness feature, and, with a little forethought, it's fairly easy to see why: Two nodes with the same text values are still distinct entities, with different siblings, parents, and ordering.

However, if you do need a list of unique entities, you can use the DOM to build such a feature.

`GetUniqueElements`, as Listing 3.21 demonstrates, works by performing an XPath search on the XML document. Each node within the returned node list is then tested against a list of nodes belonging to an unassociated root element. If the test node has the same node name and text (even if attributes are different), then it is passed over; otherwise, a new node with that name and text is added to the root element. When the search is completed, the children of the root node are then returned as a node list. The routine is written in Visual Basic, but you can adapt it to VBScript by removing the `As XXX` in the function headers and `Dim` statements.

Listing 3.21: *GetUniqueElements* Retrieves Unique Nodes from an XML Document Based on an XPath Search. (*Listing3.21.bas*)

```
Visual Basic:
Public Function GetUniqueElements(_
       xmlDoc As DOMDocument,_
       queryStr As String) As IXMLDOMNodeList
    Dim nodeList As IXMLDOMNodeList
    Dim node As IXMLDOMElement
    Dim newNode As IXMLDOMElement
    Dim parentNode As IXMLDOMNode

    Set parentNode = xmlDoc.createElement("root")
    Set nodeList = xmlDoc.selectNodes(queryStr)

    For Each node In nodeList
        If parentNode.selectSingleNode(_
                node.nodeName + "[.='" + CStr(node.text)_
                 + "']") Is Nothing Then
            Set newNode = parentNode.appendChild(_
                node.cloneNode(False))
            newNode.text = node.text
        End If
    Next
    Set GetUniqueElements = parentNode.childNodes
End Function

Public Function GetUniqueAttributes(_
        xmlDoc As DOMDocument,_
        queryStr As String,_
        attributeName as String) As IXMLDOMNodeList
    Dim nodeList As IXMLDOMNodeList
    Dim node As IXMLDOMElement
    Dim newNode As IXMLDOMElement
    Dim parentNode As IXMLDOMNode

    Set parentNode = xmlDoc.createElement("root")
    Set nodeList = xmlDoc.selectNodes(queryStr)

    For Each node In nodeList
```

```
            If parentNode.selectSingleNode(_
                    node.nodeName + "[@"+attributeName+"='"_
                    + CStr(node.getAttribute(attributeName)) +_
                    "']") Is Nothing Then
                Set newNode = parentNode.appendChild(_
                    node.cloneNode(False))
                NewNode.setAttribute _
                    attributeName,node.getAttribute(attributeName)
            End If
        Next
        Set GetUniqueElements = parentNode.childNodes
    End Function

    ' Example showing retrieval of managers names from the approval list:
    Function GetProjectTableByManager(projectFile as String) as String
    dim managerNameNode as IXMLDOMNode
    dim managerName as String
    dim projectNode as IXMLDOMNode
    dim projectDoc as DOMDocument
    dim buf as String

    set projectDoc=createObject("Microsoft.XMLDOM")
    projectDoc.load projectFile
    buf="<table>"
    for each managerNameNode in GetUniqueElements(projectDoc,_
          "//manager/name")
       managerName=managerNameNode.text
       buf=buf+"<tr>"
       buf=buf+"<td colspan='3'><b>"+managerName+"</b></td>"
       buf=buf+"</tr>"
       for each projectNode in projectDoc.selectNodes(_
                      "//project[manager/name='"+managerName+"']")
           buf=buf+"<tr><td></td>"
           buf=buf+"<td>"+projectNode.selectSingleNode("name").text
           buf=buf+"</td>"
           buf=buf+"<td>"+projectNode.selectSingleNode("status").text
           buf=buf+"</td></tr>"
       next
       buf=buf+"</table>"
       GetProjectTableByManager=buf
    End Function
    'When called from an ASP file
    Response.Write GetProjectTableByManager("Projects.xml")
```

The function ends up displaying the table shown in Table 3.6, in HTML.

There is one major caveat with this approach: What you are doing here is creating a floating node to temporarily store names or attribute values; the nodes returned from the node list are dummy placeholders and don't correspond to any nodes that are actually in the tree.

TABLE 3.6: Result of `GetProjectTableByManager` when Displayed in a Web Browser

John Locke	Super Duper Rocket	Approved
	Big Red Button	Approved
	Pyrotechnics	Approved
James Horner	Super Duper Rocket	Approved
	Big Red Button	Rejected
	Pyrotechnics	Pending
Karen Fowler	Pyrotechnics	Pending

Information Functions

XSL Pattern also provides a number of core functions that let you work with various aspects of the XML document. These offer some functionality and are covered here for review, but, in general, they are definitely inferior to the XPath functions, which are covered far more extensively in Chapter 5, "The New XML Parser." The XSL Pattern functions are described in Table 3.7.

TABLE 3.7: XSL Pattern Information Functions

Name	Description
`end()`	Always returns the last child element of a given node.
`index()`	Returns the index number of the element within the `selectNodes` query. (Note that this will only be the same as the position of the node within its parent child's collection if the query returns simply the children of the parent node.)
`nodeName()`	Returns the name of the node (its tag name).
`nodeType()`	Returns the number of the node type. (See Table 2.4 in the preceding chapter.)
`date()`	Converts the text value of the node into a date, if possible.
`text()`	Returns the text content of the node.
`value()`	Returns the value of the node. If no schema has been defined, this defaults to the text of the node; otherwise, it returns the data-typed value.

The following statement, for example, retrieves the fourth stock in the collection from our fictional stock listings (remember that the `index()` is always zero based):

```
//stock[index()=3]
```

Whenever a numeric value is passed into the predicate qualifier, the XPath parser assumes that it should be compared to the `index()` function. That is to say that `//stock[index()=3]` is the same as `stock[3]`.

You can also use the ! operator to specify that the function applies to a different node within the predicate operator. Thus, you could use the following expression to retrieve the stock for Parallel, Inc:

```
//stock[name!value()='Parallel, Inc.']
```

When you don't specify an information function within a predicate context, in fact, the `value()` is the default function used. That is, the preceding example is equivalent to the following:

```
//stock[name='Parallel, Inc.']
```

Default Information Function Behaviors

It's worth making a distinction here. The `text()` function retrieves the text content of a node, while `value()` retrieves the typed value of the node, which is the value that the node has if the text is converted to the type indicated by the XML Schema. When known schemas are present, the scoping parser takes its cue from the right-hand expression; if it's a number, then the node's value on the left side is converted into a number as well (likewise if it's a date).

In most cases where there is no schema, however, the `value()` implicitly assumes the contents to be of the `text()` type. Thus, in general, you're probably unlikely to need to use any of the information functions very often.

The `end()` function retrieves a pointer to the last item in the scoping context's list. In general, it is an expression that should only be used by itself; it doesn't return a number. If you want to return the last stock in the stock list, you'd just use the following expression:

```
//stock[end()]
```

WARNING `end()` may not do what you think it does. It retrieves the actual node associated with the context, rather than simply provide a count of the context size. Unfortunately, this leaves no clean mechanism to get the total count within XPath itself, although from DOM you can always do a `.length` count on the result of a `.selectNodes` statement to do this.

You can also use `end()`with preexisting collections. For example, revisiting the preceding stock market example, suppose that you want to retrieve the name of the last stock listed that had a current price under $50 per share. You could do this as follows:

```
//stock[currentPrice<50][end()]/name
```

The first predicate filters all stock prices under $50, while the second returns the last of these items. Note that order is important here. The following expression would only return a node if the last node in the stock's document happens to have a current price under $50.

```
//stock[end()][currentPrice<50]/name
```

Comparing dates has always been one of the more complicated actions that any programmer has to contend with when using databases, and, unfortunately, it is also one of the more common. The MSXML XSL Pattern implementation supports comparing dates, with or without a schema specification.

Just as `number()` forces a value into a numeric representation, `date()` forces a value into a date format (specifically the ISO8601 date representation, in the form YYYY-MM-DD). For example, if you want to find out the companies that have only been trading since January 1, 2000, you could write the following query:

```
set stockdoc=new DOMDocument
stockdoc.load "code3-8.stocks.xml"
set newStocks=stockDoc.selectNodes(_
   "//stock[dateFirstTraded >= date('2000-01-01')]")
```

Similarly, you could compare two stock's trading dates to retrieve all of the stocks that have come available since that stock, as shown in Listing 3.22.

Listing 3.22: *GetStocksAfterStockTrade* VB Function (*Listing3.22.vbs*)

```
Function GetStocksAfterStockTrade(stockDoc as DOMDocument,_ stockSymbol as
String) as IXMLDOMNodeList
     Dim newStocks as IXMLDOMNodelist
     Dim testDate as String
     Set testDate=stockDoc.selectSingleNode(_
       "//stock[symbol='"+stockSymbol+"']/dateFirstTraded")_
       .text
     Set newStocks=stockDoc.selectNodes(_
       "//stock[dateFirstTraded $gte$ _
       date('"+testDate+"')]")
     set GetStocksAfterStockTrade=newStocks
End Function
```

NOTE Date and number explicitly map the text value of a string to a typed representation, even if a schema hasn't been declared for that value. However, by including a schema, you can (and should) bypass these two functions, as the type conversions take place implicitly.

Summary

XPath and SQL share a number of similarities: they are optimized for locating information within their respective environments, they have a fairly easy-to-use syntax, and they deal with data as collections rather than as individual pieces of information. Perhaps most importantly, they abstract the process of dealing with complex, sometimes-Byzantine data constructs so that people don't need to worry about the exact implementation of the parser or DBMS.

The limitations that both face are also similar: Neither XPath nor SQL can truly be said to be a full programming language. Over time, SQL has developed implementations that support stored procedures, but these are not truly intrinsic to the power of the language. This is also true of XPath, which can quickly locate information within an XML structure but doesn't have the ability to process information outside the scope of the document itself.

As mentioned earlier, trying to write a book on emerging technology is always fraught with peril. When this chapter was first written, the newer parser had not yet come out even in beta. In the interim, the vastly improved (and XPath and XSL compliant) parser did finally come out, and the differences were enough to warrant covering them in their own chapter. I've tried here to provide much of the commonality between the two XPath-oriented parsers. In Chapter 4, "XSL Transform," I look at the XSL side of the older XML parser (the November 1998 version) and show how the utility of XSL patterns can enhance your output on Internet Explorer 5.

In Chapter 5, "The New XML Parser," I cover the more-advanced features of XPath as they apply to XSL, including the manipulation of strings, more sophisticated (and easier) node-handling functions, basic formatting, the use of variables, and more.

XPath is intimately tied to the Extensible Stylesheet Language, or XSL. Indeed, much of the power of XSL derives from its use of XPath, both for matching specific items and for choosing the items to be selected. Together, XSL and XPath provide much of the programming power to make XML a globally useful language.

CHAPTER 4

XSL Transform

- Seeing the power of transformation
- Understanding templates
- Creating elements and attributes
- Understanding conditional XSL
- Scripting
- Using regular expressions

While XML is a useful mechanism for storing data, its hierarchical structure makes building output for it difficult and time-consuming. The Extensible Stylesheet Language-Transform, or XSLT, fills this gap by providing an XML-based transformation language that can be used to turn XML into a wide variety of other formats.

This chapter both explores the mechanisms by which XSLT creates structured output and looks at a number of generalized XSLT filters for producing tables, trees, and other HTML and XML constructs.

Why Do We Need Transforms?

At times I find it handy to envision XML as quantum blobs zipping from one location to another through an abstract sea. This is typically after a little too much coffee at Starbucks, mind you, but the analogy is actually rather useful to understand the concept of XSL Transforms.

Throughout the 30-year history of database development, it has been conventional (and useful) to think of data as explicit values—numbers, strings, and maybe the occasional date or Boolean data type. Yet XML lets us change that viewpoint, to see data as the constituent parts of objects. By moving away from the atomic viewpoint of data and seeing it instead as a much more amorphous concept, as an entity that *describes* an object or objects, we can start thinking about information in a more holistic way.

The term "description" here is important. How do you describe a table, for example? I'm not talking here about a columnar set of data, but rather a physical table, made of wood. The one on which my laptop sits is round, with a light-colored brown grain, a moderately reflective surface, supported by a single metallic column. This is one description—a map, if you will—of this table object.

Of course, that is not the only description we can apply to the table. The same table could be described through its material composition: 20 pounds of pine and 32 pounds of iron, with assorted trace metals to provide strength to the support column and base. Or the table can be described graphically, via a rendering, a wire-mesh model, or perhaps even a fractal space-filling curve.

All of these are descriptions of the same object. While XML doesn't normally afford such a rich variety of descriptions, the same basic principle applies: an XML document is an object or a collection of objects that have an internal systematic consistency. The same object may have a number of different views, or representations, depending on the specific requirements at the time.

Traditional programming languages (even object-oriented ones) run into significant problems when dealing with the issue of representation. Typically, there will be a fairly limited number of ways that a given object can be expressed. An object can be serialized, rendered into an interim binary format. An object will typically have a few methods for drawing the object, within the constraints of the object's internal properties. Yet for the most part the mechanism used for describing that object is essentially generated internally, or is a part of a global system description (you can change the background color of an editing pane to gray in Windows, for example, but it affects every editing pane in every application).

At the most atomic level, you can change specific properties of an object one at a time. This is the principle on which almost all procedural languages are built, and it's perhaps not insignificant that the vast majority of code that's written is designed to set or retrieve individual property values of objects.

Between the atomic and the system level, there is a curious void—there are very few tools that can describe objects at the object level and thus transform an object from one representation to another. However, one of the benefits of XML is that it is essentially an object description language, something that can be used to provide a unique representation of the object at the object's level of granularity.

To use the Document Object Model to manipulate XML documents is akin to building a complex organic molecule one atom at a time. It can certainly be done. However, in most natural processes, a complex molecule such as DNA is built up holistically, with specific amino acids building whole sections of the molecule simultaneously. In a similar fashion, you can create new "views" of an XML document holistically by applying XSL Transforms.

Creating Basic XSL Templates

The principle behind XSL transforms can take a little while to appreciate fully, but it isn't terribly complicated. In essence, the transform is an XML document broken up into a set of templates. The XSL parser attempts to match the top node in the document to a given template pattern. Within the matching template, an XPath expression is used to select subordinate items within the XSL document, which are then matched against in turn. This process continues until no more matches can be found within the document.

XSL documents are probably the first documents you will encounter that make heavy use of namespaces. The XSL namespace is used to tell the parser how to interpret the tags in the XSL document—because such a document is typically used to transform an XML document from one (default) namespace to another, the XSL namespace has to be declared explicitly.

A simple example can illustrate both of these principles. Consider the organizational chart from Chapter 3; the code for it is displayed again in Listing 4.1. I've added to the listing a processing instruction, or PI, which specifies the location of an XSL filter (`managers1.xsl`) along with the style sheet type (`text/xsl`).

Listing 4.1: The Acme Rocket Company Org Chart (*code4-01.xml*)

```
<?xml:stylesheet href="manager1.xsl" type="text/xsl"?>
<company>
        <name>Acme Rocket Company</name>
        <manager>
            <name>Phil Schwarts</name>
            <title>Chief Executive Officer</title>
            <canHire>yes</canHire>
            <vested/>
        </manager>
        <division>
            <name>Finance</name>
            <manager>
                 <name>James Galway</name>
                 <title>Chief Financial Officer</title>
                 <canHire>yes</canHire>
                 <vested/>
            </manager>
        </division>
        <division>
            <name>Marketing</name>
            <manager>
                 <name>Cynthia Dresler</name>
                 <title>VP, Marketing</title>
                 <canHire>yes</canHire>
            </manager>
        </division>
        <division>
             <name>Research</name>
             <manager>
                 <name>Benny Jocum</name>
                 <title>Chief Technical Officer</title>
                 <canHire>yes</canHire>
             </manager>
             <manager>
                 <name>Allison Hart</name>
                 <title>Vice President, Year 2000 Issues</title>
                 <canHire>no</canHire>
                 <vested/>
             </manager>
             <section>
                 <name>COBOL Programming</name>
                 <manager>
                     <name>Jerry Garcia</name>
                      <title>Director, COBOL Systems</title>
                 </manager>
```

```
            </section>
        </division>
</company>
```

Suppose you wanted to create an HTML listing of all the managers by name and title, with the title appearing first, in boldface, followed by a comma and then the name. While you could use DOM to do this, you can also create an XSL template (in this case the aforementioned `managers.xsl`) to do the same thing, as shown in Listing 4.2. Figure 4.1 shows how it is displayed in Internet Explorer 5.

Listing 4.2: The Managers Transform (*manager1.xsl*)

```
<xsl:stylesheet xmlns:xsl="http://www.w3.org/TR/WD-xsl">
   <!-- Match the XML #document node -->
   <xsl:template match="/">
      <!-- find all manager nodes in the document -->
      <xsl:apply-templates select="//manager"/>
   </xsl:template>
   <!-- For any manager node found -->
   <xsl:template match="manager">
      <!-- format and output the result -->
      <p><b><xsl:value-of select="title"/>,</b>
      <xsl:value-of select="name"/></p>
   </xsl:template>
</xsl:stylesheet>
```

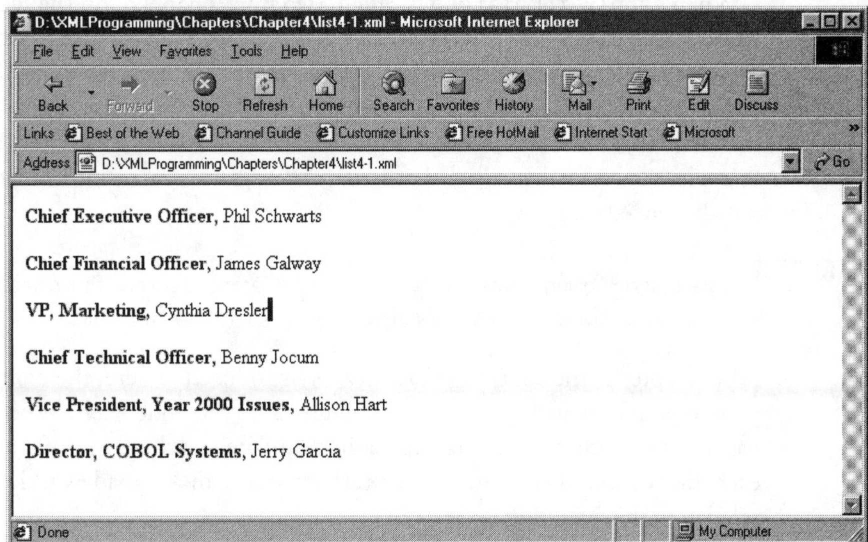

FIGURE 4.1
The result of running the managers transform in Internet Explorer 5

One of the problems with namespaces is that they can frequently make things look more complicated than they really are. Pull out comments, XSL brackets and the XSL namespace elements, and the template looks something like this:

```
Stylesheet
   Template(match="/")
      ApplyTemplates("//manager")
   End Template

   Template(match="manager")
      <p><b>(valueOf("title"),</b>
      (valueOf("name")</p>
   End Template
End Stylesheet
```

A style sheet thus consists of a set of templates to match given patterns. The first pattern that the XSL document will match is the root node of the XML document (/). Once this node has been matched, an XPath query can be used to select other nodes such as `//manager` through the `<xsl:apply-templates>` tag.

WARNING The first node in any XML document (the one matched by /) is not the first element of the document. Instead, it is the virtual node `#document`. In turn, `#document` has only one child, the `documentElement`, such as `<company>` in the above example. Forgetting this rule can make your XSL parser fail to match anything properly.

When `<apply-templates>` is called, two things happen internally. The XSL parser executes the XPath provided in the select portion of the `<apply-templates>` tag. This creates a node list of elements that satisfy the XPath query. For each node in the node list, the XSL parser compares the node to each template in turn. If a match is found, the node is passed to the template to be processed. Once processed, that node is consumed; even if there is another template match further down that satisfies the query, any result from an XPath queried will only be parsed once.

TIP Note that any given element may actually be referenced several times in a document—however, it may appear only once for a given `<apply-templates>` command.

In Chapter 3, the concept of *context* was introduced. There, the context was the starting point of a node's query, and was by default set to the node itself. With XSLT, each template has its own context. In essence, once the template matches a specific node, then (with some exceptions covered later in this chapter) any query that is made within the template is made relative to the matching node.

To see this in action, it's worth looking at the manager template again:

```
<xsl:template match="manager">
   <!-- format and output the result -->
   <p><b><xsl:value-of select="title"/>,</b>
   <xsl:value-of select="name"/></p>
</xsl:template>
```

The first match the template finds is with the CEO of the company, Phil Schwartz. Specifically, the matching node is:

```
<manager>
    <name>Phil Schwarts</name>
    <title>Chief Executive Officer</title>
    <canHire>yes</canHire>
    <vested/>
</manager>
```

Once the node is matched, then the ensuing `select` statements apply relative to the manager node—title retrieves the child `title` node, name retrieves the child `name` node and so forth by using the `<xsl:value-of>` element. This element retrieves either the text of the first child that meets the criterion set up in the `select` statement or the text of the current node if no select is specified. In other words, for the manager node:

```
<xsl:value-of/>
```

is the same as

```
<xsl:value-of select="."/>
```

which in both cases would retrieve as output the concatenated string

```
Phil SchwartzChief Executive Officeryes
```

NOTE It's worth stressing that `<xsl:value-of>` only retrieves the value of the *first* node that satisfies the `select` criterion, not of all nodes. In essence, its behavior is roughly the same as `node.selectSingleNode(selectStr).text`.

XSL Style Sheet Namespaces and Staying Updated

Before we progress too much farther, it's worth looking in a little more depth at the issue of namespaces with regard to XSL. As I write this, the W3 specification for XSL-Transform (`http://www.w3.org/TR/xslt`) has just been officially endorsed by the members of the W3C. However, the current Microsoft parser was developed for use with the 10-Dec-1998 XSL specification, which was current at the time that Internet Explorer 5.0 was released, and a significant number of products have made their way to production using the older XSL DOM.

XSL Style Sheet Namespaces and Staying Updated *(continued)*

Because of this issue, Microsoft has officially said that they will support both the 10-Dec-1998 standard and the 15-Nov-1999 standard with MSXML. However, in order to tell the parser which version of XSL is currently supported, you need to set the namespace for the appropriate XSLT parser in the `<xsl:stylesheet>` tag. Specifically, the namespace designation should be given as:

- For 10-Dec-1998: `xmlns:xsl="http://www.w3.org/TR/WD-xsl"`
- For 16-Nov-1999: `xmlns:xsl="http://www.w3.org/TR/xslt"`

One of the problems with writing a book in the fast-paced environment of the Internet is that in the time between when a manuscript is submitted and it sees print, a product can change radically. As I write this, Microsoft has not yet announced specific plans for a parser that complies with the 16 Nov XSL-T Recommendation, except that they will release a compliant version.

Most XSL transforms aren't quite so simple that they can be expressed in a single template, but even given that, XSL can give you a surprisingly compact notation for modifying your data. Consider a variation of the above example: building a tree showing the managers and their positions relative to one another.

In this case you have three distinct cases to consider—the manager of the company, the managers of each division and the section managers within each division. One approach that you can take is to create a template for each layer in the company, as shown in Listing 4.3.

Listing 4.3: Revisiting the Managers Transform (*manager2.xsl*)

```
<xsl:stylesheet xmlns:xsl="http://www.w3.org/TR/WD-xsl">
   <!-- Match the XML #document node -->
   <xsl:template match="/">
      <ul>
      <xsl:apply-templates select="company"/>
      </ul>
   </xsl:template>

   <xsl:template match="company">
   <li>
      <span><b><xsl:value-of select="name"/></b></span>
      <xsl:apply-templates select="manager"/>
      <ul>
      <xsl:apply-templates select="division"/>
      </ul>
   </li>
   </xsl:template>

   <xsl:template match="division">
      <li>
      <span><b><xsl:value-of select="name"/></b></span>
```

```
      <xsl:apply-templates select="manager"/>
      <ul>
      <xsl:apply-templates select="section"/>
      </ul>
   </li>
   </xsl:template>

   <xsl:template match="section">
      <li>
      <span><b><xsl:value-of select="name"/></b></span>
      <xsl:apply-templates select="manager"/>
      </li>
   </xsl:template>

   <xsl:template match="manager">
      <!-- format and output the result -->
      <span><xsl:value-of select="name"/>
      <i><xsl:value-of select="title"/></i></span>,
   </xsl:template>
</xsl:stylesheet>
```

However, there's also a fair amount of duplication between the different groupings. By taking advantage of some of the properties of XPath, we can collapse the list from five nodes to three (Listing 4.4).

Listing 4.4: Another Take on the Managers Transform (*manager3.xsl*)

```
<xsl:stylesheet xmlns:xsl="http://www.w3.org/TR/WD-xsl">
   <!-- Match the XML #document node -->
   <xsl:template match="/">
      <ul>
      <xsl:apply-templates select="company"/>
   </ul>
   </xsl:template>

   <xsl:template match="*">
      <li>
      <span><b><xsl:value-of select="name"/></b></span>
      <xsl:apply-templates select="manager"/>
      <ul>
      <xsl:apply-templates select="division|section"/>
      </ul>
   </li>
   </xsl:template>

   <xsl:template match="manager">
      <!-- format and output the result -->
      <span><xsl:value-of select="name"/>
```

```
        <i><xsl:value-of select="title"/></i></span>,
    </xsl:template>
</xsl:stylesheet>
```

In this case, the root template looks for a company node template but doesn't find an explicit match. However, the asterisk wildcard character does match company, so that template is used. When <apply-templates> is called for manager, the parser has a quandary: Both the wildcard character and the manager template satisfy this node. The parser resolves this by using a reverse lookup. In essence, it walks the templates from bottom to top until it finds a node that matches, then the parser terminates the search. Since <xsl:template match= "manager"> is the first node encountered from the bottom, it's the one that's applied (if you had inverted the order of the match="manager" and match="*", then the wild card would become the selected node).

NOTE To reiterate, template conflicts in XSL structures are resolved from the bottom of the document up.

Finally, within the wildcard node, the expression <xsl:apply-templates select="division|section"> is encountered. As you saw in the last chapter, this is equivalent to saying "Select either a division or a section node from the context's children." Because there is neither a division nor a section node, the wildcard is again chosen, in what amounts to a recursive process. This process is repeated until no other items can be selected.

To see the result of this transform, set the first line of the org chart XML document (code4-01.xml) to the following:

```
<?xml:stylesheet href="manager3.xsl" type="text/xsl"?>
```

The XSL Parser

So far, we haven't addressed the question of what specifically is generated by the XSL parser as it wends its way through the various nodes of the XML document. The short answer (although not completely accurate) is that the transform produces text. The long answer is a little more complicated.

When an XSL document reference is encountered by the XSL parser in the header of an XML document, the XSL document is loaded into a DOM of its own. Once the XML document itself is also loaded into a DOM, an invisible third agent comes into play: the XSL parser, a small program that can render the XML into to a specific style-sheet format. Internet Explorer 5 has a built-in XSL parser that is automatically invoked whenever an XML document is loaded into the browser.

NOTE More accurately, the XSL parser is invoked whenever a document has a text/xml MIME type, which files with .XML and .XSL have by default. This distinction is important when XML documents come from ASP sources, where the MIME type has to be set explicitly in order for the XML document to be recognized properly.

If the document in question doesn't have an explicit style-sheet processing instruction (the `<?xml:stylesheet ?>` instruction displayed earlier), IE5 will automatically invoke its own internal style sheet to display the document in a collapsible tree-view structure. It is possible to override this, but in general you're better off adding the PI to the document to change the style sheet explicitly.

How the XSL Parser Creates Its Output

After both XML and XSL documents are in DOM form, the XSL parser gets to work, performing the following actions:

1. The XSL parser loads both XML and XSL documents into separate DOMs.
2. A base document buffer is created, with empty text.
3. The parser scans through the list of templates until it encounters one that satisfies the root node (this is typically the template `<xsl:template match="/">`).
4. Each text node is transferred directly to the new document as it is encountered.
5. Non-XSL nodes are likewise transferred as text elements into the buffer.
6. When an XSL node is encountered, one of two actions can occur, depending upon whether the node is context changing or not. If not (for example, an `<xsl:value-of>` tag), then the results are evaluated and inserted into the stream.
7. On the other hand, if the context is changed (through an `<xsl:apply-templates>`, for example), then the XSL parser pushes the current context onto a stack and changes to the new context.
8. The above actions are then applied until the close tag for the context is encountered. At this point, the current context is popped off the stack and the old context is reset.
9. Once the final context (the root node's context) is popped off the stack, the processing is assumed to be completed, and the XSL parser returns the buffer as a Unicode string.
10. In IE5, this string is in turn passed onto the HTML renderer, which converts the resulting output into an HTML document.

NOTE Note that if the resulting document doesn't start with a <HTML><HEAD/><BODY>, IE5 will automatically wrap these around the output. This is why the HTML output from the manager XSL documents was still valid, even though the HTML wasn't well formed.

TIP Even the final HTML conversion is just the default action, by the way. In theory, you could set the MIME type of the output to any accepted MIME type value, and IE will then attempt to display the document as that type. For example, you could set your MIME type to `image/gif` and have your XML output GIF data to the browser.

Using the *TransformNode* and *TransformNodeToObject* Properties

While adding a style-sheet processing instruction to the top of an XML file may work for static documents, it's a fairly impractical way to handle XML documents that were created dynamically or that may need multiple transforms. Fortunately, there are other alternatives for working with XSL in the DOM. Specifically, the `IXMLDOMNode` interface has two very useful properties designed for XSL: `transformNode` and `transformNodeToObject`.

`TransformNode` could more properly be called "applyXSLTransform," since that is precisely what it does. It is *the* interface into the XSL parser. It takes as an argument an XSL document and produces as output the buffered string described above.

For example, consider again the org chart XML in Listing 4.1. By removing the initial style sheet PI, you can see the result from the application of all three style sheets by using the `transformNode` property in a script (Listing 4.5).

Listing 4.5: A Sample HTML Page Showing the Code Produced by the Respective XSL Transforms (*manager.htm*)

```
<html>
<head><title>Manager XSL Output</title></head>
<body>
<xmp>
<script language="VBScript">

function getXSLOutput(xmlDoc,xslfilepath)
   dim xslDoc
   dim buffer
   set xslDoc=createObject("Microsoft.XMLDOM")
   xslDoc.load xslFilePath
   buffer=""
   buffer=buffer+"<h2>Output for "+xslfilepath+"</h2>"
   buffer=buffer+xmlDoc.transformNode(xslDoc)
   buffer=buffer+"<h4>HTML Code for "+xslfilepath+"</h4>"
   buffer=buffer+ "<xmp>"
   buffer=buffer+xmlDoc.transformNode(xslDoc)
   buffer=buffer+ "</xmp>"
   buffer=buffer+ "<hr>"
   getXSLOutput=buffer
end function

function main()
   dim xmlDoc
   set xmlDoc=createObject("Microsoft.XMLDOM")
   xmlDoc.load "list4-4.xml"
   document.write getXSLOutput(xmlDoc,"manager1.xsl")
```

```
        document.write getXSLOutput(xmlDoc,"manager2.xsl")
        document.write getXSLOutput(xmlDoc,"manager3.xsl")
        set  node=xmlDoc.selectSingleNode("//division[name='Research']")
        document.write getXSLOutput(node,"manager3.xsl")
    end function

    main
    </script>
    </body>
    </html>
```

The fact that the end product of the XSL parser is text rather than a DOM has some interesting implications. One of the most important is that the output doesn't have to be XML or HTML; you could use the results of the XSL parser to create generic text files, Rich Text Format (RTF) files, Adobe Acrobat PDF files, SQL files, Visual Basic class definitions, or very nearly anything else. I'll explore this technique in far more detail later, but for the moment, the important thing to remember is that you are not limited to XML or HTML output when using the XSL parser.

NOTE This translation is, of course, one-way only. An XSL document can create an RTF file, but XSL isn't equipped to read an RTF file (which is built on a similar stack-based system but treats its tag enclosures differently). To go to XML from a different format, you'll probably have to use the DOM.

Sometimes, however, you want to transform from one XML format to another and need to minimize the number of string conversions. To expand upon an earlier qualification, the XSL parser doesn't actually keep a string buffer internally. Instead, it uses a C++ IStream object. Explicitly converting from IStreams to strings can be a very time-consuming operation (it's actually one of the biggest bottlenecks when dealing with XML).

To get around this, you can take advantage of the alternate method `transformNodeToObject`. This takes as arguments an XSL DOM and either a variant object or an XML DOM object. In essence, `transformNodeToObject` performs the same conversion as `transformNode` does, but it then passes the result as an IStream directly to the new DOM object. This new DOM is then validated, and the DOM's `parseError` object gets updated to reflect any errors from the conversion, as follows:

```
function main()
   dim xmlDoc as DOMDocument
   dim xslDoc as DOMDocument
   dim resultDoc as DOMDocument
   set xmlDoc=createObject("Microsoft.XMLDOM")
   set xslDoc=createObject("Microsoft.XMLDOM")
   set resultDoc=createObject("Microsoft.XMLDOM")
```

```
      xmlDoc.load "list4-4.xml"
      xslDoc.load "manager3.xsl"
      ' Pass the result of an XSL transform to resultDoc
      xmlDoc.transformNodeToObject xslDoc,resultDoc
      if resultDoc.parseError.errorCode=0 then
         msgbox resultDoc.xml
      else
         msgbox "XSL Transform failed because "_
            +resultDoc.parseError.reason
      end if
   end function
```

Unlike `TransformNode`, by the way, `TransformNodeToObject` is considerably more finicky about the output—it must be a valid XML object. If you're just transforming from one XML format to another, generally `TransformNodeToObject` is far more efficient, but if you need generalized output, them stick to `TransformNode`.

It's worth noting that both `transformNode` and `transformNodeToObject` are interfaces on `IXMLDOMNode`. As a consequence, you can call an XSL transform on a subnode of a document, although you should of course take care to ensure that the transform will in fact provide meaningful output (if the node is farther down the tree than any of the templates provide for, then the output will be simply a blank string). For example, you can apply the `manager3` transform just to the division node (this is, somewhat indirectly, what was done with the last output in Listing 4.5):

```
set node=xmlDoc.selectSingleNode(_
          "//division[name='Research']")
document.write node.transformNode("manager3.xsl")
```

Debugging XSL Transforms

XSL Transforms can be something of a black box, and when something goes wrong within the XSL parser, it can be hard to understand why you only receive a blank string as output. One way around this is to take advantage of `transformNodeToObject` and the `ParseError` object, as shown in the function `DebugTransform` (Listing 4.6).

Listing 4.6: The *DebugTransform* Function (*Listing4-06.txt*)

```
Function DebugTransform _
     (xmlNode as Variant,xslDoc as DOMDocument, _
     optional byRef buffer as String="") _
     as String
   Dim resultDoc as DOMDocument
   Dim xmlDoc as DOMDocument
   Dim MsgStr as String
   Dim localStr as String
   Set resultDoc=createObject("Microsoft.XMLDOM")
```

```
    xmlNode.transformNodeToObject xslDoc,resultDoc
    msgStr= "Source Document"+vbCRLF
    msgStr=msgStr+ErrorDump(xmlNode)
    msgStr=msgStr+"Transform Document"+vbCRLF
    msgStr=msgStr+ErrorDump(xslDoc)
    msgStr=msgStr+ "Result Document"+vbCRLF
    msgStr=msgStr+ErrorDump(resultDoc)
    buffer=msgStr
    Debug.print msgStr
    DebugTransform=xmlNode.transformNode(xslDoc)
End Function

Function ErrorDump(xmlSource as Variant) as string
    Dim errorMsg as String
    Dim xmlDoc as DOMDocument
    Select case typename(xmlsource)
        Case "DOMDocument"
            Set xmlDoc=xmlSource
        Case Else
            Set xmlDoc=xmlSource.ownerDocument
    End Select
    If xmlDoc.parseError.errorCode>0 then
        ErrorMsg="An Error occurred (Error "
        ErrorMsg=ErrorMsg+cstr(xmlDoc.parseError.errorCode)+")"+vbCRLF
        ErrorMsg=ErrorMsg+ xmlDoc.parseError.reason+vbCRLF
        ErrorMsg=ErrorMsg+" at char "+cstr(xmlDoc.parseError.linePos)
        ErrorMsg=ErrorMsg+" of line "+cstr(xmlDoc.parseError.line)
        ErrorMsg=ErrorMsg+" in file "+xmlDoc.parseError.url+vbCRLF
        ErrorMsg=ErrorMsg+"Text of line:"+xmlDoc.parseError.srcText
    Else
        ErrorMsg="OK"
    End if
    ErrorDump=ErrorMsg
End Function
```

`DebugTransform` can be used to determine the error states of all of the documents, even with a non-XML `TransformNode` call. However, you should restore these to `transformNode` or `transformNodeToObject` when you release your live code.

Note that if your transform produces non-XML results, then both your source document and transform document may be OK but your result document will generate an error, so you should examine those results carefully to determine if there really is a problem.

To debug the code, replace the `TransformNode` functions with the `DebugTransform` functions. If you want to keep a log, you can pass a string as an optional parameter, and the function will place a copy of the error log into the string. The output of `DebugTransform` is the transformed text.

Outputting HTML and Copying Nodes

HTML can prove to be a frustrating challenge for XSL coders. The examples we've looked at so far have been oriented toward XML documents, which have very definite known structures. Unfortunately, most HTML documents are (to use the SGML vernacular) *irregular*; while they follow definite rules, the tags in HTML can appear pretty much anywhere in a document.

Furthermore, HTML is not even guaranteed to be XML compliant. Indeed, one of the ironies of Microsoft's HTML implementation in IE5 is that even though it is built around the XML engine, the code that most internal Microsoft editors use (including the DHTML Editor component and the FrontPage Office application) actually generates code that is *not* XML compliant (see Chapter 7, "XML and the Browser," for a rather scathing criticism of this particular implementation policy). As a consequence, in some cases the HTML you will want to include within your XML documents would cause the XML parser to choke if represented as normal tags.

For example, consider a slide-presentation application that describes information about XML. One slide from this presentation might have a `<para>` tag that contains a block of paragraph text. If the paragraph has the potential to contain some HTML markup, the XML might look something like this:

```
<slide id="eraPCNetwork">
    <title>The Era of the PC Network (1974-1989)</title>
    <para><b>Two <i>inventions</i></b> changed the nature
    of computing -- the <i>personal computer</i> and the
    <i>modem</i>, which appeared within a few years of one
     another</para>
    <!-- more elements here -->
</slide>
```

The bold and italic tags within the text present an interesting problem. In order to pass these tags into the target stream, you need some mechanism to catch and handle these tags. A sample XSL document for displaying the text of this slide might look something like Listing 4.7.

Listing 4.7: One Way of Handling HTML Markup (*list04-07.xsl*)

```
<xsl:stylesheet xmlns:xsl="http://www.w3.org/TR/WD-xsl">
   <xsl:template match="/">
   <div>
      <xsl:apply-templates select="//para"/>
    </div>
   </xsl:template>
   <xsl:template match="para">
      <div>
```

```
      <xsl:apply-templates select="text()|b|i"/>
      </div>
   </xsl:template>
   <xsl:template match="b">
      <b><xsl:value-of/></b>
   </xsl:template>
   <xsl:template match="i">
      <i><xsl:value-of/></i>
   </xsl:template>
   <xsl:template match="text()">
      <xsl:value-of/>
   </xsl:template>
</xsl:stylesheet>
```

The `text()` operator comes from XPath, and here I specifically set up a condition such that when a text node is thrown (with `<apply-templates>`), there is a template to catch it (`<xsl:template match="text()">`). However, there's a problem. In the example above, the phrase `<b>Two <i>inventions</i></b>` has an italics tag contained within a bold tag. `value-of` automatically removes any formatting (in essence, it is the XSL equivalent of the DOM `.text` property), so that when this expression is evaluated, the XSL parser never sees the embedded italics.

One way around this is to make the `<b>` and `<i>` recursive, by using the `<xsl:apply-templates>` tag instead of the `value-of` tag. When applied without any qualifying `select` tag, `apply-templates` will pass all of the children of a given node, not just the specified elements, as shown in Listing 4.8.

Listing 4.8: A Slightly Better Way of Handling HTML Markup (*list04-08.xsl*)

```
<xsl:stylesheet xmlns:xsl="http://www.w3.org/TR/WD-xsl">
   <xsl:template match="/">
   <div>
      <xsl:apply-templates select="//para"/>
    </div>
   </xsl:template>
   <xsl:template match="para">
      <div>
      <xsl:apply-templates select="text()|b|i"/>
      </div>
   </xsl:template>
   <xsl:template match="b">
      <b><xsl:apply-templates/></b>
   </xsl:template>
   <xsl:template match="i">
      <i><xsl:apply-templates/></i>
```

```
    </xsl:template>
    <xsl:template match="text()">
       <xsl:value-of/>
    </xsl:template>
 </xsl:stylesheet>
```

Since the <b> and <i> tags can theoretically stay as themselves (directly or indirectly), this makes it possible to include nested expressions. However, you can still do better. If the para tag implies that anything contained therein is either some markup that is appropriate to the original XML schema and should be parsed or HTML markup meant for final output, then ideally you don't want to set up a complex nested loop to catch every item. Instead, you just want to pass the node on as is.

To do that, you need the <xsl:copy> tag. This incredibly useful tag acts like a gate to pass the node directly onto the output stream. Thus we can simplify the code as follows (Listing 4.9).

Listing 4.9: The Best Way of Handling Well-Formed HTML Output (*list04-09.xsl*)

```
<xsl:stylesheet xmlns:xsl="http://www.w3.org/TR/WD-xsl">
   <xsl:template match="/">
   <div>
      <xsl:apply-templates select="//para"/>
    </div>
   </xsl:template>
   <xsl:template match="para">
      <xsl:apply-templates select="*|@*|text()"/>
   </xsl:template>
   <xsl:template match="*|@*|text()">
      <xsl:copy>
      <xsl:apply-templates/>
      </xsl:copy>
   </xsl:template>
</xsl:stylesheet>
```

The template matches any element (*), attribute (@*), or text node (text()), and copies that node to the output stream. It then reapplies the template to all the children of that node, if any. This also lets you expand your output to include any nonstandard elements. For example, suppose you wanted to include a redline tag to indicate obsolete text, as in Listing 4.10.

Listing 4.10: Introducing a "Custom" Tag into the Paragraph Demonstrates how Normal HTML Can Be Extended through XSL Filters. (*Listing4-10.txt*)

```
<slide id="eraPCNetwork">
    <title>The Era of the PC Network (1974-1989)</title>
    <para><b>Two <i>inventions</i></b> changed the nature
    of computing -- the <i>personal computer</i> and the
    <i>modem</i>, which appeared within a few years of one
```

```
    another. <redline>Here's a line of <b>text</b> that you
    no longer need.</redline></para>
    <!-- more elements here -->
</slide>
```

The XSL document to transform it would need to include a redline template, as in Listing 4.11, to catch that particular bit of formatting, but otherwise doesn't need to be changed. (Figure 4.2 shows the result of the transform.)

Listing 4.11: The XSL Transform that Includes the Redline Template (*list04-11.xsl*)

```
<xsl:stylesheet xmlns:xsl="http://www.w3.org/TR/WD-xsl">
   <xsl:template match="/">
   <div>
      <xsl:apply-templates select="//para"/>
    </div>
   </xsl:template>
   <xsl:template match="para">
      <xsl:apply-templates select="*|@*|text()"/>
   </xsl:template>
   <xsl:template match="*|@*|text()">
      <xsl:copy>
      <xsl:apply-templates/>
      </xsl:copy>
   </xsl:template>
   <xsl:template match="redline">
      <span style="color:red;
      text-decoration:underline"><xsl:apply-templates
      select="*|@*|text()"/></span>
   </xsl:template>
</xsl:stylesheet>
```

WARNING Note that the redline template has to be placed below the general match template, since otherwise the general match will be encountered first (bottom-up searching) and the redline template code will never be applied.

NOTE If you use `<xsl:apply-templates/>` with no `select` block, it acts only upon the set of elements within its scope, not attributes or text. If you want to retrieve other elements, you should indicate them explicitly, with a tag like `<xsl:apply-templates select="*|@*|text()|pi()|comments()"/>` to choose all possible items in the template's scope, or `"*|@*|text()"` to choose only elements, attributes, and text.

FIGURE 4.2
Sample output from the redline template

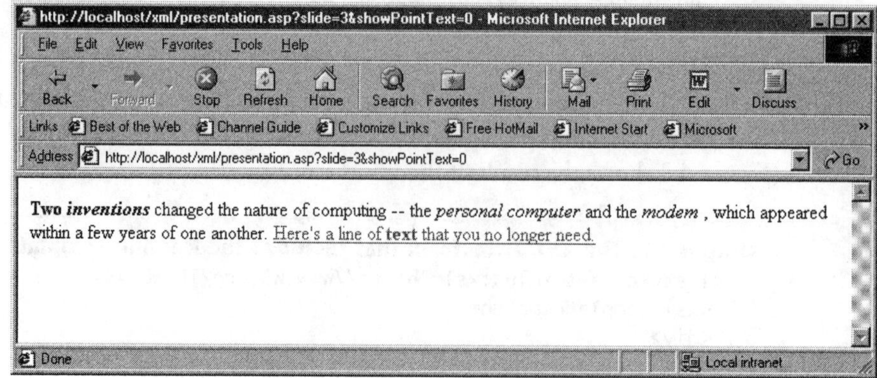

This transformation paradigm is incredibly powerful. By permitting a pass-through mechanism (`<xsl:copy>`) with the `<apply-templates>` tag, it allows you to create XSL transforms that either enhance the current HTML or override the existing HTML with different behavior. Similarly, you can use XSL to modify existing XML in places without having to write handlers for every single tag, making it easier to maintain different versions of similar but not identical XML documents.

Iterating with *xsl:for-each*

While the template model is quite powerful, the fact that it employs recursion can make it difficult for many programmers to work with. Additionally, there will be times when applying a set of templates can be overkill. These are situations where `xsl:for-each` comes into play, such as when you need to display XML data in tables. For example, consider the stock market document from Chapter 3 (repeated for convenience in Listing 4.12).

Listing 4.12: XML Stock Data (*Code4-12.Stocks.xml*)

```
<stockReport>
    <stock>
        <symbol>ACME</symbol>
        <name>Acme Rocket Company</name>
        <openPrice>22.30</openPrice>
        <currentPrice>21.92</currentPrice>
        <sharesTraded>210</sharesTraded>
        <dateFirstTraded>1956-03-01</dateFirstTraded>
    </stock>
    <stock>
        <symbol>MER</symbol>
        <name>Mermaid Tails, Inc.</name>
        <openPrice>17.24</openPrice>
```

```
        <currentPrice>18.39</currentPrice>
        <sharesTraded>912</sharesTraded>
        <dateFirstTraded>2000-03-01</dateFirstTraded>
    </stock>
    <stock>
        <symbol>MIC</symbol>
        <name>Micronaut, Consolidated</name>
        <openPrice>5.25</openPrice>
        <currentPrice>9.32</currentPrice>
        <sharesTraded>87</sharesTraded>
        <dateFirstTraded>2000-02-03</dateFirstTraded>
    </stock>
    <stock>
        <symbol>LOG</symbol>
        <name>Logarhythmics, Inc.</name>
        <openPrice>93.12</openPrice>
        <currentPrice>85.12</currentPrice>
        <sharesTraded>2140</sharesTraded>
        <dateFirstTraded>1998-02-01</dateFirstTraded>
    </stock>
    <stock>
        <symbol>SYM</symbol>
        <name>Sym-Shares, LLC.</name>
        <openPrice>124.92</openPrice>
        <currentPrice>89.50</currentPrice>
        <sharesTraded>92</sharesTraded>
        <dateFirstTraded>2000-04-12</dateFirstTraded>
    </stock>
    <stock>
        <symbol>PAR</symbol>
        <name>Parallel Solutions, Inc.</name>
        <openPrice>49.95</openPrice>
        <currentPrice>47.50</currentPrice>
        <sharesTraded>42</sharesTraded>
        <dateFirstTraded>2000-01-01</dateFirstTraded>
    </stock>
</stockReport>
```

If you wanted to tabularize this, you could write the XSL filter using an `apply-templates` approach (see Listing 4.13). Note that the element wildcard match template must appear before the stock match, or the stock table will never be matched.

Listing 4.13: The *apply-templates* Approach to Building a Stock Table (*Code4-13.ApplyTemplates.xsl*)

```
<xsl:stylesheet xmlns:xsl="http://www.w3.org/TR/WD-xsl">
   <xsl:template match="/">
      <table><xsl:apply-templates select="//stock"/></table>
```

```
    </xsl:template>
    <xsl:template match="*">
       <td><xsl:value-of/></td>
    </xsl:template>
    <xsl:template match="stock">
       <tr><xsl:apply-templates select="*"/></tr>
    </xsl:template>
 </xsl:stylesheet>
```

If we use the <xsl:for-each> statement, however, we can generate the same table using only one template and with a flow that more closely matches procedural languages (see Listing 4.14, as well as Figure 4.3 to see what the output looks like).

Listing 4.14: The *for-each* Approach to Building a Stock Table (*Code4-14.ForEach.xsl*)

```
<xsl:stylesheet xmlns:xsl="http://www.w3.org/TR/WD-xsl">
   <xsl:template match="/">
      <table>
      <xsl:for-each select="//stock">
      <tr>
         <xsl:for-each select="*">
            <td><xsl:value-of/></td>
         </xsl:for-each>
         </tr>
   </xsl:for-each>
   </table>
   </xsl:template>
</xsl:stylesheet>
```

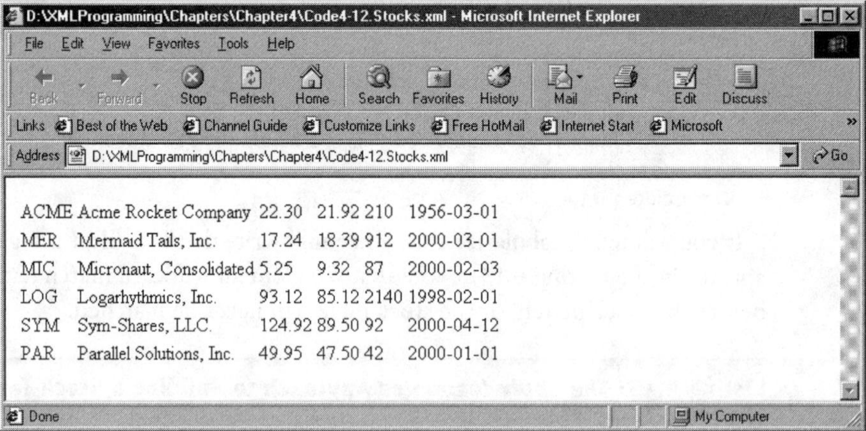

FIGURE 4.3
The table as displayed using the `for-each` XSL filter

Structurally, this is much closer to the DOM approach. Indeed, it's instructive to look at the DOM equivalent (Listing 4.15), which differs only in that the context is made explicit in variables such as stock (the stock nodes) or prop (each stock's properties).

Listing 4.15: A DOM Equivalent to Listing 4.14 (*Listing4-15.txt*)

```
Function getStockTable(stocks as DOMDocument) as String
   Dim buffer as string
   Dim stock as IXMLDOMNode
   Dim prop as IXMLDOMNode

   buffer=""
   buffer=buffer+"<table>"
   for each stock in stocksDoc.selectNodes("//stock")
      buffer=buffer+"</tr>
      for each prop in stock.selectNodes("*")
          buffer=buffer+"<td>"+prop.text+"</td>"
      next
      buffer=buffer+"</tr>"
   next
   buffer=buffer+"</table>"
   getStockTable=buffer
End Function
```

The `for-each` tag is one of the XSL nodes that force a change of context. All XPath references within the `for-each` scope have the context of each of the items found in the `for-each` select query. Thus, the outer `for-each` tag forced the context to go from one stock to the next, while the inner `for-each` tag iterated through each of the stock properties, giving each one the context in turn.

So which is better? It's typically a toss-up—`for-each` will make your code appear more procedural than `apply-templates`, hence a little easier to read and debug. It also lets you change the context more readily. However, `for-each` doesn't work as well when the data is irregular, while `apply-templates` is tailor-made for such situations. Both forms have their uses.

Template Sets

Context is very important when dealing with XML. A tag that is part of one node may need to have a very different interpretation when placed at some other point in the document. To handle this possibility, XSL lets you define *template sets*. If you think of a template as a global function, then a template set lets you create a template that applies only within a given context—the declarative equivalent of private or local functions.

For example, suppose that in the Managers example, you wanted to differentiate visually between the manager of a company (for example, make the font bold), the manager of a division (italic), and the manager of a section (underline). One way (although not the best way) to do this would be to use an XSL filter with a template set:

```
<xsl:stylesheet xmlns:xsl="http://www.w3.org/TR/WD-xsl">
<xsl:template match="/">
  <ul><xsl:apply-templates/></ul>
</xsl:template>
<xsl:template match="company">
   <li>
   <xsl:define-template-set>
      <xsl:template match="manager">
         <b><xsl:value-of select="name"/></b>
      </xsl:template>
      <xsl:template match="division">
         <ul><xsl:apply-templates/></ul>
      </xsl:template>
   </xsl:define-template-set>
   <xsl:apply-templates/>
   </li>
</xsl:template>
<xsl:template match="division">
   <li>
   <xsl:define-template-set>
      <xsl:template match="manager">
         <i><xsl:value-of select="name"/></i>
      </xsl:template>
      <xsl:template match="section">
         <ul><xsl:apply-templates/><ul>
      </xsl:template>
   </xsl:define-template-set>
   <xsl:apply-templates/>
   </li>
</xsl:template>
<xsl:template match="section">
   <li>
   <xsl:define-template-set>
      <xsl:template match="manager">
         <b><xsl:value-of select="name"/></b>
      </xsl:template>
   </xsl:define-template-set>
   <xsl:apply-templates/>
   </li>
</xsl:template>
</xsl:stylesheet>
```

WARNING Template sets have at best very limited utility. They were designed in part to mimic local functions, but in doing so they have the danger of giving the same element multiple possible interpretations (which is bad from a contextual standpoint), they can make the size of code balloon (which is bad from a coding standpoint), and can make it difficult to determine which scope is currently in effect (which is bad from a debugging standpoint). In general, there are better ways of accomplishing the same task, such as the judicious use of `xsl:choose`, covered in the section on XSL Conditionals later in this chapter.

Sorting and Ordering

As mentioned in Chapter 3, one of the curious limitations of the XPath language is that it doesn't provide any way of specifying the order of elements. Oddly, rather than placing this ability in XPath, the designers of the language felt that it should more properly be tied to the XMLT specification.

The specific syntax for sorting has changed considerably since the Dec 1998 XSL Working Draft upon which the IE5 parser is based. In the older syntax, sorting is performed using the `order-by` attribute that's part of both the `<xsl:apply-templates>` and `<xsl:for-each>` nodes. Specifically, the format for `order-by` is:

```
<xsl:apply-templates select="expr" order-by="[+|-]orderExpr"/>
```

or

```
<xsl:for-each select="expr" order-by="[+|-]orderExpr"/>
```

In both cases, the `orderExpr` is a standard XPath expression indicating the characteristic that you're wishing to order your elements by, while the optional plus or minus sign shows whether the sort is in ascending (+) or descending order (–), respectively.

Taking as an example the stock chart from the last section, you can create a table sorted by stock symbol by modifying either one of the XSL table transforms (Listing 4.16) to produce the table shown in Table 4.1.

Listing 4.16: The Stock Table Sorted by Symbol (*Code4-16.Ordered.xsl*)

```
<xsl:stylesheet xmlns:xsl="http://www.w3.org/TR/WD-xsl">
   <xsl:template match="/">
      <table>
      <xsl:for-each select="//stock" order-by="symbol">
         <tr>
         <xsl:for-each select="*">
            <td><xsl:value-of/></td>
         </xsl:for-each>
```

```
        </tr>
      </xsl:for-each>
      </table>
    </xsl:template>
  </xsl:stylesheet>
```

TABLE 4.1: The Results of an Ordered Transform on the Stock Market Data

ACME	Acme Rocket Company	22.30	21.92	210	1956-03-01
LOG	Logarhythmics, Inc.	93.12	85.12	2140	1998-02-01
MER	Mermaid Tails, Inc.	17.24	18.39	912	2000-03-01
MIC	Micronaut, Consolidated	5.25	9.32	87	2000-02-03
PAR	Parallel Solutions, Inc.	49.95	47.50	42	2000-01-01
SYM	Sym-Shares, LLC.	124.92	89.50	92	2000-04-12

In addition to ordering by text (the default) you can also create XSL transforms that order by numeric value or by date, by using the `number()` or `date()` operator. Thus, if you wanted to see the stocks listed in descending order based upon the number of shares traded, you would use the expression `"-number(sharesTraded)"` as your `order-by` parameter (see Listing 4.17).

Listing 4.17: The Stock Table Sorted in Descending Order by Number of Shares Traded (*Code4-17.OrderedStocksTraded.xsl*)

```
<xsl:stylesheet xmlns:xsl="http://www.w3.org/TR/WD-xsl">
  <xsl:template match="/">
    <table>
    <xsl:for-each select="//stock" order-by=      "-number(sharesTraded)">
      <tr>
        <xsl:for-each select="*">
          <td><xsl:value-of/></td>
        </xsl:for-each>
        </tr>
    </xsl:for-each>
    </table>
  </xsl:template>
</xsl:stylesheet>
```

Similarly, the expression `"-date(dateFirstTraded)"` would order the table by the date the stock was first traded, from the most recent to the oldest.

You can take advantage of some of the flexibility that XPath offers by combining filtering and ordering in the same expression. For example, you can set up a query that will return only those stocks for which the share price is less than $50, sorted by the number of stocks traded in descending order (Listing 4.18).

Listing 4.18: The Stock Table Showing Mixed Filtering and Ordering (*Code4-18.Mixed.xsl*)

```
<xsl:stylesheet xmlns:xsl="http://www.w3.org/TR/WD-xsl">
   <xsl:template match="/">
      <table>
      <xsl:for-each select="//stock[currentPrice<50]" order-by=
          "-number(sharesTraded)">
         <tr>
         <xsl:for-each select="*">
             <td><xsl:value-of/></td>
         </xsl:for-each>
         </tr>
   </xsl:for-each>
   </table>
   </xsl:template>
</xsl:stylesheet>
```

The current XSLT specification, on the other hand, defines a different mechanism for sorting, by introducing the `<xsl:sort>` tag with the following attributes:

```
<xsl:sort
   select = "orderExpr"
   lang = { nmtoken }
   data-type = { "text" | "number" | qname-but-not-ncname }
   order = { "ascending" | "descending" }
   case-order = { "upper-first" | "lower-first" } />
```

The `select` attribute is the same as for an `order-by` statement (without the + or –, which is specified instead by the `order` attribute). `Case order` indicates whether lowercase or uppercase characters are considered to start the sort. `Data-type` consists of one of the types defined within the XML-Schema Data-type specification, considered in the next chapter. Finally, `lang` is the two-character language token indicating which language the sort order is performed with.

NOTE Ordering and sorting are typically features that are in demand within user interfaces. Thus, you'll probably want to set these parameters programmatically. Some techniques for doing this are covered in the "XSL Scripting" section later in this chapter.

The advantage of the newer syntax is that you can create multiple sort keys. For example, if you wanted to have a primary sort key that listed stocks by `sharesTraded` and a secondary sort key that sorted by stock `name` (effectively listing those shares that had the same number of shares traded in alphabetical order), you could do so by specifying two keys:

```
<xsl:template match="/">
   <xsl:apply-templates match="//stock">
```

```
        <xsl:sort select="number(sharesTraded)" order="descending"/>
        <xsl:sort select="name"/>
    </xsl:template>
```

Using XSLT to Sort XML Documents

The IE5 XML parser (December 1998) lacks a few key features that have since been added into the W3C specs, including support for variables to make sorting fairly easy. However, you can use an embedded XSLT script to transform an unsorted XML document into a different sorted one with the SortXMLDoc function (Listing 14.19).

Listing 14.19: The *SortXMLDoc* Function Lets You Create a New Sorted DOM from an Unsorted DOM through an Embedded XSL Script. (*Listing14-19.txt*)

```
Function SortXMLDoc(xmlDoc as DOMDocument,sortItem as String,sortStr _
    as String) as DOMDocument
   Dim bf as String
   Dim xslDoc as DOMDocument
   Dim rsltDoc as DOMDocument
   bf = "<xsl:stylesheet xmlns:xsl='http://www.w3.org/TR/WD-xsl'>"
   bf = bf+ "<xsl:template match='/'><xsl:apply-templates/>
   bf = bf+ "</xsl:template>"
   bf = bf+ "<xsl:template match='*|@*|text()|pi()|comment()'>"
   bf = bf+ "<xsl:copy><xsl:apply-templates"
   bf = bf+ "    select='*|@*|text()|pi()|comment()'/></xsl:copy>"
   bf = bf+ "</xsl:template>"
   bf = bf+ "<xsl:template match='*["+sortItem+"]'>"
   bf = bf+ "<xsl:copy><xsl:apply-templates select='"+sortItem+"'"
   bf = bf+ "    order-by='"+sortStr+"'/></xsl:copy>"
   bf = bf+ "</xsl:template>"
   bf = bf+ "</xsl:stylesheet>"
   set xslDoc=new DOMDocument
   xslDoc.loadXSL bf
   xmlDoc.transformNodeAsObject(xslDoc,rsltDoc)
   set sortXMLDoc=rlstDoc
End Function

'Usage
set xmlDoc=createObject("Microsoft.XMLDOM")
xmlDoc.load "stocks.xml"
set xmlDoc=sortXMLDoc(xmlDoc,"stock","-number(SharesTraded)")
```

The embedded XSL script is also a good candidate for storage as a resource, or it can be rewritten as an external file. Using the Windows 2000 XML parser will give you another solution to the conundrum of replacing expressions in an XSL filter, as discussed in the "XSL Scripting" section later in this chapter.

Creating Elements and Attributes

When XML is transformed, the destination is not always HTML. Indeed, some of the more common transformations are what are called *orthogonal transforms*—they retain the same information as before, but the structure in which they keep the data changes somewhat. Two orthogonal transformations that are extremely common are transforming a node in which each tag contains all of its information as attributes into a corresponding form where the attributes become elements and the reverse transformation from element-specific to attribute-specific forms.

For example, consider an XML document that contains employee records. There are essentially two different ways that the records can be kept—one way, as displayed in the element-structured format of Listing 4.1, maintains each property of a manager's record as a separate element. Another way, as displayed in Listing 4.20, instead describes a manager's record as a "row" element where the attributes of the row contain the manager's pertinent information.

Listing 4.20: A Selection of Employees' Records, in Attribute Format (*Listing 4-20.txt*)

```
<recordSet>
<row name="Phil Schwarts" title="Chief Executive Officer" canHire="yes"
vested=""></row>
<row name="James Galway" title="Chief Financial Officer" canHire="yes"
vested=""></row>
<row name="Cynthia Dresler" title="VP, Marketing" canHire="yes"></row>
<row name="Benny Jocum" title="Chief Technical Officer" canHire="yes"></row>
<row name="Allison Hart" title="Vice President, Year 2000
    Issues" canHire="no" vested=""></row>
<row name="Jerry Garcia" title="Director, COBOL Systems"></row>
</recordSet>
```

So how do you transform from one format to the other? XSL supports two other tags that can help you with that chore: `<xsl:element>` and `<xsl:attribute>`, which let you create elements and attributes, respectively, in your documents. In their simplest forms (with no attributes), each of these tags takes the name of the current context and uses it as the name of the newly created element or attribute, respectively. The contents of these tags then become the interior contents of the new attribute or element.

For example, to create a `title` attribute from a `title` element (assuming you're working with the Managers list), you'd use the following template:

```
<xsl:template match="manager">
    <row><xsl:apply-templates select="title"/></row>
</xsl:template>
<xsl:template match="title">
   <xsl:attribute><xsl:value-of/></xsl:attribute>
</xsl:template>
```

You could also create a new attribute (say `income`), by setting a name to the attribute:

```
<xsl:template match="manager">
    <row><xsl:attribute name="income">125000</xsl:attribute></row>
</xsl:template>
```

This would give you a `row` element with an `income` attribute:

```
<row income="125000"/>
```

Listing 4.21 shows the XSL script to transform the manager's list into the attribute list given in Listing 4.20; as you can see, it's remarkably simple as a consequence of these defaults.

Listing 4.21: The Remarkably Short XSL Script for Transforming Manager Elements into Manager Attributes (*Code4-21.Elem2Attr.xsl*)

```
<xsl:stylesheet xmlns:xsl="http://www.w3.org/TR/WD-xsl">
   <xsl:template match="/">
      <recordSet>
         <xsl:apply-templates select="//manager"/>
      </recordSet>
   </xsl:template>
   <xsl:template match="manager">
      <row><xsl:for-each select="*">
         <xsl:attribute><xsl:value-of/></xsl:attribute>
      </xsl:for-each></row>
   </xsl:template>
</xsl:stylesheet>
```

The attribute-to-element script (Listing 4.22) is just as compact.

Listing 4.22: The Inverse Transformation (*Code4-22.Attr2Elem.xsl*)

```
<xsl:stylesheet xmlns:xsl="http://www.w3.org/TR/WD-xsl">
   <xsl:template match="/">
      <recordSet>
         <xsl:apply-templates select="//row"/>
      </recordSet>
   </xsl:template>
   <xsl:template match="row">
      <manager><xsl:for-each select="@*">
         <xsl:element><xsl:value-of/></xsl:element>
      </xsl:for-each></manager>
   </xsl:template>
</xsl:stylesheet>
```

Here the `for-each select` statement retrieves the list of all attributes (`"@*"`) for the given row node and sets each of them respectively to the default context. Without this defaulting mechanism, this becomes a vastly more complicated problem.

Assigning elements and especially attributes this way comes in handy when the values are generated programmatically. In general, if you are creating an attribute to a node using XSL, you should think seriously about using the `<xsl:attribute>` tag instead of creating the attribute explicitly.

Creating Other XML Types

Given that XSL echoes the DOM in most ways, it's perhaps not surprising that you can create all of the standard XML DOM types using XSL. Table 4.2 indicates the syntax for all of the DOM types.

TABLE 4.2: DOM Syntax

Tag name	Description
`xsl:attribute`	Creates an attribute in the output stream, with the interior contents becoming the attribute contents. Its single parameter is `name="attribute-name"`.
`xsl:cdata`	Creates a new CDATA section with the node's contents transferred to the new document as part of the CDATA section.
`xsl:comment`	Creates a new comment in the target document, with the interior contents becoming the body of the content.
`xsl:element`	Creates an element in the output stream, with the interior contents becoming the element contents. Its single parameter is `name="element-name"`.
`xsl:entity-ref`	Creates a new entity-reference. Its single parameter is name="`entity-reference-name`".
`xsl:node-name`	Inserts the name of the current node into the output stream as text.
`xsl:pi`	Inserts a processing instruction into the output stream. Single parameter: `name="processing-instruction-name"`.

Thus, you could convert a specific commentary tag into an HTML (or XML comment) using the `xsl:comment` node. For example, the `cmnt` tag in the following HTML contains commentary about the slide:

```
<slide>
   <name>Creating New XSL Elements</name>
   <cmnt>This needs to be revised</cmnt>
</slide>
```

Applying the following XSL Style sheet:

```
<xsl:stylesheet ..>
   ..
   <xsl:template match="slide">
      <h1><xsl:value-of select="name"/></h1>
      <xsl:comment><xsl:value-of select="cmnt"/></xsl:comment>
```

```
    </xsl:template>
  </xsl:stylesheet>
```

produces the following output:

```
<h1>Creating New XSL Elements</h1>
<!-- This needs to be revised -->
```

NOTE Remember that the <xsl:comment> tag creates a comment in the output stream. If you want to comment your XSL document itself, just use a standard comment tag, i.e., <!-- -->.

XSL Scripting

Templates make up a major part of most XSL transforms, but you may have begun to notice that there are a number of similarities between XSL and procedural languages, such as the existence of `for-each` statements, and the similarities between templates and functions. However, the utility of XSL would be sorely limited if no means of creating more sophisticated language elements into the transforms existed.

Fortunately, the XSL-Transform specification defines a number of elements that can considerably enhance the capabilities of the language as a programming tool. Additional tags that are part of the Microsoft XSL extension set may radically change the way that CGI is done on the Web, and they have a good chance of displacing Active Server Pages as the preferred way of presenting Web information through IIS.

The *xsl:if* and *xsl:choose* Tags

Practically all programming languages have the ability to take an action based upon the result of some comparison. Conditional statements, switches, loops, and fall-through statements can be used to build sophisticated routines in any computer language, and XSL has all of these. (Let's ignore, for now, the widespread contention that XML is simply a data format.) If templates can be thought of as the "functions" of an XSL template, then `<xsl:if>` and `<xsl:choose>` are the conditionals that make it possible to create powerful "applications."

The `<xsl:if>` tag performs a test to determine if some condition is true. If that is the case, then the contents of the tag are added to the stream (with appropriate down-level parsing). Note that `xsl:if` does not change the current context (unlike the `for-each` or `apply-templates` XSL nodes), so any XPath expression within the `if` node relies on the same context as the `if` node itself.

The syntax for `<xsl:if>` differs somewhat between the W3C and Microsoft implementations. The version of `<xsl:if >` supported by the MSXML DOM can actually take two distinct comparison tests, one based upon XPath and the second based upon a scripted expression. Its syntax is fairly simple:

```
<xsl:if test="XpathExpr" expr="ScriptExpression" language="scriptLanguage">
   <!-- Do something here if both test and expr are true-->
</xsl:if>
```

The W3C `<xsl:if>` only supports the `test` parameter and doesn't handle scripting languages per se. However, because the W3 XML-T specification also defines internal variables and parametric expressions, this is not as much of a limitation as it may appear at first.

NOTE The XML team from Microsoft has explicitly stated that they will support the scripting extensions to XSLT that were introduced in the Dec 1998 specification as well as the W3C architecture.

The stock market listing provides a good example of how the `<xsl:if>` statement can be used. Suppose that you are outputting all of the stocks to a table, but any time that the `dateFirstTraded` attribute returns a date after 1 January 2000, a spherical, green icon pops up next to the stock name. The code to do this is given in Listing 4.23, with the result shown in Figure 4.4.

Listing 4.23: An XSL Filter to Show All Stocks, with New Stocks Highlighted by an Icon (*Code4-23.NewStock.xsl*)

```
<xsl:stylesheet xmlns:xsl="http://www.w3.org/TR/WD-xsl">
   <xsl:template match="/">
      <table>
      <tr><th>Name</th><th>Date First Traded</th></tr>
      <xsl:apply-templates select="//stock"/>
      </table>
   </xsl:template>
   <xsl:template match="stock">
      <tr><td>
         <xsl:value-of select="name"/>
         <xsl:if test=".[dateFirstTraded $ge$ date('2000-01-01')]">
            <img src="new.jpg" align="top"/>
         </xsl:if>
         </td>
         <td><xsl:value-of select="dateFirstTraded"/></td>
         </tr>
   </xsl:template>
</xsl:stylesheet>
```

FIGURE 4.4
Icons indicate new files, as determined by the xsl:if test condition.

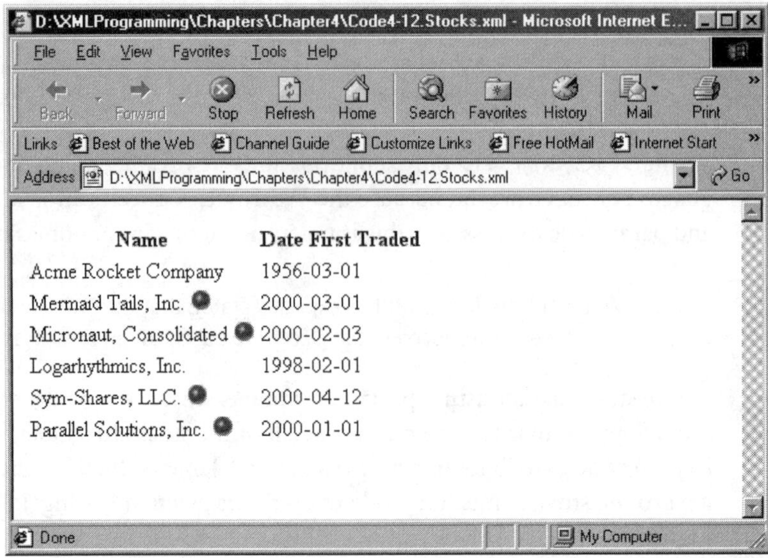

The principal problem with the `<xsl:if>` element is that it contains no provisions for processing code if the test fails. As such, it's useful for instances where material needs to be added to the stream, but it doesn't have the full functionality of something like a Visual Basic `if ... then ... else` construct.

However, you *can* get similar functionality by using the `<xsl:choose>` element. This element lets you set up a number of conditional statements, each one of which is indicated with an `<xsl:when>` tag, but also includes an `<xsl:otherwise>` option for handling cases that don't satisfy any of the `when` clauses. This differs from a Visual Basic `select case` statement in that the VB conditional looks at various cases of a specific variable, while each `<xsl:when>` element is independent of the others.

For a given `<xsl:choose>` block, the first `xsl:when` block that satisfies its respective test is the option that is selected. Upon completion of that clause, the `xsl:choose` block terminates. If none of the `when` blocks test true, then the optional `otherwise` node is executed instead. The `xsl:when` block has the same attributes as the `xsl:if` block.

Using the same stock data, a slightly different filter (Listing 4.24) on the set determines whether a given stock was a low performer (shares traded under 100), a high performer (shares traded above 500), or a moderate performer (shares traded somewhere in between).

Listing 4.24: An XSL Filter to Show Performance of Stocks by Trading Levels (*Code4-24.TradingLevels.xsl*)

```
<xsl:stylesheet xmlns:xsl="http://www.w3.org/TR/WD-xsl">
   <xsl:template match="/">
      <table>
      <tr><th>Name</th><th>Date First Traded</th>
      <th>Performance</th></tr>
      <xsl:apply-templates select="//stock"/>
      </table>
   </xsl:template>
   <xsl:template match="stock">
      <tr><td>
         <xsl:value-of select="name"/>
         <xsl:if test=".[dateFirstTraded $ge$ date('2000-01-01')]">
            <img src="new.jpg" align="top"/>
         </xsl:if>
         </td>
         <td><xsl:value-of select="dateFirstTraded"/></td>
         <td>
         <xsl:choose>
              <xsl:when test=".[sharesTraded $lt$ 100]">
              Poor Performer
              </xsl:when>
              <xsl:when test=".[sharesTraded $gt$ 500]">
              Good Performer
              </xsl:when>
              <xsl:otherwise>
              Moderate Performer
              </xsl:otherwise>
         </xsl:choose>
         </td>
         </tr>
   </xsl:template>
</xsl:stylesheet>
```

TIP You can nest an **xsl:if** or **xsl:choose** within another **xsl:if** or **xsl:when** statement for fine-tuning your decision tree.

TIP You can use an empty **xsl:when** statement to select a subset of the current context, then use the **<xsl:otherwise>** to choose the inverse of that set.

The *xsl:eval* Tag

Of course, XPath is not always the ideal tool for working with expressions. There are times when it becomes useful to pass information into the XSL structure, such as indicating to the XSL document what the consumer (e.g., browser) of the document will be. Since this can often affect how the output will look, being able to retrieve or compare that information is fairly vital.

To help facilitate that, Microsoft introduced a number of extensions to the XSL format, although they have not been adopted by the W3C in the Nov 1999 XSL recommendation. These recommendations focus around the area of additions to scripting.

Formally, there are two tags and two attributes that have been added to the Microsoft XSL parser: `<xsl:eval>`, `<xsl:script>`, the attribute `expr`, and the scripting `language` attribute.

The `language` attribute lets you take advantage of whatever scripting languages you have currently available on your system (at a minimum VBScript and JavaScript, although PerlScript, Lisp, and other scripting modules are available from third-party vendors) to do additional processing. You can specify the language that you're using within the XSL; the language defaults to JavaScript if you don't specify one.

This attribute can be attached as a floating attribute at most levels of the document, though typically it will be used in the following scenarios:

- `<xsl:stylesheet language="scriptLanguage">`. In this case the specified language becomes the default for the entire document.
- `<xsl:eval language="scriptLanguage">`. The expression contained within the `eval` tag uses the syntax of the ***`scriptLanguage`***. The expression must be in a form that evaluates to a string value.
- `<xsl:script language="scriptLanguage">`. Indicates that any code contained within the `xsl:script` block uses the ***`scriptLanguage`*** syntax. Functions may be defined within this block, and any variables defined within the block but outside the function are treated as global values.
- `<xsl:if expr="scriptExpr" language="scriptLanguage">`. The ***`script-Expression`*** must be in the specified language (or use the default if no language is defined). The value should evaluate to a Boolean value but can contain functions or variables defined in an `xsl:script` block.
- `<xsl:when expr="scriptExpr" language="scriptLanguage">`. The ***`script-Expression`*** must be in the specified language (or use the default if no language is defined). The value should evaluate to a Boolean value but can contain functions or variables defined in an `xsl:script` block.

NOTE Typically, because some languages such as VBScript have code line breaks specified by carriage returns (which aren't typically preserved in XML documents), you should get into the habit of enclosing the content of your scripts in a CDATA section.

Integrating scripting into XSL is not always completely straightforward, and sometimes it forces you into interesting kludges. Consider the following scenario. For the stock market data, you want to sort the stocks by name and then have them numbered sequentially. Finally, you want to display the number of stocks traded, and if that number exceeds 1000 you want to format the number with a thousands delimiter (Listing 4.25).

Listing 4.25: Numbering and Formatting Using *xsl:eval* and *childNumber* (*Code4-25.Numbering.xsl*)

```
<xsl:stylesheet xmlns:xsl="http://www.w3.org/TR/WD-xsl"
language="JavaScript">
   <xsl:template match="/">
      <table>
      <tr>
      <th>Number</th>
      <th>Name</th>
      <th>Shares Traded</th>
      </tr>
      <xsl:eval>var ct=0;""</xsl:eval>
         <xsl:apply-templates select="//stock" order-by="+name"/>
      </table>
   </xsl:template>
   <xsl:template match="stock">
         <tr>
            <td align="right">
            <xsl:eval>ct=ct+1</xsl:eval></td>
            <td>
            <xsl:value-of select="name"/>
            </td>
            <td align="right"><xsl:for-each select="sharesTraded">
            <xsl:eval>
            this.formatNumber(this.text,"###,###")
            </xsl:eval>
         </xsl:for-each>
         </td>
         </tr>
   </xsl:template>
</xsl:stylesheet>
```

The XSL script code in Listing 4.25 shows how you can create a numbering index with scripting (in this case, JavaScript) in conjunction with the `xsl:eval` tags. This example demonstrates a number of principles. The `xsl:eval` element will evaluate the expression and then place the result into the output stream.

In the first such statement, `<xsl:eval> var ct=0;"" </xsl:eval>`, a new variable (`ct`, for count) is created and assigned the value 0. Since you don't want the `0` to propagate into the output, you can execute a second JavaScript statement that places a blank character, instead of the 0, into the output stream.

The `apply-templates` statement illustrates the power of scoping. When the `select="stock"` template is applied, the `ct` variable retains its value. When the next `eval` statement is encountered

```
<xsl:eval> ct=ct+1 </xsl:eval>
```

`ct` is increased by one and this value is then placed into the stream. This lets you keep a running tally until you move outside of the initial scope where `ct` was declared.

The final `xsl:eval` statement

```
<xsl:eval> this.formatNumber(this.text,"###,###") </xsl:eval>
```

uses one of the built-in formatting functions to make the number of shares traded a thousands-delimited number. The most important item to notice in the `eval` statement, however, is the use of the keyword `this`, which contains a reference to the current context. It supports the primary `IXMLDOMNode` interface, as well as a few additions to the interface such as `formatNumber()`, `formatIndex`, and so forth, which are covered in Table 4.3.

TABLE 4.3: IXTLRuntime Properties and Methods

Property or Method	Description
`absoluteChildNumber(this_node)`	Returns the index of the given node within its parent's `childNodes` list. Note that this "absolute" number is not necessarily the order in which the item would appear as the result of a `for-each` or `apply-templates` selection, especially if the nodes were ordered. Values start at 1.
`ancestorChildNumber(nodeName,this_node)`	Returns the position of the named ancestor within its parent's `childNodes` list. Values start at 1. This is a useful function for finding the specific object with the current node as a given property.
`childNumber(this_node)`	Returns the number of the first node in the parent's `childNodes` collection that has the same name as the current node. Note that if `this_node` is the first node (or the only one), this will retrieve the node's position. Values start at 1.
`depth(this_node)`	Returns the number of steps from the current node up to the root node. The root node has a depth of 0.

TABLE 4.3: IXTLRuntime Properties and Methods *(continued)*

Property or Method	Description
`formatDate(date,format,locale)`	This formats the date according to the specified format, with the *`locale`* indicating the order of the month and day in the final string. Also see the section "Regular Expressions" later in this chapter for alternative ways to format dates.
`formatIndex(number,format)`	Formats the supplied number using the specified numerical system.
`formatNumber(number,format)`	Formats the supplied number using the specified format.
`formatTime(time,format,locale)`	This formats the time according to the specified format, with the locale setting the proper separator characters.

NOTE In addition to its native properties and methods, IXTLRuntime also supports the `IXMLDOMNode` interface properties and methods.

Why Mixing VBScript and JavaScript is Not a Good Idea

VBScript is not well optimized for use within `xsl:eval` statements, in part because the default VB line separator (the colon) doesn't appear to interpret properly. VB can work within `xsl:script` statements, but its use for simpler `eval` statements should be kept to a minimum.

Both `eval` and `script` statements automatically cause the parser to load in the scripting engine for every language. Thus, while you can have an XSL document include both VBScript and JavaScript code in the same document, be forewarned that this will double the amount of memory necessary to parse the document.

If you define a global variable (in either an `xsl:eval` or an `xsl:script` block), you cannot reference that variable from a different scripting language. In other words, VBScript and JavaScript maintain their own variable stacks. However, you can access functions from the other script partition.

Finally, while JavaScript uses the `this` keyword to indicate the current context, Visual Basic uses `me`, instead. Especially because it is standard programming practice when referencing the context keyword through a parameter to interchange `this` and `me`, switching from one language to another in midstream is apt to cause problems with the context variable.

The *expr* Attribute and *xsl:script*

There are times (at least for the older MSXML parser) when XPath is inadequate. In some cases, the situations involve parameterization—you are trying to change your output based upon whether the output is going to Internet Explorer 5, IE4, Netscape, or some other consumer, or you're passing information from an ASP page into the XSL structure. At other times you need to deal with information that XPath simply doesn't have the mechanisms to handle. Finally, there are times when you want to use XSL to validate the integrity of the data. All of these involve a test against a non-XPath expression, which the Microsoft parser handles with the `expr` attribute.

For example, consider a situation where you want to tailor your XML output depending on whether it's going to Internet Explorer or Netscape Navigator. Ignoring for the moment how the parameters are set, you can set up the browser type in a script variable, and then reference it through an `expr` attribute. That's what Listing 4.26 does.

Listing 4.26: Setting the Link Attribute of an HTML File through the *eval* Attribute (*code4-26.xsl*)

```
<xsl:stylesheet xmlns:xsl="http://www.w3.org/TR/WD-xsl" language="JavaScript">
   <xsl:script><![CDATA[
      var browser="IE";
      var version="5.01";
   ]]></xsl:script>
   <xsl:template select="/">
      <html><head>
<title>Stocks</title>
<link>
<xsl:choose>
   <xsl:when expr="browser=='IE'">
   <xsl:choose>
      <xsl:when expr="version gte 5">
         <xsl:attribute name="type" > text/xsl</xsl:attribute>
         <xsl:attribute name="href">IE5Doc.xsl</xsl:attribute>
      </xsl:when>
      <xsl:otherwise>
         <xsl:attribute name="type" > text/css</xsl:attribute>
      <xsl:attribute name="href">IEDoc.css</xsl:attribute>
      </xsl:otherwise>
   </xsl:choose>
   </xsl:when>
   <xsl:when expr="browser='NS'">
   <xsl:attribute name="type" > text/css</xsl:attribute>
```

```
    <xsl:attribute name="href">NSDoc.css</xsl:attribute>
    </xsl:when>
    <xsl:otherwise>
       <!-- Don't apply any stylesheet info -->
    </xsl:otherwise>
 </xsl:choose>
 </link>
 </head>
       <body>
       <xsl:apply-templates select="//stock"/>
       </body></html>
    </xsl:template>
    <xsl:template select="stock">
       <!-- process the individual stocks -->
    </xsl:template>
 </xsl:stylesheet>
```

In this code, the XSL script will end up converting the stocks listing into an HTML format. The actual presentation is handled by importing style sheets through the HTML `<link>` tag (which is part of the output stream). When the browser is IE5 or greater, the current style sheet invokes a second style sheet that will make the browser more interactive for the given page. On the other hand, an older IE browser or a Navigator browser will use a CSS style sheet and may require additional parsing on the server before being output.

Note that the `expr` attribute is highly language-dependent; the expressions that are invoked here are JavaScript comparisons (e.g. `browser == "IE"`). As with `<xsl:eval>`, you can specify an additional language attribute or apply a language to the whole document at the style sheet level, as I've done previously.

TIP You can have both an `expr` and a `test` attribute within either `<xsl:if>` or `<xsl:when>`. If both are present, both the XPath `test` and the `expr` must be true in order for the conditional to run.

I've also introduced an `xsl:script` block here. The purpose of the `xsl:script` block is simple—it gives you a way of creating routines and holding variables that can be used by the `xsl:eval` block or the `expr` attribute. In Listing 4.26, the `xsl:script` node simply lets you assign the browser type and version number.

You could also use it in a slightly different fashion. Suppose, for example, that you needed to find the total number of nodes that a given XSL query generates. Within Listing 4.27, you can create two functions, called `Count` and `Index`, to return the number of nodes from a given query and the index of the current item in the count.

Listing 4.27: Using the User-Defined *Count* and *Index* Functions in an XSL Script (*Code4-27.VBScript.xsl*)

```
<xsl:stylesheet xmlns:xsl="http://www.w3.org/TR/WD-xsl"
     language="VBScript">
   <!-- note: This is done in VBScript to demonstrate the
     use of that language in scripts -->
   <xsl:script language="VBScript"><![CDATA[
      Class CSelectNodeCount
      Dim nodeList

      Function Initialize(parentNode,query)
          Set nodeList=parentNode.selectNodes(query)
          Initialize=""
      End Function

      Function Count()
          Count=nodeList.length
      End function

      Function Index(this)
          Dim Idx
          Dim node
          Idx=-1
          For each node in nodeList
               Idx=Idx+1
               ' This is a kludge, see the warning below
               If node is _
  this.parentNode.childNodes(absoluteChildNumber(this)-1)_
     then
                   Exit for
               End if
          Next
          Index=Idx
      End Function

      Function PreviousSibling(this)
          Dim PrevIndex
          PrevIndex=Index(this)-1
          If PrevIndex>-1 then
             Set PreviousSibling=nodeList(PrevIndex)
          Else
             Set PreviousSibling=Nothing
          End if
      End Function
```

```
        Function NextSibling(this)
            Dim NextIndex
            NextIndex=Index(this)+1
            If NextIndex>=Count then
               Set NextSibling=nodeList(NextIndex)
            Else
               Set NextSibling=Nothing
            End if
        End Function

        Function GetSibling(this,pos)
            If (pos>-1) and (pos<Count) then
               Set GetSibling=nodeList(pos)
            Else
               Set GetSibling=Nothing
            End if
        End Function
      End Class

      set StockList=new CSelectNodeCount

   ]]></xsl:script>
   <xsl:template select="/">
   <xsl:eval>
   Stocklist.Initialize(me,"//stock")
   </xsl:eval>
   <xsl:apply-templates select="//stock"/>
   </xsl:template>
   <xsl:template match="stock"><xsl:value-of
      select="name"/>
    (<xsl:eval>Stocklist.Index(me)+1</xsl:eval> of
    <xsl:eval>Stocklist.Count()</xsl:eval>)
</xsl:template>
</xsl:stylesheet>
```

When run, this produces the following text output (not an XML document):

```
Acme Rocket Company (1 of 6)
Mermaid Tails, Inc. (2 of 6)
Micronaut, Consolidated (3 of 6)
Logarhythmics, Inc. (4 of 6)
Sym-Shares, LLC. (5 of 6)
Parallel Solutions, Inc. (6 of 6)
```

This code uses the VBScript 5.0 Class constructs, which I highly recommend if you are putting together VBScript (such as ASP scripts) in your own applications. The example illustrates a crucial difference between `xsl:script` and `xsl:eval` blocks: an `xsl:eval` script sends the result of the last evaluation to an internally stored variable, while `xsl:script` does not. Aside from that, the two are essentially the same object.

NOTE To reiterate the point: an `<xsl:eval>` block executes the script block and then returns the last result, while the `<xsl:script>` block executes the block but doesn't place anything on the flow stack. Except for this distinction, the two are essentially the same entity. Think of this as the difference between a function (`eval`) and a subroutine (`script`).

A Node-Mapping Kludge

One embarrassing kludge from Script 4.27 is the line:

```
If node is this.parentNode.childNodes(absoluteChildNumber(this)-1) then
```

Unfortunately, internally the XML parser treats the current node as being of a slightly different type than the standard IXMLDOMNode (it is, in fact, an IXTLRuntime object), and the XSL runtime parser doesn't handle the mapping between the two objects terribly well. The **`absoluteChildNumber`** gets the position of the item relative to the object's parent's siblings, so it can be used to retrieve the node as an IXMLDOMNode. However, because **`childNodes`** uses zero-based numbering and **`absoluteChildNumber`** uses one-based, you need to subtract one to refer to the node itself. This may be fixed by the time you read this book, but currently it is a work-around to a frustrating bug.

Script Blocks and ActiveX Controls

One feature of the Windows 2000 MSXML parser extends what you can do with XML under Windows: the ability to load ActiveX Controls into Script blocks. This has a wide number of applications, and ultimately may end up becoming the substrate under which future ASP development takes place (Microsoft evangelists have made it known that they expect future versions of IIS to be much more XML oriented, and this is a logical step in that direction).

You load an ActiveX control into an XSL document in exactly the same manner as you would in a normal script—through the use of the VBScript `CreateObject()` function or the new `ActiveXObject()`. For example, you could actually create another XML DOM within your XSL script, as follows:

```
<xsl:script language="VBScript"><![CDATA[
    dim xmlDoc
    set xmlDoc=createObject("Microsoft.XMLDOM")
    xmlDoc.load "myFile.xml"
]]></xsl:script>
```

Unfortunately, one of the limitations of the December 98 MSXML parser is that you can only use the normal XSL mechanisms for outputting XML. The `<xsl:eval>` block will automatically convert any XML produced into entity-replaced text (< gets replaced with `<`, > gets replaced with `>` and so forth). This can make it frustrating to do things like pull XML data from a data source (using ADO), convert it with an XSL file, and place the resulting output into the output stream.

However, if you're willing to do a little bit of post-processing there is a way around this conundrum. For example, suppose you want a program that will read an index of XML files and load them all into a single document, with each file being processed through an XSL document that's dependent upon the node type. The initial XML document might look something like Listing 4.28.

Listing 4.28: Book Table of Contents (*code4-28.bookTOC.xml*)

```
<document>
     <intro src="docs/myintro.xml" title="Introduction"/>
     <chapter src="docs/chapters/chapter1.xml" title="Getting started
       with XML">
            <sidebar src=docs/sidebars/newXML.xml" title="The New XML"/>
     </chapter>
     <chapter src="docs/chapters/chapter2.xml" title="XML and the DOM"/>
     <chapter src="docs/chapters/chapter3.xml" title="XPath"
       filter="newChapterFilter.xsl"/>
     <appendix src="docs/appendix/appendixA.xml" title="XML API"/>
</document>
```

You can then write a filter (Listing 4.29) that will expand those references to a fill document.

Listing 4.29: The *MakeDocument* XSL Filter (*Code4-29.MakeDocument.xsl*) Integrates All of the Documents Referenced in the Document into a Single Document through an ActiveX Component.

```
<document>
     <intro src="docs/myintro.xml" title="Introduction"/>
     <chapter src="docs/chapters/chapter1.xml" title="Getting started
       with XML">
            <sidebar src=docs/sidebars/newXML.xml" title="The New XML"/>
     </chapter>
     <chapter src="docs/chapters/chapter2.xml" title="XML and the DOM"/>
     <chapter src="docs/chapters/chapter3.xml" title="XPath"
      filter="newChapterFilter.xsl"/>
     <appendix src="docs/appendix/appendixA.xml" title="XML API"/>
</document>
```

```
<xsl:stylesheet xmlns:xsl="http://www.w3.org/TR/WD-xsl" language="VBScript">
   <xsl:script><![CDATA[
        dim xmlDoc
        dim xslDoc
        set xmlDoc=createObject("Microsoft.XMLDOM")
        set xslDoc=createObject("Microsoft.XMLDOM")

        function GetDocument()
           dim filterName

           xmlDoc.load me.getAttribute("src")
           if isNull(me.getAttribute("filter")) then
                xslDoc.load me.nodeName+".xml"
           else
                xslDoc.load me.getAttribute("filter")
           end if
           GetDocument=xmlDoc.transformNode(xslDoc)
        end function
   ]]></xsl:script>
   <xsl:template match="/">
        <document>
        <xsl:apply-templates/>
        </document>
   </xsl:template>
   <xsl:template match="*">
        <xsl:copy>
        <xsl:attribute name="title"><xsl:value-of
         select="@title"/></xsl:attribute>
        <xsl:if test="@src">
        <xsl:cdata>%<xsl:eval>GetDocument</xsl:eval>%</xsl:cdata>
        </xsl:if>
        </xsl:copy>
        <xsl:apply-templates/>
   </xsl:template>
</xsl:stylesheet>
```

When you run the document through the filter, because of the highlighted CDATA section, each subdocument comes through as part of a CDATA section, looking something like this:

```
<![CDATA[%<document>This is a sub-document</document>%]]>
```

If this transformation is run from a script (Listing 4.30), you can then do a search-and-replace on the result string to remove the expressions `<![CDATA[%` and `%]]`. This will give you an XML document (assuming the subdocument output was well formed). (The use of the % sign is a way to ensure that only CDATA sections that were specifically created by `MakeDocument.xsl` will be filtered—internal CDATA sections will still be retained.)

Listing 4.30: The *MakeDocument* VBS Script (*Code4-31.MakeDocument.vbs*) Calls the Transformation and Then Performs a Global Search-and-Replace to Remove the CDATA Boundaries. (*Listing4-30.txt*)

```
dim xmlDoc
dim xslDoc
dim rslt
set xmlDoc=createObject("Microsoft.XMLDOM")
set xslDoc=createObject("Microsoft.XMLDOM")
xmlDoc.load "Code4-28.bookTOC.xml"
xslDoc.load "Code4-29.MakeDocument.xsl"
rslt=xmlDoc.transformNode(xslDoc)
rslt=replace(rslt,"<![CDATA[@","")
rslt=replace(rslt,"@]]>","")
```

One final point to note: This program works on the assumption that there is an XSL filter corresponding to each of the node names of the `bookToc` section (i.e, a `document.xsl`, a `chapter.xsl`, a `sidebar.xsl`, an `appendix.xsl`, and so forth), unless that value is explicitly overridden with the filter attribute.

TIP Microsoft does implement an unsupported way of turning off the HTML Encoding. The expression `<xsl:eval no-entities="t"></xsl:eval>` disables the encoding, although it is definitely nonstandard and, in future implementations, will almost certainly be replaced with the `disable-output-escaping` attribute recommended by XSLT instead.

Parameterization and Entities

XML started out as a document format, a variation on a theme of SGML. One of the most important components of SGML was its ability to define *entities*, which could essentially be blocks of text ranging from a single character to entire documents. You could incorporate these entities into your own document by reference, rather than explicitly incorporating them.

Entities are not well suited for the role of passing parameters into a document, in part because they are built around references to file streams rather than around the argument format that most procedural languages use. Still, especially if you are forced into the older Dec 98 MSXML parser, entities are about your only real options.

When working with XML in programs, you have a choice of two forms of entities: internal or external (a third form, parametric, will be covered in Chapter 6, "XML Schema."). An internal entity is defined to be part of a validating DTD, but at least with the MSXML parser you don't need to define the entire DTD of the document in order to specify entity definitions. Here's an example:

```
<!DOCTYPE xsl:stylesheet [
   <!ENTITY browser 'IE'>
```

```
    <!ENTITY version '5.1'>
    ]>
<xsl:stylesheet xmlns:xsl="http://www.w3.org/TR/WD-xsl">
    <xsl:template match="/">
        <xsl:if expr="'&browser;'='IE'>
             <xsl:if expr="&version; gte 5">
                  <!-- do IE5 related output -->
              </xsl:if>
        </xsl:if>
    </xsl:template>
</xsl:stylesheet>
```

The entities use the entity definitions in the DTD to expand any text within the bracketing characters & and ; before anything else gets parsed. Thus, from the standpoint of the application, the above style sheet looks like this:

```
<xsl:stylesheet xmlns:xsl="http://www.w3.org/TR/WD-xsl">
    <xsl:template match="/">
        <xsl:if expr="'IE'='IE'>
             <xsl:if expr="5.1 gte 5">
                  <!-- do IE5 related output -->
              </xsl:if>
        </xsl:if>
    </xsl:template>
</xsl:stylesheet>
```

with `&browser;` expanded (in an abstract sense, of course) to IE and `version` to the value 5.1. Note that the quotation marks surrounding each entity declaration are of course not expanded; it's easy to forget this when writing entity references.

In a similar fashion, you can create references to external entities. In an external reference, the DTD is still defined locally, but the string to which the entity definition points is not literal text, it's the URL to an external file. Thus, the partial DTD reference for an external entity would look something like this:

```
<!DOCTYPE xsl:stylesheet [
    <!ENTITY chapter1 SYSTEM  "http://www.vbxml.com/cagle/chapter1.xml">
    <!ENTITY notes SYSTEM  "notes.xml">
    ]>
```

The `SYSTEM` keyword indicates that the information is located on a system file somewhere (not necessarily the local system, by the way). When a file is referenced, the entire content of the referenced file will be loaded into the document.

Finally, you can make the entire DTD external, which in the case of parameterization is probably the best procedure. For example, the browser entities could be saved in an external text file called `browserParams.dtd`, which would basically consist of the DTD without any specific document associated.

Listing 4.31: The *browserParamsTemplate.dtd* File Contains the DTD Entities Exclusively. (*Listing4-31.txt*)

```
<!DOCTYPE xsl:stylesheet [
   <!ENTITY browser '$browser'>
   <!ENTITY version '$version'>
   ]>
```

The XML file (Listing 4.32) would access this information through a SYSTEM DTD declaration (which, like a SYSTEM ENTITY call, retrieves the DTD from an external rather than an internal source).

Listing 4.32: The *browserTransform.xsl* Function Calls the *browserParamsTemplate*...or Does It? (*Listing4-32.txt*)

```
<!DOCTYPE xsl:stylesheet SYSTEM "browserParams.dtd">
<xsl:stylesheet xmlns:xsl="http://www.w3.org/TR/WD-xsl">
   <xsl:template match="/">
       <xsl:if expr="'&browser;'='IE'>
            <xsl:if expr="&version; gte 5">
                 <!-- do IE5 related output -->
              </xsl:if>
       </xsl:if>
   </xsl:template>
</xsl:stylesheet>
```

Okay, I admit it—I pulled a fast one here. The DTD declaration actually loads a file called `browserParams.dtd`, not `browserParamsTemplate.dtd`. This lies at the heart of a method to add parameters using XML technology exclusively. In essence, before the XSL document is even loaded, the template DTD is loaded into a text file, the parameters (in Listing 4.31, those expressions that start with a $ symbol—my notation, not XML's) are text replaced with their corresponding values, the DTD is saved as the file `browserParams.dtd`, and the XSL file is then opened with the right entities, through the use of this little bit of DOM code:

```
Dim xslDoc as DOMDocument
Dim dtdDoc as TextFile
Dim fs as FileSystemObject
Dim text as String
Set xslDoc=createObject("Microsoft.XMLDOM")
' Get a handle to the file system
Set fs=createObject("Scripting.FileSystemObject")
' Open the template file
Set ts=fs.OpenTextFile("browserParamsTemplate.dtd")
' Get the template text
text=ts.readFile
' Close the template file
ts.Close
```

```
' Replace each template item with its appropriate value
Text=replace(text,"$browser","IE")
Text=replace(text,"$version","5.1")
' Open the browserParams file
Set ts=fs.OpenTextFile("browserParams.dtd",ForWriting)
' Replace the contents with the new contents
ts.Write Text
'Close that text file
ts.Close
Set fs=Nothing
' Now load the xsldoc which has a SYSTEM pointer to
' the browserParams.dtd
xslDoc.validateOnParse=false
XslDoc.load "browserTransform.xsl"
```

Everyone raise their hand if they believe this is absurd! I know I do! The simple act of passing parameters requires us to open those three files, search and replace string contents, and turn validation off just so that the parser doesn't realize that we're trying to pull a fast one on the DTD!

A variation on this theme can be accomplished without the use of a DTD, if you're willing to take advantage of the `xsl:script` and `xsl:eval` functions. In essence, instead of using entity structures, you define a string within a script block that can be searched and replaced. For example, Listing 4.33, creates the XSL structure in a fairly familiar manner.

Listing 4.33: A Simplified Parameterization Model (*Code4-33.SimpleParam1.xsl*)

```
<xsl:stylesheet xmlns:xsl="http://www.w3.org/TR/WD-xsl" language="VBScript">
   <xsl:script id="template">
        browser="$browser"
        version="$version"
   </xsl:script>
   <xsl:script id="target"/>
   <xsl:template match="/">
       <xsl:if expr="'browser'='IE'>
            <xsl:if expr="version gte 5">
                 <!-- do IE5 related output -->
            </xsl:if>
       </xsl:if>
   </xsl:template>
</xsl:stylesheet>
```

This document includes two script blocks, one with an ID of `template`, the other with an ID of `target`. Within the template block, I designate my parameters by starting them with a dollar sign ($). This block will serve as the model for the other block, allowing me to use the same XSL file without having to reload it.

I still need a little bit of external code to be able to handle the parameterizations, but I can get away with far less using this model (Listing 4.34).

Listing 4.34: The VBScript Code to Pass Parameters into the XSL Document—the First Version (*Listing4-34.txt*)

```
dim xslDoc as DOMDocument
dim script as String
set xslDoc=createObject("Microsoft.XMLDOM")
xslDoc.load "Code4-33.SimpleParam1.xsl"
script=xslDoc.selectSingleNode_
      ("//xsl:script[@id='template']")
script=replace(script,"$browser","IE")
script=replace(script,"$version","5.1")
xslDoc.selectSingleNode("script[@id='target']")._
   text=script
```

The code here is simple—take the script text from the template script, replace the parameters, and then place this new script into the target node. The next time `transformNode` is called with the XSL script, it will assign the variables twice: once for the template and once for the target—but as the target is the last script called, the variables will have the target's values, not the template's.

There are still a few minor problems. In an ideal world we'd like to take the process one step farther and have the whole mess handled internally, perhaps by handing off an XML blob that handles all of the parameters at once. Furthermore, if you had two variables called `$browser1` and `$browser2`, this technique wouldn't work. To take care of that case, as well as to show how to *really* enhance the power of your XSL, I want to proceed to our next major topic, *regular expressions*.

Is All This Really Necessary?

While the Microsoft parser is reasonably powerful, it missed the boat on a number of areas. One of the biggest weaknesses was the lack of any implicit mechanism to handle passing parameters into XSL for processing. When the Dec 98 XSL specification came out, the focus of the model was on introducing some form of scripting solution. In the interim, a number of new features, including the explicit declaration of parameters and variables in an XSL-T structure, became part of the standard. These will have a profound impact on the ease of passing information back and forth through an XSL wall.

As the specific Microsoft implementation of this technology is still at least months away as I write this, its difficult to tell how this will be implemented. Check on the XSL-T section of the Web/CD Application for up-to-date information about parameterization in XSL-T.

Regular Expressions

XPath and XSLT are remarkably good at handling information at levels down to the node, but they are not especially good about the stuff within the node. If you want to find all managers named Smith, you're fine, but if you want to find all managers whose name starts with the letter *S*, then you're in serious trouble.

Fortunately, there is a technology that is, because of the `xsl:script` blocks, perfectly accessible, and remarkably well adapted for the tasks of fine-grain searching and manipulating: *regular expressions*. If you aren't familiar with them, you can think of regular expressions (or *regexes*, as they are popularly known) as templates that describe one or more patterns of characters in a string. Regexes form the foundation of such scripting languages as Perl, but they have only started migrating recently into the realm of JavaScript and VBScript.

JavaScript actually has the cleanest implementation of regular expressions (although the IE5.*x* release of both VBScript and JavaScript include some form of regexes). A regular expression in JavaScript is delimited by forward slashes rather than quotation marks. For example, you can create a regular expression to search for all names that begin with the letter *S* by using this syntax:

```
var reSmith=\^[sS].*\
```

The period indicates a general match of any character other than a newline, the caret signals that the search expression must start at the beginning of a line, and the asterisk indicates a search for zero or more characters following the *S*. Of course, if the text that you're searching starts with the letter *S*, then this particular pattern will match the entire string.

The expression `[sS]` indicates that the match can select either *s* or *S*. In order to select a range of characters—for example, all uppercase letters—you can also hyphenate from the start to the end of the range within the brackets: `[A-Z]`. You can also combine character searches: `[A-Za-z0-9]`, for example, will search for any alphanumeric character.

You can also invert a selection by using the carat as the first symbol within the braces (this is one of several instances where the same symbol pulls double duty depending upon whether it is within or outside a brace). Thus, `[^A-Za-z]` will match *2* or = but not *X*.

The syntax of regular expressions can become quite cryptic, but in general the characters for matching fall into two categories: regular literal characters, which are characters that match exactly with their values, and escaped characters (also called *metacharacters*), which each have a special meaning. Escaped alphanumeric characters are created by placing a reverse slash ("\") before the character and are shown in Table 4.4. Because punctuation is much less frequently matched, the sequence is reversed for most punctuation; a punctuation metacharacter is one that *doesn't* start with a slash, while the literal representation of the character must always have a slash before it (Table 4.5).

For example, the character `w` will always match a *w* in the search string, but a `\w` metacharacter is a shorthand symbol for any alphanumeric character. On the other hand, the + symbol by itself indicates that the preceding character is repeated one or more times, while \+ creates a match with any + character in the search string.

TABLE 4.4: Alphanumeric Metacharacters

Metacharacter	Meaning
`[\b]`	Matches a backspace.
`\b`	Matches a word boundary. For example, `/\bt/` matches the *t* in *big top* but not the *t* in *install.*
`\B`	Matches a non-word boundary. For example, `/\Bt/` matches the *t* in *install* but not in *big top.*
`\cX`	Matches a control character (where X is an uppercase letter). For example `\cI` matches the tab character (ASCII character 9 or Ctrl + I).
`\d`	Matches a digit; same as `[0-9]`.
`\D`	Matches a non-digit character; same as `[^0-9]`.
`\f`	Matches a form-feed.
`\n`	Matches a line-feed.
`\o` octal	Matches any octal escape value. (For example, `\o7` is the bell character.)
`\r`	Matches a carriage return.
`\s`	Matches a single white-space character such as a space or a tab; equivalent to `[\f\n\r\t\b]`.
`\S`	Matches a single character other than a whitespace character; equivalent to `[^\f\n\r\t\b]`.
`\t`	Matches a tab.
`\w`	Matches an alphanumeric character, including the underscore character. This is the same as `[A-Za-z0-9_]`.
`\W`	Matches any character other than an alphanumeric. Same as `[^A-Za-z0-9_]`.
`\x` hex	Matches any hex escape value. (For example, `\x20` is a space character.)

TABLE 4.5: Qualifiers and Punctuation Metacharacters

Qualifier or Metacharacter	Meaning
`^`	Matches the beginning of input or line. For example, ^S matches the *S* in *Smith*, but neither *S* in *ASSOCIATION*.
`$`	Matches the end of the input or line. For example, `Smith$` matches *James Smith* but not *Smith, James*.
`.`	Matches any character except a newline character.
`(x)`	Matches *x* and remembers the match.

TABLE 4.5: Qualifiers and Punctuation Metacharacters *(continued)*

Qualifier or Metacharacter	Meaning
`a|b`	Matches either expression *a* or expression *b*. For example `/new|used/` will match both *new car* and *used car*.
`[xyz]`	A character set, matching any of the characters. You can also set a range, such as `[0-9A-Fa-f]`, matching only those characters that are found in a hexadecimal string.
`[^xyz]`	Matches any character that is *not* in the indicated set. Note that this is contingent upon the character sets used.
`\n`	Where *n* is a positive integer, this provides backward reference to the *n*th parenthetic expression. For example, `([0-9A-Fa-f])\1` will match any two-digit hexadecimal number. If the number is greater than the number of parentheses, then this expression defaults to the octal value instead. (Octal is a base-7 number.)
*	Matches the previous character or parenthetic expression 0 or more times.
+	Matches the previous character or parenthetic expression one or more times.
?	Matches the previous character or parenthetic expression 0 or 1 time.
`{n}`	Where *n* is a positive integer, will match exactly *n* occurrences of the previous character or parenthetic expression.
`{n,}`	Where *n* is a positive integer, matches at least n occurrences of the previous character or expression.
`{n,m}`	Matches from *n* to *m* occurrences, where *n* is a positive expression and *m* is an integer greater than *n*.
`\`	The Escape character. This indicates that the next character is "escaped" from its normal sense (for alphanumeric characters, this means that the characters become metacharacters; for punctuation marks, this means that the next character is treated as a literal for matching purposes). To search against a backslash character, use the expression \\.

Validation with Regular Expressions

Within the JavaScript language (at least the version included with Internet Explorer 5), regular expressions can be accessed through the RegExp class. In addition to handling the ability to create such regular expressions, the RegExp class also gives you a way to test a string to see if the regular expression finds a match (the `test()` method), replace the results of a regular expression match with another string (`replace()`), and retrieve an array of strings that match the regular expression (`exec()`).

To see this in action, consider the problem of determining the validity of a zip code in an XML document. A zip code has a very well-known structure, but it is not an easy one to test using normal string processing functions. The basic characteristics are as follows:

- A zip code has a minimum of five digits.

- A zip code can have a maximum of nine digits.
- If the number of digits is greater than five, then the remaining four digits must be separated by a hyphen.

On the basis of these three conditions, its possible to create a regular expression for matching all possible zip codes:

```
/^\d{5}(-\d{4})?$/
```

Unraveling this fairly cryptic string isn't that hard—start from left to right:

1. The ^ character indicates that the search string must match from the beginning of the source string.
2. `\d` is a shortcut for a digit from 0 to 9.
3. `{5}` says that there must be five digits to be valid.
4. `(-\d{4})` indicates that there is a second group of four digits, preceded by a hyphen.
5. The question mark shows that this expression can occur either 0 or 1 time.
6. The final dollar sign, $, shows that there can be no more characters in the line of text.

Now to apply it. Assume that the source XML file is a simple name-and-address block (Listing 4.35). (Note that the zip code in the second `info` block is invalid.)

Listing 4.35: A Small XML Document that Contains Basic Name and Address Information (*Code4-35.Address.xml*). (*Listing4-35.txt*)

```
<form>
   <info>
      <name>Aleria Delamare</name>
      <street>3284 N. Hawthorne St.</street>
      <city>Olympia</city>
      <state>WA</state>
      <zipcode>98502</zipcode>
   </info>
   <info>
      <name>Shendra Marconi</name>
      <street>4291 SE. Daedalus Rd.</street>
      <city>Olympia</city>
      <state>WA</state>
      <zipcode>983122</zipcode>
</info>
</form>
```

The XSL file here needs to perform a validating function: It looks at each of the fields in turn and determines whether or not the field is valid, as demonstrated by Listing 4.36. If so, then the info block is placed into an `<accepted>` category; otherwise, it is placed in a `<rejected>` category.

Listing 4.36: An XSL Filter that Reads the Previous Form Document Format and Accepts or Rejects the Blocks as Valid (*Code4-36.ValidZipCode.xsl*)

```
<xsl:stylesheet xmlns:xsl="http://www.w3.org/TR/WD-xsl" language="JavaScript">
   <xsl:script>
      // Note here that the expression is delimited with
      slashes, not quotation marks. This automatically
      makes it into a regular expression if the search
      query is valid.

      isValidZipCode=/^\d{5}(-\d{4})?$/
   </xsl:script>
   <xsl:template match="/">
      <results>
      <xsl:apply-templates select="//info"/>
      </results>
   </xsl:template>

   <!-- This creates a pass-through for each record -->
   <xsl:template match="*|@*|text()">
      <xsl:copy>
         <xsl:apply-templates select="*|@*|text()"/>
      </xsl:copy>
   </xsl:template>

   <xsl:template match="info">
      <xsl:for-each select="zipcode">
      <xsl:choose>
         <xsl:when expr="isValidZipCode.test(this.text)">
         <accepted><info>
            <xsl:apply-templates select="../*"/>
            </info></accepted>
            </xsl:when>

         <xsl:otherwise">
         <rejected>
           <xsl:attribute name="reason">Invalid Zip
               Code</xsl:attribute>
               <info>
             <xsl:apply-templates select="../*"/>
             </info></rejected>
           </xsl:otherwise>
      </xsl:choose>
   </xsl:template>
</xsl:stylesheet>
```

When the filter is applied to the source document, it produces the output shown in Listing 4.37. Once the `isValidZipCode` object is instantiated (through the use of the slash delimiters), you can apply any string to it with the `test()` operator, which will return a True or False value depending on whether the particular expression was valid or not.

Listing 4.37: The Results of Applying the Address XSL Filter to the Data Set (*Listing4-37.txt*)

```
<results>
   <accepted>
    <info>
        <name>Aleria Delamare</name>
        <street>3284 N. Hawthorne St.</street>
        <city>Olympia</city>
        <state>WA</state>
        <zipcode>98502</zipcode>
    </info>
</accepted>
<rejected>
     <info reason="Invalid Zip Code">
        <name>Shendra Marconi</name>
        <street>4291 SE. Daedalus Rd.</street>
        <city>Olympia</city>
        <state>WA</state>
        <zipcode>983122</zipcode>
     </info>
</rejected>
</form>
```

Using XSL Templates to Create XSL

You can apply a similar methodology to the task of searching within a document for all nodes that satisfy a given regular expression. This type of search can be really powerful when performed in conjunction with XPath, because in a search you're typically less concerned about which node the data appears in than with matching the data to meaningful criteria.

For example, in the organization chart that started out this chapter (repeated for convenience in Listing 4.38), you might want to get a list of all managers who are officers of the company (that is, who have the term *officer* in their title).

Listing 4.38: The Acme Managers List Once Again (*Code4-01.xml*)

```
<?xml:stylesheet href="manager1.xsl" type="text/xsl"?>
<company>
        <name>Acme Rocket Company</name>
        <manager>
```

```
            <name>Phil Schwarts</name>
            <title>Chief Executive Officer</title>
            <canHire>yes</canHire>
            <vested/>
        </manager>
        <division>
            <name>Finance</name>
            <manager>
                 <name>James Galway</name>
                 <title>Chief Financial Officer</title>
                 <canHire>yes</canHire>
                 <vested/>
            </manager>
        </division>
        <division>
            <name>Marketing</name>
            <manager>
                 <name>Cynthia Dresler</name>
                 <title>VP, Marketing</title>
                 <canHire>yes</canHire>
            </manager>
        </division>
        <division>
             <name>Research</name>
             <manager>
                 <name>Benny Jocum</name>
                 <title>Chief Technical Officer</title>
                 <canHire>yes</canHire>
             </manager>
             <manager>
                 <name>Allison Hart</name>
                 <title>Vice President, Year 2000 Issues</title>
                 <canHire>no</canHire>
                 <vested/>
             </manager>
             <section>
                 <name>COBOL Programming</name>
                 <manager>
                     <name>Jerry Garcia</name>
                     <title>Director, COBOL Systems</title>
                 </manager>
             </section>
        </division>
</company>
```

Rather than just creating a specialized query, I want to create a generalized (parameterized) XSL script that could work for any combination of regular expression and XPath expression.

Listing 4.39 illustrates how you can create just such a filter. This code also demonstrates the third option for creating parameterized filters, an option that is perhaps a little more complex but considerably more powerful than regular text substitution. In essence, what I'm doing here is creating an XSL filter that creates an XSL filter, which in turn gets applied to the output stream.

This technique isn't terribly complicated, but it does require a re-examination of namespaces. The name of the namespace (for example, the "`xsl:`" used ubiquitously throughout this chapter) doesn't have any intrinsic magic; it is simply a label. To create a filter that outputs an XSL namespace, you can change the base namespace to some other namespace label ("`a:`" in this instance) and then output the `xsl:` namespace directly without having to worry about collisions.

The template in listing 4.39 is unusual in that you set the parameters to this template first (in this case, in the text of the nodes `<re/>`,`<returnObj/>`, and `<xpath/>`), and then you apply the template to itself. The result of this transformation is a new XSL filter that handles the specific code instances. Listing 4.40 shows the DOM script that calls this object, and Listing 4.41 shows the result of the template's transformation on itself.

Listing 4.39: A General XPath and Regular Expression Filter (*Code4-39.XPathRE.xsl*)

```
<a:stylesheet xmlns:a="http://www.w3.org/TR/WD-xsl"
   language="JavaScript" xmlns:xsl="http://www.w3.org">
   <a:template select="/">
      <xsl:stylesheet>
      <a:attribute name="xmlns:xsl">http://www.w3.org/TR/WD-xsl</a:attribute>
      <a:attribute name="language">Javascript</a:attribute>
     <xsl:script>
         re=/<a:value-of select="//parameters/re"/>/;
     </xsl:script>
   <xsl:template match="/">
       <results>
       <xsl:apply-templates>
       <a:attribute name="select">//<a:value-of
     select="//parameters/returnObj"/>[<a:value-of
     select="//parameters/xpath"/>]</a:attribute>
       </xsl:apply-templates>
       </results>
   </xsl:template>
   <xsl:template match="*|@*|text()|pi()|comment()">
         <xsl:copy>
      <xsl:apply-templates select="*|@*|text()|pi()|comment()"/>
      </xsl:copy>
   </xsl:template>
```

```
        </xsl:template><a:attribute name="match"><a:value-of select="//parameters/
returnObj"/></a:attribute>
            <xsl:if><a:attribute
        name="expr">re.test(this.selectSingleNode('<a:value-of
        select="//parameters/xpath"/>').text)</a:attribute>
                <xsl:copy><xsl:apply-templates
            select="*|@*|text()|pi()|comment()"/></xsl:copy>
          </xsl:if>
        </xsl:template>
      </xsl:stylesheet>
      </a:template>
      <parameters>
          <re>.*</re>
           <xpath>*[text()]</xpath>
           <returnObj>*[text()]</returnObj>
      </parameters>
    </a:stylesheet>
```

Listing 4.40: The VBScript Code for Processing this Transformation (*Code4-40.Transform.html*)

```
<html>
<head>
   <title>Transform</title>
</head>
<body>
<script language="VBScript">
dim xslTemplateDoc
dim xslDoc
dim xmlDoc
set xslTemplateDoc=CreateObject("Microsoft.XMLDOM")
set xslDoc=CreateObject("Microsoft.XMLDOM")
set xmlDoc=CreateObject("Microsoft.XMLDOM")
xslTemplateDoc.load "Code4-39.XPathRE.xsl"
' Set the regular expression to /Officer/
xslTemplateDoc.selectSingleNode("//re").text="Officer"
' Set the object to be returned to manager
xslTemplateDoc.selectSingleNode("//returnObj").text="manager"
' Set the node to search for the text to title
' Note that this node is relative to the return object.
xslTemplateDoc.selectSingleNode("//xpath").text="title"
call xslTemplateDoc.transformNodeToObject(xslTemplateDoc,xslDoc)
xmlDoc.load "List4-1.xml"
document.write "<xmp>"
document.write xmlDoc.TransformNode(xslDoc)
document.write "</xmp>"
</script>
</body>
</html>
```

Listing 4.41: The Interim XSL File Produced by Applying the Template to Itself after Setting the Parameters (*Code4-41.Interrim.xsl*)

```
<xsl:stylesheet xmlns:xsl="http://www.w3.org/TR/WD-xsl" language="Javascript">
   <xsl:script>
         re=/Officer/;
     </xsl:script>
   <xsl:template match="/">
      <results>
         <xsl:apply-templates select="//manager[title]"/>
      </results>
   </xsl:template>
   <xsl:template match="*|@*|text()|pi()|comment()">
      <xsl:copy>
         <xsl:apply-templates select="*|@*|text()|pi()|comment()"/>
      </xsl:copy>
   </xsl:template>
   <xsl:template match="manager"><xsl:if
   expr="re.test(this.selectSingleNode('title').text)"><xsl
   :copy><xsl:apply-templates
    select="*|@*|text()|pi()|comment()"/></xsl:copy>
      </xsl:if>
   </xsl:template>
</xsl:stylesheet>
```

Okay, so maybe this *is* pretty complicated. Creating self-referential templates is not for the faint of heart, but of all the techniques for creating XML output, it is one of the closest to the philosophy of XSL and reveals the fundamental power of the language—you can set values on an XSL transform document using just the DOM and then, using a series of XSL transforms on XML or XSL objects, you can create nearly any output you need. Additionally, once you build this template, it will give you the ability to apply any regular expression to any XML document to produce any result; the result of the interim transform on the original XML document (the manager's list, in our example) can in turn have another XSL transform applied to it to create HTML output.

Summary

XSL is the workhorse of XML. It provides the means to change one XML document into another, to display XML, to perform searches and queries on the data, and, in general, to take the object/data paradigm embedded in XML a step further.

The implementation of XSL that shipped within Internet Explorer 5 is seriously flawed in a number of critical respects: it doesn't allow for easy parameterization, it has little support for searches involving substrings of text, it has only limited capacity to deal with external objects, and it doesn't scale easily.

The material covered in this chapter targets the Microsoft browser implementation of XSL, which was valid as of December 1998. Roughly a year later, the W3C finalized the XSL-Transform specification. As this book was being written, Microsoft released their MSXML2.6 parser, which will form the cornerstone of most of Microsoft's XML development for the next several years. In the next chapter, I look at the changes in this browser, how they significantly improve life for XML developers, and why it is still necessary to understand both the old and new namespaces.

CHAPTER 5

The New XML Parser

- Using parameters, variables, and Processors
- Working with XPath functions
- Implementing object scripting
- Sorting and controlling output

Microsoft has received a fair amount of heat for a number of practices over the years, and, while working on an XML book firsthand, I have continually pounded my head against one of the more frustrating of these: the lack of a W3C-compliant XSL parser. While the parser that is based upon the December 1998 XML query language submission has done an inestimable amount to make people more cognizant of the power of XML and XSL, the differences between that parser and the one based on the November 1999 W3C XSL and XPath recommendations have caused a lot of code to be written to an out-of-date standard.

The recent release of the MSXML 2.6 parser has changed that, bringing Microsoft's technology up to a level consonant with their claims to being a major player in the XML field, and opening up to developers a much richer, more subtle, and generally more useful tool for Web development. In this chapter, I look at how you can leverage a number of features from the newest release, especially, though not exclusively, with the XSL and XPath improvements.

Parameters, Variables, and Processors

Is XSL a programming language? This is a fairly hotly debated point among both traditional and XML developers, although the emerging consensus is that it *is* a programming language, with a few caveats. A principle limitation of the earlier version of XSL is that it does not lend itself easily to *parameterization* (the ability to pass information into an XSL document prior to processing, other than the XML document itself). In some ways, this isn't a major limitation; you can actually load information that you need about the external environment into the XML source document, but this has a tendency to strongly couple the XSL filter to a given XML format.

The W3C XSL Transformations recommendation includes a number of features designed to simplify this process, and the Microsoft XSLT parser, in turn, provides a few additional features that extend XSLT without compromising the language's integrity. Among these is the ability to pass parameters (and even objects) into XML documents that can, in turn, be referenced through internal variables. The impact this has on programming is profound, because it turns XSL transformations into fully encapsulated objects, letting them play nicely in the world of object-oriented programming without compromising their inherent strength in manipulating complex data structures. The key to using such parameterization with the MSXML object is the innovation of the *XSL Processor*.

Creating XSL Processors

One of the long-standing complaints of developers about the older XSL parser is the fact that whenever you wanted to apply an XSL transformation to an XML document you needed to recompile the XSL code. This compilation took place within the DOMDocument's `.transformNode` or `.transformNodeToObject` methods. Understanding this process can help you better appreciate the current parser's improvements.

When the XSL code was compiled, the various XSL tags were tokenized, substitutions were performed recursively, and then the whole document was sent to an output stream. In other words, every time you transformed an XML document, you recreated the transformation code as well, which is a relatively slow and costly operation.

The current parser provides an alternative to this. While `.transformNode` and `.transformNodeToObject` both still work, you can also create an XSL Processor directly. An XSL Processor converts the XSL into compiled binary code that can be applied to any number of XML structures. Because it makes the costly XML compilation a one-time cost, designing around the XSL Processor makes for far faster code. Additionally, it simplifies the use of third-party components, encapsulates the XSL code so that it acts more like a component, and provides a much cleaner mechanism for parameterization.

To create an XSL Processor, you need to instantiate an XSL template object. This particular object has only one property, `styleSheet`, and one method, `createProcessor`. The sole purpose of the XSL template object is to create XSL Processors. In order to do this, you need to create a free-threaded XML object first, and load it with the XSL document that you want to make into a Processor.

Note the emphasis on *free-threaded*; in order to properly scale, the compiled XSL Processor has to be able to work effectively in a separate thread, which can only be achieved if it is passed a properly threaded source. For example, the ASP code in Listing 5.1 loads an XSL document that converts that document into an XSL Processor and then applies the newly created Processor to a set of employees to get a listing by department.

Listing 5.1: An ASP Script that Uses the XSL Processor to Output a List of Employees by Department (*showEmp.asp*)

```
<%@ Language=VBScript %>
<HTML>
<HEAD><TITLE>Show Employees By Department</TITLE
</HEAD>
<BODY>
<%
dim xslDoc
dim template
dim proc

set xslDoc=createObject("MSXML2.FreeThreadedDOMDocument")
xslDoc.load server.MapPath("params1.xsl")
set template=createObject("MSXML2.XSLTemplate")
set template.stylesheet=xslDoc
set proc=template.createProcessor
```

```
set xmlDoc=createObject("MSXML2.FreeThreadedDOMDocument")
xmlDoc.load server.MapPath("employees.xml")
proc.input=xmlDoc
proc.output=response
proc.transform
%>
</BODY>
</HTML>
```

Once the XSL document and template objects are created, the template's `.stylesheet` property is set to the document itself. You have to assign a style sheet before creating the Processor; otherwise, you'll generate an error. The Processor itself has a fairly rich set of properties and methods, which are outlined in Table 5.1.

TABLE 5.1: XSL Processor Properties

Property or Method	Description
`Sub addObject(obj As Object, namespaceURI As String)`	Adds an object into a namespace within the XSL document
`Sub addParameter(baseName As String, parameter, [namespaceURI As String])`	Sets a parameter within the XSL transform
`Property input As Variant`	Sets the input XML source
`Property output As Variant`	Sets the output XML target
`Property ownerTemplate As XSLTemplate`	Returns the template object that created the style sheet
`Property readyState As Long`	Contains the ready state of the XSL transform
`Sub reset()`	Resets parametric information and terminates active XSL transformations
`Sub setStartMode(mode As String, [namespaceURI As String])`	Sets the active XSL mode
`Property startMode As String`	Retrieves the current `startMode`.
`Property startModeURI As String`	Retrieves the URI of the current `startMode`.
`Property stylesheet As IXMLDOMNode`	Returns the style sheet as an XML document.
`Function transform() As Boolean`	Performs a transformation and sets the results to the designated output stream.

The Processor encapsulates the XSL transformation; once you've created the Processor, it really does act like a black box function in that you can set specific parameters, input and output streams, and modes, but you no longer have to worry about the XSL object as an XML entity.

Indeed, from the standpoint of programming, the XSL Processor becomes an `IStream` object. What this means is that in order to use the Processor you assign a source stream (through the `input` property) and a target stream to it (through the `output` property) and then call the `transform` method to read the source stream, transform it to the final output, and then send it on to the target stream (see Figure 5.1).

FIGURE 5.1
Streaming and the XSL Processor

In Microsoft's parlance, a stream is effectively a collection of bytes that come from some external source and can be anything from a file, a database record set, a request stream from an IIS 5 server, the contents of an HTML element, and so forth. By abstracting streams from their providers, it is possible to deal with the streams in a generic fashion, something with an obvious impact on XML. Much of the most-recent technology that Microsoft has introduced in the last year is XML-stream enabled, meaning that if an XML stream is requested from the object (either for reading or for writing) then the components that produce that stream will oblige.

Older technologies may not necessarily support the same streaming capabilities, by the way, but that doesn't mean that you still can't use streams. The streaming interface provided through XML will automatically convert an internal stream into a string (and vice versa) if it encounters an object that isn't stream enabled. Thus, at the very least, you can output an XML stream to a variable as text.

NOTE Because of the possibility that the stream may come from any number of sources, both the `input` and `output` properties are defined as variants, so you don't need to (and shouldn't) use the `set` keyword to assign the streams.

The `transform` method is both like and unlike the DOMDocument `transformNode` method. When called, it applies the XSL transform to the input stream and sends the result to the output stream. Unlike `transformNode()`, however, `transform()` does not return either a string or an object; it simply initiates the transformation object. In that respect, it can almost be thought of as a pump that moves the data from one location to another, modifying it in the process.

You can recover the style sheet from the object through the `.stylesheet` property, although this is a read-only property; if you need to run a different transform, you should create a different Processor. The style sheet is returned as an XSL document; however, it may not be quite identical to your initial style sheet document, as the Processor strips spurious white space and optimizes the output somewhat. Functionally, it should be equivalent to the initial document.

Defining Parameters and Variables

The XSL Processor provides an efficient way to assign parameters to the XSL transformation, but, in order to work with the Processor, you need to understand how XSL parameters are set up. In earlier chapters, parameters were passed through a number of kludges, either assigning IDs to XSL elements and then retrieving these and setting specific values for their attributes or text fields, or putting the information into the XML source document. Parameters do away with all of these kludges and are a much easier way to automate your XSL.

A parameter is defined via the `<xsl:param>` tag, specifically as the following example demonstrates:

```
<xsl:param name="paramName" select="xpathStr">
   paramValue</xsl:param>
```

The parameter name should follow the same rules as for naming IDs: an alphanumeric string (or the underscore character) starting with a letter. The `paramValue` and `select` attributes, on the other hand, are optional, although if you have one you shouldn't use the other. The `paramValue` can contain any valid XML code; it isn't just confined to a string, as Listing 5.2 shows.

Listing 5.2: Valid and Invalid Text Parameter Definitions (*Listing5-2.txt*)

```
<xsl:param name="department">Research</xsl:param>

<xsl:param name="message">
   <message>
        <from/>
        <to/>
        <body/>
   </message>
</xsl:param>

<xsl:param name="boilerplate">
<p>Acme Rocket Company has undertaken the services of the
legal firm <i>Dewey, Cheatem, and Howe</i>, and all
contracts are binding within their jurisdiction.</p>
```

```
</xsl:param>

<xsl:param name="markup"><![CDATA[
<script>
    function min(a,b)
        if a<b then
            test=a
        else
            test=b
        end if
        min=test
    end function
 </script>
]]></script>
</xsl:param>
```

However, the following are invalid parameters:

```
<xsl:param name="cdataStart"><![CDATA[</xsl:param>

<xsl:param name="fragment"><div>This is a test</xsl:param>
```

The `select` attribute, on the other hand, works very similar to the way that the `select` attribute in `<xsl:apply-templates>` behaves: it retrieves a set of nodes from the XML document and assigns them to the parameter. One consequence of this is that you can store the results of an XPath query for retrieval at some other point in processing, or you can pass a selection of nodes generated by a DOM query into the XSL document.

However, in addition to that, the XSLT processor will also let you place an expression to be evaluated in the `<xsl:param>` `select` attribute. For example, for the following set of parameter nodes, the value of parameter **a** evaluates to 7, or 3 + 4, while the value of parameter **b** is 12, or 5 + 7.

```
<xsl:param name="a" select="3+4"/>
<xsl:param name="b" select="5+$a"/>
```

In the case of the second parameter, the expression **$a** retrieves the value of parameter **a** and passes it on; in general, the **$** character is an operator that evaluates the parameter specified immediately thereafter.

WARNING Note that this usage differs from that of the XSL Pattern syntax described in Chapter 4, "XSL Transform." There, the **$** sign is used to escape comparison operators in XPath strings; here, it is used to evaluate parameters or variables.

You can similarly introduce strings into such parameters, but they should be delimited, using the alternating string syntax from what is used to define the attribute in the first place.

The following sample, for example, will attempt to find the nodes associated with the XPath expression "Hello" and will likely fail.

```
<xsl:param name="greeting" select="Hello"/>
```

To set greeting to the string "Hello" rather than the XPath expression "Hello", you would delimit it with single quotes:

```
<xsl:param name="a" select="'Hello'"/>
```

The XSL specification also provides a number of functions that can manipulate strings, which can be employed within select statements. For example, the following expression will concatenate (join) the first and second specified string together:

```
<xsl:stylesheet
   xmlns:xsl="http://www.w3.org/TR/1999/XSL/Transform"
   version="1.0">
   <xsl:param name="greeting" select="'Hello'"/>
   <xsl:param name="username" select="'Kurt'"/>
   <xsl:variable name="salutation"
   select="concat($greeting,', ',$username,'!')"/>
<!-- more code -->
```

The value of $salutation, then, is the string "Hello, Kurt!". The concat() function combines each of the strings contained within its functional braces and is one of a number of different functions described in the "XPath Functions" section later in this chapter.

NOTE If you've worked much with languages like VB or Java, you may wonder why the strings aren't added together using a + or & operator. The principal problem is that both of these characters have distinct meanings in XSL already, with the & character marking the beginning of entities and the + sign handling numeric addition. Moreover, the concat() function can handle the aggregation of any number of strings, so it was just not deemed sufficient by the W3C to have both a concat() function and a concatenation operator.

You can see the contents of a variable in your output by using the <xsl:value-of> element and the dereferencing $ operator. For example, once the variables are defined as above, you can display the output of the expression within a template, as Listing 5.3 demonstrates.

Listing 5.3: A Simple XSL Transform that Outputs a Tiny XML Greeting (*greetUser.xsl*)

```
<!-- greetUser.xsl -->
<xsl:stylesheet
   xmlns:xsl="http://www.w3.org/TR/1999/XSL/Transform"
   version="1.0">
   <xsl:param name="greeting" select="'Hello'"/>
   <xsl:param name="name" select="'Kurt'"/>
   <xsl:variable name="salutation"
      select="concat($greeting,', ',$name,'!')"/>
```

```
    <xsl:template match="/">
       <document>
       <xsl:value-of select="$salutation"/>
       </document>
    </xsl:template>
 </xsl:stylesheet>
```

Notice that the `salutation` block is defined as a variable (`<xsl:variable>`). The differences between parameters and variables in XSL are fairly minor: A parameter is a value that is defined from outside the XSL document, while a variable holds information that is defined within the document itself. In this case, the `salutation` variable shouldn't be defined by any external calls, so it doesn't need to be given as a parameter.

A good way to think about the distinction between parameters and variables is to look at an ActiveX control. The properties that the control exposes to you are `public`: They can be read (and sometimes modified) by other controls; a parameter is like this. On the other hand, a variable is like an internal variable in the same ActiveX control: It holds information relevant to the control itself but doesn't expose that information to the outside world and can't be changed outside of the component itself.

Passing Parameters

In addition to defining aspects of the language, the various XML specifications are also very clear about those aspects of the language that are outside the focus of the recommendation. About the use of parameters, the XSLT document is quite clear:

> Both `xsl:variable` and `xsl:param` are allowed as top-level elements. A top-level variable-binding element declares a global variable that is visible everywhere. A top-level `xsl:param` element declares a parameter to the stylesheet; *XSLT does not define the mechanism by which parameters are passed to the stylesheet* ("11.4 Top-level Variables and Parameters," `http://www.w3.org/TR/xslt`).

Setting a parameter from the older XML DOM is generally pretty simple. However, because you have two different ways of assigning parameter values (through text and through the `select` attribute), you're better off creating two distinct functions: `setTextParameter`, for assigning values to the text node of the parameter node, and `setSelectParameter`, for assigning values to the `select` attribute (see Listing 5.4).

Listing 5.4: Setting Parameters with *SetTextParameter* and *SetSelectParameter* (*Listing5-4.txt*)

```
Visual Basic:
Sub setTextParameter(xslDoc as DOMDocument,
      ParamName as String,paramValue as String)
```

```
      as IXMLDOMNOde
   Dim paramNode as IXMLDOMNode
```

VBScript:

```
Sub setTextParameter(xslDoc,paramName,paramValue)
   Dim paramNode

   Set paramNode=xslDoc.selectSingleNode("//xsl:param/[_
      name='"+paramName']")
   if not (paramNode is Nothing) then
      paramNode.removeAttribute("select")
      paramNode.text=paramValue
   else
      set paramNode=xslDoc.documentElement.appendChild(_
         xslDoc.createElement("xsl:param"))
      paramNode.text=paramValue
   end if
   set setTextParameter=paramNode
End Sub

   Set paramNode=xslDoc.selectSingleNode("//xsl:param/[_
      name='"+paramName']")
   if not (paramNode is Nothing) then
      paramNode.removeAttribute("select")
      paramNode.text=paramValue
   else
      set paramNode=xslDoc.documentElement.appendChild(_
         xslDoc.createElement("xsl:param"))
      paramNode.text=paramValue
   end if
   set setTextParameter=paramNode
End Sub
```

Visual Basic:

```
Sub setSelectParameter(xslDoc as DOMDocument,_
      paramName as String,_
      paramValue as String) as IXMLDOMNode
   Dim paramNode as IXMLDOMNode
```

VBScript:

```
Sub setSelectParameter(xslDoc,paramName,paramValue)
   Dim paramNode

   Set paramNode=xslDoc.selectSingleNode("//xsl:param/[_
      name='"+paramName']")
   if not (paramNode is Nothing) then
      set paramNode=xslDoc.documentElement.appendChild(_
```

```
            xslDoc.createElement("xsl:param"))
    end if
    paramNode.setAttribute "select",paramValue
    set setSelectParameter=paramNode
End Sub
```

Using these parameters then involves passing the name and value of the parameter with the XSL document. The short program shown in Listing 5.5 demonstrates this usage.

Listing 5.5: Displaying a Greeting Using the User-Defined *SetTextParameter* Function (*Listing5-5.txt*)

```
Set xmlDoc=createObject("MSXML2.DOMDocument")
XmlDoc.load "anyXMLDoc.xml"
Set xslDoc=createObject("MSXML2.DOMDocument")
XslDoc.load "greeting.xsl"
SetTextParameter xslDoc,"username","Aleria"
Msgbox xmlDoc.transform(xslDoc)
```

The primary situation to use either of those functions (`setTextParameter` or `setSelectParameter`) is when you don't have any need to call the XSL Processor object and you want to continue working with the XML DOM `.transformNode()` method. However, except in cases where you may need to be working with both the newer and older DOM interchangeably, any time you want to use parameters, you should probably take advantage of the XSL Processor's `addParameter()` method. This method, called prior to invoking the `transform()` method, overwrites the current parameter with the given name, if it already exists, and adds it to the XSL structure if it doesn't. The same code from Listing 5.5 can be rewritten to take advantage of the Processor, as shown in Listing 5.6.

Listing 5.6: Displaying the Greeting Using the Processor's *AddParameter* Function (*Listing5-6.txt*)

```
set xslDoc=createObject("MSXML2.FreeThreadedDOMDocument")
XslDoc.load "greeting.xsl"
set template=createObject("MSXML2.XSLTemplate")
set template.stylesheet=xslDoc
set proc=template.createProcessor

set xmlDoc=createObject("MSXML2.FreeThreadedDOMDocument")
XmlDoc.load "anyXMLDoc.xml"
proc.input=xmlDoc
proc.addParameter "username","Aleria"
proc.transform
msgbox proc.output
```

While it might appear more complicated to use the XSL Processor, there are a number of advantages to deploying it. One of the biggest is that it handles the choice of whether to use the text node or the `select` attribute automatically. It also lets you pass a list of nodes from a `selectNodes` call on the source XML (or from nodes passed within a function). Moreover, in environments, such as ASP pages, where the same XSL transform may be called repeatedly with differing parameters, storing the Processor in a session variable will result in a significant improvement in performance over recompiling the XSL with each call.

Processing Parameters through ASP

Inside of the XSL document, parameters and variables are treated in very similar fashions, the primary difference being that parameters are typically defined as global entities, while variables are typically either based upon parameters or defined internally. This is very analogous to the way that procedural functions are called.

For example, consider the problem of adding a record to an already-existing XML structure; consider an employee directory that gives essential work information for each employee, a listing that isn't all that different from the XML documents shown in Chapter 3, "Extracting Information with XSL Pattern and XPath."

Listing 5.7: A Partial Listing of Employee Information (*msdn-employees1.xml*)

```
<employees>
   <employee id="101">
      <firstName>John</firstName>
      <lastName>Janus</lastName>
      <title>President</title>
      <dateStarted>1997-11-12</dateStarted>
      <salary>324021</salary>
      <department>Administration</department>
   </employee>
   <employee id="102">
      <firstName>Kitara</firstName>
      <lastName>Milleaux</lastName>
      <title>Chief Executive Officer</title>
      <dateStarted>1997-08-12</dateStarted>
      <salary>329215</salary>
      <department>Administration</department>
   </employee>
   <employee id="103">
      <firstName>Shelley</firstName>
      <lastName>Janes</lastName>
      <title>Chief Financial Officer</title>
      <dateStarted>1998-03-16</dateStarted>
```

```
    <salary>232768</salary>
    <department>Finance</department>
  </employee>
  <employee id="104">
    <firstName>Marissa</firstName>
    <lastName>Mendez</lastName>
    <title>Chief Technical Officer</title>
    <dateStarted>1998-09-16</dateStarted>
    <salary>242768</salary>
    <department>Information Technologies</department>
  </employee>
  <employee id="105">
    <firstName>Kace</firstName>
    <lastName>Juriden</lastName>
    <title>Vice President, Marketing</title>
    <dateStarted>1998-11-03</dateStarted>
    <salary>210359</salary>
    <department>Marketing</department>
  </employee>
  <employee id="106">
    <firstName>James</firstName>
    <lastName>Marsden</lastName>
    <title>Senior Analyst</title>
    <dateStarted>1999-03-16</dateStarted>
    <salary>160204</salary>
    <department>Information Technologies</department>
  </employee>
  <employee id="107">
    <firstName>Henry</firstName>
    <lastName>Moore</lastName>
    <title>Senior Analyst</title>
    <dateStarted>1998-07-01</dateStarted>
    <salary>192142</salary>
    <department>Information Technologies</department>
  </employee>
  <employee id="108">
    <firstName>Karen</firstName>
    <lastName>LeBlanc</lastName>
    <title>Analyst</title>
    <dateStarted>1999-03-01</dateStarted>
    <salary>176245</salary>
    <department>Information Technologies</department>
  </employee>
  <employee id="109">
    <firstName>Cynthia</firstName>
    <lastName>Neville</lastName>
```

```
    <title>Marketing Analyst</title>
    <dateStarted>1999-04-07</dateStarted>
    <salary>159259</salary>
    <department>Marketing</department>
  </employee>
  <employee id="110">
    <firstName>Leonard</firstName>
    <lastName>Capacnik</lastName>
    <title>Creative Director</title>
    <dateStarted>1999-07-12</dateStarted>
    <salary>101242</salary>
    <department>Marketing</department>
  </employee>
  <employee id="111">
    <firstName>Art</firstName>
    <lastName>Sirtis</lastName>
    <title>Art Director</title>
    <dateStarted>1999-06-01</dateStarted>
    <salary>98552</salary>
    <department>Marketing</department>
  </employee>
  <employee id="112">
    <firstName>Steve</firstName>
    <lastName>Ruddell</lastName>
    <title>Senior Account Manager</title>
    <dateStarted>2000-01-05</dateStarted>
    <salary>125221</salary>
    <department>Marketing</department>
  </employee>
  <employee id="113">
    <firstName>Kiri</firstName>
    <lastName>Tekanewa</lastName>
    <title>Senior Programmer</title>
    <dateStarted>1999-10-04</dateStarted>
    <salary>102582</salary>
    <department>Information Technologies</department>
  </employee>
  <employee id="114">
    <firstName>Kace</firstName>
    <lastName>Moreaux</lastName>
    <title>Programmer</title>
    <dateStarted>2000-02-01</dateStarted>
    <salary>83024</salary>
    <department>Information Technologies</department>
  </employee>
  <employee id="115">
    <firstName>Michael</firstName>
```

```
      <lastName>Nesbit</lastName>
      <title>Graphic Designer</title>
      <dateStarted>2000-01-10</dateStarted>
      <salary>65253</salary>
      <department>Information Technologies</department>
   </employee>
   <employee id="116">
      <firstName>Sean</firstName>
      <lastName>Finnigen</lastName>
      <title>Web Designer</title>
      <dateStarted>2000-02-05</dateStarted>
      <salary>45023</salary>
      <department>Information Technologies</department>
   </employee>
   <employee id="117">
      <firstName>Missy</firstName>
      <lastName>Jerod</lastName>
      <title>Administrative Assistant</title>
      <dateStarted>1999-04-07</dateStarted>
      <salary>52003</salary>
      <department>Administration</department>
   </employee>
   <employee id="118">
      <firstName>Corey</firstName>
      <lastName>Woods</lastName>
      <title>Network Administrator</title>
      <dateStarted>2000-04-02</dateStarted>
      <salary>102225</salary>
      <department>Information Technologies</department>
   </employee>
   <employee id="119">
      <firstName>Severn</firstName>
      <lastName>Malcestis</lastName>
      <title>Public Relations</title>
      <dateStarted>2000-03-01</dateStarted>
      <salary>76224</salary>
      <department>Marketing</department>
   </employee>
   <employee id="120">
      <firstName>Rick</firstName>
      <lastName>Frain</lastName>
      <title>Programmer</title>
      <dateStarted>2000-03-06</dateStarted>
      <salary>55224</salary>
      <department>Information Technologies</department>
   </employee>
</employees>
```

Using traditional DOM methods, writing a routine to create a new entry in this list can get ugly. You either can create and set each node individually, which is both complex and extremely non-portable, or can load a template file, retrieve each node, set the value of the node, and then add it to the list. This latter method isn't much better than the former option because it still requires custom code. However, the use of the term *template* hints that maybe an XSL solution could be used.

As it turns out, by using an identity transform and parameters, XSL is actually quite up to the task, as shown in Listing 5.8. In essence, the principle is as simple as following these steps:

1. Retrieve the parameters.
2. Use these parameters to create a variable that holds a new `<employee>` "object."
3. Copy the `<employees>` node.
4. Copy all of the child `<employee>` nodes into the output `<employees>` node.
5. Pass a copy of the new employee in after the other nodes are created.
6. Close and terminate the `<employee>` node.

Listing 5.8: *AddNewEmployee1.xsl*, a Style Sheet to Add a New Employee to a Record (*addNewEmployee.xsl*)

```
<!-- addNewEmployee.xsl -->
<xsl:stylesheet xmlns:xsl="http://www.w3.org/1999/XSL/Transform" version="1.0">
   <xsl:output method="xml"/>
   <!-- retrieve the parametric information -->
   <xsl:param name="ID"/>
   <xsl:param name="FirstName"/>
   <xsl:param name="LastName"/>
   <xsl:param name="Title"/>
   <xsl:param name="DateStarted"/>
   <xsl:param name="Salary"/>
   <xsl:param name="Department"/>

   <!-- create a new variable called "NewEmployee"
        which holds an entire employee structure,
        and load the parameter values into the
        record -->
   <xsl:variable name="NewEmployee">
      <employee>
      <xsl:attribute name="id"><xsl:value-of
       select="$employeeID"/></xsl:attribute>
         <firstName>
         <xsl:value-of select="$FirstName"/>
```

```
            </firstName>
            <lastName>
            <xsl:value-of select="$LastName"/>
            </lastName>
            <title>
            <xsl:value-of select="$Title"/>
            </title>
            <dateStarted>
            <xsl:value-of select="$DateStarted"/>
            </dateStarted>
            <salary>
            <xsl:value-of select="$Salary"/>
            </salary>
            <department>
            <xsl:value-of select="$Department"/>
            </department>
         </employee>
      </xsl:variable>

      <!-- match the root node and retrieve the
            employees list -->
      <xsl:template match="/">
         <xsl:apply-templates select="//employees"/>
      </xsl:template>

      <!-- this is the identity transform, which
            copies the node passed and all of its children -->
      <xsl:template match="*|@*|text()">
         <xsl:copy><xsl:apply-templates select="*|@*|text()"/></xsl:copy>
      </xsl:template>

      <!-- copy the employees node -->
      <xsl:template match="employees">
         <xsl:copy>
         <!-- copy all of the current children into the output
               stream -->
         <xsl:apply-templates select="employee"/>
         <!-- put a copy of the newly created node into
               the output as a child of employees -->
         <xsl:copy-of select="$NewEmployee"/>
         </xsl:copy>
      </xsl:template>

   </xsl:stylesheet>
```

This sample uses one familiar and one not-so-familiar XSL element: `<xsl:value-of>` and `<xsl:copy-of>`. As mentioned in the "Defining Parameters and Variables" section, `<xsl:value-of>` can output a parameter's or a variable's value by putting the dereferencing `$` operator before the name of the parameter or variable within the `select` attribute of the element. `<xsl:value-of>` evaluates the result as text, dropping the tags in the process.

NOTE `<xsl:value-of select="expression">` retrieves the text value of the first node that satisfies the expression. If the expression is defined as a node set (the parameter or value selected a set of nodes into itself), then `<xsl:value-of>` will retrieve the text expression of the first node in that set.

This technique is fine for the parameter values, which are either text or can be represented as text (e.g., the `dateStarted` and `salary` fields). However, the variable, which contains an XML structure, will be destroyed by `<xsl:value-of>`, which is why `<xsl:copy-of>` is such an important part of the XSL lexicon. `<xsl:copy-of>` drops an exact duplicate of the node set defined by its `select` statement.

NOTE `<xsl:copy-of select="expression">` creates an exact duplicate of the node set indicated by `expression`. Thus, if a variable or value has selected a node set into itself (or, as in the example given previously, has a node set defined for it), then the result is streamed into the output.

WARNING `<xsl-copy-of>` is not the same as `<xsl:copy>`. The latter duplicates the current node name and value and can include additional `<xsl:apply-templates>` within its body. `<xsl:copy-of>`, on the other hand, copies the entire subtree; it is the most efficient way to duplicate an XML structure.

The code to actually call the transformation on the data set looks a little complicated (see Listing 5.9), but most of it is involved in loading and initializing the various XML documents. The block is given as ASP code.

Listing 5.9: *AddNewEmployee.asp*, a Script Passing Parameters and Formatting the Output (*addnewemployee1.asp*)

```
<%
' AddNewEmployee1.asp
' create the addEmployeeDoc XSL transform, a template to
 generate processors, a document to hold the source data,
 and an interrim XML document

function addEmployee(
    employees,id,firstName,lastName,title,dateStarted,
    salary,department)
```

```
  set addEmployeeDoc=createObject("MSXML2.FreeThreadedDOMDocument")
  set template=createObject("MSXML2.XSLTemplate")
  set newEmployeesDoc=createObject("MSXML2.FreeThreadedDOMDocument")

   ' create the addNewEmployee processor
  addEmployeeDoc.load server.mapPath("addNewEmployee1.xsl")
  set template.stylesheet=addEmployeeDoc
  set addNewEmployee=template.createProcessor
   ' load the XML source into the processor
  addNewEmployee.input=employees
   ' add the parameters; note they must be case identical to
   ' the XSL structure.
  addNewEmployee.addParameter "ID",id
  addNewEmployee.addParameter "FirstName",firstName
  addNewEmployee.addParameter "LastName",lastName
  addNewEmployee.addParameter "Title",title
  addNewEmployee.addParameter "DateStarted",dateStarted
  addNewEmployee.addParameter "Salary",salary
  addNewEmployee.addParameter "Department",department
   ' set the output to an interim document.
  addNewEmployee.output=newEmployeesDoc
  ' perform the transform
  addNewEmployee.transform
  set employees=newEmployeesDoc
  set addEmployee=employees.selectSingleNode("//*[@id='"+cstr(id)+"']")
end function

function main()
set employees=createObject(_
     "MSXML2.FreeThreadedDOMDocument")
  employees.load server.mapPath("employees.xml")
  id=request("id")
  firstName=request("firstName")
  lastName=request("lastName")
  title=request("title")
  salary=request("salary")
  dateStarted=request("dateStarted")
  department=request("department")
  addEmployee
    employees,id,firstName,lastName,title,dateStarted,
        salary,department
  employees.save server.mapPath("employees.xml")
  response.write employees.xml
end function

main
%>
```

The `main()` function loads in the set of employees to change and then passes the list and the set of new parameters (obtained by reading the ASP request string) to the **addEmployee** function. This, in turn, loads in the XSL transform, sets the parameters, and then applies the transform, returning the **employee** node just created.

Keep in mind that in VBScript all objects are passed by reference. This means that the XML employees document now reflects the newly added employee without it having to be retrieved explicitly as the result of the function; thus, in this particular case, the **employee** node is ignored, but the changed elements list is used instead.

NOTE Because this takes place on a server running IIS, the **server.mapPath()** function is necessary to inform the ASP interpreter that it should look on the local system for the specific file rather than attempting to treat it as a URL.

The **Request()** method is one of several ASP objects. Its purpose is to parse information sent from the client and make it available to the server. In our example, the client has a form that sends the information about a new employee to the server, as shown in Listing 5.10.

TIP The **Request()** object plays heavily in both regular and XML-centric ASP, to the extent that it is generally better to convert the **Request()** object into an XML structure. This is covered in much more detail in Chapter 8, "XML and ASP."

Listing 5.10: A Simple ASP Form for Adding New Employees (*addnewemployee.asp*)

```
<!-- AddNewEmployee.asp -- >

<%@LANGUAGE="VBScript"%>
<%response.expires=-1 %>
<!DOCTYPE HTML PUBLIC "-//W3C//DTD HTML 4.0 Transitional//EN">

<html>
<head>
   <title>Add New Employee</title>
</head>

<body>
<h1>Add Employee</h1>
<p>Please Enter the information for the new employee.</p>
<form method="POST" action="AddNewEmployee1.asp">
<table cellspacing="2" cellpadding="2" border="0">
```

```
<tr>
    <td>Employee ID</td><td><input type="Text" name="id" id="id"/></td>
</tr>
<tr>
    <td>First Name</td><td><input type="Text"
    name="firstName" id="firstName"/></td>
</tr>
<tr>
    <td>Last Name</td><td><input type="Text"
    name="lastName" id="lastName"/></td>
</tr>
<tr>
    <td>Title</td><td><input type="Text" name="title" id="title"/></td>
</tr>
<tr>
    <td>Salary</td><td><input type="Text" name="salary" id="salary"/></td>
</tr>
<tr>
    <td>DateStarted</td><td><input type="Text"
    name="dateStarted" id="dateStarted" value="<%=now%>"></td>
</tr>
<tr>
    <td>Department</td>
   <td><select name="department" size="1" id="department" value="">
       <option value="Administration">Administration</option>
         <option value="Information Technology">Information
          Technology</option>
         <option value="Finance">Finance</option>
         <option value="Marketing">Marketing</option>
        </select>
   </td>
</tr>
<tr>
    <td colspan="2"><input type="Submit" value="Submit Employee"/></td>
</tr>
</table>
</form>
</body>
</html>
```

When the preceding form is submitted (see Figure 5.2), it sends a URL to the server containing the names and values of each of the input fields, which are, in turn, read by the `Request()` object.

FIGURE 5.2
New employee form

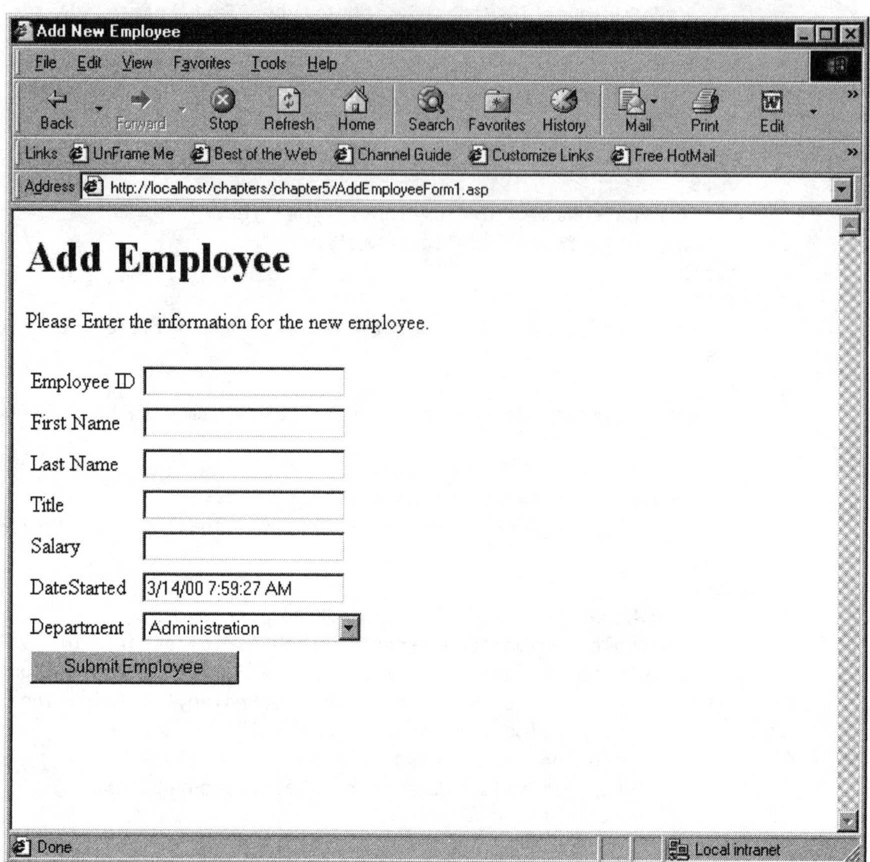

Is This Any Way to Run a Web Page?

No. The preceding example is typical of the way that many ASP sites are built, but, in fact, it suffers from a number of limitations that the use of XML and XSL can readily ameliorate. For starters, the XSL style sheet, as it exists when this book is being written, is specialized to the task of adding employees, but the task that it solves—adding an object to a collection of like objects—occurs all the time in programming settings. Instead of creating a style sheet for handling the addition of employees, an ideal solution is to define an employee-creation template (in XSL) and pass that as a subordinate style sheet into a more generic XSL structure for handling the addition of objects to collections. The template would be generated from an XML schema describing the object.

Is This Any Way to Run a Web Page? *(continued)*

That same creation template can be used to generate the HTML form in the first place, passing the requested field names and types, and can also serve to validate the submitted form prior to the new object being added to the collection. Finally, the template can even be used to determine the parameters that are needed from the request object—in essence, going full circle.

Notice how the discussion has moved into generic terms here; what you're seeing is the emergence of *patterns,* structural templates that mirror the XPath-matching patterns of XSL. With a few minor exceptions (primarily for COM initialization of objects), the system discussed here involves the flow of XML in a loop, pumped by the engine of XSL, and structured by objects described in XML Schema. This is programming at the system level and is one of the most powerful aspects of XML.

XML architecture is discussed throughout the rest of this book but is a major part of Chapter 8, "XML and ASP," and especially Chapter 11, "XML and Programming."

XPath Functions

Microsoft introduced the notion of scripting into their version of the XML component because there was a simple problem with the earlier version of the XSL parser: It was incapable of doing much beyond basic pattern matching on its own, severely limiting the utility of XSL. However, the `<xsl:eval>` and `<xsl:script>` blocks introduced a number of complications of their own, including the following:

- They are dependent upon the parser having access to some external programming language. This dependency made XSL solutions much more proprietary, since, for example, a Linux system running Java would be unlikely to work with VBScript, and the likelihood that either would want to mess with PerlScript made this even more problematic.
- The interfaces between the scripting and XSL partitions were awkward and problematic; you couldn't use the result of a scripted expression to significantly modify the XSL structure itself.
- Script isn't XML. This meant that you couldn't manipulate it, couldn't cleanly pull it into the environment, and couldn't readily parameterize it.
- Finally, the script capabilities that were available tended to break down the object environment that is becoming a hallmark of XML development.

The November 1999 XSL parser specification focuses on a number of the shortcomings of the December 1998 parser, and it addresses the scripting problem in particular through the following several changes to the technology:

Node Functions The older XSL parser didn't handle context nodes terribly well; getting a count of nodes that satisfied a given XPath expression was difficult, if not impossible, and you had to use specialized Microsoft extensions functions to perform a number of types of queries. The node functions specified in the newer XPath specification provide much-more-natural functions for handling node sets.

Text Manipulation Functions A significant amount of text matching builds around searching for or altering strings of text. By including functions to search for substrings and start strings and to handle basic transformations, the specification reduces the need for a significant amount of the scripting code that had been essential in the older version.

Expression Evaluation You can now evaluate numeric expressions directly in XSL `select` attributes with some degree of sophistication. The specification also makes provisions for numeric formatting, although this has not yet been implemented in the Microsoft parser.

Numeric Functions In addition to evaluating numeric expressions directly, XPath now also gives you a number of basic functions for manipulating numbers, performing sums, and rounding.

Parameters and Variables As discussed in previous sections, the ability to retain information in a variable can make for some remarkably powerful code. Additionally, because you can store node sets in variables, you can actually perform XSL transformations based upon multiple XML documents simultaneously.

Scripting Scripting is not dead. Microsoft realized that the functions that XPath provides still supply a relatively limited subset of all the capabilities needed to make XSL work in a production environment. Frankly, the solution they came up with is brilliant, and it is covered in the "Object Scripting" section later in this chapter.

Modes You can define a global characteristic called a mode that lets you use the same XPath pattern to refer to different templates. Thus, you can create one mode for outputting to IE, another for outputting to Navigator, and a third for outputting to a Palm Pilot browser.

NOTE It's worth noting that all of the functions introduced in the new XSL parser are technically not part of XSLT but, rather, are part of XPath. This is important as it means that you can use these functions outside of the context of XSLT.

Node Functions

Before delving into the wild world of node functions, let's reexamine the concept of a *node set*. A node set is, as the name implies, a collection of nodes, and it corresponds to the XML DOM node list. In other words, a node set does not necessarily consist of nodes that are siblings of a given parent node in the XML document structure. In fact, there is no strict requirement that the contents of a node set necessarily even belong to the same document, nor is there a requirement that all nodes in a node set be of the same type. In practice, of course, they usually are, but some of the most sophisticated XSL programming techniques have their basis in the ability to work with very disparate nodes simultaneously.

You can see this illustrated in the following expression that appears fairly often in this book:

```
"//*|@*|text()"
```

In this case, the XPath expression retrieves a node set that consists of all nodes that are elements, attributes, or text nodes. There is no requirement that these elements be contiguous; indeed, it is almost certain that they aren't. Because of this, however, when you're working with node functions, you should keep in mind that the node set that you're working with consists of a set of pointers to nodes throughout one (or conceivably more) documents. To readers working with the older XSL Pattern syntax, some of the node functions that are available to XSLT should look familiar, though not necessarily identical (see Table 5.2). However, they differ somewhat significantly as the set of nodes that they work with extends beyond a given node's immediate siblings and, instead, becomes any node in a node set.

TABLE 5.2: Node Functions

Function Type	Function Name	Description
Number	`last()`	Returns the number corresponding to the size of the XPath expression (the ***`context size`***) describing the current context.
Number	`position()`	Returns the position of the current node relative to the expression context.
Number	`count(node-set)`	Returns the number of nodes in any node set specified by the node set expression.
Node-set	`id(object)`	Converts the object specified into a string and then locates the node with that ID. (Note that a schema or DTD must be defined that explicitly declares a schema in order for this to return any set.)
String	`local-name(node-set?)`	Returns the name of the local part (the last expression in an XPath string) of the node context. If no node set is provided, the node set is the local context.

TABLE 5.2: Node Functions *(continued)*

Function Type	Function Name	Description
String	`name(node-set?)`	Returns the expanded name of the node context. If no node set is provided, the node set is the local context.
String	`namespace-uri(node-set?)`	Returns the URI of the namespace that covers the current node set context.

If some of the descriptions seem a little cryptic, don't feel bad. In point of fact, most of these functions are both powerful and fairly easy to use, but they are not immediately intuitive. I concentrate in this section on the `position()`, `last()`, and `count()`functions first, as they typically work together.

The *position()* and *last()* Functions

One of the hardest things to do with XSL Pattern is something that should be simple: taking a set of nodes and converting them into a comma-delimited list. This isn't a big requirement for outputting to XSL, but if you're attempting to generate SQL or comma-delimited files for output to interfaces that don't yet support XML (the vast majority, to be honest), then this ability is crucial.

For example, suppose that you want to output a list of all of the fields of all employees that belong to the Information Technologies division from Listing 5.11 (which reprises a few records from Listing 5.7), making the list comma delimited.

Listing 5.11: Part of the *employees.xml* Employees List

```
<employees>
   <employee id="101">
      <firstName>John</firstName>
      <lastName>Janus</lastName>
      <title>President</title>
      <dateStarted>1997-11-12</dateStarted>
      <salary>324021</salary>
      <department>Administration</department>
   </employee>
   <employee id="102">
      <firstName>Kitara</firstName>
      <lastName>Milleaux</lastName>
      <title>Chief Executive Officer</title>
      <dateStarted>1997-08-12</dateStarted>
      <salary>329215</salary>
      <department>Administration</department>
   </employee>
   <employee id="103">
```

```
      <firstName>Shelley</firstName>
      <lastName>Janes</lastName>
      <title>Chief Financial Officer</title>
      <dateStarted>1998-03-16</dateStarted>
      <salary>232768</salary>
      <department>Finance</department>
   </employee>
   <employee id="104">
      <firstName>Marissa</firstName>
      <lastName>Mendez</lastName>
      <title>Chief Technical Officer</title>
      <dateStarted>1998-09-16</dateStarted>
      <salary>242768</salary>
      <department>Information Technologies</department>
   </employee>
```

You can now use `position()` and `last()` to do the conversion, as is shown in the XSL `getCSVListByDepartment()` file in Listing 5.12. The `position()` function returns the position of the node relative to the current node set—its *position* in the node set, if you will. The `last()` function is a little more complex: it retrieves the position of the last element in the node set. You can then compare `position()` to `last()` to determine whether you've completed the set.

Listing 5.12: The XSL *getCSVListByDepartment.xsl* Transform

```
<xsl:stylesheet
   xmlns:xsl="http://www.w3.org/1999/XSL/Transform"
   version="1.0">

<xsl:output method="text"/>

<!-- retrieve the parametric information -->

<xsl:param
  name="Department">Information Technologies</xsl:param>

<!-- match the root node and retrieve the
      employees list for the parametric department -->

<xsl:template match="/">
      <xsl:apply-templates
        select="//employee[department=$Department]"/>
   </xsl:template>

<!-- for each employee property, attach a comma
      after the property itself if the property isn't
      the last in the employee. -->
```

```
<xsl:template match="*">
       <xsl:value-of/>
       <xsl:if test="not(position()=last())">,</xsl:if>
</xsl:template>

<!-- for each employee, retrieve the comma delimited
        names, then insert a carriage return after the
        properties list if the employee isn't the last
        in the list -->

<xsl:template match="employee">
    <xsl:if test="position()=1">
       <xsl:for-each select="*">
           <xsl:value-of select="name()"/>
           <xsl:if test="not(position()=last())">,</xsl:if>
       </xsl:for-each>
       <xsl:text xml:spacing="preserve">
</xsl:text>
   </xsl:if>
       <xsl:apply-templates select="*"/>
       <xsl:if test="not(position()=last())">
           <xsl:text xml:space="preserve">
</xsl:text>
       </xsl:if>
   </xsl:template>
</xsl:stylesheet>
```

There are, in fact, three distinct situations where the counting mechanism in the preceding example is used. Most comma-separated value files (CSVs) require that the names of the fields be given as the first line of the file. Thus, a test is made to determine whether the employee is the first in the collection. If it is, then the node names are passed as field information, through the use of the `name()` function, which retrieves the name of the node for the current context, as in the following example:

```
<xsl:if test="position()=1">
   <xsl:for-each select="*">
       <xsl:value-of select="name()"/>
```

Once the name is retrieved and put into the output stream, then a comma should also be output, but, again, only if the item isn't the last element in the node set:

```
<xsl:if test="not(position()=last())">,</xsl:if>
```

Finally, when the line is completed, a carriage return should be sent to the stream to start a new line. This makes use of a new node not yet discussed: the `<xsl:text>` node. `<xsl:text>` returns the text contained within exactly as shown. You can apply a special attribute (`xml:spacing="preserve"`) to the node to indicate that white space should be preserved rather than stripped. This gives you the following rather unusual-looking construct:

```
        <xsl:text xml:spacing="preserve">
</xsl:text>
```

This sample is sending a carriage return to the output stream. (Note that if the closing </ xsl:text> element was indented, the indenting space would also end up in the output stream, which is why it breaks the normal indenting.) Once outside of the scope, you can continue indenting as normal.

After the node names are sent to the output stream, you can output the actual values. Because this is a general case, I placed the routine to handle this in a separate * template, which uses the same counting mechanism to position the employee properties with commas, as in the following example:

```
<xsl:template match="*">
        <xsl:value-of/>
        <xsl:if test="not(position()=last())">,</xsl:if>
</xsl:template>
```

When control returns to the calling employee template, a test is made to determine if this is, in fact, the last record. If it's not, then a carriage return is added to the line, and the whole process starts over again. The reason for testing this is because many CSV-based programs don't automatically skip over empty lines. Here is an example:

```
        <xsl:if test="not(position()=last())">
            <xsl:text xml:space="preserve">
</xsl:text>
        </xsl:if>
```

After applying this template to the employee list, the output is exactly what we would hope to see, as shown in Listing 5.13.

Listing 5.13: Sample CSV Output when *getCSVListByDepartment* Is Applied to *employees.xml* (*getCSVListByDepartment_output.txt*)

```
firstName,lastName,title,dateStarted,salary,department
Marissa,Mendez,Chief Technical Officer,1998-09-16,242768,_
    Information Technologies
James,Marsden,Senior Analyst,1999-03-16,160204,_
    Information Technologies
Henry,Moore,Senior Analyst,1998-07-01,192142,_
    Information Technologies
Karen,LeBlanc,Analyst,1999-03-01,176245,_
    Information Technologies
Kiri,Tekanewa,Senior Programmer,1999-10-04,102582,_
    Information Technologies
```

```
Kace,Moreaux,Programmer,2000-02-01,83024,_
    Information Technologies
Michael,Nesbit,Graphic Designer,2000-01-10,65253,_
    Information Technologies
Sean,Finnigen,Web Designer,2000-02-05,45023,_
    Information Technologies
Corey,Woods,Network Administrator,2000-04-02,102225,_
    Information Technologies
Rick,Frain,Programmer,2000-03-06,55224,_
    Information Technologies
```

Notice that I've used `last()` rather than `count()` in this example. The `last()` function always reflects the last item in the current context set, while `count()`takes an XPath expression and returns the number of items that satisfy that expression. The difference here is subtle but important. For a given node, it's basically impossible to retrieve the context that called it. Thus, the expression `count(.)` will always return a value of `1` since that's what the template sees: only one node of the node set. (The `length()` function, on the other hand, keeps track of the last context that was called and returns the count of the nodes that satisfy that context; internally, `length()` almost certainly calls `count()`, but the context object itself is essentially inaccessible.)

The *count()* Function

So where would you use `count()`? Essentially, anywhere where you need to get the count of items in a different context. For example, suppose that you want an XSL transform that provides a count of the number of people in each department. Assuming that you have a list of the departments in a parameter (getting such a list is a considerably more-complex task), the `getEmployeeCount.xsl` transform (Listing 5.14) shows one way that you can easily do this.

Listing 5.14: The *getEmployeeCount.xsl* Transform Returns a List of Employees by Department.

```
<xsl:stylesheet
    xmlns:xsl="http://www.w3.org/1999/XSL/Transform"
    version="1.0">

<xsl:output method="html"/>
<xsl:param name="departments">
   <department>Administration</department>
   <department>Information Technology</department>
   <department>Finance</department>
   <department>Marketing</department>
   <department>Recruiting</department>
</xsl:param>
```

```
<xsl:template match="/">
<ul>
   <xsl:for-each select="$departments/*">
      <xsl:variable name="departmentName"><xsl:value-of/>
      </xsl:variable>
      <li>
      <xsl:value-of/>:
      <xsl:value-of select=
       "count(//employee[department=$departmentName])"/>
     <xsl:text xml:space="preserve"> employees</xsl:text>
      </li>
   </xsl:for-each>
</ul>
</xsl:template>

</xsl:stylesheet>
```

This example does illustrate an important technique for working with XSL transforms: The `$departments` parameter essentially takes the place of a node containing the various `<department>` children. Because it is a valid node, you can actually include it as part of an XPath expression and even iterate over the children with an `<xsl:for-each` statement:

```
<xsl:for-each select="$departments/*">
```

Thus, you essentially have two documents controlling the output, one being the list of employees who are being counted and the second being a list of the available departments in a given order. Within the `for-each` block, you then define a variable called `$departmentName`, which, in turn, contains the name of each document. By placing this in a variable, you can keep your code easier to read and spend less time trying to build complex context expressions.

The use of the `count()` here is simple; it takes the expression retrieving the employees in each department and retains the count of the resulting node set:

```
<xsl:value-of select=
 "count(//employee[department=$departmentName])"/>
```

The *name(), local-name(),* and *id()* Functions

The functions of `name()` and `local-name()` retrieve the name of either the current context or the first item in that context, depending upon whether or not the node set is a single item. You can also pass a distinct node set and either function will return the name. The real distinction between `name()` and `local-name()` has to do with the notion of *expanded name*. An expanded name is the name with its namespace designator. For example, for the expression `<xsl:if>`, the name of the node is `xsl:if`, while the `local-name` is `if`. The `namespace-uri`, in turn, returns the namespace itself.

Similarly, the `id()` function provides another means of retrieving a node. If the XML document has an associated schema or DTD in which IDs are defined, then the `id()` function returns, when passed a string, the object that is associated with the string. If the current node has an ID associated with it, then, when `id()` is called on the node (with no arguments), the result is a node set consisting of just that node.

TIP The `id()` is a powerful function, but it is best demonstrated in larger applications. The message board application in Chapter 8, "XML and ASP," uses the `id()` function extensively.

Text-Manipulation Functions

Given the fact that much of the functionality of XML derives from the string-oriented characteristics of SGML, the lack of native string functions in XSL Pattern has been a source of constant irritation to XML developers. How do you search for a given string in the old parser? Essentially, you need to search through each node in the scope, call a scripting function to retrieve the text of that node, perform whatever string queries you need (either directly with the JavaScript or VBScript string-handling functions or indirectly with Regular Expressions), and then pass a Boolean value back to the expression indicating that a match has been found. This makes for some incredibly ugly-looking XSL code.

The XPath string functions described in the November 1999 specification very nicely addresses this issue. Although the actual text-handling functions are a little weak, they are adequate for performing most basic string-searching tasks that you're likely to encounter, and the XSL extension mechanisms provide a direct means to expand that capability. The functions are summarized in Table 5.3.

TABLE 5.3: Text-Manipulation Functions

Function Type	Function Name	Description
String	`string(object?)`	For a node set (or the current context), returns the text value of the string (i.e., the same value you would see in the DOM's `.text()` method). For numeric values, converts the number into a decimal-string representation of that number. Boolean values are converted to true or false.
String	`concat(string,string,string*)`	Combines two or more strings into a single string with no delimiters and returns that string.
String	`starts-with(string,string)`	Returns true if the first string starts with all of the characters in the second string (false otherwise). This was designed to help implement look-ahead type functions.

TABLE 5.3: Text-Manipulation Functions *(continued)*

Function Type	Function Name	Description
String	`contains(string,string)`	Returns true if the first string contains the second string somewhere in its body.
String	`substring-before(string,string)`	Returns the string consisting of all characters in the first string up to the first match of the second string. Useful for parsing expressions. (For example `substring-before ("1999/04/01","/")` returns the string `"1999"`.)
String	`substring-after(string,string)`	Returns the string consisting of all characters in the first string following the first match of the second string. Useful for parsing expressions. (For example, `substring-after ("1999/04/01","/")` returns the string `"04/01"`).
String	`substring(string,startnumber,count?)`	For the given string, returns the first character specified by `startnumber`, for the count given by the argument `count`. If `count` is not included, then the entire string from the `startnumber` on is returned. (Thus, `substring("12345",2,3)` returns the string `"234"`, while `substring("12345",2)` returns `"2345"`. Note that the first character in the string is character `1`, not character `0`.)
String	`string-length(string?)`	Returns the number of characters in the passed string or the text of the current context if no string is provided.
String	`normalize-space(string?)`	Strips leading and trailing space characters from a given string and converts all white space between characters into a single space. If no string is provided, normalize-space returns the normalized text of the current context.
String	`translate(srcText,srcMap,targetMap)`	Searches through the `srcText` for characters in the `srcMap` function and replaces those characters with the ones in the same position of the `targetMap` function. If no character can be found in the target map for a character in the source map, the character is not mapped. (For example, `translate("--aaa--","abc-","ABC")` has no map for the dash character, so it doesn't translate these. However, it does have a direct map for the **a** character—**a** to **A**—so the expression `"--aaa--"` maps to `"AAA"`. Notice that characters not mentioned in the `srcMap` are automatically translated as is.)

The functions can be used in a number of different circumstances. As a simple example, suppose that you want to create an XSL filter that returns a list of all employees for which one of their fields starts with a specific set of characters. Take a look at the easiest case first, in Listing 5.15, where you want to match the first characters of the last name of an employee and return the corresponding records.

Listing 5.15: *getEmployeesFromLastName1.xsl*

```
<!-- getEmployeesFromLastName1.xsl -->
<xsl:stylesheet
   xmlns:xsl="http://www.w3.org/1999/XSL/Transform"
   version="1.0">
   <xsl:output method="xml"/>

   <xls:param name="fragment"></xsl:param>

   <xsl:template match="/">
      <employees>
         <xsl:apply-templates select=
   "//employee[start-of(string(lastName),$fragment)]"/>
      </employees>
   </xsl:template>

   <xsl:template match="employee">
      <xsl:copy-of/>
   </xsl:template>
</xsl:stylesheet>
```

This is beginning to show the real advantages of the XPath model over the older XSL Pattern model: The same task would have taken twice as much code and been a tenth as fast in the older version. In this case, there are two string functions used: `string()` and `start-of()`, although `string()` is actually optional here. The `string()` function retrieves the text contents of the current employee's `lastName` node and uses this as the source text. The fragment, passable as a parameter from DOM, contains the search string.

Of course, there's one flaw in this code: The code as given is case sensitive; finding all employees whose names start with *j* will likely not yield a match since XSL sees `j` and `J` as distinct characters. However, there is a fairly easy way around this, by using the `translate` function, as shown in Listing 5.16 in the `getEmployeesFromLastName2.xsl` file.

Listing 5.16: *getEmployeesFromLastName2.xsl*

```
<!-- getEmployeesFromLastName2.xsl -->
<xsl:stylesheet
   xmlns:xsl="http://www.w3.org/1999/XSL/Transform"
```

```
   version="1.0">
   <xsl:output method="xml"/>

   <xsl:param name="fragment"></xsl:param>
   <xsl:variable
      name="ucase","'ABCDEFGHIJKLMNOPQRSTUVWXYZ'"/>
   <xsl:variable
      name="lcase","'abcdefghijklmnopqrstuvwxyz'"/>
   <xsl:variable name="lcFragment"><xsl:value-of
   select="translate($fragment,$ucase,$lcase)"/>

   <xsl:template match="/">
      <employees>
          <xsl:apply-templates select=
   "//employee[start-of(
   translate(string(lastName),$ucase,$lcase),
   $lcFragment)]"/>
      </employees>
   </xsl:template>

   <xsl:template match="employee">
      <xsl:copy-of/>
   </xsl:template>
</xsl:stylesheet>
```

This example is a case where variables can make your code far more legible. The `$ucase` and `$lcase` variables are defined to include the uppercase and lowercase characters, respectively. The employee match then performs translations to convert both strings to lowercase. This way, there will always be a match regardless of how the user types the search string.

NOTE Note that this comes at a penalty: Even in highly optimized code, doing this kind of character mapping is not instantaneous. For this reason, I defined `$lcFragment` (lowercase *fragment*) to contain the pretranslated parametric fragment; this significantly reduces the number of translations that the parser needs to make.

Making Your Search Code Generic

Of course, it would be ideal to have the specific property within the employee object itself be specifiable; in other words, to be able to arbitrarily ask for all employees by first name or all departments that start with given characters. This, unfortunately, can be very difficult to do directly since the XPath specification doesn't have a mechanism to convert a string back into an XPath expression. However, you can do this indirectly by understanding that there is one very significant difference between XSL Pattern and XPath.

In XSL Pattern, a predicate can't contain an expression with another predicate. In other words, the following expression is illegal because it nests predicates:

```
//employer[*[nodeName()='firstName']]
```

However, XPath overcomes this limitation. This means that you can work with variables or parameters to pass the properties that you want specified and then create a second predicate that performs the tests on the resultant nodes, as shown in Listing 5.17 in the final search routine, `getEmployeesFromProperty.xsl`.

Listing 5.17: *getEmployeesFromProperty.xsl*

```
<!-- getEmployeesFromProperty.xsl -->
<xsl:stylesheet
   xmlns:xsl="http://www.w3.org/1999/XSL/Transform"
   version="1.0">
   <xsl:output method="xml"/>

   <xsl:param name="fragment"></xsl:param>
   <xsl:param name="property" select="'lastName'"/>
   <xsl:variable
      name="ucase","'ABCDEFGHIJKLMNOPQRSTUVWXYZ'"/>
   <xsl:variable
      name="lcase","'abcdefghijklmnopqrstuvwxyz'"/>
   <xsl:variable name="lcFragment"><xsl:value-of
      select="translate($fragment,$ucase,$lcase)"/>

   <xsl:template match="/">
      <employees>
          <xsl:apply-templates select=
   "//employee[start-of(
   translate(string(*[name=$property]),$ucase,$lcase),
   $lcFragment)]"/>
      </employees>
   </xsl:template>

   <xsl:template match="employee">
      <xsl:copy-of/>
   </xsl:template>
</xsl:stylesheet>
```

Notice, though, that the code given in this example now has only two elements that are specifically declared: the `<employees>` node and the `//employee` node in the search path. The `<employees>` node is essentially a generic collection node; it holds objects, and the name is really secondary. In other words, it can be passed as a parameter. The `//employee` nodes, on the other hand, are a node set, but if you pass the node set as an expression, that can also be parameterized.

In other words, with a little intelligent thought, you can make your search routine completely parameterized and generic so that it will work on any set of nodes. An example of exactly such a routine is shown in Listing 5.18.

Listing 5.18: *getObjectsFromPartialQuery.xsl*

```
<!-- getObjectsFromPartialQuery.xsl -->
<xsl:stylesheet
   xmlns:xsl="http://www.w3.org/1999/XSL/Transform"
   version="1.0">
   <xsl:output method="xml"/>

   <xsl:param name="objects" select="/*/*"/>
   <xsl:param name="collectionName" select="'collection'"/>
   <xsl:param name="fragment"></xsl:param>
   <xsl:param name="property" select="'lastName'"/>
   <xsl:variable
      name="ucase","'ABCDEFGHIJKLMNOPQRSTUVWXYZ'"/>
   <xsl:variable
      name="lcase","'abcdefghijklmnopqrstuvwxyz'"/>
   <xsl:variable name="lcFragment"><xsl:value-of
      select="translate($fragment,$ucase,$lcase)"/>

   <xsl:template match="/">
      <xsl:element name="$collectionName">
         <xsl:apply-templates select=
   "$objects[start-of(
   translate(string(*[name()=$property]),$ucase,$lcase),
   $lcFragment)]"/>
      </xsl:element>
   </xsl:template>

   <xsl:template match="*">
      <xsl:copy-of/>
   </xsl:template>

</xsl:stylesheet>
```

Okay, time to catch your breath for a bit to realize what exactly this transform does. A great deal of effective programming comes in seeing emergent patterns and programming for those patterns rather than for specific instances of the patterns. In the preceding listing, a pattern that seems to frequently emerge is that of the collection/object/property (COP) model, in which a single collection node holds a set of similar object nodes. Each object node, in turn, contains one or more properties that are themselves represented by element nodes. The employee list is one example; a recordset (transformed from an attribute to an element model) is another.

By abstracting out the class of XML patterns, you can then develop XSL transforms that act at the class level; the following is one of those transforms:

```
<collection>
   <object ...>
       <property1>propertyVal1</property1>
       <property2>propertyVal1</property2>
       ..
   </object>
   <object ...>
       <property1>propertyVal1</property1>
       <property2>propertyVal1</property2>
       ..
   </object>
      ...
</collection>
```

If your XML falls into the preceding form, then you can use `getObjectsFromPartialQuery.xsl` to generate a list of the items for which one of the properties starts with a given string. Similarly, you can modify that transform to search within a string (using the `contains()` function) or, really, to do any other comparison and retrieve a result set. Listing 5.19 shows how such a command would be called.

Listing 5.19: Demonstrating the Use of *getObjectsFromPartialQuery.xsl* (*Listing5-19.txt*)

```
<%

' Get property name and property search string
' From request object
prop=request("property")
fragment=request("fragment")

' Initialize the processor
set PartialQueryXSL=createObject(_
   "MSXML2.FreeThreadedDOMDocument")
set transformFactory=createObject(_
   "MSXML2.XSLTransform")
PartialQueryXSL.load _
   server.mapPath("getObjectsFromPartialQuery.xsl")
set transformFactory.stylesheet=PartialQueryXSL
set getPartialQuery=transformFactory.createProcessor

'load the data
set employees=createObject(_"
   "MSXML2.FreeThreadedDOMDocument")
employees.load server.mapPath("employees.xml")
```

```
'transform the data
with getPartialQuery
   .input=employees
   .output=response
   .addParameter "collectionName","employees"
   .addParameter "objects",_
      employees.selectNodes("//employee")
   .addParameter "property",prop
   .addParameter "fragment",propVal
   .transform
end with
%>
```

Note that this code could be further encapsulated into functions, but I wanted to keep the path of what was actually taking place fairly obvious. Ultimately, the intention is to get to the point where there will be nearly no obvious ASP code, but I leave elaborating on that point to Chapter 8, "XML and ASP."

Numeric and Boolean Expressions and Functions

Given that XML is moving into the realm of being a data format, more and more information in XML documents are becoming encoded not as straight data but as calculated data instead. This was, in fact, one of the primary reasons for working with the `<xsl:eval>` node in the older XML parser; manipulating numbers directly was not a feature of the XSL language.

However, that's changed considerably with the latest release. As with modifying text, you can evaluate numeric expressions through the `<xsl:value select="">` tag. In its simplest case, this can be basic numerics:

```
<xsl:value-of select="3*(100+(25 div 5)) mod 60"/>
```

This sample places the value `15` into the output stream; the `div` token replaces the / token for division (since the parser interprets the forward-slash character as an XPath node), while `mod` is the modulus operator, which returns the remainder of a division operation. Thus, the preceding expression is interpreted as `3*(100+5) mod 60 => 315 mod 60 =>15`.

Typically, though, you'll be more inclined to create expressions that incorporate node-text values or variables. For example, Listing 5.20 calculates the tax on salary. (I'm assuming a flat-tax rate here, which is unrealistic; I'll show how to get around that problem later in this chapter.)

Listing 5.20: The XSL *getTaxes.xsl* Transform

```
<!-- getTaxes.xsl -->
<xsl:stylesheet
   xmlns:xsl="http://www.w3.org/1999/XSL/Transform"
   version="1.0">
   <xsl:output method="xml"/>
```

```
<xsl:param name="taxRate" select="0.25"/>

<xsl:template match="/">
   <h1>Taxes</h1>
   <h4>Tax Rate:
   <xsl:value-of select="$taxRate *100"/>%
   </h4>
   <ul>
      <xsl:apply-templates select="//employee"/>
   </ul>
</xsl:template>

<xsl:template match="employee">
   <li><xsl:value-of select="lastName"/>,
       <xsl:value-of select="firstName"/>:
       $<xsl:value-of select="$taxRate * salary"/>
    </li>
</xsl:template>

</xsl:stylesheet>
```

In this case, I created a parameter for tax rate. (Increases in taxes are practically as inevitable as taxes themselves, unfortunately, so parameterizing this variable makes sense.) The variable can then be used in an expression such as the one that converts the tax rate to a percentage. It can also be used with the result of an XPath query; the expression `$taxRate * salary`, for example, has a number of unstated conversions, including the following:

1. It retrieves the contents of the variable or parameter named `taxRate`.
2. When the multiply operator (*) is found, the `taxRate` expression is then converted into a number.
3. The `salary` XPath expression evaluates as a node.
4. The `multiply` operator forces that node to return the text type of the node.
5. This, in turn, is converted into a number.
6. The tax rate is multiplied against the resulting salary.
7. The result is converted back into a string and sent to the output string.

You can also assign expressions to variables in this same way. For example, you can set the result to a variable and then output the variable directly, keeping that information for other computations later:

```
<xsl:template match="employee">
   <xsl:variable name="employeeTax"
    select="$taxRate*salary"/>
   <li><xsl:value-of select="lastName"/>,
```

```
            <xsl:value-of select="firstName"/>:
            $<xsl:value-of select="$employeeTax"/>
        </li>
    </xsl:template>
```

These local variables also make it possible to separate your computational code from your output code by storing intermediate results. While this is not necessarily a good practice in normal programming, it makes more sense in a declarative notation.

There are also a number of basic numeric functions that you can incorporate into your code, as described by the W3C XPath specification. These elements are shown in Table 5.4.

TABLE 5.4: Numeric and Boolean Functions

Function Type	Function Name	Description
Boolean	`boolean(object)`	Converts its argument into a Boolean expression. For the most part, is called implicitly; empty contexts, empty strings, the number 0, or the implicit `false()` function all generate a Boolean value of false (most everything else returns true).
Boolean	`not(boolean)`	Converts a Boolean expression to its inverse; true becomes false, and vice versa. Performs an implicit conversion for non-Boolean objects into a Boolean type before inversion.
Boolean	`true()`	Returns the value true.
Boolean	`false()`	Returns the value false.
Boolean	`lang(language?)*`	Returns true if the language specified in the `xml:lang` attribute is the same as (or is a sublanguage of) the language specified in the argument as a string. If no language is specified in either the node or any ancestor nodes of the current node, `lang()`implicitly returns `false()`.
Number	`number(object?)`	Converts the object into a number if the number is a numeric string, the first node of a node set with numeric text, a numeric expression, or (if object is left blank) the current context node with a numeric value. If the number cannot be converted, then the value `NaN` (not a number) is returned. Note that this argument is typically called implicitly.
Number	`sum(node-set)*`	Converts each node's text element into a number and then adds these values together. Returns `NaN` if the number cannot be converted
Number	`floor(number)*`	Returns the largest integer (closest to positive infinity) that is less than or equal to the specified number.
Number	`ceiling(number)*`	Returns the smallest integer (closest to negative infinity) that is greater than or equal to the specified number.
Number	`round(number)*`	Returns the integer that is closest to the current number. If this value is halfway between two integers (such as 2.5), then `round()` always returns the number closest to positive infinity (For example, `round(2.5) ==> 3`, while `round (-2.5) ==> -2`).

WARNING The functions denoted by an asterisk (*) in Table 5.4 were not supported in the preview release of the MSXML 2.6 parser, and documentation at the time this book is being written suggests that they may not be supported in the final release. If you need to use these functions, you can take advantage of scripting objects defined in the "Object Scripting" section later in this chapter to create namespace alternatives that can be switched if and when the functions become supported.

Most functions in Table 5.4 are straightforward, with the possible exception of the `sum()` function, which takes a node set as an argument and attempts to convert each node's text field, in turn, to a number. If all numbers convert, then the values are summed together. This behavior is very similar to the way that a spreadsheet program such as Excel operates. In Excel, for example, the expression `SUM(C2:C12)` sums up all of the elements in column C, rows 2 through 12. A simple XSL transform—`showSalaries.xsl` in Listing 5.21—demonstrates how the `sum()` function works.

Listing 5.21: The XSL *showSalaries.xsl* Transform

```
<!-- showSalaries.xsl -->
<xsl:stylesheet
   xmlns:xsl="http://www.w3.org/1999/XSL/Transform"
   version="1.0">
   <xsl:output method="xml"/>

   <xsl:param name="taxRate" select="0.25"/>

   <xsl:template match="/">
      <h1>Salaries</h1>
      <h4>Total Payroll:
      $<xsl:value-of select="sum(//employee/salary)"/>%
      </h4>
      <ul>
         <xsl:apply-templates select="//employee"/>
      </ul>
   </xsl:template>

   <xsl:template match="employee">
      <li><xsl:value-of select="lastName"/>,
          <xsl:value-of select="firstName"/>:
          $<xsl:value-of select="salary"/>
       </li>
   </xsl:template>

</xsl:stylesheet>
```

Expressions in Attributes

Attributes provide a particularly sticky conundrum with respect to evaluating expressions. Consider, for example, the following expression:

```
<img src="<xsl:value-of select="concat($filePath,image)"/>">
```

This sample will raise a definite error in the XSL parser because it is bad XML. There are ways around this problem, of course, such as the use of the `<xsl:attribute>` tag, as in the following example:

```
<img><xsl:attribute name="src"><xsl:value-of
select="concat($filePath,image)"/></xsl:attribute></img>
```

Unfortunately, this tends to make for large and ungainly code. (Trust me on this one; I've written far too much code like this, and it's both difficult to write and difficult to maintain).

However, XSL offers an alternative: the evaluate operators `{ and }`. These can be used within attribute strings, and they basically indicate that everything within the brackets should be evaluated, converted into a string, and sent to the output string. The expression from the preceding example can be written as the following:

```
<img src="{concat($filePath,image)}"/>
```

TIP The brackets can also be used in some, but not all, of the XSL elements themselves. The biggest exception to this rule is in the use of the `select` attribute, principally because it implicitly performs such an evaluation anyway. However, brackets can be used (but aren't explicitly required) in the name attributes of elements or attributes.

You can actually create some interesting special effects when combining embedded expressions with style sheets. For example, suppose that you want to graphically show the differences in salaries among people in a corporation. Assuming the previous employee list, the code in Listing 5.22 creates a horizontal bar chart in DHTML that shows relative wealth, as shown in Figure 5.3.

Listing 5.22: The XSL *showSalaryRange.xsl* Transform

```
<!-- showSalaryRange.xsl -->
<xsl:stylesheet
   xmlns:xsl="http://www.w3.org/1999/XSL/Transform"
   version="1.0">
   <xsl:output method="xml"/>
   <xsl:param name="scale" select="2.0"/>
   <xsl:template match="/">
      <h1>Salary Range</h1>
```

```
        <xsl:apply-templates select="//employee"/>
    </xsl:template>

    <xsl:template match="employee">
        <div style="
            background-color:yellow;
            position:relative;
            width:{($scale*salary) div 1000}px;
            border:outset 3px yellow;">
             $<xsl:value-of select="salary"/>
        </div>
    </xsl:template>

</xsl:stylesheet>
```

FIGURE 5.3
Salary Ranges in DHTML

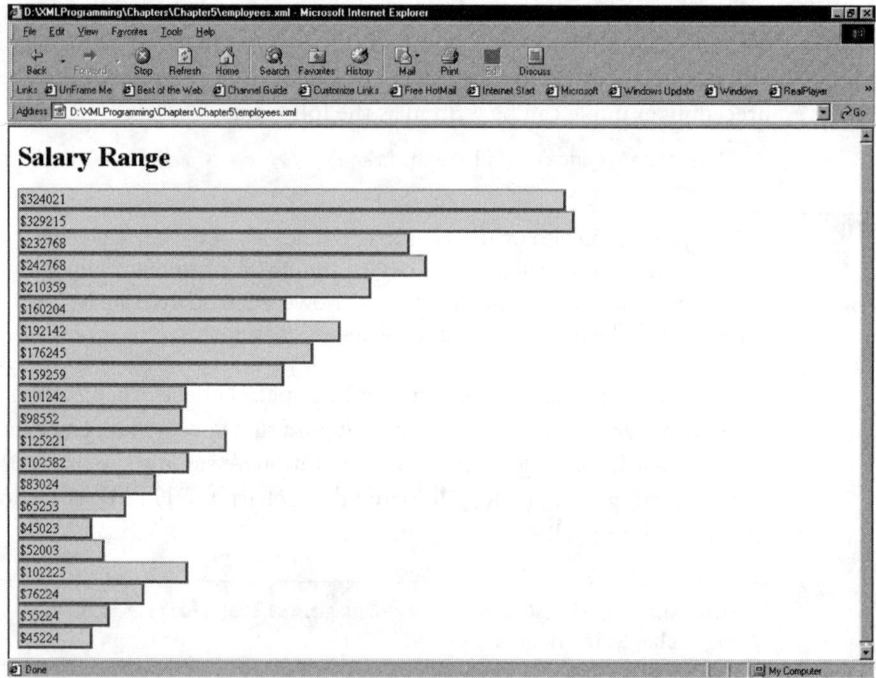

In this particular bar graph, the width is calculated by the following expression:

```
width:{($scale* salary div 1000}px;
```

The expression `salary div 1000` takes each salary and divides it by 1,000, which means that the sample widths range from 45 pixels to 324 pixels. The scale factor, in turn, is used to increase or decrease the width of this overall, and is a parameter.

Note that this solution is workable but is not especially ideal; a better calculation would be to determine the maximum salary, normalize all of the other salaries to percentages of the maximum, and then multiply these numbers by the maximum number of pixels in the graph. To do this, however, you need to determine the maximum salary dynamically, and we don't have the tools to do this yet since the XPath specifications don't directly support min or max functions.

Object Scripting

Extensibility is always an interesting conundrum—how to provide the best means to extend the capabilities of your technology without sacrificing the underlying ease of use. With XSLT, this has taken on an added twist: The language itself is a standard, which means that any solution that you come up with should additionally conform to this architecture. The older XSL Pattern architecture exposed a fundamental flaw in that XSL code required too much other coding language to be effective cross-platform, and, in the process, it ended up with highly fragmented code.

The strength of languages such as Visual Basic only really became apparent when the notion of objects became a core part of them. If you break your code into discrete objects that have a life of their own and that are furthermore encapsulated as distinct entities, then you make your code more modular and flexible. This holds true for such declarative languages as XSL.

XML has the concept of a namespace. A namespace is a way of defining a unique class and, in some respects, is as important a concept as the notion of XSL transforms or schemas. If you pull back from the code that defines all XML entities and start looking at them from a more global perspective, you can begin defining some of the critical classes at play: the default class (XML itself), the transform class, and the schema definition class. Moreover, a transform class is, in itself, a catalyst; in the main, it is unchanged from one transformation to the next. That means that one way of thinking about this transform class is as a way to map namespaces: An XML namespace gets mapped to an XHTML namespace, a data-set namespace gets mapped to a different data-set namespace, and employees tax records become HTML display.

TIP To reiterate, a transform converts one or more namespaces into another namespace.

Given this concept of transformation, the solution that the Microsoft XML development team came up with to handle non-XML objects seems simple, albeit brilliant: Turn COM or Java objects of all sorts into namespaces that can be manipulated within XSL using XSL mechanisms. In other words, with the new XSL Processor object, everything is XML.

One of the new namespaces that Microsoft introduced into their implementation of the XSL parser is the `msxsl` namespace, which is associated with the `urn:schemas-microsoft-com:xslt` URN. This namespace lets you define objects within XSL documents. For example, consider the problem from the previous section: How do you determine the maximum (or minimum) value from a set of nodes? This is a class of problems that's difficult to do in XSL; primarily because XSL doesn't readily retain state well; it's fairly easy to solve in procedural languages, however.

To that end, I created a basic `math:` namespace that contains a couple of functions that weren't included in the XSL specification: `max()` and `min()`. In this case, I knew that I was working with integer values (actually `long` values), so I designed it around this type. If you are creating a more general-purpose routine, take that into account. The code to handle this is shown in Listing 5.23.

Listing 5.23: An XSL Transform to Display Salaries Relative to the Smallest Salary (*sampleTransform.xsl*)

```
<xsl:stylesheet
    xmlns:xsl="http://www.w3.org/1999/XSL/Transform"
    version="1.0"
    xmlns:math="http://www.vbxml.com/cagle/math"
    xmlns:msxsl="urn:schemas-microsoft-com:xslt">
<xsl:output method="xml"/>
   <msxsl:script language="VBScript" implements-prefix="math"><![CDATA[
      function max(nodelist)
          dim m_max
         m_max=-2^31+1
         for each node in nodelist
             if m_max<clng(node.nodeTypedValue) then
               m_max=clng(node.nodeTypedValue)
            end if
         next
         max=m_max
      end function

      function min(nodelist)
          dim m_min
         m_min=2^31-1
         for each node in nodelist
             if m_min>clng(node.nodeTypedValue) then
```

```
                m_min=clng(node.nodeTypedValue)
             end if
          next
          min=m_min
       end function

       function floor(expr)
          floor=clng(expr)
       end function

   ]]></msxsl:script>

   <xsl:variable name="ct" select="count(//employee)"/>

<xsl:template match="/">
   <employees>
   <xsl:apply-templates select="//employee"/>
   </employees>
</xsl:template>

<xsl:template match="employee">
    <div style="position:relative;background-
   color:red;border:outset 3px red;width:{(salary div
   math:min(//employee/salary))*50}px;height:20px;">
   <xsl:value-of select="salary"/> (<xsl:value-of
   select="math:floor(math:max(//employee/salary) div
   salary)"/> to 1)</div>
</xsl:template>
</xsl:stylesheet>
```

If you've worked with the `<xsl:script>` nodes in Chapter 4, "XSL Transform," the preceding code may look eerily dissimilar. Instead of creating general functions, this code creates an object and associates it with a namespace called `math:`. This is done through the namespace call in the `<xsl:stylesheet node>`, as in the following sample:

```
xmlns:math="http://www.vbxml.com/cagle/math">
```

This declaration, in essence, creates a new class with the namespace designation of `math:` pointing to the `http://www.vbxml.com/cagle/math` URN. The importance of this URN is that it is a label, a way of uniquely identifying the object. It doesn't have to (and in most cases doesn't) point to a specific block of code or object definition.

Another URN is also defined for the XSL object:

```
xmlns:msxsl="urn:schemas-microsoft-com:xslt"
```

This URN defines the `msxsl` namespace. This namespace essentially lets you create an object within a script block, with the namespace taking the place of the object variable. This looks similar to the older `<xsl:script>` block but now includes the `implements-prefix="math"` attribute. What this says is that the functions contained in the script block define the interface for the `math:` namespace; it creates a math object with two methods (`math:min()` and `math:max()`), as shown here:

```
<msxsl:script language="VBScript" implements-prefix="math"><![CDATA[
   function max(nodelist)
```

The `max()` function itself takes as its sole parameter a node list. If the function is called from within a `select` statement or evaluation block, then the node list is passed in exactly the same way that the `count()` statement would pass it: through an XPath string. Thus, the following XSL statement calls the `max` function and passes the XPath expression through the `//employee/salary` context:

```
<xsl:value-of select="math:max(//employee/salary)"/>
```

There are no quotes here, by the way; you're passing an XPath expression, not a string. The internal code is similar to most DOM code within this book:

```
function max(nodelist)
    dim m_max
   m_max=-2^31+1
   for each node in nodelist
       if m_max<clng(node.nodeTypedValue) then
         m_max=clng(node.nodeTypedValue)
      end if
   next
   max=m_max
end function
```

If this function had an XML schema, the `nodeTypedValue` expressions wouldn't need the `clng` function to convert them into long values, but, in this case, it's good coding form if nothing else. The output is then the result of the winnowing to produce a maximum value.

External Components

While you can create an object (or several objects, using multiple `<msxsl:script>` blocks with different namespaces), the real benefit of using this particular notation is that it makes the use of external components possible. By associating a given namespace URL with an object, you can essentially bring that object "inside," letting the XSL have access to that object both for reading and for writing data. This has a number of ramifications for Visual Basic development, as it means that you can effectively build XSL filters into all of your favorite interface controls, and its effects on working with interfaces, such as ADO 2.5, cannot be underestimated.

However, it's worth looking at a fairly simple example of component interactions to understand how to work with the technology. Consider a simple class that performs a number of basic math functions on collections of nodes, such as averaging, getting standard deviation, determining mode, and similar activities, as shown in Listing 5.24. This could just as readily be an ActiveX DLL, but, for convenience sake, I'm creating a generic Math class in VBScript. (This assumes you are using VBScript 5 or better.)

Listing 5.24: A VBScript Math Class (*Math.vbs*)

```
<%
' Math.vbs
Class CMath
      function max(nodelist)
          dim m_max
         m_max=-2^31+1
         for each node in nodelist
             if m_max<clng(node.nodeTypedValue) then
               m_max=clng(node.nodeTypedValue)
            end if
         next
         max=m_max
      end function

      function min(nodelist)
          dim m_min
         m_min=2^31-1
         for each node in nodelist
             if m_min>clng(node.nodeTypedValue) then
               m_min=clng(node.nodeTypedValue)
            end if
         next
         min=m_min
      end function

      function floor(expr)
         floor=clng(expr)
      end function

      function sum(nodelist)
         dim m_sum
         m_sum=0
         for each node in nodelist
            m_sum=m_sum+clng(node.nodeTypedValue)
         next
```

```
            sum=m_sum
        end function

        function average(nodelist)
            average=sum(nodelist)/clng(nodelist.length)
        end function

        function stdev(nodelist)
            mean=average(nodelist)
            m_sum=0
            for each node in nodelist
                diffMean=mean-(node.nodeTypedValue)
                m_sum=m_sum+diffMean*diffMean
            next
            stdev=sqr(m_sum/(nodelist.length-1))
        end function
end class
%>
```

The preceding class, in turn, would be passed as an object in an ASP script (Listing 5.25) into the `showStatisticalInfo` XSL transform (Listing 5.26). The following line creates an instance of the CMath class, which can then be passed into the `showStatisticalInfo.xsl` transform object before the transform itself is performed:

```
Set math=new CMath
```

The call to do this (associated with the XSL Processor) is `addObject`, which takes both the object itself and a namespace as an argument. The namespace must match a namespace definition within the `<xsl:stylesheet>` tag, at which point the namespace prefix becomes associated with the object itself. The output is shown in Figure 5.4.

Listing 5.25: The ASP *showStatisticalInfo.asp* Script, Incorporating the *Math.vbs* Class (*Listing5-25.txt*)

```
<!--#include FILE="Math.vbs" -->
<%
set math=new CMath
set xslDoc=createObject("MSXML2.FreeThreadedDOMDocument")
set xslTemplate=createObject("MSXML2.XSLTemplate")
xslDoc.load server.mapPath("showStatisticalInfo.xsl")
set xslTemplate.stylesheet=xslDoc
set showStats=xslTemplate.createProcessor
set employees=createObject(_
    "MSXML2.FreeThreadedDOMDocument")
employees.load server.mapPath("employees.xml")
showStats.input=employees
showStats.output=response
```

```
showStats.addObject Math,"http://www.vbxml.com/math"
showStats.transform
```

Listing 5.26: The XSL *showStatisticalInfo.xsl* Transform

```
<xsl:stylesheet
   xmlns:xsl="http://www.w3.org/1999/XSL/Transform"
   version="1.0"
   xmlns:math="http://www.vbxml.com/math">
   <xsl:output method="html"/>

   <xsl:variable name="employeeSet"
      select="//employee/salary"/>

   <xsl:template match="/">
      <h1>Salary Analysis</h1>
      <table>
      <tr>
      <td>Total Payroll:</td>
      <td>$<xsl:value-of
           select="math:sum($employeeSet)"/></td>
      </tr>
      <tr>
      <td>Maximum Salary:</td>
      <td>$<xsl:value-of
           select="math:max($employeeSet)"/></td>
      </tr>
      <tr>
      <td>Minimum Salary:</td>
      <td>$<xsl:value-of
           select="math:min($employeeSet)"/></td>
      </tr>
      <tr>
      <td>Average Salary:</td>
      <td>$<xsl:value-of
           select="math:average($employeeSet)"/></td>
      </tr>
      <tr>
      <td>Standard Deviation:</td>
      <td>$<xsl:value-of
           select="math:stDev($employeeSet)"/></td>
      </tr>
      </table>
   </xsl:template>
</xsl:stylesheet>
```

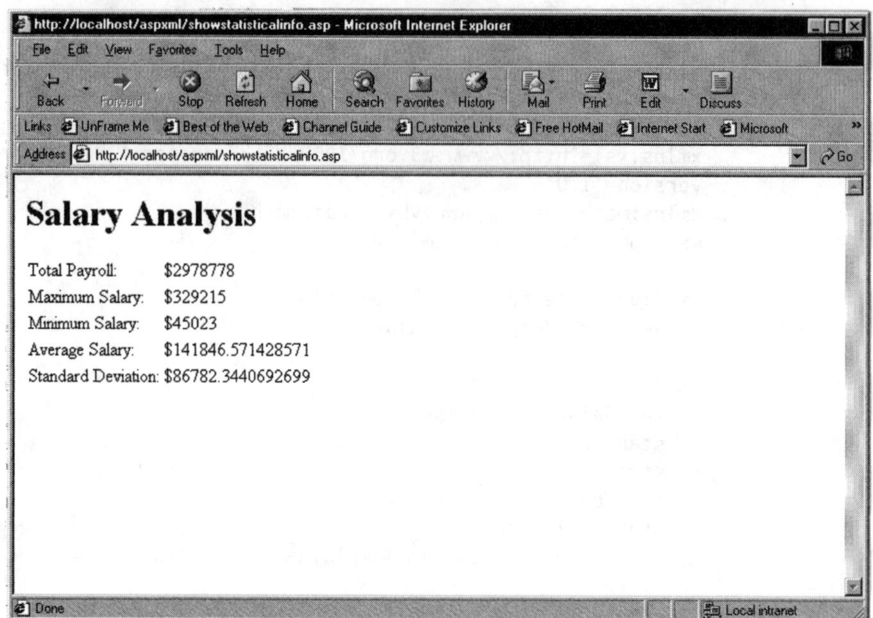

FIGURE 5.4
A statistical analysis of salaries

Sorting and Controlling Output

Sorting can be a fairly complicated process; beyond the issues of defining how you sort a column (whether a column of numbers is sorted as numbers or as strings; how to handle uppercase versus lowercase characters, and so forth), the problem of sorting seldom occurs in a vacuum. Given the easy redundancy of data that XML can introduce, you may end up needing to sort one property alphabetically, such as a name, and then sort a subset of that numerically, such as salaries for identical names.

The sorting capability offered by the older XSL parser has two other limitations: You can effectively only sort <xsl:apply-templates> nodes, and the mechanism for reversing a sort, an extremely common operation when dealing with visual interfaces, requires that you parse and test the starting character to determine whether it is a - or not. While this doesn't make the sort useless, it does limit its functionality greatly. Fortunately, the newer parser provides for a much more sophisticated sorting operation.

In the new parser, sort is handled through a special `<xsl:sort>` tag that is a child of either the `<xsl:apply-templates>` element or the `<xsl:for-each>` element, as the following example demonstrates:

```
<xsl:sort
select = string-expression
lang = { token }
data-type = { "text" | "number" |dataTypeName }
order = { "ascending" | "descending" }
case-order = { "upper-first" | "lower-first" } />
```

Most of these properties are defaulted to the first state given in the stub. For example, consider a simple case: sorting the list of employees by their last names (Listing 5.27).

Listing 5.27: Sorting the Employees by Last Name (*lastname.xsl*)

```
<xsl:stylesheet
   xmlns:xsl="http://www.w3.org/1999/XSL/Transform"
   version="1.0"
   xmlns:math="http://www.vbxml.com/math">
   <xsl:output method="xml"/>

   <xsl:template match="/">
       <employees>
       <xsl:apply-templates select="//employee">
           <xsl:sort select="lastName"/>
       </xsl:apply-templates>
       </employees>
   </xsl:template>

   <xsl:template match="employee">
       <xsl:copy-of/>
   </xsl:template>

</xsl:stylesheet>
```

In this particular situation, the default values for the sort all apply: `order="ascending"`, `lang="en"` (for English), `data-type="text"`, `case-order="upper-first"`. On the other hand, if you want to show a list of employees by salary from the highest to the lowest, you need to specify more attributes, as in Listing 5.28.

Listing 5.28: Sorting the Employees by Salary (*salary.xsl*)

```
<xsl:stylesheet
   xmlns:xsl="http://www.w3.org/1999/XSL/Transform"
   version="1.0"
```

```
    xmlns:math="http://www.vbxml.com/math">
    <xsl:output method="xml"/>

    <xsl:template match="/">
        <employees>
        <xsl:apply-templates select="//employee">
            <xsl:sort select="salary"
                      order="descending"
                      data-type="number"
            />
        </xsl:apply-templates>
        </employees>
    </xsl:template>

    <xsl:template select="employee">
        <xsl:copy-of/>
    </xsl:template>

</xsl:stylesheet>
```

The support for data types currently extends to those specified in the Microsoft Reduced Data XML Schema, so you can sort by `date`, `dateTime`, and so forth. However, it is likely, with the final release, that the parser will support the full W3C XML Schema recommendations, and the sort mechanism would then be able to support these instead.

NOTE One interesting question that has yet to be fully resolved at the level of the W3C deals with the issue of archetypes and sorting. An archetype allows for the creation of a complex data type, which is useful for definition, but one of the more interesting quandaries comes when you have to decide how one instance of an archetype (such as an address) is larger than another instance. Sort keys of some sort are likely to be a feature of the full XML Schema specification, but, at the time this book is being written, it is not clear what form they will take.

What about the situation where you want to sort data by last name but with identical last names being further sorted by first name? All that you need to do is add a separate sort key after the first. Each subsequent key orders the results at ever-finer levels of granularity, as Listing 5.29 demonstrates.

Listing 5.29: Sorting the Employees by Last Name, Then by First Name (*lastnamefirstname.xsl*)

```
<xsl:stylesheet
    xmlns:xsl="http://www.w3.org/1999/XSL/Transform"
    version="1.0"
    xmlns:math="http://www.vbxml.com/math">
    <xsl:output method="xml"/>
```

```
    <xsl:template match="/">
        <employees>
        <xsl:apply-templates select="//employee">
            <xsl:sort select="lastName"/>
            <xsl:sort select="firstName"/>
        </employees>
    </xsl:template>

    <xsl:template match="employee">
        <xsl:copy-of/>
    </xsl:template>

</xsl:stylesheet>
```

The sort mechanism is not actually tied into the `<xsl:apply-templates>` or `<xsl:for-each>` objects but rather into the `select` attribute. This means that it can actually be invoked from within the `<xsl:variable>` or `<xsl:parameter>` tags as well. Thus, Listing 5.30, in which employees are actually sorted ahead of time, is a valid, if somewhat unorthodox, approach to sorting.

Listing 5.30: Parametric Sorting (*sort.xsl*)

```
<!-- sort.xsl -->
<xsl:stylesheet
    xmlns:xsl="http://www.w3.org/1999/XSL/Transform"
    version="1.0"
    xmlns:math="http://www.vbxml.com/math">
    <xsl:output method="xml"/>
    <xsl:parameter name="sortKey" select="'lastName'"/>
    <xsl:parameter name="sortOrder" select="'ascending'"/>
    <xsl:parameter name="sortType" select="'text'"/>

    <xsl:variable name="employeeList" select="//employees">
        <xsl:sort select="*[name()=$sortKey]"
                  order="$sortOrder"
                  data-type="$sortType"/>
        </xsl:sort>
    </xsl:variable>

    <xsl:template match="/">
        <employees>
        <xsl:apply-templates select="$employeeList"/>
        </employees>
    </xsl:template>
```

```
    <xsl:template match="employee">
        <xsl:copy-of/>
    </xsl:template>

</xsl:stylesheet>
```

You can then sort the employee list by any property of the `employees` object with a simple script. For example, to sort, in descending order, the employees by their start date, you would run the script shown in Listing 5.31.

Listing 5.31: The ASP *SortEmployees.asp* Script (*sortEmployees.asp*)

```
<%
set xslDoc=createObject("MSXML2.FreeThreadedDOMDocument")
set xslTemplate=createObject("MSXML2.XSLTemplate")
xslDoc.load server.mapPath("sort.xsl")
set xslTemplate.stylesheet=xslDoc
set sortProc=xslTemplate.createProcessor
set employees=createObject(_
      "MSXML2.FreeThreadedDOMDocument")
employees.load server.mapPath("employees.xml")
sortProc.input=employees
sortProc.output=response
sortProc.addParameter "sortKey","dateStarted"
sortProc.addParameter "sortOrder","descending"
sortProc.addParameter "sortType","date"
sortProc.transform
%>
```

Setting Output Type

So far in this book, I've been using a concept that I haven't fully clarified: the notion of an *output type*, through the use of the `<xsl:output>` node. The output node lets you define the characteristics of how the result of the transform is interpreted. The output node is, strictly speaking, unnecessary if you are just sending the results of the transform to XML. Additionally, this is the most efficient mechanism for performing transformations because it keeps the XML stream intact. However, the full specification for the output is considerably more complex, with attributes given in Table 5.5.

TABLE 5.5: Output Node Attributes

Attribute Name	Attribute Values	Description
`Method`	`xml|html|text`	Indicates the formatting type of the output.
`Version`	Version of the method used	Provides the version of the output method and usually should be `1.0`.

TABLE 5.5: Output Node Attributes *(continued)*

Attribute Name	Attribute Values	Description
`Encoding`	Encoding string	Gives the encoding format for the output. The default format for the MSXML parser is `UTF-16`.
`Omit-xml-declaration`	`yes|no`	Specifies whether the `<?xml version="1.0"?>` header should be included in the output. The default is not to include it.
`Standalone`	`yes|no`	Determines whether the document can exist without a DTD or XML schema. The default is that it can (e.g., `standalone="yes"`).
`Doctype-public`	String	Gives the public DTD declaration if the XML document uses one (a document using XML Schema can assign this as an attribute to the node explicitly).
`Doctype-system`	String	Gives the system DTD declaration if the XML document uses one (a document using XML Schema can assign this as an attribute to the node explicitly).
`Cdata-section-elements`	Element names	Tells which nodes within the output document are given as CDATA sections. The names are given as a string of elements with a single white space between elements (e.g., `cdata-section-elements="description title quote"`).
`Indent`	`yes|no`	Specifies whether white space should be added to the output to indent child nodes. The default is yes.
`Media-type`	`mime-type` string	Indicates that the output should be presented with the indicated mime type. (For example, if the output method is `xml`, the mime-type could be `text/xml` for outputting an XML document, `text/xsl` for outputting an XSL document, `text/xhtml` for outputting an XHTML document, and so forth.)

The output node can actually solve a problem that many developers encountered with the older XML parser. In that parser, you couldn't use a DOM method to append a `DOCTYPE` header to an XML document, because this declaration wasn't one of the standard types. (You could get around this by passing in a `DOCTYPE` declaration as part of a string into the `loadXML` method, but this very definitely falls into the category of a kludge.)

Of the attributes in Table 5.5, one of the more important is `encoding`. As many of the readers of this book can attest, the Web extends far beyond the confines of the United States. XML output is used in Tokyo, Oslo, Bangalore, and Pretoria. The `encoding` mechanism can be used to guarantee that the output uses the proper character set for the language in question.

For example, if you want to make sure that output is encoded to use the Japanese katakana character set (with the Microsoft extension to support the use of kanji), then you set the output tag's encoding value to `Shift-JIT`, as in the following example:

```
<xsl:output method="xml" encoding="Shift-JIT"/>
```

TIP The full list of valid encoding tags is maintained by the Internet Assigned Numbers Association, or IANA, at `ftp://ftp.isi.edu/in-notes/iana/assignments/character-sets/`.

You can also set the media type to determine the use of the output stream. For example, you may very well want the media type of the output of an XSL script that produces a different XSL script to be set to `text/xsl`; this will tell devices that recognize the `xsl` type to display it in the appropriate fashion.

TIP As an avenue of exploration, you can, in theory, save both GIF and JPEG images in their mime-type encoding formats as CDATA sections within an XML document (an admittedly large XML document), use XSL to select the appropriate block of mime-encoded graphics, and output the result with a media type of `image/gif` or `image/jpeg`.

Controlling Spacing and Escaping

If you have ever tried controlling the way that space gets sent to the output stream of the older XSL parser, you've probably discovered that it is a difficult (if not impossible) process. The newer parser, on the other hand, gives you an option to control the process more cleanly through the use of the `xml:space` attribute.

The `xml:space` attribute can be assigned to nearly all XSL nodes. When set to `"preserve"`, this attribute specifies that all of the space within the scope of the node is preserved upon output. When set to `"default"` (which is, not surprisingly, the default), leading and trailing spaces are stripped and extended white space within the give element is replaced with a single space.

You can use this to good effect in conjunction with variables. As in the following example, if you want to create a carriage return in your output but otherwise want the text to normalize, you can define a variable to hold the carriage return space:

```
<xsl:variable name="cr" xml:space="preserve"/>
</xsl:variable>

<xsl:template match="/">This is line one.
    <xsl:value-of select="$cr"/>This is line two.
    <xsl:value-of select="$cr"/>
    <xsl:value-of select="$cr"/>This is line 3
  . <xsl:template>
```

When output, this would produce the following result:

```
This is line one.
This is line two

This is line three
```

You can also nest `xml:space` elements so that a template preserves text but subordinate elements don't, as in the following example:

```
<xsl:template match="/" xml:space="preserve">
This is line one.
<xsl:for-each select="//employee" xml:space="default"/>
   <xsl:value-of select="lastName"/>,<xsl:value-of select="firstName"/>;
</xsl:for-each>
<xsl:template>
```

The output for this example looks like the following:

```
This is line one.
Janus,John;Milleaux,Kitara;Janes,Shelley;Mendez,Marissa;
```

A problem similar to that involving the preservation of space comes in situations when outputting CDATA sections. The default behavior of the `<xsl:value-of/>` node when it sends characters such as the < and > brackets is to convert the characters into their escaped notations `<` and `>`. However, if the information that the CDATA holds happens to be HTML data (as may be the case from a discussion board or similar application), this escaping isn't desirable.

You can disable this escaping mechanism with the `disable-output-escaping` attribute. When set to `yes`, then the contents of the CDATA sections aren't escaped, making for live data; the HTML code is output as HTML code. On the other hand, if set to `no` (the default), then the resulting output is converted into "safe" code.

Thus, if you have an XML document that contains live HTML data, such as the `MessageBoard.xml` document in Listing 5.32, then you can output the bodies of a given message to HTML using disable-output escaping, as shown in Listing 5.33.

Listing 5.32: An XML Document that Contains Live HTML Data (*MessageBoard.xml*)

```
<?xml-stylesheet type="text/xsl"
                 href="showMessage.xsl"?>
<messages>     <message id="vbxmlProg0">
        <title><![CDATA[Welcome to <VB-XML Programming>]]></title>
        <date>2/6/2000 5:50:13 PM</date>
        <from>Kurt Cagle</from>
        <email>cagle@olywa.net</email>
```

```
        <body><![CDATA[<p><b>XML</b> is becoming a
  pervasive part of Web programming. This discussion
  board, itself written using <i>XML</i> and <i>ASP</I>,
  is intended for the working professional who has
  questions about XML, XSL, Schemas, programming, and
 more. If you want to know more about a topic (or,
  conversely, have an answer to a topic), feel free to ask
  it here.</p>

  <p>Also, if you have any questions about the
  construction or maintenance of this particular board,
  please feel free to contact me, Kurt Cagle, at
  cagle@olywa.net (or just click on the CAGLE tab in the
  menu bar).</p>

  <cite>-- Kurt Cagle</cite>
]]></body>
          </message>
  </messages>
```

Listing 5.33: The XSL *showMessage.xsl* Transform

```
<xsl:stylesheet
  xmlns:xsl="http://www.w3.org/1999/XSL/Transform"
  version="1.0"
  xmlns:math="http://www.vbxml.com/math">
  <xsl:output method="html"/>

  <xsl:template match="/">
      <xsl:apply-templates select="//message"
  </xsl:template>

  <xsl:template match="message">
      <h1><xsl:value-of select="title"/></h1>
      <div>
      <xsl:value-of select="body"
                          disable-output-escaping="yes"/>
      </div>
  </xsl:template>

</xsl:stylesheet>
```

This produces the HTML output shown in Listing 5.34.

Listing 5.34: HTML Output from *showMessage.xsl*

```
<h1>Welcome to &lt;VB-XML Programming&gt;</h1>
<div>
<p><b>XML</b> is becoming a pervasive part of Web
programming. This discussion board, itself written using
<i>XML</i> and <i>ASP</I>, is intended for the working
professional who has questions about XML, XSL, Schemas,
 programming, and more. If you want to know more about a
topic (or, conversely, have an answer to a topic), feel free
to ask it here.</p>

<p>Also, if you have any questions about the
construction or maintenance of this particular board,
please feel free to contact me, Kurt Cagle, at
cagle@olywa.net (or just click on the CAGLE tab in the menu
bar).</p>

<cite>-- Kurt Cagle</cite>
</div>
```

Notice how the < and > characters are escaped in the `<h1>` title but not in the body (contained in the `<div>` tag).

Importing Style Sheets

In most programming languages, the definition for an object does not necessarily reside in a single page of code. More typically, especially with languages such as Java or C++, you have the notion of inheritance. For example, rather than designing all of the code for a class from scratch, you create a base class and then inherit the properties and methods of that class in a child class.

A similar, though not quite as powerful, model exists for XSL. Specifically, it is possible to include one style sheet within another—in essence, inheriting the characteristics of one of the sheets. The method for handling this is the `<xsl:include>` tag. `xsl:include` takes a URL as an argument to its `HREF` attribute, at which point the style sheet specified is loaded into the host style sheet and treated as if part of the original document.

Consider the `AddNewEmployee.xsl` style sheet discussed in the "Processing Parameters through ASP" section earlier in this chapter, reprised in Listing 5.35. The problem of adding an employee to a list of employees is, in fact, a manifestation of the more general problem of adding an object to a list of similar objects.

Listing 5.35: The *AddNewEmployee.xsl* Style Sheet, Reprised

```
<!-- addNewEmployee.xsl -->
<xsl:stylesheet
   xmlns:xsl="http://www.w3.org/1999/XSL/Transform"
   version="1.0">
   <xsl:output method="xml"/>
   <!-- retrieve the parametric information -->
   <xsl:param name="ID"/>
   <xsl:param name="FirstName"/>
   <xsl:param name="LastName"/>
   <xsl:param name="Title"/>
   <xsl:param name="DateStarted"/>
   <xsl:param name="Salary"/>
   <xsl:param name="Department"/>

   <!-- create a new variable called "NewEmployee"
        which holds an entire employee structure,
        and load the parameter values into the
        record -->
   <xsl:variable name="NewEmployee">
      <employee>
      <xsl:attribute name="id"><xsl:value-of
       select="$employeeID"/></xsl:attribute>
         <firstName>
         <xsl:value-of select="$FirstName"/>
         </firstName>
         <lastName>
         <xsl:value-of select="$LastName"/>
         </lastName>
         <title>
         <xsl:value-of select="$Title"/>
         </title>
         <dateStarted>
         <xsl:value-of select="$DateStarted"/>
         </dateStarted>
         <salary>
         <xsl:value-of select="$Salary"/>
         </salary>
         <department>
         <xsl:value-of select="$Department"/>
         </department>
      </employee>
   </xsl:variable>

   <!-- match the root node and retrieve the
        employees list -->
```

```
    <xsl:template match="/">
       <xsl:apply-templates select="//employees"/>
    </xsl:template>

    <!-- this is the identity transform, which
         copies the node passed and all of its children -->
    <xsl:template match="*|@*|text()">
       <xsl:copy><xsl:apply-templates select="*|@*|text()"/></xsl:copy>
    </xsl:template>

    <!-- copy the employees node -->
    <xsl:template match="employees">
       <xsl:copy>
       <!-- copy all of the current children into the output
            stream -->
       <xsl:apply-templates select="employee"/>
       <!-- put a copy of the newly created node into
            the output as a child of employees -->
       <xsl:copy-of select="$NewEmployee"/>
       </xsl:copy>
    </xsl:template>

</xsl:stylesheet>
```

There are two different approaches that can be taken in code like this to code reuse. One approach is to define the object as a separate entity and load it into a generic `addItem` style sheet. However, the problem with this is that you can't use the normal parameterization methods to change the source of the include, something that makes it generic. The other approach, in which the code to create a generic object is included in the XSL source for that particular object, makes more sense from a programmatic standpoint; it is essentially the declarative analog to inheriting a base class rather than extending it to handle a more specialized scenario, and it is the approach I use here.

Listing 5.36, which shows the new `AddEmployee.xsl` transform, shows one way that the `addItem.xsl` transform can be incorporated.

Listing 5.36: The *addEmployee.xsl* Transform, Incorporating the *addItem.xsl* Transform

```
<!-- addEmployee.xsl -->
<xsl:stylesheet
 xmlns:xsl="http://www.w3.org/1999/XSL/Transform"
 version="1.0">
   <xsl:output method="xml"/>
   <!-- retrieve the parametric information -->
   <xsl:param name="ID"/>
```

```
    <xsl:param name="FirstName"/>
    <xsl:param name="LastName"/>
    <xsl:param name="Title"/>
    <xsl:param name="DateStarted"/>
    <xsl:param name="Salary"/>
    <xsl:param name="Department"/>

    <!-- create a new variable called "NewEmployee"
         which holds an entire employee structure,
         and load the parameter values into the
         record -->
    <xsl:variable name="NewEmployee">
       <employee>
       <xsl:attribute name="id"><xsl:value-of
        select="$employeeID"/></xsl:attribute>
          <firstName>
          <xsl:value-of select="$FirstName"/>
          </firstName>
          <lastName>
          <xsl:value-of select="$LastName"/>
          </lastName>
          <title>
          <xsl:value-of select="$Title"/>
          </title>
          <dateStarted>
          <xsl:value-of select="$DateStarted"/>
          </dateStarted>
          <salary>
          <xsl:value-of select="$Salary"/>
          </salary>
          <department>
          <xsl:value-of select="$Department"/>
          </department>
       </employee>
    </xsl:variable>

    <xsl:include "addItem.xsl"/>

    <xsl:parameter name="objects" select="//employees"/>
    <xsl:parameter name="collectionName"
          select="'employees'"/>
    <xsl:parameter name="itemAdded"
          select="$NewEmployee"/>
</xsl:stylesheet>
```

The new code performs only one action: It adds a new object to an existing set of objects, placing the object at the end, as specified in Listing 5.37. Notice how the variables shadow the parameters in the calling structure; this is analogous to the initialization of a class in a procedural module. In this sense, `AddEmployee.xsl` inherits from `addItem.xsl` and implements the parameters set up there in the subordinate transform class.

Listing 5.37: The Generic *addItem.xsl* Transform

```
<xsl:stylesheet
   xmlns:xsl="http://www.w3.org/1999/XSL/Transform"
   version="1.0">

<!--
       These parameters must be instantiated
       In the calling transform
       <xsl:param name="collectionName"
        select="name(*)"/>
       <xsl:param name="objects" select="/*/*"/>
       <xsl:param name="itemAdded" />
-->

   <xsl:template match="/">
      <xsl:element name="{$collectionName}">
      <xsl:apply-templates select="$objects"/>
      </xsl:element>
      <xsl:copy-of select="$itemAdded"/>
   </xsl:template>

   <xsl:template match="*">
      <xsl:copy-of/>
   </xsl:template>
```

Note that order is critical here. One of the limitations of XSL parameters is that you can't declare the same variable (or parameter) twice in the same scope. Thus, it is not possible to create default stub properties; your calling transform must assign the parameters required by the included transform in order for the transform to work.

NOTE At the time of this writing, the XSL specification has a way around this, with the use of the `with-parameters` tag. However, the current documentation indicates that this functionality will probably not end up in the final release.

The Mode Attribute

Internet Explorer and Mozilla are two very different applications. While they both speak HTML, the dialectic differences between them are severe enough that writing good code that works well on both platforms is well nigh impossible.

The mode attribute was designed partly in response to this particular need. You can think of this mode as a descriptor that indicates some global condition about the XSL structure, such as the fact that the output is going to a Mozilla browser instead of to Internet Explorer.

Modes can be incorporated into `<xsl:template tags>`, and, in that function, they act as filters: If the mode is not set to the indicated value, then, even if the searched-for context is found, it's not evaluated. Thus, you can actually have the same pattern with two or more distinct modes, and the mode value will act as a switch to ensure that the right mode is selected.

In Listing 5.38, a stylesheet is shown that uses the mode attribute.

Listing 5.38: Displaying Based Upon the Mode (*mode.xsl*)

```
<xsl:stylesheet
 xmlns:xsl="http://www.w3.org/1999/XSL/Transform"
 version="1.0">

<xsl:template select="/">
   <html>
      <head>
         <title>Employees<title>
      </head>
      <body>
      </body>
   </html>
   <xsl:template match="//employee"
</xsl:template>

<xsl:template match="employee" mode="IE">
    <div><xsl:value-of select="lastName"/>, <xsl:value-of
    select="firsNameName"/></div>
</xsl:template>

<xsl:template match="employee" mode="NS">
    <layer><xsl:value-of select="lastName"/>,
    <xsl:value-of select="firsNameName"/></layer>
</xsl:template>

</xsl:stylesheet>
```

Summary

With the introduction of variables, parameters, sorting, and includes, the new MSXML 2.6 parser both radically simplifies XSL transforms and vastly extends its reach. Couple this with the ability to add objects dynamically into the XSL environment and you have a remarkably robust mechanism for handling a large cross section of the programming problems that currently plague both Web applications and database applications.

Writing a book like this, especially when a new technology is introduced, can make for some interesting problems in terms of when things get done. Chapter 6, "XML Schema," returns to the older parser to concentrate on the Microsoft XML Schema implementation and point to the development that is taking place in the W3C XML Schema recommendation, while Chapter 7, "XML and the Browser," focuses on XML on the client, where the parser is much more likely to be that of Internet Explorer 5 (the older XML parser) rather than the upgraded parser that will be shipped with Internet Explorer 5.5.

Chapter 8, "XML and ASP," returns to the new XSL parser for a look at how XML can be incorporated into ASP applications on the Web, specifically for the task of building a job-listing board and resume service. It uses the new parser extensively and should be looked at as a case study for working with the power of XSL transforms and true XPath.

Chapter 6

XML Schema

- Understanding XML Schema
- Examining datatypes in XML
- Understanding the W3C Schema
- Programming with XML Schema

A database, regardless of its type, needs to retain three critical pieces of information: the data itself, the structure of given fields of data relative to other fields, and descriptive information (typically known as *metadata*) that describes the characteristics of the data (the type of data, boundary conditions, default values, and so forth).

XML is no different in this regard. Because XML is a text-based format, the need for maintaining this type of information is perhaps stronger than it is in binary formats. XML Schema is an XML-based schema (or metadata) description language that actually provides two pieces of critical data: a definition of the acceptable structure of the elements that make up a valid type of XML document, and a representation of the datatype used by the document.

XML actually does have a second internal definition language called the Document Type Definitions (DTD), which is based on the older SGML DTD standards. While DTD implementations are more prevalent in the XML community, they suffer from a number of limitations compared to schemas, and by the time this book is published, they will probably be on their way out as means to represent XML, in favor of the W3C XML Schema Recommendation. (Refer to the "Why DTDs Aren't Covered" sidebar.)

This chapter looks at some techniques for using XML schemas beyond the simple process of document validation and explores some of the latest thinking about schemas.

Why DTDs Aren't Covered

To many in the XML community, the decision not to cover Document Type Definitions in an XML book would seem the height of heresy. After all, XML is a subclass of SGML, and DTDs are the language of SGML. Nearly every book out there has been written with a big, thick section on getting to know the intricacies of building DTDs, working with parametric entities and PCDATA sections, and all of the other detritus that comes with any SGML-based language.

And that, to me, is at the heart of the problem. XML is not SGML. It is an internally consistent language where all of the critical pieces are either written in XML or are geared toward working with the element/attribute structure that defines the language. XML schemas are written in XML and are thus accessible to XML programming. A DTD, on the other hand, requires a separate parser, adding both to the cost of implementing an XML solution and to the complexity of programming in what is already a fairly complex language. The notation used in DTDs is terse and cryptic and, worse, is geared toward a class of problems that XML is moving away from: the management of large, messy documents.

DTDs handle text, not any datatype. There is no way from the XML DOM or XSL to retrieve sets of enumerated constraints, no way to set default values, no way to treat XML in an object-oriented manner. In short, DTDs add little to the value of the XML language that isn't currently handled by better mechanisms, and its potential for misuse makes it an awkward, cumbersome choice for programmers to work with.

Just say no to DTDs.

Understanding XML Schemas

Not surprisingly, the big database companies—Microsoft, Oracle, InfoSys, IBM, and others—have been the biggest motivators in developing a data-centric implementation of XML. The language has obvious benefits to both a database company and to a database developer: it's a non-proprietary solution for passing data between two machines, and, using fairly simple tools, it can be readily transformed into a presentation format or into another data format.

However, by themselves, XML documents have some serious limitations as well. One of the most significant is that, to XML, everything is text. The language has no intrinsic notion of a datatype beyond strings of character text. The danger that this presents can be seen by looking at a simple XML document:

```
<!-- Sum.xml -->

<sum>
   <a>2</a>
   <b>3</b>
</sum>
```

When you apply

```
xmlDoc.load "sum.xml"
debug.print xmlDoc.selectSingleNode("//a").text+
 xmlDoc.selectSingleNode("//b").text
```

you will get "23" (not "5," as might be expected).

Furthermore, there is no way to distinguish between a floating point number and an integer, dates are highly problematic, and more complex datatypes (such as a point) are simply not possible.

Another problem is one of document definition. Creating ad hoc data structures can prove troublesome pretty quickly; without a clear-cut map, it is impossible to tell whether a given node does, in fact, belong as a child of another node, whether a specific attribute (or its value) is appropriate for the given node, or even whether a spelling variation for a given node was intentional (it's a different node altogether) or accidental (not enough caffeine this morning).

Finally, in a typical data structure, a great deal of the information may be redundant. In most databases, you can specify a default value for a given field. Defaults help optimize the database, since you need only store a given value if it differs from the default. Raw XML doesn't include this defaulting optimization, so you have to use some sort of convention for defaults or bypass this feature altogether. Similarly, there may be whole standard default node trees that only come into play in very specialized circumstances, so storing them as part of a generic XML structure can be very costly, especially if the XML has to be transmitted over the Web.

Document Type Definitions are one solution to this problem, but they are far from ideal. For starters, a DTD doesn't contain any datatype information. Couple that with the need to use a specialized DTD parser when dealing with DTDs (as they are not written in XML) and you can see that while they may solve the structure problem they don't resolve the rest of the issues.

Another solution, XML Schema, gets around these issues. Specifically, XML schemas offer the following benefits over traditional DTDs:

- They are written in XML and can be referenced through a standard XML parser.
- They maintain data information about given node contents.
- They let you explicitly place limits on the number of elements contained within a structure, as well as whether a given XML node's contents is closed (can only contain the specifically declared subelements) or open (can contain any subelements).
- They are tied into namespaces, letting you load multiple schemas into the same document. (DTD-based documents, on the other hand, must be declared through a command node, and a document can only have one DTD, although that DTD can provisionally include or exclude other DTDs.)
- You can define entities within XML Schemas using XML, making them easier to manipulate (W3C specification only).
- You can define archetypes within an XML schema, giving you the basis for inheritance, encapsulation, and other OOP features (W3C specification only).

NOTE As with almost everything else in the XML world, Microsoft has a different XML Schema representation than the W3C specification, although this will almost certainly change with the publication of XML Schema as a recommendation. The current differences (as of when this chapter was written) are covered in this chapter.

A Basic Schema

An XML Schema has essentially two types of actions: definition and declaration. In *definition*, a node's characteristics are defined—the node's name, the datatype, the type of enclosing content it can contain, and the order in which that content appears. Within an element's definition, there may very well be one or more child-element declarations. The *declaration* indicates how many times the given element can appear, within its parent and such a declaration, in turn, must have a definition for the given element further down the tree.

TIP The definition for an XML Schema is somewhat analogous to a template definition in an XSL document, while a declaration is closer in spirit to an `<xsl:apply-templates />` statement.

For example, consider both part of an XML structure that holds detailed records for all of the employees of a company (Listing 6.1) and its corresponding XML schema (Listing 6.2).

Listing 6.1: Part of an XML Document Containing a List of Employees at Acme Rockets (*Listing6-1.txt*)

```
<employees xmlns="x-schema:employees.dtd">
   <employee>
      <id>1249</id>
      <lastName>Yokum</lastName>
      <firstName>Benny</firstName>
      <title>Manager, Y2K Systems</title>
      <department>Research</department>
      <salary>85000</salary>
      <canHire>yes</canHire>
      <managerID>1024</managerID>
   </employee>
   <!-- More employees -->
</employees>
```

NOTE Note the use of the `x-schema:` prefix before `employees.dtd`. Any time that you declare an explicit schema from a file or URL reference, you must use the `x-schema:` designation.

Listing 6.2: An XML Schema that Defines the *employees.xml* Structure (*Code6-2.employees.dtd*)

```
<?xml version ="1.0"?>
<Schema name = "employees.dtd"
   xmlns = "urn:schemas-microsoft-com:xml-data"
   xmlns:dt = "urn:schemas-microsoft-com:datatypes">

   <!-- employees is the root node, and includes one or
   more employee nodes -->
   <ElementType name = "employees" content = "eltOnly" order = "seq">
      <element type = "employee" minOccurs = "1" maxOccurs = "*"/>
   </ElementType>

   <!-- the employee element defines the structure for an employee -->
   <ElementType name = "employee" content = "eltOnly" order = "seq">
      <element type = "id"/>
      <element type = "lastName"/>
      <element type = "firstName"/>
      <element type = "title"/>
      <element type = "department"/>
      <element type = "salary"/>
```

```
      <element type = "canHire"/>
      <element type = "managerID"/>
   </ElementType>

   <!-- Everything from here on define the properties of
   the employee object -->
   <ElementType name = "id" content = "textOnly" dt:type="id"/>
   <ElementType name = "lastName" content = "textOnly"/>
   <ElementType name = "firstName" content = "textOnly"/>
   <ElementType name = "title" content = "textOnly"/>
   <ElementType name = "department" content = "textOnly"/>
   <ElementType name = "salary" content = "textOnly"/>
   <ElementType name = "canHire" content = "textOnly"/>
   <ElementType name = "managerID" content = "textOnly" dt:type="id"/>
</Schema>
```

The schema can look a little daunting at first glance, but as long as you keep the distinction between definition and declaration firmly in your mind, the meaning of the schema falls out pretty quickly. In the preceding listing, the definitions are made with the `ElementType` tag. For example, the `<lastName>` element is defined by the following tag:

```
<ElementType name = "lastName" content = "textOnly"/>
```

This basically indicates that the name of the tag is `lastName` and that it can only contain text, not elements or mixed text and elements. The `<employee>` tag, on the other hand, is a little more complex:

```
<ElementType name = "employee" content = "eltOnly" order = "seq">
   <element type = "id"/>
   <element type = "lastName"/>
   <element type = "firstName"/>
   <element type = "title"/>
   <element type = "department"/>
   <element type = "salary"/>
   <element type = "canHire"/>
   <element type = "managerID"/>
</ElementType>
```

In this example, the `ElementType` tag indicates that this is a definition for the `employee` tag, and `eltOnly` indicates that this tag can only contain elements, not text nodes. (Note that this doesn't place any restrictions one way or the other on attributes.) The tag then contains declarations of the eight child elements with the `element` tag, with the `type` attribute naming the specific element. Finally, the `ElementType` tag's `order` attribute indicates how these elements are arranged, with `seq` indicating that the items will appear exactly in the sequence shown within the definition (`lastName` follows `id` and precedes `firstName`, for example); any other order would generate an error when the XML document is loaded.

The definition for the employees node is even a little more complex than the <employee> tag, as you will note in the following example:

```
<ElementType name = "employees" content = "eltOnly" order = "seq">
   <element type = "employee" minOccurs = "1" maxOccurs = "*"/>
</ElementType>
```

This node is a container: it will contain one or more employee nodes. This is indicated in the employee element declaration by the minOcccurs (1 in this example) and maxOccurs (* in this sample) attributes. The asterisk means that there may be any number of occurrences of the declared element, down to the indicated minimum; for example, you must have a minimum of one employee in your employees list, but you can have as many beyond that as is needed.

NOTE In theory, there's nothing stopping you from declaring, for example, that you have a minOccurs of 3 and a maxOccurs of 8, though this isn't likely to come up in most cases.

With one exception, any time a node is declared, there must be a definition for that node somewhere within your schema, although more than one element definition may refer to a defined element. That is to say that if an <employee> node is defined somewhere within the schema then both the <managers> and <contractors> nodes could reference the same employee definition.

NOTE A definition, such as an ElementType node, can only occur once in a document for any given node name, but any number of declarations, such as element, can reference that definition.

TIP The mechanism of referencing definitions may strike you as being similar to the way that object-oriented programming works: a class (ElementType) is used to define multiple instances (element) of that class. This resemblance is not accidental. The current W3C XML Schema includes a mechanism to make these associations stronger, as discussed in the "The W3C XML Schema" section later in this chapter.

So What's the Parser Doing?

Note that while an element node requires an ElementType node to exist somewhere in the document, there is no explicit requirement that all ElementType nodes be referenced. In particular, the root node of an XML schema will never be referenced explicitly. Although not strictly required, as a general guideline you should place this node first in your schema, both because it's the most efficient structure programmatically and because it makes it easier to see what's going on in the document. Afterward, you should generally define elements in the order that they will be traversed by the parser (i.e., next child, then next sibling, then next parent); again, this is not an explicit requirement but makes the design easier to maintain.

So What's the Parser Doing? ***(continued)***

To a certain extent, the way that a schema works is very closely tied to the way that an XSL document works: the top-most node indicates which nodes are processed next, and they, in turn, process their child nodes, throughout the document. When an element declaration is encountered, the parser searches through the schema (probably using XPath or XSL Pattern), finds an associated definition, implements the definition, and then resolves any new declarations that it encounters in the subelement's definition.

One upshot of this is that it really doesn't matter in which order `ElementType` nodes are placed in the document so long as there are no duplicates. Indeed, some XML schemas will not allow multiple definitions at all.

XML Schema Elements

Of course, many XML structures are more complicated than the data list in the preceding section, and XML Schema needs to be robust enough to handle this complexity. Table 6.1 describes the various tags that schemas can use to define XML documents.

TABLE 6.1: XML Schema Tags

Name	Description
`schema`	Defines the encompassing element for the schema document, which also identifies the name of the schema.
`ElementType`	Defines an element in the schema and, typically, includes text node information and the element's child elements and attribute.
`AttributeType`	Defines an attribute in the schema, including the attribute's datatype and constraints.
`element`	References an `ElementType` that is defined somewhere within the schema.
`attribute`	References an `AttributeType` that is defined somewhere within the schema.
`datatype`	Defines the type of data that an element or attribute can contain. (Note that you can use an alternate form, where `datatype` is defined as an attribute, in `ElementTypes` or `AttributeTypes`.)
`description`	Provides information about an element or attribute.
`group`	Collects elements together to define a specific sequence of elements.

NOTE Letter casing is important: `ElementType` and `AttributeType` must always be capitalized, while all other elements must be lowercased.

The `<Schema>` tag holds the schema document together and also defines the name of the schema. In order to use the MSXML schema that is built into the Internet Explorer 5 XML parser, you need to specifically declare it as being of the namespace `urn:schemas-microsoft-com:xml-data`, just as you would for an XSL document. This alerts the parser that the schema conforms to the Microsoft schema. As with many schemas, this URN doesn't specifically refer to a location on the Web but, rather, is a unique tag for identifying the schema; the parser holds its own internal schema that it refers to when checking the validity of any Microsoft-based XML Schema. Here is an example:

```
<Schema name = "employees.dtd"
   xmlns = "urn:schemas-microsoft-com:xml-data"
   xmlns:dt = "urn:schemas-microsoft-com:datatypes">
```

The name of the schema can conceivably be anything, although, in general practice, you are best off calling the schema the same name as the document containing the schema. Thus, as the schema defined in the preceding example is in the `employees.dtd` file, the schema is similarly named.

The final namespace declaration points to the datatypes specification that was first put forward by Microsoft, and lies at the foundation of the Reduced Data Set specification (and a significant portion of the datatype specifications within the W3C Schema Datatypes specification as well.) Without this declaration, the schema won't be able to interpret the names of various datatypes that are used throughout the document.

The XML Schema typically doesn't have the same namespace requirements that XSL does (that is, the need to manipulate one namespace through tags described by another namespace), so it defines schemas using the default namespace. You could change this, however, by setting the namespace name to a specific string and then making sure that every tag within the particular schema starts with that tag. Consider the following example:

```
<kc:Schema name = "employees.dtd"
    xmlns:kc = "urn:schemas-microsoft-com:xml-data"
    xmlns:dt = "urn:schemas-microsoft-com:datatypes">
   <kc:ElementType name="document">
   </kc:ElementType>
   <!-- more elements
</kc:Schema>
```

The full specification for the `ElementType` declaration, in turn, describes the elemental characteristics of each node, as shown in the following example (and explained further in Table 6.2):

```
<ElementType name="eltID"
             content="empty|textOnly|eltOnly|mixed"
             dt:type="xml_data_type"
             model="open|closed"
             order="one|seq|many"
             >
```

TABLE 6.2: XML `ElementType` Tag for the Microsoft XML Schema Parser

Name	Description
`name`	Identifies the name of the element.
`content`	Determines whether the element contains elements, text, or both.
`dt:type`	Defines the specific datatype of the element. (This is covered more extensively in the "Datatypes in XML" section later in this chapter.)
`model`	Indicates whether the elements specified as children in the `ElementType` definition are the only ones that can appear (`closed`) or whether other elements may also appear (`open`).
`order`	Specifies that the children of the current element either must appear within a given sequence (`seq`), must form a mutually exclusive set (`one`), or must appear in any order (`many`).

The attribute name should be a valid XML token—i.e., one or more alphanumeric characters (with the first character alphabetic), as well as dashes (-) and underscores (_). The name is a required attribute.

`content` refers to the type of content that the element contains, and it can either be `empty` (the element has no child elements or text), contain text only (`textOnly`), contain elements only (`eltOnly`), or contain both text and elements (`mixed`).

NOTE Attributes are independent of this model. An element can be empty and still have attributes associated with it.

NOTE CDATA sections are considered as text within this model. Processing instructions and comments, on the other hand, are considered to exist outside the boundaries of the schema and don't impact the schema in any way.

The *ElementType model* Attribute

The `ElementType model` attribute indicates whether the child elements contained within the `ElementType` are exclusive (no other elements are allowed). If this is the case, the model is described as being `closed` for the element. If the model is `open`, on the other hand, then the list of element declarations within the `ElementType` form a minimum set, but there can be more elements that are not specifically declared.

An open model is typically used to describe document structures, where the child elements may not even be part of the same schema or namespace. A good example of this is an XHTML document, where there actually may be several distinct namespaces in play at the same time.

WARNING Note that this can be a disadvantage. If an element is described as **open**, then you know less about its internal contents than if it were closed, so you actually have to query the XML document rather than just referring to the schema to find out what's happening within any given element.

The *ElementType order* Attribute

The `ElementType order` attribute can be a little confusing at first glance. It defines the set characteristics of the element. An order of `one`, for example, means that only one of the elements listed within an `ElementType` definition can be included in the XML structure; otherwise, when you validate the document, the validation parser generates an error. As another example, consider the case of a manager's description. The qualifications for an IT manager would include the computer languages that he or she knows, while the qualifications for an administrative manager would include his or her business credentials, and a marketing manager would list successful product campaigns, as follows:

```
<ElementType name="qualifications"
             content=" eltOnly"
             model=" closed"
             order="one"
             >
    <element type="computerLanguages"/>
    <element type="businesses"/>
    <element type="campaigns"/>
</ElementType>
```

Only one of these elements can appear as a child of `qualifications`:

```
<qualifications>
     <computerLanguages>
          <computerLanguage>C++</computerLanguage>
          <computerLanguage>Java</computerLanguage>
          <computerLanguage>Visual Basic</computerLanguage>
     </computerLanguages>
</qualifications>
```

The preceding example is valid, but the following one is not:

```
<qualifications>
     <computerLanguages>
          <computerLanguage>Visual Basic</computerLanguage>
     <computerLanguages>
     <campaigns>
          <campaign>Acme Rocket Company Big Bang</campaign>
     </campaigns>
</qualifications>
```

NOTE By the way, note that there is no way to perform conditional logic here; determining whether a person with an attribute of `marketing` can, in fact, have a `<computerLanguages>` node is not possible from the XML Schema itself. Typically, though, if this situation comes up, you may want to rethink the architecture of the schema that you're using.

An order of `seq`, on the other hand, specifies that the elements must occur in a specific sequence and only that sequence. One of the most familiar examples of this case is the use of the `<head>` and `<body>` elements of an XHTML document, which must always appear in the following order:

```
<ElementType name="HTML"
             content="eltOnly"
             model="closed"
             order="seq"
             >
    <element type="head"/>
    <element type="body"/>
</ElementType>
```

A sequential set of child elements is more meaningful when the model is closed; if the model is open, then, while the specified elements must occur in the given order, there is nothing saying that there may be other elements that appear before or after these elements. For example, consider the following `ElementType` document:

```
<ElementType name="document"
             content="eltOnly"
             model="open"
             order="seq"
             >
    <element type="a"/>
    <element type="b"/>
    <element type="c"/>
</ElementType>
```

The following XML fragment is considered valid because the highlighted elements do match the proper sequence, even with intervening (and repeating elements).

```
<document>
    <d/>
    <b/>
    <a/>
    <c/>
    <b/>
    <b/>
    <c/>
    <e/>
</document>
```

Finally, you can specify an order of many, which indicates to the schema that the enclosed declarations can appear in any order and that any number of declarations (including none) can appear within the document. A typical HTML <div> element, for example, has a fairly wide number of subordinate items that can appear within it, coming in any order whatsoever. Similarly, the <div> can be empty. In the closed case, only the items defined within the schema can appear, but in the open case, the many order essentially indicates that there is no real bar or requirement on a specific child appearing, and elements that do appear are there more for convenience (i.e., the subelements have their own definitions) than anything else.

The *attribute* and *AttributeType* Tags

The AttributeType element performs the same function for attributes that ElementType does for elements: It defines an attribute's characteristics, delimits its values, and provides a means for validation, as shown in the following example (and further explained in Table 6.3):

```
<AttributeType name="eltID"
               default="defaultValue"
               model="open|closed"
               required="yes|no"
               dt:type="xml_data_type"
               dt:values="set_of_tokens"
             >
```

TABLE 6.3: XML AttributeType Tag for the Microsoft XML Schema Parser

Name	Description
name	Identifies the name of the attribute.
model	In a closed model, indicates that the attribute can only hold a value that is specified within the schema. In an open model, indicates that the attribute may hold any value.
default	Indicates the value that is used for the attribute if the attribute is not included in the element. (If the attribute has a set of enumerated dt:values–see below—and the attribute model is closed, then the default must be one of these attributes.)
required	Indicates that the attribute must be specified within the element to be valid. (Note that if required is yes then the attribute cannot simultaneously define a default value, and vice versa.)
dt:type	Identifies the specific datatype of the attribute. (This is covered more extensively in the "Datatypes in XML" section later in this chapter.)
dt:values	Spaces separated tokens that specify the possible values of the attribute. This is the mechanism that XML Schema uses for enumeration.

The model definition of the AttributeType is a little bit more restrictive than it is for an element; an attribute either can contain a previously specified value (i.e., one of an enumerated set of tokens) or can potentially have any value that is consistent with its datatype. In the first case, the model is described as closed (note that this is different from the ElementType definition of a closed model), while the latter case describes an open model.

Enumerated tokens are given in the `dt:values` set and follow the same rules as for the creation of a node name: The token must consist only of alphanumeric characters or the underscore character and cannot have spaces or other white-space characters (tabs, carriage returns, and so forth). The following example defines a set of enumerated tokens that describe a manager's specific division:

```
<AttributeType name="division" dt:type="nmtokens"
   dt:values="administration marketing development finance"
    model="closed"/>
```

If you do define a set of `dt:values`, then the `dt:type` should be set to `nmtokens` (short for *name tokens*), which is how XML Schema designates an enumerated type. Note that because the model is closed the `division` attribute can only take one of the four values specified in `dt:values`, and no other values will be acceptable.

A number of attributes typically are going to have one value 80 percent of the time and then have another value the remainder of the time. In this particular case, creating a default value for the attribute makes sense. For example, in the now-familiar case of Acme Rocket Company, most of the employees are actually part of the development division, with only a few support personnel handling the day-to-day maintenance of the company. In this case, the `division` attribute could have the default value of `development` and wouldn't need to be explicitly included in the XML declaration:

```
<AttributeType name="division" dt:type="nmtokens"
   dt:values="administration marketing development finance"
   model="closed" default="development"/>
```

The default value does have to be consistent with the datatype specified in `dt:type` but doesn't have to be part of an enumerated type if the attribute isn't defined as an enumerated type itself. In other words, the default value for the `itemsShipped` attribute of a purchase order may be set to `1` *if* the attribute isn't specified; then it's assumed to refer to only one item. For another way of looking at this, consider the following schema:

```
<AttributeType name="itemsShipped" dt:type="number"
   model="closed" default="1"/>
```

And note the following corresponding element:

```
<item name="BigRocket"/>
```

This element is the same as the following:

```
<item name="BigRocket" itemsShipped="1"/>.
```

This ability to specify default values for given attributes is extremely powerful since it can significantly reduce the size of an XML file, either in production or when sent across the wire. From the standpoint of the parser, by the way, an attribute for which a default value exists looks exactly the same as if you had set the attribute explicitly. Note that if you do set the attribute (even to the same value), this value will override the attribute for that element but not for the default of the attribute.

NOTE One way to understand how the defaulting mechanism of XML Schema works is to think of it as a default definition that provides a global value for the attribute. If you redefine the attribute's value locally, then that local value will always take precedence over the global one.

The `default` attribute provides a way of giving a default value to an attribute that isn't there. The `required` attribute, on the other hand, forces a given attribute to be explicitly included in the associated tag. In general, if you include the `required` tag, then you can't have a default value.

Just as an `element` tag references an `ElementType` definition, so does an `attribute` tag reference an `AttributeType` definition. The exact position of the `AttributeType` in the document as a consequence doesn't really matter that much from the parser's standpoint; there are some schools of thought that recommend placing all attribute definitions near the beginning or end of the document, while others recommend keeping them close to the place where they are first referenced. (An attribute needs to be defined only once—in fact should be defined only once—but can be referenced any number of times.)

The Schema attributes for the `attribute` tag are straightforward—the `type` attribute indicating the name of the attribute being referenced, the optional `default` value providing a default at the level of the specified tag's attribute (rather than the default for all attributes of that type), and `required` value indicating whether the given attribute must be given explicitly (which overrides the `AttributeType` `required` attribute).

By being given the ability to override global attributes with local ones, you can make your schemas more flexible. For example, in the schema fragment given in Listing 6.3 (the full schema is contained in the `Code6-3.managers.dtd` file on the accompanying CD-ROM), the `AttributeType` definition for `prefix` (near the bottom of the listing) is set to default to the value MNG, for manager. (I'm assuming that `prefix` is some kind of object designator.) However, in each of the `<company>`, `<division>`, and `<section>` schema nodes, the default `prefix` attribute is changed to CMP, DIV, and SEC, respectively.

Listing 6.3: Part of an XML Schema Showing how Local Attributes Can Override Global Declarations (*Listing 6-3.txt*)

```
<?xml version ="1.0"?>
<Schema name = "managers.dtd"
    xmlns = "urn:schemas-microsoft-com:xml-data"
    xmlns:dt = "urn:schemas-microsoft-com:datatypes">
```

```
   <!-- company is the root node -->
   <ElementType name = "company" content = "eltOnly" order = "many">
      <element type = "division" minOccurs = "0" maxOccurs = "*"/>
      <element type = "title" minOccurs = "1" maxOccurs = "1"/>
      <element type = "manager" minOccurs = "1" maxOccurs = "*"/>
      <attribute type="prefix" default="CMP"/>
   </ElementType>

   <ElementType name = "division" content = "eltOnly" order = "many">
      <element type = "section" minOccurs = "0" maxOccurs = "*"/>
      <element type = "title" minOccurs = "1" maxOccurs = "1"/>
      <element type = "manager" minOccurs = "1" maxOccurs = "*"/>
      <attribute type="prefix" default="DIV"/>
   </ElementType>

   <ElementType name = "section" content = "eltOnly" order = "many">
      <element type = "group" minOccurs = "0" maxOccurs = "*"/>
      <element type = "title" minOccurs = "1" maxOccurs = "1"/>
      <element type = "manager" minOccurs = "1" maxOccurs = "*"/>
      <attribute type="prefix" default="SEC"/>
   </ElementType>

   <AttributeType name="prefix" dt:type="string" default="MNG" model="closed"/>

   <!-The XML Schema continues -->
</Schema>
```

One upshot of assigning default attribute values in this type of schema is that the following XML structure:

```
<company>
    <manager/>
    <division>
      <manager/>
         <section>
               <manager/>
          </section>
    </division>
</company>
```

is the same as the following sample:

```
<company prefix="COM">
    <manager prefix="MNG"/>
    <division prefix="DIV">
        <manager prefix="MNG"/>
        <section prefix="SEC">
            <manager prefix="MAN"/>
```

```
        </section>
    </division>
</company>
```

WARNING It can be argued that inconsistent attribute defaults can be very confusing, both from a documentation standpoint and from a development standpoint. On the other hand, setting default values in this way is fairly consistent with a vision of XML being an object framework. As with everything else in the language, weigh the gains that attribute scoping offers (reduced file size, cleaner code, etc.), with the disadvantages (maintainability, documentation, etc.) to determine whether such techniques work for you.

group Tag Dynamics

Ordinarily, placing `element` references within an `ElementType` tag can be done without any sort of explicit grouping. However, in some cases, you'll have two or more elements that must always appear together or must always appear in an explicit order. This is precisely what the `group` tag is designed for.

The `group` tag's syntax is an abbreviated form of the `ElementType` syntax, as the following example demonstrates:

```
<ElementType ...>
   <group minOccurs="0|1" maxOccurs="1|*"
          order="one|seq|many">
       <element/>
       <element/>
   </group>
   <element/>
</ElementType>
```

Typically, the `group` tag is used with the `seq` order to designate a set of common elements. For example, consider the case where an invoice contains one of three sets of invoice codes (each code has an associated description); only one of the three sets of codes can be contained in the invoice, but both the code and the description for that set must be included. The XML Schema to do that would look something like Listing 6.4.

Listing 6.4: Grouped Elements (*code6-4.invoiceGroup.dtd*)

```
<?xml version ="1.0"?>
<Schema name = "invoice.dtd"
    xmlns = "urn:schemas-microsoft-com:xml-data"
    xmlns:dt = "urn:schemas-microsoft-com:datatypes">
   <!-- Various other elements -->
   <ElementType name="invoice" >
       <element type="invoiceID"/>
```

```
            <!-- Create a group to ensure that only one
                 of the sets is chosen -->
            <group order="one" minOccurs="1" maxOccurs="1">
                 <!-- each sub-group in turn contains the
                      relevant invoice code and description -->
                 <group order="seq" minOccurs="0" maxOccurs="1">
                      <element type="primaryCode"/>
                      <element type="primaryCodeDescr"/>
                 </group>
                 <group order="seq" minOccurs="0" maxOccurs="1">
                      <element type="firstAltCode"/>
                      <element type="firstAltCodeDescr"/>
                 </group>
                 <group order="seq" minOccurs="0" maxOccurs="1">
                      <element type="secondAltCode"/>
                      <element type="secondAltCodeDescr"/>
                 </group>
            </group>
       </ElementType>
       <!-- Various other elements -->
  </Schema>
```

The outer group ensures that there can only be one set of code and description as a child to the <invoice> schema, while the internal groups define what makes up a particular set, including both the specific elements in the set and the order in which they're given. Thus, according to this schema, the following sample is valid:

```
<invoice>
     <primaryCode/>
     <primaryCodeDescr/>
</invoice>
```

But the next example is not valid:

```
<invoice>
     <primaryCode/>
     <primaryCodeDescr/>
     <firstAltCode/>
     <firstAltCodeDescr/>
</invoice>
```

Nor is the following example:

```
<invoice>
     <primaryCodeDescr/>
     <primaryCode/>
</invoice>
```

The latter two samples aren't valid because the `order="seq"` attribute forces the XML tags to appear in a given order.

NOTE Staggered grouping like this is the primary reason for using the **group** tag at all. In most circumstances, the **group** tag is implicit: You can think of the `ElementType` tag object inheriting it, although that's something of a simplification.

A Brief *description*

The `description` tag provides a mechanism for documenting the various `ElementType` and `AttributeType` nodes within the XML Schema. Description content is explicitly open, and you can include XML-compliant HTML within it, making it a useful way to provide some basic information about a given tag to either a developer or a development tool.

Descriptions are primarily useful from the DOM. See the "Programming with XML Schemas" section later in this chapter to see how you can use `description` tags to help document an XML structure.

Datatypes in XML

A primary limitation of the older Document Type Definitions relates directly to their text-based legacy. A DTD for an XML document is, not surprisingly, document-centric, treating all of the information within an XML document as being simply strings of character information.

However, because of XML's simplified structure, the need for manipulating XML data as, well, data has become a central reason for its popularity. As data typically comes in flavors more complex than just text, many of the W3C members who had strong database presences (Microsoft, Oracle, IBM, etc.) pushed for a new version of the DTD that could be manipulated programmatically and would have some means of representing datatypes.

The resulting specifications were broken up into two distinct standards: the XML Schema Structure specification and the XML Schema Datatype specification. The latter specification defines a number of accepted datatypes and gives some hints as to their implementations.

Note that this "hinting" process is very important; one of the goals of XML is to make the language itself independent of any given processor, operating system, or development environment. Since different systems may implement the same kind of datatype in different ways (one may represent an integer as four 8-bit bytes, while another may represent an integer as four 16-bit words), the goal of the datatype specification is to ensure that both systems can describe the data in a consistent fashion that can be communicated from one to the other.

The XML Schema Datatype document makes a number of distinctions in its terminology that are worth understanding before working with datatypes. Typically, a given datatype can be described as being either an `atomic` datatype or an `aggregate` datatype. An `atomic` type is an indivisible one: it can't be decomposed into other datatypes. (For example, an `integer` type is considered an atomic type.) An `aggregate` datatype, on the other hand, is composed of one or more other datatypes (the parent datatypes can also be aggregates). (For example, a `3Dpoint` is a datatype that can consist of three integers and, hence, is considered an aggregate type.)

Subtly different is the distinction between a `primitive` and a `generated` datatype. A `primitive` datatype cannot be defined in terms of any other datatype, while a `generated` datatype is a subtype of an existing datatype (known as the basetype). For example, in the W3C recommendation, a `decimal` datatype is considered `primitive`, while an `integer` is derived from a decimal type and is thus considered `generated`.

NOTE Note that, programmatically, there is no real difference in the action of a `generated` datatype compared to that of a `primitive` datatype. The parser treats them the same.

Finally, a `built-in` datatype is one that is specified in the W3C recommendation, while a `user-generated` datatype is one created in an external schema. Note that this distinction is of much greater import in the W3C specification than it is with Microsoft's Reduced Data Set (RDS), which is covered next, since, in the RDS schema, the datatypes themselves are fixed and you can't create extended datatypes from data primitives.

WARNING The terms *primitive* and *built-in* may imply that these datatypes have some corollaries with programming language types. This is not the case; a datatype defined as a primitive in the W3C specification may or may not be a primitive datatype in C++ or Java. In general, the terminology should be seen as a generic abstraction of a datatype, not as any given implementation of that abstraction.

Microsoft Reduced Data Set Datatypes

As with many of the XML specifications, Microsoft was involved early with proposals and recommendations, especially those revolving around the use of XML as a data transport mechanism. Much of the current architecture of the XML Schema specification derives explicitly from Microsoft's Reduced Data Set proposal, which first laid out the architecture for representing different datatypes. While the W3C recommendation has evolved somewhat since then (especially in the area of archetypes and custom definable types), the Reduced Data Set proposal still forms the foundation of most of Microsoft's own XML data efforts.

The datatype attributes in the Reduced Data Set are fairly explicitly defined in the specification and are covered in Table 6.4. Note that these do not necessarily reflect the types defined in the W3C, and if you are planning on working with older XML data that will communicate with non-Microsoft XML parsers, you should translate the datatypes into the latest specification.

TABLE 6.4: Microsoft XML Reduced Data Set Types

Name	Parsed As	Internal Representation	Description
`String`	PCData	Unicode String	This is the default datatype.
`Number`	A number without constraints on number of digits or signs	String	Internally, this type is kept as a string and converted into a numeric value only when retrieved. This is especially useful for handling extremely large numbers.
`Int`	An integer number without constraints	32-bit signed binary	Note that while the standard recognizes an arbitrarily large value, in practice the size is limited to $\pm2^{31-}1$.
`Float`	Same as for **`number`**	64-bit IEEE 488	You can express numbers using exponential notation in this format (i.e., 6.24E-5 is the same as 0.0000624).
`fixed`	Same as **`number`** but with no more than four digits to the right of the decimal and no more than 14 digits to the left	64-bit signed binary	This is frequently used for currency calculations.
`Boolean`	**`1`** or **`0`**	Bit	Note that VB has **`true=-1`**, so, in general, you're safer not testing for **`0`** conditions.
`DateTime.iso8601`	A date in ISO 8601 format, having optional time and no time zone. Fractional seconds may be as precise as nanoseconds.	Internal data structure	**`2000-11-05T06:25:16.22`** (16.22 seconds after 6:25 A.M. on November 5, 2000)
`Date`	Same as **`dateTime.iso8601`**	Internal data structure	**`2000-11-05T06:25:16.22`** (16.22 seconds after 6:25 A.M. on November 5, 2000)
`DateTime.iso8601.tz`	A date in ISO 8601 format, having optional time and time zone. Fractional seconds may be as precise as nanoseconds.	Internal data structure	**`2000-11-05T06:25:16.22-08`** (16.22 seconds after 6:25 A.M. on November 5, 2000, in the eighth time zone—Pacific time)
`date.iso8601`	A date in ISO 8601 format, without given time or time zone	Internal data structure	**`2000-11-05`** (November 5, 2000)

TABLE 6.4: Microsoft XML Reduced Data Set Types *(continued)*

Name	Parsed As	Internal Representation	Description
`time.iso8601`	A time in ISO 8601 format, without time zone. Fractional seconds may be as precise as nanoseconds.	Internal data structure	`6:25:16.22` (16.22 seconds after 6:25 A.M.)
`time.iso8601.tz`	A time in ISO 8601 format, with optional time zone. Fractional seconds may be as precise as nanoseconds.	Internal data structure	`6:25:16.22-08:00` (16.22 seconds after 6:25 A.M. in the eighth time zone—Pacific time)
`i1`	An integer, with option sign but without exponent and fractional part	8-bit binary	Range of –128 to 127
`i2`	As with `i1`	16-bit	Range of –32,768 to 32,767
`i4`	As with `i1`	32-bit	Range of –2,147,483,648 to 2,147,483,647
`i8`	As with `i1`	32-bit	Range of –9,223,372,036,854,775,808 to 9,223,372,036,854,775,807
`ui1`	An integer, without sign, exponent, and fractional part	8-bit binary	Range of 0 to 255
`ui2`	As with `ui1`	16-bit	Range of 0 to 65,535
`ui4`	As with `ui1`	32-bit	Range of 0 to 4,294,967,295
`ui8`	As with `ui1`	32-bit	Range of 0 to 18,446,744,073,709,551,615
`r4`	Same as `number`	IEEE 488 4-byte float	Same as `number`
`r8`	Same as `number`	IEEE 488 4-byte float	Same as `number`
`float.IEEE.754.32`	Same as `number`	IEEE 754 4-byte float	Same as `number`
`float.IEEE.754.64`	Same as `number`	IEEE 754 8-byte float	Same as `number`
`Uuid`	Hexadecimal numbers representing octets. Optional embedded hyphens are ignored.	128-byte Unix UUID structure	For GUID representations
`url`	Universal Resource Locator	As defined by the W3C	`http://www.ietf.org/html.charters/urn-charter.html`

TABLE 6.4: Microsoft XML Reduced Data Set Types *(continued)*

Name	Parsed As	Internal Representation	Description
bin.hex	Hexadecimal digits representing octets	No specified size	Used for encoding binary information in an XML document
Char	String	One 16-bit Unicode character	Used for representing a single character
String.ansi	String containing only ASCII characters	Unicode or single-byte string	Should generally be avoided in favor of the default string format, primarily for localization reasons

In addition to these datatypes, the Microsoft XML Reduced Data Set Schema also supports a number of XML primitives that are part of the W3C specification, as shown in Table 6.5.

TABLE 6.5: Primitive W3C Data Types

Name	Description
entity	Indicates that the type is an entity object.
entities	Indicates the type is a collection of entity objects.
id	Defines the attribute as a unique ID. (Note that no two objects within the XML structure can have the same ID.)
idref	Determines that the value contained therein is a token that explicitly points to some ID in the document (an ID reference). There can be more than one `idref` in the document, but the `idref` must point to some ID in the document.
idrefs	Indicates a collection of `idref` objects.
nmtoken	A name token (or **`nmtoken`**) is a collection of alphanumeric characters that can also include an underscore or period but no other punctuation or white space.
nmtokens	Indicates a collection of **`nmtoken`** objects. Note that if you use the **`dt:values`** attribute, you should also include a **`dt:type="nmtokens"`** to help the schema parser resolve the tokens.
notation	Indicates that the value is a notation reference.
string	A string is a primitive datatype (discussed in Table 6.4).

The *datatype* Tag and the *dt:* Namespace

Similar to the Reduced Data Set, the `dt:` namespace is a Microsoft convention, and it represents the Microsoft datatype namespace. In order to use these datatype tokens, you should explicitly declare the namespace, as in the following example:

```
<Schema name = "mySchema.dtd"
    xmlns = "urn:schemas-microsoft-com:xml-data"
    xmlns:dt = "urn:schemas-microsoft-com:datatypes">
```

As with groups, it's possible to move the datatype information for a given element or attribute into a separate XML node, the datatype node. The datatype node has a number of attributes (detailed in Table 6.6) that can, as with the group, be inherited by the parent ElementType or AttributeType nodes.

TABLE 6.6: Attributes of the datatype Node

Attribute Name	Description
dt.type	One of the datatypes listed in Table 6.4 and 6.6.
dt:min	Indicates the minimum inclusive value that the element or attribute can hold and still be considered valid.
dt:minExclusive	Same as dt:min, except the specific value is excluded.
dt:max	Indicates the maximum inclusive value that the element or attribute can hold and still be considered valid.
dt:maxExclusive	Same as dt:max, except the specific value is excluded.
dt:maxLength	For a string, indicates the maximum number of characters that the value can hold. For any other type, indicates the maximum number of bytes that can be used to support the value.
dt:values	Defines an enumerated set of tokens that can be valid values. (Note that this is the same as dt:values for the Attribute token.)

The datatype attributes are specifically designed to create constrained types, limiting the range over which defined types can extend. The simplest constraint is the dt:values constraint. For example, you can set up an attribute that lets you use only days of the week, as in the following example:

```
<AttributeType name="weekday">
    <datatype dt:type="nmtokens" dt:values="Sunday Monday
    Tuesday Wednesday Thursday Friday Saturday"/>
</AttributeType>
```

This particular attribute can then only take one of the seven values, Sunday through Saturday. On the other hand, using numeric values, you can limit the bounds of a datatype's range as well:

```
<AttributeType name="itemsRequested">
   <datatype dt:type="int" dt:min="1" dt:max="99"/>
</AttributeType>
```

The itemsRequested attribute is thus limited to being an integer between 1 and 99 inclusive; attempting to get no items, a negative number of items, or a hundred or more items would all make the XML document invalid. Similarly, you can constrain dates in the same fashion:

```
<AttributeType name="datePurchased">
   <datatype dt:type="date" dt:min="2000-01-01"
    dt:maxExclusive="2001-01-01"/>
</AttributeType>
```

This example constrains the `datePurchased` attribute to a time between January 1, 2000, and December 31, 2000. (The maximum value is exclusive, meaning that the `2001-01-01` date is not included in the range.)

You can also set up constraints in character length. For example, a number of EDI field codes are fixed in length to a certain maximum size, as in the following `invoiceShipCode` element, which is limited to a maximum of six characters:

```
<ElementType name="invoiceShipCode">
   <datatype dt:type="string" dt:maxLength="6"/>
</ElementType>
```

NOTE Note that the `dt:maxLength`, when applied to non-string data, restricts (according to the W3C recommendation) the number of bytes used to represent an object. As most operating systems have very definite formats for representing such things as floating-point or integer numbers, the `dt:maxLength` is itself more of a hint that may or may not be followed than a binding requirement.

The W3C XML Schema

The Microsoft XML Schema language was devised originally as an extension of their proposal for integrating XML into database applications, the Microsoft XML Reduced Data Set Schema, in mid-1998. The original schema was fine for what it was (a mechanism to indicate preexisting datatypes in a consistent format), but it lacked any serious capability to extend these datatypes or to create custom types. Furthermore, it lacked the ability to handle mainstays of traditional SGML documents, such as entities and notations, and it provided no way to include one schema within another, which was a critical part of any inheritance mechanism.

The W3C XML Schema grew out of this and other proposals. In its main goals, it resembles the initial Microsoft proposal, but it has added archetypes (ways of extending datatypes) and entity and notation references into the language. It does differ slightly in syntax here and there as well (the `eltOnly` token becomes `elemOnly`, as one small example), so the two schema-description languages are not quite identical.

At the time this book was written, the W3C XML Schema was still in Working Group status, with some major holes in terms of the final implementation of given features. As a consequence, the material presented here may be somewhat out of date by the time you read this. Check the two primary Schema reference documents `http://www.w3.org/TR/xmlschema-1/` and `http://www.w3.org/TR/xmlschema-2/`, which discuss the structure and the datatypes of the schema language, respectively.

W3C Archetypes

Although not yet supported by the Microsoft XML parser (this may change by the time this book is published), the W3C XML Schema specification includes a number of features to radically extend the scope of what can be done with XML schemas. Perhaps one of the most exciting of these is the inclusion of the `archetype` element.

Archetypes are mechanisms that let you define complex datatypes and refer to them as a single unit. Put another way, with archetypes the object-oriented nature of XML gets strengthened considerably. Consider, for example, the problem of *addresses*. In most financial transactions, addresses may occur several times within an XML schema. If, instead of specifying all of the subordinate tags that support an address (street, city, state, etc.), you could dictate that a given tag is an address type, you would go a long way toward building a more encapsulated version of your objects.

The `archetype` tag does just that. It lets you create an XML "object" in your XML Schema document and then make references to the object in the same way that a Visual Basic class would build an instance of the class. Returning to the problem of building an address, an archetype approach might be written in a manner similar to that in Listing 6.5.

Listing 6.5: An Address Archetype (*Listing6-5.dtd*)

```
<archetype name="address">
   <element type="street" minOccurs="1" maxOccurs="1"/>
   <element type="street2" minOccurs="0" maxOccurs="1"/>
   <element type="city" minOccurs="1" maxOccurs="1"/>
   <group order="one">
      <group order="seq">
         <element type="state" minOccurs="1" maxOccurs="1">
         <element type="zipcode" minOccurs="1" maxOccurs="1">
      </group>
      <group order="seq">
         <element type="province" minOccurs="1" maxOccurs="1">
         <element type="regionalCode" minOccurs="1" maxOccurs="1">
      </group>
      <group order="seq">
         <element type="region" minOccurs="1" maxOccurs="1">
         <element type="regionalCode" minOccurs="1" maxOccurs="1">
         <element type="country" minOccurs="1" maxOccurs="1">
      </group>
   </group>
</archetype>
```

This listing assumes that all the elements contained in the archetype have been previously defined with `ElementType` tags. Once the archetype is defined, you can reference the archetype as a datatype of an element:

```
<ElementType name="Shipping Address" type="address"/>
```

A key mechanism that is currently being reviewed by the W3C is a way to incorporate one schema within another. With archetypes, you could thus define a set of core archetypes within one schema, reference them within a second schema, and then use that to validate your XML documents. If this technique seems eerily reminiscent of referencing a DLL or object library, you can understand why archetypes are currently such tantalizing technology.

Archetypes can also be used in more subtle ways. Suppose, for example, that you have a 3-D–graphics package that you want to convert into an XML format. One of the most frequently used primitives is a 3-D point. Rather than defining the coordinates of each specialized point explicitly, you can use an archetype to define a standard `point3d` type (Listing 6.6).

Listing 6.6: An Archetype Showing the *point3d* Definition (*Listing6-6.dtd*)

```
<Schema name="Shapes">
   <ElementType name="x" type="real" minInclusive="-1000.0"
    maxInclusive="1000.0" default="0.0"/>
   <ElementType name="y" type="real" minInclusive="-1000.0"
    maxInclusive="1000.0" default="0.0"/>
   <ElementType name="z" type="real" minInclusive="-1000.0"
    maxInclusive="1000.0" default="0.0"/>
   <AttributeType name="unit" type="nmtoken" values="vx in
    cm px pt" default="vx"/>
   <archetype name="point3d" order="seq">
       <attribute type="unit"/>
       <element type="x"/>
       <element type="y"/>
       <element type="z"/>
   </archetype>
   <!-- Some examples -->
   <ElementType name="point1" type="point3d"/>
   <archetype name="triangle3d" order="seq">
       <element type="pointA"/>
       <element type="pointB"/>
       <element type="pointC"/>
   </archetype>
   <ElementType name="triangle" type="triangle3d"/>
   <ElementType name="shapes" type="elemOnly">
      <element type="triangle" minOccurs="0" maxOccurs="*"/>
   </ElementType>
</Schema>
```

The point3d archetype, as defined here, serves much the same function as a constructor in a language like Java or C++ by providing both default values for the points (all points start out at the origin p(0,0,0) until positioned elsewhere) and default units (the vx unit, for voxel), and boundaries are placed upon the extent to which the points can be set. To illustrate this last point, I created lower and upper bounds for each coordinate at –1,000 and 1,000, respectively.

Once defined, an archetype can serve as the basis for other archetypes. In the example in Listing 6.6, three point3d points are defined, and then these points, in turn, make up a triangle3d object. Initially, such a triangle exists as a singularity, because all three points are at the origin. However, as Listing 6.7 shows, the XML document that the schema describes will specify all the points.

Listing 6.7: An XML Shapes Document that the Shapes Schema Describes (*Listing6-7.xml*)

```
<shapes>
   <triangle>
      <pointA unit="cm">
           <x>1.2</x>
           <y>3.4</y>
           <z>4.2</z>
      </pointA>
      <pointB unit="cm">
           <x>3.2</x>
           <y>1.4</y>
           <z>6-5</z>
      </pointB>
      <pointC unit="cm">
           <x>3.1</x>
           <y>9.4</y>
           <z>6.3</z>
      </pointC>
  </triangle>
   <triangle>
      <pointA unit="cm">
           <x>1.2</x>
           <y>3.4</y>
           <z>4.2</z>
      </pointA>
      <pointB unit="cm">
           <x>-2.5</x>
           <y>3.5</y>
           <z>2.0</z>
      </pointB>
      <pointC unit="cm">
```

```
            <x>3.1</x>
            <y>9.4</y>
            <z>6.3</z>
        </pointC>
    </triangle>
</shapes>
```

The *datatype* Element

While archetypes are useful as a way to define complex data structures, one must often deal with a single datatype that occurs in a number of places. For example, consider the `point3d` class described in the previous section. The three initial coordinates each must have their constraints specified, even though, in all three cases, the constraints are the same:

```
<ElementType name="x" type="real" minInclusive="-1000.0"
   maxInclusive="1000.0" default="0.0"/>
```

As the following example demonstrates, you can simplify this constraint process through the use of the `datatype` tag, which lets you create *generated* tags based upon a preexisting, or *base*, datatype:

```
<datatype name="coordinate">
   <basetype>real</basetype>
   <minInclusive="1000.0"/>
   <maxInclusive="1000.0"/>
</datatype>

<ElementType name="x" type="coordinate" default="0.0"/>
<ElementType name="y" type="coordinate" default="0.0"/>
<ElementType name="z" type="coordinate" default="0.0"/>
```

The `datatype` tag is also a useful way to set up a range of enumerated tokens. For example, rather than specifying the various possible kinds of units in the `unit` attribute, you could create a datatype that contains these enumerations, creating the equivalent of global, VB-enumerated types:

```
<datatype name="unit_of_measure">
   <basetype>nmtoken</basetype>
   <enumeration>vx px pt cm in twip</enumeration>
</datatype>

<AttributeType name="unit" type="unit_of_measure" default="vx"/>
```

The primary limitation of the `datatype` tag is that it can't set an explicit default value, but this is not typically a major problem since you can set defaults through the `AttributeType` or `ElementType` tags anyway.

WARNING Note the subtle differences between the datatype declaration used within the Microsoft Schema and that used within the W3C Schema. In the former case, the datatype simply acts to encapsulate some of the data characteristics of an element or attribute, while in the latter case the datatype actually creates a new type that can be subsequently referenced.

Entities

Entities were discussed briefly in Chapter 2, "Modeling the XML Document Object," but, to recapitulate, they are essentially blocks of text or XML nodes that are given a specific name. The simplest entities are those that refer to individual characters, such as the `<` entity to designate the less-than (<) symbol or the `&` entity to indicate an ampersand (&). More complex entities can include blocks of text or XML nodes, or can even contain the contents of whole documents.

The new XML Schema recognizes the following three distinct kinds of entities:

- Internal parsed entities
- External parsed entities
- Unparsed entities

Internal Parsed Entities

An *internal parsed entity* is an entity where the contents are contained within the schema itself. For example, in a legal document, you may want to include a copyright notice in a number of places. You could define such a notice as an internal parsed entity using the `textEntity` tag:

```
<textEntity name="copyright">This document is copyright
  1999 by Kurt Cagle.</textEntity>
```

In the XML document described by the schema, you could then reference this entity using the notation `©right;`, as follows:

```
<legalese>&copyright;</legalese>
```

Typically, though, rather than using the term `copyright`, most documents use the © symbol for indicating copyright. This symbol is defined as character 169 in the standard English encoding and can be represented within the entity declaration as another entity, as the following example demonstrates:

```
<textEntity name="copyright">This document &#169;1999 by
   Kurt Cagle.</textEntity>
```

As the name indicates, a text or internal parsed entity can be parsed, which means that its contents will be expanded when the schema is instantiated before validation takes place. Thus, the `textEntity` node can contain additional XML text:

```
<textEntity name="icon"><img src="icon.gif" align="left"/></textEntity>
```

When the parser encounters the expression `&icon;`, it replaces `icon` with its entity's contents:

```
&icon; The Next Point
```

The preceding line becomes the following:

```
<img src="icon.gif" align="left"/> The Next Point
```

External Parsed Entities

External parsed entities, not surprisingly, come from an outside file or data source and are defined by the `<externalEntity>` tag. External entities include the system attribute for specifying the location of the data store, and that value can either be a file reference or a URL of some sort, so long as it points to a valid XML source. For example, you can define a set of chapters from a book in your XML:

```
<externalEntity name='FrontMatter'
                system='FrontMatter.xml' />
<externalEntity name='Chapter1'
                system='chapter1.xml' />
<externalEntity name='Chapter2'
                system='Chapter2.xml' />
<externalEntity name='BackMatter'
                system='BackMatter.xml' />
```

Once the entities are defined, you can then use the familiar &XXX; format to specify them. To tie all of these chapters into a single book, for example, you simply include the entities by name:

```
<book>
   &FrontMatter;
   &Chapter1;
   &Chapter2;
   &BackMatter;
</book>
```

When the XML document is instantiated in memory, these entities expand into their full form; unless something is seriously wrong, you shouldn't see the entities at all in the final XML output.

Unparsed Entities

The final form of entities, *unparsed entities*, are retrieved from a file or stream and inserted directly into the XML document without being parsed or rendered. One typical use of this is to include binary information directly in the XML document. For example, you can transport a binary image, such as the bits of an icon, by specifying the location of the bits from the system tag of the <unparsedEntity> object:

```
<unparsedEntity name="icon" system="http://www.vbxml.com/cagle/icon.gif"/>

<image><![CDATA[&icon;]]></image>
```

Entity Controversy

The inclusion or exclusion of entities in the W3C deliberations has been extremely contentious. Entities form a critical component of the older SGML specifications, since one of the principle uses for SGML is to provide a way of integrating disparate blocks of text. However, entities introduce a number of problems in a data-oriented environment: they don't follow normal XML "element and attribute" notation, they add another layer of abstraction onto an already-complex structure, they are indifferently supported by parsers, and they duplicate functionality that is already included with the XLink specification.

In general, if you are looking at including external documents in your XML, look at XLink or XInclude instead of resorting to entities. The former gives you much finer grain control over retrieving resources, and the latter is easier to work with than entities, especially when combined with XSLT.

Programming with XML Schemas

One of the principal advantages that comes from working with XML schemas can be summarized in three words: *Schemas are XML*. Put another way, a schema exists as part of the document, can be accessed from the document, and can be used to provide underlying characteristics of the document's structure that would be impossible to express with a Document Type Definition.

The following points demonstrate the advantages to this approach:

- Default values for a document from the schema are passed transparently; thus, you can cut down on the amount of information you need to specify.
- You can document your XML documents with schema description tags; by storing this information in the schema, you keep the size of the individual XML files down to a minimum.
- You can store all the possible enumerated values that a given element or attribute can hold and then retrieve these values for a list box or table.
- You can combine schemas with XSLT to simplify your templates (and, not coincidentally, form the cornerstone of most of your XML development efforts).

In this section, I focus on these points. However, programming with schemas can address a host of other issues, and references to schema programming permeate this book.

TIP The following examples are built around the older Microsoft XML Schema implementation.

NOTE One of the most significant aspects of any schema or DTD is validation. However, validation in and of itself also extends far beyond whether the document is well formed.

Working with Typed Values

The Microsoft XML Document Object Model contains a number of features geared toward working with schemas. At the node level, these include the `datatype`, `nodeTypedValue`, and `specified` properties, as well as the two `setAttribute` and `getAttribute` attribute properties. As Listing 6.8 and Listing 6.9 demonstrate, these properties and methods are best illustrated by looking at a simple purchase order and its associated schema.

Listing 6.8: A Simple Purchase Order (*Code6-8.PurchaseOrder.xml*)

```
<! Code6-7.PurchaseOrder.xml -->
<purchaseOrder xmlns="x-schema:Code6-8.POSchema.xml>
   <taxRate>6.5</taxRate>
   <lineItems>
       <lineItem>
           <itemName>Big Bang Rocket</itemName>
           <itemCode>KBOOM</itemCode>
           <quantity>10</quantity>
           <unitPrice>24.95</unitPrice>
       </lineItem>
       <lineItem>
           <itemName>Extravaganza</itemName>
           <itemCode>XTRAV</itemCode>
           <quantity>32</quantity>
           <unitPrice>14.95</unitPrice>
       </lineItem>
       <lineItem>
           <itemName>Mini-Rockets</itemName>
           <itemCode>MINI</itemCode>
           <quantity>75</quantity>
           <unitPrice>4.95</unitPrice>
       </lineItem>
  </lineItems>
</purchaseOrder>
```

Listing 6.9: A Simple Purchase Order Schema (*Code6-9.POSchema.xml*)

```
<Schema name = "Code6-8.POSchema.xml"
   xmlns = "urn:schemas-microsoft-com:xml-data"
   xmlns:dt = "urn:schemas-microsoft-com:datatypes">
    <ElementType name="purchaseOrder" content="eltOnly" model="closed">
         <element type="taxRate" content="textOnly" dt:type="fixed.14.4"/>
         <attribute type="totalPrice" content="textOnly"
           dt:type="fixed.14.4" default="0"/>
         <element type="lineItems" minOccurs="1" maxOccurs="1"/>
    </ElementType>
    <AttributeType name="totalPrice"
    <ElementType name="lineItems" content="eltOnly">
         <element type="lineItem" minOccurs="0" maxOccurs="*"/>
    </ElementType>
    <ElementType name="itemName" content="textOnly"
      dt:type="string" maxLength="32"/>
    <ElementType name="itemCode" content="textOnly"
      dt:type="string" maxLength="6"/>
    <ElementType name="quantity" content="textOnly"
      dt:type="int" min="0" max="9999"/>
    <ElementType name="unitPrice" content="textOnly"
      dt:type="fixed.14.4" minExclusive="0.0"
      max="99999.99"/>
</Schema>
```

In order to find out what your total cost is for the purchase order, you need to add each item's quantity by its unit price, and then add the sum multiplied by the tax rate. As Listing 6.10 demonstrates, the `computeTotalCost` function does two things: It retrieves the total cost, and it sets the value of the `totalCost` attribute, which is declared as a default on the `purchaseOrder` node.

Listing 6.10: The Visual Basic *computeTotalCost* Function Demonstrates how Typed Values Can Be Retrieved to Calculate the Cost of a Purchase Order Request. (*Listing6-10.txt*)

```
Function computeTotalCost(poDoc as DOMDocument)
   Dim sum as double
   Dim item as IXMLDOMNode

   Sum=0
   For each item in poDoc.selectNodes("//lineItem")
     Sum=sum+_
       item.selectSingleNode("quantity").nodeTypedValue *_
        item.selectSingleNode("unitPrice").nodeTypedValue
```

```
    Next
   Sum=sum*(1+poDoc.selectSingleNode("//taxRate")._
     nodeTypedValue
    PoDoc.selectSingleNode("purchaseOrder/@totalCost")._
       nodeTypedValue=sum
    ' Note that this could also have been written
    ' PODoc.selectSingleNode("purchaseOrder").setAttribute
      "totalCost",sum
    ComputeTotalCost=Sum
End Function

' Example of Usage
Dim purchaseOrder as DOMDocument
Dim cost as double
PurchaseOrder.async=false

PurchaseOrder.load "PurchaseOrder.xml"
Cost=computeTotalCost(PurchaseOrder)
```

The `nodeTypedValue` property retrieves the text content of the node and attempts to convert it to the indicated datatype. When a value is assigned, the conversion is reversed: The XML parser attempts to interpret the expression passed to it and then converts it to the appropriate type. This assigned value is held in memory as the specified type but will be converted into a string again if the document is serialized back out to an XML string using the `.xml` method. The XML parser attempts to convert the value to the closest C++-equivalent datatype (as specified in the "Internal Representation" column of Table 6.4).

However, there may be times when you want to handle the conversion yourself. The `dataType` property can help you with that conundrum. The `dataType` property retrieves the name of the type for a given element or attribute. Note that this is a read-only property; you can't change the expressed datatype of an element on the fly once the schema has been loaded.

The `specified` property of the `IXMLDOMNode` interface can tell you whether the value for the given node has been explicitly given in the XML data document (which makes it true) or whether it was provided as a default (which makes it false). The principle reason you may want to use this is to make sure that you're not writing the same value as the default back to the node in question. A default value doesn't take up any space in the XML document but only in the schema; however, any time you write a value to a node, that value will be stored in the document, even if the value is the same as the default. If you have an XML document with a number of default values and you read and then rewrite the node values back to the document, the size of the XML file can jump dramatically.

Documenting XML Schema

XML documents of any sort provide an interesting conundrum when it comes to describing what it is that they mean. Describing, or documenting, these documents within the documents themselves means that a great deal of information needs to be transmitted that doesn't contain relevant data. Moreover, this information would be highly redundant if each document (such as a purchase order) had to include its own set of descriptions on top of the contained data.

One of the more useful tags found within the XML Schema declaration (as well as the Microsoft XML Schema) is `description`. With the `description` tag, you can describe what a given node does without having to actually include the description in the source document. Moreover, you can actually place XML code within a `document` block, letting you retrieve any number of descriptive labels, HTML blocks, or anything else from your schema.

The `description` tag comes in handy especially for display documents such as HTML tables, where you may want to include headers for each column of information without including the header information in the document itself. Similarly, you may want to include pop-up help text that appears when your mouse hovers over a given cell, describing what the cell does in greater detail.

In Listing 6.11, the purchase order schema has been expanded to include a description block for each element. The `description` tag itself contains two child nodes: a `title` node, which provides a short title for the purchase order node in question, and a `body` node, which includes text that may appear in a pop-up or status-bar text block.

NOTE Note that neither `title` nor `body` is part of the XML Schema specification; however, the `description` tag is declared as open, letting you add tags as need be without having to formally include them within the XML Schema specification itself.

Listing 6.11: A Modified Purchase Order Schema that Includes Descriptions (*Code6-11.PurchaseOrder.xml*)

```
<Schema name = "Code6-10.POSchemaDescr.xml"
   xmlns = "urn:schemas-microsoft-com:xml-data"
   xmlns:dt = "urn:schemas-microsoft-com:datatypes">
    <AttributeType name="totalPrice" dt:type="fixed.14.4">
        <description>
            <title>Total Price</title>
            <body>Contains the total cost of the purchase
              order, including sales tax and
              surcharges.
            </body>
```

```
            <format>$###,###.00</format>
         </description>
      </AttributeType>
    <ElementType name="taxRate" content="textOnly" dt:type="fixed.14.4">
       <description>
          <title>Tax Rate</title>
          <body>The rate used for local taxes and surcharges.</body>
          <format>##.#%</format>
       </description>
    </ElementType>
     <ElementType name="itemName" content="textOnly" dt:type="string">
       <description>
          <title>Item Name</title>
          <body>The name that identifies the item in the
             product catalog.
          </body>
       </description>
    </ElementType>
     <ElementType name="itemCode" content="textOnly" dt:type="string">
       <description>
          <title>Item Code</title>
          <body>A six character code that uniquely
             identifies the item in the catalog database.
          </body>
       </description>
    </ElementType>
     <ElementType name="quantity" content="textOnly" dt:type="int">
       <description>
          <title>Quantity</title>
          <body>The quantity of a given item being purchased.</body>
             <format>###,###</format>
       </description>
    </ElementType>
    <ElementType name="unitPrice" content="textOnly" dt:type="fixed.14.4">
       <description>
          <title>Unit Price</title>
          <body>The price for one of the specified items.</body>
             <format>$###,###.00</format>
       </description>
    </ElementType>
    <ElementType name="lineItemCost" content="textOnly" dt:type="fixed.14.4">
       <description>
          <title>Line Item Cost</title>
          <body>The cost of a single line item purchase</body>
             <format>$###,###.00</format>
       </description>
    </ElementType>
```

```
<ElementType name="subTotal" content="textOnly" dt:type="fixed.14.4">
   <description>
      <title>Sub-total</title>
      <body>The total cost of the purchase order before taxes.</body>
         <format>$###,###.00</format>
   </description>
</ElementType>
<ElementType name="taxAmount" content="textOnly" dt:type="fixed.14.4">
   <description>
      <title>Tax Amount</title>
      <body>The additional cost for the purchase order due to taxes</body>
         <format>$###,###.00</format>
   </description>
</ElementType>
<ElementType name="total" content="textOnly" dt:type="fixed.14.4">
   <description>
      <title>Total</title>
      <body>The total cost of the purchase order, including taxes.</body>
         <format>$###,###.00</format>
   </description>
</ElementType>
 <ElementType name="lineItem" content="eltOnly">
    <description>
      <title>Line Item</title>
      <body>One specific item, of given quantity, to be purchased.</body>
   </description>
   <element type="itemName"/>
   <element type="itemCode"/>
   <element type="quantity"/>
   <element type="unitPrice"/>
</ElementType>
 <ElementType name="purchaseOrder" content="eltOnly" model="closed">
    <description>
      <title>Purchase Order</title>
      <body>A document requesting the purchase of one or more items.</body>
   </description>
      <element type="taxRate" minOccurs="1" maxOccurs="1"/>
      <attribute type="totalPrice" default="0"/>
      <element type="lineItems" minOccurs="1" maxOccurs="1"/>
 </ElementType>
 <ElementType name="lineItems" content="eltOnly">
    <description>
      <title>Line Items</title>
      <body>A collection of line item objects.</body>
   </description>
   <element type="lineItem" minOccurs="0" maxOccurs="*"/>
 </ElementType>
</Schema>
```

Of course, once these description elements have been added to the schema, the most obvious question is how to retrieve them again. The key here is the `definition` property, a DOM element that was discussed only in passing in Chapter 2, "Modeling the XML Document Object." This property, part of the `IXMLDOMNode` interface, returns a pointer to the schema node that specifically defines the node in question.

For example, consider the XML purchase order document shown in Listing 6.12. This example demonstrates one logical use for an XSL filter, one that turns the purchase order into a receipt that shows the subtotals from each item and the final total (at the bottom of the table), as well as providing header information and roll-over "tool-tips."

Listing 6.12: A Purchase Order for Acme Rocket Products (*Code6-12.PurchaseOrder.xml*)

```
<!-- Code6-11.PurchaseOrder.xml -->
<purchaseOrder xmlns="x-schema:Code6-10.POSchema.xml">
   <taxRate>.065</taxRate>
   <lineItems>
       <lineItem>
           <itemName>Big Bang Rocket</itemName>
           <itemCode>KBOOM</itemCode>
           <quantity>10</quantity>
           <unitPrice>24.95</unitPrice>
       </lineItem>
       <lineItem>
           <itemName>Extravaganza</itemName>
           <itemCode>XTRAV</itemCode>
           <quantity>32</quantity>
           <unitPrice>14.95</unitPrice>
       </lineItem>
       <lineItem>
           <itemName>Mini-Rockets</itemName>
           <itemCode>MINI</itemCode>
           <quantity>75</quantity>
           <unitPrice>4.95</unitPrice>
       </lineItem>
       <lineItem>
           <itemName>Sky Writers</itemName>
           <itemCode>SKY</itemCode>
           <quantity>16</quantity>
           <unitPrice>26-95</unitPrice>
       </lineItem>
       <lineItem>
           <itemName>Sparklers</itemName>
           <itemCode>SPRK</itemCode>
           <quantity>45</quantity>
```

```
            <unitPrice>1.95</unitPrice>
        </lineItem>
        <lineItem>
            <itemName>Chrysanthemum</itemName>
            <itemCode>CRYS</itemCode>
            <quantity>3</quantity>
            <unitPrice>41.95</unitPrice>
        </lineItem>
    </lineItems>
</purchaseOrder>
```

To get the header and descriptive information, such as the tax rate's name and description, you can use the `definition` property to retrieve the corresponding schema node, and then query the description block, as shown in Listing 6.13 (which also contains output).

Listing 6.13: Sample Code from *Code6-13.PORoutines.bas* Demonstrating how to Retrieve Information Elements from the *definition* Property

```
Dim purchaseOrder as DOMDocument
Dim taxRateNode as IXMLDOMNode
Dim taxRateDefNode as IXMLDOMNode
Dim title as String
Dim body as String

' Create a new DOM Document
Set purchaseOrder=new DOMDocument
' Load the purchase order
purchaseOrder.load "Code6-11.PurchaseOrder.xml"
' Retrieve the tax rate node
set taxRateNode=purchaseOrder.selectSingleNode("//taxRate")
' Retrieve the node's definition
set taxRateDefNode=taxRateNode.definition
Debug.Print taxRateDefNode.xml
' Output from the debug.print is as follows

   <ElementType name="taxRate" content="textOnly"
   dt:type="fixed.14.4" xmlns="x-schema:Code6
    -10.POSchema.xml" >
      <description>
         <title>Tax Rate</title>
         <body>The rate used for local taxes and surcharges.</body>
         <format>##.#%</format>
      </description>
   </ElementType>
```

```
' Get the title of the node
title=taxRateDefNode.selectSingleNode(_
     "//description/title").text
Debug.print title

"Tax Rate"
body=taxRateDefNode.selectSingleNode(_
     "//description/body").text
"The rate used for local taxes and surcharges."
```

NOTE When the `.xml` method is applied to a schema-based node, then the schema declaration (the `xmlns=""` part) is automatically inserted into the top node of the resulting text.

You can apply this principle to the task of creating the receipt, either through DOM or through XSL. For example, a Visual Basic solution for creating such a result (which consists of a table in HTML) can query the nodes directly, as in the `DisplayPurchaseOrderDisplay()` function shown in Listing 6.14, with the sample purchase order using this format displayed in Figure 6.1.

FIGURE 6.1
The purchase order data displayed as an HTML table

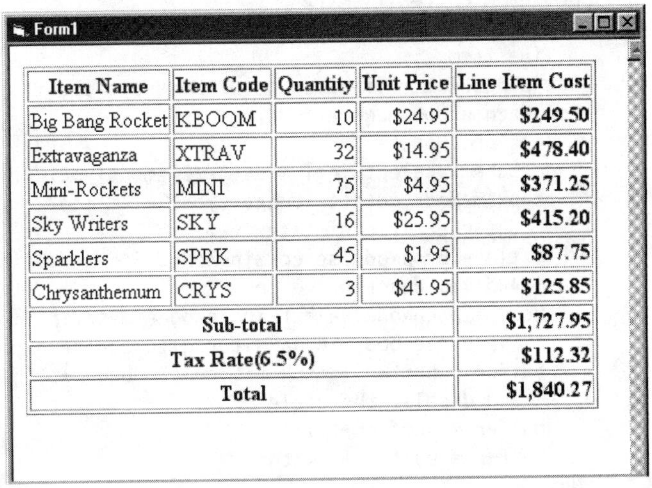

Form1

Item Name	Item Code	Quantity	Unit Price	Line Item Cost
Big Bang Rocket	KBOOM	10	$24.95	**$249.50**
Extravaganza	XTRAV	32	$14.95	**$478.40**
Mini-Rockets	MINI	75	$4.95	**$371.25**
Sky Writers	SKY	16	$25.95	**$415.20**
Sparklers	SPRK	45	$1.95	**$87.75**
Chrysanthemum	CRYS	3	$41.95	**$125.85**
Sub-total				**$1,727.95**
Tax Rate(6.5%)				**$112.32**
Total				**$1,840.27**

Listing 6.14: The Visual Basic *DisplayPurchaseOrder()* Function, Designed to Work on the Previous Purchase Order Schema (*DisplayPurchaseOrderListing.vbs*)

```
Function DisplayPurchaseOrder(poDoc As DOMDocument) As String
   Dim docSchema As IXMLDOMNode
   Dim buffer As String
   Dim propsList As IXMLDOMNodeList
```

```
Dim lineItem As IXMLDOMNode
Dim propNameNode As IXMLDOMElement
Dim propNode As IXMLDOMElement
Dim title As String
Dim body As String
Dim cellValue As Variant
Dim sum As Double
Dim taxRate As Double
Dim taxAmount As Double
Dim liTitle As String
Dim liBody As String
Dim formatNode As IXMLDOMNode
Dim formatMask As String

buffer = "<table border='1'>"
' Get a reference to the document's schema
Set docSchema = poDoc.documentElement.definition.parentNode
' Get the line item definition
Set lineItem = _
  docSchema.selectSingleNode _
  ("//ElementType[@name='lineItem']")
buffer = buffer + "<tr>"
' Retrieve the name of all elements in a typical
' line item
Set propsList = lineItem.selectNodes("element")
For Each propNameNode In propsList
   Set propNode =
  docSchema.selectSingleNode("//ElementType[@name='" + _
  propNameNode.getAttribute("type") + "']")
   ' Get the title of each item
   title = propNode.selectSingleNode("description/title").Text
   ' And its descriptive body
   body = propNode.selectSingleNode("description/body").Text
   ' Place the body in an alt tag to create a pop-up
   buffer = buffer + "<th title='" + body + "'>"
   ' and display the title
   buffer = buffer + title
   buffer = buffer + "</th>"
Next
' Create another cell for the line item cost
Set liCostNode = _
  docSchema.selectSingleNode _
  ("//ElementType[@name='lineItemCost']")
liCostTitle = liCostNode.selectSingleNode("description/title").Text
liCostBody = liCostNode.selectSingleNode("description/body").Text
Set liformatNode = liCostNode.selectSingleNode("description/format")
```

```
If Not (liformatNode Is Nothing) Then
   liformatMask = liformatNode.Text
End If
buffer = buffer + "<th title='" + liCostBody + "'>"
buffer = buffer + liCostTitle + "</th>"
buffer = buffer + "</tr>"
' Zero out an accumulator
sum = 0
' Retrieve each line item in turn
For Each lineItem In poDoc.selectNodes("//lineItem")
   buffer = buffer + "<tr>"
   ' From the properties list generated above
For Each propNameNode In propsList
   Set propNode = _
  docSchema.selectSingleNode("//ElementType[@name='" +_
 propNameNode.getAttribute("type") + "']")
   ' Retrieve the title and descriptive body
   body = propNode.selectSingleNode("description/body").Text
   Set formatNode = propNode.selectSingleNode("description/format")
   If Not (formatNode Is Nothing) Then
        formatMask = formatNode.Text
   Else
        formatMask = ""
   End If
   buffer = buffer + "<td title='" + body + "'"
   cellValue = _
     lineItem.selectSingleNode(propNode. _
     getAttribute("name")).nodeTypedValue

   If IsNumeric(cellValue) Then
     buffer = buffer + "align='right'>"
   Else
     buffer = buffer + "align='left'>"
   End If
   ' Use then name of the property to get
   ' the cell's contents.
   If formatMask = "" Then
       buffer = buffer + cellValue
   Else
       buffer = buffer + Format(cellValue, formatMask)
   End If
   buffer = buffer + "</td>"
Next
' Retrieve the quantity and unit price,
' multiply them together and add them to the sum
subTotal =
```

```
lineItem.selectSingleNode("quantity").nodeTypedValue *
lineItem.selectSingleNode("unitPrice").nodeTypedValue
   sum = sum + subTotal
   ' Display the body description as pop-up text
    buffer = buffer + "<th title='" + liCostBody + "' align='right'>"
      ' And show the subtotal amount

    If Not (liformatNode Is Nothing) Then
       liformatMask = liformatNode.Text
    End If

    buffer = buffer + Format(subTotal, formatMask) + "</td>"
    buffer = buffer + "</tr>"
Next
' Span the column so that there are only two columns
' in the subtotal row, then display the subtotal
Set tempNode = docSchema.selectSingleNode("//ElementType[@name='subTotal']")
title = tempNode.selectSingleNode("description/title").Text
body = tempNode.selectSingleNode("description/body").Text
buffer = buffer + "<tr>"
buffer = buffer + "<th colspan='" + CStr(propsList.length) + "'>"
buffer = buffer + title
buffer = buffer + "</th>"
buffer = buffer + "<th title='" + body + "' align='right'>"
buffer = buffer + Format(sum, formatMask) + "</th>"
buffer = buffer + "</tr>"

' Show the tax rate and tax amount
buffer = buffer + "<tr>"
   Set tempNode = _
     docSchema.selectSingleNode _
     ("//ElementType[@name='taxRate']")
   title = tempNode.selectSingleNode("description/title").Text
   body = tempNode.selectSingleNode("description/body").Text
   Set formatNode = tempNode.selectSingleNode("description/format")
   If Not (formatNode Is Nothing) Then
      formatMask = formatNode.Text
   End If
taxRate = poDoc.selectSingleNode("//taxRate").nodeTypedValue
buffer = buffer + "<th colspan='" + CStr(propsList.length) + "' "
buffer = buffer + "title='" + body + "'>"
buffer = buffer + title + "(" + Format(taxRate, formatMask) + ")"
buffer = buffer + "</th>"

   Set tempNode = _
     docSchema.selectSingleNode _
     ("//ElementType[@name='taxAmount']")
```

```
        body = tempNode.selectSingleNode("description/body").Text
        Set formatNode = tempNode.selectSingleNode("description/format")
        If Not (formatNode Is Nothing) Then
           formatMask = formatNode.Text
        End If

    taxAmount = sum * taxRate
    buffer = buffer + "<th title='" + body + "' align='right'>"
    buffer = buffer + Format(taxAmount, formatMask) + "</th>"
    buffer = buffer + "</tr>"

    ' Add the tax amount to the subtotal to get the total
    buffer = buffer + "<tr>"
    Set tempNode = docSchema.selectSingleNode("//ElementType[@name='total']")
        title = tempNode.selectSingleNode("description/title").Text
        body = tempNode.selectSingleNode("description/body").Text
        Set formatNode = tempNode.selectSingleNode("description/format")
        If Not (formatNode Is Nothing) Then
           formatMask = formatNode.Text
        End If
    buffer = buffer + "<th colspan='" + CStr(propsList.length) + "'>"
    buffer = buffer + title
    buffer = buffer + "</th>"
    buffer = buffer + "<th title='" + body + "' align='right'>"
    buffer = buffer + Format(sum + taxAmount, formatMask) + "</th>"
    buffer = buffer + "</tr>"
    buffer = buffer + "</table>"
    ' Set the resulting HTML table to output to the
    ' function
    DisplayPurchaseOrder = buffer
    End Function
```

This is a large (and somewhat unwieldy) function, but it illustrates a number of important programming techniques. For example, if you want to retrieve the schema of a document as a separate DOM object, you can use the following expression:

```
Set docSchema=xmlDoc.documentElement._
    .definition.parentNode
```

The definition for the `documentElement` will always be an `ElementType` node located as a child of the Schema node; thus, if you grab the definition of this root node and ask for its parent, you will get a pointer to the Schema node; from here, you can query for any node in the tree.

One of the problems with generating a table from a standard XML document (sans Schema) is that you can run into the degenerate case where the document contains no items of the type that you're looking for but you still want to display header information. For example, in the purchase order document, it is entirely possible that a purchase order has no line items at all but is being sent simply as a template for future line items.

Thus, rather than relying upon the purchase order source document, you can query the schema to get the names of the header elements. (I'll use a similar technique to generate new line items in the next section.) One consequence of this is that you can set up in your schema the order in which you want the output to appear. In this case, the order was set by the elements in the following `lineItem ElementType` declaration:

```
<ElementType name="lineItem" content="eltOnly">
   <description>
      <title>Line Item</title>
      <body>One specific item, of given quantity, to be purchased.</body>
   </description>
   <element type="itemName"/>
   <element type="itemCode"/>
   <element type="quantity"/>
   <element type="unitPrice"/>
</ElementType>
```

You may notice that there are a number of elements that are defined in the schema that aren't specifically used, such as `taxAmount`. I put these into the schema specifically for their description information; instead of hard coding the names of specific headers and titles in the VB function, I referred to these otherwise-unused elements.

TIP

By placing the descriptive information for a given **`output`** tag into the schema (if it is not explicitly used by the source document), you create a powerful tool for localizing your display code. You could change the contents of the **`description`** node from English to German, Japanese, or Arabic and not have to alter any of your program code or XML source.

TIP

One technique used in this section is to include **`title`** attributes for each cell that contains the description body information. In IE4 and IE5, setting the title attribute to a non-empty string causes a "tool-tip" type box to appear over the designated element. This trick doesn't work with Netscape Navigator, however.

One additional element that I included in the description element is the `format` tag. The purpose of this tag is to display the format of the associated element using a mask that works with the Visual Basic `Format()` function. For example, the `total` element has a format mask of `$###,###.00`, which tells the `Format()` function to format the result as comma separated, with two decimal places always appearing in the displayed result.

An advantage to placing the formatting procedures in the schema is that it, in general, is the same as placing descriptive information in the schema; you can change the schema to reflect differences in formatting based upon locale. If you wish to set the formatting to German standard, for example, you can change the formatting mask in a German schema to `###.###,0dm`, which, for the value 23,259.24 deutsche marks, would be displayed as `23.259,2dm`. Similar formatting can be done using dates and times.

Retrieving Enumerations

Enumerations (sets of tokens that represent valid values for a given attribute) can sometimes prove problematic for developers. With the older style DTDs, you were limited to only knowing when the token that you had was valid within the given set of tokens; at least with the MSXML parser, it has not been possible to retrieve these tokens explicitly.

Fortunately, XML schemas are much more friendly in this regard. Since the values themselves are contained in attributes, they can be retrieved from the schema through the DOM. For example, if you have an attribute that can hold one of eight colors—red, blue, yellow, green, orange, violet, white, or black—then you can set up an `AttributeType` definition, like the following, that lists these properties in the `dt:values` tag:

```
<AttributeType name="color" dt:values="red blue yellow green orange violet white
black" dt:type="nmtokens"/>
```

You can then use the `definition` tag for the `attribute` node to retrieve the `dt:values` attribute. For example, for the simple `colors.xml` file (Listing 6.15) and its associated `colorSchema.xml` schema (Listing 6.16), you can access the `dt:values` node and then use the `split` function to create an array of tokens, as in Listing 6.17 (which also contains output).

Listing 6.15: The *colors.xml* file, which Contains a Number of Color Items (*Code6-15.Colors.xml*)

```
<!-- Colors.xml -->
<items xmlns="Code6-14.ColorSchema.xml">
   <item id="fire" color="red">Fire</item>
   <item id="water" color="blue">Water</item>
   <item id="earth" color="green">Earth</item>
   <item id="nightsky" color="black">Night Sky</item>
   <item id="ice" color="white">Ice</item>
</items>
```

Listing 6.16: The Associated *colorSchema.xml* Schema, Showing how Enumerations Can Be Expanded (*Code6-16.ColorSchema.xml*)

```
<!-- ColorSchema.xml -->
<Schema name = "Code6-14.ColorSchema.xml"
   xmlns = "urn:schemas-microsoft-com:xml-data"
   xmlns:dt = "urn:schemas-microsoft-com:datatypes">
    <AttributeType name="id" dt:type="id">
        <description>
            <title>ID</title>
            <body>A unique identifier for an item.</body>
        </description>
    </AttributeType>
<AttributeType name="color" dt:values="red blue yellow
```

```
green orange violet black white" dt:type="nmtokens" >
        <description>
            <title>Color</title>
            <body>The tokenized color of the item.</body>
            <options>
                <option id="red">Bright Red</option>
                <option id="blue">Ocean Blue</option>
                <option id="yellow">Solar Yellow</option>
                <option id="green">Verdant Green</option>
                <option id="orange">Pumpkin Orange</option>
                <option id="violet">Violet</option>
                <option id="black">Abyssal Black</option>
                <option id="white">Pure White</option>
            </options>
        </description>
    </AttributeType>
  <ElementType name="item" content="textOnly">
     <attribute type="id"/>
     <attribute type="color"/>
     <description>
        <title>Item</title>
        <body>An unique object that has an associated color.</body>
     </description>
  </ElementType>
  <ElementType name="items" content="eltOnly">
     <element type="item" minOccurs="0" maxOccurs="*"/>
     <description>
        <title>Items</title>
        <body>A collection of item objects</body>
     </description>
  </ElementType>
</Schema>
```

Listing 6.17: The *GetTokens()* Function, which Retrieves the List of Tokens for a Given Node, or Nothing if the Node's Schema Contains No Tokens for That Node (*Code6-17.GetTokens.bas*)

```
Function GetTokens(srcNode as IXMLDOMNode) as Variant
   Dim defNode as IXMLDOMElement
   Dim tokensStr as String
   Dim tokenList() as Variant

   Set defNode=srcNode.definition
   If isNull(defNode.getAttribute("dt:values")) or
        (defNode.getAttribute("dt:values")="") then
      tokenList=Nothing
```

```
    else
       tokenList=split(defNode.getAttribute("dt:values"),_
          " ")
    end if
    GetTokens=tokenList
End Function

' Usage

dim xmlDoc as DOMDocument
dim colorNode as IXMLDOMNode
dim colors() as Variant
dimcolor as Variant
xmlDoc.load "Code6-14.Colors.xml"
colors=GetTokens(xmlDoc.selectSingleNode("//item[0]/ @color")
for each color in colors
    Debug.Print color
Next
' Output
red
blue
yellow
green
orange
violet
black
white
```

If you have ever had a requirement to output a list box to DHTML, you may have discovered one fairly major problem with working with enumerations. Typically, enumerated tokens are fairly short keywords rather than displayed values. A token can't have any internal spaces, making it useless, for example, if you want to display a list of states. Another way of putting this is that most selection boxes and similar interface devices need two pieces of information for each item: a token to readily identify the item in a compact form and a title for making the token easy to understand from a human standpoint.

You can take advantage of the open nature of the `<description>` tag, however, to significantly expand the capabilities of your enumerations. In Listing 16.18, I created a set of `<option>` tags that are contained within an `<options>` block. Note that these are not standard schema tags; they can only be included because the `<description>` tag's model is `open`.

Consider the problem of displaying a drop-down list box, or a `select` box as it is described in HTML. Displaying an item in a list box with its own associated alternative values becomes fairly simple, at least from the DOM, as shown in Listing 16.18 (which also contains output).

Listing 6.18: The *DisplayListBox()* Function Generates HTML for a List Box when Passed an Attribute with a Set of Enumerated Values in *option* Format, as Shown in Listing 6.16. (*Code6-18.DisplayListBox.bas*)

```
Function DisplayListBox(enumNode as IXMLDOMNode,id as _
  String,optional numItemsDisplayed as Integer = 0) as _
  String
    Dim optionNode as IXMLDOMElement
    Dim optionsNodeList as IXMLDOMNodeList
    Dim Buffer as String
    Set optionsNodeList=enumNode.definition.selectNodes(_
          "option/options")
    Buffer="<SELECT id='"+id+ size='"+cstr(numItemsDisplayed)+"' _
        "' value='"+enumNode.nodeTypedValue+"'>
    for each optionNode in optionsNodeList
        Buffer=buffer+"<OPTION value='"+_
            optionNode.getAttribute("id")+"' "
        if optionnode.getAttribute("id")=enumNode.nodeTypedValue then
           buffer=buffer+"SELECTED='SELECTED'"
        end if
        buffer=buffer+">"+optionNode.text+"</OPTION>"
    next
    buffer=buffer+"</SELECT>"
    DisplayListBox=buffer
End Function

' Usage
Dim xmlDoc as new DOMDOcument
Dim redNode as IXMLDOMNode

xmlDoc.load "Code6-13.Colors.xml"
Set redNode=xmlDoc.selectSingleNode("//item/@color='red'")
Debug.Print DisplayListBox(redNode,"MyItemID")

<SELECT id='MyItemID' size='0' value='red'>
    <OPTION value='red' SELECTED='SELECTED'>Bright Red</OPTION>
    <OPTION value='blue'>Ocean Blue</OPTION>
    <OPTION value='yellow'>Solar Yellow</OPTION>
    <OPTION value='green'>Verdant Green</OPTION>
    <OPTION value='orange'>Pumpkin Orange</OPTION>
    <OPTION value='violet'>Violent Violet</OPTION>
    <OPTION value='black'>Deep Black</OPTION>
    <OPTION value='white'>Ice White</OPTION>
</SELECT>
```

When `DisplayListBox` is passed any node that has a collection of `option` objects within the `<description>` tag, it iterates through that collection and converts the result into a `select` box format. You can also pass in a parameter that sets the number of items being displayed.

TIP The size parameter in an HTML **select** box determines the basic characteristics of the box. If size is 4, for example, then the list box is displayed as a list box with four items; if size is 0, on the other hand, then the box becomes a drop-down list box instead.

This particular technique gets around one of the significant problems of both schemas and DTDs: neither recognizes the possibility that an element can contain a set of enumerations. By placing the enumerations directly into the schema as XML elements, you can leverage the advantages of enumerations without having to worry about the limitations.

WARNING Make sure that if you do use the technique described in this section you still make the **ID** tokens correspond to the enumerated set (if you're using an attribute); the parser will do a certain amount of validation for you if you follow this rule, but it doesn't know anything about the <option> elements.

Combining Schemas and XSL

Schemas and XSL can be made to work together; indeed, by placing much of the onus of definition for an XML file on the schema, you can radically simplify your XSL scripts. The purchase order is a good example of where XSL may be superior to using the DOM in conjunction with XML Schema, although it does require a little bit of interior scripting to make it work well (see Listing 6.19).

NOTE Listing 6.19 uses the older Microsoft XSL parser, although it can easily port to the newer format.

Listing 6.19: Outputting the Purchase Order through XSL (*Code6-19.PurchaseOrderTable.xsl*)

```
<xsl:stylesheet xmlns:xsl="http://www.w3.org/tr/wd-xsl" language="VBScript">
   <xsl:script><![CDATA[
       function getTitle(this)
          dim title
          getTitle=this.definition.selectSingleNode(_
               "description/title").text
       end function

       function getBody(this)
          dim title
          getTitle=this.definition.selectSingleNode(_
               "description/body").text
       end function

       function getMask(this)
          dim title
```

```
   getTitle=this.definition.selectSingleNode(_
        "description/format").text
end function

function getFormattedOutput(this)
   dim maskNode
   dim mask
   dim output
   set maskNode=this.definition.selectSingleNode(_
        "description/format")
   if (maskNode is nothing) then
       output=this.text
   else
       output=format(this.nodeTypedValue,_
           maskNode.text)
   end if
   getFormattedOutput=output
end function

function getElemDefNode(eltName)
   set defRoot=me.definition.parentNode
   set getEltDefNode=defRoot.selectSingleNode(_
      "//ElementType[@name='"+eltName+"']")
end function

dim sum ' This is a global value
sum=0   ' Initialize it globally

function getLineItemCost(this)
   dim itemCost
   dim itemCostNode
   dim itemMask
   itemCost=this.selectSingleNode(_
        "quantity").nodeTypedValue *_
        this.selectSingleNode(_
        "unitPrice").nodeTypedValue
   sum=sum+itemCost
   set itemCostNode=getElemDefNode("lineItemCost")
   itemMask=getMask(itemCostNode)
   getLineItemCost=format(itemCost,itemMask)
end function

function getTax()
   tax=sum*me.selectSingleNode(_
        "//taxRate").nodeTypedValue
   set taxNode=getElemDefNode("taxRate")
   taxMask=getMask(taxNode)
   getTax=format(tax,taxMask)
end function
```

```
]]></xsl:script>
<xsl:template match="/">
   <table>
      <tr>
      <xsl:for-each select="//lineItem[0]/*">
          <th>
          <xsl:attribute name="title">
               <xsl:eval>getBody(me)</xsl:eval>
          </xsl:attribute>
          <xsl:eval>getTitle(me)</xsl:eval>
          </th>
      </xsl:for-each>
      <th><xsl:eval>
          <xsl:attribute name="title">
               <xsl:eval>
               getBody(getElemDefNode("lineItemCost"))
               </xsl:eval>
          </xsl:attribute>
          <xsl:eval>
              getTitle(getElemDefNode("lineItemCost"))
          </xsl:eval>
      </th>
      </tr>
      <xsl:apply-templates select="//lineItem"/>
      <tr>
          <th>
          <xsl:attribute name="colSpan">
             <xsl:eval>me.selectNodes(_
                 "//lineItem/*").length
             </xsl:eval>
          <xsl:attribute name="title">
             <xsl:eval>
              getTitle(getElemDefNode("subTotal"))
             </xsl:eval>
          </xsl:attribute>
          </xsl:attribute>
          <xsl:eval>
            getBody(getElemDefNode("subTotal"))
          </xsl:eval>
          </th>
          <th>
          <xsl:attribute name="align">right
          </xsl:attribute>
          <xsl:eval>
      format(sum,getMask(getElemDefNode("subTotal"))
          </xsl:eval>
          </th>
      </tr>
```

```
<tr>
    <th>
    <xsl:attribute name="colSpan">
       <xsl:eval>me.selectNodes(_
           "//lineItem/*").length
       </xsl:eval>
    <xsl:attribute name="title">
       <xsl:eval>
         getTitle(getElemDefNode("taxRate"))
       </xsl:eval>
    </xsl:attribute>
    <xsl:eval>
      getBody(getElemDefNode("taxRate"))
    </xsl:eval>
    (<xsl:eval>format(this.nodeTypedValue,
         getMask(me))</xsl:eval>)
    </th>
    <th>
    <xsl:attribute name="align">right
    </xsl:attribute>
    <xsl:eval>getTax</xsl:eval>
    </xsl:eval>
    </th>
</tr>
<tr>
    <th>
    <xsl:attribute name="colSpan">
       <xsl:eval>me.selectNodes(_
           "//lineItem/*").length
       </xsl:eval>
    <xsl:attribute name="title">
       <xsl:eval>
         getTitle(getElemDefNode("total"))
       </xsl:eval>
    </xsl:attribute>
    </xsl:attribute>
    <xsl:eval>
      getBody(getElemDefNode("total"))
    </xsl:eval>
    </th>
    <th>
    <xsl:attribute name="align">right
    </xsl:attribute>
    <xsl:eval>
      format(sum+clng(getTax()),
             getMask(getElemDefNode("total"))
```

```
                </xsl:eval>
                </th>
            </tr>
        </table>
    </xsl:template>
    <xsl:template match="lineItem">
        <tr>
        <xsl:for-each select="*">
    <td>
        <xsl:attribute name="align">
            <xsl:choose>
            <xsl:when expr="IsNumeric(me.nodeTypedValue)
  or IsDate(me.nodeTypedValue)">right</xsl:when>
            <xsl:otherwise>left</xsl:otherwise>
            </xsl:attribute>
            <xsl:attribute name="title">
            <xsl:eval>getBody(me)</xsl:eval>
            </xsl:attribute>
                <xsl:eval>getFormattedOutput(me)</xsl:eval>
    </td>
        </xsl:for-each>
          <th><xsl:eval>
              <xsl:attribute name="title">
                   <xsl:eval>
                   getBody(getElemDefNode("lineItemCost"))
                   </xsl:eval>
              </xsl:attribute>
     <xsl:eval>getLineItemCost(me)</xsl:eval>
          </th>
        </tr>
    </xsl:template>
</xsl:stylesheet>
```

It's perhaps not very surprising that the majority of the code in the XSL script is geared toward the exceptions to the general rule: determining the line item costs and displaying the subtotals, tax rate, and final total. Indeed, you could probably make a compelling argument that they don't belong in the final output at all but should be computed (and displayed) through their own XSL filter.

However, the important point to consider here is that you can use an XSL filter rather than DOM directly to output schema-based information. Again, one of the principal benefits of this is that you can, as in the preceding examples, actually separate the display of the invoice information into the following three distinct areas:

Data The province of the original XML document. This should contain just this information, rather than labels, formatting markup, or similar output considerations.

Semantical Information This is the province of the schema, indicating relationships between nodes and also providing descriptive information about the elements and attributes. In other words, this *describes* the XML.

Transformational Data This is the province of XSL transform. It takes the data and converts into a usable form, using the semantic information to provide some contextual meaning for the user.

Note that one implication of the separation of transformational and structural information is that the transform alters the form without needing to know anything about the content or the semantics of the data—a real boon when it comes to handling localization issues. The triad of provinces from the preceding list appears repeatedly throughout this book and should be the foundation upon which you build all of your XML development efforts.

Summary

When working with XML from a programmatic standpoint, you need to be able to handle a number of different aspects of the application (in other words, XML is more than just tags and attributes), including the following:

- Representation of data, through XML
- Working with XML programmatically, via the XML DOM
- Locating resources in XML, through the agency of XPath and XLink
- Transforming data into different forms, with the use of XSL transform
- Describing data semantically, through XML Schema

This effectively describes the core "canon" of XML; with these five different technologies, you can essentially work with XML in the abstract, without necessarily being tied to any specific implementation, platform, or company.

However, with that stated, most of the principal applications of XML don't exist in a vacuum; the language is seen as a bridge between two or more programs, databases, or computer systems. In following chapters, I explore ways in which you can start integrating the powerful capabilities that XML gives you in a number of different venues. As the focus of this book is on Microsoft's implementation of XML, many (though not all) of these applications are either Microsoft products or are written with Microsoft tools. I want you to keep in mind as you are reading this, however, that most of the techniques can be modified to work within a Java or Perl context with a W3C-compliant parser, and, as I am presenting examples for you to work with, I hope to include some recommendations on how you can take the same code and apply it outside of that domain.

So it's time to put what you've learned so far to some use—onward to Chapter 7, "XML and the Browser," to start applying XML in the wild world of Internet client development.

CHAPTER 7

XML and the Browser

- Using XML and CSS
- Understanding data islands
- Introducing behaviors
- Focusing on XML-centric behaviors

When XML was first being created, the primary purpose of the language was to replace the creaking HTML standard, which had been seriously wounded in the browser wars. Ironically, XML has not really taken off on the browser, in part because, at the time this book is being written, only one company, Microsoft, seriously supports an XML implementation on the browser. However, the next-generation, open-source Mozilla browser will provide a base-level support for the language.

However, if you have the luxury of using Internet Explorer 5 or higher as your only browser (for example, as an Intranet-based application), then, by all means, you should take advantage of the power that XML brings to the Web page. From markup to data sourcing, and from graphics creation to synchronization of time-based events, XML permeates the IE5 browser.

Finally, whether you can use IE5 exclusively or not, you can still leverage XML on your Web pages through the use of server-side code that duplicates much of the functionality of client-side components. Because of the wide diversity of clients in use, the use of server-side HTML components are increasing in popularity. Chapter 8, "XML and ASP," covers the creation of such code on the server side.

XML and CSS

Do you remember the `<big>` tag? This particular artifact of HTML popped up during the struggle between Microsoft and Netscape for dominance of the browser market, and it illustrates one of the big pitfalls of attempting to develop a standard through marketing pressures. The sole purpose of `<big>` was to make text, well, bigger. It provided no significant information about why the text should be bigger, nor did it describe exactly how big such a display should be. In short, it was a fairly useless tag that provided no semantic information, exercised very little control over visual appearance, and, despite migrating into the specifications of JavaScript, never really did gain much acceptance in the Web developer's toolkit.

I bring this up to point out why Cascading Style Sheets (CSS) were developed in the first place. It had become obvious by 1996 that adding more tags to the HTML specification only caused further fragmentation, especially when such tags imparted nothing but stylistic information. CSS was introduced to start separating the content of a Web page from its presentation.

Internet Explorer 5 supports style sheets through the `<style>` tag directly or the `<link>` tag indirectly. Style sheets themselves consist of various rules that describe sets of CSS properties that can be applied to a given tag. For example, if you want to indicate that a paragraph should be rendered in 8-point Arial font and colored blue, you would essentially use a paragraph rule such as the following:

```
<style>
   P {font-family:Arial;font-size:8pt;color:blue;}
```

```
</style>
<P>This should be blue text in 8pt Arial.</P>
```

NOTE Note that the style block doesn't need to be in the <head> block of an HTML document and that there can be more than one such style in the document.

You can similarly define a `style` attribute on an HTML tag, letting you apply CSS properties specifically to that tag, as in the following sample:

```
<P style="color:red;">This should be red text</P>
<P style="color:green;">This should be green text</P>
```

However, the danger that you run into with such style references is that you create visual distinctions in the output that may not necessarily exist in the source document. For example, the green text may be some kind of a note, while the red text may be a warning. You can make this association more explicit (and generally should do so) by creating classes in your style sheets. A class is defined by a token starting with a period in the style sheet and is applied to a given tag through the `class` attribute, as the following example demonstrates:

```
<style>
   .note {color:green;}
   .warning {color:red;}
</style>

<P class="note">This is a note, and it should be rendered in green.</P>
<P class="warning">This is a warning, and it should be rendered in red.</P>
```

By abstracting the styles as distinct classes, you begin to impart semantic information into your HTML. Now, instead of having two generic paragraph elements, you have a `note` element and a `warning` element. Indeed, there is nothing stopping you from applying the same class to other elements:

```
<DIV class="warning">This is a warning, and it should be
  rendered in red.</DIV>
<H2 class="warning">This section contains sensitive information.</H2>
```

However, you may also want to have the same level of abstraction use different visualizations, depending upon the HTML tag being used as a container. To do this, you can qualify the class, as in the following example:

```
<style>
   .note {color:green;}
   .warning {color:red;}
   H1.warning {font-size:36pt;font-style:bold;color:red;}
   P.warning {font-size:12pt;font-style:plain;color:red;}
</style>
```

```
<H1 class="warning">Dangerous Information</H1>
<P class="warning">This section contains dangerous information.</P>
<H3 class="warning">Authored by Kurt Cagle</H3>
```

Finally, you can have more than one rule apply to a given tag simultaneously. This can happen in one of two ways (at least with Internet Explorer 5 and higher). First, the children of an element with a given style or class inherit many of the CSS properties (such as font size and color) of their parent, unless those properties are explicitly overridden. For example, you can define a `.super` class that changes by the color and the size of a container and two `.sub` classes that only modify one or the other property, as the following example demonstrates:

```
<style>
    .super {font-size:24pt;color:blue;}
    .sub1 {font-size:12pt;}
    .sub2 {color:red;}
</style>
<div class="super">This should be both blue and at a size of 24pt, however,
   <span class="sub1">this will be blue but only 12pt text</span>,
   <span class="sub2">while this will be 24pt text but will be red.</span></div>
```

Second, you can apply two distinct classes to the same tag directly, by separating the rule names by a space (just as you would separate XML tokens by a space), as in the following example:

```
<style>
    .sub1 {font-size:12pt;}
    .sub2 {color:red;}
</style>
<p class="sub1 sub2">This text will have both red text and be 12pt high.</p>
```

TIP The ability to apply two templates at once comes in handy when disabling an element, especially when behaviors are involved. (See the "Behaviors" section later in this chapter.)

By now, you may have noted the similarity in theory between classes and XML tags. Both provide some kind of contextual information to HTML documents that transcends the HTML structure. This similarity was not lost on the IE5 design team, which included a mechanism within style sheets to define extended tags, which must be conformant to XML. The one caveat in using these tags is that the tags must be defined in a namespace separate from the HTML tags. For example, you can create distinct `warning` and `note` tags, each of which would include borders (red and green, respectively, in the preceding example) around a block of text, as Listing 7.1 demonstrates.

Listing 7.1: An Example of Creating Custom Tags in HTML (*Code7-1.CustomTags.htm*)

```
<html xmlns:x="http://www.vbxml.com">
<style>
    x\:warning {border:inset 3p red;width:300px;
         display:block;}
    x\:note { border:outset 3p lightGreen;width:300px;
         display:block;
</style>
<body>
<h1>XML "Custom" Tags</h1>
<x:warning>This is a warning block, used to indicate
 information that could potentially cause problems.  It has
 a declaration of <br/>
    x\:warning {border:inset 3p red;width:300px;display:block;}
</x:warning>
and
<x:note>This is a note block, used to provide general
 information that is noteworth to a reader.  It has a
 declaration of <br/>

    x\:note {border:outset 3p
 lightGreen;width:300px;display:block;}</x:note>
</body>
</html>
```

In this case, the namespace `x` points to a unique namespace designator (`http://www.vbxml.com`). As with many such namespaces, it doesn't have to explicitly point to any actual document; the namespace exists just to uniquely identify the tag labels.

In the `<style>` element, tags are specifically defined with the namespace prefix. The backslash escapes the colon, which has a very specific meaning in CSS (otherwise as a separator of CSS properties). Once these items are defined, they can be used in the document as if they were default HTML document elements.

Such elements can take additional CSS elements as well. Thus, if you want to change the font family of one distinct `note` tag to Verdana, you can do it by adding a `style` attribute, as in the following example:

```
<x:note style="font-family:Verdana;">This note is rendered in the Verdana font-
face</x:note>
```

NOTE Typically, the changes that are made to such a tag are more often behaviors than visual modifications, but both are certainly possible.

CSS in XML Documents

Can CSS be applied to XML? This would seem a natural extension of the CSS language: An extensible tag in DHTML is nothing more than an XML tag, right? Well, sort of. The reality, in most cases, is that CSS is not a terribly good fit for XML as a stand-alone descriptor, for quite a number of reasons:

- Currently, CSS is supported for XML on only two browsers: Internet Explorer 5 and the alpha version of Mozilla.
- The IE5 implementation of CSS support doesn't include support for list-style display elements or tabular elements. As this makes up a significant portion of the kind of output that you'll probably want to make with XML, what's left as production capabilities is rather limited.
- The W3C recently split the XSL Formatting Objects (XSL-FO) language from the XSL Transformations specifications. XSL-FO contains many of the formatting elements that are likely to make up an alternative description to HTML for formatting XML information, with CSS being an integral part of this.

Despite the preceding points, you still can apply CSS style sheets to an XML document, in a fashion that is similar to how you would do it in HTML. The one difference is that you can't define inline CSS style sheets since there is no specific way of differentiating a tag as the one that handles style-sheet information.

Thus, to use CSS in an XML document, you need to create an external style sheet (see the following "The `HTML:` Namespace" section). Such a style sheet is identical to the contents of an HTML sheet as long as you remember that element-style rules (unlike class-style rules) don't require beginning periods. For example, suppose that you have a list of employees, such as the one in Listing 7.2, and that you want to make "business cards" to show each one.

Listing 7.2: A Listing of Employees Who Work for Acme, Inc. (*Code7-2.Employees.xml*)

```
<employees>
   <employee>
      <id>101</id>
      <firstName>John</firstName>
      <lastName>Janus</lastName>
      <title>President</title>
      <dateStarted>1997-11-12</dateStarted>
      <salary>324021</salary>
      <department>Administration</department>
      <company>Acme, Inc.</company>
      <phone>(360)951-6159</phone>
      <email>janus@acme.com</email>
   </employee>
```

```
  <employee>
     <id>102</id>
     <firstName>Kitara</firstName>
     <lastName>Milleaux</lastName>
     <title>Chief Executive Officer</title>
     <dateStarted>1997-08-12</dateStarted>
     <salary>329215</salary>
     <department>Administration</department>
     <company>Acme, Inc.</company>
     <phone>(360)352-7439</phone>
     <email>milleaux@acme.com</email>
  </employee>
  <employee>
     <id>103</id>
     <firstName>Shelley</firstName>
     <lastName>Janes</lastName>
     <title>Chief Financial Officer</title>
     <dateStarted>1998-03-16</dateStarted>
     <salary>232768</salary>
     <department>Finance</department>
     <company>Acme, Inc.</company>
     <phone>(360)357-5555</phone>
     <email>janes@acme.com</email>
  </employee>
  <employee>
     <id>104</id>
     <firstName>Marissa</firstName>
     <lastName>Mendez</lastName>
     <title>Chief Technical Officer</title>
     <dateStarted>1998-09-16</dateStarted>
     <salary>242768</salary>
     <department>Information Technologies</department>
     <company>Acme, Inc.</company>
     <phone>(360)555-1212</phone>
     <email>janus@acme.com</email>
  </employee>
</employees>
```

To add a CSS style sheet, you use exactly the same mechanism that you would for an XSL one, adding the processing instruction before the first line of the XML, as follows:

```
<?xml-stylesheet type="text/css" href="Code7-3.bizCards.css"?>
<employees>
   <!-- and so forth -->
```

In the preceding sample, `bizCards.css` is the style sheet presented in Listing 7.3.

Listing 7.3: A CSS Style Sheet for Displaying Employee Business Cards (*Code7-3.BizCards.css*)

```
employee {
   display:block;
   font-size:10pt;
   font-family:sans-serif;
   border:outset 3px #C0C0C0;
   width:3.25in;
   height:2.5in;
   background-image:url(acmeLogo.jpg);
   }
firstName {display:inline;
   font-size:12pt;
   font-weight:bold;
   color:blue;
   font-family:serif;
   }
lastName {display:inline;
   font-size:14pt;
   font-weight:bold;
   color:blue;
   font-family:serif;
   }
title {display:block;}
department {display:block;}
company {display:block;
   margin-bottom:1.25in;
   }
phone {display:block;}
email {display:block;}
id {display:none;}
salary {display:none;}
dateStarted {display:none;}
```

Perhaps the most important CSS attribute that you need to know if you work with CSS and XML directly is the `display` attribute, which can hold one of the following four possible values:

`block` Element Has a bounding rectangle surrounding the entire element, which changes the flow so that the next element starts outside of the entire block. It is analogous to the HTML `DIV` element, and such blocks as `<H1>` and `<P>` are block elements.

`inline` Element Stays within the flow of the output. It is analogous to the HTML `SPAN` element, and such tags as `<B>` and `<I>` are inline elements.

`list-item` Element Is something like a bullet point and is not natively supported in IE; they default to block elements.

none Element Indicates that the element is not included in the flow of the output at all. (For example, in the preceding business-card example, the `salary`, `id`, and `dateStarted` were all irrelevant properties for the business card, so their `display` property was set to `none` to make sure they didn't appear in the flow.)

Note that if a tagged element doesn't have a `display` attribute, it inherits most of the CSS properties of its container element. The one exception to this is the `display` element. Unless explicitly declared as having a display of `block`, most elements automatically are assigned a `display` attribute value of `inline`. This guarantees that text elements will be contiguous if the parser doesn't recognize the markup.

Incorporating Graphic Elements into XML

If you want to incorporate known images into your XML, you can take advantage of the CSS `background-image` attribute. When passed a `url` parameter (that is, a parameter of the form `url(myImage.jpg)` or `url(http://www.myServer.com/images/myImage.jpg"))`, the `background-image` loads within the element but doesn't displace text or otherwise take up "flowspace." All you need to do is set the width and height of the container to the size of the image to display the full picture, but this isn't necessary if you are just using the image as a background. Note that the `background-image` works for both `block` and `inline` elements.

The *HTML:* Namespace

One of the big problems that I have with CSS and XML together is that the combination always strikes me as somewhat anemic. You can produce stylistic elements that are similar to fairly basic Web pages but lack the richness of the event model, the scripting, and the depth of the DOM that you'd normally have access to in HTML. Worse, you have to spend a lot of time putting together style sheets for what is, in essence, your own private HTML. (If this seems like an unfair criticism, think about the fact that there are nearly 100 HTML elements, perhaps half that many attributes, plus a significant number of capabilities that open up when you incorporate scripted DOM; that's *a lot* of elements to define.)

However, as in the preceding section, there is a way around this anemia if you are using IE5. When you work with HTML, the IE5 parser treats the HTML as an implicitly defined namespace—the default namespace, if you will. In an XML document, on the other hand, HTML is no longer the default namespace, but that doesn't mean that it is completely unavailable.

In fact, you can define a special namespace with the prefix of `HTML:` (or `html:`). (While namespaces are case sensitive, both the uppercase and the lowercase namespaces have been reserved by IE5.) These two namespaces are built into Internet Explorer 5. You still need to set the namespace declaration in your document to *some* namespace URN, but its specific content doesn't really matter.

Once the namespace has been declared, any element that uses the namespace prefix essentially acts like an HTML element. In particular, there are four HTML elements for which this capability can prove useful: images (through the `<html:img>` tag), objects (`<html:object>`), styles (`<html:style>`), and scripts (`<html:script>`). Because these objects are both so rich and provide interfaces into formatting that transcends normal CSS attributes, you may find that incorporating them within your XML can significantly add to the capabilities of CSS-driven XML.

As a simple example, suppose that you want to add e-mail support to the online business cards discussed previously. This capability isn't normally possible with CSS (at least as supported under IE5), which simply doesn't support that level of linkage. However, using script, you can access the XML tags as if they were HTML tags, as in Listing 7.4.

Listing 7.4: Incorporating Scripting into XML (*Code7-4.Employees.xml*)

```
<?xml-stylesheet type="text/css" href="Code7-3.BizCards.css"?>
<employees xmlns:html="http://www.w3.org/TR/HTML">
   <html:script language="JavaScript">
       function launchLink(){
           var elt=event.srcElement;
           eltName=elt.nodeName;
           if (eltName=="email"){
               location="mailto:"+elt.innerText;
               }
           }

        document.body.onclick=launchLink;
   </html:script>
   <html:style>
       email {text-decoration:underline;cursor:hand;}
   </html:style>
   <employee>
      <id>101</id>
      <firstName>John</firstName>
      <lastName>Janus</lastName>
      <title>President</title>
      <dateStarted>1997-11-12</dateStarted>
      <salary>324021</salary>
      <department>Administration</department>
      <company>Acme, Inc.</company>
      <phone>(360)951-6159</phone>
      <email>janus@acme.com</email>
   </employee>
   <!--continued as before -->
```

The new <html:style> block sets the default specification for the email node to something more similar to an HTML link, underlining it and setting the cursor automatically whenever the mouse moves over the link. In turn, the <html:script> uses a global approach to handling mouse clicks. Rather than attempting to identify and attach event handlers to each email tag, it associates the document's onclick event (which is passed onto the body) with the launchLink function.

When launchLink is called, it looks at the event.srcElement object to find out the HTML element that first intercepted the event (the srcElement in this example). (That this element isn't a "real" HTML element is immaterial to the window event object; internally, it is represented in the same way.) A test is then run on the element object to determine whether it is the <email> tag (i.e., has the nodeName of email); if so, launchLink prefaces the <email> tag's text with a mailto: tag to let the browser know that the link is an e-mail link, and it sets the location of the page to that link. Typically, this means that the browser launches your specified e-mail program with the given e-mail address as the *To:* address.

One consequence of incorporating script is that you gain a level of control in your documents that approaches that of XSL. For example, imagine that after the acquisition of a new, high-resolution printer, the president of Acme, Inc., decided that each employee should have a business card with his or her image on it. Kace Moreaux, their resident XML expert, created a simple style sheet and modified the employee list just a wee bit, as in Listing 7.5.

Listing 7.5: A Modified Style Sheet (*Code7-5.BizCards2.css*)

```
employee {
   display:block;
   font-size:10pt;
   font-family:sans-serif;
   border:outset 3px #C0C0C0;
   width:3.25in;
   height:2.5in;
   position:relative;
   }
firstName {display:inline;
   font-size:12pt;
   font-weight:bold;
   color:blue;
   font-family:serif;
   }
lastName {display:inline;
   font-size:14pt;
   font-weight:bold;
   color:blue;
   font-family:serif;
   }
```

```
title {display:block;}
department {display:block;}
company {display:block;
   margin-bottom:1.25in;
   }
phone {display:block;}
email {display:block;
   text-decoration:underline;
   cursor:hand;
   }
id {display:none;}
salary {display:none;}
dateStarted {display:none;}
```

To avoid complications, the background logo was removed from the `employee` node definition. Also, the `position` attribute of the element was changed to `relative`; this let the element flow in its normal manner but also made it possible for the browser to determine coordinates for the element. Kace then added a new script into `EmployeeCards.xml`, as in Listing 7.6.

Listing 7.6: *EmployeeCards.xml*, Which Includes the Requisite Image Display Code (*Code7-6.EmployeeCards.xml*)

```
<?xml-stylesheet type="text/css" href="code7-5.bizCards2.css"?>
<employees xmlns:html="http://www.w3.org/TR/HTML">
   <html:script language="JavaScript">
       function launchLink(){
           var elt=window.event.srcElement;
           eltName=elt.nodeName;
           if (eltName=="email"){
             location="mailto:"+elt.innerText
               }
           }

      function showImages(){
         var numIDs=document.getElementsByTagName("id").length;
         for (var index=0;index!=numIDs;index++){
          var idElt=document.getElementsByTagName("id")(index);
         var employeeNode=idElt.parentElement
         var img=new Image();
         employeeNode.insertBefore(img,employeeNode.childNodes(0));
         img.src="acme"+idElt.innerText+".jpg"
         img.style.position="absolute"
         img.style.left=145;
         img.style.top=80+employeeNode.style.pixelTop;
           }
         }
```

```
      document.body.onclick=launchLink;
    window.onload=showImages;
  </html:script>
  <html:style>
  </html:style>
  <employee>
     <id>101</id>
     <firstName>John</firstName>
    <lastName>Janus</lastName>
     <title>President</title>
     <dateStarted>1997-11-12</dateStarted>
     <salary>324021</salary>
     <department>Administration</department>
    <company>Acme, Inc.</company>
     <phone>(360)951-6159</phone>
     <email>janus@acme.com</email>
  </employee>
  <employee>
     <id>102</id>
     <firstName>Kitara</firstName>
    <lastName>Milleaux</lastName>
     <title>Chief Executive Officer</title>
     <dateStarted>1997-08-12</dateStarted>
     <salary>329215</salary>
     <department>Administration</department>
    <company>Acme, Inc.</company>
     <phone>(360)352-7439</phone>
     <email>milleaux@acme.com</email>
  </employee>
  <employee>
     <id>103</id>
     <firstName>Shelley</firstName>
    <lastName>Janes</lastName>
     <title>Chief Financial Officer</title>
     <dateStarted>1998-03-16</dateStarted>
     <salary>232768</salary>
     <department>Finance</department>
    <company>Acme, Inc.</company>
     <phone>(360)357-5555</phone>
     <email>janes@acme.com</email>
  </employee>
  <employee>
     <id>104</id>
     <firstName>Marissa</firstName>
    <lastName>Mendez</lastName>
     <title>Chief Technical Officer</title>
     <dateStarted>1998-09-16</dateStarted>
```

```
        <salary>242768</salary>
        <department>Information Technologies</department>
       <company>Acme, Inc.</company>
        <phone>(360)555-1212</phone>
        <email>janus@acme.com</email>
    </employee>
 </employees>
```

The `showImages()`function demonstrates how you can change multiple elements simultaneously as well as how to incorporate HTML elements into the XML output. The `getElementsByTagName()` function, which is a method on most HTML tags, retrieves an array of elements that satisfy the given condition, something akin to the `selectNodes()` function in the XML DOM. In the preceding example, the `getElementsByTagName()` function retrieves all nodes with the `id` tag (which are still in the structure, just not shown) and uses the node to retrieve both the `id` for the employee and the `employee` node itself.

With this information, the routine creates a new `Image` object, assigns the `src` to an element that looks like `acme102.jpg`, adds the picture to the element object (using `insertBefore`), and sets the position of the image itself. The outcome is shown in Figure 7.1.

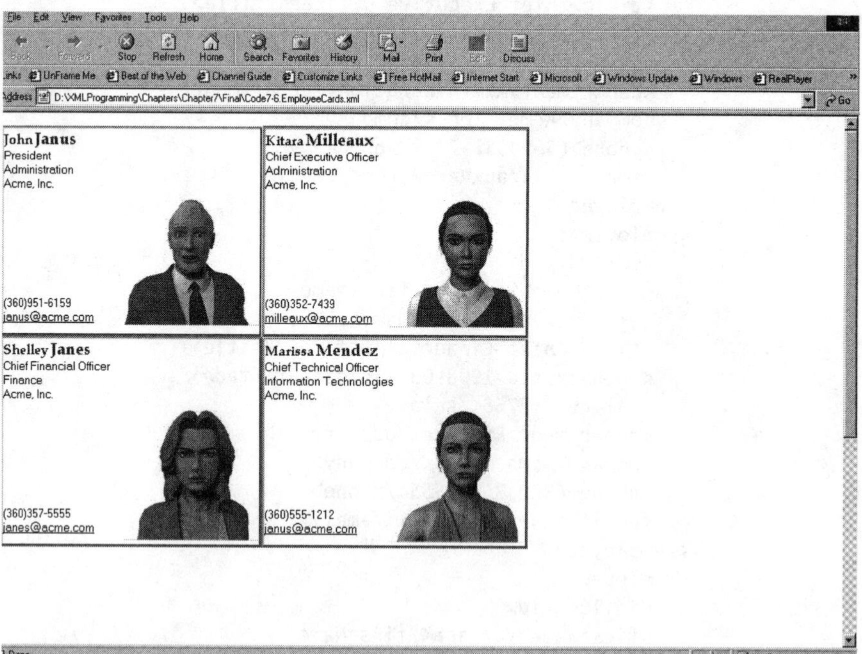

FIGURE 7.1 Business cards, showing the use of XSL to associate employee photographs with their cards

In general, using CSS and the HTML: namespace, you can create XML-based Web pages with nearly the same depth and complexity of a regular Web page. Furthermore, you can take advantage of behaviors (discussed in the "Behaviors" section later in this chapter) to hide a lot of the code that you'd otherwise have to struggle with.

Before digging into the topic of behaviors, however, it's worth looking at one other capability that the IE5 browser in particular (and, with some work, most other browsers) can use to store information local to the page: data islands.

Data Islands

A *data island* is a little bit of XML in a sea of HTML. It's actually a way to keep XML inline instead of loading it from an external source, and it works best when you need a bit of XML for configuration information or when you want to let the Web designer retrieve XML parametrically without messing with scripts.

An XML data island is an Internet Explorer 5 construct only; it won't even work with older versions of IE. To use it, you enclose the XML that you want to incorporate within an <xml> tag. For example, suppose that you want to store the preceding employee information for a simple search application: A list box is populated with the names of all of the employees in the company. When the user selects a name in the list, the full record for that employee appears, along with his or her picture. This application, shown in Listing 7.7, demonstrates one way of working with data islands.

Listing 7.7: An Employees Application Showing how a Data Island Can Be Used to Store Data Locally (*Code7-7.Employees.htm*)

```
<html>
<head>
<title>Employees Application</title>
<style>
.employee {
   display:block;
   font-size:10pt;
   font-family:sans-serif;
   border:outset 3px #C0C0C0;
   width:3.25in;
   height:2.5in;
   position:relative;
   }
.firstName {display:inline;
   font-size:12pt;
   font-weight:bold;
```

```
    color:blue;
    font-family:serif;
    }
.lastName {display:inline;
    font-size:14pt;
    font-weight:bold;
    color:blue;
    font-family:serif;
    }
.title {display:block;}
.department {display:block;}
.company {display:block;}
.phone {display:block;}
.email {display:block;
    text-decoration:underline;
    cursor:hand;
    }
.id {display:none;}
.salary {display:none;}
.dateStarted {display:none;}
</style>
</head>
<body>
<script language="VBScript">
    function loadNames()
        set xmlDoc=employees.XMLDocument
        for each employeeNode in xmlDoc.selectNodes("//employee")
            firstName=employeeNode.selectSingleNode("firstName").text
            lastName=employeeNode.selectSingleNode("lastName").text
            id=employeeNode.selectSingleNode("id").text
            set opt=document.createElement("OPTION")
            opt.value=id
            opt.text=lastName+","+firstName
            employeeNames.options.add opt
        next
    end function

    function display()
        if not (document.all("placeholder") is nothing) then
            employeeNames.options.remove(0)
        end if
        set xmlDoc=employees.XMLDocument
        id=employeeNames.value
        set employeeNode=xmlDoc.selectSingleNode("//employee[id='"+id+"']")
        set employeeDiv=document.createElement("DIV")
        employeeDiv.className="element"
        set img=document.createElement("IMG")
```

```
        img.src="acme"+id+".jpg"
        img.align="left"
        employeeDiv.appendChild img
        for each propNode in employeeNode.selectNodes("*")
           set propDiv=document.createElement("DIV")
           propDiv.className=propNode.nodeName
           select case propNode.nodeName
              case "email"
                 propDiv.innerHTML="<a
        href='mailto:"+propNode.text+"'>"+
        propNode.text+"</a>"
              case else
              propDiv.innerText=propNode.text+" "
           end select
           employeeDiv.appendChild propDiv
        next
        employeeDisplay.innerHTML=""
        employeeDisplay.appendChild employeeDiv
     end function
     window.onload=getRef("loadNames")
  </script>
  <div>Select an employee:
  <select id="employeeNames" onchange="display()">
    <option id="placeholder" value="">-- Employees
      --</select></div><br clear="all">
  <div id="employeeDisplay"></div>

  <xml id="employees">
  <employees>
      <employee>
         <id>101</id>
         <firstName>John</firstName>
        <lastName>Janus</lastName>
         <title>President</title>
         <dateStarted>1997-11-12</dateStarted>
         <salary>324021</salary>
         <department>Administration</department>
        <company>Acme, Inc.</company>
         <phone>(360)951-6159</phone>
         <email>janus@acme.com</email>
      </employee>
      <employee>
         <id>102</id>
         <firstName>Kitara</firstName>
        <lastName>Milleaux</lastName>
         <title>Chief Executive Officer</title>
         <dateStarted>1997-08-12</dateStarted>
```

```
        <salary>329215</salary>
        <department>Administration</department>
       <company>Acme, Inc.</company>
        <phone>(360)352-7439</phone>
        <email>milleaux@acme.com</email>
     </employee>
     <employee>
        <id>103</id>
        <firstName>Shelley</firstName>
       <lastName>Janes</lastName>
        <title>Chief Financial Officer</title>
        <dateStarted>1998-03-16</dateStarted>
        <salary>232768</salary>
        <department>Finance</department>
       <company>Acme, Inc.</company>
        <phone>(360)357-5555</phone>
        <email>janes@acme.com</email>
     </employee>
     <employee>
        <id>104</id>
        <firstName>Marissa</firstName>
       <lastName>Mendez</lastName>
        <title>Chief Technical Officer</title>
        <dateStarted>1998-09-16</dateStarted>
        <salary>242768</salary>
        <department>Information Technologies</department>
       <company>Acme, Inc.</company>
        <phone>(360)555-1212</phone>
        <email>mendez@acme.com</email>
     </employee>
  </employees>
  </xml>

  </body>
  </html>
```

There are several points of note in the preceding example. One of them is that most data islands are accessed through `ids` (in this example, the `"employees" id`). This underscores a subtle aspect about data islands: *A data island is not an XML element; it is an HTML element.* The `<XML>` tag is part of IE5's HTML implementation. It's what's inside of the XML island that makes up the XML document.

Because `<XML>` is an HTML element, in order to retrieve its contents in XML, you can't just use the `innerHTML` property; this would retrieve the code in HTML, which is similar but not identical. Instead, you should use the `.XMLDocument` property. This property gives you a DOMDocument object, and you can do XML operations on that.

One advantage of working with data islands is that they can be used to abstract connections to XML data sources. The `src` attribute of the data island loads in an XML document from a URL and passes that as the `.XMLDocument` if it's used. In other words, the code works identically if you replace the preceding data island with the following one:

```
<xml id="employees" src="employees.xml"/>
```

WARNING If you do use the `src` attribute, the data island becomes asynchronous. In other words, you can only use it when the data island's `readystate=4` (i.e., complete). This means that if you have any external dependency on the data island being complete, you should call that event when the `ondatasetcomplete` event fires or when the `window.onload` event fires.

TIP Data islands work well in conjunction with data binding, which is discussed in detail in Chapter 9, "XML and MS Databases."

Behaviors

One of the reasons that HTML has been stretched to the limits is due to the fact that different people have differing requirements for presenting information on the Web. Especially as Web pages have turned from simple, written documents into complex, data-driven applications, the language itself has been strained well past its breaking point.

Scripting, originally intended as a way of enhancing HTML, has, in its own way, become a key part of the problem. Blocks of code interspersed throughout a Web page are more difficult to maintain, and, in many cases, the code also obscures the general semantic description of the page. By moving the generation of HTML into JavaScript and VBScript sections, you make it much more difficult to change the code easily—in turn, making the page more fragile. Finally, by working with scripting code in this manner, you force an overlap between the Web-page designer, who is frequently a graphic artist concerned with the look and feel of the page, and the Web developer, who is typically a programmer more concerned with whether things work than with whether things are aesthetic. Not surprisingly, the result is often less than sterling.

Scriptlets were originally designed to ameliorate this situation. A *scriptlet* is an object that is defined in a separate script document and was first incorporated into Internet Explorer 4. However, the scriptlet engine ran into a number of problems: It consumed a significant amount of memory, it didn't integrate cleanly with the browser in many ways, and it used the generic `<object>` tag to instantiate an instance. For these reasons, scriptlets never really caught on with Web developers.

Behaviors are an attempt to rethink scriptlets in the context of how people actually code. Their most significant limitation is that behaviors only work within Internet Explorer 5, although Microsoft has been pressing to create a behaviors standard within the W3C that other browser manufacturers could also endorse.

A behavior can be thought of as a way to add functionality to an HTML (or XML) tag without having to petition the W3C to add the tag. Once manifested, a behavior exposes properties (either through code or set from attributes), methods, and events, and it also receives events from the containing browser. The behavior itself is an XML file that contains scripting code and declarations of elements, referenced through the CSS `behavior` property. For example, the following sample turns a normal HTML `div` tag into a digital clock:

```
<div style="behavior:url(dclock.htc);font-size:24pt;font-
family:Haettenschweiler" format="long" />
```

The behavior in this situation is contained in the `dclock.htc` file, which is located in the same folder as the Web page calling it. Behaviors are also known as *hypertext components* (HTCs), after their identifying suffix. When the browser draws the Web page, it also instantiates any behaviors that are defined in the page. Once instantiated, the behaviors act like Java applets or ActiveX controls and can be refreshed independently of the main page.

In addition to instantiating a behavior within a `style` tag, you can also call it as part of a CSS class definition in a style sheet. For example, the preceding clock behavior can be declared within a previously defined style sheet rule, as in the following example:

```
<style>
   .clock {behavior:url(dclock.htc);)
</style>
<div class="clock" format="long"/>
```

Similarly, it can be defined as a custom HTML tag:

```
<style xmlns:kc="http://www.vbxml.com/cagle">
   kc\:clock {behavior:url(dclock.htc);)
</style>
<kc:clock format="long"/>
```

You can similarly use behaviors in XML through an externally defined style sheet. For example, to incorporate a clock into your XML, your initial XML document needs to declare the style sheet that incorporates the behavior, as in the following sample:

```
<?xml:style sheet type="text/css" href="code7-8.clock.css"?>
<document>
<clock id="c1" format="long"
style="display:block;font-size:24pt;color:green;"/>
<clock id="c2" format="short" style="display:span;
;font-size:24pt;color:green;/>
</document>
```

The CSS style sheet referenced here, `clock.css`, associates the styles with tags defined in the XML document. Since the only tag that is explicitly declared here is the `<clock>` tag, the CSS document has only one line (two counting the comment), as shown in Listing 7.8.

Listing 7.8: Calling the Clock Behavior from XML (*Listing7-8.txt*)

```
// Code7-8.Clock.css - Style sheet for the XML clock Test page.
clock {behavior:url(Code7-9.dclock.htc); }
```

When the XML page is displayed in an IE5 browser, the `clock` attribute is replaced with a clock that updates its own time once a second. The two format values `short` and `long` indicate that the time is displayed as hours and minutes only or as hours, minutes, and seconds, respectively (i.e., `2:25 PM` or `2:25:16 PM`).

TIP Note the use of the `style` attributes within the `<clock>` tag. You can apply additional CSS styles to an attribute over a behavior, either in the same rule where the behavior was initially defined or in a separate style sheet or `style` attribute.

TIP You can apply more than one behavior to a given element, either in CSS or XML. Within a `style` attribute or class definition, you would list each of the URLs of the behaviors, separated by a space (`<myTag style="behavior:url(behavior1.htc) url(behavior2.htc) url(behavior3.htc)">`, e.g.). If more than one behavior affects the same attribute (such as the color of text), the last behavior that changed the attribute has precedence.

The technique of creating behaviors provides a number of benefits to Web developers:

- You can separate the layout and functional aspects of your code. The Web designer can drop in a `behavior` tag without needing to know how it works, and the Web developer, in turn, doesn't have to be concerned with the visual appearance of the total page but can concentrate on writing code.
- Code is much easier to maintain, since you can make changes to the implementation file independent of the Web page that calls it.
- For non-IE5 browsers, you can filter out the `behavior` tags with XSLT and replace them with server-side code. (For example, a server-side XSLT script might determine that the browser doesn't support behaviors. Instead, the `<clock/>` tag is replaced with the current time before being sent to the client.)
- You can combine behaviors with XSLT to create completely different views of data in real time. (For example, you can create a dynamic table that lets you sort items, change the visual display, and filter out specific information from the table—all within a single behavior.)
- Because behaviors are intrinsically supported in Internet Explorer 5, you don't have to digitally sign them or worry about security restrictions on them.

Of course, like any technology, there are a few drawbacks to consider when deploying behaviors as well:

- Behaviors are usually script, not binary code. (Although they can be written using binary code in C++, that is beyond the scope of this book.) This means that they run more slowly than compiled script. Moreover, they tend to be resource intensive.
- Behaviors are only supported by Internet Explorer 5. This makes them useful only in those places where you can exclusively restrict your browser market.
- It is easy enough to follow a browser link back to its source and view the browser code. However, there are ways that you can obfuscate the code, rendering it unintelligible to a human being even though it can be read by the computer.

Behavior Elements and Attributes

A behavior is an ActiveX component. Actually, this is a little misleading. When you install Internet Explorer on your system, one of the elements that is also added is the `MSScript.dll` component. This particular library handles all of the scripting on your machine, from the VBScript and JavaScript found in HTML code to the scripting performed within XSL to the Windows Scripting architecture. Not surprisingly, it also handles behaviors.

When a behavior is called from a CSS style or class, the browser retrieves the corresponding HTC file, which is, in fact, a native XML file with a HTC extension. The script engine then interprets the XML to help it create an interface, and temporarily defines the interface as a COM object. This means that working with a behavior, from the standpoint of the browser, is remarkably similar to working with an ActiveX control or Java class.

What this means from the standpoint of the XML code is that its primary purpose is to define both the interface and the implementation of the interface for the behavior. It does this by working within the `PUBLIC:` namespace. This (reserved) namespace gets interpreted by the script engine to define specific properties, methods, events, and event sinks (also known as *attachments*) that are available to the browser. (Since the only consumer of HTCs is the browser, Microsoft didn't include a namespace declaration at the root of the document.) Table 7.1 discusses the elements used to define an HTC, while Table 7.2 discusses the attributes.

TABLE 7.1: HTC Interface Elements

Element Name	Associated attribute(s)	Description
`<PUBLIC: COMPONENT/>`	`NAME, URN, ID`	Determines the containing node for a behavior.
`<PUBLIC: PROPERTY/>`	`NAME, GET, PUT, INTERNAL_NAME, VALUE, PERSIST`	Defines a public property for the behavior. Can correspond to an attribute in the element declaration tag of the HTML source.

TABLE 7.1: HTC Interface Elements *(continued)*

Element Name	Associated attribute(s)	Description
<GET/>	InternalNAME	Declares the function called when a property is retrieved via code in the host document. If only PUT is included as a child of <PUBLIC:PROPERTY>, the property is write-only. Element is optional.
<PUT/>	InternalNAME	Declares the function called when a property is retrieved via code in the host document. If only GET is included as a child of <PUBLIC:PROPERTY>, the property is read-only. Element is optional.
<PUBLIC: METHOD/>	NAME	Declares the name of a public method of the behavior. If a function or subroutine is defined but not declared, then it is only accessible from within the behavior itself, not from the host document.
<PUBLIC: ATTACH/>	EVENT, ONEVENT, FOR, ID	Creates an event sink. Whenever the event specified in the EVENT attribute occurs in the host document, the behavior calls the function given in the ONEVENT attribute. This is useful for intercepting mouse, keyboard, creation, and destruction events.
<PUBLIC: EVENT/>	NAME, ID	Defines an event for the behavior. Whenever this event is fired, the host document receives the event and can act on it if a handle for the event exists.
<SCRIPT>	LANGUAGE, SRC	Defines a script block within the behavior, using the specified language. The <SCRIPT> block, in turn, can be loaded from an external file, making it suitable for loading code from a common code base. (Note that because the HTC is itself an XML document, you should get into the habit of placing the contents of the SCRIPT element within a <![CDATA[ ]]> section.)
Other elements	Various	So long as you respect the integrity of the XML structure, you can include any HTML code within the component, including XML data islands. (Examples of this are shown in subsequent sections.)

TABLE 7.2: HTC Interface Attributes

Element Name	Associated attribute(s)	Description
NAME	NMToken	Identifies the name of the property, method, or event specified in the appropriate tags. (Note that in the host document the name is the attribute name for the calling element.)

TABLE 7.2: HTC Interface Attributes *(continued)*

Element Name	Associated attribute(s)	Description
InternalNAME	NMToken	Comprises the name that is used within the document to define a property or method. It's not exposed as a public interface.
VALUE	Any	Sets the initial value of a property if not otherwise specified in the host document. (Note that GET overrides VALUE.)
EVENT	onContentReady	Indicates the name of the event to attach to the behavior. When the behavior receives this event from the host document, it fires the function listed in ONEVENT.
ONEVENT	initialize()	Comprises the function that's called when the event specified in <ATTACH/> takes place in the host document.
ID	NMToken	Uniquely identifies the component, property, method, or event within the component itself. This is analogous to a DHTML id.
LANGUAGE	JavaScript (default), VBScript, PerlScript	Indicates the language used to evaluate the script block.
SRC	URL	Specifies an optional URL that points to the source of the <SCRIPT> tag. (Note that any elements defined in the <SCRIPT> tags override the same methods and other elements defined in the SRC document.)
GET	FunctionName	Specifies the name of the function that returns a result when a property is queried. This is the same as the NAME property for the GET element.
PUT	FunctionName	Specifies the name of the function that receives a property value when it is assigned in the host document.
PERSIST	true|false	Ensures that the property persists its value. (In IE5, you can persist a page from code.)
URN	Any valid URN	Uniquely identifies the component.
FOR	document|element|window	Identifies the source of events for an ATTACH element.

The clock example described in the previous section actually serves as a good introduction to behaviors as it provides examples of nearly all of the elements within the behavior vocabulary. Listing 7.9 shows an alarm clock behavior. You can set the style of the digital clock's display in either *hour:minute* or *hour:minute:second* format. You can also specify a time in the appropriate format for when you want an alarm event to fire; when this event fires, you can catch it in your HTML document with an onalarm event handler.

Listing 7.9: The Digital Clock Behavior (*Code7-9.Dclock.htc*)

```
<PUBLIC:COMPONENT>

   <!-- format describes whether the time is given in the
        form HH:MM AM (short) or HH:MM:SS AM (long). The
        default is long. The sub-elements GET and PUT
        handle sending the contents of the format property
        back to the calling document and receiving content
        from that document through attributes or DOM
        properties -->
   <PUBLIC:PROPERTY NAME="format">
      <GET internalNAME="get_format"/>
      <PUT internalNAME="put_format"/>
   </PUBLIC:PROPERTY>

   <!-- alarmTime is the time, expressed in long notation,
   when the onAlarm event is fired.  You can disable
   the alarm by setting the AlarmTime to an empty
   string (""), or not listing it in the attributes
   of the calling element. -->

   <PUBLIC:PROPERTY NAME="alarmTime">
      <GET internalNAME="get_AlarmTime"/>
      <PUT internalNAME="put_AlarmTime"/>
   </PUBLIC:PROPERTY>

   <!-- currentTime is a read-only property that returns
   the time formatted in the current format. -->
   <PUBLIC:PROPERTY NAME="currentTime">
      <GET internalNAME="get_CurrentTime"/>
   </PUBLIC:PROPERTY>

   <!-- updateClock repaints the clock. It is normally
   called automatically once a second, but it can be called
   manually as well to force a change in
   format or alarmTime. -->

   <PUBLIC:METHOD NAME="updateClock"/>
   <!-- onContentReady is automatically called
   once the behavior has been fully instantiated. In this
   case, the behavior will start the clock running once all
   the code is in memory. -->

   <PUBLIC:ATTACH EVENT="oncontentready" ONEVENT="startClock()"/>
```

```
   <PUBLIC:METHOD NAME="resize"/>

   <PUBLIC:ATTACH EVENT="onresize" FOR="window" ONEVENT="resize()"/>

    <!-- onAlarm is an event that the behavior
   itself generates, whenever the time is the same as the
   alarmTime.   -->
   <PUBLIC:EVENT NAME="onalarm" ID="alarmID"/>

   <!-- onClockStart is fired once the clock
   itself has begun.   -->
   <PUBLIC:EVENT NAME="onclockstart" ID="clockStartID"/>

   <!-- Note that the script element is not a public
element - it does not expose any interfaces to the outside
container. Further note the syntax of the CDATA section -
the script block here will automatically interpret anything
within it as a script, so you need to comment out the
<![CDATA[ ]]> declaration with a VBScript comment. -->

   <script language="VBScript">'<![CDATA[
dim m_format
dim m_timeID
dim m_alarmTime
function get_format()
   if m_format="" then
      m_format="long"
   end if
   get_format=m_format
end function

function put_format(pFormat)
   m_format=pFormat
end function

function get_AlarmTime()
   get_AlarmTime=m_alarmTime
end function

function put_AlarmTime(pAlarmTime)
   m_AlarmTime=pAlarmTime
end function

function get_CurrentTime()
   get_CurrentTime=me.innerHTML
end function
```

```
function startClock()
   m_fontSize=me.currentStyle.fontSize
   m_fontSize=left(m_fontSize,len(m_fontSize)-2)
   if me.id="" then
      me.id=document.uniqueID
   end if   m_timeID=setInterval(me.id+".updateClock",1000,_
         "VBScript")
   set evt=CreateEventObject()
   clockStartID.fire evt
end function

function updateClock()
   dim tm
   dim subTime
   dim formattedTime
   tm=split(now," ")
   select case m_format
      case "long"
         formattedTime=tm(1)+" "+tm(2)
      case "short"
         subTime=split(tm(1),":")
         formattedTime=subTime(0)+":"+subTime(1)+" "+tm(2)
   end select
   me.innerHTML=formattedTime
   if m_AlarmTime=tm(1)+" "+tm(2) then
      me.style.color="blue"
      set evt=CreateEventObject()
      alarmID.fire evt
   end if
end function

function resize()
   dim ratio
   ratio=window.event.clientX/480
   me.style.fontSize=m_fontSize*ratio
end function

']]>  </script>
</PUBLIC:COMPONENT>
```

The component description is broken into two primary pieces in the preceding example, although the division is purely arbitrary. The top portion contains the interface declarations, specifically the interface defining the `format`, `alarmTime`, and `currentTime` properties, the `startClock` method, the `onContentReady` attachment, and the `onAlarm` event.

Behavior Properties

When a Web page is first instantiated, the behavior parser reads the attributes from the page and passes them to the properties set up in the behavior. If the `<PUBLIC:PROPERTY>` tag has a `<PUT>` child, then the method specified by that child in its `internalName` attribute is called, and the attribute value from the calling document gets passed as a parameter. Consider the following sample:

```
<clock format="long" alarmTime="5:00:00 PM"/>
```

In the document calling the behavior, if you have a tag like this preceding example, then when the behavior parser creates the behavior, it checks to see the following:

- Whether a `<PUBLIC:PROPERTY NAME="format">` tag exists. This tag means that the `format` attribute specified in the `<clock>` tag belongs to this behavior.
- Whether the `PROPERTY` tag includes a `PUT` child element. If so, then the parser calls the function specified by the `internalName` (for `format`, the function is `put_format`), passing the value (`long`) as a parameter. Notice that the `put_format()` function has a placeholder parameter called `pFormat`, similar to a Visual Basic `property` assignment. In this particular case, the values of the HTML attributes are assigned to local variables as well (`m_format` and `m_alarmTime`, respectively).

  On the other hand, if no `PUT` element is found, then the property's value is automatically assigned to a variable with the same property name (i.e., it would be a variable entitled `format` in this example). In general, it is better to use `PUT` and `GET` for property declarations rather than declaring the property value directly, as it makes it easier to validate the data. It also makes it easier to initialize data or to change the UI in response to a user change.

The `PUT` and `GET` tags serve a purpose similar to `Property Let/Set` and `Property Get` in Visual Basic: They assume that in most cases public properties actually change some aspect of the component—the user interface, the data content, or the events that the object reacts to.

TIP Even if you don't think you'll need to change anything on the basis of a property change, you should get into the habit of using `GET` and `PUT` and keeping the results in a local (private) variable.

TIP If you want to make your property read-only, include only a `GET` tag but not a `PUT` tag. This technique is especially useful when the information being returned is derived from some source (such as the `currentTime` property being derived in the preceding example from the `innerHTML` of the element).

WARNING On the other hand, be careful about using just a PUT tag or attribute without a corresponding GET. This makes the property write-only: You can change it, but you can't read it.

Behavior Methods and Attachments

The <PUBLIC:METHOD> element defines a public method in the component. METHOD has a required NAME property, which is the name of the function as it is seen to the outside world. METHOD also has a potential INTERNALNAME property, which gives the name that the function is referred to within the component itself; this defaults to the NAME as well if it isn't otherwise provided.

The principal reason for an Internal Name is to avoid naming conflicts with potential functions that have already been defined by the scripting language. For example, if you have a method called Format and you are using Visual Basic as a scripting language, the parser generates an error since Format is already a predefined function in VB. However, setting the internalName to _Format and keeping the name attribute as Format will get around this problem, as in the following example:

```
<PUBLIC:METHOD NAME="Format" INTERNALNAME="_Format"/>
<script language="VBScript">
   function _Format(expr,formatStr)
      '… This formats an expression
   end function
</script>
```

Note that unlike more conventional COM interfaces, the parameters for the method call are not contained in the declaration. You can still pass parameters, of course, but you need to be aware of the fact that anyone who uses your tools will need to have some form of documentation indicating what the parameters are.

Attachments can seem a little confusing at first, but they are the engines that make behaviors work, so it's important to be familiar with them. To better understand attachments, it's worth looking at the way that events work within Internet Explorer. When you click on an element with the mouse, type a character on the keyboard, gain or lose the focus, or perform nearly any other action, you generate an event within the browser. However, in order to process that event, you need to have an event sink within your component; this sink notifies the browser that the component should be told when the event occurs.

Sinks, or attachments, can trap any event coming from one of three sources: the element that the behavior is attached to, the document that holds this element, or the window that the document is in. This source is specified using the FOR attribute of the <PUBLIC:ATTACH/> element and can hold the value of element, document, and window. The fact that nearly all of the events within a browser pass through one of these three objects effectively means that an HTC component can act on almost any event that might take place.

For one example of a sink, consider the attachment for the `onContentReady` event. This event is automatically fired by an element when all of the HTML within it has been loaded and initialized, and it is typically the one that you will want to sink in order to initialize a behavior. In the code in Listing 7.9, the `onContentReady` attachment calls the `startClock()` method within the script, as the following sample demonstrates:

```
<PUBLIC:ATTACH EVENT="oncontentready" ONEVENT="startClock()"/>
<SCRIPT language="VBScript">
' .. Other code

function startClock()
   m_fontSize=me.currentStyle.fontSize
   m_fontSize=left(m_fontSize,len(m_fontSize)-2)
   if me.id="" then
      me.id=document.uniqueID
   end if
   m_timeID=setInterval(me.id+".updateClock",1000,_
         "VBScript")
end function

</SCRIPT>
```

This function, in turn, performs some initialization procedures (in this case, retrieving the font size of the clock for use in the `resize` function, described later in this section). It also calls the `setInterval` method, which is a window method from the DOM that executes the statement given as the first parameter once every 1,000 milliseconds (the second parameter), using VBScript as the executing language (the third parameter).

Before going on, I will explain the first expression in the `setInterval` statement, as it is far from obvious what is happening there, and that points out the complicated activity going on beneath the surface of an apparently simple behavior. `setInterval` and its counterpart `set-Timeout` are examples of *forking methods*. In essence, what they do is schedule an event to occur after a certain predefined period—`setTimeout` performing the action once and then dying, and `setInterval` calling it repeatedly until being explicitly turned off.

However, since you don't want to hold up everything else while waiting for the interval to complete, the browser actually launches the specified action as a completely separate thread. This thread has no knowledge of the current thread, can't work with any currently defined variables, and is essentially asynchronous. Thus, in order to tell the browser which specific element called the action, you need to pass the `id` of the element as part of the expression being evaluated. The following code snippet checks to see whether the element that the behavior is attached to has been defined with a specific `id`:

```
if me.id="" then
    me.id=document.uniqueID
end if
```

The behavior inherits the `id` if that is the case; otherwise, its `id` is blank. The `uniqueID` method is extraordinarily useful in this circumstance because it generates `id`s that are unique from anything currently defined. Once the `id` is generated, it is assigned to the instance variable and becomes the name by which the element is referred from then on.

Attachments can, as explained previously, come from events other than those acting on the element itself. For example, the clock discussed in a previous example is set up so that if the browser is resized the font size of the clock itself is enlarged or reduced accordingly. To do this, it creates an event sink for the `onresize` event, which is associated with the window object, as the following example demonstrates:

```
<PUBLIC:ATTACH EVENT="onresize" FOR="window" ONEVENT="resize()"/>

<script language="VBScript">
' .. Other code

function resize()
   dim ratio
   ratio=window.event.clientX/480
   me.style.fontSize=m_fontSize*ratio
end function
</script>
```

One benefit of attachments is that when they call the function given in the `ONEVENT` attribute, the `window.event` object has automatically been set for that event. Thus, in this case, the `window.event.clientX` will contain the position of the mouse cursor's horizontal position at the time the `onresize` event was called. As `resize` is called whenever the user clicks and drags on the right-hand tab, this action should fairly closely approximate the width of the window.

Events

Just as attachments are event sinks, the `<PUBLIC:EVENT>` tag defines an event source. For example, one feature of any clock is its ability to raise an alarm when a certain time is reached. This alarm is an event, which can, in turn, be trapped in the calling HTML document through the use of an `onalarm` event handler.

When you define a <PUBLIC:EVENT> tag, you are not creating an event. Instead, think of the element as a launching pad for events or as an event factory. When you need to send an event up to the hosting document, you do the following:

1. Create the <PUBLIC:EVENT> tag. Set its NAME attribute to the name of the event you want to create (for example, NAME="onalarm"), and set its ID to something that uniquely identifies the element (typically, something like ID="alarmID"). This ID now defines the factory; this happens once, when the component is instantiated.
2. When you want to actually launch the event, create an `event object` with the `CreateEventObject` function. This creates a generic object:
   ```
   Set evt=CreateEventObject()
   ```
3. You can attach attributes to the event object with the `setAttribute` method. For example, to include the current time, create a new "`time`" attribute with the current time:
   ```
   setAttribute "time",tm(0)+" " +tm(1)
   ```
4. `Fire` the event with the event factory, specifying the event factory `id` and passing it the newly created event object:
   ```
   alarmID.fire evt
   ```
5. In your calling document, create an event handler to intercept this event, similar to how you'd intercept any other event:
   ```
   <clock alarmTime="3:24:00 PM" format="long"
    onalarm="alert('The time is now
    '+window.event.getAttribute('time');"/>
   ```

NOTE Note that while the event factory is persistent, once you fire an event, that event is consumed and can't be fired again. That's why you need to use `CreateEventObject()` prior to every firing.

Coding with Simple Behaviors

Once you have a behavior defined, coding against that behavior is relatively simple. For example, in the previous alarm clock example, you can take advantage of the fact that a behavior looks like any other HTML element, ActiveX object, or Java applet. The code in Listing 7.10 demonstrates a sample HTML page that uses the `clock` behavior.

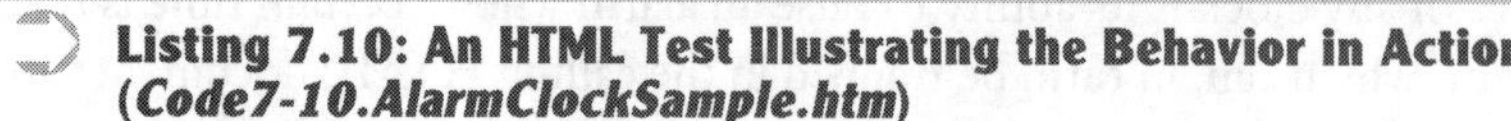

Listing 7.10: An HTML Test Illustrating the Behavior in Action (*Code7-10.AlarmClockSample.htm*)

```
<html>
<head>
<style>
```

```
clock {behavior:url(Code7-8.dclock.htc);font-size:24pt;}
</style>
   <title>Alarm Clock</title>
<script language="VbScript">

function alarmCalled()
   ' This should be called when the alarm is reached.
   alert "Time's Up"
end function

function setAlarm()
   tm=alarmText.value
   ' If the input time has no AM/PM designator, assume it
   'is in the same
   ' meridian as the current time.
   if lcase(right(tm,1)) <> "m" then
      tm=tm+" "+right(clock.currentTime,2)
   end if
   ' Set the alarm time
   clock.alarmTime=tm
   report.innerHTML="Alarm is now set for "+clock.alarmTime
end function

</script>
</head>
<body>
<div class="clock" id="clock" onalarm="alarmCalled()"> Initializing</div>
<div>Enter alarm time as <b>HH:MM:SS AM</b>:<input
 type="text" id="alarmText" value=""/>
<input type="button" onclick="setAlarm" value="Set Alarm"/></div>
<div id="report"/></div>
</body>
</html>
```

The `div` with the `id` of `clock` in this example creates an event handler for the `onalarm` function, but since the `alarmTime` is not explicitly set, the handler isn't called until after the `clock.alarmTime` property is also defined. Note how both the read and write aspects of `alarmTime` are used—writing to set the alarm, reading to get the meridian zone if the candidate alarm string doesn't have an AM or PM at the end.

Additionally, I put a small `Initializing` tag inside of the `<div>` element of `clock`. Behaviors are not necessarily lightning fast, and including placeholders in your text can often spell the difference between an apparently responsive and an unresponsive Web page.

NOTE How about an `onclockupdate` event handler? While it would be easy to add such a thing (you'd actually just place it into the `updateClock` method), the one danger to keep in mind with behaviors is that they are comparatively slow, especially when handling events. You would receive updates once a second; however, you would also notice the responsiveness of the rest of the page begin to lag, especially on slower machines. As a consequence you should use custom events sparingly.

The Dynamic Table Behavior

The *behavior declaration script* is an XML document. However, this is really only a convenience for the behavior parser; it could be written in script just as easily, and, in fact, it used to be for older versions of scriptlets. The fact that it is an XML document does have a number of interesting implications, including that a behavior can integrate XML into its own structure, can readily handle XML introduced as streams, can leverage XML data islands, and can be used in conjunction with XSL to simplify production of code.

In this overall section, I demonstrate a useful behavior that you can leverage from HTML or within XML documents; designed primarily for use in Internet Explorer 5, Dynamic Table is detailed here, beginning with the following definition:

Dynamic Table Is used as both a display and a selection device, and lets you sort each column independently. This is especially useful for displaying records obtained from a database.

As with Dynamic Table, the following two workhorses can prove to be indispensable on most e-commerce sites:

Dynamic Tree Implements low-bandwidth collapsible trees that still provide plenty of power. (Collapsible trees have become a common and well-liked interface element in most applications.)

Dynamic Form Generates an input form that lets you populate a given schema although it does include techniques for validating input as well.

Behaviors are generally useful components. They are easy to write, they don't require working with binary code, and they can often emulate more traditional components but with considerably richer functionality because they can take advantage of the robust IE environment. Hopefully, the examples in this chapter will help you write your own behaviors, tailored to your particular situation.

NOTE The code in this section uses the older Microsoft XSL implementation, as it is the one that has the greatest distribution with browsers.

Determining Data Structure

Tables are a staple of Web pages, but most tables are fairly static entities. With the use of behaviors and a decent XSL script, you can create a table that lets you filter information, change the order of columns, create alternating bands, respond to mouse-over and mouse-click movements, and, in general, more closely resemble programmatic grids than the static tables of yore.

The architecture used in the upcoming example (as well as most of the others in this section) works something like this:

1. The behavior instantiates and reads a property to determine both the data source (either a data island, DOMDocument variable, or external XML stream) and the primary XSL filter.
2. The XML document, in turn, contains a reference to an XML schema. This schema is used principally to pull description and type information about the elements rather than for its structural information. This document is loaded into a larger control XML document that maintains state information for the table.
3. The script applies the XSL transform to the XSL script and inserts the result into the body of the `behavior` element. The XML and XSL documents are retained in memory.
4. The behavior is set up to accept a number of mouse actions through attachments, forwarding these events to subelements within the table to determine the precise course of action.
5. Events are defined on the element rather than on its children. While this necessitates a small amount of internal processing, it also simplifies the number of code objects at play and improves responsiveness.
6. The user can access the data portion of the table, change the data on the fly, and then refresh the table to reflect the changes to the internal data.
7. Finally, a mechanism is constructed to retrieve records that have been selected as an XML document. Additionally, you can set the selection mode; either one item is selected at any given time, multiple items are selected simultaneously, or no selection takes place at all.

TIP

This component, like the others discussed in this section, is self documenting: You can query it to get information about the component's interfaces.

One of the things I've learned over the years is that every time you attempt to make a problem more generic you will also make the application more complex. In the following listing, the Dynamic Table component can work with XML documents without necessarily needing to know the names of specific elements in the document. To do this, it works on the assumption that the information it is displaying consists of a collection of records, each record of which is, in turn, made up of a set of properties, such as the list of employees shown in Listing 7.11.

Listing 7.11: A List of Employees at the Acme Company (*Code7-11.Employees.xml*)

```
<employees xmlns="x-schema:Code7-12.EmployeesSchema.xml">
   <employee>
      <id>101</id>
      <firstName>John</firstName>
      <lastName>Janus</lastName>
      <title>President</title>
      <dateStarted>1997-11-12</dateStarted>
      <salary>324021</salary>
      <department>Administration</department>
   </employee>
   <employee>
      <id>102</id>
      <firstName>Kitara</firstName>
      <lastName>Milleaux</lastName>
      <title>Chief Executive Officer</title>
      <dateStarted>1997-08-12</dateStarted>
      <salary>329215</salary>
      <department>Administration</department>
   </employee>
   <employee>
      <id>103</id>
      <firstName>Shelley</firstName>
      <lastName>Janes</lastName>
      <title>Chief Financial Officer</title>
      <dateStarted>1998-03-16</dateStarted>
      <salary>232768</salary>
      <department>Finance</department>
   </employee>
   <employee>
      <id>104</id>
      <firstName>Marissa</firstName>
      <lastName>Mendez</lastName>
      <title>Chief Technical Officer</title>
      <dateStarted>1998-09-16</dateStarted>
      <salary>242768</salary>
      <department>Information Technologies</department>
   </employee>
   <employee>
      <id>105</id>
      <firstName>Kace</firstName>
```

```
    <lastName>Juriden</lastName>
    <title>Vice President, Marketing</title>
    <dateStarted>1998-11-03</dateStarted>
    <salary>210359</salary>
    <department>Marketing</department>
</employee>
<employee>
    <id>106</id>
    <firstName>James</firstName>
    <lastName>Marsden</lastName>
    <title>Senior Analyst</title>
    <dateStarted>1999-03-16</dateStarted>
    <salary>160204</salary>
    <department>Information Technologies</department>
</employee>
<employee>
    <id>107</id>
    <firstName>Henry</firstName>
    <lastName>Moore</lastName>
    <title>Senior Analyst</title>
    <dateStarted>1998-07-01</dateStarted>
    <salary>192142</salary>
    <department>Information Technologies</department>
</employee>
<employee>
    <id>108</id>
    <firstName>Karen</firstName>
    <lastName>LeBlanc</lastName>
    <title>Analyst</title>
    <dateStarted>1999-03-01</dateStarted>
    <salary>176245</salary>
    <department>Information Technologies</department>
</employee>
<employee>
    <id>109</id>
    <firstName>Cynthia</firstName>
    <lastName>Neville</lastName>
    <title>Marketing Analyst</title>
    <dateStarted>1999-04-07</dateStarted>
    <salary>159259</salary>
    <department>Marketing</department>
</employee>
<employee>
    <id>110</id>
    <firstName>Leonard</firstName>
    <lastName>Capacnik</lastName>
    <title>Creative Director</title>
```

```
    <dateStarted>1999-07-12</dateStarted>
    <salary>101242</salary>
    <department>Marketing</department>
  </employee>
  <employee>
    <id>111</id>
    <firstName>Art</firstName>
    <lastName>Sirtis</lastName>
    <title>Art Director</title>
    <dateStarted>1999-06-01</dateStarted>
    <salary>98552</salary>
    <department>Marketing</department>
  </employee>
  <employee>
    <id>112</id>
    <firstName>Steve</firstName>
    <lastName>Ruddell</lastName>
    <title>Senior Account Manager</title>
    <dateStarted>2000-01-05</dateStarted>
    <salary>125221</salary>
    <department>Marketing</department>
  </employee>
  <employee>
    <id>113</id>
    <firstName>Kiri</firstName>
    <lastName>Tekanewa</lastName>
    <title>Senior Programmer</title>
    <dateStarted>1999-10-04</dateStarted>
    <salary>102582</salary>
    <department>Information Technologies</department>
  </employee>
  <employee>
    <id>114</id>
    <firstName>Kace</firstName>
    <lastName>Moreaux</lastName>
    <title>Programmer</title>
    <dateStarted>2000-02-01</dateStarted>
    <salary>83024</salary>
    <department>Information Technologies</department>
  </employee>
        <employee>
    <id>115</id>
    <firstName>Michael</firstName>
    <lastName>Nesbit</lastName>
    <title>Graphic Designer</title>
    <dateStarted>2000-01-10</dateStarted>
    <salary>65253</salary>
    <department>Information Technologies</department>
```

```
    </employee>
    <employee>
        <id>116</id>
        <firstName>Sean</firstName>
        <lastName>Finnigen</lastName>
        <title>Web Designer</title>
        <dateStarted>2000-02-05</dateStarted>
        <salary>45023</salary>
        <department>Information Technologies</department>
    </employee>
    <employee>
        <id>117</id>
        <firstName>Missy</firstName>
        <lastName>Jerod</lastName>
        <title>Administrative Assistant</title>
        <dateStarted>1999-04-07</dateStarted>
        <salary>52003</salary>
        <department>Administration</department>
    </employee>
    <employee>
        <id>118</id>
        <firstName>Corey</firstName>
        <lastName>Woods</lastName>
        <title>Network Administrator</title>
        <dateStarted>2000-04-02</dateStarted>
        <salary>102225</salary>
        <department>Information Technologies</department>
    </employee>
    <employee>
        <id>119</id>
        <firstName>Severn</firstName>
        <lastName>Malcestis</lastName>
        <title>Public Relations</title>
        <dateStarted>2000-03-01</dateStarted>
        <salary>76224</salary>
        <department>Marketing</department>
    </employee>
    <employee>
        <id>120</id>
        <firstName>Rick</firstName>
        <lastName>Frain</lastName>
        <title>3D Artist</title>
        <dateStarted>2000-03-06</dateStarted>
        <salary>55224</salary>
        <department>Information Technologies</department>
    </employee>
</employees>
```

This particular structure is built exclusively around elements without attributes. While there are advantages to using attribute-driven record sets, you can transform an attribute-based XML structure to an element-based XML structure quite easily with a simple XSL transform, as in Listing 7.12.

Listing 7.12: The Attributes-to-Elements Transformation (*Code7-12.AttribToElem.xsl*)

```
<xsl:style sheet xmlns:xsl="http://www.w3.org/TR/WD-xsl">
   <xsl:template match="/">
       <xsl:apply-templates select="*"/>
   </xsl:template>
   <xsl:template match="*">
       <xsl:element>
       <xsl:apply-templates select="*|@*"/>
       </xsl:element>
   </xsl:template>
   <xsl:template match="@*">
       <xsl:element>
       <xsl:value-of/>
       </xsl:element>
   </xsl:template>
</xsl:style sheet>
```

This listing would thus transform the original employee list into the following code:

```
<?xml:style sheet type="text/xsl" href="AttribToElem.xsl"?>
<employees>
   <employee
      id="101"
      firstName="John"
      lastName="Janus"
      title="President"
      dateStarted="1997-11-12"
      salary="324021"
      department="Administration"
      />
   <employee
      id="102"
      firstName="Kitara"
      lastName="Milleaux"
      title="Chief Executive Office"
      dateStarted="1997-08-12"
      salary="329215"
      department="Administration"
      />
   <employee
      id="103"
      firstName="Shelley"
```

```
        lastName="Janes"
        title="Chief Financial Officer"
        dateStarted="1998-03-16"
        salary="232768"
        department="Finance"
        />
    <!-- More employee records. -->
</employees>
```

One of the keys to making interface elements is to remember that while XML structures are designed to be legible to humans, they aren't necessarily sympathetic to humans. When I look at a table, I like to read the labels formatted in a way I expect—words capitalized and spaced, with rollover hints to give me some idea about what a given column represents, and so forth.

In addition to the cosmetic issues of user interfaces, working from a schema provides another benefit, deriving from the question "What happens if you have a table but no data?" For a specific table, you know the corresponding table headers, but for a generic routine, an empty data set means you have no idea what headers you need to apply. With a schema, however, you can query the structure to make some intelligent guesses about what the data is supposed to look like, even without specific data at hand.

TIP

Here's another case where you can see a parallel between traditional programming classes and XML schemas. Both essentially are templates for generating new objects and should be relied on for that task rather than for copying existing objects.

The schema for the `Employees` collection is straightforward, although I have taken the liberty of incorporating by the `<TITLE>` and `<BODY>` tags discussed in the last chapter into the schema itself, as shown in Listing 7.13.

Listing 7.13: The Schema for Defining and Describing the *Employees.xml* Document (*Code7-13.EmployeesSchema.xml*)

```
<Schema name = "Code7-12.EmployeesSchema.xml"
    xmlns = "urn:schemas-microsoft-com:xml-data"
    xmlns:dt = "urn:schemas-microsoft-com:datatypes">
    <ElementType name="id" content="textOnly" dt:type="string">
          <description>
          <title>Employee ID</title>
          <body>This identifies the employee.</body>
       </description>
    </ElementType>
    <ElementType name="firstName" content="textOnly" dt:type="string">
          <description>
          <title>First Name</title>
          <body>The first, or given, name of the employee.</body>
       </description>
```

```
</ElementType>
<ElementType name="lastName" content="textOnly" dt:type="string">
      <description>
      <title>Last Name</title>
      <body>The last, or family, name of the employee.</body>
   </description>
</ElementType>
<ElementType name="title" content="textOnly" dt:type="string">
      <description>
      <title>Title</title>
      <body>The job title of the employee.</body>
   </description>
</ElementType>
<ElementType name="dateStarted" content="textOnly" dt:type="date">
      <description>
      <title>Date Started</title>
      <body>The date that the employee started with the company.</body>
   </description>
</ElementType>
<ElementType name="salary" content="textOnly" dt:type="fixed.14.4">
      <description>
      <title>Salary</title>
      <body>The annual salary of the employee.</body>
   </description>
</ElementType>
<ElementType name="department" content="textOnly" dt:type="string">
      <description>
      <title>Department</title>
      <body>The department the employee belongs to.</body>
   </description>
</ElementType>
<ElementType name="employee" content="eltOnly" model="closed">
      <description>
      <title>Employee</title>
      <body>The employee record.</body>
   </description>
     <element type="id" minOccurs="1" maxOccurs="1"/>
     <element type="firstName" minOccurs="1" maxOccurs="1"/>
     <element type="lastName" minOccurs="1" maxOccurs="1"/>
     <element type="title" minOccurs="1" maxOccurs="1"/>
     <element type="dateStarted" minOccurs="1" maxOccurs="1"/>
     <element type="salary" minOccurs="1" maxOccurs="1"/>
     <element type="department" minOccurs="1" maxOccurs="1"/>
</ElementType>
<ElementType name="employees" content="eltOnly" model="closed">
      <description>
      <title>Employees</title>
```

```
        <body>The employee recordset</body>
      </description>
        <element type="employee" minOccurs="0" maxOccurs="*"/>
    </ElementType>
</Schema>
```

If your XML data contains a collection/object/property architecture at deep levels, you may want to extract the tree from just the collection node, although structures with deeper data than this typically should either be decomposed into subtables or be transformed into flatter structures for output purposes. The one advantage of such an approach is that it is usually the form that (differences between property attributes and property elements aside) most XML database servers now generate because it best represents the flat view structure so common in SQL recordsets.

Creating Envelopes

Once you have normalized your data and created a schema, you can begin the fun work of building an XSL transform...almost. While the newer XML parser allows for parameterization, the older parser (the one found in all IE5 browsers) doesn't have as convenient a mechanism. While you can fall back on entities, an easier solution to work with is to build what's called an *envelope*. The envelope contains crucial information for use by the XSL parser about the particular instance of data, and it also holds the data set as a subtree.

In this section's example, the envelope holds the following three critical sets of information:

IDColumn Uniquely identifies a row in the table and corresponds to a primary key in a database table.

Column Set Tells you which columns appear in what order. (Ideally, as the Web designer, you want to specify the columns in a specific order, and only those columns that are of interest to you.)

Styles Lets you incorporate your own behaviors on the elements or the interactions. (I have been accused of having absolutely no taste when it comes to colors. Partially because of this, I incorporated a mechanism for letting the developer designate the styles used for everything in the table from row patterns and column headers to rollover and click effects.)

The envelope for the table is actually contained as part of the Table behavior definition, but, in practice, it looks something like Listing 7.14.

Listing 7.14: The Envelope for the Table Behavior (*code7-14.xml*)

```
<document>
   <head>
      <idColumn>id</idColumn>
      <columns/>
```

```
        <styles>
            <!-- style of the table element -->
            <style id="table">cursor:hand;</style>
            <!-- style of each header cell -->
            <style id="header">
background-color:blue;color:white;border:outset
3pt blue;</style>
            <!-- style of each odd row in the table's body -->
            <style id="row1">background-color:#C0C0FF</style>
            <!-- style of each even row in the table's body-->
            <style id="row2">background-color:white</style>
            <!-- style of a header is pressed -->
            <style id="depressed">border:inset 3pt blue;</style>
            <!-- style of a row when selected -->
            <style id="selected">color:blue;font-weight:bold;</style>
            <!-- style of a row when rolled over -->
            <style id="highlighted">text-decoration:underline;</style>
        </styles>
    </head>
    <body>
    <!-- The actual data (such as the contents of
        Listing7-11.Employees.xml) goes here. -->
    </body>
</document>
```

The `style` elements contain an `id` that corresponds to elements created by the XSL structure. If you incorporate your own XSL structures, you should either change the names of the styles to match each of the styles in the transformed outlets or use the previously listed styles in your XSL. The text of the `style` elements are CSS rules as you would see in a <STYLE> block of an HTML document. Note that you can incorporate behaviors into each of these styles if you so choose, although you certainly should experiment to make sure that the interactions with the existing code work.

The behavior is responsible for adding the data set you want to display into the envelope. It also exposes the styles so that you can modify them from script once the browser instantiates the behavior, giving you even more flexibility with your user interface.

Transforming Your Data

The purpose of the XSL structure is to lay out the table and to redraw it as necessary to accommodate changes in data or style. It assigns CSS classes to specific elements but doesn't deal with any dynamic code at all; this is all handed via event attachments in the behavior. The transform is shown in Listing 7.15.

Listing 7.15: An XSL Filter to Create a Dynamic Table (*Code7-15.TableFilter.xsl*; also *DynamicTable.xsl*)

```
<xsl:stylesheet xmlns:xsl="http://www.w3.org/TR/WD-xsl" language="VBScript">
   <xsl:script language="VBScript"><![CDATA[
   ' Retrieve the schema and store it in a global variable
   set schema=me.selectSingleNode("//body/*"_
         ).definition.ownerDocument
   ' This retrieves the id column name
   idName=me.selectSingleNode("//head/idColumn").text
   ' This initializes the row id
   id=""
   ' This initializes the row count
   ct=-1

   ' updateCount() is used to determine whether a given
   ' row is even or odd
   function updateCount()
      ct=ct+1
      updateCount=ct
   end function

   ' getColumnName will return the friendly name of the
   ' column corresponding to the current cell in
   ' the table
   function getColumnName()
      colName=me.text
      set schemaDescrNode=schema.selectSingleNode(_
       "//ElementType[@name='"+colName+_
       "']/description")
      getColumnName=schemaDescrNode.selectSingleNode(_
         "title").text
   end function

   ' getColumnDescription returns the description
   ' of the current column when users roll over a column
   ' header
   function getColumnDescription()
      colName=me.text
      set schemaDescrNode=schema.selectSingleNode(_
         "//ElementType[@name='"+colName+"']/description")
      getColumnDescription=_
         schemaDescrNode.selectSingleNode(_
         "body").text
   end function
```

```
' getRowID returns the id of the row that the current
' cell is from. This id is the same as shown in the
' element's IDColumn element.
function getRowID()
   id=me.selectSingleNode(idName).text
   getRowID=id
end function

' getAlignment returns the alignment of elements within
' the table, based upon the datatype of the cell (for
' example, a string aligns left, while a date or number
' aligns to the right.
function getAlignment(pID)
   set node=getCurrentNode(pID)
   select case node.datatype
      case "string"
         getAlignment="left"
      case "date"
         getAlignment="right"
      case else
         getAlignment="right"
   end select
end function

' getCurrentNode retrieves the node of the source XML
' document corresponding to the currrent row. In the
' case of the employees.xml sample, that row is the
' <employees> node.
function getCurrentNode(pID)
   set getCurrentNode=
me.selectSingleNode("//body/*/*["+idName+"='"+pID+"'
]/"+ me.text)
end function

' This formats the data based upon its data type.
' The fixed.14.4 notation is assumed in this case to
' correspond to currencies, so is formatted with the
' system currency designator. If you want to apply
' custom formatting, you should subclass this routine.
function getFormattedValue(pID)
   dim curValue
   set node=getCurrentNode(pID)
   tValue=node.nodeTypedValue
   select case node.dataType
      case "fixed.14.4"
         curValue=FormatCurrency(tValue)
      case "string"
```

```
            curValue=tValue
         case "date"
            curValue=FormatDateTime(tValue,vbShortDate)
         case else
            curValue=FormatNumber(tValue)
      end select
      getFormattedValue=curValue
   end function

]]>   </xsl:script>
   <xsl:template match="/">
      <xsl:apply-templates select="document"/>
   </xsl:template>

   <!-- Match the envelope document node,
        build the table, then apply appropriate
        style sheets from the envelope -->
   <xsl:template match="document">
<table cellpadding="5" cellspacing="0" class="table">
<!-- build the style sheet and populate it -->
<style>
<xsl:for-each select="//head/styles/style">
   .<xsl:value-of select="@id"/> {<xsl:value-of/>}
</xsl:for-each>
</style>
<!-- build the header cells, including setting class, title
     and id tags for each cell.  The id is the same as the
     property nodeName (i.e., "firstName","lastName",etc.
     All header cells have a class of "header". -->
<tr><xsl:for-each select="//head/columns/column">
<th>
      <xsl:attribute name="id"><xsl:value-of/></xsl:attribute>
      <xsl:attribute name="class">header</xsl:attribute>
      <xsl:attribut
   name="title"><xsl:eval>getColumnDescription</xsl:eval>
      </xsl:attribute>
<xsl:eval>getColumnName()</xsl:eval>
</th>
</xsl:for-each>
</tr>
<!-- Call to build the body of the table -->
<xsl:apply-templates select="body/*"/>
</table>
   </xsl:template>

   <!-- The body of the table contains each of the
        actual rows of the table. -->
```

```
      <xsl:template match="body/*">
         <!-- Retrieve each row and assign it id
              and class. Classes alternate "row1" and
              "row2" to give the striped effect -->
         <xsl:for-each select="*" id="order">
         <tr>
         <xsl:attribute name="id"><xsl:eval>getRowID</xsl:eval></xsl:attribute>
         <xsl:attribute name="class">
         <xsl:choose>
            <xsl:when expr="updateCount mod 2 = 0">row1</xsl:when>
            <xsl:otherwise>row2</xsl:otherwise>
         </xsl:choose>
         </xsl:attribute>
      <!-- Using the column names in the envelope
           retrieve each column cell in the order given,
           assign it a tag corresponding to the column name,
           and place the aligned and formatted value of
           the row and column into the appropriate cell. -->
      <xsl:for-each select="//head/columns/column">
         <td>
         <xsl:attribute name="title">
             <xsl:eval>getColumnName</xsl:eval>
         </xsl:attribute>
         <xsl:attribute name="align">
             <xsl:eval>getAlignment(id)</xsl:eval>
         </xsl:attribute>
         <xsl:eval>getFormattedValue(id)</xsl:eval></td>
      </xsl:for-each>
         </tr>
         </xsl:for-each>
      </xsl:template>

   </xsl:stylesheet>
```

There's a fair amount of indirection in this example. In order to specify that the columns be drawn in a specific order, you can't just select the children elements of the `<employee>` node. Instead, you need to retrieve the names of the columns from the envelope and then iterate through that list and reference the XML structure in that manner. Because you're essentially breaking the normal parent/child relationship, you actually need to know the `id` of the row in order to locate it uniquely, which is the primary reason the `id` exists (although it also helps identify selections, as discussed in the upcoming "Writing the Behavior" section).

Once again, notice in the preceding script that the XSL transform is not concerned with the visual appearance of the resulting HTML, other than at the gross structural level of building the table. The eye candy is passed on to CSS through the use of CSS classes; they determine such factors as colors, font size, borders, backgrounds, and so forth. Indeed, even without CSS, this transform would create a credible table that would work on nearly any browser (as shown in Chapter 8, "XML and ASP," where a nearly identical script is used to build server-side tables).

TIP Separate the structural and visual aspects of your outputs into XSL and CSS, respectively. This lets you more easily modify the visual appearance of the behavior without forcing you to change its underlying structure. Put another way, you should always *decouple* the structural and decorative aspects of your XML. (More and more, this decoupling should be a familiar aspect of XML to you.)

Writing the Behavior

The table behavior looks fairly imposing (okay, it *is* fairly imposing), but the principle behind it is similar to the smaller clock behavior discussed earlier in this chapter. The behavior is broken up into the following three distinct sections:

Interface Declaration Defines public properties, methods, events, and attachments. This part tells the behavior component what specifically is in the interface and is independent of any specific implementation.

Functional Implementation Implements the various interface methods and properties, associates attachments with event handlers, and fires events. This is typically contained in a `<script>` node (which is not technically part of the behavior, by the way).

XML Data Islands Contain internal XML and XSL style sheets and are shown here primarily to demonstrate how XML can be stored natively within a behavior.

NOTE The comments that are contained within the `DESCRIPTION` attribute describe the function of each interface element, not just for internal documentation but also for use by one of the interface methods, `getInfo()`. In essence, the behavior contains a second behavior used to describe itself.

As you'll soon notice, Listing 7.16 is a doozie. It's been broken up into six different chunks that are interspersed between here and the end of this section, providing for a more manageable, understandable discussion. (After all, several smaller bites are easier to swallow than one giant one!)

Listing 7.16: The Dynamic Table Behavior, Showing the Public Interfaces (*Code7-16.DynamicTable.htc*; also *DynamicTable.htc*)

```
<PUBLIC:COMPONENT ID="DynamicTable" name="DynamicTable">
  <DESCRIPTION>
The Dynamic Table Component Copyright 2000 Cagle
 Communications. For more information about this component,
```

```
please visit the VBXML Web site at
http://www.vbxml.com/cagle.
  </DESCRIPTION>

  <PUBLIC:PROPERTY name="XMLSource">
     <GET internalName="getXMLSource"/>
     <PUT internalName="putXMLSource"/>
     <DESCRIPTION>This contains the location of the xml
source. To set this to a url (say for the file
"resources/myDoc.xml"), use
XMLSource="url(resources/myDoc.xml)". To use a data
island, just pass the id of that island.
     </DESCRIPTION>
  </PUBLIC:PROPERTY>

  <PUBLIC:PROPERTY name="XSLSource">
     <GET internalName="getXSLSource" value="url(DynamicTable.xsl)"/>
     <PUT internalName="putXSLSource"/>
     <DESCRIPTION>This contains the location of the xsl
source. To set this to a URL (say, for the file
"resources/transform.xsl"), use
XSLSource="url(resources/myDoc.xml)". To use a data
island, just pass the id of that island.</DESCRIPTION>
  </PUBLIC:PROPERTY>

  <PUBLIC:PROPERTY name="XMLDocument">
     <GET internalName="getXMLDocument"/>
     <DESCRIPTION>Retrieves an instance of the full XML
document, which can be modified accordingly. Note that
once a change is made to the document, you can use the
Refresh method to update the table.</DESCRIPTION>
  </PUBLIC:PROPERTY>

  <PUBLIC:PROPERTY name="XSLDocument">
     <GET internalName="getXSLDocument"/>
     <DESCRIPTION>Retrieves an instance of the XSL
transformation document, which can be modified
accordingly. Note that once a change is made to the
document, you can use the Refresh method to update the
table. </DESCRIPTION>
  </PUBLIC:PROPERTY>

  <PUBLIC:PROPERTY name="Columns">
     <GET internalName="getColumns"/>
     <PUT internalName="putColumns"/>
     <DESCRIPTION>Sets or retrieves the columns to be used
```

```
in the table. To set the columns you wish to display,
pass the names of each element that you want to make into
a column, separated by a space. For example,
columns="firstName lastName dateOfBirth occupation" would
display as columns those elements that have the names
given, in that order. Note that if columns is not
included, the parser will either attempt to read the
document schema or, if that is unsuccessful, will read
the first record to display the columns.
     </DESCRIPTION>
  </PUBLIC:PROPERTY>

  <PUBLIC:PROPERTY name="IDColumn">
     <GET internalName="getIDColumn"/>
     <PUT internalName="putIDColumn"/>
     <DESCRIPTION>Sets or retrieves the column name used
to uniquely identify a given record. If column name is
missing, the first column is assumed to be the ID column.
     </DESCRIPTION>
  </PUBLIC:PROPERTY>

  <PUBLIC:PROPERTY name="SelectMode">
     <GET internalName="getSelectMode"/>
     <PUT internalName="putSelectMode"/>
     <DESCRIPTION>Determines whether the table lets you
select one item exclusively (SelectMode="option"), lets
you select multiple items simultaneously
(SelectMode="multiple"), or turns off selection altogether
(SelectMode="none"). If the SelectMode is turned off,
rollovers will be disabled as well.
     </DESCRIPTION>
  </PUBLIC:PROPERTY>

  <PUBLIC:PROPERTY name="SelectedRecords">
     <GET internalName="getSelectedRecords"/>
     <DESCRIPTION>This returns an XML structure containing
all of the records that are currently selected. Note that
this is a read-only property, and changing these records
will not change the component.
     </DESCRIPTION>
  </PUBLIC:PROPERTY>
        <style id="table">cursor:hand;</style>
        <style id="header">background
-color:blue;color:white;border:outset 3pt blue;</style>
        <style id="row1">background-color:#C0C0FF</style>
        <style id="row2">background-color:white</style>
```

```
        <style id="depressed">border:inset 3pt blue;</style>
        <style id="selected">color:blue;font-weight:bold;</style>
        <style id="highlighted">text-decoration:underline;</style>

  <PUBLIC:PROPERTY name="Styles">
     <GET internalName="getStyles"/>
     <PUT internalName="putStyles"/>
     <DESCRIPTION>Styles lets you set or change the styles
of each of the CSS classes that are used within the
behavior. The styles are given as tokenized functions
separated by spaces, e.g. "table(cursor;hand)
header(background-color:blue;color:white;border:outset 3pt
blue;)" etc. To change a given class style, simply pass a
string containing the stylenames and CSS style strings in
the same format: styles="row1(background-color:#C0C0FF)
row2(background-color:white);"</DESCRIPTION>
  </PUBLIC:PROPERTY>

  <PUBLIC:METHOD name="Refresh" internalName="draw">
     <DESCRIPTION>This method should be called whenever
you need to update the visual contents of this component.
     </DESCRIPTION>
  </PUBLIC:METHOD>

  <PUBLIC:METHOD name="getInfo">
     <DESCRIPTION>Invoke this method to get interface
information about this component.
     </DESCRIPTION>
  </PUBLIC:METHOD>

  <PUBLIC:ATTACH event="onload" for="window" onEvent="initialize()">
  </PUBLIC:ATTACH>

  <PUBLIC:ATTACH event="onmousedown" onEvent="handleMouseDown()">
  </PUBLIC:ATTACH>

  <PUBLIC:ATTACH event="onmouseup" onEvent="handleMouseUp()">
  </PUBLIC:ATTACH>

  <PUBLIC:ATTACH event="onmouseover" onEvent="handleMouseOver()">
  </PUBLIC:ATTACH>

  <PUBLIC:ATTACH event="onmouseout" onEvent="handleMouseOut()">
  </PUBLIC:ATTACH>

  <PUBLIC:ATTACH event="onclick" onEvent="handleClick()">
  </PUBLIC:ATTACH>
```

```
    <PUBLIC:EVENT name="onselected" id="selectedID">
       <DESCRIPTION>When a row is selected, the onselected
  event gets fired. Note that if SelectedMode is set to
  "none" then this event doesn't fire.
       </DESCRIPTION>
    </PUBLIC:EVENT>

    <PUBLIC:EVENT name="onrefresh" id="refreshID">
       <DESCRIPTION>This event is fired every time the
  screen is refreshed, either automatically or through the
  Refresh method.
       </DESCRIPTION>
    </PUBLIC:EVENT>
```

The first part of the behavior defines each interface element. Typically, even if it doesn't seem necessary, you should assign internal functions to handle all of your properties, and you can conceivably do the same thing for your internal events. Note that although it's not strictly required with behaviors (unlike with more formalized languages such as Visual Basic) you should try to make sure that the object returned by your GET function implementor is the same as that used as a parameter by your PUT parameter; this makes documentation easier and is less likely to result in errors down the road.

NOTE Behaviors make no distinction between assigning objects to properties and assigning text or other "scalar" values to properties. As a consequence, rather than having different LET and SET keywords as in Visual Basic, behaviors use the comprehensive PUT keyword instead.

WARNING Behaviors recognize the <DESCRIPTION> tag, but, unlike schemas, don't recognize any subelements. As a consequence, any HTML you write within the description will simply get stripped in favor of its equivalent text when the `description` tag is read.

The "Using the Behavior" section contains the actual implementation of the behavior. One thing that may not be immediately obvious when looking at the behavior, however, is that it's not really an XML document. Internally, the behavior sees itself as a specialized HTML document. It can use the IE5 Document Object Model, seeing CDATA sections as foreign entities, which is why the CDATA section in the upcoming script declaration line is commented out with a VBScript constant. (You'll need to see the document as an XML document, which does recognize the CDATA section.)

NOTE To reiterate, a behavior is a form of HTML document, not an XML document. You can use the HTML DOM to manipulate it, but, with very few exceptions, you can't use the XML DOM to do the same.

The first block of code in the upcoming script block declares all of the variables that are global to the script block but are private; they are not seen by the public interface at all, and attempting to use them in that capacity will generate an error. After that, the code handles the direct interface connections with the public properties and methods. The `SelectMode`, for example, handles whether clicking on an item turns off all of the other selections, adds to an existing list of selected items, or does nothing at all.

This section, "Writing the Behavior," also contains the code for determining which columns are displayed by the table. The behavior first goes to the properties and sees if the `Columns` attribute has been set with a space-separated list of column `id`'s, and it uses them if it has; if not, it goes to the schema and attempts to recreate the schema output from some basic patterns in the schema.

Finally, the following listing builds the envelope from the initial data inside the `MakeColumns()` method. This is an internal method (it's not declared in the public interface), but it is critical nonetheless. `MakeColumns()` reads the `envelope` data island located at the end of the behavior, converts the data island into an XML document, and then inserts the XML data to be displayed into the body of the envelope XML. The continuation of Listing 7.16 shows how this is done.

WARNING A bug in the older MS XML parser makes retaining schemas when XML documents are joined in this manner somewhat problematic. The only solution I've found around this quandary is to build the envelope, insert the data, convert the document to text, and use `loadXML` to reinsert the data (now with proper schema references) back into the containing XML document.

Listing 7.16, Continued: The Dynamic Table Behavior, Showing the Private Implementation (*Code7-16.DynamicTable.htc*)

```
<script language="VBScript">'<![CDATA[
dim xmlDoc
dim xslDoc
dim m_xmlSource
dim m_xmlSourceType
dim m_xslSource
dim m_xslSourceType
dim m_selectMode
dim m_selectedDoc
dim m_columns
dim m_IDColumn
dim lastOrder
dim lastRollover

function getSource(pDocSource,pDocSourceType)
   dim tempDoc
```

```
   select case pDocSourceType
      case "url"
         set tempDoc=createObject("Microsoft.XMLDOM")
         tempDoc.validateOnParse=true
         resolveExternals=true
         tempDoc.async=false
         tempDoc.load pDocSource
   end select
   set getSource=tempDoc
end function

function getSelectMode()
   if m_selectMode="" then
      m_selectMode="option"
   end if
   getSelectMode=m_SelectMode
end function

function putSelectMode(mode)
   if mode="" then
      m_selectMode="option"
   else
      m_SelectMode=mode
   end if
end function

function initialize()
   set lastRollover=nothing
   set m_selectedDoc=createObject("Microsoft.XMLDOM")
   m_selectedDoc.loadXML "<keys/>"
   draw
end function

function getXMLSource()
   getXMLSource=m_xmlSource
end function

function putXMLSource(srcPath)
   if lcase(left(srcPath,4))="url(" then
      if right(srcPath,1)=")" then
         m_xmlSource=mid(srcPath,5,len(srcPath)-5)
         m_xmlSourceType="url"
         set bodyDoc=getSource(m_xmlSource,m_xmlSourceType)
         set xmlDoc=createObject("Microsoft.XMLDOM")
         set tempDoc=envelope.XMLDocument
         set bodyNode=tempDoc.selectSingleNode("//body")
         bodyNode.appendChild bodyDoc.documentElement
```

```
            xmlDoc.resolveExternals=true
            xmlDoc.validateOnParse=true
            xmlDoc.loadXML tempDoc.xml
            set bodyNode=xmlDoc.selectSingleNode("//body/*")
         end if
      end if
   end function

   function putColumns(columnList)
      m_columns=columnList
   end function

   function getColumns()
      getColumns=m_columns
   end function

   function putIDColumn(pIDColumn)
      m_IDColumn=pIDColumn
   end function

   function getIDColumn()
      getIDColumn=m_IDColumn
   end function

   function makeColumnCollection()
            set columnsNode=xmlDoc.selectSingleNode("//columns")
            for each columnNode in columnsNode.selectNodes("column")
               columnsNode.removeChild columnNode
            next
            set root=xmlDoc.selectSingleNode("//body/*")
            rowName= _
    root.definition.selectSingleNode("element" _
    ).getAttribute("type")
            set elTypeNodes=root.definition.selectNodes _
   ("//ElementType[@name='"+ rowName+"']/element")
            if getColumns<>"" then
               for each column in split(getColumns," ")
               set columnNode=columnsNode.appendChild( _
               xmlDoc.createElement("column"))
                  columnNode.text=column
               next
            else
               buf=""
               for each elNode in ElTypeNodes
                  column=elNode.getAttribute("type")
                  set columnNode=columnsNode.appendChild( _
                   xmlDoc.createElement("column"))
```

```
                columnNode.text=column
                buf=buf+column+" "
             next
             buf=left(buf,len(buf)-1)
             putColumns buf
          end if
          set idColumnNode=xmlDoc.selectSingleNode("//idColumn")
          if idColumnNode is nothing then
             set
        idColumnNode=columnsNode.parentNode.appendChild( _
        xmlDoc.createElement("idColumn"))
          end if
          if getIDColumn<>"" then
             idColumnNode.text=getIDColumn
          else
             idColumnNode.text=elTypeNodes(0).getAttribute("type")
             putIDColumn idColumnNode.text
          end if
end function

function getXSLSource()
   getXSLSource=m_xslSource
end function

function putXSLSource(srcPath)
   if lcase(left(srcPath,4))="url(" then
      if right(srcPath,1)=")" then
         m_xslSource=mid(srcPath,5,len(srcPath)-5)
         m_xslSourceType="url"
         set xslDoc=getSource(m_xslSource,m_xslSourceType)
      end if
   end if
end function

function getXMLDocument()
   set getXMLDocument=xmlDoc
end function

function getXSLDocument()
   set getXSLDocument=xslDoc
end function
```

The `OrderProperty` indicates which column is used to sort the output, using the – attribute to reverse the order. This provides a simple example of how to build a reordering mechanism into your behaviors and will be used in a slightly modified form when discussing server-side components in Chapter 8, “XML and ASP.”

XML is used in a number of different ways within the behavior. One way that has no bearing on the outside interface is the use of an XML document to store selection keys. As you select items in the table, the item's key (its row `id` in this case) is added to or removed from the list, depending upon whether the item has previously been selected. In the case where the `SelectedMode` is `"option"`, the key's XML structure only holds one key node, but if `"multiple"` is selected, it can hold as many elements as it needs to. This keys list contains only the `id`s, not the complete item record, so when a request is made to get the selected items, the behavior converts this document into an expended list of nodes. The next continuation of Listing 7.16 shows how this is done.

Listing 7.16, Continued: The Dynamic Table Behavior, with Ordering and Key Interfaces (*Code7-16.DynamicTable.htc*)

```
function setOrderProperty(propName)
   if lastOrder=propName then
      propName="-"+propName
   end if
   set orderNode=xslDoc.selectSingleNode("//*[@id='order']")
   orderNode.setAttribute "order-by",propName
   lastOrder=propName
end function

function setSelectProperty(propName,propValue)
   set orderNode=xslDoc.selectSingleNode("//*[@id='order']")
   if propName="" then
      expr="*"
   else
      expr="*["+propName+"='"+propValue+"']"
   end if
   orderNode.setAttribute "select",expr
end function

function addKey(id)
   set node=m_selectedDoc.selectSingleNode("//key[@id='"+id+"']")
   if node is nothing then
      set node=m_selectedDoc.documentElement.appendChild( _
      m_selectedDoc.createElement("key"))
      node.setAttribute "id",id
   end if
end function

function removeKey(id)
   set node=m_selectedDoc.selectSingleNode("//key[@id='"+id+"']")
   if not (node is nothing) then
      m_selectedDoc.documentElement.removeChild node
```

```
      end if
   end function

   function clearKeys()
      m_selectedDoc.loadxml "<keys/>"
   end function

   function keys()
      buf=""
      for each node in m_selectedDoc.selectNodes("//key")
         buf=buf+node.getAttribute("id")+","
      next
      if len(buf)>0 then
         buf=left(buf,len(buf)-1)
      end if
      keys=split(buf,",")
   end function

   function updateSelectedItems()
      for each key in keys
         set row=element.all(key)
         row.className=row.className+" selected"
      next
   end function

   function getSelectedRecords()
      dim recordsDoc
      set recordsDoc=createObject("Microsoft.XMLDOM")
      recordsDoc.loadXML "<records/>"
      set recordsNode=recordsDoc.documentElement
      for each key in keys
         recordsNode.appendChild xmlDoc.selectSingleNode("//
*[id='"+key+"']").cloneNode(true)
      next
      set getSelectedRecords=recordsDoc
   end function
```

The `draw` function lies at the heart of the behavior. While it doesn't handle the special-effects functions (the color and style changes introduced by the various mouse events, for example), `draw` creates the table itself and draws it into the element that contains the behavior. Additionally, it refreshes the table any time a column is reordered and launches an `onrefresh()` event whenever it is called, letting external consumers of the control update their own states when the contents or order of the table changes.

The mouse events, on the other hand, rely on a few techniques to minimize the amount of processing necessary to handle events. Rather than placing an event handler on each table cell, each row, and each column head, I place one event handler that the entire table uses for each type of event. When an event happens (such as a click event) on the behavior, the behavior calls the `handleClick` method handler.

The `handleClick` function, in turn, uses the `event.srcElement` object to determine which HTML element was actually clicked. With this object known, the specific node name of the element in question determines its disposition. In the case of the click, for example, a node name of `TD` indicates that element is a cell in the body of the table, and the routine thus goes up to the cell's row to get the `id` of the row (which, in turn, can be used to retrieve the XML record corresponding to that `id`).

On the other hand, if the element is a `TH`, then the cell is known to be a column head, which has already been assigned an `id` corresponding to the `nodeName` of the column in the XML document (i.e., the `Last Name` column header has an `id` of `lastName`, which is the same name as the `<lastName>` property node in the source XML structure). The next continuation of Listing 7.16 shows this concept.

Classy Tricks for Making Buttons and Rollovers

Look closely at how HTML classes are used within the event handlers. As discussed earlier in this chapter, a CSS `class` attribute can actually contain more than one class name, with the effect that the classes are cumulative. In the case of the table head elements, when the mouse is clicked over the cell, the routine adds a `"depressed"` class, which switches the border style from `outset` (pushed up) to `inset` (pushed down). As the mouse is released, the `"depressed"` class is removed from the class string and the style of the cell reverts back to the original `outset` appearance again.

This same technique is used for the rollovers, except for the fact that the element rolled over (a <TD> cell element) is not the element that needs to be changed. To change the appearance of an entire row on the basis of a mouse click, get the `parentNode` of the cell clicked to retrieve the row reference, and then set the class or style attributes of that element instead.

Listing 7.16, Continued: The Dynamic Table Behavior, with Drawing and Mouse Interactions (*Code7-16.DynamicTable.htc*)

```
function draw()
    makeColumnCollection
    me.innerHTML=xmlDoc.transformNode(xslDoc)
    updateSelectedItems
    set evt=createEventObject
    refreshID.fire evt
end function
```

```
function handleMouseDown()
   dim elt
   set elt=window.event.srcElement
   select case elt.nodeName
      case "TH"
         id=elt.id
         if instr(elt.className,"depressed")=0 then
            elt.className=elt.className+" depressed"
         else
            elt.className=replace(elt.className," depressed","")
         end if
      case "TD"
         id=elt.parentElement.id
         set row=elt.parentElement
         select case SelectMode
            case "multiple"
               if instr(row.className,"selected")=0 then
            row.className=row.className+" selected"
                   addKey id
               else
                  row.className=replace(row.className," selected","")
                  removeKey id
               end if
               set evt=CreateEventObject()
               selectedID.fire evt
            case "option"
               for each key in keys
                  if key<>id then
'                     alert(element.all(key).nodeName)
                     element.all(key).className= _
 replace(element.all(key).className," selected","")
                  end if
               next
               clearKeys
               if instr(row.className,"selected")=0 then
                  row.className=row.className+" selected"
                   addKey id
               else
                  row.className=replace(row.className," selected","")
                  removeKey id
               end if
               set evt=CreateEventObject()
               selectedID.fire evt
         end select
      case else
         id=""
```

```
   end select
'   alert id
end function

function handleMouseUp()
   dim elt
   set elt=window.event.srcElement
   select case elt.nodeName
      case "TH"
         id=elt.id
         elt.className=replace(elt.className," depressed","")
      case "TD"
         id=elt.parentElement.id
      case else
         id=""
   end select
'   alert id
end function

function handleClick()
   dim elt
   set elt=window.event.srcElement
   handleMouseup
   select case elt.nodeName
      case "TH"
         id=elt.id
         setOrderProperty id
         'document.body.style.cursor="wait"
         draw
      case "TD"
         id=elt.parentElement.id
      case else
         id=""
   end select
'   alert id
end function

function handleMouseOver()
   dim elt
   set elt=window.event.srcElement
   select case elt.nodeName
      case "TH"
      case "TD"
         if m_selectMode="none" then
            exit function
         end if
```

```
         if instr(elt.parentElement.className," highlighted")=0 then
            elt.parentElement.className=elt.parentElement._
             className+" highlighted"
         end if
         set lastRollover=elt.parentElement
      case else
         id=""
   end select
end function

function handleMouseOut()
   if (not (lastRollover is nothing)) then
      lastRollover.className=replace( _
lastRollover.className," highlighted","")
    end if
   set lastRollover=nothing
end function
```

In a relatively complex behavior such as this one, the ability to change styles becomes very important. One of the reasons I used classes rather than styles explicitly was to ensure that I could change the style of a given component (a highlight color, the background color of a row, the color or texture of buttons, and so forth) from the interface without having to know more than a minimal amount about the inner workings of the behavior. In the next section of Listing 7.16, I show how you can use styles to customize the appearance of this table without having to touch the behavior code itself. The following continuation of Listing 7.16 shows this technique.

Listing 7.16, Continued: The Dynamic Table Behavior, Retrieving and Setting Styles (*Code7-16.DynamicTable.htc*)

```
function getStyle(styleKey)
   set
 styleNode=xmlDoc.selectSingleNode("//head/styles/style[
@id='"+styleKey+"']")
   if not (styleNode is Nothing) then
      getStyle=styleNode.text
   else
      getStyle=""
   end if
end function

function setStyle(styleKey,newStyle)
   set
 styleNode=xmlDoc.selectSingleNode("//head/styles/style[
```

```
@id='"+styleKey+"']")
   if not (styleNode is Nothing) then
      styleNode.text=newStyle
   end if
   draw
end function

function getStyles()
   dim buf
   buf=""
   for each styleNode in xmlDoc.selectNodes("//head/styles/style")
      buf=buf+styleNode.getAttribute("id")+","
   next
   if buf<>"" then
      buf=left(buf,len(buf)-1)
   end if
   getStyles=split(buf,",")
end function
```

Documentation for a behavior is critical. The people working with your code as a component are often likely to be non-programmers. They will want to know what attributes to set (or, at most, what functions are supported by the interface) when they write HTML code using your component. The `getInfo()` function provides a bare-bones mechanism for, at the very least, displaying the valid attributes, methods, and events on the component, in essence by loading the behavior as an HTML document (using the `ID="DynamicTable"` attribute from the `<PUBLIC:COMPONENT>` tag at the start of the document) and then converting the output into XML.

However, the IE5 HTML DOM has a rather maddening peculiarity. The DOM doesn't enclose certain attributes (such as the critical `id` attributes) in quotation marks when it converts the DOM back into text. To head off this problem (and to also skirt the problem of declaring the `PUBLIC:` namespace, which, again, is an IE5 implementation), I built several regular expressions in the following listing to replace attributes without quotes with those that have them, to strip off the `PUBLIC:` namespace, and to remove script and XML nodes (primarily to avoid the problems having to do with embedded CDATA sections).

With what was left, I pulled in a second XML data island called `documentor`. The XML contained herein is a style sheet and demonstrates a technique that I could have used on the larger behavior document as well. (If you want to have a style sheet always associated with a behavior, make it a data island and embed it in the document itself.)

This smaller style sheet is used to filter the stripped results of the behavior's source code and break it up into properties, methods, and events (attachments are largely unimportant since they can't be viewed or modified by the user of the behavior). This is also where the <DESCRIPTION> tags come into play, since they are recognized by the HTML object model, even though other tags contained within the PUBLIC: namespace don't seem to. The next continuation of Listing 7.16 shows how this is done.

TIP Embed style sheets within your behaviors as data islands to handle default behaviors. By keeping the style sheets constrained in this fashion, you lessen the risk of disassociating the crucial display information from the behavioral interface.

Listing 7.16, Continued: The Dynamic Table Behavior, with *getInfo* Function (*Code7-16.DynamicTable.htc*)

```
function getInfo()
   dim infoDoc
   set infoDoc=createObject("Microsoft.XMLDOM")
   infoDoc.validateOnParse=false
   set re=new RegExp
   src=replace(DynamicTable.outerHTML,"PUBLIC:","")
   re.ignoreCase=true
   re.global=true
   re.pattern=" ([A-Za-z0-9]+)=(\w+)"
   src=re.replace(src," $1='$2'")
   re.pattern="(<SCRIPT[\w\W]+SCRIPT>)"
   src=re.replace(src,"")
   re.pattern="(<xml[\w\W]+xml>)"
   src=re.replace(src,"")
   infoDoc.loadXML src
   set documentorXSL=documentor.XMLDocument
   getInfo=infoDoc.transformNode(documentorXSL)
end function

']]></script>
<xml id="envelope">
<document>
   <head>
      <idColumn>id</idColumn>
      <columns/>
      <styles>
         <style id="table">cursor:hand;</style>
         <style id="header">
background-color:blue;color:white;border:outset 3pt blue;
         </style>
         <style id="row1">background-color:#C0C0FF</style>
```

```
            <style id="row2">background-color:white</style>
            <style id="depressed">border:inset 3pt blue;</style>
            <style id="selected">color:blue;font-weight:bold;</style>
            <style id="highlighted">text-decoration:underline;</style>
         </styles>
      </head>
      <body/>
   </document>
   </xml>

   <xml id="documentor">
      <xsl:style sheet xmlns:xsl="http://www.w3.org/TR/WD-xsl">
         <xsl:template match="/">
            <xsl:apply-templates select="COMPONENT"/>
         </xsl:template>
         <xsl:template match="COMPONENT">
            <div>
            <h1><xsl:value-of select="name"/></h1>
            <div><xsl:value-of select="DESCRIPTION"/></div>
            <h2>Properties</h2>
            <ul><xsl:apply-templates select="PROPERTY"/></ul>
            <h2>Methods</h2>
            <ul><xsl:apply-templates select="METHOD"/></ul>
            <h2>Attachments</h2>
            <ul><xsl:apply-templates select="ATTACH"/></ul>
            <h2>Events</h2>
            <ul><xsl:apply-templates select="EVENT"/></ul>
            </div>
         </xsl:template>

         <xsl:template match="PROPERTY">
         <LI><b><xsl:value-of select="@name"/>.</b>
         <xsl:choose>
            <xsl:when test=".[GET $and$ not(PUT)]">(read-only)</xsl:when>
            <xsl:when test=".[PUT $and$ not(GET)]">(write-only)</xsl:when>
         </xsl:choose>
         <xsl:value-of select="DESCRIPTION"/>
         </LI>
         </xsl:template>

         <xsl:template match="METHOD">
         <LI><b><xsl:value-of select="@name"/>.</b>
         <xsl:value-of select="DESCRIPTION"/>
         </LI>
         </xsl:template>
```

```
        <xsl:template match="EVENT">
        <LI><b><xsl:value-of select="@name"/>.</b>
        <xsl:value-of select="DESCRIPTION"/>
        </LI>
        </xsl:template>

    </xsl:style sheet>
</xml>
</PUBLIC:COMPONENT>
```

Using the Behavior

After all of that, you might expect that using the behavior might also be depressingly complex. However, an old adage in software design is appropriate to this situation: The simplicity of the interface is inversely proportional to the complexity of the implementation. In this case, the interface is pretty much Plug and Play.

To display data such as the `Employees.xml` sample file discussed earlier in this chapter, you need to make sure that the `DynamicTable.htc` and `DynamicTable.xsl` files are located in the same directory as the HTML page the behavior is embedded in. Once you do this, then about all you need to do is specify the source of the data. Listing 7.17 demonstrates how to do that.

Listing 7.17: Displaying the Behavior (*Code7-17.DynamicTable.htm*)

```
<html>
    <head>Employees List</head>
    <style>
      .dynamicTable {behavior:url(DynamicTable.htc);}
    </style>
    <body>
    <h1>Employees</h1>
    <div    id="employeeTable"
       class="dynamicTable"
       xmlSource="url(employees.xml)"/>
    </body>
</html>
```

That's it. The result of this code is shown in Figure 7.2. Of course, like most interfaces, you can do a lot more with the control than just this, but the idea here is that in a well-defined interface you should be able to have the behavior work with a minimal set of attributes.

The full set of properties, methods, and events are given in the following respective sections. (Note that this list was actually generated directly from the behavior itself.)

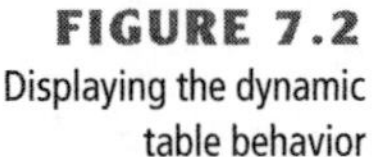

FIGURE 7.2
Displaying the dynamic table behavior

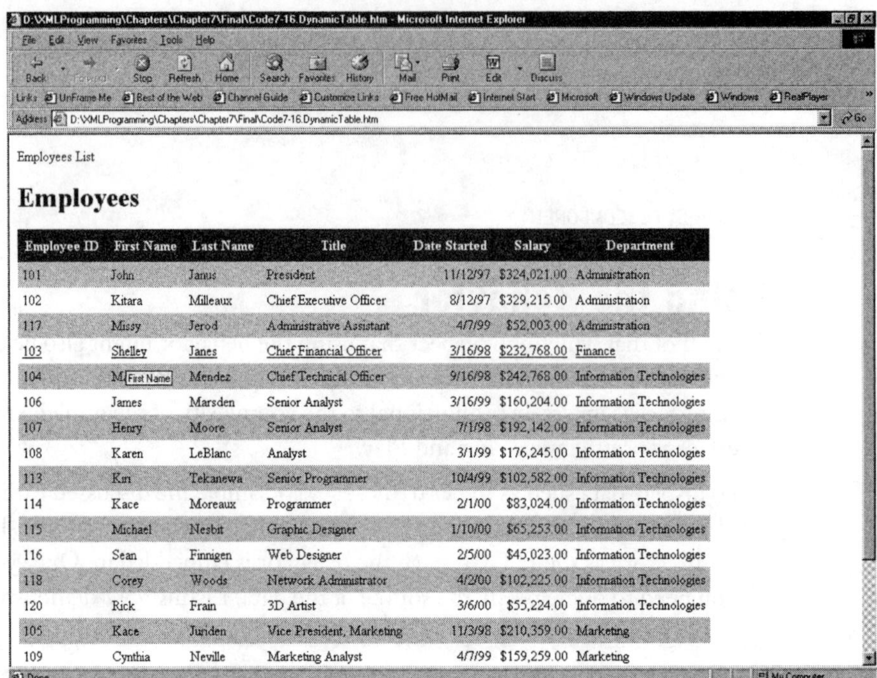

Employees

Employee ID	First Name	Last Name	Title	Date Started	Salary	Department
101	John	Janus	President	11/12/97	$324,021.00	Administration
102	Kitara	Milleaux	Chief Executive Officer	8/12/97	$329,215.00	Administration
117	Missy	Jerod	Administrative Assistant	4/7/99	$52,003.00	Administration
103	Shelley	Janes	Chief Financial Officer	3/16/98	$232,768.00	Finance
104	M First Name	Mendez	Chief Technical Officer	9/16/98	$242,768.00	Information Technologies
106	James	Marsden	Senior Analyst	3/16/99	$160,204.00	Information Technologies
107	Henry	Moore	Senior Analyst	7/1/98	$192,142.00	Information Technologies
108	Karen	LeBlanc	Analyst	3/1/99	$176,245.00	Information Technologies
113	Kim	Tekanewa	Senior Programmer	10/4/99	$102,582.00	Information Technologies
114	Kace	Moreaux	Programmer	2/1/00	$83,024.00	Information Technologies
115	Michael	Nesbit	Graphic Designer	1/10/00	$65,253.00	Information Technologies
116	Sean	Finnigen	Web Designer	2/5/00	$45,023.00	Information Technologies
118	Corey	Woods	Network Administrator	4/2/00	$102,225.00	Information Technologies
120	Rick	Frain	3D Artist	3/6/00	$55,224.00	Information Technologies
105	Kace	Junden	Vice President, Marketing	11/3/98	$210,359.00	Marketing
109	Cynthia	Neville	Marketing Analyst	4/7/99	$159,259.00	Marketing

Properties

XMLSource Contains the location of the XML source. To set this to a URL (say for the `resources/myDoc.xml` file), use `XMLSource="url(resources/myDoc.xml)"`. To use a data island, just pass the `id` of that island.

XSLSource Contains the location of the XSL source. To set this to a URL (say for the `resources/transform.xsl` file), use `XSLSource="url(resources/myDoc.xml)"`. To use a data island, just pass the `id` of that island.

XMLDocument (read-only) Retrieves an instance of the full XML document, which can be modified accordingly. Note that once a change is made to the document, you can use the `Refresh` method to update the table.

XSLDocument (read-only) Retrieves an instance of the XSL transformation document, which can be modified accordingly. Note that once a change is made to the document, you can use the `Refresh` method to update the table.

columns Sets or retrieves the columns to be used in the table. To set the columns you wish to display, pass the names of each element that you want to make into a column, separated by a space. For example, `columns="firstName lastName dateOfBirth occupation"` displays as columns those elements that have the names given, in that order. Note that if `columns` is not included, the parser will either attempt to read the document schema or, if that is unsuccessful, will read the first record to display the columns.

`idColumn` Sets or retrieves the column name used to uniquely identify a given record. If the column name is missing, the first column is assumed to be the `ID` column.

`SelectMode` Determines whether the table selects one item exclusively (`SelectMode="option"`), selects multiple items simultaneously (`SelectMode="multiple"`), or turns off the selection altogether (`SelectMode="none"`). If the `SelectMode` is turned off, rollovers are disabled as well.

`SelectedRecords` (read-only) Returns an XML structure containing all of the records that are currently selected. Note that this is a read-only property, and changing these records will not change the component.

`styles` Retrieves a selection of tokenized functions, with each function name corresponding to a CSS class name (i.e., `"row1(background-color:#C0C0FF) row2(background-color:white) table(..) …"`). If you pass one or more classes back to the `styles` property in this notation, it sets the appropriate classes in the table.

Methods

`Refresh` Updates the visual contents of this component.

`getInfo` Retrieves interface information about this component.

Events

`onselected` Gets fired when a row is selected. Note that if `SelectedMode` is set to `"none"` this event doesn't fire.

`onrefresh` Fires every time the screen is refreshed, either automatically or through the `Refresh` method.

Suppose you want to set a table so that it displays the first name, last name, job title, and department, with rows showing alternatively as white text on a navy background and black text on a white background. When you click on an entry, it should display the XML for that particular record. The code to do this would then look like that shown in Listing 7.18.

Listing 7.18: Displaying the Behavior (*Code7-18.DynamicTable2.htm*)

```
<html>
<head>Employees List</head>
<style>
    .dynamicTable {behavior:url(DynamicTable.htc);}
```

```
</style>
<script language="VBScript">
   function showRecords()
      alert(employeeTable.selectedRecords.xml);
   end function
</script>
<body>
<h1>Employees</h1>
<div    id="employeeTable"
class="dynamicTable"
xmlSource="url(employees.xml)"
columns="firstName lastName title department"
idColumn="id"
styles="row1(color:white;
background-color:navy;)
row2(color:black;background-color:white;)"
            selectMode="multiple"
            onselected="showRecords()"
/>

   </body>
</html>
```

TIP The best way to learn about behaviors is to play with as many as you can.

Summary

This is a tough chapter. XML is definitely coming into its own in the browser, but it will take a while before it becomes standard fare—thus the emphasis in this chapter on Internet Explorer 5 and on the building of behaviors. You can use XML in conjunction with CSS (something that the Mozilla 5 browser will also permit, if the alpha release at the time this book is being written is any indication), but to really take advantage of it you need the ability to script your code. Data islands, likewise, are exclusively IE5 inventions, though with a little work you can incorporate data islands into other browsers using a few HTML tricks.

XML probably won't be a part of the standard Web developer's toolkit on the client for quite some time if they're dealing with browsers other than Explorer. However, that doesn't mean that XML can't be used in conjunction with HTML. Much of the development that is occurring at the time of this writing explores how XML can be leveraged to build distributed components, with the results displayed using basic HTML on the client but much of the logic (resulting from links passing URL strings) taking place on the server. In Chapter 8, "XML and ASP," I show how you can build highly interactive, server-based applications with XML and how you can reduce some of the ugly complexity of behaviors into more easily manageable, server-side components.

CHAPTER 8

XML and ASP

- Designing server-side XML
- Integrating XML and the IIS objects
- Building XML-based components

XML started out as the ultimate client technology ("Build your own documents with your own structured language!"), but over time, most developers have come to realize that this original view of XML was both simplistic and naïve. Most people have neither the time nor the resources to create an entire markup language. As the data-centric view of XML has begun to permeate the XML development community, the language has increasingly moved to the server or even farther back into the database stores.

Perhaps not surprisingly, XML has made significant inroads in two server-side technologies: Java and Active Server Pages. Entire books have been written about Java and XML, to the extent that many in the Java camp have proclaimed that XML and Java were made for one another. While I'd dispute this (see Chapter 11, "XML and Programming," for my take on the whole "best languages" issue), the ability to leverage XML on the server in most languages makes it far more suited for its role there.

In this chapter, I look at XML as a server technology as well as its relationship to Microsoft's Active Server Pages. The two form an uneasy alliance, although the most recent version of IIS provides somewhat better support for XML. I concentrate here on baseline solutions (as the adoption of Windows 2000 is still far from common in the marketplace as of when this chapter was written).

Designing Server-Side XML

The term *Web application* is a relatively new one in the lexicon of developers. Applications that run on a single machine typically have very tightly coupled architectures, to such an extent that they seem largely seamless and monolithic. Programs such as Microsoft Word or Excel tend to best exemplify this principle: While Word, for example, actually consists of a fairly large number of discrete components, in practice most of the core functionality resides within a single application executable.

Client/server applications represent the next level of abstraction when dealing with programs. In this case, you're typically dealing with two primary programs: a server program, which provides the data (and occasionally, but not often, the formatting of that data), and a client program that takes that data and places a user interface on it. The vast majority of accounting and inventory management systems out there fall into this category.

The Web application moves the level of abstraction up yet one more level. In this case, the client application is a browser that provides a rendering engine for some type of code (HTML, XML, or several others) while the server is a generalized program providing data based upon HTTP requests and posts. In other words, the client and server are both very generalized applications. Between client and server resides the application layer, where application calls are translated (usually through an interface such as Active Server Pages, Java Server Pages, CGI, or ultimately XML) into client-viewable code.

As a developer, you are undoubtedly familiar with most of this at the level of using the technology, but it's worth thinking about this architecture a bit in light of XML. If you work upon the assumption that even the HTML that you are dealing with is, in fact, XML (that is, if you are working with XHTML), then some interesting possibilities begin to emerge for application design, either within an ASP script or as part of a component:

1. An HTTP request is made against the server, passing a number of parameters in the form of name/value pairs. *Suppose that the request information is then transformed into an XML document.*
2. Specific parameters within the request are used to determine which specific action the ASP code will take. This action is expressed in the form of an XSL script.
3. The requested action, in turn, loads in other actions, perhaps through some kind of a "job" script written in XSL.
4. Data from external sources would, in turn, be output based upon the input from the job scripts and the initial request parameters.
5. Similarly, at various points along the path, resultant information (for example, the contents of a form) could be written out to external XML files or data sources.
6. Finally, the resultant information is formatted in a manner appropriate to the browser and sent back to it.

This is a very abstract view of the process of using XML on the server. In essence, this is the pipeline view; the XML flows along one or more pipes in this model, from the input based upon the `Request` object from the client to the output sent back to the client. This model works well when all of the elements are XML sources, although it can even be used with external data providers or consumers through the use of XML Servers, which are primarily programs or DLLs that can communicate through either the XSL script interface or through XML parameters.

Building such an application can take more time to set up than would one ASP page (or even a couple of them), but the flexibility and strength that this model offers more than pays for itself in the long run. Some specific advantages to the pipeline view include:

Modularity You can use the same data stream and application interface to handle any number of different tasks.

Targetability You can target your output to any number of different sources simply by swapping one XSL transformation for another.

Portability By dealing with abstract operations, you can port your XML code to work with any W3C XSL server, regardless of operating system, browser, or platform.

Encapsulation The result of any such job is itself an XML stream that can, in turn, be incorporated into other XML clients.

One interesting upshot of all of this is that once you begin building a pipeline model your ASP or JSP code becomes much smaller and more manageable (and may, in time, disappear completely as specialized servers come into play) and that the development environment begins to look pretty exclusively like a single cohesive XML system.

Integrating the IIS Objects and XML

A significant amount of the processing in any ASP script goes to a simple process: retrieving and interpreting the parameters that come from forms or query strings in browsers. Some of this activity focuses on validation—is the data coming in well-formed or within bounds?—while much of it also deals with converting null values (unpassed parameters) to their default values.

The use of XML here can be a little problematic. In an ideal world, most of the processing should be able to take place within an XSL script, but even with the benefits of the `addParameter` method in the compiled XSL object, this still means a lot of procedural code needs to be written just to handle the simple act of setting up parameters. For example, Listing 8.1 shows a sample of code that is typically used for setting up an XSL script for processing, in this case for a page that shows the various messages available on a given message board.

Listing 8.1: Bad ASP Parameterization (*Listing8-1.txt*)

```
<%
' showListPageBad.asp
page=request.queryString("page")
if page="" then
   page=1
end if
recordSize=request.queryString("recordSize")
if recordSize="" then
   recordSize=20
end if
board=request.queryString("board")
set xslDoc=createObject("MSXML2.DOMDocument")
xslDoc.load server.mapPath("showListPageBad.xsl")
set param=xslDoc.selectSingleNode(_
     "xsl:param[@name='page']")
param.setAttribute "select",page
```

```
set param=xslDoc.selectSingleNode(_
     "xsl:param[@name='board']")
param.setAttribute "select",board
set xmlDoc=createObject("MSXML2.DOMDOcument")
xmlDoc.load server.mapPath(board+".xml")
response.write xmlDoc.transformNode(xslDoc)
```

So why is this kind of a page a problem? There are actually several problems here. The first and most pressing is a lack of modularity. The ASP page will only work for the situation where you want to show a list page, and only for the specific data contained therein. If you wanted to show the data in a different way, you would need a separate ASP page to handle this, which both degrades performance (since it increases the number of documents to cache) and makes management of the site more complex.

A second problem has to do with implementation of the `Request` object. Here, I have to know that the `Request` object has a specific set of interfaces and, moreover, that the information was specifically sent via either a `GET` or a `POST` command on the server. If I wanted to change the data source of this information (perhaps for testing purposes or maybe to cache commonly accessed pages automatically), I would have to provide an alternative `Request` object with identical interfaces.

Finally, the parameterization shown here is DOM based: XSLT is supposed to minimize the interaction of DOM with the host environment, but if you have to spend all your time writing DOM parameter calls then somewhere along the line you've lost sight of the advantages that XSLT offers. Since the DOM described here is very much a Microsoft implementation, the less reliance you have on the DOM in your XSLT code, the easier that it is to port to other systems (or vice versa).

Rethinking the *Request* Object

The `Request` object is a very useful (and surprisingly complex) component; while most people tend to use it to retrieve just form or query-string information, it, in fact, controls four distinct collections:

Form The form collection contains information sent from HTML forms (and more generically contains information sent via the HTTP `POST` method). This is the most common way of sending large or complex data and can be used to send binary data as well as text data.

Query String The query string collection contains information sent from URL requests with query strings (the name/value pairs given after the `?` character in URLs, and separated by an `&` character. More generically, `QueryString` contains information sent via the HTTP `GET` method. Query strings are the oldest HTTP command, but they are limited in length to 1,024 characters (give or take a few per implementation).

Cookies Cookies are bits of information that are kept by the client browser and are indexed by the same key mechanism that forms and query strings use.

Server Variables These contain information that either the server itself retains or that is sent as part of the header information from the client. Unlike the other properties, these are typically a fixed set of tokens.

One useful characteristic of each of these collections is that you don't necessarily need to know the name of each key to invoke it; instead, you can enumerate through each of these collections and retrieve the keys directly, which, in turn, lets you retrieve the values associated with each key. This implies that it should be possible to make the `Request` object more generic, even conceivably turning it into an XML object.

If a mechanism exists to turn the `Request` object into XML, this means that the entire contents of the `Request` object can be passed directly into the XSL document without needing onerous ASP code to do the conversions. This simplifies the ASP code to such an extent as making it (almost) unnecessary. It also makes it easy to swap out this `Request` object with a different one (or an XML file that emulates such an object). The `passRequestObjectTo()` function and its two supporting functions, `getRequestXML()` and `setKeysCollection()` (Listing 8.2), do just this.

Listing 8.2: XML Response Creator Functions (*Listing8.2.asp*)

```
function getRequestXML(collectionsString)
    dim xmlDoc
    set xmlDoc=server.createObject("Microsoft.XMLDOM")
    xmlDoc.loadXML "        <keys/>"
    if collectionsString="" then
        collectionsString="all"
    end if
    collections=split(lcase(collectionsString),",")
    if collections(0)="all" or collections(0)="" then
        setKeysCollection xmlDoc,"querystring"
        setKeysCollection xmlDoc,"form"
        setKeysCollection xmlDoc,"cookies"
        setKeysCollection xmlDoc,"servervariables"
    else
        for each collection in collections
            setKeysCollection xmlDoc,collection
        next
    end if
    set getRequestXML=xmlDoc
end function
```

```
function setKeysCollection(xmlDoc,collectionName)
    set collectionNode=xmlDoc.createElement("collection")
    collectionNode.setAttribute "id",collectionName
    for each key in eval("request."+collectionName)
        set keyNode=xmlDoc.createElement("key")
        keyNode.setAttribute "id",key
        keyNode.text=request(key)
        collectionNode.appendChild keyNode
    next
    xmlDoc.documentElement.appendChild collectionNode
    set setKeysCollection=collectionNode
end function

function passRequestObjectTo(xslDoc)
    collectionsString="all"
    set requestDoc=getRequestXML(collectionString)
    set param=xslDoc.selectSingleNode("//xsl:param[@name='request']")
    if param is nothing then
        set param=xslDoc.documentElement.insertBefore _
(xslDoc.createElement("xsl:param"), _
xslDoc.selectSingleNode _
("//xsl:template"))
        param.setAttribute "name","request"
    end if
    while param.childNodes.length>0 then
        param.removeChild param.childNodes(0)
    wend
    param.appendChild requestDoc.documentElement
end function
```

To use `passRequestObjectTo()`, you define and load your XSL document, and then call it as an argument to `passRequestObjectTo`. This will, in turn, generate an XML `Request` object and place it into the `$request` parameter definition. At that point, the object is part of your XSL and can be referenced in the same manner that you reference other parametric information. (I use this extensively throughout the chapter, so there will be many useful examples shortly.)

The way the code is set up, the keys are automatically assigned to the `$request` parameter, replacing whatever previous code had been in place. To simplify placement, I also explicitly create a request parameter node as part of the `RequestUtils.xsl` file, which can then be imported into any XSL filter through the `<xsl:include mechanism>`. The whole script for `RequestUtils.xsl` is shown later in this chapter in Listings 8.4 and 8.5.

The core of the code, `setKeysCollection`, performs the actual XML creation: It enumerates through each collection in turn, retrieves the keys for that collection, and then uses the keys to get to the values associated with those keys. For a typical machine, this generates output that looks something like Listing 8.3. The query string that was sent to the server to generate this was given as the following:

```
http://localhost/xmlpro/getRequestKeys.asp?key1=This+is+key
   +1&key2=Here+is+another+key.
```

Listing 8.3: XML Request Format (*listing8.3.xml*)


```
      <keys>
         <collection id="querystring">
           <key id="key1">This is key 1</key>
           <key id="key2">Here is another key.</key>
      </collection>
        <collection id="form" />
        <collection id="cookies" />
        <collection id="servervariables">
                   <key id="ALL_HTTP">HTTP_ACCEPT:image/gif,
image/x-xbitmap, image/jpeg, image/pjpeg, application/ms
-bpc, application/vnd.ms-powerpoint, application/vnd.ms
-excel, application/msword, */* HTTP_ACCEPT_LANGUAGE:en
-us,da;q=0.5 HTTP_CONNECTION:Keep-Alive HTTP_HOST:localhost
 HTTP_USER_AGENT:Mozilla/4.0 (compatible; MSIE 5.5; Windows
 98) HTTP_COOKIE:ASPSESSIONIDFFFEMOBX=LMLNIAFBJJBEPLFBIIHCBD
ME HTTP_ACCEPT_ENCODING:gzip, deflate</key>
         <key id="ALL_RAW">Accept: image/gif, image/x-
xbitmap, image/jpeg, image/pjpeg, application/ms-bpc,
 application/vnd.ms-powerpoint, application/vnd.ms-excel,
 application/msword, */* Accept-Language: en-us,da;q=0.5
 Connection: Keep-Alive Host: localhost User-Agent:
 Mozilla/4.0 (compatible; MSIE 5.5; Windows 98) Cookie:
 ASPSESSIONIDFFFEMOBX=LMLNIAFBJJBEPLFBIIHCBDME Accept
-Encoding: gzip, deflate</key>

         <key id="APPL_MD_PATH">/LM/W3SVC/1/ROOT/xmlpro</key>
         <key id="APPL_PHYSICAL_PATH">d:\xmlPro\</key>
         <key id="AUTH_PASSWORD" />
         <key id="AUTH_TYPE" />
         <key id="AUTH_USER" />
         <key id="CERT_COOKIE" />
         <key id="CERT_FLAGS" />
         <key id="CERT_ISSUER" />
         <key id="CERT_KEYSIZE" />
         <key id="CERT_SECRETKEYSIZE" />
         <key id="CERT_SERIALNUMBER" />
         <key id="CERT_SERVER_ISSUER" />
```

```
        <key id="CERT_SERVER_SUBJECT" />
        <key id="CERT_SUBJECT" />
        <key id="CONTENT_LENGTH">0</key>
        <key id="CONTENT_TYPE" />
        <key id="GATEWAY_INTERFACE">CGI/1.1</key>
        <key id="HTTPS">off</key>
        <key id="HTTPS_KEYSIZE" />
        <key id="HTTPS_SECRETKEYSIZE" />
        <key id="HTTPS_SERVER_ISSUER" />
        <key id="HTTPS_SERVER_SUBJECT" />
        <key id="INSTANCE_ID">1</key>
        <key id="INSTANCE_META_PATH">/LM/W3SVC/1</key>
        <key id="LOCAL_ADDR">127.0.0.1</key>
        <key id="LOGON_USER" />
        <key id="PATH_INFO">/xmlpro/getRequestObject.asp</key>
        <key id="PATH_TRANSLATED">d:\xmlPro\getRequestObject.asp</key>
        <key
 id="QUERY_STRING">key1=This+is+key+1&key2=Here+is+anoth
er+key.</key>
        <key id="REMOTE_ADDR">127.0.0.1</key>
        <key id="REMOTE_HOST">127.0.0.1</key>
        <key id="REMOTE_USER" />
        <key id="REQUEST_METHOD">GET</key>
        <key id="SCRIPT_NAME">/xmlpro/getRequestObject.asp</key>
        <key id="SERVER_NAME">localhost</key>
        <key id="SERVER_PORT">80</key>
        <key id="SERVER_PORT_SECURE">0</key>
        <key id="SERVER_PROTOCOL">HTTP/1.1</key>
        <key id="SERVER_SOFTWARE">Microsoft-IIS/4.0</key>
        <key id="URL">/xmlpro/getRequestObject.asp</key>
        <key id="HTTP_ACCEPT">image/gif, image/x-xbitmap,
image/jpeg, image/pjpeg, application/ms-bpc,
 application/vnd.ms-powerpoint, application/vnd.ms-excel,
 application/msword, */*</key>
        <key id="HTTP_ACCEPT_LANGUAGE">en-us,da;q=0.5</key>
        <key id="HTTP_CONNECTION">Keep-Alive</key>
        <key id="HTTP_HOST">localhost</key>
        <key id="HTTP_USER_AGENT">Mozilla/4.0
 (compatible; MSIE 5.5; Windows 98)</key>

        <key
id="HTTP_COOKIE">ASPSESSIONIDFFFEMOBX=LMLNIAFBJJBEPLFBI
IHCBDME</key>
        <key id="HTTP_ACCEPT_ENCODING">gzip, deflate</key>
    </collection>
 </keys>
```

Note that the bulk of the XML code is actually dedicated to server variables and that these same server variables frequently contain highly useful information. For example, the HTTP_USER_AGENT key contains information about the browser client and can be used to customize output within your XSL transformations. Similarly, HTTP_ACCEPT_LANGUAGE can tell you what the standard written language is for the browser, making it easier to internationalize your content. You can retrieve path information, making it possible for XSL scripts to retrieve potential information about their file and directory environments. Finally, you can access information such as the IP address of the remote host, making it possible to identify machines that have been visited before without using cookies (but see the sidebar "The Onus of Privacy.")

The Onus of Privacy

If you ask people who use the Internet regarding their biggest concerns about the medium, one topic that frequently comes up is invasion of privacy. People are rightly uncomfortable giving information over the Internet that may fall into the hands of unscrupulous people (not to mention direct marketing firms), and are much more uncomfortable when information is interpolated from the user without their permission or knowledge.

Ironically, though, being able to track machines is an integral part of the Internet, and the supposition that one user will typically use the same machine is true in almost every case. When combined with the ability to analyze structured data that XML provides, this means that it is possible to store and discern patterns of behavior for a given person without necessarily having detailed information about that person—when you go to a large, complex site, what you buy, how much you buy, where you visit, and more could be observed by keeping salient information keyed to an IP address, meaning that this information could form the basis for both good (providing a better user experience by customizing the interface to preferred settings, keeping contextual references handy) and not so good (targeted marketing, surveillance, and the like).

The genie, unfortunately, is out of the bottle, and only by using this information ethically can we, as developers, expect to continue to receive the support from our ultimate employers, the people who use our applications.

Working with Request Information

Once you have the Request object's information in XML and attached to the XSL document, retrieving the information internally does require a little legerdemain. Suppose, for instance, that you had an XSL script where you wanted to know whether the browser was Internet Explorer 5 or above so you could use advanced features if it was IE and deprecate the code accordingly if it wasn't.

If you've done any major server development at all, you know that answering this question (at least under IIS) is not anywhere near as straightforward as it should be. One solution that has evolved has been to keep a file with various browser capabilities associated with the HTTP_USER_AGENT string. The downside to this is that the file must be periodically updated to reflect more recent browsers coming into the market; otherwise, any code built upon this will revert back to the default browser in the list, which generally reflects the state of the art as of 1994.

TIP You can find more information about the Browser Capabilities DLL at `http://msdn.microsoft.com/workshop/server/Default.asp`. Additionally, the file itself, shipped with both PWS and IIS, is called `browscap.ini` and should be located in your Windows System or System32 folder.

Short of incorporating this component, you can still attempt to parse the HTTP_USER_AGENT, and XPath now offers basic tools to let you do that. On my machine, running Microsoft's Personal Web Server, my Internet Explorer 5.5 client returned the HTTP_USER_AGENT of `Mozilla/4.0 (compatible; MSIE 5.5; Windows 98)`, while Netscape returned `Mozilla/4.7 [en] (Win98; I)`. The key sequence for identifying Internet Explorer is the expression `MSIE 5.`, which serves to identify any 5.0 versions (IE 4 is likewise designated with the `MSIE 4.` sequence). Thus, we can use these as markers.

Rather than incorporating the test directly into the working templates, it would be better to define the browser type and version ahead of time, and place the resulting values into variables. Note that variables in XSL are not quite the same as for procedural variables: Once you define a given variable at a specific scope, you can't redefine that variable again at the same scope. Listing 8.4 demonstrates one technique for handling detection of the browser.

Listing 8.4: Defining Browser Types (*Listing8-4.txt*)

```
<xsl:variable name="userAgent">
    <xsl:value-of
     select="$request//key[@id='HTTP_USER_AGENT']"/>
</xsl:variable>

<xsl:variable name="browser">
    <xsl:choose>
        <xsl:when
 test="contains($userAgent,'MSIE')">IE</xsl:when>
        <xsl:otherwise>NS</xsl:otherwise>
</xsl:variable>

<xsl:variable name="version">
    <xsl:choose>
```

```
            <xsl:when test="contains($browser,"IE")">
                <xsl:value-of select="number(substring-
        before(substring-after($userAgent,'MSIE '),';'))"/>
            </xsl:when>
            <xsl:otherwise>
                <xsl:value-of select="number(substring-
  before(substring-after($userAgent,'Mozilla/'),' '))"/>
            </xsl:otherwise>
        </xsl:choose>
  </xsl:variable>
```

The expression `<xsl:value-of select= "$request//key[ @id = 'HTTP_USER_AGENT']"` demonstrates how to retrieve a specific defined value from the `Request` object; simply replace HTTP_USER_AGENT with the name of the query string property, the form property, or the server variable name that you want to request.

NOTE The preceding code is obviously somewhat simplistic in that it recognizes only Netscape and Internet Explorer browsers. As there are something on the order of 135 different browsers currently on the market, you could, in fact, expand this considerably. The default assumption, though, is that if there is no match with Internet Explorer then the browser is assumed to be Netscape Navigator.

You can also see some of the power of the XPath functions through the combined use of `substring-before` and `substring-after`, which together can parse out the HTTP_USER_AGENT string to retrieve browser make and version information. For Internet Explorer 5.5, the variable `$browser` will contain the string `IE`, and `$version` will have a numeric value of `5.5`. For Netscape Navigator 4.7, the same variables will hold the values NS and `4.7`, respectively.

Retrieving Documents Internally

When you write computer books, you get used to dealing with products before they actually see the shrink-wrapped stage, and the Microsoft XML parser is no exception. Certain core features of the XSL model were not implemented when this chapter was written, and there isn't necessarily a reason to anticipate that they will be before the product ships.

One of the more frustrating of these features is the `document()` function. This function retrieves the contents of an XML document and makes it available for processing with the XSL filter. However, it is possible to make both a script-based function that will emulate this and another (more powerful) one that will let you pull in an XML document and transform it with either an external XSL document or a local XSL template. This transform-within-a-transform mechanism can prove quite powerful because it essentially lets you create transformational scripts.

You can create a script in the newer XSLT format that lets you add functions into your XSLT XPath expressions. For example, you could create a JavaScript block, as shown in Listing 8.5, that includes both a `document()` function, a `transformTree()` function, and a `transformDocument()` function. `document()` lets you pass a URL to retrieve the contents of an external document, while `transformTree()` lets you transform a node source from an XSL filter node, and `transformDocument()` loads the respective documents, converts them into XML trees, and then transforms them with `transformTree()`.

Listing 8.5: The *document()*, *transformTree()*, and *transformDocument()* Inline Definitions—Part of *RequestUtils.xsl* (*Listing8.5.xsl*)

```
<xsl:stylesheet xmlns:xsl="http://www.w3.org/1999/XSL/Transform"
        xmlns:utils="http://www.vbxml.com/utils"
        xmlns:msxsl="urn:schemas-microsoft-com:xslt"
        version="1.0">
    <xsl:output method="xml" omit-xml-declaration="yes"/>
    <msxsl:script implements-prefix="utils" language="Javascript"><![CDATA[
    function document(url){
        var xmlDoc=new ActiveXObject("MSXML2.DOMDocument")
        xmlDoc.async=false;
        xmlDoc.load(url);
        return xmlDoc;
        }

    function transformTree(xmlDoc,xslDoc){
        var target=""+xmlDoc.transformNode(xslDoc);
        return target;
        }

    function transformDocument(sourceUrl,filterUrl){
        var xmlDoc=document(sourceUrl);
        var xslDoc=document(filterUrl);
        var target=transformTree(xmlDoc,xslDoc);
        return target;
        }
]]>    </msxsl:script>
<!-- more inline code -->
</xsl:stylesheet>
```

Once these are defined, you can then use them to load external XML files and store them in variables, where they, in turn, can be manipulated using similar techniques as you would use for the initial XML stream. For a simple example, suppose that you had an XML document that served as a table of contents to other XML documents, such as that shown in Listing 8.6.

Listing 8.6: A Simple Table of Contents (*Listing8-6.txt*)

```
<book title="XML Developer's Handbook">
    <chapter src="chapter1.xml" title="Why XML?"/>
    <chapter src="chapter2.xml" title="XML and DOM"/>
    <chapter src="chapter3.xml" title="XML and XPath/>
    <chapter src="chapter4.xml" title="XML Patterns"/>
    <chapter src="chapter5.xml" title="XPath"/>
</book>
```

You could combine all of the chapters into a single document through an XSL script that uses the preceding `utils:document()` definition, as shown in Listing 8.7.

Listing 8.7: Combining Chapters (*Listing8.7.xsl*)

```
<xsl:stylesheet xmlns:xsl="http://www.w3.org/1999/XSL/Transform"
        xmlns:utils="http://www.vbxml.com/utils"
        xmlns:msxsl="urn:schemas-microsoft-com:xslt"
        version="1.0">
    <xsl:output method="xml" omit-xml-declaration="yes"/>
    <msxsl:script implements-prefix="utils" language="Javascript"><![CDATA[
    function document(url){
        if (typeof(url)!="string"){
            url=url.text
        end if
        var xmlDoc=new ActiveXObject("MSXML2.DOMDocument")
        xmlDoc.async=false;
        xmlDoc.load(url);
        return xmlDoc;
        }
]]>     </msxsl:script>
   <xsl:template match="/">
       <book>
            <xsl:apply-templates select="//chapter"/>
       </book>
   </xsl:template>

   <xsl:template match="chapter">
       <xsl-copy-of select="utils:document(@src)" disable-
output-escaping="yes"/>
   </xsl:template>
</xsl:stylesheet>
```

TIP

While the code here is meant to showcase the use of scripting for acquiring documents, you should test your code to see if `document()` has, in fact, been implemented before defining your own; the code will be faster and more robust.

This is a fairly easy application. For a more typical use of such code, let's return to the example that started out this chapter: the creation of a message board system. Each board is a separate file, with the messages contained in a hierarchical tree that shows primary messages and responses to those messages. The boards themselves have a table of contents file that lists all of the boards in the system, as shown in Listing 8.8.

Listing 8.8: Table of Contents for Boards (*Listing8.8.xml*)

```
<boards>
    <category id="site" public="yes">
        <board id="general">
            <title>General Site Board</title>
            <descr>This is essentially the "welcoming
                   board" for the site.  Come here to
                   introduce yourself, find out more about
                   the site, or bring up important points
                   to the general membership.
            </descr>
            <readAccess>0</readAccess>
            <writeAccess>1</writeAccess>
            <src>general.xml</src>
            <admin idref="cagle@olywa.net">
            <msgCount>3<msgCount>
            <baseMsgCount>2</baseMsgCount>
            <msgIndex>4</msgIndex>
        </board>
        <board id="announcements">
            <title>Announcements</title>
            <descr>This board contains notices from the
                   site administrator concerning new
                   features, technical problems, scheduled
                   maintainence and the like.
            </descr>
            <src>announcements.xml</src>
            <readAccess>0</readAccess>
            <writeAccess>3</writeAccess>
            <admin idref="cagle@olywa.net">
            <msgCount>85<msgCount>
            <baseMsgCount>85</baseMsgCount>
            <msgIndex>86</msgIndex>
        </board>
        <board id="bugreport">
            <title>The Bug Report</title>
            <descr>This board is for use by members to
                   report problems, bugs, and similar
                   issues.
```

```
            </descr>
            <src>bugreport.xml</src>
            <readAccess>3</readAccess>
            <writeAccess>1</writeAccess>
            <admin idref="cagle@olywa.net">
            <msgCount>32<msgCount>
            <baseMsgCount>32</baseMsgCount>
            <msgIndex>33</msgIndex>
        </board>
     </category>
    <category id="xml" public="yes">
        <board id="xmlfaq">
            <title>XML Frequently Asked Questions</title>
            <descr>This site contains articles and
                   information pertinent to XML, written by
                   our selected group of gurus.
            </descr>
            <readAccess>0</readAccess>
            <writeAccess>2</writeAccess>
            <src>xmlfaq.xml</src>
            <admin idref="jean@halcyon.com">
            <msgCount>124<msgCount>
            <baseMsgCount>15</baseMsgCount>
            <msgIndex>129</msgIndex>
        </board>
        <board id="xmlstandards">
            <title>XML Standards</title>
            <descr>This board focuses on the latest actions
                   of the W3C and relevent XML based
                   standards.
            </descr>
            <readAccess>0</readAccess>
            <writeAccess>1</writeAccess>
            <src>xmlstandards.xml</src>
            <admin idref="jean@halcyon.com">
            <msgCount>252<msgCount>
            <baseMsgCount>76</baseMsgCount>
            <msgIndex>261</msgIndex>
        </board>
        <board id="xmldom">
            <title>XML Document Object Model</title>
            <descr>Learning the XML document object model?
                   Got some cool tricks or effective
                   programming techniques? This is the
                   place to be.
            </descr>
            <readAccess>0</readAccess>
```

```
            <writeAccess>1</writeAccess>
            <src>xmldoc.xml</src>
            <admin idref="jean@halcyon.com">
            <msgCount>985<msgCount>
            <baseMsgCount>258</baseMsgCount>
            <msgIndex>1002</msgIndex>
        </board>
        <board id="xslt">
            <title>XSL Transformations</title>
            <descr>Discuss the use of XSL Transformations,
                   show off your transforms or get help
                   dealing with XSLT related programming.
            </descr>
            <readAccess>0</readAccess>
            <writeAccess>1</writeAccess>
            <src>xslt.xml</src>
            <admin idref="jean@halcyon.com">
            <msgCount>392<msgCount>
            <baseMsgCount>125</baseMsgCount>
            <msgIndex>400</msgIndex>
        </board>
        <board id="xmlschemas">
            <title>XML Schemas</title>
            <descr>Learn how to leverage the XML schema or
                   Microsoft's reduced dataset, DTDs and
                   More.
            </descr>
            <readAccess>0</readAccess>
            <writeAccess>1</writeAccess>
            <src>xmlschemas.xml</src>
            <admin idref="kc@halcyon.com">
            <msgCount>125<msgCount>
            <baseMsgCount>28</baseMsgCount>
            <msgIndex>129</msgIndex>
        </board>
    </category>
    <category id="services" public="yes">
        <board id="joboffers">
            <title>Offering Employment</title>
            <descr>Search this board for available
                   XML and development related positions.
            </descr>
            <readAccess>1</readAccess>
            <writeAccess>1</writeAccess>
            <src>joboffers.xml</src>
            <admin idref="cagle@olywa.net">
            <msgCount>65<msgCount>
```

```
            <baseMsgCount>56</baseMsgCount>
            <msgIndex>67</msgIndex>
        </board>
        <board id="componentoffers">
            <title>Component Needs</title>
            <descr>If you are a freelance developer and
                   want to work on specific components
                   check out this site.
            </descr>
            <readAccess>1</readAccess>
            <writeAccess>1</writeAccess>
            <src>componentoffers.xml</src>
            <admin idref="cagle@olywa.net">
            <msgCount>64<msgCount>
            <baseMsgCount>62</baseMsgCount>
            <msgIndex>65</msgIndex>
        </board>
    </category>
    <!-- more categories and boards as needed -->
</boards>
```

Before you can enter a message board, you need to be able to see basic information about the board—its category and title, for example, as well as how many messages are currently on the board and, ideally, whether the message boards have changed since you last visited. The XML structure described here contains some of that information, but, as you may have noticed, it doesn't contain any information about the number of messages that the board contains, nor does it contain date information. The filter that displays this information, then, will actually need to query the files that contain the actual message boards to retrieve this data.

The actual message board files have names that initially correspond to the ID of the board, but there's no strict requirement for this; it's an artifact of the way that the boards are set up in the first place. The `<src>` field could contain a fully qualified URL that points to a message board located on a different machine (or through a different interface, such as a SQL Server 2000 query filtered by a template).

Access Permissions

Access permissions can be a fairly complicated problem to handle, especially when you are trying to build such systems across multiple platforms. While fairly primitive, the message boards contain a way of handling such permissions. A message board assumes that there are four classes of users on the system:

- Anonymous Users (0), who can often read messages on the site but can't post them.
- Registered Users (1), who can both read and write messages. Registered users are maintained in a user database.

Access Permissions *(continued)*

- Authors (2), who have permission to read or write to specific message boards (the boards are contained in their user profiles). These may be content developers for something like a Frequently Asked Question (or FAQ) board or may be members of a limited-access message board.
- Admin (3), who have the ability to read or write at all levels.

The attributes cascade: An Author can read any Registered User or Anonymous User message. A board can (and typically will) have different attributes for reading and writing. For example, even the most open board, one available to anonymous users, would only allow users to read the message board; they would have to register to write to it. In most cases, the Write permission is equal to or higher than the Read permission, but areas such as bug reports can actually serve as mailing services that are effectively write only, since you're sending a message to an administrator. Finally, only the creator of a message (by definition a Registered User or above) can delete that message—the only exception to that being an administrator, who can delete any messages (or boards, for that matter).

Saving Documents Internally

I concentrate in this section on the mechanism in the `showBoards.xsl` script that determines both the number of messages and the ID of the most recent message within the board. Each message board retains an index generator that increments automatically when a new message is added. Although messages can be deleted, the generator won't be decremented again, so there is a guarantee that the index of any new messages will always be higher than that of existing messages. This is also a convenient way of bypassing the issue of date conversions, an issue that can prove awkward and error prone.

The message boards themselves are hierarchical in nature: A message can contain one or more messages that are responses to the initial message, which can, in turn, contain one or more messages, and so forth. A (small) part of one message board is shown in Listing 8.9, a message board fragment:

Listing 8.9: A Message Board Fragment (*Listing8.9.xml*)

```
<board id="general" indexKey="4">
        <title>General Site Board</title>
        <descr>This is essentially the "welcoming
                board" for the site.  Come here to
                introduce yourself, find out more about
                the site, or bring up important points
                to the general membership.
        </descr>
```

```
        <date>2/5/2000 2:25:15</date>
        <moderator>Kurt Cagle</moderator>
        <moderatorEmail>cagle@olywa.net</moderatorEmail>
        <messages>
            <message id="1">
                <title><![CDATA[A starting message]]></title>
                <date>2/6/2000 5:50:13 PM</date>
                <from>Kurt Cagle</from>
                <email>cagle@olywa.net</email>
                <isLive>yes</isLive>
                <body><![CDATA[This is a basic message.]]></body>
                <message id="2">
                    <title><![CDATA[Re:A starting message]]></title>
                    <date>2/6/2000 5:56:13 PM</date>
                    <from>Kurt Cagle</from>
                    <email>cagle@olywa.net</email>
                    <isLive>yes</isLive>
                    <body><[CDATA[!This is a response to
the previous message, and is actually contained in the
 message this is a response to.]]></body>
                </message>
            </message>
            <message id="3">
                    <title><![CDATA[A second message]]></title>
                <date>2/6/2000 6:15:13 PM</date>
                <from>Kurt Cagle</from>
                <email>cagle@olywa.net</email>
                <isLive>yes</isLive>
                <body><![CDATA[This is another message at
the same scope as the first message in the board.]]></body>
            </message>
        </message>
    </messages>
</board>
```

This example gives a basic idea about how the structure is set up, although it's worth remembering that a typical board may have hundreds or even thousands of messages associated with it. The XML does give rise to two distinct pieces of information worth knowing: the number of messages in total and the number of base messages, those that are not written in response to some other message, given in the table of contents XML as <msgCount> and <baseMsgCount>, respectively.

While the number of either message or base message can be calculated easily from the boards, you wouldn't want to retrieve this every time someone comes to the table of contents page. To see why, consider that a message board system may contain several dozen (or even several hundred) distinct boards. Opening up each of these large files, performing a count on their indices, then closing them again would be a significant hit even if you had only one person interacting with the message boards at any given time, and it is far more likely that there will, in fact, be dozens of people pulling from the boards simultaneously.

Instead, the most logical way of handling the problem is to update the table of contents whenever a change is made to any given board, changing only the information for the board that was modified. In that sense, the table of contents file begins to take on some of the capabilities of a registry, a comparison that I intend to exploit further. The XSLT filter `updateToC.xsl` (Listing 8.10) does this update by taking as a parameter the ID of the message board to be updated, opening up the message board in question, retrieving the count of messages, base messages, and the index key, opening the TOC, recording the changes, and then saving the TOC from where it was loaded.

Listing 8.10: Updating the Table of Contents (*Listing8.10.xsl*)

```
<!-- This assumes that toc.xml is the input stream -->
<xsl:stylesheet xmlns:xsl="http://www.w3.org/1999/XSL/Transform"
        xmlns:utils="http://www.vbxml.com/utils"
        xmlns:msxsl="urn:schemas-microsoft-com:xslt"
        version="1.0">
    <xsl:output method="xml" omit-xml-declaration="yes"/>

    <xsl:param name="boardID"/>

    <msxsl:script implements-prefix="utils"
    language="Javascript"><![CDATA[
    function document(url){
        if (typeof(url)!="string"){
            url=url(0).text;
            }
        var xmlDoc=new ActiveXObject("MSXML2.DOMDocument");
        xmlDoc.async=false;
        xmlDoc.load(url);
        return xmlDoc;
        }

    function persistDocumentTo(url,context){
        if (typeof(url)!="string"){
            url=url(0).text;
            }
        var xmlDoc=new ActiveXObject("MSXML2.DOMDocument");
        xmlDoc.documentElement=context(0).cloneNode.true;
        xmlDoc.save(url);
```

```
                return xmlDoc;
                }
        ]]>     </msxsl:script>

           <xsl:template match="/">
              <xsl:variable name="boardRef"
                  select="//board[@id=$boardID]"
              <xsl:variable name="board" select="utils:document($boardRef/src)"/>
              <xsl:variable name="newToc">
                  <boards>
                     <xsl:apply-templates select="//category"/>
                  </boards>
              </xsl:variable>
              <xsl:copy-of select="utils:persistDocumentTo(
                  'toc.xml',$newToc)" disable-output-escaping="yes"/>
           </xsl:template>

           <xsl:template match="category">
                <xsl:choose>
                     <xsl:when test=".[board[@id=$boardID]]">
                          <category id="{@id}" public="{@public}">
                               <xsl:apply-templates
                                    select="board"/>
                          </category>
                     </xsl:when>
                     <xsl:otherwise>
                          <xsl:copy-of select="."/>
                     </xsl:otherwise>
                </xsl:choose>
           <xsl:template>

           <xsl:template match="board">
                <xsl:choose>
                     <xsl:when test=".[@id=$boardID]">
                          <board id="{@id}">
              <xsl:variable name="msgCount"
                   select="count($board//message)"/>
              <xsl:variable name="baseMsgCount"
                   select="count($board//messages/message)"/>
              <xsl:variable name="msgIndex"
                   select="count($board//messages/@indexKey)"/>
                   <title>
                      <xsl:value-of select="$board/title"/>
                   </title>
                   <descr>
                      <xsl:value-of select="$board/descr"/>
                   </descr>
```

```
            <readAccess>
                <xsl:value-of select="$board/readAccess"/>
            </readAccess>
            <writeAccess>
                <xsl:value-of select="$board/readAccess"/>
            </writeAccess>
            <src>
                <xsl:value-of select="$board/src"/>
            </src>
            <admin>
                <xsl:copy-of select="$board/admin"/>
            </readAccess>
            <msgCount>
                <xsl:value-of select="$msgCount"/>
            </msgCount>
            <baseMsgCount>
                <xsl:value-of select="$baseMsgCount"/>
            </baseMsgCount>
            <msgIndex>
                <xsl:value-of select="$msgIndex"/>
            </msgIndex>
                  </board>
             </xsl:when>
             <xsl:otherwise>
                  <xsl:copy-of select="."/>
             </xsl:otherwise>
        </xsl:choose>
    <xsl:template>

  </xsl:stylesheet>
```

To borrow a line from the movie *Ghostbusters*, the one thing you must avoid doing is crossing the streams; this is bad. To explain this, consider the difference between procedural and declarative languages. In a procedural language, you are dealing with objects with explicit properties that you can change. In declarative languages, you are dealing with streams; the XML coming in (from the `toc.xml` file) cannot be changed, but it can be duplicated (this is one of the reasons that an XSL variable cannot be changed once created).

This is essentially the technique that is used here: A stream is assigned to the variable `$newToc`, which duplicates the effects of the normal output stream. Thus, the template matches for category and board aren't, in fact, streaming to the default output stream but instead are being sent to the `$newToc` stream. This stream can then be persisted using the previously defined `utils:persistDocumentTo()` method. With a judicious bit of planning, the output of this object is the changed table of contents, which can, in turn, be passed back to the default output stream.

From Properties to Plumbing

The procedural programmers among you may be squirming a little bit about this last transformation. It seems like an incredible amount of work just to change a few properties, something that could be handled with a JavaScript or a VBScript code in perhaps half the number of lines of code. It is a valid criticism, in this simple case in particular, but with the exception of the actual persistence code (an artifact of the current implementation, not of the language itself, and one that's not really all that necessary), the principles displayed here are handled completely within an XML context. You could swap out the category and message templates and replace them with any other matches you need without ever leaving an XML environment.

Moreover, it becomes possible (although more complex than I deal with in this chapter, so see Chapter 11, "XML and Programming") to create handlers that are very generic. Since the structure involved here—an index file that contains references to other XML content files—is very common, this means that with some work you can essentially abstract out the whole process and create a mechanism for updating the index whenever any of its child files changes. As you read the other examples contained in this chapter (and in the book hereafter), start thinking about abstraction; it's one of XML's greatest strengths and an advantage that XML holds over the more objectified reality of OOP programming.

Persisting Session Data

The `Session` object is a staple of most ASP programming, but it runs into a number of limitations—specifically the following—that make it less than ideal in the XML/XSL world:

Cookies Sessions are highly reliant on client-side cookies. If such a cookie mechanism doesn't exist (or if the user turns cookies off), then there is no clear-cut mechanism to retain state on the server.

Session Timeout A session keeps a connection "alive" so that the client and server know about one another. However, if a user leaves a connection inactive for too long, the session times out and relevant information gets lost.

Session Is an Object The `Session` object is just that: an object, which makes it awkward (though not impossible) to work within the context of XSL. It can, however, have its values retrieved through keys in a manner that is similar to the way that the `Request` object works.

Session Is External The `Session` object is a distinct part of the ASP environment and can't be queried through an internal XSL mechanism without passing it in from the outside.

Thus, a solution that either bypasses or enhances the capabilities of the `Session` object needs to be examined before any architecture is built onto it, since session maintenance is a key part of any server setup.

The first solution to this, and one that's already been alluded to in the previous section, is to design your architecture in such a way that you don't need to worry about state, by simply passing state information through query string or form. Unfortunately, this mechanism only really works for relatively simple state information; an anchor tag on an HTML form isn't going to have the depth to transmit large chunks of information, and it makes the code awkward to both write and debug.

The second solution is to convert the session state information into XML when the page instantiates and then convert it back into a `Session` object when the session terminates. This can actually work well for XML information when a session state is guaranteed, and this solution would use a mechanism similar to that of the `Request` object, as shown in Listing 8.11.

Listing 8.11: Session State Functions (*Listing8.11.vb*)

```
function getSessionXML()
    dim xmlDoc
    set xmlDoc=server.createObject("Microsoft.XMLDOM")
    xmlDoc.loadXML "<keys/>"
    set collectionNode=xmlDoc.createElement("collection")
    collectionNode.setAttribute "id","session"
    collectionNode.setAttribute "sessionID",session.sessionID
    for each key in session.contents
        set keyNode=xmlDoc.createElement("key")
        keyNode.setAttribute "id",key
        keyNode.text=session(key)
        collectionNode.appendChild keyNode
    next
    set getSessionXML=xmlDoc
end function

function passSessionObjectTo(xslDoc)
    collectionsString="all"
    set sessionDoc=getSessionXML()
    set param=xslDoc.selectSingleNode("//xsl:param[@name='session']")
    if param is nothing then
        set _
param=xslDoc.documentElement.insertBefore _
(xslDoc.createElement("xsl:param"), _
xslDoc.selectSingleNode("//xsl:template"))
        param.setAttribute "name","session"
    end if
    while param.childNodes.length>0 then
        param.removeChild param.childNodes(0)
    wend
    param.appendChild sessionDoc.documentElement
end function
```

This function will end up passing a keys collection to the XSL filter under the parameter `<xsl:param name="session">`:

```
<keys>
   <collection id="session" sessionID="748945042">
      <key id="key1">This is the first session variable</key>
      <key id="key2">Here's the second.</key>
</collection>
</keys>
```

This collection can be accessed in exactly the same way that the `Request` keys can—through the XPath expression `$session//key[@id='token']`—where *`token`* can take the name of any session key.

Setting new keys within an XSL document is a little more complex, and lies at the heart of why session state is such a pain to maintain effectively. There is no easy way to pass any XML out of an XSL filter except through persisting and retrieving it or through passing it to the generic output stream. However, ASP sessions don't take place in a vacuum: There are typically any number of users accessing the server simultaneously. If an XML stream is persisted to a standard file, there is no way to make sure that the file saved within the XSL filter has not been overwritten by another session before the current session has a chance to retrieve the file, short of uniquely identifying the file as belonging to this particular session.

Thus, a way of identifying the user uniquely is still required in this scenario. As it stands, in addition to the session tokens, the session XML stream also contains a unique `sessionID` attribute, attached to the `<collection>` node. This attribute is also used by the `Session` object itself and can be used to retrieve the XML file from its temporary storage place once the XSL script terminates.

With this information, you can create a local XML document in the XSL structure in script, then define four functions: `initializeSession()`, `setSessionVariable()`, `getSessionVariable()`, and `persistSession()`. `initializeSession()` takes the `Session` object as a parameter and creates a read/write version of the same object. `setSessionVariable()` passes the name of the variable and the given XML context into the session XML structure, either creating a new variable with the name or changing the contents of an existing variable. `getSessionVariable()` retrieves the named variable, and `persistSession()` saves the current state to a file called `_temp_sessionID.xml`, where `sessionID` is the current session ID (e.g., `_temp_748945042.xml`). The implementations of these four functions are shown in Listing 8.12.

Listing 8.12: XML Session Object Code (*Listing8.12.xsl*)

```
<!-- This assumes that toc.xml is the input stream -->
<xsl:stylesheet xmlns:xsl="http://www.w3.org/1999/XSL/Transform"
        xmlns:session="http://www.vbxml.com/utils"
        xmlns:msxsl="urn:schemas-microsoft-com:xslt"
        version="1.0">
    <xsl:output method="xml" omit-xml-declaration="yes"/>

    <xsl:param name="session"/>

    <msxsl:script implements-prefix="session"
    language="Javascript"><![CDATA[

    Var session=new ActiveXObject("MSXML2.DOMDocument")
    function initializeSession(sessionContext){
        session.documentElement=
            sessionContext(0).selectSingleNode(
            "//keys").cloneNode(true);
         var keyNode=session.selectSingleNode(
              "//key[@id='"+key+"']");
         return keyNode.getAttribute("sessionID")
         }

    function setSessionVariable(key,context){
         var keyNode=session.selectSingleNode(
              "//key[@id='"+key+"']");
         if (keyNode==null){
             var collectionNode=session.selectSingleNode(
                  "//collection");
             keyNode=collectionNode.appendChild(
                   collectionNode.createElement("key"))
             keyNode.setAttribute("id")=key
             }
         for (childNode in keyNode.childNodes){
             keyNode.removeChild(childNode);
             }
         for (childNode in context){
             keyNode.appendChild(childNode);
             }
         }

    function getSessionVariable(key){
         var keyNode=session.selectSingleNode(
              "//key[@id='"+key+"']");
```

```
        if (keyNode!=null){
           return keyNode;
           }
        else {
            return "#ERROR: No key named '"+
               key+"'#";
            }
        }

    function persistSession(){
        var sessionID=session.selectSingleNode(
            "//@sessionID").text
        persistDocumentTo("_temp_"+sessionID+".xml",
            session);
        }

    function document(url){
        if (typeof(url)!="string"){
            url=url(0).text;
            }
        var xmlDoc=new ActiveXObject("MSXML2.DOMDocument");
        xmlDoc.async=false;
        xmlDoc.load(url);
        return xmlDoc;
        }

    function persistDocumentTo(url,context){
        if (typeof(url)!="string"){
            url=url(0).text;
            }
        var xmlDoc=new ActiveXObject("MSXML2.DOMDocument");
        xmlDoc.documentElement=context(0).cloneNode.true;
        xmlDoc.save(url);
        return xmlDoc;
        }
]]>     </msxsl:script>
    <!-- more code -->

    <xsl:param name="session">
        <keys>
            <collection id="session" sessionID="0"/>
        </keys>
    </xsl:param>

    <xsl:variable name="sessionID"
      select="session:initializeSession($session)"/>
```

Note the declaration of the <xsl:param> and <xsl:variable> tags at the end of the script. If the session isn't otherwise defined, then a dummy parameter value is set up that contains a collection but no keys. The sessionID isn't actually likely to be required in the XSL structure itself, but it serves as an excuse to invoke the initializeSession() method, which returns the session ID anyway and prepares the session XML object for use.

The getSessionVariable() takes a key name as a parameter and returns an XML context object, while setSessionVariable accepts both a key name and a context object:

```
<xsl:value-of select=
    "session:getSessionVariable('formInfo')"/>
<xsl:value-of select=
    "session:setSessionVariable('formInfo',.)"/>
```

SetSessionVariable(), by the way, returns a null string, so it has no impact on the output stream. Finally, persistSession() automatically saves as indicated earlier, likewise returning a null string to the output stream. persistSession() should be invoked prior to the XSL script terminating, as any changes made to the session state will not get reflected into the temporary file.

TIP

You can use these session variables to work with writeable variables in your XSL, although for both performance and portability reasons you should keep the use of such variables to a minimum.

Once the XSL filter terminates and you return to the ASP environment, you can use the function updateSession() to convert the XML file back into session variables, as in Listing 8.13. Note that if no initial session was supplied, then the session XML will be contained in the file named _temp_0.xml. Both the session ID file and the default file are automatically deleted.

Listing 8.13: Session State Functions (*Listing8-13.txt*)

```
function updateSession()
    dim xmlDoc
    set xmlDoc=server.createObject("Microsoft.XMLDOM")
    xmlDoc.async=false
    dim fso
    set fso=server.createObject(
          "Scripting.FileSystemObject")
    filename=server.mapPath(
         "_temp_"+server.serverID+".xml")
    if fso.fileExists(filename) then
        xmlDoc.load filename
        fso.deleteFile filename
```

```
        else
        filename=server.mapPath("_temp_0.xml")
            if fso.fileExists(filename) then
                xmlDoc.load filename
                fso.deleteFile filename
            end if
        end if
        if not (xmlDoc is nothing) then
            for each keyNode in xmlDoc.selectNodes("//key")
                session(keyNode.getAttribute("id"))=keyNode.xml
            next
        end if
    end function
```

Can You Do Sessions without a *Session* Object?

The `Session` object is a fairly heavily used part of most ASP development, but there is a hint here that you can get by without it.

The most difficult part of maintaining session state is retaining unique information about the user on the other end of the server. While server applications such as ASP maintain a unique ID that identifies a specific user profile, you can at least determine if the same machine is used in a transaction by looking at its REMOTE_ADDR (remote address) property in the `Request` object. Since that is passed in as part of the request XML structure, you can actually load a file with a reference to the IP address (such as `_temp_127.0.0.1.xml`), use the methods discussed in this section for referencing stored elements, and then persist the file back to the server's hard drive.

There are three minor problems with this technique. The first has to with the fact that a machine may have more than one user profile but only one IP address. This is not likely a major issue, by the way; the purpose of the `Session` object is to maintain state during a session, and a person disconnecting and another person reconnecting on the same machine during the same session is fairly unlikely.

A more serious issue comes from the fact that session timeouts exist for a reason: If your Web site takes a significant number of hits then your hard drive may quickly fill up with interim state files. If you do want to go this route, you should think about inserting a time stamp into an XML index file, then periodically removing all sessions older than a certain period.

Finally, file access is far slower than keeping `Session` objects in memory. If performance is an issue, you may be better off parameterizing the information you need from the session variables and passing that data in directly rather than building a `Session` object indirectly, at least at this point in the evolution of XML.

Working with Output Streams

Active Server Pages were originally designed for the purpose of "serving" Web pages, and they still perform that task admirably. However, as with most such Web servers, they do far more than just dish out HTML code. It is useful to switch contexts with ASP, moving it away from being a program that returns HTML upon request and focusing it instead on being a program that serves data streams upon request.

The `Response` object acts as the conduit that transmits formatted information to the client from the server, and as such it works well into the stream architecture that's been discussed in this chapter. `Response` has a number of properties and methods of interest to the XML developer, which are covered in Table 8.1.

TABLE 8.1: `Response` Properties and Methods

Property or Method	What It Does	Importance for XML
`AddHeader(bstrHeader-Name,bstrHeaderValue)`	Adds an HTTP header to the response stream.	Useful for sending document information to client.
`AppendToLog(bstrLogEntry)`	Adds a string to the IIS log session.	Useful for debugging.
`BinaryWrite(varInput)`	Writes out binary information to the client.	Principally useful with XMLHTTP.
`Buffer`	If true, then buffers output. Otherwise, page is sent at the termination of the ASP script.	Useful for controlling amount of XML sent to client for display. Used in conjunction with `Flush()`.
`CharSet`	Sets the character set used by the output.	Ditto.
`Clear`	Empties the buffer without transmitting any information.	Useful for controlling output on errors.
`ContentType`	Sets the MIME type of the document.	This usually will need to be set explicitly to `"text/xml"`.
`Cookies`	Lets you write cookies to the client.	Useful for storing general information; in theory, you could send an XML document into a cookie, though this is generally not recommended.
`End`	Terminates the ASP session and transmits the information to the client.	Usually only required with buffered output.
`Expires`	Gives the time in minutes until the page must refresh itself.	Setting expires to –1 will automatically force a refresh of the page, something that's essential to an ASP XML server.

TABLE 8.1: Response Properties and Methods *(continued)*

Property or Method	What It Does	Importance for XML
`ExpiresAbsolute`	Gives an absolute time before the current page should no longer be cached.	Of minimal importance.
`Flush`	Clears the output buffer after sending the contents of the buffer.	Used heavily with buffered output, this can let you fine tune your output time.
`IsClientConnected`	Returns true if a client session is active.	Useful for determining if you need to refresh your state.
`Pics`	Collection for controlling content ratings for your page.	Minimally useful.
`Redirect(bstrURL)`	Redirects the source of the output stream to a new location.	This can prove handy with an XML server, as it allows techniques to perform conditional output based upon parameters rather than filenames.
`Status`	Sets the error status text of the page.	This can be useful for handling XML errors on the server, as you can modify this string to reflect errors in the object itself.
`Write(varText)`	Sends the specified text to either the output stream or to a text buffer.	*The* `Response` method that you will use for most XML output, unless you're working with XMLHTTP.

ASP code falls into two basic categories: code in which the page is relatively static and content that changes with each query, even given the same initial parameters. The `Response.Expires` property controls this, and understanding its use with XML is even more important than it is for HTML. `Expires` gives the number of minutes until the page expires (i.e., until a request to the server will force ASP to rerun the script instead of relying on a copy cached on the client).

If your content is relatively static—if you're serving up XML that doesn't have frequent updates, for example, you can get by without even setting the `expires` property—the client-side cache will maintain this information for the user's desired period. However, if the data changes frequently, you should set `response.expires = -1`. This will automatically force the page to refresh itself.

The `ContentType` property should also be set when outputting XML pages, although things get a little more complicated here. The `<xsl:output>` element can take as values either `xml`, `html`, or `text`, each of which sets the type of the XML stream to the appropriate MIME type (`text/xml`, `text/html` and `text/plain`, respectively). However, the ASP content type (which is also set to the MIME type) will override this in all cases. With the current implementation of ASP, you should execute the line

```
Response.ContentType="text/xml"
```

prior to sending any data into the body of the output stream, if you want the output to be XML. If you're sending this to a browser, by the way, the `ContentType` header should control whether the browser displays the result as an HTML document or as an XML document.

Buffering output makes a great deal of sense when used in conjunction with XML. To turn buffering on, you should declare `Response.Buffer=true` before sending any information (header declarations or body content). This tells the ASP engine to save the building content into a text buffer rather than just sending it to the default output stream. You can fill a buffer partially (say, by writing a record in XML to the output stream via `Response.Write`) and then call `Response.Flush` to send the data to the client and clear the buffer. This works especially well when dealing with asynchronous XML structures on the client since you can catch updates via the `onreadystatechange` event to start processing your structure even before the whole document has been downloaded.

Buffering lets you do something else, too: handle errors effectively. Periodically, errors happen—the server for a critical piece of information has just busted a hard drive, a bad parameter was passed, and so forth. In this case, you can use buffering to halt the output production at the point where the error occurred, clear the buffer, then send an XML error message to indicate that a problem occurred, as shown in the following listing:

```
<%@LANGUAGE="VBSCRIPT%>
xmlDoc.buffer=true
xmlDoc.async=true
xmlDoc.load server.mapPath("myMisnamedFile.xml")
if xmlDoc.parseError.errorCode <> 0 then
    'create a quick object, then send it
    set errorDoc=createObject("Microsoft.XMLDOM")
    errorDoc.loadxml "<error/>"
    with xmlDoc.parseError
        errorDoc.setAttribute "erroreode",.errorcode
        errorDoc.setAttribute "charpos",.charpos
        errorDoc.setAttribute "linepos",.linepos
        errorDoc.setAttribute "line",.charpos
        errorDoc.setAttribute "srctext",.srctext
        errorDoc.setAttribute "url",.url
        errorDoc.text=.reason
    end with
    Response.Clear
    Response.Write errorDoc.xml
```

```
        Response.Flush
    else
        ' Handle the code
    end if
```

TIP Establishing regular error-handling routines for your XML should be designed in from the start. While they don't improve the performance of the final Web application, they are crucial when developing.

Constructing XML Servers with ASP

Parametric XML is cool, but in many (if not most) cases, if you're trying to retrieve XML (or, for XHTML, see the "Building XHTML Components" section), loading several objects, setting up parameterization, and then dealing with the output can beg the question of why XML is so advantageous. However, you can take advantage of ASP to encapsulate this function not as a procedural function but as a URL with query-string or form parameters.

For example, consider that most of the XML operations that you are going to be dealing with will likely center around two areas: transforming an XML document with an XSL filter that has parameters and querying an XML document for a specific XML node set. I faced this problem myself, and while the logical solution to the problem of transforming an XML document would be to use query-string name/value pairs as parameters, I couldn't think of a clean way of building an interface that differentiated parameters from filenames, for instance. Then it occurred to me that filtering out filenames to those that started with a unique token would do it.

Listing 8.14 is one of my workhorse functions: You pass the name of the XML resource in the `source` parameter, the name of the XSL resource in the `filter` parameter, and the `type` (content type) of the output as parameters in a form or a query string (where `type` defaults to `xml` but can also take the values of `html` or `text`).

Listing 8.14: *XMLserver* Lets You Filter an XML Source with a Parameteric XSL Source. (*Listing8.14.asp*)

```
<%@LANGUAGE="VBSCRIPT"%>
<%
response.expires=-1
function processXML()
    src=request("source")
    xfilter=request("filter")
    mimetype=request("type")
    if mimetype="" then
        mimetype="xml"
    end if
```

```
    Response.ContentType="text/"+mimetype
    set xmlDoc=createObject("Microsoft.XMLDOM")
    set xslDoc=createObject("Microsoft.XMLDOM")
    xmlDoc.async=false
    xslDoc.async=false
    xmlDoc.load server.mapPath(src)
    xslDoc.load server.mapPath(xfilter)
    for each key in request.queryString
       setParameter xslDoc,key,request(key)
    next
    for each key in request.form
       setParameter xslDoc,key,request(key)
    next
    response.write xmlDoc.transformNode(xslDoc)
end function

function setParameter(xslDoc,key,keyValue)
        if left(key,6)="param_" then
           key=lcase(mid(key,7))
           set
keynode=xslDoc.selectSingleNode("//xsl:param _
[@name='"+key+"']")
           if not keynode is nothing then
              keynode.setAttribute "select","'"+cstr(keyValue)+"'"
           end if
        end if
        if left(key,6)="param*" then
           key=lcase(mid(key,7))
           set
keynode=xslDoc.selectSingleNode _
("//xsl:param[@name='"+key+"']")
           if not keynode is nothing then
              keynode.setAttribute "select",".["+cstr(keyValue)+"]"
           end if
        end if

end function

processXML
%>
```

Thus, for the message board example, I have a TreeView XSL control that displays the messages and their responses (the details of which are covered in the following "Building XHTML Components" section). To be able to apply to a message board a file that produces the list of messages in a tree-like structure (assuming both are in the same directory as the ASP file), you would need to use the following URL:

```
http://www.myserver.com/xmlserver.asp?
    source=general.xml&filter=simpleTreeView.xsl
```

The specific XSL transform, contained in the file `simpleTreeView.xsl`, employs a number of parameters that can determine the characteristics of the resulting tree. The parameters for the XSL function are passed using two prefixes: `param_` and `param*`. The distinction between the two is subtle but important. The expression `param_` points to a parameter that gets passed as a string into the XSL filter (`param_caption=body`, for example, translates into `<xsl:param name="caption" select="'body'"/>`). On the other hand, `param*` actually passes an XPath expression, with `param*object=//message` translating as `<xsl:param name="object" select="//message"/>`.

For example, the `$caption` property determines what specific property in the message block is displayed (with the default being the `title` node). To change this to `body`, which would display the text of each message rather than the titles as the control's captions, you'd change the preceding URL to the following:

```
http://www.myserver.com/xmlserver.asp?source=general.xml&
    filter=simpleTreeView.xsl&param_caption=body
```

Note that while this URL could be typed in at a browser window or generated from an anchor tag, it could just as easily be an argument passed to an XML load method (either on the client or, more importantly, on the server):

```
dim xmlDoc
set xmlDoc=createObject("Microsoft.XMLDOM")
xmlDoc.async=false
xmlDoc.load "http://www.myserver.com/xmlserver.asp?_
   source=general.xml&filter=simpleTreeView.xsl&_
   param_caption=body"
```

Additionally (at least in theory), as the following snippet demonstrates, the XPath `document()` method could also call the URL to retrieve such content into the XSL filter, although that feature wasn't implemented in the most recent MSXML component (though it should be in the final version).

```
<xsl:variable name="dynList"
   select="document(http://www.myserver.com/xmlserver.asp?_
   source=general.xml&filter=simpleTreeView.xsl&_
   param_caption=body)"/>
<xsl:copy-of select="$dynList" disable-output-escaping="yes"/>
```

As XSL becomes more mainstream, using ASP to serve it up in this fashion will likely become a common option. The same process can be used to retrieve a set of nodes, such as the set of all messages written by Kurt Cagle, sorted by date. Rather than placing this functionality in the ASP script, use the `xmlserver.asp` script, and call an XSL filter (`getFilteredRecords.xsl`) with the appropriate parameters, as shown in Listing 8.15.

Listing 8.15: *getFilteredRecords* Can Be Used to Retrieve Nodes from an XML Document. (*Listing8.15.xsl*)

```
<xsl:stylesheet
xmlns:xsl=http://www.w3.org/1999/XSL/Transform
 version="1.0">
    <xsl:output method="xml" omit-xml-declaration="yes"/>
    <xsl:param name="collectionname" select="'messages'"/>
    <xsl:param name="objectname" select="'message'"/>
    <xsl:param name="sortby" select="'title'"/>
    <xsl:param name="sorttype" select="'text'"/>
    <xsl:param name="sortorder" select="'ascending'"/>
    <xsl:template match="/">
        <xsl:element name="{$collectionname}">
            <xsl:apply-templates select="//*[name(.)=$objectname]">
                    <xsl:sort select="$sortby" data-
type="{$sorttype}" order="{$sortorder}"/>
            </xsl:apply-templates>
        </xsl:element>
    </xsl:template>
    <xsl:template match="*">
        <xsl:param name="criterion" select=".[from='Mark Wilson']"/>
        <xsl:for-each select="$criterion">
            <xsl:copy-of select="."/>
        </xsl:for-each>
    </xsl:template>
</xsl:stylesheet></xsl:stylesheet>
```

To retrieve the aforementioned set of all messages written by Kurt Cagle, sorted by date, you could call the following URL:

```
http://www.myserver.com/xmlserver.asp?source=messages.xml&
   filter=getFilteredRecords&param_collectionname=messages&
    param_objectname=message&param_sortorder=descending&
param*criterion=from='Kurt+Cagle'
```

Being able to combine the XML and XSL in a remote process, especially parameterized in this way, gives you a high degree of flexibility. Indeed, this best illustrates the concept of the remote server: By encapsulating the XML output of any operation behind a URL to an ASP or a related provider (such as a SQL Server or an Oracle database), you change these connections into anonymous sources—you know that they produce XML but, beyond that, you shouldn't know (or need to know) the specific implementation that generates that XML in the first place.

While the code discussed here has focused on the IIS objects and how they relate to XML, knowing how to be able to work with this information is as critical as knowing the API. In the next section, I look at a few sample applications for XML and ASP, returning first to the XML replacement for HTML: XHTML.

Building XHTML Components

One of the great ironies of XML development is that three years after the XML standard first saw the light of day the principal reason for creating it in the first place is still largely unfulfilled. The original intent of XML was to serve as a means to create output in browsers that was better suited to specific document requirements rather than relying on the context-poor HTML structure.

Unfortunately, only Internet Explorer 5.*x* supports the ability to view XML with a filter, although only with the browser, not when printed or displayed in source form (this will likely change with Internet Explorer 5.5). Netscape Navigator 4.*x* can't understand XML at all, although Navigator 6 looks like it may be capable of displaying information in a few different, well-defined XML formats. For the vast majority of Internet users out there, client-side support of XML simply won't be a standard state of affairs for several years to come.

In a way, however, this state of affairs may actually have a silver lining. The wide diversity of different browsers that are currently in circulation, plus those yet undreamed, makes it difficult to create Web pages that can target more than the most dominant ones. If, however, a core HTML standard that were compliant with XML emerged from the W3C, it would be possible to use server-side code to customize the output for the appropriate browser.

Such a standard exists and is called XHTML. Approved in January, 2000, the XHTML 1.0 Recommendation creates a version of HTML 4 that is fully compliant with the XML standard—quote-delimited attributes, properly terminated tags, the elimination of singleton tags, such as the `<OPTION>` attribute's `SELECTED` tag, in favor of fully resolved attributes (i.e., `SELECTED="yes"`). The changeover from HTML to XHTML is largely transparent; indeed, all of the HTML code in this book has been written using XHTML.

Catching Namespace Tags

From the standpoint of the server developer, XHTML offers two primary benefits. First of all, since XHTML is, in fact, also XML, it is easy to create XHTML as part of a pipeline process: XHTML gets generated by one XSL transform, incorporates additional XHTML through a second XSL transform, and can then be tweaked to best fit the client browser.

A second advantage to XHTML is that you can actually create XHTML "`behaviors`": tags (with attributes or other interior content) that can be trapped by an XSL filter and replaced with other XHTML code. This is a mechanism that is becoming increasingly common with languages like Java Server Pages, where XML tags incorporated into the body of XHTML code trigger Java classes that modify the code, and is something that has been a staple of Allaire's ColdFusion Server for years (albeit using proprietary tags rather than XML).

In essence, XML tag replacement involves a slight variation on the Identity Transformation. The simplest Identity Transformation is one in which the result stream is an exact duplicate of the source stream, as shown in Listing 8.16.

Listing 8.16: The Identity Transformation (*Listing8.16.xsl*)

```
<xsl:stylesheet
   xmlns:xsl="http://www.w3.org/1999/XSL/Transform"
   version="1.0">

   <xsl:template match="/">
      <xsl:apply-templates select="*"/>
   </xsl:template>

   <xsl:template name="identity"
   match="*|@*|text()|comment()|processing-instruction()">
      <xsl:copy><xsl:apply-templates
      select="*|@*|text()|comment()|processing-
      instruction()"/><xsl:copy>
   </xsl:template>
</xsl:stylesheet>
```

In and of itself, the Identity Transformation is rather useless. However, by placing additional template matches after the identity template, you can catch exceptions to the general rule, so that when you run the script you will end up with the starting document but with the flagged tags converted into new XML (or XHTML) code. In short, you have the server-side analog of a client-side DHTML behavior.

As a simple example, consider an XHTML document that contains a tag for retrieving page hits, as shown in Listing 8.17. The tag is defined as part of the `serv:` namespace, a namespace that I specifically made up to contain some of the server-side tags of general utility to readers.

Listing 8.17: A Sample Page-Hits Page (*Listing8-17.txt*)

```
<html xmlns:serv="http://www.vbxml.com/serv">
     <head>
        <title>Page Visits</title>
     </head>
```

```
    <body>
        <h1>Page Visits</h1>
        <p>This page has been visited <serv:pagehits
            href="pagehittest.htm"/> times.</p>
    </body>
</html>
```

The page-hits data itself is contained in another XML file called pageHits.xml (Listing 8.18). This is indexed so that each page has its own page count.

Listing 8.18: The Page Hits XML Source File (*Listing8-18.txt*)

```
<pagehits>
    <pagehit href="pagehittest.htm" counter="415"/>
    <pagehit href="main.htm" counter="6215"/>
    <pagehit href="index.htm" counter="42814"/>
</pagehits>
```

The XSL script that then replaces the <serv:pagehits> tag is a modified Identity Transformation that also updates the appropriate counter information (Listing 8.19). Note that you do need to declare the serv: namespace in the filter, as otherwise the XSL parser will complain vociferously.

Listing 8.19: A Limited *serv:* Filter (*Listing8.19.xsl*)

```
<xsl:stylesheet
   xmlns:xsl="http://www.w3.org/1999/XSL/Transform"
   xmlns:serv="http://www.vbxml.com/serv"
   xmlns:service="http://www.vbxml.com/servimpl"
   xmlns:msxsl="urn:schemas-microsoft-com:xslt"
   version="1.0">
    <xsl:output method="xml" omit-xml-declaration="yes"/>
    <msxsl:script implements-prefix="service"
    language="Javascript"><![CDATA[
function getPageHitCount(pageURL){
    var xmlDoc=new ActiveXObject("Microsoft.XMLDOM");
    xmlDoc.async=false;
    xmlDoc.load("pageHits.xml")
    var pageNode=xmlDoc.selectSingleNode(
        "//pagehit[@href='"+pageURL+"']");
    if (pageNode==null){
        pageNode=xmlDoc.documentElement.appendChild(
        xmlDoc.createElement("pagehit"));
        pageNode.setAttribute("href",pageURL)
        pageNode.setAttribute("counter",0)
        }
    pageHitCount=pageNode.getAttribute("counter")
```

```
        pageNode.setAttribute("counter",
              parseInt(pageHitCount)+1)
       xmlDoc.save("pageHits.xml")
       return pageHitCount
       }
 ]]>    </msxsl:script>

    <xsl:template match="/">
        <xsl:apply-templates select="*"/>
    </xsl:template>

    <xsl:template name="identity"
    match="*|@*|text()|comment()|processing-instruction()">
        <xsl:copy><xsl:apply-templates
        select="*|@*|text()|comment()|processing-
        instruction()"/></xsl:copy>
    </xsl:template>

    <xsl:template name="pagehits" match="serv:pagehits">
        <xsl:value-of
         select="service:getPageHitCount(string(@href))"/>
    </xsl:template>
 </xsl:stylesheet>
```

You can the use the `xmlserver.asp` script discussed in the last section (Listing 8.14) to perform the server filtering, with the following URL:

```
http://localhost/messageboards/xmlserver.asp?
source=pagehitstest.xml&filter=servFilter1.xsl&mimetype=html
```

When this runs, it will return a sample page showing the number of times the page has been accessed. Additionally, if the page has never been referenced before, then the code actually creates a new `<pagehits>` node in the `pagehits.xml` document and initializes it.

TIP Note that it would take relatively little effort to retrieve the page count number, convert the number to a string, then map each digit to a GIF filename (`coolNumber0.gif`, `coolNumber1.gif`, etc.). This gives you a quick-and-dirty cool counter, which could be parameterized for any number of different image "fonts."

While such a script obviously works, the danger in creating such a server XSL script implementation is that you'll probably want the `serv:` namespace to represent a number of different services, and as the script for the page counter showed, such an XSL filter could get huge quickly. However, by taking advantage of the pipeline architecture, you could actually simplify the process immensely. The document containing the identity transform could also act as a switching station, where each service, in turn, used `xmlserver.asp` to perform the actual calls against the `document()` object, as shown in Listing 8.20.

Listing 8.20: A Switching *serv:* Filter (*Listing8.20.xsl*)

```
<xsl:stylesheet
   xmlns:xsl="http://www.w3.org/1999/XSL/Transform"
   xmlns:serv="http://www.vbxml.com/serv"
   xmlns:service="http://www.vbxml.com/servimpl"
   xmlns:msxsl="urn:schemas-microsoft-com:xslt"
   version="1.0">
    <xsl:output method="xml" omit-xml-declaration="yes"/>

   <xsl:template match="/">
       <xsl:apply-templates select="*"/>
   </xsl:template>

   <xsl:template name="identity"
   match="*|@*|text()|comment()|processing-instruction()">
       <xsl:copy><xsl:apply-templates
       select="*|@*|text()|comment()|processing-
       instruction()"/></xsl:copy>
   </xsl:template>

   <xsl:template name="pagehits" match="serv:pagehits">
       <xsl:variable name="path">xmlserver.asp?
        source=stub.xml&filter=pagehits.xsl&
        param_href=<xsl:value-of select="string(@href)"/>
       </xsl:variable>
       <xsl:value-of
        select="document($path)"/>
   </xsl:template>
</xsl:stylesheet>
```

In essence, this delegates the responsibility of generating the `pagehits` update to a separate filter (called `pagehits.xsl`) and parameterizes the `@href` attribute. Because the source XML at this point is unimportant—the `pagehits.xsl` file just works off the root node to generate its output—the path loads in a `stub.xml` file, which simply contains the single tag `<stub/>`. The new `pagehits` filter file (Listing 8.21) is also simpler, since it doesn't have to include the Identity Transformation.

Listing 8.21: The *pageHits* Filter (*Listing8.21.xsl*)

```
<xsl:stylesheet
   xmlns:xsl="http://www.w3.org/1999/XSL/Transform"
   xmlns:serv="http://www.vbxml.com/serv"
   xmlns:service="http://www.vbxml.com/servimpl"
   xmlns:msxsl="urn:schemas-microsoft-com:xslt"
   version="1.0">
```

```
    <xsl:output method="xml" omit-xml-declaration="yes"/>
    <msxsl:script implements-prefix="service"
    language="Javascript"><![CDATA[
function getPageHitCount(pageURL){
    var xmlDoc=new ActiveXObject("Microsoft.XMLDOM");
    xmlDoc.async=false;
    xmlDoc.load("pageHits.xml")
    var pageNode=xmlDoc.selectSingleNode(
         "//pagehit[@href='"+pageURL+"']");
    if (pageNode==null){
        pageNode=xmlDoc.documentElement.appendChild(
        xmlDoc.createElement("pagehit"));
        pageNode.setAttribute("href",pageURL)
        pageNode.setAttribute("counter",0)
        }
    pageHitCount=pageNode.getAttribute("counter")
     pageNode.setAttribute("counter",
           parseInt(pageHitCount)+1)
    xmlDoc.save("pageHits.xml")
    return pageHitCount
    }
]]>    </msxsl:script>

    <xsl:parameter name="href"/>

    <xsl:template name="pagehits" match="/">
        <xsl:value-of
         select="service:getPageHitCount($href)"/>
    </xsl:template>
</xsl:stylesheet>
```

In this way, `servFilter2.xsl` could contain templates matching as many `serv:` tags as you choose to define, in turn delegating the actual implementation of the tags to different XSL filters. Of course, there is no requirement that you use the `xmlserver.asp` implementation; the URL could point to anything that generates a known XML stream, although parameterization methods will obviously be different.

Consider, for instance, a tag set that points to a URL that retrieves an XML block from a mobile server that returns the position of a laptop given by a global positioning satellite. The remote calls decouple the requirement that complex code exist on your server; indeed, the tags could call an XML-generating ASP script that, in turn, calls an XML-generating ASP script (or Java applet or related code) on another server that, in turn, calls the XML-generating code on the laptop. All you need to worry about is the immediate URL and the format of the XML code being received from the remote server.

Furthermore, your ASP code, in turn, may be used by another program to aggregate the locations of the laptops of the entire sales force and display them through a map drawn in SVG. This is one of the reasons that XSLT (and, consequently, XML) is so important. Everything becomes a stream, which is far more scalable in a distributed network than in an object-oriented environment.

A Configurable Outline Component

The code for setting up behaviors on the client can be immensely complicated. In addition to spending a great deal of time designing a component that can only be used on 20 percent of all browsers, development requires some intensely complex code for generating the output and really doesn't fit well into the XML paradigm. It would be far more satisfying to create something like a collapsible hierarchical view (for example) by placing the simpler tag

```
<serv:treeview source="generalMessages.xml"
 container="messages" object="message"
 caption="title"/>
```

into the XHTML code and preprocessing it on the server. Not only do you not have to worry about burdening your client with behaviors, but it's easier to make sure that the right code would be sent to the Netscape Navigator browser (or the Nokio XHTML component, or even the voice browser embedded into your client's car).

Creating a simple outline from XSLT is child's play; because XML is essentially hierarchical anyway, if you are outputting to XHTML, then you can use the HTML <LI> list element and either the <OL> or the <UL> tags for creating ordered (i.e., numbered) or unordered (i.e., bulleted) lists. What is not commonly appreciated, in part because HTML is very forgiving about not properly terminating a list element, is that the <LI> element is a container element: If you put another list element inside the first one, then that second list element will appear as a subordinate element.

Even better, if you put a list element inside of a <UL> or <OL> tag within another list element, then you have a transparent container that you can show or hide as a unit, which forms the basis for most collapsible tree implementations.

Thus, at its core, one of the more useful HTML structures looks something like Listing 8.22. The use of the <SPAN> element here is twofold: It makes it easy to apply styles just to the text without affecting any subordinate text, and it makes it easier to identify the children of a given node as elements (the <SPAN> is element 0, and the <UL> node is element 1).

Listing 8.22: A Sample HTML Outline (*Listing8-22.txt*)

```
<UL>
    <LI><SPAN>Chapter 1</SPAN>
        <UL>
            <LI><SPAN>Section 1</SPAN>
                <UL>
                    <LI><SPAN>Topic 1</SPAN>
                    <LI><SPAN>Topic 2</SPAN>
                </UL>
            </LI>
            <LI><SPAN>Section 2</SPAN>
                <UL>
                    <LI><SPAN>Topic 3</SPAN>
                    <LI><SPAN>Topic 4</SPAN>
                </UL>
            </LI>
        </UL>
    </LI>
    <LI><SPAN>Chapter 2</SPAN>
        <UL>
            <LI><SPAN>Section 3</SPAN>
                <UL>
                    <LI><SPAN>Topic 5</SPAN>
                    <LI><SPAN>Topic 6</SPAN>
                </UL>
            </LI>
            <LI><SPAN>Section 4</SPAN>
                <UL>
                    <LI><SPAN>Topic 7</SPAN>
                    <LI><SPAN>Topic 8</SPAN>
                </UL>
            </LI>
        </UL>
    </LI>
</UL>
```

I wanted to be able to create a simple outline transform that would take a class of XML hierarchical structures and render them in the same way, regardless of the actual names of the elements being displayed. As an additional set of features, I wanted to have the ability to parameterize the output so that it could equally be able to render output both as bulleted points and as a classical outline (remember the I.A.i.a.1 format from your high school English classes?).

I also wanted to have the ability to display any field in the outline that I was dealing with in the original XML, not just the obvious title or caption field. By parameterizing this caption attribute, I could switch from seeing a message's title to a message's body, with the press of a button.

Finally, I wanted to be able to specify a JavaScript function that would get called any time a particular item in the outline was selected; I didn't yet want to add collapsible capability, but I did want the outline to be sufficiently intelligent that it could be interactive rather than static. The result that I came up with is shown in Listing 8.23.

Listing 8.23: A Parametric Outline Filter (*Listing8.23.xsl*)

```
<xsl:stylesheet
 xmlns:xsl="http://www.w3.org/1999/XSL/Transform"
version="1.0">
<xsl:output type="html"/>
<xsl:param name="containername" select="'messages'"/>
<xsl:param name="objectname" select="'message'"/>
<xsl:param name="caption" select="'title'"/>
<xsl:param name="listtype" select="'ordered'"/>
<xsl:variable name="listContainer">
     <xsl:choose>
          <xsl:when
test="$listtype='unordered'">UL</xsl:when>
          <xsl:otherwise>OL</xsl:otherwise>
     </xsl:choose>
</xsl:variable>
<xsl:param name="clickevent"><![CDATA[
     //alert(me.id);
     window.status=me.id;
]]></xsl:param>
<xsl:param name="ordered1" select=
      "'list-style-type:upper-roman'"/>
<xsl:param name="ordered2" select=
      "'list-style-type:upper-alpha'"/>
<xsl:param name="ordered3" select=
      "'list-style-type:lower-roman'"/>
<xsl:param name="ordered4" select=
      "'list-style-type:lower-alpha'"/>
<xsl:param name="ordered5" select=
      "'list-style-type:numeric'"/>
<xsl:param name="unordered1" select=
      "'list-style-type:disc'"/>
<xsl:param name="unordered2" select=
      "'list-style-type:circle'"/>
<xsl:param name="unordered3" select=
      "'list-style-type:square'"/>
<xsl:param name="unordered4" select=
      "'list-style-type:diamond'"/>
```

```
<xsl:param name="unordered5" select=
     "'list-style-type:disc'"/>

<xsl:variable name="treelevelstylesheet">
    .ordered1 {<xsl:value-of
           select="$ordered1"/>;cursor:hand;}
    .ordered2 {<xsl:value-of select="$ordered2"/>}
    .ordered3 {<xsl:value-of select="$ordered3"/>}
    .ordered4 {<xsl:value-of select="$ordered4"/>}
    .ordered5 {<xsl:value-of select="$ordered5"/>}
    .unordered1 {<xsl:value-of
       select="$unordered1"/>;cursor:hand;}
    .unordered2 {<xsl:value-of select="$unordered2"/>}
    .unordered3 {<xsl:value-of select="$unordered3"/>}
    .unordered4 {<xsl:value-of select="$unordered4"/>}
    .unordered5 {<xsl:value-of select="$unordered5"/>}
</xsl:param>

<xsl:template match="/">
    <xsl:apply-templates
       select="//*[name(.)=$containername]"/>
</xsl:template>

<xsl:template match="*">
    <xsl:param name="treeLevel"/>
    <li>
    <xsl:attribute name="class"><xsl:value-of
       select="$listtype"/><xsl:value-of
       select="$treeLevel"/></xsl:attribute>
    <xsl:attribute name="id"><xsl:value-of
       select="@id"/></xsl:attribute>
    <xsl:attribute
  name="onclick">handleTreeClick(this)</xsl:attribute>
    <span><xsl:value-of
       select="*[name(.)=$caption]"/>(<xsl:value-of
       select="$treeLevel"/>)</span>
    <xsl:call-template name="drawNode">
        <xsl:with-param name="objectRef" select="*"/>
        <xsl:with-param name="treeLevel"
       select="number($treeLevel)+1"/>
    </xsl:call-template>
    </li>
</xsl:template>

<xsl:template match="*[name(.)=$containername]">
    <script language="JavaScript">
    function handleTreeClick(me){
```

```
        <xsl:value-of select="$clickevent"/>
        event.cancelBubble=true;
        }
        </script>
        <style>
        <xsl:value-of select="$treelevelstylesheet"/>
        </style>
        <xsl:call-template name="drawNode">
            <xsl:with-param name="objectRef" select="*"/>
            <xsl:with-param name="treeLevel" select="1"/>
        </xsl:call-template>
    </xsl:template>

    <xsl:template name="drawNode">
        <xsl:param name="objectRef"/>
        <xsl:param name="treeLevel"/>
        <xsl:element name="{$listContainer}">
        <xsl:apply-templates
           select="$objectRef[name(.)=$objectname]">
        <xsl:with-param name="treeLevel" select="$treeLevel"/>
                </xsl:apply-templates>
        </xsl:element>
    </xsl:template>
    </xsl:stylesheet>
```

To handle the requirements for customization rather than using the name of elements in the templates (say, `message`), I used a parameter (`$objectname`, for example) and then performed a match with the test `.[name(.)=$objectname]`. This is not efficient (in fact, it's hideously inefficient since it forces a match attempt on every node rather than using the optimized code for working with preexisting tokens), but it has the advantage of working for a fairly wide class of XML examples, essentially any code that has the following structure:

```
<category>
     <object @id="id1">
          <caption>A Caption</caption>
          <!-- other elements -->
          <object @id="id2">
               <caption>A Caption</caption>
               <!-- other elements -->
               <!-- other objects -->
          </object>
      </object>
      <!-- other objects -->
</category>
```

where `category`, `object`, and `caption` are all parametric in nature.

When dealing with XSLT scripts, parameters essentially take the role that public properties and methods do in procedural languages—because the results of XSLT transformations can be so much more extensive than is usually the case with functions, there tend to be more parameters than you would normally expect for just a function. The parameters for the outline filter are given in Table 8.2. Keep in mind that XSLT parameters, like those of Java but not of Visual Basic, are case-sensitive.

TABLE 8.2: Parameters for the Parametric Outline Component

Parameter Name	Values	What It Does	Required
`Container-name`	String	Determines the name of the element that contains the elements to be displayed (for example, `messages`).	Yes
`Objectname`	String	Comprises the name of the object itself (for example, `message`).	Yes
`Caption`	String	the name of the element that holds the caption or title for each item.	No (Defaults to `title`.)
`Listtype`	'ordered'|'unordered'	If ordered, the outline will display classical outline format (I.A.i.a.1. format). If unordered, the outline will be displayed using various bullet symbols.	No (Defaults to `ordered`.)
`Clickevent`	JavaScript code as String	Contains code that gets executed when a user clicks on an item. It can either be a block of JavaScript code or a function call to other code in the surrounding page. Use the `me` object to get access to the `list` element, or `me.id` to get access to the ID of the corresponding element in the source.	No (If no code is given, then clicking on an item performs no action.)
`Ordered1-5`	CSS rule as String	Provide the CSS rules that describe the nodes in ordered view. You can change the numbering character by setting the `list-style-type: CSS property`.	No (See code for assigned defaults.)
`Unordered1-5`	CSS rule as String	Provide the CSS rules that describe the nodes in unordered view. You can set the default bullets to one of the other standard bullet types using `list-style-type`, or assign the level a graphic as a bullet with `list-style-image: url(myImage.gif)`.	No (See code for assigned defaults.)

Thus, if you had a collection of `<note>` objects contained in a `<folder>` object, wanted to have the outline use bulleted points instead of numbers, and wanted to display the `<body>` node instead of the `<title>` node from your notes list, you could do this by calling the `xmlserver.asp` function as follows:

```
http://www.myserver.com/xmlserver.asp?
source=notes.xml&filter=drawoutline.xsl&mimetype=html&
param_collectionname=folder&param_objectname=note&
param_listtype=unordered&param_caption=body
```

One noteworthy point about the XSL script: The code includes a named template called `$drawNode`, which actually builds the `UL` or `OL` container for the `LI` elements. The advantage to using named templates is that they can be parameterized and can thus cut down on duplication in your code.

WARNING Outline structures such as the one dealt with here are highly recursive in nature: They push information onto a stack every time the XSLT parser progresses from a parent level to a child level. While stock processing is an integral part of XSLT, system limitations can cause the stack to overflow, usually with fatal results. If you run into problems with large, deep data sets, you may want to limit the number of levels deep a message response can go (or work with an indexed hierarchical structure that points to a linear set of rich data).

A Dynamic TreeView Component

While outlines are useful, they can also be overwhelming. The collapsible TreeView structure has become a staple of most user interfaces. You can click on a folder to open or close it, displaying or hiding the contents of that folder and revealing the files and subfolders contained within. In this way, you can hide detailed information about topics until the user specifically requests it, which is especially useful for complex, XML-related structures.

The most difficult part of working with TreeView controls isn't implementing them; they are not all that much more complex than creating an outline control. Rather, it's in understanding where they work best. A TreeView control should be considered a structure of nested objects. Thus, in the message-board view, a message board system holds multiple message boards, which in turn hold multiple messages, which in turn hold multiple responses. By selecting any of these items, you should see in a different display window some representation of that object—in essence the properties associated with that object.

Too many people look at the hierarchical view of XML and automatically assume that such a structure maps easily to a TreeView structure. In practice, it usually doesn't because even though an element referencing an object and an element referencing a property are identical in implementation, conceptually they are two very different things.

The TreeView component given here works on this assumption. This assumes a container/contained relationship along the lines of the previous outline control: a `<messages>`-type collection can contain multiple `<message>` objects, which can, in turn, contain `<message>` `Response` objects.

NOTE A response is still considered a message, by the way—the only real difference between the two being whether the message is connected to the root object (`<messages>`) or are children of other messages.

The Parametric Dynamic Tree (Listing 8.24) borrows considerably from the outline but is more suited for more formal applications. In the form as it exists right now, the Dynamic Tree only works in Internet Explorer 4 and above. (It requires the use of the CSS `display` property, which is not well supported in Netscape Navigator.) Unlike the outline, however, it can do such things as track the position of the cursor as it passes over items (the default is to underline them, but that is customizable) and select an item if clicked, and it can be set to both begin at a node other than the root and start with a given item visible.

Listing 8.24: A Parametric Dynamic Tree Filter (*Listing8.24.xsl*)

```
<xsl:stylesheet
   xmlns:xsl="http://www.w3.org/1999/XSL/Transform"
   version="1.0">
<xsl:output type="html"/>
<xsl:param name="containername" select="'messages'"/>
<xsl:param name="objectname" select="'message'"/>
<xsl:param name="caption" select="'title'"/>
<xsl:param name="childname" select="'message(s)'"/>
<xsl:param name="visibleid" select="''"/>
<xsl:param name="selectedid" select="''"/>
<xsl:param name="treeid" select="'tree'"/>
<xsl:param name="startfromid" select="''"/>
<xsl:param name="clickevent"><![CDATA[
    window.status=me.id;
]]></xsl:param>
<xsl:param name="folderstyle"
    select="'list-style-type:none;
    list-style-image:url(folder.gif);cursor:hand;'"/>
<xsl:param name="filestyle"
    select="'list-style-type:none;
    list-styleimage:url(file.gif);'"/>
<xsl:param name="selectedstyle"
select="'background-color:navy;color:white;'"/>
<xsl:param name="highlightstyle"
```

```
select="'text-decoration:underline;'"/>
<xsl:param name="defaultstyle"
select="'font-size:11pt;font-family:Arial;'"/>
<xsl:variable name="treelevelstylesheet">
    .defaultstyle {<xsl:value-of select="$defaultstyle"/>}
    .folder {<xsl:value-of select="$folderstyle"/>}
    .file {<xsl:value-of select="$filestyle"/>}
    .selected {<xsl:value-of select="$selectedstyle"/>}
    .highlight {<xsl:value-of select="$highlightstyle"/>}
</xsl:param>

<xsl:template match="/">
    <xsl:choose>
         <xsl:when test="$startfromid != ''">
             <xsl:apply-templates
      select="//*[name(.)=$objectname][@id=$startfromid]"/>
         </xsl:when>
         <xsl:otherwise>
             <xsl:apply-templates
               select="//*[name(.)=$containername]"/>
         </xsl:otherwise>
    </xsl:choose>
</xsl:template>

<xsl:template match="*">
    <xsl:param name="treeLevel"/>
    <li>
    <xsl:choose>
         <xsl:when test="*[name(.)=$objectname]">
            <xsl:attribute
      name="class">folder</xsl:attribute>
         </xsl:when>
         <xsl:otherwise>
            <xsl:attribute
      name="class">file</xsl:attribute>
         </xsl:otherwise>
    </xsl:choose>
    <xsl:attribute name="id"><xsl:value-of
    select="@id"/></xsl:attribute>
    <xsl:if test="@id=$selectedid">
        <xsl:attribute name="onload">
 handleTreeClick(this,<xsl:value-of
               select="$treeid"/>)
        </xsl:attribute>
    </xsl:if>
    <xsl:attribute
```

```
   name="onclick">handleTreeClick(this,<xsl:value-of
   select="$treeid"/>)</xsl:attribute>
    <xsl:attribute
    name="onmouseover">handleTreeOver(this)</xsl:attribute>
    <xsl:attribute
      name="onmouseout">handleTreeOut(this)</xsl:attribute>
    <xsl:attribute
      name="onmousedown">handleTreeDown(this,<xsl:value-of
      select="$treeid"/>)</xsl:attribute>
    <xsl:variable name="childObjects"
      select="*[name(.)=$objectname]"/>
    <span><xsl:value-of select="*[name(.)=$caption]"
      xml:preserve-space="yes"/><xsl:if
        test="count($childObjects) &gt; 0"> (<xsl:value-of
        select="count($childObjects)"/>
      <xsl:text> </xsl:text><xsl:value-of
        select="$childname"/>)</xsl:if></span>
    <xsl:call-template name="drawNode">
        <xsl:with-param name="objectRef" select="*"/>
        <xsl:with-param name="treeLevel"
           select="number($treeLevel)+1"/>
    </xsl:call-template>
    </li>
</xsl:template>

<xsl:template match="*[name(.)=$containername]">
    <xsl:call-template name="writeIEEventHandlers" />
    <style>
    <xsl:value-of select="$treelevelstylesheet"/>
    </style>
    <xsl:call-template name="drawNode">
        <xsl:with-param name="objectRef" select="*"/>
        <xsl:with-param name="treeLevel" select="1"/>
        <xsl:with-param name="treeID" select="$treeid"/>
    </xsl:call-template>
</xsl:template>

<xsl:template name="drawNode">
    <xsl:param name="objectRef"/>
    <xsl:param name="treeLevel"/>
    <xsl:param name="treeID" select="false()"/>
    <ul>
    <xsl:if test="$treeID">
         <xsl:attribute name="id"><xsl:value-of
            select="$treeID"/></xsl:attribute>
    </xsl:if>
```

```
    <xsl:attribute name="style">
    display:<xsl:choose>
        <xsl:when test="number($treeLevel)=1 or
          $objectRef//@id[.=$visibleid]">block</xsl:when>
        <xsl:otherwise>none</xsl:otherwise>
    </xsl:choose>
    </xsl:attribute>
    <xsl:apply-templates
       select="$objectRef[name(.)=$objectname]">
        <xsl:with-param name="treeLevel"
           select="$treeLevel"/>
    </xsl:apply-templates>
    </ul>
</xsl:template>

<xsl:template name="writeIEEventHandlers" >
    <script language="JavaScript">
    var oldNode=new Array();
    function handleTreeClick(me,treeID){
    if (me.className=="folder"){
        var container=me.children(1);
        if (container.style.display=="none"){
            container.style.display="block";
            }
        else {
            container.style.display="none";
            }
        }

    <xsl:value-of select="$clickevent"/>
    event.cancelBubble=true;
    }

    function handleTreeDown(me,treeID){
    if (oldNode[treeID]!=null){
        oldNode[treeID].className="";
        }
    span=me.children(0)
    span.className="selected"
    oldNode[treeID]=span;
    event.cancelBubble=true;
    }

    function handleTreeOver(me){
        span=me.children(0);
        if (span.className.charAt("highlight")!=-1){
            span.className+=" highlight";
            }
```

```
            event.cancelBubble=true;
            }

        function handleTreeOut(me){
            span=me.children(0);
            span.className=span.className.replace(
                " highlight","")
            event.cancelBubble=true;
            }
        </script>
    </xsl:template>

    </xsl:stylesheet>
```

This example demonstrates both the advantage and the dangers of working with XSL—one of the principal problems is that JavaScript code is contained within the body of the script. The same rules apply to such code as apply to client code in ASP:

- You should refrain as much as possible from mixing the two blocks of code together.
- Client script code does not run in the same process as the XSL code output, unless encapsulated in an `<msxsl:script>` block.
- Because scripting code incompatibility is the largest area of difference between the major browsers, you should always make sure if you support multiple versions of code that you have them clearly delineated, preferably in different templates (or perhaps matching templates but with different modes).

Thus, I extracted the event-handling code that would be used by the nodes and placed them into a distinctly named template (`writeIEEventHandlers`). One modification that I could have made to the code would have been to retrieve the browser, then add the appropriate event-handling code for each distinct browser configuration; since the JavaScript is a separate template in each case, it makes the code much easier to handle (and one that becomes more amenable to `<xsl:include>` elements).

The results of processing the component again fall somewhere between the results generated by a function and the sophistication of an object. The parameters of the Dynamic Tree are given in Table 8.3; the list is similar to, but a little richer than, the list for the outline.

TABLE 8.3: Parameters for the Dynamic TreeView Component

Parameter Name	Values	What It Does	Required
`Containername`	String	The name of the element that contains the elements to be displayed (for example, `messages`).	Yes
`Objectname`	String	The object itself (for example, `message`).	Yes
`Caption`	String	The name of the element that holds the caption or title for each item.	No (Defaults to `title`)

TABLE 8.3: Parameters for the Dynamic TreeView Component *(continued)*

Parameter Name	Values	What It Does	Required
`Childname`	String	The control indicates the number of child responses that the given message has.	No (If not included, the string showing this information is not displayed.)
`Clickevent`	JavaScript code as String	Contains code that gets executed when a user clicks on an item. It can either be a block of JavaScript code or a function call to other code in the surrounding page. Use the `me` object to get access to the `list` element, or `me.id` to get access to the ID of the corresponding element in the source.	No (If no code is given, then clicking on an item performs no action.)
`Visibleid`	String	If a value is given and an item has this ID, then the control will start with this item (and hence all of its parents) open.	No (If not included, then the tree only displays the topmost children and hides the rest.)
`Selectedid`	String	If a value is given and an item has this ID, then the item will automatically be selected. Note that such an item could still be invisible.	No (If not included, no item is initially selected.)
`Treeid`	String	If two or more such tree controls are included on the page, it is necessary to set `treeid` for each of them so that they are unique. This is required for maintaining state information.	No (Unless two or more controls are present, then yes.)
`Startfromid`	String	If this item is given and an item in the tree has this ID, then this will be displayed as the root node.	No (If this isn't given, then it is assumed that the container object is the root node of the tree.)
`Folderstyle`	CSS String	Gives the CSS rule that describes the folder list item. Note that in the example it is assumed that the file `folder.gif` is in the same directory.	No (Defaults to a folder icon view, if the GIF is available.)
`Filestyle`	CSS String	Gives the CSS rule that describes the file list item. Note that in the example it is assumed that the file `file.gif` is in the same directory.	No (Defaults to a file icon view, if the GIF is available.)
`Selectedstyle`	CSS String	Gives the CSS rule that describes the appearance of the span when this item is selected.	No (Defaults to white text on a navy rectangle.)
`Highlightstyle`	CSS String	Gives the CSS rule that describes the appearance of the span when the mouse moves over the item.	No (Defaults to underlined text.)
`Defaultstyle`	CSS String	Gives the CSS rule that describes the default state of the text in all of the spans.	No

The principles behind this and the outline are similar, although this takes more advantage of DHTML to produce the visual effects such as the rollover. That, however, brings up a good point about construction: In this case, the primary purpose of the XSLT is not to set up the eye candy but rather to create the underlying structure that supports the interactive elements. The XSLT script doesn't actually know about the behavior of the object, per se (with one minor exception); instead, it lets the browser take over this task while assigning the relevant CSS classes to each of the list elements.

The one exception to this rule comes from the use of the `visibleid` and `selectid` parameters. The `visibleid` property indicates that a given node should automatically be visible when the control starts, and the only way to do that is to make sure that its parent-container `<UL>` tags are also all visible. This is one of the reasons that the `display` property is kept distinct from the normal `SPAN` or `LI` style, since the CSS `display` property will be set or not set independent of any other class associations. Similarly, the `selectid` parameter determines what item should be selected, but rather than changing the visual appearance of that node it instead notifies the page (through the `onload` event) that when all of the elements for that section of the tree are completely rendered the `LI` element with the `selectid` ID value should be handled as if it were clicked.

In other words, use the XSLT capabilities to set up the structural elements of the control, but turn over the interactive and rendering components of the control to a different language (such as CSS or JavaScript). This is consistent with the paradigm used throughout this book on XSLT: Transform your data into structures with XSLT, decorate it with CSS, and enliven it with script (all of which can be delivered via the XSLT, of course).

Summary

ASP and XML exist in an uneasy alliance; clearly, ASP was never intended to serve as a host for XML, but it performs this task moderately well nonetheless. It has the necessary tools to provide XML streams from remote servers, to tie those streams together through XSLT or DOM, and it can provide a suitable environment for building distributed applications by making incoming, outgoing, and state-maintenance pipes available, although not necessarily in a clean fashion.

In this chapter I deliberately stayed away from the most advanced features of IIS, both because the adoption of IIS5 is still not widespread and because its capabilities really shine only when working in conjunction with XMLHTTP. Up until now, most of the concentration in working with code has been oriented towards scripting environments. However, XML offers a number of significant advantages to the compiled environment of Visual Basic as well, and certain VB features, such as Web Classes, can significantly enhance XML's native flexibility and can radically simplify the pipeline architecture that will likely be the primary way of working with XML in the future.

CHAPTER 9

XML and MS Databases

- Introducing RDS and data binding
- ADO 2.5 support for XML
- Creating and binding hierarchical recordsets
- SQL Server 2000 support for XML

XML is a language for representing structured information, and as such it's an ideal mechanism for exchanging information between different database management systems, or for building front ends for database applications that run on thin clients. Internet Explorer 5 supports XML, and Microsoft is adding XML support to its databases. ADO (ActiveX Data Objects), Microsoft's data access technology, supports XML already. The new version of SQL Server, which is in beta right now, will also support XML natively.

In addition to adding XML features to the databases, Microsoft is enhancing XML support in Internet Explorer. As you probably know, any features added to Internet Explorer are also available to any language, like VBScript or Visual Basic. At this point, there are many XML tools, both on the database side and on the client side, but these tools are still rough around the edges. For one thing, you must write programs (or scripts, in the case of Internet Explorer) to parse XML documents. Eventually, XML must become transparent to developers so that we won't have to write code to manipulate the XML document itself. At this point, you must not only write code to process XML data, but you must use JavaScript to make sure your client applications will run in both browsers.

In this chapter, you'll learn how to retrieve XML-formatted data from a database, pass them to the client, and bind them to HTML controls. In the first part of the chapter, I discuss the Remote Data Services (RDS) and data-binding techniques. Once you learn how data binding works and you can bind a recordset to the HTML controls on a Web page, you'll be able to apply the same techniques to XML recordsets as well. You'll also learn how to use the XML Data Control and how to create data islands.

In the second half of the chapter, you'll learn how to use ADO's methods to persist recordsets in XML format and how to update the tables in the database through an XML recordset. You'll see the syntax used to mark changes in a recordset and how the modified recordset is submitted to the database and committed there. In the last section of the chapter, you'll learn about the new XML features of SQL Server 2000. You'll see how you can query SQL Server remotely through an HTTP connection and how to execute stored procedures against a SQL Server database remotely. As you will see, it is possible to directly access and manipulate SQL Server databases from within your browser.

RDS and Data Binding

Before examining the specifics of ADO's XML support, it is important to understand the basics of data binding. *Data binding* is the process of associating a control to a data field. When the underlying field changes value, the control is updated automatically. Likewise, when the viewer edits the control, the underlying field is updated automatically. The recordset whose fields are bound to the controls of a Form on a Web page is a disconnected recordset, and the changes are not immediately reflected to the database. The disconnected recordset is one of the most prominent features of ADO 2.1 and later versions; unlike the regular recordset we've been using for years, a disconnected recordset does not require an open connection to the database. It's populated through an open connection, but it maintains its data even after the connection to the database has been closed. Disconnected recordsets are updateable. You can edit their rows, and the changes can be committed to the database after the connection to the database has been established again. In this section, you'll see how to move a disconnected recordset to the client and display its fields on HTML controls.

HTML is nothing more than a language for formatting text to be displayed on a browser. Yet modern Web applications do not rely on static content that can be stored in HTML pages and transmitted to the client. For example, we want to be able to display field values on certain controls, but the exact fields that will be displayed on the controls are not known ahead of time. Thus we need a technique to bind the fields of a database to elements of a page, so that when we connect to the database, the elements will be populated automatically.

Visual Basic programmers have been doing this for years, but they can have a quick link to the database. However, Web applications can't assume that they have immediate access to a database. Despite this, it is possible for a Web page to "see" the fields of a database through the *Remote Data Services (RDS) Data Control.* The RDS Data Control connects to a database server, such as SQL Server, and retrieves the data from tables. The viewer can then edit the data and update the database en masse.

If you're familiar with database programming, you already see the similarities between the usual Data Controls used in building database front ends with VB or other high-level languages (the DAO and ADO Data Controls) and the RDS Data Control. The main difference is that the RDS Data Control connects to the database over the HTTP protocol. Because dial-up connections are not fast enough for database operations, the RDS Data Control maintains the data in a disconnected recordset and updates the database only when requested. This happens at the end of a session. Now you'll see how to bind the fields of the recordset to HTML elements.

Binding Fields to HTML Elements

The RDS Data Control can bind HTML elements to database fields, but it can also bind them to XML data. The following lines insert an RDS Data Control onto a page and specify the database it connects to, as well as a query to retrieve the desired data:

```
<OBJECT
    CLASSID="clsid:BD96C556-65A3-11D0-983A-00C04FC29E33"
    ID="Products" WIDTH = 0 HEIGHT = 0>
    <PARAM NAME="Connect" VALUE="DSN=NWindDB">
    <PARAM NAME="Server" VALUE = "PROTO">
    <PARAM NAME="SQL" VALUE="SELECT * FROM Products">
</OBJECT>
```

This <OBJECT> tag tells the RDS Data Control to connect to a local database—the NorthWind database—and retrieve all the rows from the Products table. PROTO is the name of the machine on which SQL Server is running, and DSN is a Data Source Name that points to the NorthWind database.

NOTE To set up a DSN, use the ODBC Data Source tool in the Control Panel (if you're using Windows 98) or in the Administrative Tools (if you're using Windows 2000).

Instead of connecting directly to a database, you can specify the name of a script with the URL attribute. The script will retrieve the data from the database server and return them to the client as a recordset. Here's the alternate <OBJECT> tag that uses the URL of a script to get the data:

```
<OBJECT
    CLASSID="clsid:BD96C556-65A3-11D0-983A-00C04FC29E33"
    ID="Products" WIDTH = 0 HEIGHT = 0>
    <PARAM NAME="URL" VALUE="GetProducts.asp">
</OBJECT>
```

Both tags create a recordset—the Products recordset—on the client. By definition, this is a disconnected recordset, and you can bind its fields to HTML elements on the page (discussed in the next section). As you navigate through the rows of the recordset with its navigational methods, the values of the bound HTML controls are updated. If you edit a field (provided that the control allows editing), the new value is committed to the local recordset as soon as you move to another row. The changes are not sent to the server.

To update the underlying tables, you must call the disconnected recordset's SubmitChanges method. Another method, Refresh, discards the changes and reloads the recordset from the database.

Data Binding Properties

To bind an HTML element to the RDS Data Control, you must use the following two properties:

DATASRC This is the name of the RDS Data Control that contains the data. You must prefix the name of the data source with the pound sign (#) to indicate that the data source is local to the client.

DATAFLD This is the name of the field in the control to which the element is bound.

Table 9.1 lists the HTML elements that support data binding as well as the name of the properties you bind to the data fields.

TABLE 9.1: The Data-Bound HTML Elements

HTML Element	Bound Property
A	HREF
BUTTON	innerText and innerHTML
DIV	innerText and innerHTML
FRAME	SRC
IFRAME	SRC
IMG	SRC
INPUT TYPE=CHECKBOX	CHECKED
INPUT TYPE=HIDDEN	VALUE
INPUT TYPE=PASSWORD	VALUE
INPUT TYPE=RADIO	CHECKED
INPUT TYPE=TEXT	VALUE
SELECT	<OPTION>
SPAN	innerText and InnerHTML
TEXTAREA	VALUE
TABLE	<TD>

To display a field on the page, use the SPAN tag as follows:

```
ProductID   <SPAN DATASRC="#Products"
             DATAFLD="ProductID">
            </SPAN>
ProductName <SPAN DATASRC="#Products"
             DATAFLD="ProductName">
            </SPAN>
Description <SPAN DATASRC="#Products"
             DATAFLD="Description">
            </SPAN>
```

The following statements display the entire recordset on a table:

```
<TABLE DATASRC="#Products">
<TR><TD>ProductID</TD>
    <TD><SPAN DATAFLD="ProductID"></SPAN>
    </TD>
    <TD>ProductName</TD>
    <TD><SPAN DATAFLD="ProductName"></SPAN>
    </TD>
    <TD>Description</TD>
```

```
        <TD><SPAN DATAFLD="Description">
            </SPAN>
        </TD>
    </TR>
    </TABLE>
```

As you can see, we don't have to specify more than a single row of the table. Since the data-bound element is a table, the browser knows that it must iterate through the entire recordset and create a new table row for each row in the recordset.

When we bind a table to a recordset, the DATASRC attribute is specified in the <TABLE> tag, so that we won't have to repeat it in every <TD> cell. The DATASRC attribute's value doesn't change from row to row.

The <TABLE> tag supports yet another attribute, DATAPAGESIZE, which specifies how many rows will be displayed on the table. The following tag will create a table with the first 20 products:

```
<TABLE ID="ProdTable"
       DATASRC="#Products" DATAPAGESIZE="20">
```

In this example, we've specified an ID for the table. This is because we want to be able to move to any group of 20 products. To do so, we must provide scripts for two buttons that take the viewer to the previous group and the next group, respectively. These buttons must call the control's PreviousPage and NextPage methods. The following statements insert two buttons after the table that implement the table's navigational methods:

```
<INPUT TYPE=Button VALUE="PREVIOUS"
    onClick="ProdTable.PreviousPage()"/>

<INPUT TYPE=Button VALUE="NEXT"
    onClick="ProdTable.NextPage()"/>
```

The ProductsTable.htm page on the accompanying CD retrieves product information from the NorthWind database and displays it in tabular format on the browser. Before you open the document, change the following two lines in the definition of the RDS Data Control:

```
<PARAM NAME="Connect" VALUE="DSN=NWindDB">
<PARAM NAME="Server" VALUE = "PROTO">
```

The Connect attribute should be the name of a DSN on your computer, and the Server attribute should be the name of the computer on which SQL Server is running. Figure 9.1 shows a small section of the Products table with the product data.

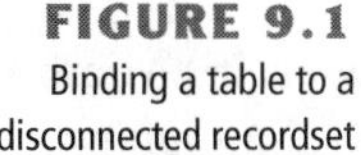

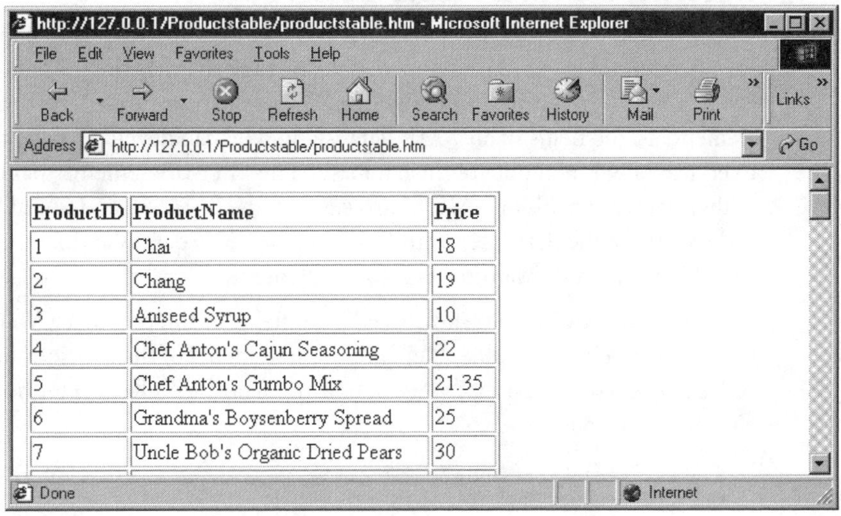

FIGURE 9.1
Binding a table to a disconnected recordset

NOTE If you only have Access on your system, set up a DSN for the NorthWind database and omit the `Server` parameter.

Retrieving Data with ASP Files

If you want to use an ASP file on the server to retrieve the data, open the `ProductsTable-Script.htm` file (on the accompanying CD). You must copy the file to the root folder of the Web server, start your browser, and connect to the address `127.0.0.1/ProductsTable-Script.asp`. The RDS Data Control will invoke the `GetProducts.asp` script (Listing 9.1), which will furnish the rows of the Products table:

Listing 9.1: The *GetProducts.asp* Script

```
<%
Set RS = Server.CreateObject("ADODB.Recordset")
RS.Open "Products", "DSN=NWINDDB"
RS.Save Response, adPersistXML
RS.Close
Set RS=Nothing
%>
```

The `Save` method places the recordset's rows directly in the `Response` stream. The `adPersistXML` argument tells ADO to save the recordset in XML format.

NOTE There is more information on the `Save` method later in this chapter.

Editing Data-Bound Controls

The problem with RDS control is that you can't use it with just any browser; it's Microsoft-specific technology. XML is a universal language that has the potential to communicate with any database (if not now, hopefully someday in the near future). By being able to bind HTML elements to the fields of an XML data island, you can develop Web pages that allow viewers to edit the fields and update the database. The HTML elements that can be bound to fields (either database fields or XML fields) support the DATASRC and DATAFLD properties. DATASRC is the name of the database, or the name of an XML data island, in our case. DATAFLD is the name of the field we want to bind to the element.

If you want viewers to be able to edit the fields of the recordset, you must place a Text control in every cell of the table. Here are the statements of the previous table, only this time each cell is a Text control so that you can edit the fields. You'll see later how to commit the changes to the database.

```
<TABLE DATASRC="#Products">
<TR><TD>ProductID</TD>
    <TD><INPUT TYPE=Text DATAFLD="ProductID"/></TD>
    <TD>ProductName</TD>
    <TD><INPUT TYPE=Text DATAFLD="ProductName"/></TD>
    <TD>Description</TD>
    <TD><INPUT TYPE=Text DATAFLD="Description"/></TD>
</TR>
</TABLE>
```

These revised pages have two drawbacks: too many rows to edit at once, and there's no mechanism to submit the changes to the database. We'll revise this page as we go along in the chapter. Also in upcoming sections, you will learn how to display a single row and allow the user to navigate through the recordset, as well as how to submit the changes to the database.

The XML Data Control

The previous section showed you how to connect an RDS Data Control to an XML recordset: You specify the URL of a script that returns a disconnected recordset. In this section, you'll learn how to do the same with the XML Data Control. In essence, the <XML> tag is the XML Data Control. The following statements will create an XML Data Control, name it Prod, and populate it with XML data:

```
<XML ID="Prod">
<Products>
  <Product>
    <ProductID>1</ProductID>
    <ProductName>ProductName1/ProductName>
    <UnitPrice>1.11</UnitPrice>
```

```
    </Product>
    <Product>
      <ProductID>2</ProductID>
      <ProductName>ProductName2/ProductName>
      <UnitPrice>2.22</UnitPrice>
    </Product>
  { XML statements for the remaining products }
  </Products>
  </XML>
```

The XML Data Control supports the same navigational methods as the RDS Data Control, and all the changes are maintained in a local XML recordset. After the viewer has edited the fields, your page should be able to transmit the modified rows to another script on the Web server that will update the database. This takes more than a call to the `SubmitChanges` method, and you'll see later in this chapter how to commit the changes to the database.

XML Data Islands

A recordset that's transmitted to the client as part of the HTML document is called a *data island*. The data island's fields can be bound to any of the HTML controls listed in Table 9.1, shown earlier. An advantage of the XML Data Control is that, technically, it's not an ActiveX control. This means you don't have to use the `<OBJECT>` tag to insert it on a page, and it can be used with any browser that supports XML—by next year, all browsers will be XML-capable.

The problem with XML data islands is how they're created. Coding XML data islands by hand is obviously out of the question. Luckily, the major data access mechanism, ADO, supports XML, which means that the databases themselves don't have to support XML natively. In the following section, you'll see how to retrieve recordsets in XML format from Access and SQL Server. First, we'll look at ADO support for XML.

ADO Support for XML

ActiveX Data Objects is a key technology and one of the cornerstones of the Windows DNA (Distributed Network Architecture). Though ADO has limited support for XML right now, future versions will provide more elaborate XML support.

One of the most important features of ADO 2.5 is its ability to retrieve recordsets in XML format. ADO 2.5 can format recordsets as XML documents and save them in a file or in a `Stream` object. The Web server's response to the client is such a stream, and ADO can save a recordset in XML format directly to the `Response` object. The data are then sent to the client, where a client-side script can traverse the XML data and display, or otherwise manipulate, the rows.

The XML format contains information about the structure of the data, so the XML recordset carries with it a description of its structure as well as the data itself. Because XML is an open standard, you should be able to use XML recordsets to exchange structured data between any two machines. This is the promise of XML, but we aren't quite there yet. There are no tools that would allow you to store the structure of an Access database as an XML document and use it to create a DB2 database populated with the Access data. This situation may change in just a year, as Microsoft is pushing this technology and wants to incorporate it into flagship products like SQL Server.

NOTE Since ADO is not database specific, the XML techniques discussed in this chapter apply to Access, SQL Server, and every other DBMS that has support for ADO.

Web developers who are not into database programming can also use an XML-formatted recordset. So long as they're familiar with XML and the DOM, they can work with this document without having to understand how the data is stored in the database, or even how to query the database.

In this section of the chapter, we'll explore how to use ADO to extract information from databases, format the recordset as an XML document, and display it on the client computer. You'll also see how to write a front end for the browser to edit the data and submit the changes back to the server in XML format.

Persisting Recordsets in XML Format

The ADO's recordset object supports the `Save` method, which stores the rows of the recordset to a file or a `Stream` object. In ADO jargon, saving the data to a file or `Stream` object is called *persisting* the recordset. The `Save` method can store the data in a proprietary binary format, in the ADTG (Advanced Data Table Gram) format, or in XML format. To store the recordset represented by the `RS` object variable to a file in XML format, use the following statement:

```
RS.Save fileName, adPersist
```

where *`fileName`* is the name of the file and *`adPersist`* is a constant that determines the structure of the file, and its value can be one of two constants: `adPersistADTG` or `adPersistXML`.

Assuming that you have Access installed on your system and you have created a Data Source Name for the NorthWind database, you can use the following VB statements to create a file with the rows of the Categories table in XML format. Just start a new VB project and enter the following lines in a button's Click event handler:

```
Dim RS As New ADODB.Recordset
FName = "C:\Temp\Categories.xml"
```

```
RS.Open "SELECT CategoryID, CategoryName, " & _
        "Description FROM Categories", "DSN=NWIND"
If Dir$(FName) <> "" Then Kill FName
RS.Save FName, adPersistXML
```

NOTE If the file created by the code above exists already, the **Save** method won't overwrite it. Instead, it will cause a runtime error. That's why you must either delete the file or prompt the user for a different filename.

The first few rows of the RS recordset in XML format are shown in Figure 9.2.

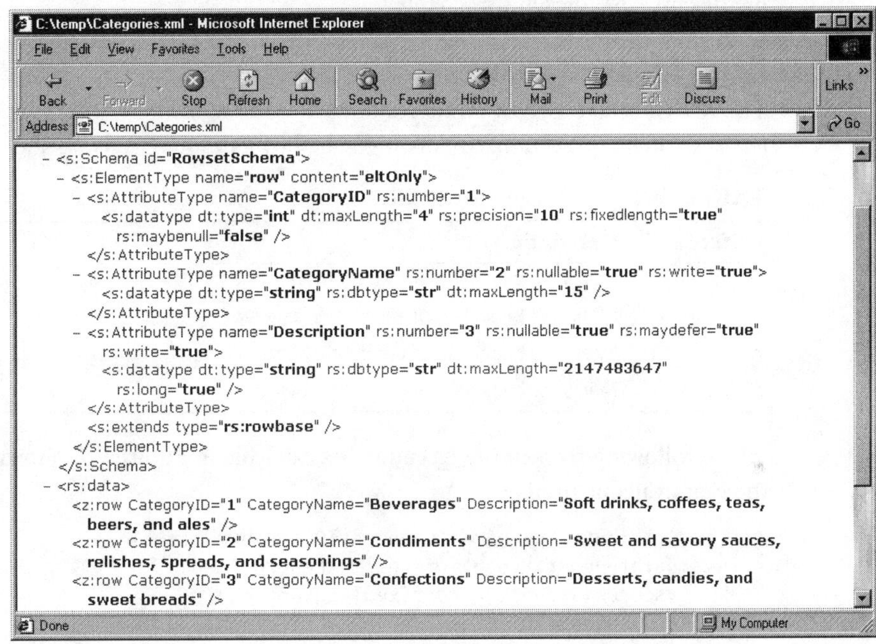

FIGURE 9.2 Persisting a table in XML format

If you want to access the database and produce XML output from within a server-side script, you can use the equivalent VBScript statements. With a server-side script, you need not save the XML-formatted recordset to a database. You can send it directly to the client by writing the output to the **Response** stream, as shown here:

```
Set RS = Server.CreateObject("ADODB.Recordset")
RS.Open "SELECT CategoryID, CategoryName, " & _
        "Description FROM Categories", "DSN=NWIND"
RS.Save Response, adPersistXML
```

TIP You should probably insert a few HTML statements above and below the XML data island, telling the client what to do with the XML data. Use the `Response.Write` method to send additional output to the client.

Though the XML document produced by the `Save` method (shown in Figure 9.2, displayed in Internet Explorer) looks quite elementary, let's take a close look at it. The appearance of the document, called `categories.xml`, may be of interest to developers, but it's not what a typical viewer would like to see on their browser. The simplest method to format the XML is to write an XSL file, as you have seen in previous chapters. Yet since this book is addressed to developers, I'm assuming you'll find it easier to write scripts rather than XSL files. Thus I will not discuss XSL files in this chapter.

Namespace Prefixes

The XML format used by ADO contains up to four sections, which in XML jargon are called *namespaces*. These sections are distinguished by a unique prefix, as shown in Table 9.2.

TABLE 9.2: XML Namespace Prefixes

Prefix	Description
s	Marks the beginning of the recordset's schema
dt	Marks the beginning of each row's data type
rs	Marks the beginning of the data section
z	Marks the beginning of each data row

The following rows in the `categories.xml` file in Figure 9.2, shown earlier, use three of the four available prefixes:

```
<s:AttributeType name="CategoryID" rs:number="1">
<s:datatype dt:type="int" dt:maxLength="4"
   rs:precision="10" rs:fixedlength="true"
   rs:maybenull="false" />
</s:AttributeType>
```

This section specifies the structure of a column. It's very unlikely that you will use this information on the client, but it's needed by ADO if you use the XML document to update a database.

The `dt` prefix appears in front of the row's data type attributes. Different data types have different attributes, of course. The *string* data type, for instance, doesn't have a precision attribute.

Later in the categories.xml file, you'll find the actual data. Each row in this section is identified with the z prefix:

```
<z:row CategoryID="2" CategoryName="Condiments"
Description="Sweet and savory sauces, relishes,
             spreads, and seasonings" >
```

(The Description line was broken to fit on the page.) If you select all the fields in the table, you'll see that the data section of the XML file contains a very long field, which is an image encoded as a sequence of characters. The image is not rendered on the client, because the content type of the file is text/html.

Although it is possible to include a textual representation of binary data in an XML-formatted recordset, it is not possible to directly bind the binary data to an <IMG> tag. To display a picture on a page with data-bound fields, use the <IMG> tag along with a URL, as shown here:

```
<IMG SRC="CategoryPicture.asp?CategoryID=XX">
```

The CategoryPicture.asp script reads the Picture column of the row in the Categories table that matched the specified Category ID. Most developers don't even store binary information in the database; they prefer to create image files in a specific folder and name them according to a key field in the database. This way they can easily match a row in the table to the corresponding file. For the Categories table, you should store each category's image to a file named xx.gif, where *xx* is the ID of the category.

The <s:datatype> attribute specifies the data type of each field, as well as other field attributes (whether the field can have a null value, for example). The data types that may appear in an XML file are shown in Table 9.3

TABLE 9.3: XML Data Types

Type	Description
bin.base64	A binary object.
bin.hex	Binary values in hex format.
Boolean	A True/False value.
Char	A string that contains a single character.
Date	A date value in the format *yyyy-mm-dd*.
DateTime	A date and time value in the format *yyyy-mm-ddThh:mm:ss*. The time value is optional; if omitted, it's assumed to be 00:00:00.
DateTime.tz	A date and time value that includes time zone information in the format *yyyy-mm-ddThh:mm:ss-hh:mm*. The time zone information is expressed in hours and minutes ahead or behind GMT.
fixed.14.4	A fixed floating-point value with up to 14 integer digits and up to four fractional digits.
Float	A floating-point value.
Int	An integer value.

TABLE 9.3: XML Data Types *(continued)*

Type	Description
`Number`	A floating-point value.
`Time`	A time value in the format *hh:mm:ss*.
`Time.tz`	A time value that includes time zone information in the format *hh:mm:ss-hh:mm*. The time zone information is expressed in hours and minutes ahead or behind GMT.
`i1`	A single-byte integer value.
`i2`	A two-byte integer value.
`i4`	A four-byte integer value.
`r4`	A four-byte fractional value.
`r8`	An eight-byte fractional value.
`ui1`	A single-byte, unsigned integer value.
`ui2`	A two-byte, unsigned integer value.
`ui4`	A four-byte, unsigned integer value.
`Uri`	A Universal Resource Indicator.
`Uuid`	A universally unique ID made up of hex digits.

The first thing to keep in mind when you work with XML recordsets generated by ADO (or SQL Server's native XML format, for that matter) is that the XML recordsets contain a description of the schema of the data. Not only that, but each row contains all the column values in a single tag, the `<z:row>` tag. As you will see later in the chapter, it takes some extra coding to get rid of the schema information. As far as the structure of the tags goes, Microsoft designers opted for a less verbose XML format: All the columns in a row are listed in the same `<z:row>` tag. For example, the line

```
<z:row CategoryID="2" CategoryName="Condiments"
Description="Sweet and savory sauces,
            relishes, spreads, and seasonings" >
```

corresponds to the following lines of straight XML code:

```
<Category>
<CategoryID>2</CategoryID>
<CategoryName>Condiments<CategoryName/>
<Description>Sweet and savory sauces, relishes,
            spreads, and seasonings<Description/>
</Category>
```

Updating XML Recordsets

The XML format used by ADO can also handle updates by storing edits, insertions, and deletions in the XML document itself. This is a very interesting feature, because it will eventually allow you to read data from any data source, edit it, and then post the changes to the original database. The software you use need not be aware of the capabilities of the database from where the data came. This is not the case right now, however. The various vendors are just beginning to add XML features to their databases, but it won't be long before XML becomes a standard feature for exchanging data between databases. But let's start by looking at the tags for updating recordsets.

Editing Rows

An edited row is specified with the `<rs:update>` and `<rs:original>` tags. The `<rs:update>` tag signifies the changes, and `<rs:original>` signifies the original row. Here's a typical example. The following lines correspond to the first row of the Customer table of the NorthWind database, after we have changed the CompanyName column from `BLAUER SEE DELIKATESSEN` to `BLAUER SEE DELIKATESSEN1` and set the `Region` field to `REGION`:

```
- <rs:update>
- <rs:original>
  <z:row CustomerID="ALFKI"
         CompanyName="BLAUER SEE DELIKATESSEN"
         ContactName="MARIA ANDERS"
         ContactTitle="Sales Representative"
         Address="Obere Str. 577" City="Berlin"
         Region="REGION" PostalCode="12209"
         Country="GERMANY"
         Phone="030-0074321" Fax="030-0076545" />
  </rs:original>
  <z:row CompanyName="BLAUER SEE DELIKATESSEN1" />
  </rs:update>
```

Notice that all the columns appear in the `<rs:update>` tag, even though only one of them was changed.

You may be wondering why ADO keeps track of the original values. ADO won't post any updates to the database if a row has been changed since it was read. If another user has already modified the same line after your application has read it, ADO will generate a runtime error and won't overwrite the edited columns. When the updates take place through a disconnected recordset, ADO needs to know what the values of the columns in the recordset were before it can commit any changes to the database.

Inserting Rows

Inserted rows appear at the end of the document in an `<rs:insert>` tag. The following lines add a new customer to the XML document:

```
<rs:insert>
  <z:row CustomerID="TEST" />
  <z:row CustomerID="TEST"
```

```
        CompanyName="TEST-CompanyName"
        ContactName="TEST-ContactName"
        ContactTitle="TEST-ContactTitle" />
</rs:insert>
```

To summarize, you must follow these steps to persist a recordset to an XML document and to edit the persisted rows:

1. Create a disconnected recordset by setting its `LockType` property to `adLockBatchOptimistic`. You can persist all types of recordsets, but ADO won't reflect the changes in the recordset to the XML document representing the recordset. Other types of recordsets update the database as soon as a row is changed. Only disconnected recordsets maintain a list of changes and submit all the changes to the database at once.
2. Persist the recordset to an XML file. Do so by calling the recordset's `Save` method with the `adPersistXML` argument. ADO will convert the current recordset into an XML document and save it to disk. The disk file is a static image of the recordset the moment you saved it (in XML format, of course).
3. Edit the recordset and resave it as an XML file. ADO maintains internally all the changes made to the recordset. It's actually the Cursor service that maintains the changes, in addition to the original data. This is the information that will be stored to the database.
4. If you update the recordset by calling its `UpdateBatch` method, the changes will be committed to the database. An updated disconnected recordset doesn't contain any `<rs:update>` tags.

NOTE If the Cursor engine can't commit the changes to the database, a runtime error will occur.

Deleting Rows

Deleted rows appear at the end of the document in an `<rs:delete>` tag. As an example, if you remove the customer with key ANTON from the Customers table of the NorthWind database, the following lines will be appended to the `<rs:data>` section of the XML file:

```
<rs:delete>
  <z:row CustomerID="ANTON"
        CompanyName="Antonio Moreno Taquería"
        ContactName="Antonio Moreno"
        ContactTitle="Owner"
        Address="Mataderos 23129"
        City="México D.F." PostalCode="05023"
        Country="México" Phone="(5) 555-3932" />
</rs:delete>
```

As you can see, the entire row, not just the primary key of the row, appears in the XML document.

Editing Disconnected Recordsets: An Example

Let's look at an example of editing disconnected recordsets persisted in XML format. This is a Visual Basic project, but you don't really need to understand Visual Basic. Because the code is quite simple, you can understand what's happening even if you're not familiar with the data-access features of Visual Basic. The project is called `DisconnectedRS`, and you will find it in a folder called DisconnectedRS on the accompanying CD.

To begin, start a new project and add a reference to the Microsoft Active Data Object 2.5 Library to the project. Then place a Command button on the form and enter the following code in the button's Click event handler:

```
Private Sub Command1_Click()
Dim RS As New ADODB.Recordset
    RS.CursorLocation = adUseClient
    RS.LockType = adLockBatchOptimistic
    RS.Open "C:\Customers.xml"
    RS.Fields(1) = RS.Fields(1) & "1"
    RS.MoveNext
    RS.Delete
    Kill "C:\Customers.xml"
    RS.Save "C:\Customers.xml", adPersistXML
End Sub
```

The code is quite simple—a real recordset-editing application would be too complicated. But if you're familiar with ADO's basic features, you can easily develop a user interface for an application that allows users to edit any row.

When the `Save` method is called to persist the recordset to a local XML file, the updates are saved along with the original data. If you call the `UpdateBatch` method, however, the changes are committed to the XML representation of the recordset. The `UpdateBatch` method will make changes in the `<rs:data>` section of the XML document.

The code shown above edits the first row (by appending a single character to the `CompanyName` field value) and then deletes the next row. To add a new row, insert the following statements:

```
RS.AddNew
RS.Fields(0)="TEST"
RS.Fields(1)="TEST-CompanyName"
RS.Fields(2)="TEST-ContactName"
RS.Fields(3)="TEST-ContactTitle"
RS.Update
```

If you persist the recordset to an XML file, the following lines will be appended to the `<rs:data>` section:

```
<rs:insert>
  <z:row CustomerID="TEST"
         CompanyName="TEST-CompanyName"
         ContactName="TEST-ContactName"
         ContactTitle="TEST-ContactTitle" />
  </rs:insert>
```

Multiple inserts appear together in as a single `<rs:insert>` section, but each row has its own `<z:row>` element.

This example uses the XML representation of a recordset, but there are no advantages to using XML with a desktop application. In the next section, you'll see how to pass the XML representation of a recordset to the client and how to get back the same recordset in XML format to update the database.

Passing XML Data to the Client

In addition to files, ADO recordsets can be persisted on `Stream` objects. A `Stream` object represents a stream of data, and the most common `Stream` object is the ASP `Response` object, which represents the stream of data from the Web server to the client. If you have ASP 3.0 installed on your server (ASP 3.0 comes with Windows 2000, and so does ADO 2.5), you can persist a recordset directly to the `Response` object. Use the following statement:

```
RS.Save Response, 1
```

where the second argument is the value of the constant `adPersistXML`. (ASP doesn't consult type libraries to resolve constant names.)

WARNING If you use constant names in your code, as you should, make sure you have declared them or have included the appropriate INC file. If not, VBScript will assume it's a variable and will initialize it to zero.

NOTE If you're using VB to create the recordset, you don't have to declare the constants.

The statement shown above will create a recordset and send it to the client. The browser will see an XML document and will display the raw data. Normally, we don't want to display raw data to the client. Therefore, we add a client-side script, or an XLS file, to display the data in a more appropriate format. The XML data that are part of an HTML page form a so-called data island. The viewer sees what you display on the browser from within your script, not the raw XML data.

Now that you have seen how to create disconnected recordsets and how you can XML format the rows of a disconnected recordset, let's switch our attention to the client and see how to bind the XML-formatted data to HTML elements.

Creating and Using Data Islands

A section of XML data enclosed in a pair of XML tags forms a data island. You can create data islands by simply retrieving the desired data from the database and sending them directly to the client by persisting the recordset to the `Response` object.

First, create the `Products.xml` file by persisting the recordset with the rows of the Products table in the NorthWind database. Then create a file with the XML data to the client with the following script:

```
<%
Const adPersistXML = 1
Set RS = Server.CreateObject("ADODB.Recordset")
RS.Open "Products", "DSN=NWINDDB"
RS.Save "C:\Products.xml", adPersistXML
%>
```

This short script generates a typical XML output. The XML output produced by the `Save` method is not really an XML island; it contains an <XML>, but this tag doesn't have an ID attribute. Thus we must surround the entire file by the following pair of <XML> tags:

```
<XML ID="Products">
...
</XML>
```

However, there is a problem with this solution: You can't have nested <XML> tags in an XML document. The correct solution is to rename the <XML> tags in the XML document generated by the `Save` method to something else and then embed the entire document in a new pair of <XML> tags. You can rename the existing <XML> tags into anything; I used the tag <ADOXML> in testing the scripts. Here are the first two and last two lines of the revised XML file:

```
<XML ID="XMLProducts">
<ADOXML    xmlns:s= ...
...
</ADOXML>
</XML>
```

Don't be concerned that if you open the edited file with Internet Explorer, you won't see anything. There's nothing wrong with the file; the XML document sent to the client has become a data island. The data are available to the client, but there's no script to tell the browser what to do with the data.

To turn the data island into an HTML page that can be displayed on the browser, let's add a few HTML statements to the XML file. To do so, we must add the following HTML elements and bind them to the fields of the recordset:

```
<HTML>
<TABLE DATASRC="#XMLProducts">
<TR><TD>
<TABLE DATASRC="#XMLProducts" DATAFLD="rs:data">
<TR><TD>
<TABLE DATASRC="#XMLProducts" DATAFLD="z:row" >
<TR>
<TD><SPAN DATAFLD="ProductID"></SPAN></TD>
<TD><SPAN DATAFLD="ProductName"></SPAN></TD>
<TD><SPAN DATAFLD="UnitPrice"></SPAN></TD>
</TR>
</TABLE>
</TD></TR>
</TABLE>
</TD></TR>
</TABLE>
</HTML>
```

If you want to be able to edit the table, replace the table's cells with Text controls. Figure 9.3 shows a section of the page with the NorthWind products displayed on a table. You will find the XML data island and the HTML code for binding the fields to a table's cells in the `ProductsXML.htm` file on the accompanying CD. To create this file, I generated the recordset with the recordset's `Save` method and then edited it a little.

I must explain the statements that bind the table to the data islands. They're quite different from the binding statements we've seen so far. The fields we want to bind to the table are the ones prefixed by the `<z:row>` tag. But these tags appear under the `<rs:data>` tag. So to skip the `<rs:data>` section, we bind the fields in the `<rs:data>` tag to a table that has no rows of its own. Then. within this table, we nest another table whose cells are bound to the fields in the `<z:row>` tag. You'll have to use this simple trick with all the data islands you create with ADO's `Recordset.Save` method. The alternative is to include an XSL file or a client-side script to exploit the XML document's DOM.

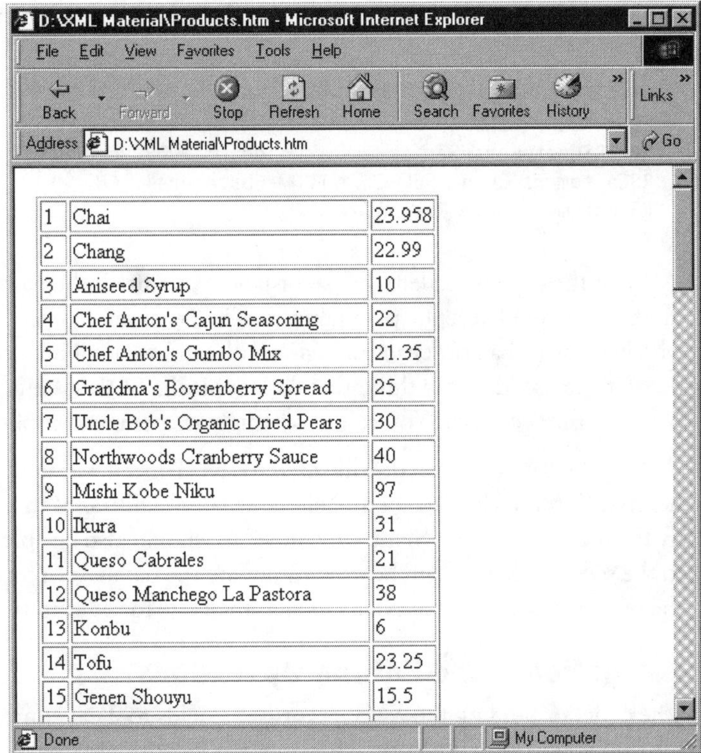

1	Chai	23.958
2	Chang	22.99
3	Aniseed Syrup	10
4	Chef Anton's Cajun Seasoning	22
5	Chef Anton's Gumbo Mix	21.35
6	Grandma's Boysenberry Spread	25
7	Uncle Bob's Organic Dried Pears	30
8	Northwoods Cranberry Sauce	40
9	Mishi Kobe Niku	97
10	Ikura	31
11	Queso Cabrales	21
12	Queso Manchego La Pastora	38
13	Konbu	6
14	Tofu	23.25
15	Genen Shouyu	15.5

FIGURE 9.3
Displaying a data island on a table

Creating Data Islands on the Fly

The example in the previous section demonstrates how to create XML data islands and process them on the client. As you have probably noticed, we had to edit the XML recordset. We persisted the recordset to an XML file, then edited it to convert the file into a form suitable for use as a data island on the client. Yet to make this technique more useful, we should be able to edit the XML data from within our server-side script. This would allow us to create XML data islands on the fly, without user intervention.

To do so, first we must insert an RDS Data Control that provides the data. The following <OBJECT> tag places an RDS Data Control on the page, which calls a script on the server to retrieve the data:

```
<OBJECT
   CLASSID="clsid:bd96c556-65a3-11d0-983a-00c04fc29e33"
   ID="DSOCustomers" WIDTH="0" HEIGHT="0">
<PARAM NAME= "URL" VALUE="GetCustomersXML.asp">
</OBJECT>
```

The name of the script is GetCustomersXML.asp, and here's what it does. First, it creates a local recordset (on the Web server) with the desired data. Then, it saves the data on the Response stream:

```
<%
CN = "DSN=NWINDDB
Set RSCustomers=Server.CreateObject("ADODB.Recordset")
RSCustomers.Open "SELECT * FROM Customers", CN
RSCustomers.Save Response, 1
%>
```

When the page is loaded, the data island contains all the rows of the Customers table. The same script could accept a parameter to select customers from a specific country, customers who have placed an order in the last month, and so on. The script that provides the data doesn't change; the only thing that changes is the SQL statement that retrieves the data to populate the recordset. You can make this statement as complicated as you wish.

Once the data has been downloaded to the client, it's bound to the HTML elements of the HTML Form. If the data-bound elements allow editing of their content, the viewer can modify the recordset on the client. Of course, we should also be able to return the edited recordset to the server, where it will be used to update the database. You'll see how to post the data to the server shortly. But first, let's look at the code for editing the recordset on the client.

Navigational and Editing Operations

The code for binding the XML recordset's fields to Text controls on the Form is fairly simple, and you've seen it before. This time, we'll use the following statements to bind one row at a time to a few Text controls:

```
Company Name
<INPUT TYPE=TEXT DATASRC="#DSOCustomers"
                 DATAFLD="CompanyName" SIZE="40">
</INPUT>
<BR>
Contact Name
<INPUT TYPE=TEXT DATASRC="#DSOCustomers"
                 DATAFLD="ContactName" SIZE="30">
</INPUT>
Contact Title
<INPUT TYPE=TEXT DATASRC="#DSOCustomers"
                 DATAFLD="ContactTitle" SIZE="25">
</INPUT>
```

This code binds the CompanyName, ContactName, and ContactTitles fields to three Text controls. You can add the statements to bind the remaining fields as well. When the page is loaded, you'll see the fields of the first row, as shown in Figure 9.4.

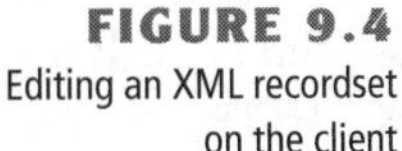

FIGURE 9.4
Editing an XML recordset on the client

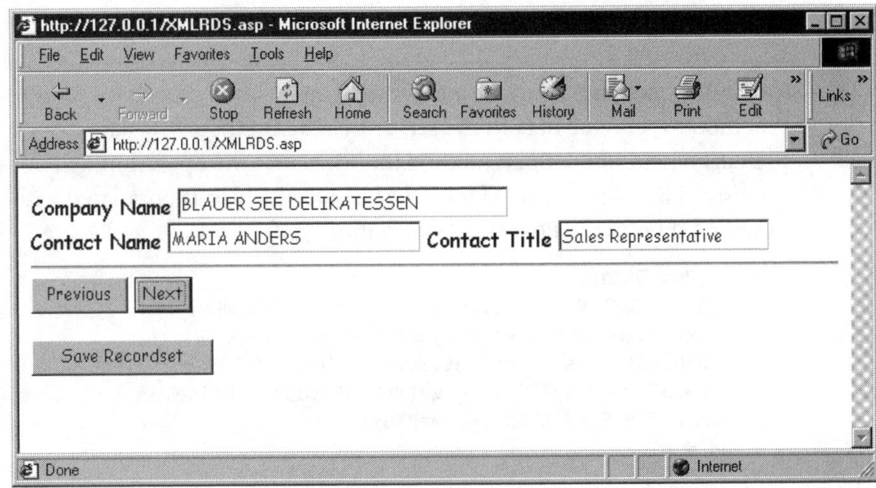

We must also add a few buttons (shown in Figure 9.4) to allow the viewer to navigate through the recordset. Add the Previous and Next buttons with the following statements:

```
<INPUT TYPE=button VALUE="Previous" ONCLICK="PrevRec">
<INPUT TYPE=button VALUE="Next" ONCLICK="NextRec">
```

We must also provide the code for the PrevRec and NextRec buttons (seen as Previous and Next). This code must simply call the `MovePrevious` and `MoveNext` methods of the RDS Data Control:

```
Sub NextRec
    If Not DSOCustomers.Recordset.EOF Then
        DSOCustomers.Recordset.MoveNext
    End If
End Sub

Sub PrevRec
    If Not DSOCustomers.Recordset.BOF Then
       DSOCustomers.Recordset.MovePrevious
    End If
End Sub
```

Notice that the code examines the `BOF` and `EOF` properties to make sure that the script doesn't attempt to move before the first row or beyond the last row in the recordset.

Finally, we must add a button for submitting the changes to the server. The definition of this button, Save Recordset, is shown here:

```
<INPUT TYPE=button VALUE="Save Recordset"
       ONCLICK="PostData">
```

The PostData subroutine, which posts the modified recordset to the server, is the most interesting part of the page. The code uses the XMLHTTP object, which uses the HTTP protocol to pass XML-encoded data to the server. This script uses two of the XMLHTTP object's methods: the Open method to establish a connection to a script on the server, and the Send method to send the data to the server by reading the XML data from a Stream object. The last argument of the Open method indicates that the operation will not take place asynchronously. This object is an ADO Stream object, which is populated with the Recordset.Save method. Here's the PostData subroutine:

```
Sub PostData()
   Set XMLHTTP = CreateObject("Microsoft.XMLHTTP")
   Set StrData = CreateObject("ADODB.Stream")
   DSOCustomers.Recordset.Save StrData, 1
   XMLHTTP.Open "POST", "GetXMLData.asp", False
   XMLHTTP.Send STRDATA.ReadText()
End Sub
```

You may have noticed that this technique requires the presence of two objects on the client: the XMLHTTP and ADO objects. XMLHTTP comes with Internet Explorer, and ADO 2.5 (the ADO version that supports the Stream object) is also installed along with Windows 2000. The bottom line is that this technique works with Internet Explorer only. For the time being, Microsoft is ahead of Netscape in using XML as a universal data exchange protocol, but it's too early to say which methods will be adopted by the industry for exchanging XML data between servers and clients, especially for posting data to the server.

Listing 9.2 shows the entire document that allows editing of recordsets on the client.

Listing 9.2: Editing Recordsets on the Client (*XMLRDS.asp*)

```
<HTML>
<OBJECT CLASSID="clsid:bd96c556-65a3-11d0-983a-00c04fc29e33"
   ID="DSOCustomers" WIDTH="0" HEIGHT="0">
<PARAM NAME= "URL" VALUE="Customers.xml">
</OBJECT>

<SCRIPT LANGUAGE=VBScript>
Sub PostData()
   Set XMLHTTP = CreateObject("Microsoft.XMLHTTP")
   Set StrData = CreateObject("ADODB.Stream")
   DSOCustomers.Recordset.Save StrData, 1
   XMLHTTP.open "POST", "GetXMLData.asp", False
   XMLHTTP.Send STRDATA.ReadText()
End Sub

Sub NextRec
    If Not DSOCustomers.Recordset.EOF Then
        DSOCustomers.Recordset.MoveNext
    End If
End Sub
```

```
Sub PrevRec
    If Not DSOCustomers.Recordset.BOF Then
       DSOCustomers.Recordset.MovePrevious
    End If
End Sub

</SCRIPT>
<FONT FACE="Comic Sans MS" SIZE=3>
Company Name <INPUT TYPE=TEXT DATASRC="#DSOCustomers" DATAFLD="CompanyName"
SIZE="40"></INPUT>
<BR>
Contact Name <INPUT TYPE=TEXT
              DATASRC="#DSOCustomers"
              DATAFLD="ContactName" SIZE="30">
</INPUT>
Contact Title
<INPUT TYPE=TEXT DATASRC="#DSOCustomers"
       DATAFLD="ContactTitle" SIZE="25"></INPUT>
<HR>
<INPUT TYPE=button VALUE="Previous" ONCLICK="PrevRec">
<INPUT TYPE=button VALUE="Next" ONCLICK="NextRec">
<P>
<INPUT TYPE=button VALUE="Save Recordset"
       ONCLICK="PostData">
</FONT>
</HTML>
```

Reading XML Data on the Server

Now we need a method to read the edited recordset on the server. The client-side script transmitted the data with the POST method, so we must use the Request object on the server to read the data. To read the data, use the recordset object's Open method, specifying that it should read from a file:

```
NewRS = Server.CreateObject("ADODB.Recordset")
NewRS.Open Request, , , , adCmdFile
```

Notice that no connection information is specified in the Open method. This technique will work only if:

- The recordset sent to the client is opened as a disconnected recordset. Only a disconnected recordset maintains the changes to the data, and not just the new values of the fields.
- The recordset is mapped to an RDS Data Control on the client, and not to an XML Data Control.
- The recordset that receives the XML data on the server is also opened as a disconnected recordset, so that you can call its UpdateBatch method to commit the changes.

Once the remote XML recordset is read into a local recordset on the server, you can call the UpdateBatch method to commit the changes to the database. The following script accepts the edited XML recordset on the server and posts the changes to the database.

```
<%
NewRS = Server.CreateObject("ADODB.Recordset")
NewRS.CursorLocation = adUseClient
NewRS.Open Request, ,adOpenKeyset , _
        adLockBatchOptimistic , adCmdFile
NewRS.ActiveConnection = "DSN=NWIND"
NewRS.UpdateBatch
NewRS.Close
Set NewRS = Nothing
%>
```

This script reads the data posted by the client. The NewRS recordset variable is opened with the adLockBatchOptimistic option, because it's a disconnected recordset. Then it connects the disconnected recordset to the database and calls the UpdateBatch method to update the database. This is the GetXMLData.asp script, which you will find on the accompanying CD.

Hierarchical Recordsets

The recordsets we used so far are uniform—each row contains the same number of columns. These recordsets are very similar to tables, although they may contain rows from multiple tables.

Another type of recordset contains not only rows from multiple tables, but the relationship between the tables they're based on. These are called *hierarchical*, or *shaped*, recordsets. They're made up of different sections, and each section has a different structure. Let's say you want a list of all customers in a city, their orders, and the items of each order. A hierarchical recordset with this information contains a row for each customer. Under each customer, there's another recordset with the customer's orders.

In this table, the customer rows have a different structure from the order rows, and the order rows have a different structure from the item rows. Thus the recordset carries with it information about the structure of the entities it includes, as shown in this example:

```
Customer 1
  Order 1
    Item 1
    Item 2
    Item 3
```

```
    Order 2
      Item1
      Item2
  Customer 2
    Order 1
      Item 1
      Item 2
      Item 3
      Item 4
    Order 2
      Item 1
      Item 2
    Order 3
      Item 1
      Item 2
```

Each customer has one or more orders, and all the orders belonging to the same customer appear under the customer's name. Likewise, each order has one or more items, and all the items (detail lines) belonging to the same order appear under the order's ID.

Hierarchical recordsets are structured, and they lend themselves to XML descriptions. You can use ADO to produce hierarchical recordsets, but these recordsets are pretty useless outside ADO. You just can't process a hierarchical recordset on a computer that doesn't support ADO. However, if you translate a hierarchical recordset to an XML document, you can process it on every computer that supports XML.

The SHAPE Language

To create hierarchical recordsets, you use a special language, the *SHAPE language*. The SHAPE language supports all of the SQL statements, plus a few more keywords, to specify the relationships between the different recordsets. Following is the SHAPE statement that produces a hierarchical recordset with the customers, their orders, and the details of each order:

```
SHAPE {SELECT * FROM Customers}  AS
Command1 APPEND (( SHAPE {SELECT * FROM Orders}
AS  & Command2 APPEND ({SELECT * " & _
    " FROM [Order Details]}  AS Command3 RELATE 'OrderID'
```

Fortunately, you don't have to learn the SHAPE language to create hierarchical recordsets. The simplest method to define a hierarchical recordset is to use the visual database tools that come with Visual Studio. You can also write the statement yourself; conceptually, it's a little more complicated than straight SQL.

Building Hierarchical Recordsets with VB

Let's build a shaped recordset with VB. To do so, start a new VB project and enter the following statements in a button's Click event handler:

```
Private Sub Command1_Click()
Dim RS As New Recordset
ShapedCommand =
    " SHAPE {SELECT * FROM Customers}  AS " & _
    " Command1 APPEND (( SHAPE {SELECT * FROM Orders}" & _
    " AS " & Command2 APPEND ({SELECT * " & _
    " FROM [Order Details]}  AS Command3 RELATE " & _
    " 'OrderID' TO 'OrderID') AS Command3) " & _
    " AS Command2 RELATE 'CustomerID' TO" & _
    " 'CustomerID') AS Command2"
RS.Open ShapedCommand, CN
RS.Save "C:\Temp\Sales.xml", adPersistXML
```

You must set the CN Connection object to point to the NorthWind database on your system. If you run the program and click the button, a recordset will be created and saved to a disk file as `Sales.xml`, which is shown in Listing 9.3.

Listing 9.3: The *Sales.xml* File

```
- <xml xmlns:s="uuid:BDC6E3F0-6DA3-11d1-A2A3-00AA00C14882"
      xmlns:dt="uuid:C2F41010-65B3-11d1-A29F-00AA00C14882"
      xmlns:rs="urn:schemas-microsoft-com:rowset"
      xmlns:z="#RowsetSchema">
- <s:Schema id="RowsetSchema">
  - <s:ElementType name="row" content="eltOnly"
          rs:CommandTimeout="30" rs:ReshapeName="Command1">
  - <s:AttributeType name="CustomerID" rs:number="1"
          rs:writeunknown="true">
    <s:datatype dt:type="string" dt:maxLength="5"
          rs:fixedlength="true" rs:maybenull="false" />
    </s:AttributeType>
  - <s:AttributeType name="CompanyName"
          rs:number="2" rs:writeunknown="true">
    <s:datatype dt:type="string" dt:maxLength="40"
          rs:maybenull="false" />
    </s:AttributeType>
  - <s:AttributeType name="ContactName"
          rs:number="3" rs:nullable="true"
          rs:writeunknown="true">
    <s:datatype dt:type="string" dt:maxLength="30" />
    </s:AttributeType>
    - <s:ElementType name="Command2" content="eltOnly"
          rs:CommandTimeout="30"
          rs:ReshapeName="Command2"
          rs:relation="010000000200000000000000">
```

```
- <s:AttributeType name="OrderID" rs:number="1">
  <s:datatype dt:type="int" dt:maxLength="4"
        rs:precision="10" rs:fixedlength="true"
        rs:maybenull="false" />
  </s:AttributeType>
- <s:AttributeType name="CustomerID" rs:number="2"
        rs:nullable="true" rs:writeunknown="true">
  <s:datatype dt:type="string" dt:maxLength="5"
        rs:fixedlength="true" />
  </s:AttributeType>
- <s:AttributeType name="EmployeeID" rs:number="3"
        rs:nullable="true" rs:writeunknown="true">
  <s:datatype dt:type="int" dt:maxLength="4"
        rs:precision="10" rs:fixedlength="true" />
  </s:AttributeType>
- <s:AttributeType name="OrderDate"
        rs:number="4" rs:nullable="true"
        rs:writeunknown="true">
  <s:datatype dt:type="dateTime" rs:dbtype="timestamp"
        dt:maxLength="16" rs:scale="3"
        rs:precision="23" rs:fixedlength="true" />
  </s:AttributeType>
  - <s:ElementType name="Command3" content="eltOnly"
        rs:CommandTimeout="30" rs:ReshapeName="Command3"
        rs:relation="010000000100000000000000">
  - <s:AttributeType name="OrderID"
        rs:number="1" rs:writeunknown="true">
    <s:datatype dt:type="int" dt:maxLength="4"
        rs:precision="10" rs:fixedlength="true"
        rs:maybenull="false" />
    </s:AttributeType>
  - <s:AttributeType name="ProductID"
        rs:number="2" rs:writeunknown="true">
    <s:datatype dt:type="int" dt:maxLength="4"
        rs:precision="10" rs:fixedlength="true"
        rs:maybenull="false" />
    </s:AttributeType>
  - <s:AttributeType name="UnitPrice"
        rs:number="3" rs:writeunknown="true">
    <s:datatype dt:type="i8" rs:dbtype="currency"
        dt:maxLength="8" rs:precision="19"
        rs:fixedlength="true" rs:maybenull="false" />
    </s:AttributeType>
    </s:ElementType>
    </s:Schema>
```

To explore the structure of this script, I'll use one of the sample pages at the Microsoft XML site. If you connect to `msdn.microsoft.com/xml/general`, you will find a list of interesting samples. Connect to this URL, click the Sync TOC button, and when the frames with the TOC appear, click the Samples and Downloads link. Select the XML Data Source

Object, and download it to your computer. After you have saved all the necessary files in a folder on your system, double-click the `dsoMap.htm` file's icon, and you will see the page shown in Figure 9.5.

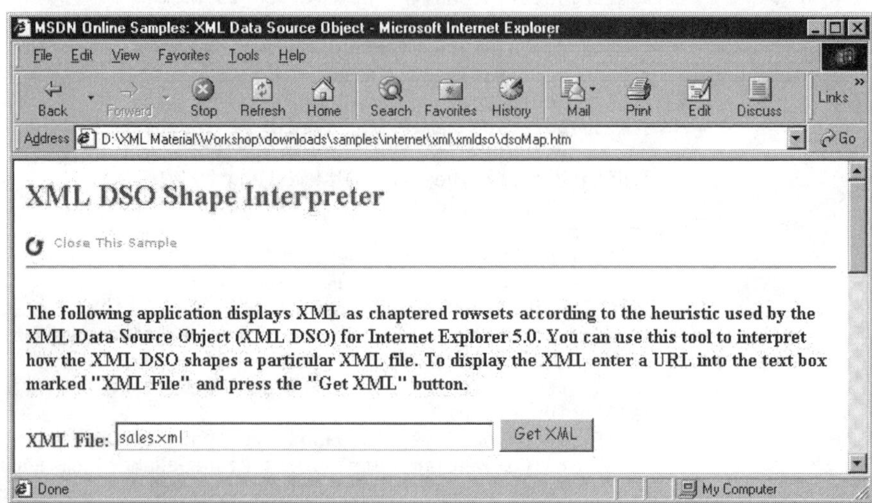

FIGURE 9.5
On this page, select the XML file to map.

Enter **Sales.xml** in the XML File textbox, and click the Get XML button. Scroll to the bottom of the XML DSO Shape Interpreter page, and you'll see the two sections in the file: the schema section and the data section. Both items are hyperlinks, and you can click the `<rs:data>` hyperlink to see the data of the hierarchical recordset. This section is made up of `<z:row>` tags.

When you click the `<rs:data>` hyperlink, you'll see another table that contains the `<z:row>` hyperlink. Click this hyperlink and you will see the nodes of the parent recordset, which contains all the customers in the database, as shown in Figure 9.6. For each customer, you see the number of orders placed by the customer (in the TotInvoices column) as well as the total revenue for the specific customer (in the CustomerTotal column).

In each customer's Orders column is another hyperlink, leading to the child recordset that corresponds to each customer and contains all of their orders. For example, if you click the Orders hyperlink for the customer ANTON, you'll see all of Anton's orders, as shown in Figure 9.7.

This recordset contains each order's ID (in the OrderID column), as well as its total (in the OrderTotal column). The order's total is not stored along with each order; it's a calculated field. Each row in the Orders recordset has its own child recordset, which contains the order's detail lines. Click an order's `Details` hyperlink to see the order's details.

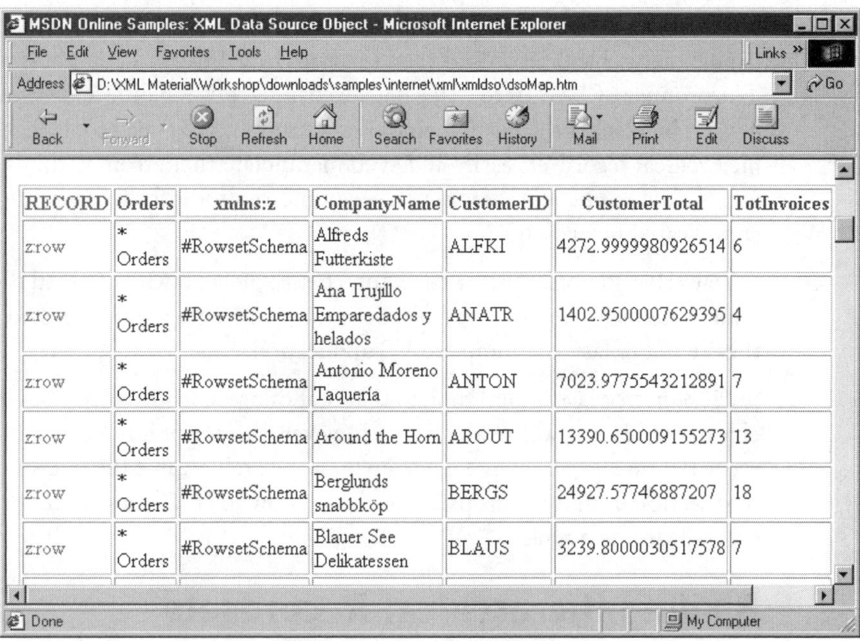

RECORD	Orders	xmlns:z	CompanyName	CustomerID	CustomerTotal	TotInvoices
zrow	* Orders	#RowsetSchema	Alfreds Futterkiste	ALFKI	4272.9999980926514	6
zrow	* Orders	#RowsetSchema	Ana Trujillo Emparedados y helados	ANATR	1402.9500007629395	4
zrow	* Orders	#RowsetSchema	Antonio Moreno Taquería	ANTON	7023.9775543212891	7
zrow	* Orders	#RowsetSchema	Around the Horn	AROUT	13390.650009155273	13
zrow	* Orders	#RowsetSchema	Berglunds snabbköp	BERGS	24927.57746887207	18
zrow	* Orders	#RowsetSchema	Blauer See Delikatessen	BLAUS	3239.8000030517578	7

FIGURE 9.6
Viewing the customers in the `Sales.xml` recordset

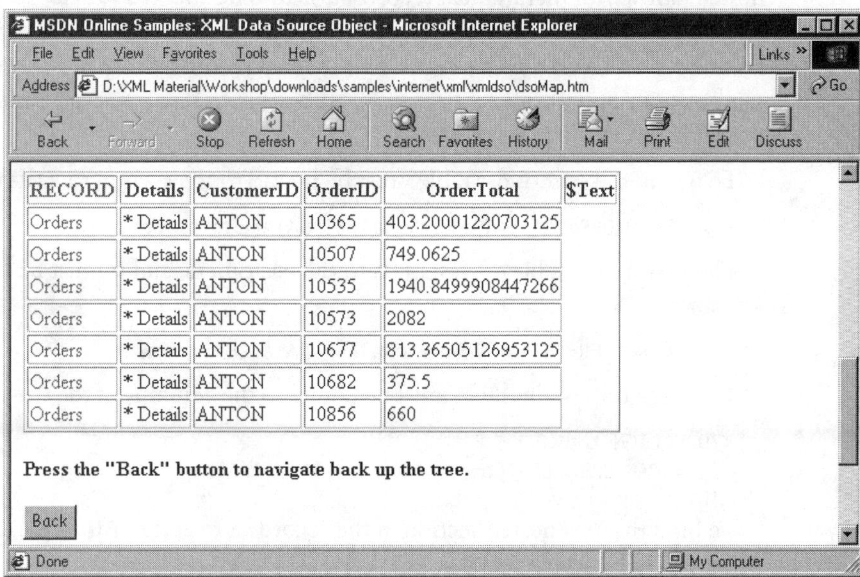

RECORD	Details	CustomerID	OrderID	OrderTotal	$Text
Orders	* Details	ANTON	10365	403.20001220703125	
Orders	* Details	ANTON	10507	749.0625	
Orders	* Details	ANTON	10535	1940.8499908447266	
Orders	* Details	ANTON	10573	2082	
Orders	* Details	ANTON	10677	813.36505126953125	
Orders	* Details	ANTON	10682	375.5	
Orders	* Details	ANTON	10856	660	

FIGURE 9.7
Viewing a customer's orders

While you're exploring hierarchical recordsets with the `DSOMap.htm` page, you can view the XML recordset by clicking the View XML button at the bottom of the page. This appends the entire XML recordset to the current page.

The Shape Interpreter page is an interesting example of a client-side script that handles complicated recordsets. However, developers shouldn't have to write complicated scripts to handle hierarchical recordsets (and DSOMap.htm deploys a complicated script on the client). The promise of XML is to make data exchange between different systems a reality. This can't happen by placing the burden on the programmer. We need tools that will allow us to display hierarchical recordsets easily and even manipulate them from within scripts with a few statements. It won't be long before you see numerous tools for interpreting and manipulating complicated recordsets.

You will also notice that it takes Internet Explorer a while to load the XML document and bind its fields to the nested tables. Scripting languages are interpreted, not compiled, and they're not as fast as a compiled VB application.

DSOMap.htm is a helpful tool, in that it allows you to visualize both the structure of a hierarchical recordset as well as the data. However, this is not how you would display a hierarchical recordset on a page. A page made up by nested tables, like the one shown in Figure 9.8 in the next section, is more appropriate. Let's see how to create nested tables by binding a hierarchical recordset to a table.

Binding Hierarchical Recordsets

Again, let's assume that the XML recordset was generated by ADO. The first step in creating nested tables with hierarchical recordsets is to bind the <rs:data> section to a table with no rows. Then we can bind the <x:row> section to a nested table. This is what we did with flat recordsets earlier in the chapter. A hierarchical recordset's <z:row> section, however, contains rows from multiple tables. We must be able to separate each child recordset's rows and display them in their own table.

To begin, the outermost table must be bound to the section <rs:data>, as usual:

```
<TABLE BORDER="1" DATASRC="#Sales" DATAFLD="rs:data">
```

The first nested table corresponds to the customers, and it must be bound to the section <z:row>:

```
<TABLE BORDER="1" DATASRC="#Sales" DATAFLD="z:row">
```

Then, the cells of this table must be bound to the columns of the Customers child recordset:

```
<TD VALIGN=top><B>
    <SPAN DATAFLD="CompanyName"></B></SPAN></TD>
<TD>
```

To bind the next nested section in the recordset to an HTML table, use the following value of the DATAFLD attribute:

```
<TABLE BORDER="1" DATASRC="#Sales"
                  DATAFLD="rs:data.z:row.Orders">
```

This table's cells must be bound to the fields of the Orders child recordset:

```
<TD VALIGN=top><SPAN DATAFLD="OrderID"></SPAN></TD>
<TD VALIGN=top><SPAN DATAFLD="OrderTotal"></SPAN></TD>
```

The details are a child recordset of the Orders recordset. Their table must be bound to the following field:

```
<TABLE BORDER="1" DATASRC="#Sales"
                  DATAFLD="rs:data.z:row.Orders.Details">
```

The Details recordset, which is a child of the Orders recordset, is in turn a child of the Customers recordset.

Now let's look at Listing 9.4, the complete `Sales.htm` file. The file is fairly lengthy, but not difficult to understand.

Listing 9.4: Binding Hierarchies to an HTML Table (*Sales.htm*)

```
<TABLE DATASRC="#Sales">
<TR>
  <TD>
    <TABLE BORDER="1" DATASRC="#Sales" DATAFLD="rs:data">
    <TR>
      <TD>
        <TABLE BORDER="1" DATASRC="#Sales" DATAFLD="z:row">
        <TR>
          <TD VALIGN=top><B>
               <SPAN DATAFLD="CompanyName"></B></SPAN></TD>
          <TD>
          <TABLE BORDER="1" DATASRC="#Sales"
                 DATAFLD="rs:data.z:row.Orders">
          <THEAD>
          <TR>
          <TD><B>OrderID</B></TD>
          <TD><B>Total</B></TD>
          </TR>
          </THEAD>
          <TBODY>
          <TR>
            <TD VALIGN=top>
                <SPAN DATAFLD="OrderID"></SPAN></TD>
            <TD VALIGN=top>
                <SPAN DATAFLD="OrderTotal"></SPAN></TD>
            <TD>
            <TABLE DATASRC="#Sales"
                   DATAFLD="rs:data.z:row.Orders.Details">
            <THEAD>
            <TR>
              <TD><B>ID</B></TD>
              <TD><B>Price</B></TD>
              <TD><B>Qty</B></TD>
              <TD><B>SubTotal</TD>
```

```
                  </TR>
                  </THEAD>
                  <TBODY>
                  <TR>
                    <TD><SPAN DATAFLD="ProductID"></SPAN></TD>
                    <TD><SPAN DATAFLD="UnitPrice"></SPAN></TD>
                    <TD><SPAN DATAFLD="Quantity"></SPAN></TD>
                    <TD><SPAN DATAFLD="LineTotal"></SPAN></TD>
                  </TR>
                  </TBODY>
                  </TD>
                </TR>
                </TBODY>
                </TABLE>
                </TD>
              </TR>
              </TABLE>
            </TD>
          </TR>
          </TABLE>
        </TD>
      </TR>
      </TABLE>
```

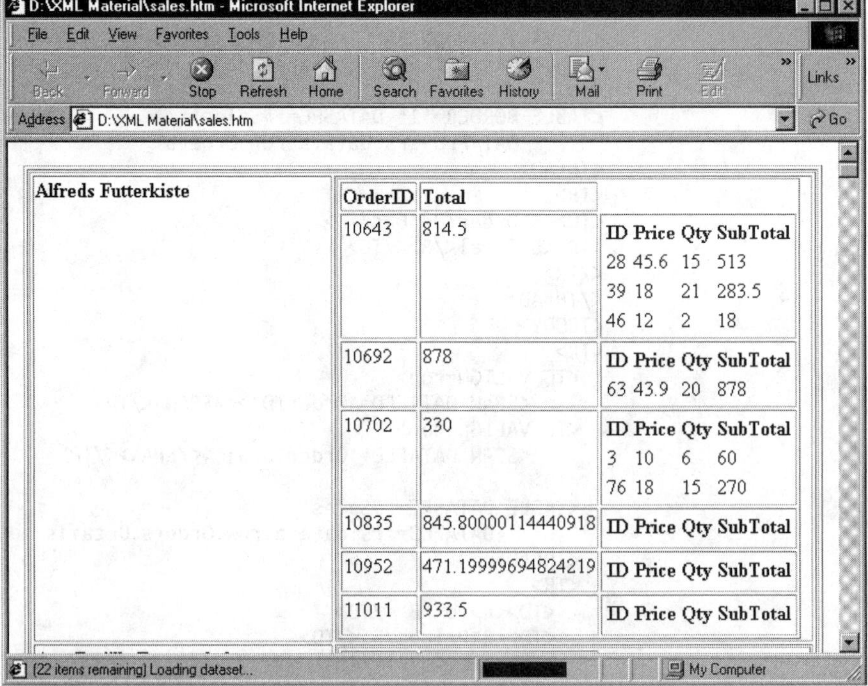

FIGURE 9.8 Binding a hierarchical recordset to nested tables on an HTML page

Viewing Reduced Recordsets

One of the most common and most useful applications of XML recordsets is to reduce the information displayed on the client. Let's say you want to display a hierarchical recordset with sales information. If you download a data island with the orders of a few customers, you are defeating the purpose of the data island. Clearly, you must download all the information in a single data island.

If you download all the information at once and display all the rows of the recordset on the same page, this page will be too long to be practical. The solution is to hide the child recordsets and let the user expand (and collapse) them as needed. This way, the viewer can quickly locate and view the desired information. When they're done with a child recordset (a customer's orders, or an orders' lines), they can simply hide it and move to another one.

To collapse and expand sections of the table, you must insert a script that reacts to the click of the mouse over a customer's name or an order ID. Assuming that the cells with the customers are named Orders and the nested tables with the orders are named OrdersTable, Listing 9.5 (`SalesTree.htm`) can be used to display and hide each customer's orders.

Listing 9.5: The Mouse Event Handlers for the Bound Recordset (*SalesTree.htm*)

```
<SCRIPT LANGUAGE=JavaScript FOR=Orders EVENT=onclick>
  rowID = this.recordNumber - 1;
  if (OrdersTable[rowID].style.display == "none")
  {
    OrdersTable[rowID].style.display = "inline";
  }
  else
  {
    OrdersTable[rowID].style.display = "none";
  }
  window.event.cancelBubble = true;
</SCRIPT>

<SCRIPT LANGUAGE=JavaScript FOR=Details EVENT=onclick>
  rowID = this.recordNumber - 1;
  if (DetailsTable[rowID].style.display == "none")
  {
    DetailsTable[rowID].style.display = "inline";
  }
  else
  {
    DetailsTable[rowID].style.display = "none";
  }
  window.event.cancelBubble = true;
</SCRIPT>
```

This file is identical to the `Sales.htm` page we saw earlier, except that some of the HTML elements have different names and styles. Also, there is some added script that expands/collapses the orders and details for each customer.

The SalesTree page is shown in Figure 9.9. As you can see, the page lets you select a customer and view their orders and their order details.

FIGURE 9.9
The SalesTree page

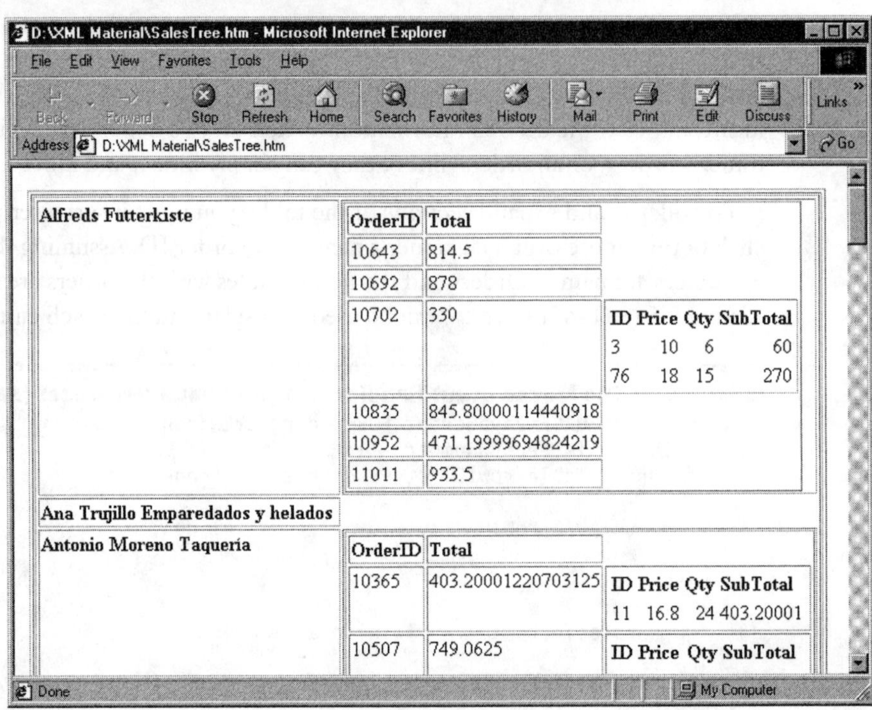

XML and SQL Server 2000

Everything we discussed in the earlier section "ADO Support for XML" applies to SQL Server as well, but SQL Server 2000 will have native support for XML. What this means is that SQL Server can produce XML-formatted cursors and transmit them directly to the client. The XML support for SQL Server is provided in the form of DLLs that sit between the DBMS and the Web server. These DLLs convert the cursors, returned by SQL Server in response to a query to XML data.

Let me start by showing you how easy it is to execute a SQL statement against a SQL Server database and retrieve a cursor in XML format. As you recall, a data island need not be included as is in an ASP file. You can use the SRC attribute of the <XML> tag to specify the URL of the XML file, or the URL of an ASP script that will return the desired data. The following lines can be entered in the browser's Address box to contact the SQL Server running on the same machine and execute a SQL statement against the NorthWind database:

```
http://127.0.0.1/NorthWind?sql=SELECT+
CategoryName,+Description+FROM+Categories
FOR+XML+RAW
```

NOTE This long line was broken to fit on the book page. Don't worry about this—you can't break lines in the browser's Address box anyway.

Any string entered in the browser's Address box must not contain any special characters. These characters must be replaced by their URL-encoded equivalents, which are shown in Table 9.1.

TABLE 9.4: The URL Encoding of Special Characters

Special Character	URL Encoding
Space	+
+	%2B
/	%2F
?	%3F
%	%25
#	%23
&	%26

Once you enter the appropriate information into the browser's Address box, SQL Server 2000 will execute the query and return the names and descriptions of the categories in the NorthWind database, as shown here:

```
<?xml version="1.0" encoding="UTF-8" ?>
<root>
<row CategoryName="Beverages"
     Description="Soft drinks …"/>
<row CategoryName="Condiments"
     Description="Sweet and Savory…"/>
<row CategoryName="Confections"
     Description="Desserts,…"/>
<row CategoryName="Dairy Products"
     Description="Cheeses"/>
<row CategoryName="Grains/Cereals"
     Description="Breads, crackers…"/>
<row CategoryName="Meat/Poultry"
     Description="Prepared meats…"/>
```

```
<row CategoryName="Produce"
     Description="Dried fruit …"/>
<row CategoryName="Seafood"
     Description="Seaweed and fish"/>
</root>
</xml>
```

Figure 9.10 shows how this file is rendered on your browser's window. This is an XML data island, and it contains row data but no information about the structure of the data in the cursor.

FIGURE 9.10
The XML-formatted cursor produced by SQL Server in response to a simple query

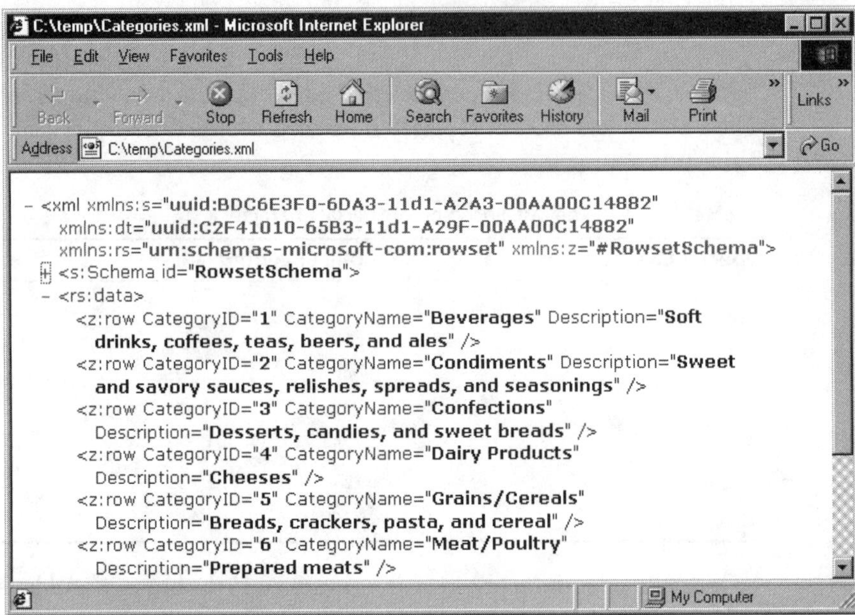

Being able to extract XML-formatted data directly from SQL Server is a very powerful feature, but we must still format the data as an HTML document. As you know very well by now, the simplest method to convert XML data to HTML documents is to use an XSL file. The XSL file should reside on the server, and you can include it in the response by simply adding its name to the previous URL:

```
http://127.0.0.1/NorthWind?sql=SELECT+
CategoryName,+Description+FROM+Categories
FOR+XML+RAW
&xsl=http://127.0.0.1/categories.xsl
```

The `categories.xsl` file must reside in the server's virtual folder.

Before you can contact SQL Server through the HTTP protocol, you must configure it accordingly with the `regxmlss` utility, which is described in the next section.

> **Microsoft's Technology Preview**
>
> You don't need the SQL Server 2000 beta to test drive the product's new features. You can download the XML Technology Preview from Microsoft's Web site and use it with SQL Server 7.5. Connect to the site `msdn.microsoft.com/SQLServer`, and select the appropriate hyperlink. As of this writing, the SQL Server 2000 beta is also available on this site.
>
> The most prominent feature of the XML Technology Preview is that you can contact SQL Server directly from a client through the HTTP protocol and execute SQL statements directly against the database. The results are returned to the client in the form of XML documents. As you can imagine, this raises some security issues, but more on this later.

The *regxmlss* Utility

The `regxmlss` utility defines a virtual folder, which is the root folder of the SQL server. SQL Server will service requests made to this folder only, and this is where SQL Server expects to find all auxiliary files (like XSL or template files). Of course, this virtual root folder can have subfolders, just like the Web server's root folder.

The SQL server's virtual root folder is different from the Web server's home page, so that the functionality of the two components is separated. I'm sure you don't want to place all the template files for accessing a database in the Web's root folder. Their place is the virtual folder of SQL Server. You can define an alias for the virtual root of SQL Server and map it to the Web server's physical root folder.

To specify the SQL server's virtual root folder, follow these steps:

1. Open the SQL server's menu and select the Configure IIS option to see the Register XML SQL Server Extensions dialog box (see Figure 9.11).
2. In the Internet Information Server section of the dialog box, specify the names of the IIS server (in the Site text box), the virtual root, and the physical folder (in the Directory text box) that will be mapped to the virtual root folder.
3. In the SQL Server section of the dialog box, set the name of the server and the name of the database. Note that all requests apply to this database, and you can't specify that a query be applied to a different database via the URL.
4. In the Connection Settings section of the dialog box, specify the type of authorization to be used.
5. To enable viewers to execute queries against a database through the HTTP protocol, select the Allow URL Queries check box at the bottom of the dialog box. To enable viewers to use templates for their queries, select the Allow Template Queries check box. (A *template* is a query that can be called by name, and it accepts parameters, just like stored procedures. Using templates and stored procedures is discussed later in this chapter.)

FIGURE 9.11
The Register XML SQL Server Extensions dialog box

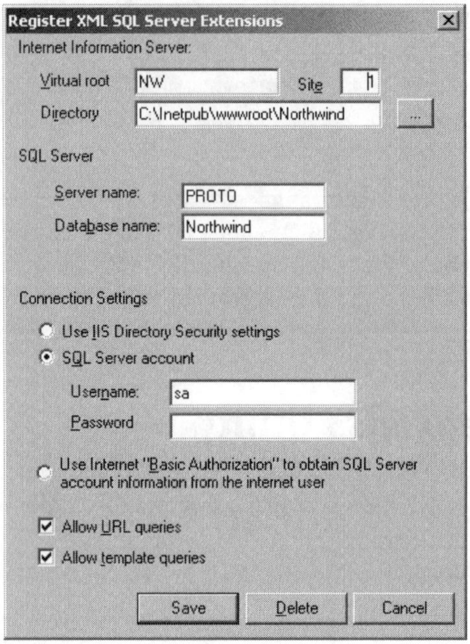

SQL Server's XML Modes

The XML returned by SQL Server in response to a query over the Web can be in one of three different flavors. These flavors are called *XML modes*, and they are RAW, AUTO, and EXPLICIT.

RAW

RAW mode converts each row into a single XML element, using the generic tag <row>. For example, the statement

```
SELECT ProductName, CategoryName
FROM Products, Categories
WHERE Products.CategoryID=Categories.CategoryID
FOR XML ROW
```

produces the following output (only the first few lines are shown):

```
<row ProductName="Chai" CategoryName="Beverages"/>
<row ProductName="Chang" CategoryName="Beverages"/>
<row ProductName="Aniseed Syrup"
        CategoryName="Condiments"/>
<row ProductName="Chef Anton&apos;s Cajun Seasoning"
     CategoryName="Condiments"/>
<row ProductName="Ikura" CategoryName="Seafood"/>
```

AUTO

AUTO mode returns a nested XML tree. Each table in the FROM clause is represented by an XML element, and the names of the fields become attributes. The same statement we used in the example of RAW mode will return the following rows, if you replace RAW with AUTO:

```
<Categories CategoryName="Beverages">
<Products ProductName="Chai"/>
<Products ProductName="Chang"/>
</Categories>
<Categories CategoryName="Condiments">
<Products ProductName="Aniseed Syrup"/>
<Products ProductName="Chef Anton&apos;s Cajun Seasoning"/>
<Products ProductName="Chef Anton&apos;s Gumbo Mix"/>
<Products ProductName="Grandma&apos;s Boysenberry Spread"/>
</Categories><Categories CategoryName="Produce">
<Products ProductName="Uncle Bob&apos;s Dried Pears"/>
</Categories>
```

As you can see, SQL Server is intelligent enough to consider the structure of the data and put together a hierarchical recordset, because this is exactly what you get in the AUTO mode. Each category section contains all the products in the category.

EXPLICIT

EXPLICIT mode allows you to define the exact shape of the XML tree. In effect, you must visualize the XML tree and write your query following specific rules. These rules are described in SQL Server's documentation, so I will not discuss them here. Since the RAW and AUTO modes are simpler, I'll use them in the following section's examples.

TIP You can use the Query Analyzer to experiment with the various XML modes and see the output they produce. However, you can't direct the XML output produced by a query in the Results Pane of the Query Analyzer to a client.

The *FOR* Clause

Here is the complete syntax of the FOR option:

```
FOR [mode][, schema][, ELEMENTS]
```

Notice that all arguments are optional. As you learned in the previous sections, the *mode* argument can be RAW, AUTO, or EXPLICIT. The *schema* argument specifies whether the recordset will contain schema information, and it can have the value DTD (Document Type Definition) or XMLDATA. The statement

```
SELECT ProductName, CategoryName
FROM Products, Categories
```

```
WHERE Products.CategoryID=Categories.CategoryID
FOR XML AUTO, DTD
```

will insert the following schema information at the beginning of the document:

```
<!DOCTYPE root
[<!ELEMENT root (Categories)*>
<!ELEMENT Products EMPTY>
<!ATTLIST Products ProductName CDATA #IMPLIED>
<!ELEMENT Categories (Products)*>
<!ATTLIST Categories CategoryName CDATA #IMPLIED>]>
<root>
```

The DTD option inserts the <root> element, and all data rows follow this tag. If you executed the same statement with the XMLDATA option, the following schema information will be inserted at the beginning of the document (the last four lines correspond to the first category):

```
<Schema xmlns="urn:schemas-microsoft-com:xml-data"
    xmlns:dt="urn:schemas-microsoft-com:datatypes">
<ElementType name="Products"
             content="textOnly" model="closed">
    <AttributeType name="ProductName" dt:type="string"/>
    <attribute type="ProductName" required="no"/>
</ElementType>
<ElementType name="Categories"
             content="mixed" model="closed">
<element type="Products"/>
    <AttributeType name="CategoryName" dt:type="string"/>
    <attribute type="CategoryName" required="no"/>
</ElementType>
</Schema>
<Categories CategoryName="Beverages">
<Products ProductName="Chai"/>
<Products ProductName="Chang"/>
</Categories>
```

NOTE If you omit the schema option, no schema information will be prepended to the document.

The ELEMENTS argument specifies that the columns will be returned as subelements. ELEMENTS can be used with AUTO mode only, and it produces straight XML code, which can be used as is in a data island. Let's try our sample statement with the ELEMENTS option:

```
SELECT ProductName, CategoryName
FROM Products, Categories
WHERE Products.CategoryID=Categories.CategoryID
FOR XML AUTO, ELEMENTS
```

The first few lines of the output produced by the preceding statement are shown here:

```
<Categories>
<CategoryName>Beverages</CategoryName>
```

```
<Products>
<ProductName>Chai</ProductName>
</Products>
<Products>
<ProductName>Chang</ProductName>
</Products>
</Categories>
<Categories>
<CategoryName>Condiments</CategoryName>
<Products>
<ProductName>Aniseed Syrup</ProductName>
</Products>
<Products>
<ProductName>Chef Anton&apos;s Cajun
           Seasoning</ProductName>
</Products>
```

OK, there's a catch here. The output produced by SQL Server doesn't contain an `<XML>` or `<ROOT>` tag, and it doesn't encode the text for transmission over the HTTP protocol.

Executing Stored Procedures

Stored procedures can be executed via a URL as easily as SQL statements. Actually, it's simpler to execute stored procedures, because the URL is simpler—it contains only the stored procedure's name and, optionally, one or more parameters. To call the `Ten Most Expensive Products` stored procedure of the NorthWind database, use the following URL:

```
http://127.0.0.1/NW?sql=execute+
[Ten+Most+Expensive+Products]
```

The square brackets are needed because the procedure's name contains spaces. This syntax uses the `execute` reserved keyword, followed by the name of the stored procedure.

If the stored procedure accepts parameters, you must supply their values either by ordinal position or by name. The `Sales by Year` stored procedure, also of the NorthWind database, expects two arguments: the beginning and ending dates, in this order. The names of the parameters are `@BeginningDate` and `@EndingDate`, respectively. Here's the definition of the Sales by Year stored procedure:

```
  create procedure "Sales by Year"
     @Beginning_Date DateTime, @Ending_Date DateTime AS
  SELECT Orders.ShippedDate, Orders.OrderID, "Order Subtotals".Subtotal,
DATENAME(yy,ShippedDate) AS Year
  FROM Orders INNER JOIN "Order Subtotals" ON Orders.OrderID = "Order
Subtotals".OrderID
  WHERE Orders.ShippedDate Between @Beginning_Date And @Ending_Date
```

To execute this stored procedure with the arguments 1/1/1998 and 12/31/1998, you can use either of the following two URLs:

```
http://127.0.0.1/NW?sql=execute+
[Sales by Year]+1/1/1998+12/31/1998
```

or

```
http://127.0.0.1/NW?sql=execute+
[Sales by Year]+@EndingDate=1/1/1998+
@BeginningDate=12/31/1998
```

Using the first form, you can specify the values of the parameters, as expected by the stored procedure. You don't have to know the names of the parameters, but you must know their order. With the second form, you use named parameters. You must know the names of the parameters, but you can specify them in any order, as you can see in the example.

Using Templates

In addition to XSL files, you can use templates to automate the process. Although it's possible to pass any statement as a URL, this requires a lot of typing, not to mention that you won't get the statement right the first time. As mentioned earlier in the chapter, it is possible to create template files with queries you want to execute against the database and call these template files by names, instead of supplying the actual SQL statement. The scripts need not be aware of the structure of the database. The database can prompt viewers for the values of some parameters and pass them as arguments to the template.

Another good reason for using template files is security. By placing a template file in the virtual root directory, you can enforce security by removing the URL query processing service on the virtual root. SQL Server will invoke the XML ISAPI to process the template file.

Finally, templates may contain other statements you want to include in your output. For example, you can insert the <XML> tags around the output, which are not produced automatically when you use the ELEMENTS argument in the FOR clause.

So, what exactly is a template file? A template is an XML file that contains SQL statements and parameters definitions like this:

```
<ROOT xmlns:sql="urn:schemas-microsoft-com:xml-sql">
<SQL:query">
enter your SQL statements here
</SQL:query>
</ROOT>
```

The first and last lines are always the same; only the SQL statements change from template to template.

Let's create a template for retrieving product categories. To begin, enter the following code in a text file and store it in the SQL Server's XML-enabled root folder:

```
<ROOT xmlns:sql="urn:schemas-microsoft-com:xml-sql">
<SQL:query">
SELECT CategoryID, CategoryName, Description
FROM Categories
FOR XML AUTO
</SQL:query>
</ROOT>
```

Assuming that the name of the template file is `AllCategories.xml`, you can execute this query against SQL Server by entering the following URL in your browser's Address Box:

```
http://127.0.0.1/NW/AllCategories.xml
```

If the template accepts parameters (and most templates do), use the following syntax:

```
<ROOT xmlns:sql="urn:schemas-microsoft-com:xml-sql">
<SQL:query
 name1='value1' name2='value2'>
{ enter your SQL statement(s) here }
</SQL:query>
</ROOT>
```

Replace the strings *`name1`* and *`name2`* with the names of the parameters. *`value1`* and *`value2`* are the default values of the parameters, and they'll be used only if no values are specified in the URL.

The following template file will select the products of a specific category. Its name is `ProdByCategory.xml`, and it must stored in SQL Server's root folder:

```
<ROOT xmlns:sql="urn:schemas-microsoft-com:xml-sql">
<SQL:query
 SelCategory='3'>
 SELECT * FROM Products
 WHERE CategoryID = ?
</SQL:query>
</ROOT>
```

This template will select all the files in the category specified by the request. If no Category ID is specified, it will return the products belonging to the category with an ID of 3. To call this template passing the Category ID 4 as the parameter, connect to the following URL:

```
http://127.0.0.1/NW/ProdsByCategory.xml?SelCategory=4
```

Using Update Grams

In the section "Updating XML Recordsets" earlier in this chapter, you saw how to post updates to a database using XML. SQL Server supports XML-based insert, update, and delete operations with a similar syntax. The statements for updating the database are called *grams*, and they can be used to post new rows and to edit or delete existing ones.

The syntax of an update gram is

```
<sql:sync xmlns:sql="urn:schemas-microsoft-com:xml-sql">
   <sql:before>
      <TABLENAME [sql:id="value"]
                 col1="value1"
                 col2="value2"/>
   </sql:before>
   <sql:after>
      <TABLENAME [sql:id="value"]
                 [sql:at-identity="value"]
                 col1="value1"
                 col2="value2"/>
   </sql:after>
</sql:sync>
```

before and after are keywords that specify field values before and after the update. The sync keyword delimits the operation, and everything between a pair of <sync> and </sync> tags is treated as a transaction. In other words, SQL Server will not update only a few of the fields if an error occurs. If one of the specified values is incompatible with the definition of the column, then the entire operation will be aborted.

In the <before> section, you specify the field values of an existing row. In the <after> section, you specify the new values for one or more fields. You must provide as many column="value" pairs as there are fields to be changed.

The <before> and <after> sections are optional. If the <before> section is missing, then it's assumed that you're inserting a new row to the database. The new row's fields must be specified in an <after> section. If the <after> section is missing, then the row identified by the field values in the <before> section is removed from the table.

It is possible to specify multiple updates in a single gram. If the <after> section contains rows with no matching entry in the <before> section, then these are new rows. The rows in the <after> section with a matching row in the <before> section are updated. Rows that appear only in the <before> section are deleted.

Inserting Rows

Following is an update gram that inserts a new row to the Customers table:

```
<ROOT xmlns:sql="urn:schemas-microsoft-com:xml-sql">
    <sql:sync>
      <sql:after>
         <Customers CustomerID="NEW"
                    CompanyName="New Company"
                    ContactName="New Contact"
                    ContactTitle="New Owner/>
      </sql:after>
    </sql:sync>
</ROOT>
```

This is quite a URL, if you're thinking about submitting it to the server.

The information you retrieve from SQL Server via a URL is not a disconnected recordset. As a result, any changes you make are not going to be embedded in the recordset. The easiest approach is to create the update grams from within a client-side script and submit them to the server, just as you would submit a normal query via URL. Alternatively, you can call a template file and pass the values of the fields as arguments.

Most applications don't add rows to unrelated tables. A practical example is the insertion of a new order to the NorthWind database. To add an order, you must add a new row to the Orders table. SQL Server will automatically assign a new ID to the order. Then, you must use this ID to insert one or more rows to the Order Details table. Each item has its own row in the Order Details table, and all the rows that belong to the same order must have the same OrderID. The following statement will add a new row to the Orders table:

```
<sql:sync>
  <sql:after>
    <Orders sql:at-identity='newID' CustomerID='ALFKI'/>
  </sql:after>
</sql:sync>
```

newID is a variable name that will be assigned the ID of the new order. The OrderID field in the Order table is an AutoNumber field, so SQL Server knows which value to assign to the *newID* variable.

Now you can use this variable to add the order's details. For each detail, add a new row to the Order Details table and set the OrderID field to the value of the *newID* variable. The following statements add a single detail for the new order:

```
<sql:sync>
   <sql:after>
   <OrderDetails OrderID='newID'
                 ProductID='11'
                 Quantity='10'/>
   </sql:after>
</sql:sync>
```

Listing 9.6 is a page that adds a new order for the customer ALFKI. The order contains three items, for the products with ID of 11, 12, and 13. To add the new order, the HTML page uses the `AddOrder()` function, which builds a template file. The contents of the template file are transmitted to the server by redirecting the script to the new URL.

Listing 9.6: The AddOrder Script

```
<HTML>
<SCRIPT>
  function AddOrder()
  {
    NewOrderXML = "http://127.0.0.1/NW/?template=
    <ROOT xmlns:sql='urn:schemas-microsoft-com:xml-sql'>
```

```
      <sql:sync>
         <sql:after>
         <Orders sql:at-identity='newID'
                     CustomerID='ALFKI'/>
         <OrderDetails OrderID='newID'
                       ProductID='11'
                       Quantity='10'/>
         <OrderDetails OrderID='newID'
                       ProductID='12'
                       Quantity='20'/>
         <OrderDetails OrderID='newID'
                       ProductID='13'
                       Quantity='30'/>
         </sql:after>
      </sql:sync>
   </ROOT>
     document.location.href = newOrderXML;
  }
</SCRIPT>
<BODY>
Click here to
<INPUT type="button" value="ADD ORDER"
       OnClick="AddOrder();">
</BODY>
</HTML>
```

You can modify this script so that it reads the values of the various fields from controls and builds the appropriate template file. This file isn't stored on the server. SQL Server simply executes it, and nothing is saved on the root folder.

An even better method to update the database is to write a stored procedure that accepts the same information we pass to the template file with the `AddOrder()` function and updates the database by adding new rows to the appropriate tables. The stored procedure should also be able to handle errors and return a True/False value indicating whether or not the operation was successful. It should also perform all the updates in the context of a transaction. The template file is also executed as a transaction, so that if a single insertion fails, the entire transaction is aborted.

Deleting Rows

To delete one or more rows in a table, specify the `<before>` section of the update gram and omit the `<after>` section. The sure method to delete the desired row is to supply its primary key. For example, the following statements remove the customers with ID TEST1 and TEST2 from the Customers table in the NorthWind database:

```
<ROOT xmlns:sql='urn:schemas-microsoft-com:xml-sql'>
  <sql:sync>
    <sql:before>
      <Customers  CustomerID="TEST1"/>
      <Customers  CustomerID="TEST2"/>
```

```
    </sql:before>
  </sql:sync>
</ROOT>
```

If the primary key of the row to be deleted is not known, supply as much information as possible to uniquely identify the row you want to remove. The following statements attempt to locate a row in the Customers table with `ContactName="Joe Doe"` and `City="NY"`:

```
<ROOT xmlns:sql='urn:schemas-microsoft-com:xml-sql'>
  <sql:sync>
    <sql:before>
      <Customers  ContactName="Joe Doe" City="NY"/>
    </sql:before>
  </sql:sync>
</ROOT>
```

If such a customer exists, it will be removed from the database. If two or more rows meet the specified criteria, then only the first row will be removed from the table. As you can understand, deleting rows with criteria other than the primary key is tricky, and you can't be sure that the deleted row was the one you intended.

Deleting Multiple Rows with One Statement

There are situations where you want to delete multiple rows with a single statement. For instance, to remove an order, you must first delete the details from the Order Details table. These are the lines whose `OrderID` field matches the ID of the order you want to remove. For example, the following statement will not remove all the rows whose `OrderID` field is `9840`. Instead, it will remove only the first row that matches the criteria:

```
<ROOT xmlns:sql='urn:schemas-microsoft-com:xml-sql'>
  <sql:sync>
    <sql:before>
      <[Order Details] OrderID="9840"/>
    </sql:before>
  </sql:sync>
</ROOT>
```

To remove multiple rows from a table with a single statement, you must repeat the statement as many times as there are rows to be removed, or execute an action query against the database. The following statements will remove all the detail lines of the order with `ID=9840`:

```
<ROOT xmlns:sql="urn:schemas-microsoft-com:xml-sql">
<SQL:query
 DELETE FROM [Order Details]
 WHERE OrderID = 9840
</SQL:query>
</ROOT>
```

As you may have guessed, the best method to remove an order is to write a stored procedure that accepts the ID of the order to be removed as an argument and that performs all the deletions as a single transaction. For example, you can define the following stored procedure that deletes the detail lines of an order:

```
USE NORTHWIND
CREATE PROCEDURE DeleteDetails
@OrderID int
AS
DELETE FROM [Order Details]
WHERE [Order Details].OrderID = @OrderID
```

You can call the `DeleteDetails` stored procedure to delete the detail lines of an order and pass the ID of the order whose details you want to delete as an argument:

```
http://127.0.0.1/NW?sql=execute+
DeleteDetails+19088
```

Templates versus Stored Procedures

It seems that templates are nearly identical to stored procedures, and you can write a stored procedure instead of a template. Although this is true in most situations, template files can be used to execute multiple SQL statements. In fact, you can use template files that call stored procedures themselves.

Another good use of templates is to define update and delete grams. As you recall from our earlier discussion, the syntax of grams is a bit peculiar, and it takes a bit of effort to implement the gram from within a client script. You can insert all the tags of the gram in a template file and pass the necessary values as parameters.

Summary

This fairly lengthy chapter introduced the basic concepts of using XML with Microsoft databases. You learned how to retrieve data from databases in XML format and how to bind individual fields to HTML controls on a Web page. You also learned how to create XML data islands and pass a lot of information to the client with a single trip to the server. (Once the information is on the client, you can control how it will be displayed with a client-side script.)

There are two methods to create XML data islands: You can either use ADO's `Recordset.Save` method or use the native XML support of SQL Server 2000. The advantage of the first method is that the DBMS need not support XML, and it works with any database that can be accessed through ADO. SQL Server's native XML support allows you to query databases through the HTTP protocol.

XML is an emerging standard, and ADO 2.5/2.6 provides rather limited support for XML-formatted data. Recently, Microsoft announced ADO+, which will provide better XML support, so you should check the Microsoft MSDN site for more information on this technology. According to recent announcements by Microsoft, XML will be one of the cornerstones of products ranging from databases to future versions of the Windows operating system.

CHAPTER 10

E-commerce with Microsoft BizTalk

- Understanding BizTalk
- Examining the BizTalk Framework
- Swapping information through `BizTalk.org`
- Using BizTalk Server 2000

One of the most obvious arenas for the use of XML is business-to-business communication, sometimes known by the acronym B2B. However, the very flexibility of XML can be its downfall. If every organization defines their own schema for carrying business information, it's impossible for any two organizations to talk. So in this area, at least, standards for schema design are very important.

In this chapter, I review one such standard, BizTalk. Originally designed by Microsoft, *BizTalk* has become a multi-organizational specification of increasing importance in the crowded B2B market.

What Is BizTalk?

Microsoft announced the BizTalk Framework for e-commerce in March 1999, with the stated goal of letting "software speak the language of business." The description of BizTalk has changed and become clearer in the intervening months. At first, it seemed as though Microsoft was promoting BizTalk as a refinement to Windows DNA, their process for creating distributed applications. But over time, the XML features of BizTalk have gradually assumed center stage. As of this book's writing in mid 2000, there are three main parts to the BizTalk initiative:

- The *BizTalk Framework* provides a methodology and set of rules for creating XML schemas and tags to enable integration of business applications. These schemas are meant to be completely independent of software implementation details such as operating system or programming language.
- *BizTalk.org* is a quasi-independent industry group that supports collaboration among business organizations with an interest in BizTalk-compliant schemas. One of their most important activities is the maintenance of a library of BizTalk schemas.
- *Microsoft BizTalk Server 2000* is being promoted as "the industrial-strength, reliable operating environment for document transformation and routing to automate electronic procurement, business-to-business portals, and extranets, as well as automating value chain processes." Microsoft has also announced that BizTalk Server 2000 will include a graphical process-modeling environment. This product isn't shipping yet, but you can download the BizTalk Server Technology Preview for an early look at parts of the BizTalk Server technology.

In this chapter, I cover each of these parts of the BizTalk initiative in detail. You'll see what Microsoft is currently offering in this area, and I'll try to give you a sense of what you can implement today.

NOTE Because BizTalk Server 2000 hasn't shipped yet, some of this chapter is necessarily speculative. There's no guarantee that the final product will include all the features of the BizTalk Server Technology Preview. Nevertheless, gaining early experience with the parts of BizTalk that are implemented now will help you come up to speed quickly when the product is released.

The BizTalk Framework

Microsoft released version 1.0a of the BizTalk Framework Independent Document Specification in January 2000. This document defines a set of XML tags that are designed to allow BizTalk-enabled applications to exchange information with one another. The specification defines an overall logical architecture for message passing between applications, defines key terms, and includes a set of XML tags that are used to encapsulate information in BizTalk messages.

In this section, I'll walk you through the details of the BizTalk Framework Independent Document Specification. At the end of the section, I'll show you a sample document that conforms to the specification.

NOTE The BizTalk Framework Independent Document Specification is still evolving as Microsoft and its partners collaborate on refining the ideas in BizTalk. You should always be able to download the current version of the specification from `www.microsoft.com/biztalk/`. This chapter is based on version 1.0a of the specification.

The BizTalk Architecture

The overall architecture for BizTalk is a layered design vaguely reminiscent of the ISO/OSI seven-tiered architecture for networking, although considerably simpler. Figure 10.1 shows the components in this architecture.

FIGURE 10.1
The BizTalk architecture

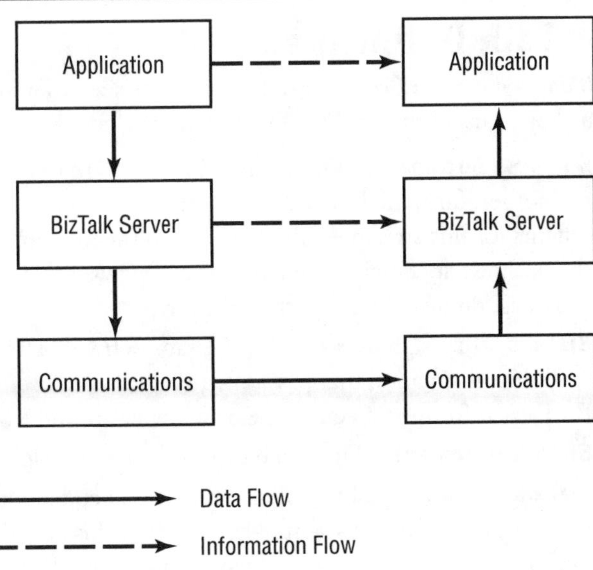

The BizTalk architecture includes three components:

The Application This is the business process that's sending or receiving data. This might be a purchasing program, a health care processing application, or any other business-specific application.

The BizTalk Server This is the server that knows how to interpret and route BizTalk messages. This might be Microsoft BizTalk Server 2000, but there's nothing to prevent other vendors from also shipping applications that function as BizTalk servers.

The Communications Layer This represents the network and communications infrastructure that moves messages from one BizTalk server to another. It might use a direct LAN connection, a dedicated dial-up line, an Internet protocol such as HTTP, or a message passing system such as Microsoft Message Queue (MSMQ). BizTalk is designed to be independent of the communications protocol used, and it doesn't care about the implementation details so long as messages actually get delivered.

In the BizTalk architecture, the logical flow of information differs from the physical flow of data. Physically, an application sends a message to the local BizTalk server, which sends it to the communications layer. This layer forwards the message to the communications layer on another computer, which passes the message up to the BizTalk server on the receiving end, which passes it to the receiving application. Logically, though, from the application's point of view, it is simply using BizTalk services to talk to another application. Similarly, the BizTalk server acts as if it's talking directly to another BizTalk server. Each layer in the architecture has its own distinct information that it processes.

BizTalk Definitions

To understand the BizTalk Framework, you need to understand the vocabulary that it uses. The key terms in the BizTalk Framework include:

Business Document This is the information that's being transferred from one application to another, formatted as an XML stream. The BizTalk Framework does not prescribe the schema for this stream. Rather, it's left to the implementers of the applications to agree on the business document schemas to use. One way to do this is by using schemas from BizTalk.org, discussed later in this chapter.

BizTags BizTags are a set of XML tags defined by the BizTalk Framework. These tags hold the information that passes from one BizTalk server to another. You can think of the BizTags as forming an envelope or wrapper around a business document.

BizTalk Document This is a business document together with the surrounding BizTags.

BizTalk Message A BizTalk document is encoded into a BizTalk message by the communications layer when it's sent. The details of this encoding can vary depending on the particular communications layer. I won't discuss BizTalk message formats in this chapter, because you're not likely to need to deal with BizTalk on this level.

Referring back to Figure 10.1, the business document passes between the two applications, the BizTalk document passes between the two servers, and the BizTalk message passes between the two communications layers.

BizTags

The BizTalk Framework defines a set of XML tags, called *BizTags*, to handle the delivery and addressing information that one BizTalk server requires in order to send a message to another BizTalk server. In this section, I'll review these tags one by one. In the next section, you'll see an example of a complete BizTalk document.

A BizTalk document must be enclosed in the <biztalk_1> tag and include a reference to the BizTalk namespace. This is what identifies the document as a BizTalk document. This tag and the namespace reference can take one of two forms:

```
<biztalk_1 xmlns="urn:biztalk-org:biztalk:biztalk_1">
     document_contents
</biztalk_1>
```

or

```
<biztalk_1
➥xmlns="http://schemas.biztalk.org/BizTalk/gr677h7w.xml">
    document_contents
</biztalk_1>
```

NOTE In the tag examples in this section, italicized text such as *document_contents* indicates variables, information that is not part of the tag itself.

The first form of the <biztalk_1> tag uses a Uniform Resource Name (URN) to specify the location of the namespace definition on the Internet. Someday, this will be the preferred method of pointing to this definition. But at the moment, the Internet Engineering Task Force (IETF) hasn't finalized a URN definition for vendors to implement.

The second form of the tag uses a standard Web address to locate the namespace definition. This format allows today's tools to validate BizTalk documents against the schema.

The <header> tag is used within the <biztalk_1> tag to identify the header of the BizTalk document (the addressing and message processing information used by the BizTalk servers). The <body> tag is used within the <biztalk_1> tag to hold the business document being transmitted as part of this BizTalk document. These three tags fit together like this:

```
<biztalk_1 xmlns="urn:biztalk-org:biztalk:biztalk_1">
    <header>
        processing_information
    </header>
    <body>
```

```
        business_document
      </body>
  </biztalk_1>
```

The other BizTags occur within the <header> tag. This makes sense, because the header section is where all of the information needed by the BizTalk server occurs. This information is precisely what BizTags are meant to contain.

The direct children of the <header> tag are the <delivery> tag and the <manifest> tag. The <delivery> tag contains delivery and addressing information for the BizTalk document. The <manifest> tag contains message content information.

The <delivery> tag is the parent of the <message>, <to>, and <from> tags. The <message> tag contains information about the message itself, while the <to> and <from> tags contain address information for the sender and recipient.

The <message> tag contains three child tags:

<messageID> This is an arbitrary message ID. It can be a sequential unique number generated by the sending BizTalk server, or a globally unique identifier (GUID). The BizTalk Framework does not specify a required format for this tag.

<sent> This tag is the time that the message was sent, according to the originating BizTalk server.

<subject> This is the subject of the message. Note that this is a subject determined by the BizTalk server, not by the originating application (which knows nothing about the content of BizTags).

The <from> and <to> tags have the same internal structure. Each of these tags can contain up to five other tags:

<address> This is a Uniform Resource Identifier (URI) describing the address of the sending or receiving system. The BizTalk server is responsible for resolving the URI address into a transport-specific address that can be understood by the communications layer in the BizTalk architecture.

<state> This tag is used by the BizTalk server to hold information used within the individual BizTalk server.

<referenceID> This is a unique identifier for the instance of the particular business process sending the message. This can be used when a reply to the message comes back to locate the destination process.

<handle> A refinement to the `referenceID`, this tag can be used to hold state information. For example, it might represent the step within a particular business process that transmitted the original business document.

<process> A refinement to the `handle`, this tag can be used to hold the account, process, or security information for the originating message.

The <manifest> tag contains information for the BizTalk server about the contents of the BizTalk message. Applications are free to send attachments along with business documents, and these attachments must be included with the message. Thus, the <manifest> tag contains the <document> tag and the <attachment> tag. The <document> tag must come before any instances of the <attachment> tag.

The <document> tag doesn't contain the document (that's in the <body> tag). Rather, it contains information about the document. The <name> tag is required and contains the name of the document. The <description> tag is optional and contains a description of the document. If there are multiple business documents within a single BizTalk document, then the <document> tag must be repeated multiple times, in the same order as the documents themselves.

The <attachment> tag can contain four child tags:

<index> This is a unique (within the context of the current BizTalk document) identifier for the attachment.

<filename> This is the filename of the attachment.

<description> This tag offers additional description of the attachment.

<type> This is a keyword identifying the type of attachment. If the attachment is itself a BizTalk document, then the type should be set to `biztalk`. Applications can define additional keywords to use here.

Putting the last several tags together, a full <manifest> section from a BizTalk document might look like this:

```
<manifest>
    <document>
        <name>PO 142787</name>
        <description>Purchase Order</description>
    </document>
    <attachment>
        <index>1</index>
        <filename>sig.jpg</filename>
        <description>Signature graphic</description>
        <type>jpg</type>
    </attachment>
<manifest>
```

Finally, the <body> tag contains the actual business document. This document will itself be an XML stream, but the tags and schema used by this stream are not dictated by the BizTalk Framework. It's important, though, that the opening tag for the business document contain namespace information for the tags within the business document. If this namespace information is omitted, then the business document tags will be interpreted as part of the BizTag namespace, which will most likely cause an error. For example, BizTalk.org defines a sample

Purchase Order schema with a schema definition located at schemas.biztalk.org/BizTalk/cfwau8qx.xml. You could use this within a <body> tag as follows:

```
<body>
    <PO xmlns="http://schemas.biztalk.org/BizTalk/cfwau8qx.xml">
        purchase_order_information
    </PO>
</body>
```

Table 10.1 lists the complete set of BizTags and shows which ones are optional and which are required.

TABLE 10.1: BizTags

Tag	Parent	Required	Occurs
Address	to or from	Yes	Once
Attachment	manifest	No	Zero or more
Biztalk_1	None	Yes	Once
Body	biztalk_1	Yes	Once
Description	document or attachment	No	Zero or once
Delivery	header	No	Once
Document	manifest	Yes	One or more
Filename	attachment	Yes	Once
From	delivery	Yes	Once
Handle	to or from	No	Zero or once
Header	biztalk_1	No	Once
Index	attachment	Yes	Once
Manifest	header	No	Zero or once
Message	delivery	Yes	Once
MessageID	message	Yes	Once
Name	document	Yes	Once
Process	to or from	No	Zero or once
ReferenceID	to or from	Yes	Once
Sent	message	Yes	Once
State	to or from	No	Zero or once
Subject	message	No	Zero or once
To	delivery	Yes	Once
Type	attachment	No	Zero or once

A BizTalk Document

At this point, you've seen all of the components of a BizTalk document. Now it's time to see how they fit together. Listing 10.1 shows a sample BizTalk document (`PurchaseOrder.xml`) encapsulating a business message that's written using the sample purchase order schema from BizTalk.org. In this listing, the BizTags are shown in boldface type. The normal type indicates the business document contained within the BizTalk document.

Listing 10.1: A BizTalk Document (*PurchaseOrder.xml*)

```
<biztalk_1 xmlns="urn:biztalk-org:biztalk:biztalk_1">
  <header>
    <delivery>
      <message>
        <messageID>134576</messageID>
        <sent>2000-07-02T22:45:30+06:00</sent>
        <subject>Purchase Order</subject>
      </message>
      <to>
        <address>http://schmoop.com/po.asp</address>
        <state>
          <referenceID/>
        </state>
      </to>
      <from>
        <address>mailto:purchasing@schmoop.com</address>
        <state>
          <referenceID>241AA6</referenceID>
        </state>
      </from>
    </delivery>
    <manifest>
      <document>
        <name>PO 142787</name>
        <description>Purchase Order</description>
      </document>
    <manifest>
  </header>
  <body>
<PO
➥xmlns="http://schemas.biztalk.org/BizTalk/cfwau8qx.xml">
      <POHeader>
        <poNumber>142787</poNumber>
        <custID>4718</custID>
        <description>
          Order for styrofoam cups
        </description>
        <paymentType>Invoice</paymentType>
        <shipType>Ground</shipType>
        <Contact>
          <contactName>Mel Schmoop</contactName>
          <contactEmail>
```

```
            Mel@schmoop.com
          </contactEmail>
        </Contact>
        <POShipTo>
          <attn>Schmoop</attn>
          <street>123 Willow Way</street>
          <city>Brook City</city>
          <stateProvince>WA</stateProvince>
          <postalCode>99999</postalCode>
          <country>USA</country>
          </POShipTo>
        <POBillTo>
          <attn>Schmoop</attn>
          <street>123 Willow Way</street>
          <city>Brook City</city>
          <stateProvince>WA</stateProvince>
          <postalCode>99999</postalCode>
          <country>USA</country>
        </POBillTo>
      </POHeader>
      <POLines>
        <count>1</count>
        <totalAmount>650.00</totalAmount>
        <Item>
          <line>1</line>
          <partno>S100</partno>
          <qty>325</qty>
          <uom>pkg</uom>
          <unitPrice>2.00</unitPrice>
          <discount>0</discount>
          <totalAmount>650.00</totalAmount>
        </Item>
      </POLines>
    </PO>
</body>
</biztalk_1>
```

BizTalk.org

Now you've seen how a BizTalk document is formed, but we haven't discussed the content of the business document that it contains. Developing and promoting standardized XML schemas to support business-to-business interchange is the mission of BizTalk.org.

BizTalk.org is an organization administered by the BizTalk Steering Committee. This is a group formed by Microsoft in conjunction with a number of partners. The charter members of the BizTalk Steering Committee are:

- American Petroleum Institute
- Ariba

- Baan
- Boeing
- Commerce One
- Concur Technologies
- Data Interchange Standards Association
- J.D. Edwards
- Merrill Lynch
- Microsoft
- Open Applications Group
- PeopleSoft
- Pivotal Software
- SAP

The main activity of BizTalk.org is to act as a repository for BizTalk schemas. The group also hosts a set of online discussion areas and provides news related to BizTalk on its Web site at `www.biztalk.org`.

The BizTalk Web Site

The BizTalk Web site (`www.biztalk.org`) is divided into six major areas:

Home The home page includes breaking news about the BizTalk initiative, as well as quick links to important BizTalk information. From this page, you can also register with BizTalk. Registration is free, but it's required for access to some parts of the Web site.

Library The library page provides access to the BizTalk library of schemas. I'll discuss this more in the next section. From this page, you can also register to become a BizTalk contributor. You'll need to do this if your company wants to place a schema into the BizTalk library.

Community The community page provides a set of discussion groups for BizTalk-related topics. These range from a Newbies corner to several expert areas. The discussion groups are moderately active, and there are knowledgeable people available to answer your questions.

News The news page highlights news about BizTalk and related areas such as XML messaging and other industry XML initiatives. You can also sign up to receive e-mail notification of news items.

Resources The resources page provides a small selection of XML tools, white papers, and links.

Help The help page provides a list of frequently asked questions (FAQ) and general help with using the BizTalk Web site.

BizTalk Schemas

The BizTalk schemas are accessible through the library page on BizTalk.org. To find a particular schema, you need to search for it. There are two ways to search for schemas:

- You can enter a keyword or a comma-separated list of keywords to find schemas containing those keywords (such as "purchase" or "invoice").
- You can drill down through a list of industrial classifications to see all schemas that have been classed with a particular industry (the organization that submits the schema determines the classification).

TIP To see a list of all schemas in the BizTalk library, enter a single space in the Keyword Search textbox and click Search.

As of April 2000, the BizTalk library contains just over 400 schemas, submitted by a wide variety of organizations. Figure 10.2 shows one of these schemas in BizTalk.org's Schema-View application.

FIGURE 10.2
BizTalk.org schema

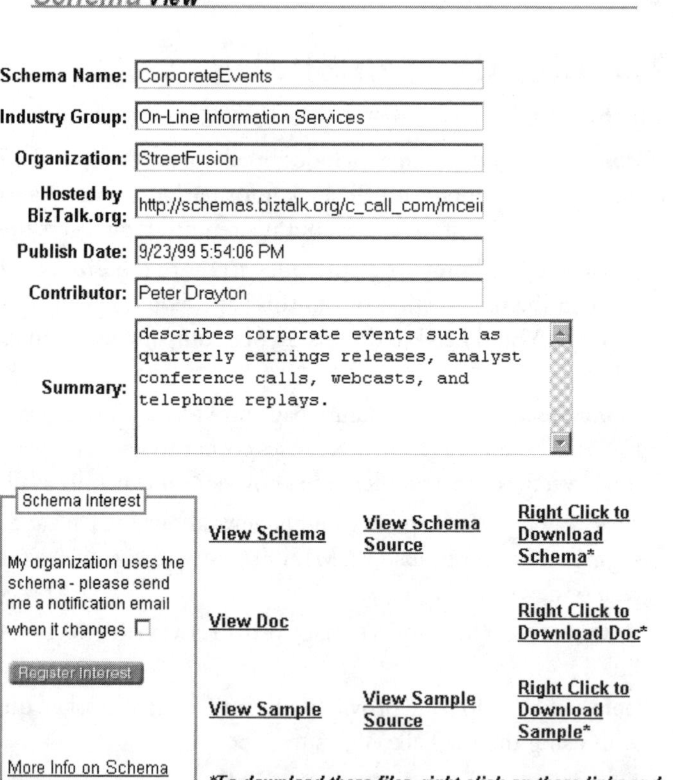

BizTalk.org lets you perform any of these operations with a schema from the library:

View Schema Displays the details of the schema in an instance of Internet Explorer, formatted with a style sheet that displays everything for easy browsing.

View Schema Source Displays the schema as raw text within an instance of Internet Explorer. This lets you see what the schema looks like as a text file rather than as formatted XML.

Download Schema Downloads the schema from the library to your local computer.

View Doc Displays a description of the schema, contact information for the submitting organization, and other information about the schema.

Download Doc Downloads a copy of the schema documentation to your local computer.

View Sample Displays a sample document conforming to the schema in Internet Explorer, formatted with Internet Explorer's default XML style sheet.

View Sample Source Displays the sample as raw text within an instance of Internet Explorer. This lets you see what the sample looks like as a text file rather than as formatted XML.

Download Sample Downloads a copy of the sample document to your local computer.

BizTalk Server 2000

BizTalk Server 2000 is a server product designed to provide the "glue" between diverse business organizations. It provides a set of services that can help translate and transmit data, as well as tools to help you manage BizTalk documents.

The services provided by BizTalk Server 2000 include:

- Receiving documents via FTP, file drop-off, or message queuing
- Transmitting documents via HTTP, HTTPS, SMTP, STP, file drop-off, fax, or message queuing
- Parsing data from XML files and other industry-standard formats, such as ANSI X12
- Validating data against a specification and raising warnings to human operators when the data fails validation
- Document security

The components of BizTalk Server 2000 include:

- BizTalk Editor for creating document specifications
- BizTalk Mapper for specifying the rules to convert documents from one specification to another

- BizTalk Management Desk for overall management of data exchange with other organizations
- BizTalk Server Administration Console for managing BizTalk server services
- BizTalk Server Tracking for following documents through the organization and beyond

In the remainder of this chapter, I'll examine the services and components provided by BizTalk Server 2000. You'll see how you can use this product to automate B2B communications that use XML as their basic vocabulary. To see how the pieces fit together, I'll follow the major steps of setting up a BizTalk application to transform data from one format to another:

- Using BizTalk Editor to create specifications
- Using BizTalk Mapper to create a mapping
- Creating organizations
- Creating document definitions
- Creating agreements
- Creating pipelines
- Submitting documents
- Tracking documents

WARNING This section of the chapter is based on the BizTalk Server Technology Preview, released in April 2000. For up-to-date information on the release of BizTalk Server, check the BizTalk Server Web site at `www.microsoft.com/biztalkserver`.

Creating Specifications with BizTalk Editor

The first step in using BizTalk Server is to define the format of the documents that I'll be using in this example. The tool for this is Microsoft BizTalk Editor. Figure 10.3 shows the process of editing a specification in BizTalk Editor. In this particular case, the Editor is showing the structure of a specification named `ProductionOrder1.xml`. The left-hand pane shows the overall structure of the specification, while the right-hand pane shows the properties of the selected node in the structure.

BizTalk Editor can design document specifications in a variety of formats:

- XML
- Edifact
- X12

FIGURE 10.3
Microsoft BizTalk Editor

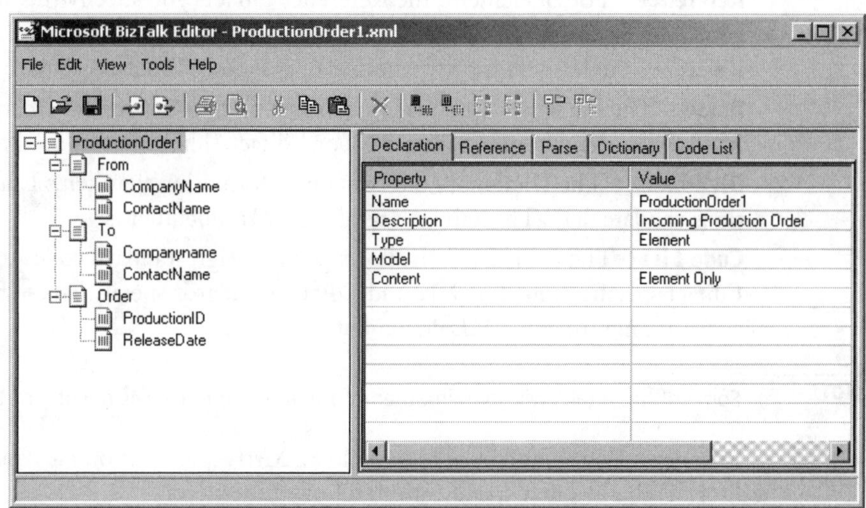

If you're supporting legacy applications, you might need to define formats for Edifact or X12 standards. For new applications, it makes sense to use XML right from the start. To create a new XML specification, open BizTalk Editor, select File ➢ New, select Blank Specification as the specification type, and click OK.

The BizTalk Editor will help you build an XML schema for your document by letting you insert element and attribute nodes. You can do this from the Edit menu with the Insert Record and Insert Field menu items, or from toolbar buttons. As you insert each item, you can define the properties for that item.

TIP

The BizTalk Editor uses *record* to refer to an XML element and uses *field* to refer to an XML attribute. *Record* and *field* are more general terms that are more familiar to people working with specifications based on legacy standards.

The right-hand pane of the BizTalk Editor is divided into five sections by tabs:

Declaration The Declaration tab contains the basic information defining the element or attribute that's currently selected in the TreeView. For an element, this includes the Name, Description, Type (always Element), Model (should be left set to Closed), and Content (will be Element Only if the element has any attributes). For an attribute, this includes Name, Description, Type (always Attribute), Data Type, Data Type Values (only available if the Data Type is set to Enumeration), Min Length, and Max Length. Generally, you should supply at least a name for every node in the tree and data types for all attributes to help BizTalk verify document contents.

Reference For an element, the Reference tab lets you specify the minimum (0 or 1) and maximum (1 or many) occurrences of the element in the document. For an attribute, the Reference tab lets you specify whether or not the attribute is required.

Parse The Parse tab contains information used to extract information from non-XML files such as delimited, flat files, X12, or Edifact. This tab isn't used for XML documents.

Dictionary The Dictionary tab contains information that helps Edifact or X12 specifications validate data. This tab isn't used for XML documents.

Code List The Code List tab allows you to assign standard codes to fields in an X12 or Edifact specification. The X12 and Edifact standards specify lists of field codes. These codes are not used in XML documents.

NOTE Some of these tabs will contain other information for non-XML document types.

In general, you should be able to build an XML specification fairly quickly with BizTalk Editor. To build a new specification, follow these steps:

1. Create the new specification.
2. Add the elements (records) to the root node or to their parent nodes.
3. Add the attributes (fields) to their parent nodes.
4. Set the minimum and maximum occurrence for each element on the Reference tab.
5. Set the data type and field size information for each attribute on the Declaration tab.
6. Set the required information for each attribute on the Reference tab.
7. Optionally, add element and attribute descriptions to the Declaration tab.

Saving a Schema with XML-DR

Once you've finished defining a schema in the BizTalk Editor, you can select File ➢ Save to save the schema in XML-Data Reduced (XML-DR) format. This format adds data type information to the XML schema information, and makes it possible for BizTalk server to validate the data in incoming documents. For example, Listing 10.2 shows the saved XML-DR file (`ProductionOrder1.xml`) for the schema shown earlier in Figure 10.3.

Listing 10.2: An XML-DR File (*ProductionOrder1.xml*)

```
<?xml version="1.0"?>
<Schema name="ProductionOrder1" b:root_reference="ProductionOrder1"
b:standard="XML" xmlns="urn:schemas-microsoft-com:xml-data"
xmlns:d="urn:schemas-microsoft-com:datatypes" xmlns:b="urn:schemas-microsoft-
com:BizTalkServer">
<b:SelectionFields/>

<ElementType name="To" content="empty" model="closed">
```

```
<b:RecordInfo/>
<AttributeType name="ContactName" d:type="string">
<b:FieldInfo/></AttributeType>
<AttributeType name="Companyname" d:type="string">
<b:FieldInfo/></AttributeType>
<attribute type="Companyname" required="yes"/>
<attribute type="ContactName" required="yes"/>
</ElementType><ElementType name="ProductionOrder1" content="eltOnly">
<description>Incoming Production Order</description>
<b:RecordInfo/>
<element type="From" maxOccurs="1" minOccurs="1"/>
<element type="To" maxOccurs="1" minOccurs="1"/>
<element type="Order" maxOccurs="1" minOccurs="1"/>
</ElementType><ElementType name="Order" content="empty" model="closed">

<b:RecordInfo/>
<AttributeType name="ReleaseDate" d:type="dateTime">
<b:FieldInfo/></AttributeType>
<AttributeType name="ProductionID" d:type="string">
<b:FieldInfo/></AttributeType>
<attribute type="ProductionID" required="yes"/>
<attribute type="ReleaseDate" required="yes"/>
</ElementType><ElementType name="From" content="empty" model="closed">

<b:RecordInfo/>
<AttributeType name="ContactName" d:type="string">
<b:FieldInfo/></AttributeType>
<AttributeType name="CompanyName" d:type="string">
<b:FieldInfo/></AttributeType>
<attribute type="CompanyName" required="yes"/>
<attribute type="ContactName" required="yes"/>
</ElementType></Schema>
```

Saving a Schema with WebDAV

While it can be useful to dump a schema to XML-DR so that you can see the XML that BizTalk Editor is creating, this is not how you should save a schema for use by BizTalk Server. Instead, you need to save your specification to a Web Distributed Authoring and Versioning (WebDAV) repository. To do this, select File ➢ Store to WebDAV in BizTalk Editor. This will open up a browse dialog showing you the folders on the WebDAV repository that your BizTalk server is currently using. You can work with this browse dialog just like any other file saving dialog box. Select or create a folder to hold your specification, assign a name, and click Save to save the specification to the repository.

WARNING In the current implementation, a WebDAV repository is simply a folder on your hard drive, at `C:\Program Files\Microsoft BizTalk Server\BizTalkServerRepository`. However, you should always use the editor interfaces designed to store and retrieve documents to the repository, rather than treating it as a file folder, because there's no guarantee that the server will always use this implementation. BizTalk Server adds this folder as an IIS virtual directory and uses the HTTP protocol to communicate with the repository.

Translating Documents

One of the primary uses of BizTalk Server is to translate documents between the formats used by two business partners. For the examples in the rest of this chapter, I'll use two different schemas for a production order. The first is the one that you already saw in Figure 10.3; the second is shown in Figure 10.4. As you can see, although the two schemas contain much of the same information, there are some differences between them. In particular, the first schema treats the originating company, the receiving company, and the production order as three separate entities. The second schema sees both companies as attributes of an element named `TradingPartners`. There's also a piece of information (the date the production order was received) that's included in the second schema rather than in the first. In the following sections, you'll see how to use BizTalk Server to seamlessly integrate documents based on these schemas despite these differences.

FIGURE 10.4
Second schema in BizTalk Editor

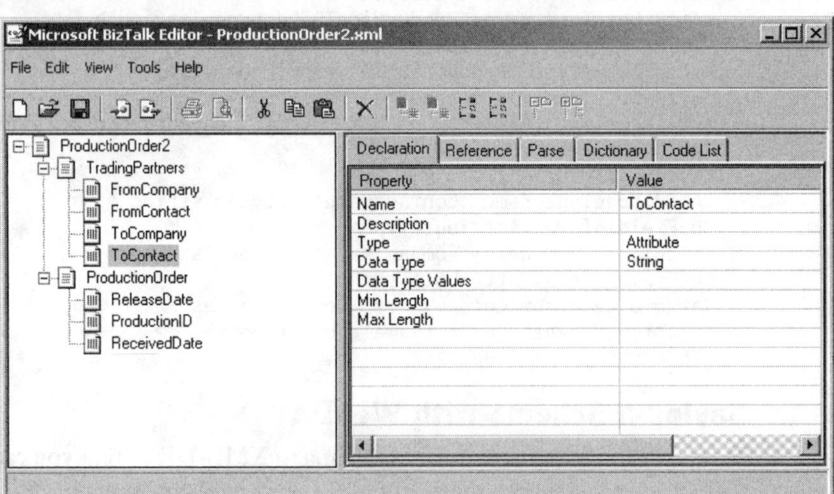

Creating a Mapping with BizTalk Mapper

To tell BizTalk Server how to convert a document from one format to another, you must create a *mapping*. A mapping is a set of instructions that tells BizTalk Server how two schemas are related. The tool for doing this is named, not surprisingly, BizTalk Mapper. Figure 10.5 shows BizTalk Mapper in action.

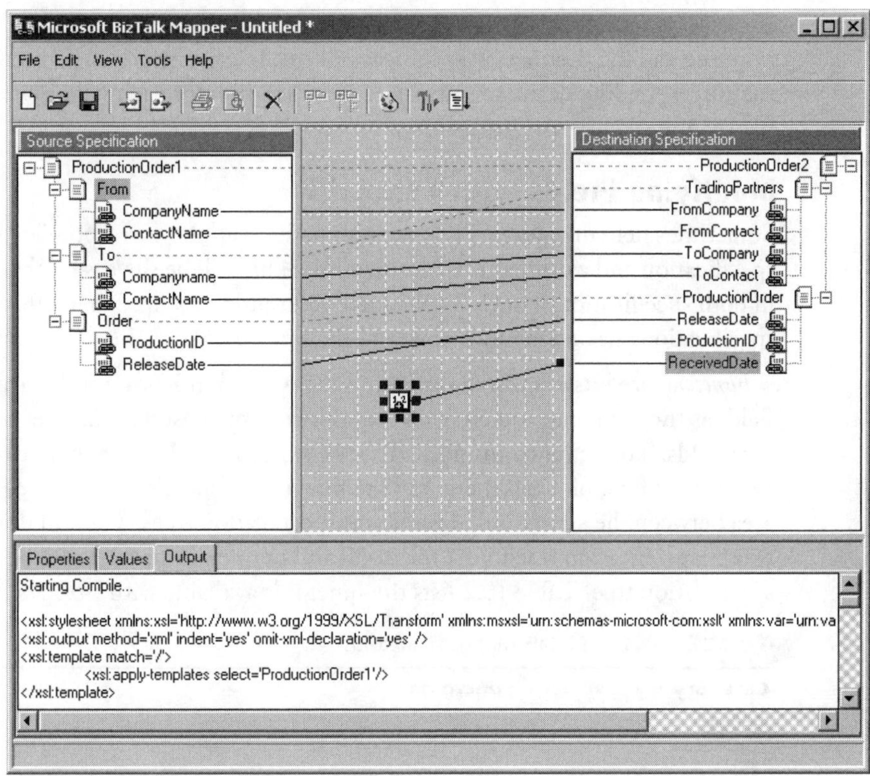

FIGURE 10.5 Microsoft BizTalk Mapper

After launching BizTalk Mapper, the first thing you'll want to do is create a new mapping. This is a multiple-step process:

1. Select File ➢ New. This will launch a series of dialog boxes to guide you through the remaining steps.
2. Select a type for the source specification. This can be a file on your computer, a template for a general class of files (Edifact, X12, or XML), or a WebDAV file.
3. Select the actual source specification.
4. Select a type for the destination specification.
5. Select the actual destination specification.

After you've selected the source and destination specifications, BizTalk Mapper will populate the Source Specification and Destination Specification panes of its interface with the node information from your chosen specifications.

Once you've loaded the source and destination specifications, the next step is to indicate the corresponding fields between the two specifications. To do this, expand the source specification tree and the destination specification tree, locate a source field, and drag and drop it to the corresponding destination field. Repeat this step for each field that exactly matches between the source and destination.

Modifying Fields with Functoids

Sometimes field mapping will be enough to indicate the correspondence between a source specification and a destination specification. This will be the case if there are the same fields in both specifications but they're named differently or stored in a different order. However, specifications are much more powerful than this thanks to the use of functoids.

Functoids are bits of custom programming written in VBScript that can be used to modify fields as they're being copied from the source to the destination, or even to create entirely new fields. To use functoids in BizTalk Mapper, select View ➢ Functoid Palette, choose a category of functoid, and then drag the individual functoid that you require to the mapping area between the source and destination specification trees. You can drag inputs from the source specification tree to the functoid, and outputs from the functoid to the destination specification tree. Table 10.2 lists the functoids available with BizTalk Mapper.

TABLE 10.2: BizTalk Mapper Functoids

Category	Functoids
String	Position of a substring, left characters, convert to lowercase, right characters, string length, extract substring, concatenate strings, remove leading spaces, remove trailing spaces, convert to uppercase
Mathematical	Absolute value, integer, maximum value, minimum value, modulus, rounding, square root, sum, difference, product, quotient
Logical	Greater than, greater than or equal, less than, less than or equal, equal, not equal, is a string, is a date, is a number, logical OR, logical AND
Date and Time	Add days, current date, current time, current date and time
Conversion	Character to ASCII, ASCII to character, decimal to hexadecimal, decimal to octal
Scientific	Arc tangent, cosine, sine, tangent, exponential, natural logarithm, power of 10, base 10 logarithm, power, arbitrary base logarithm
Advanced	Custom VBScript function

Functoids can also be chained to perform multiple operations. For example, you can remove leading and trailing space from a string field by following these steps:

1. Drag the remove leading spaces functoid to the mapping area.
2. Drag the remove trailing spaces functoid to the mapping area.
3. Drag from the source field to the remove leading spaces functoid.

4. Drag from the remove leading spaces functoid to the remove trailing spaces functoid.
5. Drag from the remove trailing spaces functoid to the destination field.

Saving a Mapping

Once you've created all the mappings that you need between the source and destination specifications, it's time to save the mapping. Before saving, you must select Tools ➢ Compile Map. This creates an XSL document describing the mapping. You can save the compiled map as an XSL file if you'd like to see the results of running BizTalk Mapper. Again, though, to be useful to BizTalk Server, the mapping must be saved into the WebDAV repository. Select File ➢ Store to WebDAV to save the mapping to the repository.

Creating Organizations with BizTalk Management Desk

After creating specifications for the source and destination documents and producing a map to transform the source into the destination, it's time to start working in Microsoft BizTalk Management Desk. BizTalk Management Desk is an integrated development environment that handles the details of BizTalk Server's operations. Figure 10.6 shows the BizTalk Management Desk. To the left are controls for selecting organizations and agreements; at the top are the current agreements and their status; below is an editor section that changes according to context.

FIGURE 10.6
BizTalk Management Desk

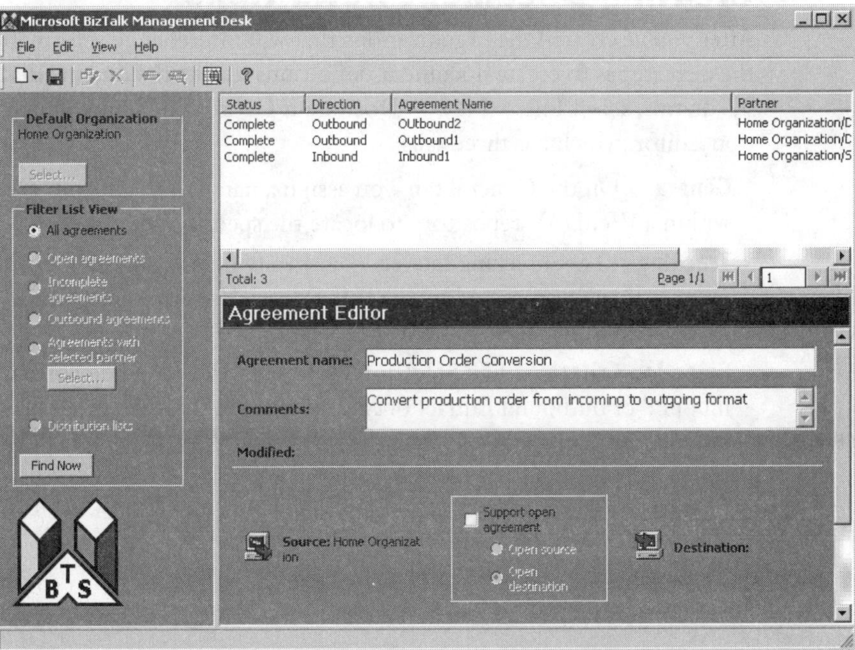

The first task you need to accomplish is creating an organization to represent your own business unit. To do this, follow these steps:

1. Select File ➢ New ➢ Organization.
2. On the General tab of the Organization Editor dialog box, enter a name for the organization.
3. On the Identifiers tab of the Organization Editor dialog box, enter your Dun & Bradstreet or other identifier. You can skip this tab if you like.
4. On the Applications tab of the Organization Editor dialog box, enter the names of all the applications that are either document sources or document destinations for this organization. These are arbitrary names that will identify the applications with which BizTalk Server will communicate.
5. Click OK to save the organization definition.

You can create as many organizations as you like with BizTalk Management Desk. For this chapter's example, I created an organization named Home Organization with a number of applications including Production Order Source and Production Order Destination.

TIP BizTalk Server can be used to transform documents within a single organization as well as to convert information sent from one trading partner to another.

Creating Document Definitions

After you've created the organizations that will interchange information via BizTalk Server, the next step is to create document definitions for the documents that will be interchanged. To do this, select File ➢ New ➢ Document Definition. This will open the Document Definition Editor, which has three tabs:

General On the General tab, you assign a name to the document definition and browse within a WebDAV repository to locate the specification for the document.

Tracking The Tracking tab lets you specify fields that you'd like to log from the document as they're processed by BizTalk Server. You can select any or all of the fields (XML Attributes) from the document specification for logging.

Selection Criteria The Selection Criteria tab lets you flag particular values within an inbound or outbound Edifact or X12 document. This tab is not used with XML documents.

When you've filled in the tabs on the Document Definition Editor, click OK to save the document definition.

Creating Agreements

After defining the organizations and document definitions involved in a business interchange, the next step is to create an agreement. An *agreement* represents the set of rules involved in moving data either into or out of BizTalk Server. All agreements have the BizTalk Server default organization as either the source or the destination. To move a document into BizTalk Server and have a transformed document come out elsewhere, you'll need to create two agreements and a pipeline. (Pipelines are discussed in the next section.)

To create a new agreement, select File ➢ New ➢ Agreement. Figure 10.7 shows an agreement being edited in the Agreement Editor, which is hosted exclusively within BizTalk Management Desk.

FIGURE 10.7
Creating an agreement

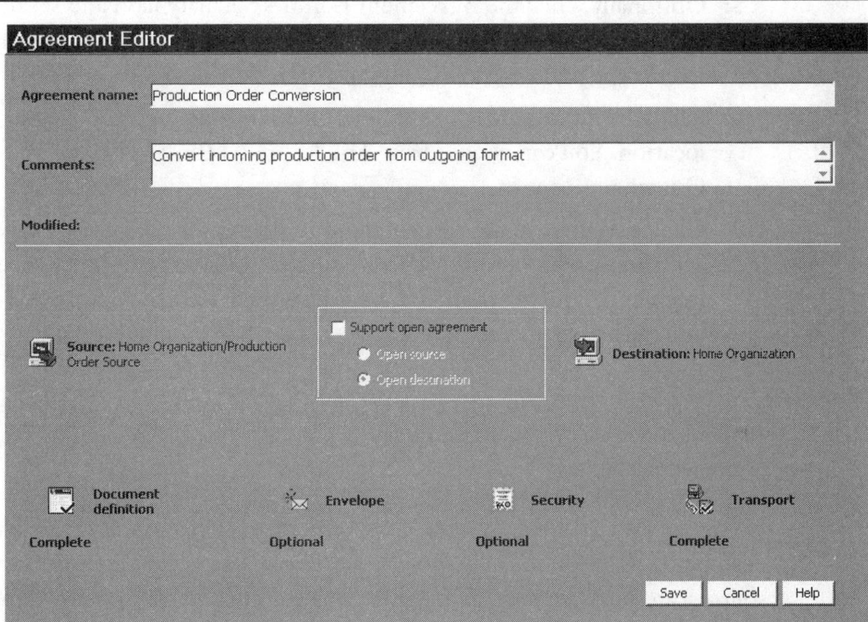

An agreement must have a source and a destination, a document definition, and a transport. Optionally, it can also have an envelope and security settings.

NOTE *Envelopes* are used to provide routing information for documents in older formats such as Edifact and X12. They're not necessary for XML documents, and I don't cover them in this chapter.

To set the properties of a newly created agreement, follow these steps:

1. In the Agreement Editor, type in a name and description of the agreement.
2. Click the Source icon. This will open the Select an Organization dialog box. Select the organization that's the source of the document and the application that supplies the document.
3. Back in the Agreement Editor, click the Destination icon. This will open the Select an Organization dialog box. Select the organization that's the destination of the document and the application that supplies the document.
4. Again in the Agreement Editor, click the Document Definition icon. Select the document definition for the document that this agreement will process.
5. Optionally, click the Agreement Editor's Security icon and set the security properties for the agreement. You can choose whether to use MIME or custom encoding, whether to encrypt, and whether to digitally sign the document as it's being moved.
6. Click the Transport icon and select a Transport type and originating or destination location. You can choose from HTTP, HTTPS, SMTP, FTP, File, Fax, and Message Queuing transports.
7. Click Save to save the agreement after defining it. When you save an agreement, you can choose whether to save it as complete or as incomplete. Once you save an agreement as complete, it can no longer be edited. Before you can actually use an agreement, you must save it as complete.

NOTE The transport type and address are only used on outbound agreements. The BizTalk Server Technology Preview requires assigning a transport to inbound agreements, but this transport is ignored by the server.

You can also use the Support Open Agreement check box to create an open-source or open-destination agreement. An *open-source agreement* can accept documents from many different sources; an *open-destination agreement* can send documents to many different sources. The source or destination that's left open must be specified when the document is submitted to BizTalk Server.

Creating Pipelines

To convert one document format to another with BizTalk Server, you need three things:

- An inbound agreement
- An outbound agreement
- A pipeline connecting the two agreements

A *pipeline* is simply the way that BizTalk stores the connection between a pair of agreements. Any given pipeline might include a map, or it might just move data from an inbound agreement to an outbound agreement with no changes. To create a pipeline, first click an outbound agreement in the upper pane of BizTalk Management Desk and then select File ➢ New ➢ Pipeline. This will open the Pipeline Editor, shown in Figure 10.8.

FIGURE 10.8
Adding a pipeline

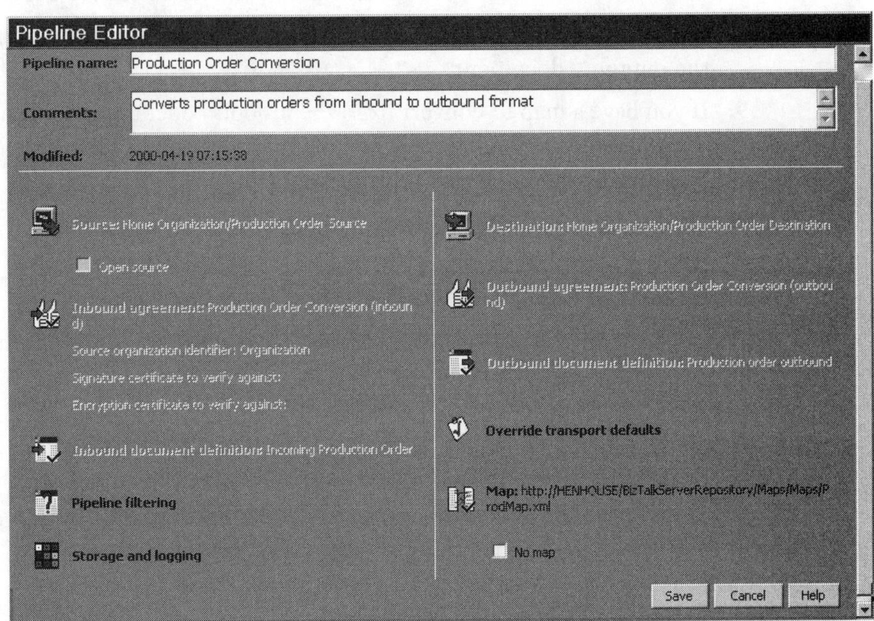

Once you've created a pipeline, follow these steps to set its properties:

1. Fill in a name and optional comments describing the pipeline.
2. Within Pipeline Editor, click the Source icon. Select the source organization and application in the Select an Organization dialog box and click OK.
3. Back in Pipeline Editor, click the Inbound Agreement icon to open the Select an Inbound Agreement dialog box. This dialog box shows the inbound agreements that are associated with the organization and application that you chose in step 2. Select the appropriate inbound agreement and click OK.
4. Again in Pipeline Editor, click the Inbound Document Definition icon and choose the document definition for the incoming document. The Select an Inbound Document Definition dialog box will show only the document definitions that match the inbound agreement that you chose in step 3.

5. The Pipeline Filtering icon allows you to look for specific values to be monitored in the inbound document. This is optional.
6. The Storage and Logging icon allows you to set storage formats and logging levels for the pipeline. This is optional.
7. In Pipeline Editor, click the Outbound Document Definition icon and select the document definition into which the document should be converted.
8. Optionally, click the Override Transport Defaults icon to modify the transport used for the outgoing document.
9. If you have a map to convert from the inbound document definition to the outbound document definition, uncheck the No Map check box, click the Map icon within Pipeline Editor, and select the appropriate map.
10. Click Save to save the pipeline.

Creating and Submitting Documents

To recap, here are the steps to using BizTalk Server 2000 that I've discussed so far:

1. Create incoming and outgoing document specifications.
2. Create a mapping.
3. Create an organization.
4. Create inbound and outbound document definitions.
5. Create inbound and outbound agreements.
6. Create a pipeline.

At this point, BizTalk Server is ready to go to work. Referring back to the architectural diagram of BizTalk in Figure 10.1, you'll see that the "plumbing" is in place. What remains is to create and submit a document.

You can use any XML editor to create the document to be submitted. The format of the document must match that defined by the incoming document specification. For example, this document matches the sample production order specification I showed you earlier in the chapter:

```
<ProductionOrder1>
   <From CompanyName = "Integrated Industries"
 ContactName = "John Banbino" />
   <To CompanyName = "Owl Group Ltd"
Contactname = "Ella Manfredi" />
   <Order ProductionID = "1425"
ReleaseDate = "2000-03-14 11:30 AM" />
</ProductionOrder1>
```

BizTalk provides a set of COM interfaces that allow you to submit documents directly from an application such as a Visual Basic program or an ASP page. In order to submit a document that will use a map, you should reference these libraries:

- Microsoft BizTalk Server Core Type Library
- Microsoft BizTalk Server Interchange 1.0 Type Library
- Microsoft BizTalk Server StateEngine Type Library

The code for submitting a document is relatively simple. Listing 10.3 shows `SubmitDoc.frm`, a Visual Basic program that opens a document and submits it to BizTalk Server for processing.

Listing 10.3: Submitting a Document (*SubmitDoc.frm*)

```
Option Explicit
'Openness flag for not open agreements
Const MODELDB_OPENNESS_TYPE_NOTOPEN = 1

Private Sub cmdSubmit_Click()
    Dim objInterchange As New Interchange
    Dim txtStream As Object
    Dim fileSysObj As Scripting.FileSystemObject
    Dim strDocument As String
    Dim strHandle As String
    Dim strPipeline As String

    ' Retrieve the contents of the file that we want to submit
    Set fileSysObj = New Scripting.FileSystemObject
    If fileSysObj.FileExists(txtFileSource.Text) Then
        Set txtStream = fileSysObj.OpenTextFile _
         (txtFileSource.Text, 1, True)
        strDocument = txtStream.ReadAll
        txtStream.Close
        Set txtStream = Nothing
    Else
        strDocument = "Empty document"
    End If
    txtSend.Text = strDocument

    ' Specify the pipeline for BizTalk to use
    strPipeline = "Production Order Conversion"

    ' And actually submit the document
    strHandle = objInterchange.Submit _
     (MODELDB_OPENNESS_TYPE_NOTOPEN, _
      strDocument, , , , , strPipeline, "", "")

    MsgBox "Document has been submitted"

End Sub
```

As you can see, the code to submit a document is straightforward. All of the work is done by calling the `Submit` method of the `Interchange` object. This method has the following arguments:

`lOpenness` A constant indicating whether the agreement is open-source or open-destination, or closed

`Document` The actual text of the document to submit

`DocName` The name of the document to submit

`SourceQualifier` Routing information to be submitted with the document

`SourceID` Routing information to be submitted with the document

`DestQualifier` Routing information to be submitted with the document

`DestID` Routing information to be submitted with the document

`PipelineName` Name of the BizTalk Server pipeline to use to convert this document

`FilePath` Override for the storage path of the converted file

`EnvelopeName` Envelope format to use for the pipeline (if any)

For most documents, you should be able to manage with just the arguments (lOpenness, Document, and PipelineName) that are used in this example.

Once you call the Submit method, BizTalk Server takes over. Assuming that you've properly defined all of the objects that it requires, the converted document will show up in the file, FTP, or other location that you've specified as part of the transport information for the outbound agreement. If anything goes seriously wrong, BizTalk Server will post a message to the Windows event log with the details.

Tracking Documents

BizTalk Server includes a Web-based tracking application that will help you see the activity on your server. This application is automatically installed at `http://servername/BizTalk-DTA/` when you install BizTalk. This application uses ActiveX controls to allow you to query and display information from the BizTalk Server's internal database. This information includes details of documents that have been sent or received by BizTalk Server and of interchanges between applications using BizTalk Server.

The tracking application allows you to perform these tasks:

- Search for interchanges and documents by agreement.
- Search for interchanges and documents by organization.
- Search for interchanges and documents by date.
- Search for data in fields captured by BizTalk Server.

- View the details and data of an interchange.
- View an activity log for an interchange.
- View document details.
- View document data in its native format or XML.

BizTalk Server Administrator

BizTalk Server Administrator is a Microsoft Management Console (MMC)–based application that gives you administrative access to the operations of a BizTalk server. Figure 10.9 shows the BizTalk Server Administrator.

FIGURE 10.9
BizTalk Server Administrator

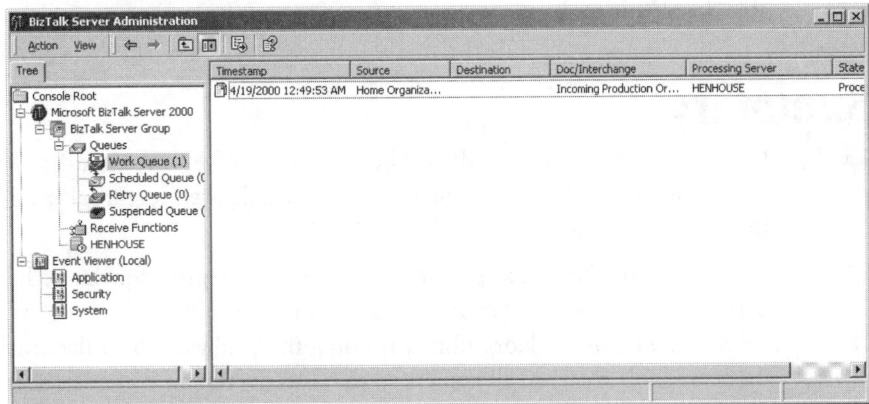

Just like any other MMC-based application, BizTalk Server Administrator arranges its functionality in a hierarchy. As you select nodes in the TreeView on the left side of the MMC window, details on those nodes appear in the list view on the right side of the window.

The topmost node is the Microsoft BizTalk Server 2000 node. This node allows you to create new BizTalk Server Groups.

The next level down is the BizTalk Server Group. A BizTalk Server Group is an arbitrary group of servers containing one or more computers. If you click a group node, the list view will show the status of all the servers in that group. A group also lets you add a new server.

The next level below the BizTalk Server Group includes three node types. These are the queues, the receive functions, and the servers themselves.

The Queues node includes work, scheduled, retry, and suspended queues. Each of these shows the documents that are currently contained in the queue when the queue node is selected. Information displayed includes a timestamp, the current state of the work item, a description of any error, the source and destination organizations, the name of the document or interchange, and the interchange ID.

The Receive Functions node shows all of the receive functions on this server. A receive function is a BizTalk Server polling job. For example, to receive documents that are dropped off on an FTP server you need to set up a receive function that polls that server looking for new documents. From this node you can create new file, FTP, or MSMQ receive functions.

The Server node shows the status of the selected server. You can start or stop the BizTalk server from this node.

Finally, the BizTalk Server Administration console also shows the Windows 2000 event logs. This is convenient because BizTalk posts errors to the application log, making it a valuable diagnostic tool.

Summary

In this chapter I've described the Microsoft BizTalk Framework. You learned about the three major components of this framework: the BizTalk architecture, BizTalk.org, and Microsoft BizTalk Server 2000.

The BizTalk architecture provides an overall blueprint for the exchange of information between diverse business processes and organizations that depends on XML as its common language. The BizTalk.org library is doing the vital work of collecting schemas and making them available freely to all comers so that less document conversion will be needed. Finally, BizTalk Server 2000 provides a completely automated solution for converting documents between formats and transporting them between line-of-business applications.

Just a reminder: The bulk of this chapter is based on unreleased and preview software in an area that's evolving rapidly. Rather than go into all the details of dialog boxes that are certain to change before the product's release, I've tried to give you a sense of what BizTalk can mean in practice. If your organization is involved in the electronic interchange of business data and documents with other organizations, this is definitely an area that you need to keep an eye on.

CHAPTER 11

XML and Programming

- Comparing streams and components
- Understanding XML-HTTP and messaging
- Using RPCs and SOAP
- Considering the future of XML

XML is here for the long term. It is not an unreasonable assessment to say that the technology that is being developed today will likely still be very much in use in 2025, and perhaps even in 2050. This is not to say that it won't be somewhat different in form (perhaps wildly different), but XML as a means of representing transactions, processing, and much more will almost certainly prove to be one of the lasting legacies of the last half century.

One comment that many developers make when first encountering XML is to dismiss the language as being simply another data format, that surely it's not a programming language. However, as I've shown throughout this book and hope to emphasize strongly in this chapter, XML technology is most certainly a programming language and, what's more, represents a profound paradigm shift in the way that we think about programming—one that may very well be moving us beyond the Object-Oriented Programming viewpoint. Just as that language has become more sophisticated and powerful as it has matured, expect that the post-OOP world of XML will likewise grow in ways that we are only just beginning to realize.

Streams versus Components

More than 30 years ago, when the C language was beginning to solidify and the Unix platform was going through its first of many convoluted growing spurts (of which Linux is only the latest version), a concept had taken hold in the arcane symbology of shell prompts and forks. The notion was a simple one: In a well-designed program, the data that was passed into a program was considered to be part of a stream, and when the program had run its course, it produced a different stream; this stream, in turn, could be passed on to other programs, could be persisted, could even be sent to devices, and could even be held in suspended animation until a process began again.

This concept worked well in the world of text manipulation functions that made up the bulk of the code at the time. Of course, there were some profound limitations with the approach: The output stream of one program needed to match the expected input stream of the next process to work properly (although it could work improperly with remarkable abandon). Moreover, streams worked less well as information began to become increasingly encoded in more efficient binary formats, and they never really extended beyond the scope of the operating system, although, given that most of these systems were slave terminals connected to a single main-frame, this was generally not a problem.

The Emergence of OOP

Languages such as Perl, which took the mantle for Unix development from C sometime in the late 1980s, managed to build remarkably sophisticated applications using a similar streaming mechanism. However, streams as a means of building programs largely disappeared from the programming lexicon as the Object-Oriented Programming (OOP) paradigm began to replace it. While OOP in and of itself is fairly neutral about streams (the C++ `cin` and `cout` elements are, of course, streams, as are many of the file-handling capabilities of Java), OOP encouraged the emergence of asynchronous event-based programming coupled with windowing systems, such as Microsoft Windows, Apple's OS, and even the recent KDE and Gnome interfaces that are emerging as the dominant windowing paradigm of Linux.

The central thesis of Object-Oriented Programming is simple: The programming environment consists of a sea of "objects," which couple one or more data structures (properties) with methods that can be used to affect the actions of these structures. Actions are announced via events that an object generates whenever a specific state changes within the object. This approach stresses three distinct facets as defining OOP entities (though, in truth, there are a fairly significant number of languages that incorporate object-like behaviors but don't fully implement all three features):

Encapsulation An object is a self-contained unit.

Inheritance An object's definition (or class) can be used to create more-specialized classes that enhance or limit the properties or behavior of the parent class.

Polymorphism If two different classes derive from one parent class, then any property or method that is common to both should implement actions appropriate to the child class.

Ironically, of the three, only encapsulation is really truly common to most OOP and object-like systems. Inheritance is important to those languages in which datatyping is important (this rather makes sense, as a datatype is fundamentally just a class reference in all but the simplest cases), while polymorphism, perhaps the hardest feature to implement in a language, is the feature that is least readily used.

When OOP is used in its purest manifestation, it can make for a remarkably powerful system, and, to a certain extent, both COM and CORBA are reflections of the OOP paradigm at the system level. Yet it is also not a terribly easy paradigm to fully understand, in part because it requires a high degree of discipline in coding to work effectively with interfaces, and in part because a significant part of OOP has been co-opted by the rise of component architectures.

Comparing OOP and Components

The principal difference between an OOP-based system and a component-based system is that components support encapsulation but do not necessarily support inheritance or polymorphism. The best example of a component-based system is Visual Basic, while pure Java could be said to be an OOP system. On the latter point, however, you could argue that the rise of Java Beans is a sign that even in Java the component nature of the language is far more important than either inheritance or polymorphism, though I will doubtless draw the ire of Java partisans and OOP purists with this statement.

There is no question that component-based systems are powerful, especially in visual environments. With drag-and-drop components, you can build a visual interface, connect it to a database or file resource, and manage all of the events associated with the interface in a very transparent fashion. Even outside of visual forms or windows, you can use components in environments such as ASP to better encapsulate sophisticated functionality without having to write extensive code on your own. This makes it easier to distribute functional expertise, to reduce the amount of rework in solving classes of problems, and it decreases the cost of developing solutions in general.

However, component-based programming also introduces problems, many of which are becoming ever more pressing as we move from the desktop to distributed systems. Key among these are the following:

Platform Dependence Many component-based systems work differently from one platform to the next (or, in some cases, don't work at all). This can make building cross-platform solutions difficult.

Binary Representations Most components are encoded as binary representations for performance and efficiency. In addition to diminishing system compatibility, such binaries are expensive to download across the Web.

Emergent Behaviors This is a more subtle, but ultimately more important, problem. As the number of components increases within a given framework or environment, the number of interactions between these components also increases. One attempt to solve this has been the rise of threaded architectures, but such architectures can still introduce bottlenecks and inefficiencies that are not direct artifacts of the components themselves.

Divergent Data Models A component typically will consume or produce data peculiar to its own implementation; this requires that a significant amount of work in building such components ends up concentrating on supporting each of these data models.

Scalability A component that works well when dealing with a low-demand environment could quickly choke in a high-demand environment. As the number of users of an application jumps from a handful to potentially millions, components need to scale effectively as well; most don't.

States Most components maintain their own internal state. Across a network, however, maintaining a state requires that a connection be kept between the two communicating systems. Each connection, in turn, consumes resources, slowing down the interaction of components and limiting the number of users that can work with the application.

Of these, the issues of divergent data models, states, and emergent behaviors are the most serious that client/server applications face, because they are systemic rather than implementation specific—even if all machines in the network use exactly the same operating system and programs, these factors will limit the efficacy of any applications built using a component-based architecture.

Ironically, it is in this environment that streams (such as those represented by XML) begin to reappear as viable programming paradigms, and XML's benefits are able to overcome most, if not all, of the limitations of the earlier Unix stream implementations. However, with the emergence of XSLT and XML Schema, XML streams are positioned to have a profound impact on the nature of programming in general, and streams may usher in a paradigm that could truly be called *post-OOP*.

To understand this, it's worth examining the advantages that an XML/XSLT/XML-Schema architecture has over a component-based one. In an XML architecture, all data sources produce XML through XML interfaces, such as XPath or XLink. Put another way, any *device* can be queried through an XML interface to produce an XML result set.

Your Different Devices

Consider the term *device* for a moment. In traditional client/server programming, the server is a specialized device that, based upon a request, produces some information to the client. The client, in turn, is the device that initiates the request and consumes the information provided by the server. This distinction is a fairly central feature even of component-based architecture, since components typically tend to fall fairly easily into either consumers or producers of information.

In a stream-based architecture, however, a device can be thought of as being both a consumer and a producer of information. Indeed, in this case, it is actually easier to think of a device as something that can consume zero or more streams of information and can similarly produce zero or more streams of information. An XSL Transformation by this definition falls into the category of such devices: It typically takes a stream of information, performs actions on that stream, and sends the resultant stream off to some other device.

This subtle shift in thinking has some profound results. The client/server operation is a very procedural concept: It concentrates on one object interacting with another object. The objects have very definite qualities to them, have very distinct protocols for communication between them, and are fairly tightly coupled. In the device/stream architecture, on the other hand, a device is simply a node in a network of streams. It is relatively anonymous: A device has a set of API calls that are intrinsic to the device but that can be accomplished via a common protocol (HTTP over TCP/IP), and the calls are implementation independent. Put another way, when a device talks to another device, it shouldn't need to know whether that device is a database, a piece of hardware, a file system, or anything else, only that it will produce a given response when queried with a specific command.

One side effect of this is that the APIs for such devices follow one of two protocols: either via the URL/URN/URI notation that has become the primary means of referencing resources (perhaps with an XLink addition once that standard becomes finalized) or via an XML block sent as a message to the target device. The first can be thought of as the GET orientation, echoing the HTTP GET command, while the second is essentially the POST orientation, echoing the HTTP POST command. The second method forms the foundation of the HTTP1.1 Extensions (also known as WebDAV, or XML-HTTP), which is covered later in this chapter.

Reviewing RPCs

Exactly what the messages being sent to the device are and what they should receive are the subject of some controversy. There are, in effect, two distinct camps of thought beginning to emerge on the subject. The first sees the messages and responses as ***Remote Procedure Calls*** (or RPCs). In a more traditional language, such as Visual Basic or Java, RPCs tend to dominate when discussions of complex distributed systems come up; in essence, you use a messaging protocol, such as CORBA, RMI, or Distributed COM, to target a remote computer with a specific method or function call on a given object.

This process, called *marshalling*, is fairly complex. Your program sends a function call request to a marshalling broker (COM or CORBA) on your machine. This service, in turn, contacts the remote computer, sends the function request to it, and waits. When the computer on the other end receives the function, that computer attempts to evaluate the function and either returns the result of the function or sends a message back saying that the attempt has failed. This message gets sent back to your computer, which consequently notifies you of the status of the command and returns data if the request succeeded. (Note that with COM much the same procedure is used internally, except that instead of distinct machines you're dealing with distinct processes, or applications, within the same machine).

I like to talk about RPCs as basically being the *envoy* approach to distributed programming. Suppose that you had two kingdoms, Localle and Remotte, within the empire of Comm that were in a touchy situation concerning their borders. The king of Localle wishes to propose a peace treaty to the king of Remotte, so he sends an envoy with the treaty. The envoy can only go to the border, at which point he has to follow a very formal request with the border guards to summon an envoy from the capital of Remotte.

When this worthy envoy comes, she takes the treaty to the king of Remotte, who must, in turn, either sign the document with appropriate amendments or decide not to sign it. (If the document doesn't have the appropriate protocols, he won't sign it, by the way, and may even misinterpret it and send back a completely erroneous treaty agreement.) In time, the other kingdom's envoy returns to the border and passes the treaty back to Localle's envoy, who then returns back to his king. The process can take place relatively quickly because the protocols are in place, but the amount of information that can be transmitted and received is relatively small.

Things break down, however, if the king of Localle wants to send a message to the queen of Iava in the empire of Corrba. You see, the problem here is that the people in Corrba speak a different language and follow a different protocol for handling envoys than the people in Comm do. A treaty sent there would be interpreted as gibberish, and the best that can be hoped for would be that the envoy would return saying that negotiations are impossible.

This is the state of affairs right now with COM and CORBA. Both are marshalling protocols, but they differ just enough that you need highly specialized code to handle the intermediation between the two. This is where XML comes in. XML is essentially vendor neutral and can pass through HTTP in a way that executable code typically can't, since it is not uncommon for RPCs to go through a different port on a server. As a consequence, there have been a number of recommendations for XML RPC standards, including XML-RPC, ZOPE, XPORT, and SOAP (among a host of others). All of these attempt to do the same thing: provide a mechanism for marshalling information using a uniform standard.

SOAP, or Simple Object Access Protocol, for example, handles RPCs by setting up a *messaging* schema. Messaging works by sending an XML block (usually using the `POST` protocol) to the remote server with the body containing both the function call to invoke and the parameters (and their data types) to pass. When the server intercepts the message block, it breaks the XML down to its constituent parts, attempts to evaluate the function in question, places the result in a return message block along with a code indicating how successful the call was, and then sends this information back to the client, which, in turn, needs to interpret the result of this.

SOAP gets around two major stumbling blocks that plague other RPC languages. First, you can send a SOAP message (or a similar RPC format) to a remote machine that uses a different messaging protocol, and still get it to conceivably work if that system recognizes SOAP. As it is much easier to write applications that can work with SOAP's XML structure, then it's likely that SOAP interpreters will be common fare on CORBA systems (or, at the very least, can be easily written). Second, working with SOAP means that the two systems can use completely different development languages, so long as the SOAP message contains the relevant object reference (for example, a Java class name) to pull the information from. This makes XML-based RPCs superior to their binary-based siblings.

Streams versus RPCs

However, there are some fundamental problems with RPCs in concert with XML. It can be argued with a great deal of validity that XML not only makes universal RPCs possible but it also makes them obsolete. This, of course, is a message that is not lost on large companies that have a significant stake in preserving messaging systems—companies that will likely continue to press for the implementation of XML-based RPCs despite a number of significant limitations compared to a stream architecture.

The stream architecture works on the precept, as described previously, that a device can return XML through a URL-based process. In this case, the URL serves as a command call to the server, which becomes the basic broker of the service. In other words, when a page is invoked (either with ASP, JSP, or CGI), that page acts as a unique server of information. The difference between an XML-RPC call and a stream call is that in the former case the call is made to an object on the server's system, whereas with a stream-based system the call is made to a more abstract entity, the page being served, which internally may make whatever calls that it needs.

This seems like a fairly trivial distinction, but in terms of architectural design it's actually quite important. The RPC model sees XML as being primarily a medium to exchange programmatic data in a procedural way: The XML serves as a bundle to contain a procedural call and its response. This technique works well when you are dealing with COM objects on the server instead of XML, but it forces you to know a great deal of information about both what the COM object is expecting as arguments and what form it will return this information.

With a device/stream architecture, on the other hand, you send a request through either a `GET` or a `POST` operation that would likely be processed through some form of XSLT script (in the `GET` case, with the parameters getting encoded into an XML structure before being passed). The XSLT script provides a barrier between the client and the server. Less XML code is wasted in messaging structures—the client is expecting XML back in a specific form, tailored to its own needs, and doesn't need to spend time extracting information from possibly proprietary messaging blocks.

This makes the device more anonymous as well: So long as the XML coming back conforms to the required code, the client doesn't need to know anything about the internal structure or capabilities of the device. If the IT department decides to replace the Windows 2000 server with a Linux one, for example, a stream-based architecture could support the change transparently, while the RPC code would almost certainly break. Moreover, the device could be changed to an embedded system (perhaps a tracking chip with a transmitter on a package being shipped), and so long as the XML coming from that device remains the same, then it won't matter to the client.

XSLT also plays a bigger part in a device/stream architecture. Indeed, in such an architecture, the XSLT script would replace procedural code, acting as a broker to mediate any number of XML streams simultaneously. Because these streams are similarly anonymous, they would likewise be requested via a URL mechanism (or perhaps through a `POST`-like mechanism, which focuses on XSLT templates being executed, not procedural code).

The primary limitation with a stream architecture is that it becomes a little more challenging when the streams are asynchronous. If you need three streams to generate a response XML structure, for example, then the time for an operation becomes the time for the stream of longest duration to arrive. To a certain extent, such a problem can be ameliorated by building in a better caching mechanism for streams, but, in all likelihood, it will take until the next generation of XSLT before the problem is solved completely.

So Which Is Better: RPCs or Streams?

This is one of those questions that really depends upon context. RPCs work well in the context where you are communicating between machines with known sets of protocols, and your primary purpose is to enable procedural code to talk with other procedural code. They can also be used to provide a POST-based solution for sending parametric information from a client to a server.

Streams use a URL-based mechanism to pass information and work well when you want to abstract your devices. They are simpler to work with in XSLT or XLink environments, they handle complex network topologies better, and they can be leveraged to form a pipeline architecture. Unfortunately, they work less well in mixed environments, where at least some of the data sources or sinks don't provide an XML-based resource link.

In general, if you're looking at using XML to bind together distributed COM or CORBA objects or to handle communication between these standards, then RPCs may be the better bet, at least for the short term. On the other hand, if you are designing a system from the ground up, you may want to look at the stream/device model as a way to more succinctly modularize your development efforts.

XML-HTTP and Messaging

One of the problems that client/server applications have when hosted over the Internet is that a Web page is basically static; once you load the page, communicating with the server is a considerably more complex proposition. You can get around this problem with ActiveX controls or Java applets, but these components force additional downloads.

However, one of the lesser-known features of the MSXML parser—the XML-HTTP component—may be about to change all of that. This interface lets you send a block of XML to the server at a specific URL and then lets you receive XML back that can be loaded into another XML document object. This XML pipe provides a way to create a dialog between client and server that can effectively make Web pages dynamic in content in a way that DHTML alone simply cannot match. Indeed, as you'll notice in the following list, applications for such a pipeline are legion and varied:

Chat Applications With XML acting as the message carrier, you can create a simple chat setup, or extend it into a full-featured gaming environment.

Real-Time Validation Front ends to databases can update and validate field entries with business rules on the server, reducing the amount of client-side code and increasing security.

Real-Time Displays You could create dynamic views of stock behaviors with a combination of XML-HTTP and VML (or SVG or 3DML, if you wanted to extend the information into three dimensions).

Interactive Audio/Video Streaming Audio or Video could communicate with the client by passing SMIL-type XML documents to provide data support for interactive entertainment.

Dynamic Documents The `XML-HTTP` component may update XHTML content in response to internal link structures (a rollover on a link might actually load in a document rather than just act as a passive link). Imagine documentation that configures itself dynamically and transparently to users' navigation.

Application Servers Imagine being able to provide a password and get access to your virtual system, files, applications, and so forth through a browser. An XML-HTTP-driven application server could give you the power of a high-end server system through a thin client.

Examining XML-HTTP

The `XML-HTTP` component is a part of the MSXML DLL, but it doesn't derive directly from an XML Document object. Instead, you need to create an object with a reference to the `MSXML2.XMLHTTP` progID. Once created, the object is a stand-alone object independent of any specific XML documents; you can think of it as being a way to create a conduit to the server from the client (via the interfaces shown in Table 11.1).

TABLE 11.1: XML-HTTP Interface Elements

Name	Type	Description
`Sub abort()`		Aborts HTTP request
`Function getAllResponseHeaders()`	as String	Gets all HTTP response headers
`Function getResponseHeader(`		
`bstrHeader as String)`	as String	Gets HTTP response header
`Property onreadystatechange`	as Object	Registers a complete event handler
`Sub open(`		
`bstrMethod as String,`		
`bstrUrl as String,`		
`varAsync as Optional Variant,`		
`bstrUser as Optional Variant,`		
`bstrPassword as Optional Variant)`		Opens HTTP connection

TABLE 11.1: XML-HTTP Interface Elements *(continued)*

Name	Type	Description
`Property readyState`	as Long (Read Only)	Gets ready state
`Property responseBody`	as Variant (Read Only)	Gets response body as an encoded object
`Property responseStream`	as Variant (Read Only)	Gets response body as an `IStream` object
`Property responseText`	as String (Read Only)	Gets response body as a string of text
`Property responseXML`	as Object)Read Only)	Gets response body as an XML document
`Sub send(`		
`varBody as Optional Variant)`		Sends HTTP request
`Sub setRequestHeader(`		
`bstrHeader as String,`		
`bstrValue as String)`		Adds HTTP request header
`Property status`	as Long (Read Only)	Gets HTTP status code
`Property statusText`	as String (Read Only)	Gets HTTP status text

To use the component, you first need to open a connection to a URL located on a remote machine with the `open()` method. This is perhaps one of the most complex XML-HTTP commands, but it also gives you considerable control over how you handle the transmission of your XML streams. The first parameter, `method`, determines the HTTP method that is used to send the information. In most cases, this will be either by `GET` or by `POST`, which pass information via the URL or by way of form post, respectively. Additionally, you could use such HTTP commands as `OPTION`, `DIR`, `NEW`, and so forth to create more sophisticated interactions, but only if the server that you're communicating with supports the `HTTP1.1 WebDAV` extensions.

The second parameter contains the URL of the resource that you're wishing to reference, and could just as readily be an ASP or a JSP page as an XML file (indeed, for posting information, it will almost certainly be a server page of some sort).

The third parameter, `async`, can be a little confusing, and controls the interactions between the XML-HTTP object and the resulting XML document that retrieves the target XML. Specifically, the `responseXML` and `responseStream` properties implement XML document and XML stream interfaces, respectively. When `async` is false, the program suspends until the XML stream arrives from the server or a timeout occurs. At that point, `responseXML` and `responseStream` both hold the actual contents of the XML returned from the server as an XML `DOMDocument` and an XML stream, respectively.

However, if you set async to true, then you can assign an XML document (or an XML-based iStream interface) to the responseXML property itself. For example, consider code in a Web page that requests information from the server through the GET command but uses the XML-HTTP object instead of the xmlDoc.load facility. In this case, the XML document becomes the recipient of the results of the query. You can use the onReadyStateChange or onContentReady events of the XML document to determine when all of the content has been loaded or otherwise processed:

```
<script language="VBScript">
function main()
     Set http=createObject("MSXML2.XMLHTTP")
     Set xmlDoc=createObject("MSXML2.DOMDocument")
     XmlDoc.async=true
     http.open "GET",
          "http://www.vbxml.com/myresource.asp",true
     set xmlDoc=http.responseXML
     xmlDoc.oncontentready=getRef("showResults")
     http.send
end function

function showResults()
   display.innerHTML=xmlDoc.xml
end function
</script>
```

WARNING This can be confusing if you're not used to working with the XML DOM in asynchronous mode. If you're running into problems with the XML-HTTP component not properly returning result sets, chances are that the async property is at fault; in general, if you want to retrieve the value in the same block as the send() command, you should set the async property of the HTTP object defined previously to false.

Finally, you can send a username and password as parameters, which get added to the HTTP header collection. These can be retrieved with the server variables AUTH_USER and AUTH_PASSWORD, respectively; that is, you can get the username and password with the following expressions:

```
UserName=request.serverVariables("AUTH_USER")
Password=request.serverVariables("AUTH_PASSWORD")
```

The subroutine SetRequestHeader() gives you a way to assign other request headers. For example, you could actually send something like a zip file to the server by setting the CONTENT_TYPE request header to the value application/x-zip-compressed, as follows:

```
http.setRequestHeader "CONTENT_TYPE","application/x-zip-compressed"
```

The server may have filters in place to process such zip files, but, if not, you could test the CONTENT_TYPE server variable to determine what's being sent. In general, the XML-HTTP component works with the assumption that XML is being sent, so it's not explicitly a requirement to set the content type or the content length.

The actual content is sent through the pipeline with the Send() method, which takes as a parameter the actual content as a variant. Thus, if you had a previously defined XML structure, you can pass that document directly as a parameter. You could also send generic text or even binary information, although if the object being sent doesn't support the IStream interface you need to make sure that your server-side code knows what to do with the object. In general, you are best off sending XML through the pipeline.

NOTE Previous versions of the XML-HTTP component required that you pass the length of the information being sent, but this is now handled implicitly by the send() command itself.

Creating a Chat Server

Using the GET HTTP command in conjunction with the XML-HTTP component would seem to be overkill. Can't you do the same thing with the xmlDoc.load() method? In fact, you can, and it really is a waste of programming to use GET with XML-HTTP. However, the one problem with the GET protocol is that it isn't really a practical way to send a block of XML; most XML blocks would exceed the 1024-byte length that GET enforces as the maximum length of records; you'd have to encode the XML in HTTP-escaped format, and soon.

POST, on the other hand, opens up all kinds of interesting possibilities. As the names imply, the primary purpose of the GET command is to simply retrieve information from a server, while the primary purpose of the POST command is to send information to the server. Thus, the fact that a POST will usually return some form of result is more of a side effect: Its primary purpose is to get a large amount of data from the client to the server.

This makes POST ideal for creating a message server. An XML message server can be thought of as a way to send a request for information to the server as a block of XML and then to pass the result of that information back to the client as another XML block (if this sounds remarkably like the RPC concept described earlier, then you are beginning to understand where all of this is leading).

For example, consider how a chat room works. You type your message into a text field, then submit that message to the server. In addition to the text, additional information is likely also sent—your identity (so that the server can identify you to others) as well as perhaps a command specifying that what you're sending is meant to be displayed to all other people in the chat room. However, you can also send information targeted to only one person, or even a message to the server requesting information about the session (who is currently in the room, what other message boards are available, a request for a transcript dump, and so forth).

The important part about such an application is that you never leave the current page. If the page had to refresh after every person in the room had a comment, the application would be distracting in the extreme. Instead, by using a messaging protocol, you can send the message and identity information through the `XML-HTTP` component and receive the response as an XML document, which can then be used to update a visual record. Moreover, you can set the component to periodically query the server for updates (other people may very well be chatting when you're not, for example).

Designing even a modestly functional chat server is not difficult, but neither is it a trivial undertaking. The application basically requires the use of both a server page (which, in this case, is an XSLT script that processes the messages, performs the appropriate updates, and then outputs resulting messages) and a VBScript-driven client application. (Note that this application must run under Internet Explorer 5 because of the limitations of WebDAV support for IE4.) The client piece is more traditional procedural code but essentially demonstrates a way that you can create a full messaging system. In essence, it works as follows:

1. A message is created of the form `@command prop1=value1;prop2=value2;prop3=value3`, etc. (The default message, `@speak`, is automatically created when a line with no command is sent.)
2. The message gets parsed into an XML structure of the form shown in Listing 11.1.

Listing 11.1: A Request Object (*Listing11-1.txt*)

```
<request>
    <chat_room>myRoom</chat_room>
    <command>@command</command>
    <user_name>myUserName</user_name>
    <params>
        <param name="prop1">value1</param>
        <param name="prop2">value2</param>
        <param name="prop3">value3</param>
    </params>
</request>
```

3. The XML-encoded message is sent via an asynchronous XML-HTTP send command to the server page `chat.asp` (see Listing 11.2), where it serves as the primary input stream. Note that the server page here is extremely simple; the majority of the work is actually accomplished by the XSL transformation `processChatRequest.xsl`, which takes the request and transforms it into the appropriate response, as shown in Listing 11.3.

Listing 11.2: The ASP Code for Handling the Page Essentially Just Invokes the XSL Script *processChatRequest.xsl* (*chat.asp*).

```
<%@LANGUAGE="VBScript"%>
<%response.expires=-1
set requestDoc=createObject("MSXML2.DOMDocument")
requestDoc.load request
set processChat=createObject("MSXML2.DOMDocument")
processChat.load server.mapPath("processChatRequest.xsl")
response.write requestDoc.transformNode(processChat)
%>
```

Listing 11.3: A Response Object (*Listing 11-3.txt*)

```
<response>
    <command>command</command>
    <status>A Status Message</status>
    <from>System</from>
    <body>
        Contents of the message.
    </body>
</response>
```

4. Depending upon the command, `processChatRequest.xsl` switches to different templates. In some cases, these templates can actually load or save XML files on the server to maintain general state information for the application. This makes use of a little internal scripting through the `MSXSL` namespace to define both a way of persisting and retrieving data and a way to handle date information.
5. Once the response object is created, it is then sent back to the client, which intercepts it through the `processMessage` command. This likewise filters the responses back to handle the appropriate interface updates and is more typical of a Web page than of an XML page. (Note that you could draft this into an XHTML-based page to simplify things somewhat, but I wanted to demonstrate the use of DOM code on the client.)

Because new messages will be added by all people in the chat rooms, one message loop is particularly important. This is the `@query` loop; it keeps track of the ID of the last message that was retrieved and then calls `@query` with that particular ID to retrieve all messages that have entered the room's message queue after the last message. This loop is invoked using a `setTimeout` method every second, so at any given time the display queue is no more than a second out of date with the server. The new messages are added at the beginning of the XML queue so that it appears that new messages always appear at the top and then scroll down. You can build a bottom-up queue as well, but this requires repositioning the display window to the bottom after every update.

When the application first fires up, it retrieves the available rooms and selects the first room in the queue. This, in turn, sends another event to retrieve the users currently logged in to the room. A user can choose at this point to log in to the room themself, where they receive a dump of the current conversation to this point. They can then write text (either commands, preceded by the @ character, or conversational chat text) into the commentary line and submit it, which causes the XML-HTTP command to send the XML-encoded command to the server.

The server code, as mentioned, simply passes the message being sent as an XML stream to the XSLT script. Note that ordinarily XSLT is viewed as being a simple transformation mechanism—the input stream is effectively filtered through the XSL to produce output. However, the design that is used here is actually much closer in design to the way that a C++ application works—the XML input stream is a message that is compared to a set of mappings within the XSLT. When a template matches the message, it either performs an operation or calls a named template to perform the operation in its stead. This is highly analogous to the Message Maps that event-driven C++ windows applications use explicitly (and languages such as Visual Basic use implicitly), but here the code is essentially handled through a server-side "component," the XSLT script hosted by ASP.

`processChatRequest.xsl` incorporates two internal "helper objects" that it uses to perform a few basic tasks that fall outside of the normal scope for XSLT. The first, contained in the namespace `state:`, effectively has two methods associated with it: `state:document()`, which retrieves an external XML document so that it can be used within the XSLT script, and `state:persistDocument()`, which, when passed an XML node, persists the node back to the server.

These two additions (one of which is meant to echo the `document()` function that should be implicit in XPath but hasn't been implemented yet in the MSXML3 parser) significantly enhance the capabilities of XSLT since it becomes possible for a single script to persist interim information or update files. This is, in fact, what is done here with such things as adding a new user to the users list, and demonstrates a useful technique for updating files, as shown in Listing 11.4.

Listing 11.4: Adding a New User to an External XML Store Becomes Possible with Variables and the Internally Defined *state:persistDocument()* Function. (*Listing11-4.txt*)

```
<xsl:template name="addNewUser">
    <xsl:param name="user_name"/>
    <xsl:param name="chat_room"/>
    <xsl:variable name="usersDoc">
        <xsl:copy-of select="state:document('users.xml')"/>
    </xsl:variable>
    <xsl:variable name="new_user">
```

```
        <user>
            <user_name><xsl:value-of select="$user_name"/></user_name>
            <chat_room><xsl:value-of select="$chat_room"/></chat_room>
        </user>
        </xsl:variable>
        <xsl:variable name="new_user_doc">
            <users>
                <xsl:copy-of select="$usersDoc//user"/>
                <xsl:copy-of select="$new_user"/>
            </users>
        </xsl:variable>
        <xsl:variable name="persist_doc"
select="state:persistDocument('users.xml',$new_user_doc)"/>
        <xsl:copy-of select="$new_user_doc"/>
    </xsl:template>
```

Additionally, a second namespace—the `date:` namespace—handles one of the minor deficiencies that XSLT itself has: no native support for dates (although it does support dates through the XML Schema). This namespace supports the two functions `date:getDate()`, which converts a date in *MM/DD/YYYY* format to the *YYYY-MM-DDTHH:MM:SS.ddd* format that XML schema currently supports, and `format-Date()`, which calls the VBScript function of the same name to convert a date into long-date notation (Monday, January 20, 2000, for example).

I included yet one more namespace in all of this, one that doesn't reference a script. The `doc:` namespace is designed to provide documentation for the XSLT document and is included to show how you can make your code more self-documenting. The advantage to putting such code in a separate namespace rather than as comments is that you can effectively query the XSLT with a different XSLT filter to produce tables or similar formatted pages that describe how the XSL document works—something that is more difficult to do with comments. You can also run the XSLT through a separate XSLT filter to remove all elements within the namespace document, as shown in Listing 11.5.

Listing 11.5: Removing the *doc:* Nodes that Support Documenting Your XSLT Involves Applying an XSL Transformation on the Primary Transformation. (*stripDocs.xsl*)

```
<!-- stripDocs.xsl -->
<xsl:stylesheet
xmlns:xsl="http://www.w3.org/1999/XSL/Transform"
 version="1.0">
    <xsl:output method="xml"/>
    <xsl:template match="/|*|@*">
        <xsl:copy><xsl:apply-templates
 select="*[not(starts
-with(string(name),'doc:']|@*"/></xsl:copy>
    </xsl:template>
</xsl:stylesheet>
```

The primary XSLT filter is shown in Listing 11.6 and provides support for a minimal set of chat functions, as described in Table 11.2. By the way, to illustrate the power of the `doc:` approach when writing larger XSL scripts, note that the table for the chat commands was generated automatically by an XSLT script that mapped the documentation elements in `processChatRequest.xsl` to an XHTML output format.

TABLE 11.2: Chat @ Commands with Their Associated Parameters

Command or Parameter	Type	Description
`@speak`	matched template	Passes the text spoken into the appropriate `chat_room` log, then sends back a simple confirmation request. Note that this doesn't handle the requests for the conversation thread; that's the role of `@query`.
`@query`	matched template	Compares the ID passed as a parameter in the request object to the current `idcounter` of the `chat_room` object, then returns those actions that haven't yet been requested from the browser in question. The browser should then update its own internal chat-room indexes, where the cycle begins again.
`Id`	number	Retrieves all actions (such as conversation lines) from the ID forward. To get a dump of the whole log, you'd use `@query id=0`.
`@createRoom`	matched template	Comprises the request interface for creating a new room.
`chat_room`	string	Determines the name of the new chat room. If such a room already exists, the room won't be created.
`user_name`	string	Determines the username of the person creating the site. Only the person who creates a room (or the system administrator) can eliminate it.
`Public`	string	Indicates whether it is publicly listed in the rooms list or can only be accessed through a known door. This is currently unimplemented.
`@deleteRoom`	matched template	Comprises the request interface for deleting a room. Only the person who creates a room or the system administrator (not yet implemented) can delete that room.
`chat_room`	string	Determines the name of the new chat room. If no such room exists, then nothing will be eliminated.
`@getRooms`	matched template	Returns a list of all currently undeleted rooms. (When a room is deleted, it is simply marked as such; a scheduled routine periodically removes all deleted rooms.)
`@login`	matched template	Makes users visible to the system and initiates the query system that retrieves messages for a given room.

TABLE 11.2: Chat @ Commands with Their Associated Parameters *(continued)*

Command or Parameter	Type	Description
chat_room	string	Determines that if a **chat_room** name is passed the user is automatically logged in at the chat room; otherwise, the user automatically starts in **_Home**.
@logout	matched template	Removes users from the system.
user_name	string	Comprises the name used for logging in and also the name displayed in the conversation threads.
@goRoom	matched template	Moves a user from one room to another and initiates code to update the status displays in the client.
user_name	string	Comprises the name of the person to move. Note that if unspecified this defaults to the current user.
chat_room	string	Determines the name of the room to move to.
@getUsers	matched template	Retrieves a list of all of the users that are currently in a specific chat room.
chat_room	string	Determines the name of the room to query.

Listing 11.6: *processChatRequest.xsl* Is an Entire Chat Server in a Single XSL Document.

```
<xsl:stylesheet xmlns:xsl="http://www.w3.org/1999/XSL/Transform"
    xmlns:state="http://www.vbxml.com/state"
    xmlns:date="http://www.vbxml.com/date"
    xmlns:msxsl="urn:schemas-microsoft-com:xslt"
    xmlns:doc="http://www.vbxml.com/documentation"
    version="1.0">
    <xsl:output method="xml"/>

<doc:document>
<doc:filename>processChatRequest.xsl</doc:filename>
<doc:abstract>
This is used in conjunction with the chatClient.asp page
 to create an XML based chat application. It was produced
 as part of the XML Developer's Handbook by Kurt Cagle for
 Sybex Press, and is copyright 2000. For questions about this
 code, please check the above mentioned book, Kurt's website
 at http://www.vbxml.com, or contact him at cagle@olywa.net.
</doc:abstract>
<doc:author>Kurt Cagle</doc:author>
</doc:document>

<doc:term>
<doc:title>state:</doc:title>
<doc:type>Namespace</doc:type>
<doc:body>The purpose of the state namespace is to manage
 the document retrieval and persistance stories.</doc:body>
</doc:term>
```

```
<doc:term>
<doc:title>state:document(url)</doc:title>
<doc:type>Scripting Addition</doc:type>
<doc:body>is meant to emulate the document function in
 XPath notation. By passing a URL to the function, you can
 retrieve the document as a node selection or store the
 result into a variable.</doc:body>
</doc:term>

<doc:term>
<doc:title>state:persistDocument(url,newDoc)</doc:title>
<doc:type>Scripting Addition</doc:type>
<doc:body>saves the structure contained in newDoc to the
 server at the given URL.</doc:body>
</doc:term>

<msxsl:script language="VBScript" implements-prefix="state">'<![CDATA[
function document(url)
    set xmlDoc=createObject("MSXML2.DOMDocument")
    xmlDoc.async=false
    xmlDoc.load url
    set document=xmlDoc
end function

function persistDocument(url,newDoc)
    set doc=createObject("MSXML2.DOMDocument")
    doc.async=false
    set node=newDoc(0).cloneNode(true)
    doc.appendChild node
    doc.save url
    set persistDocument=doc
end function

']]></msxsl:script>

<doc:term>
<doc:title>date:</doc:title>
<doc:type>Namespace</doc:type>
<doc:body>The date: namespace contains scripting utilities
 for working with dates.</doc:body>
</doc:term>

<doc:term>
<doc:title>date:getDate(dateExpr)</doc:title>
<doc:type>Scripting Addition</doc:type>
<doc:body>
This expression retrieves the date in the notation YYYY-MM
-DDTHH:MM:SS.DDD when passed an expression of the form
 "MM/DD/YY". If dateExpr is blank ("") then the current
 date is retrieved.
</doc:body>
</doc:term>
```

```
<doc:term>
<doc:title>date:formatDate(dateText,style)</doc:title>
<doc:type>Scripting Addition</doc:type>
<doc:body>This formats the date given in the YYYY-MM
-DDTHH:MM:SS.DDD format into any of a number of notations,
 as detailed in the Visual Basic Script
 specifications.</doc:body>
</doc:term>

<msxsl:script implements-prefix="date" language="VBScript">'<![CDATA[
function getDate(dateExpr)
    if dateExpr="" then
        getDate=date
    else
        getDate=dateValue(dateExpr)
    end if
end function

function formatDate(dateText,style)
    datestr=mid(dateText,6,2)+"/"+mid(dateText,9,2)+"/"+mid(dateText,1,4)
    dt=dateValue(datestr)
    formatDate=formatDateTime(dt,style)
end function

']]></msxsl:script>


<doc:term>
<doc:title>logfile</doc:title>
<doc:type>Variable</doc:type>
<doc:body>Contains the name of the session to act as the
 log and repository for the session (not including the .xml
 extension). This is the same as the current chat room
 name.</doc:body>
</doc:term>
        <xsl:variable name="logfile"
 select="concat(string(//chat_room),'.xml')"/>

<doc:term>
<doc:title>sessionLog</doc:title>
<doc:type>variable</doc:type>
<doc:body>Contains a copy of the active session log for
 reference in query calls.</doc:body>
</doc:term>
        <xsl:variable name="sessionLog"><xsl:copy-of
 select="state:document($logfile)"/></xsl:variable>

<doc:term>
<doc:title>getResponseBlock</doc:title>
<doc:type>Named Template</doc:type>
<doc:body>Contains the name of the session to act as the
```

```
 log and repository for the session (not including the .xml
 extension). This is the same as the current chat room
 name.</doc:body>
<doc:param>
<doc:name>command</doc:name>
<doc:type>string</doc:type>
<doc:descr>Contains the command to use to send information
 back to the client.</doc:descr>
</doc:param>
<doc:param>
<doc:name>status</doc:name>
<doc:type>string</doc:type>
<doc:descr>Contains the return status text. Default is "OK".</doc:descr>
</doc:param>
<doc:param>
<doc:name>from</doc:name>
<doc:type>string</doc:type>
<doc:descr>The originator of the command. With the
 exception of @speak (where it contains the user_name of
 the person who spoke, this will usually be
 "system".</doc:descr>
</doc:param>
</doc:term>

    <xsl:template name="getResponseBlock">
        <xsl:param name="command"/>
        <xsl:param name="status" select="'OK'"/>
        <xsl:param name="from" select="'system'"/>
        <xsl:param name="content"/>
        <response>
            <command><xsl:value-of select="$command"/></command>
            <status><xsl:value-of select="$status"/></status>
            <from><xsl:value-of select="$from"/></from>
            <body>
                <xsl:copy-of select="$content"/>
            </body>
        </response>
    </xsl:template>

<doc:term>
<doc:title>Root Node Template (/)</doc:title>
<doc:type>Matched Template</doc:type>
<doc:body>The root node template, when matches requests and
sends them off to their appropriate filter.</doc:body>
</doc:term>

    <xsl:template match="/">
        <xsl:apply-templates select="//request"/>
    </xsl:template>

<doc:term>
<doc:title>@speak</doc:title>
```

```
<doc:type>Matched Template</doc:type>
<doc:body>This passes the text spoken into the appropriate
 chat_room log, then sends back a simple confirmation
 request. Note that this doesn't handle the requests for
 the conversation thread -- that's the role of
 @query.</doc:body>
</doc:term>

    <xsl:template match="request[command='@speak']">
        <xsl:variable name="currentID"
 select="number($sessionLog//@idcounter)"/>
        <xsl:variable name="text" select="params/param[@name='text']"/>
        <xsl:variable name="actionObject">
            <action><xsl:attribute name="id"><xsl:value-of
 select="$currentID"/></xsl:attribute>
                <command>speak</command>
                <from><xsl:value-of select="//user_name"/></from>
                <to>*</to>
                <status>OK</status>
                <body>
                    <text><xsl:value-of select="$text"/></text>
                </body>
            </action>
        </xsl:variable>
        <xsl:variable name="newSessionDoc">
            <session><xsl:attribute
 name="idcounter"><xsl:value-of
 select="$currentID+1"/></xsl:attribute>
                <xsl:copy-of select="//chat_room"/>
                <xsl:copy-of select="$actionObject"/>
                <xsl:copy-of select="$sessionLog/session/action"/>
            </session>
        </xsl:variable>
        <xsl:variable name="session">
            <xsl:copy-of
 select="state:persistDocument($logfile,$newSessionDoc)"/>
        </xsl:variable>
        <xsl:call-template name="getResponseBlock">
            <xsl:with-param name="command" select="'speak'"/>
            <xsl:with-param name="content" select="$text"/>
        </xsl:call-template>
    </xsl:template>

<doc:term>
<doc:title>@query</doc:title>
<doc:type>Matched Template</doc:type>
<doc:body>@query compares the id passed as a parameter in
 the request object to the current idcounter of the
 chat_room object,then returns those actions that haven't
 yet been requested from the browser in question. The
 browser should then update its own internal chatroom
 indexes, where the cycle begins again.</doc:body>
```

```
<doc:param>
<doc:name>id</doc:name>
<doc:type>number</doc:type>
<doc:descr>This retrieves all actions (such as conversation
 lines) from the id forward.  To get a dump of the whole
 log, you'd use '@query id=0'.</doc:descr>

</doc:param>
</doc:term>

    <xsl:template match="request[command='@query']">
        <xsl:variable name="current_id" select="//param[@name='id']"/>
        <xsl:variable name="session">
            <session><xsl:attribute
 name="idcounter"><xsl:value-of
 select="$sessionLog//@idcounter"/></xsl:attribute>

            <chat_room><xsl:value-of
 select="//param[@name='chat_room']"/></chat_room>

            <user_name><xsl:value-of
 select="//param[@name='user_name']"/></user_name>

                <xsl:for-each
 select="$sessionLog//action[number(@id) &gt;=
 number($current_id)]">

                    <xsl:sort select="@id" order="descending"/>
                    <xsl:copy-of select="."/>
                </xsl:for-each>
            </session>
        </xsl:variable>
        <xsl:call-template name="getResponseBlock">
            <xsl:with-param name="command" select="'query'"/>
            <xsl:with-param name="content" select="$session"/>
        </xsl:call-template>
    </xsl:template>

<doc:term>
<doc:title>makeNewChatRoom</doc:title>
<doc:type>Named Template</doc:type>
<doc:body>Creates a new chat room object to be dropped into
 the chatRooms.xml file, which maintains the current state
 of the system's chat rooms.</doc:body>
<doc:param>
<doc:name>title</doc:name>
<doc:type>string</doc:type>
<doc:descr>The name of the chat room.</doc:descr>
</doc:param>
<doc:param>
<doc:name>created_by</doc:name>
```

```
<doc:type>string</doc:type>
<doc:descr>The user_name of the person creating the site.
 Only the person who creates a room (or the system
 administrator) can eliminate it.</doc:descr>
</doc:param>
<doc:param>
<doc:name>public</doc:name>
<doc:type>string</doc:type>
<doc:descr>Indicates whether it is publicly listed in the
 rooms list, or can only be accessed through a known door.
 This is currently unimplemented. </doc:descr>
</doc:param>
</doc:term>

    <xsl:template name="makeNewChatRoom">
        <xsl:param name="title"/>
        <xsl:param name="created_by"/>
        <xsl:param name="public" select="'yes'"/>
        <chat_room>
            <title><xsl:value-of select="$title"/></title>
            <created_by><xsl:value-of select="$created_by"/></created_by>
            <date_created><xsl:value-of
 select="date:getDate('')"/></date_created>
            <public><xsl:value-of select="$public"/></public>
        </chat_room>
    </xsl:template>

<doc:term>
<doc:title>@createRoom</doc:title>
<doc:type>Matched Template</doc:type>
<doc:body>@createRoom is the request interface for creating
 a new room. </doc:body>
<doc:param>
<doc:name>chat_room</doc:name>
<doc:type>string</doc:type>
<doc:descr>The name of the new chat room. If such a room
 already exists, the room won't be created.</doc:descr>
</doc:param>
<doc:param>
<doc:name>user_name</doc:name>
<doc:type>string</doc:type>
<doc:descr>The user_name of the person creating the site.
 Only the person who creates a room (or the system
 administrator) can eliminate it.</doc:descr>

</doc:param>
<doc:param>
<doc:name>public</doc:name>
<doc:type>string</doc:type>
<doc:descr>Indicates whether it is publicly listed in the
 rooms list, or can only be accessed through a known door.
```

```
  This is currently unimplemented. </doc:descr>
 </doc:param>
 </doc:term>

     <xsl:template match="request[command='@createRoom']">
         <xsl:variable name="chatRoomName"
  select="string(//params/param[@name='chat_room'])"/>
         <xsl:variable name="newChatRoomNode">
         <xsl:call-template name="makeNewChatRoom">
             <xsl:with-param name="title"
 select="//params/param[@name='chat_room']"/>
             <xsl:with-param name="created_by" select="//user_name"/>
             <xsl:with-param name="public"
  select="//params/param[@name='public']"/>
         </xsl:call-template>
         </xsl:variable>
         <xsl:variable name="OldChatRoomDoc">
             <xsl:copy-of select="state:document('chatrooms.xml')" disable-
output-escaping="yes"/>
         </xsl:variable>
         <xsl:variable name="newChatRoomDoc">
             <chat_rooms>
                 <xsl:for-each
  select="$OldChatRoomDoc//chat_room[title!=$chatRoomName]">
                     <xsl:copy-of select="."/>
                 </xsl:for-each>
                 <xsl:choose>
                 <xsl:when
  test="$OldChatRoomDoc//chat_room[title=$chatRoomName]">
                     <xsl:for-each select=".">
                         <xsl:choose>
                         <xsl:when
  test="string(created_by)=string(//user_name)">
                             <xsl:copy-of select="$newChatRoomNode"/>
                         </xsl:when>
                         <xsl:otherwise>
                             <xsl:copy-of select="."/>
                         </xsl:otherwise>
                         </xsl:choose>
                     </xsl:for-each>
                 </xsl:when>
                 <xsl:otherwise>
                     <xsl:copy-of select="$newChatRoomNode"/>
                 </xsl:otherwise>
                 </xsl:choose>
             </chat_rooms>
         </xsl:variable>
         <xsl:variable name="saveChatRoomIndex"
  select="state:persistDocument
 ('chatRooms.xml',$newChatRoomDoc)"/>
         <xsl:variable name="chatRoomFile">
             <session idcounter="0"><chat_room>
```

```
<xsl:value-of select="$chatRoomName"/>
</chat_room></session>
        </xsl:variable>
        <xsl:variable name="saveChatRoomFile"
 select="state:persistDocument
(concat($chatRoomName,'.xml'),$chatRoomFile)"/>
        <xsl:variable name="responseObject">
            <response id="-1">
                <command>createRoom</command>
                <status>OK</status>
                <from>system</from>
                <body><xsl:copy-of select="$newChatRoomNode"/></body>
            </response>
        </xsl:variable>
        <xsl:copy-of select="$responseObject" disable-output-escaping="yes"/>
    </xsl:template>

<doc:term>
<doc:title>@deleteRoom</doc:title>
<doc:type>Matched Template</doc:type>
<doc:body>@deleteRoom is the request interface for deleting
 a room. Only the person who creates a room or the system
 administrator (not yet implemented) can delete that
 room.</doc:body>
<doc:param>
<doc:name>chat_room</doc:name>
<doc:type>string</doc:type>
<doc:descr>The name of the new chat room. If no such room
 exists, then nothing will be eliminated.</doc:descr>

</doc:param>
<doc:param>
<doc:name>user_name</doc:name>
<doc:type>string</doc:type>
<doc:descr>The user_name of the person creating the site.
 Only the person who creates a room (or the system
 administrator) can eliminate it.</doc:descr>
</doc:param>
</doc:term>

    <xsl:template match="request[command='@deleteRoom']">
        <xsl:variable name="chatRoomName"
 select="string(//params/param[@name='chat_room'])"/>
        <xsl:variable name="OldChatRoomDoc">
            <xsl:copy-of
 select="state:document('chatrooms.xml')"
disable-output-escaping="yes"/>
        </xsl:variable>
        <xsl:variable name="newChatRoomDoc">
            <chat_rooms>
                <xsl:for-each
```

```
    select="$OldChatRoomDoc//chat_room[title!=$chatRoomName]">
                        <xsl:copy-of select="."/>
                    </xsl:for-each>
                    <xsl:choose>
                    <xsl:when test="$OldChatRoomDoc//
chat_room[title=$chatRoomName]">
                        <xsl:for-each select=".">
                            <xsl:choose>
                            <xsl:when
   test="string(created_by)=string(//user_name)">
                                <chat_room>
                                <xsl:copy-of select="*"/>
                                <delete/>
                                </chat_room>
                            </xsl:when>
                            <xsl:otherwise>
                                <xsl:copy-of select="."/>
                            </xsl:otherwise>
                            </xsl:choose>
                        </xsl:for-each>
                    </xsl:when>
                    <xsl:otherwise>
                        <xsl:copy-of select="."/>
                    </xsl:otherwise>
                    </xsl:choose>
                </chat_rooms>
            </xsl:variable>
            <xsl:variable name="saveChatRoomIndex"
    select="state:persistDocument
   ('chatRooms.xml',$newChatRoomDoc)"/>
            <xsl:variable name="chatRoomFile">
                <session idcounter="0"><chat_room>
   <xsl:value-of select="$chatRoomName"/>
   </chat_room></session>
            </xsl:variable>
            <xsl:variable name="saveChatRoomFile"
    select="state:persistDocument(concat
   ($chatRoomName,'.xml'),$chatRoomFile)"/>
            <xsl:variable name="responseObject">
                <response id="-1">
                    <command>deleteRoom</command>
                    <status>OK</status>
                    <from>system</from>
                    <body><xsl:copy-of select="$newChatRoomDoc"/></body>
                </response>
            </xsl:variable>
            <xsl:copy-of select="$responseObject" disable-output-escaping="yes"/>
        </xsl:template>

   <doc:term>
   <doc:title>@getRooms</doc:title>
```

```
<doc:type>Matched Template</doc:type>
<doc:body>@getRooms returns a list of all currently
 undeleted rooms (when a room is deleted it is simply
 marked as such -- a scheduled routine periodically removes
 all deleted rooms..</doc:body>
</doc:term>

    <xsl:template match="request[command='@getRooms']">
        <xsl:variable name="chat_rooms">
<xsl:copy-of select="state:document('chatrooms.xml')"/>
</xsl:variable>
        <response id="-1">
            <command>getRooms</command>
            <status>OK</status>
            <from>system></from>
            <body>
                <chat_rooms>
                    <xsl:for-each select="$chat_rooms//chat_room">
                        <xsl:copy-of select=".[not(deleted)]"/>
                    </xsl:for-each>
                </chat_rooms>
            </body>
        </response>
    </xsl:template>

<doc:term>
<doc:title>@login</doc:title>
<doc:type>Matched Template</doc:type>
<doc:body>@login makes users visible to the system, and
 initiates the query system that retrieves messages for a
 given room.</doc:body>
<doc:param>
<doc:name>user_name</doc:name>
<doc:type>string</doc:type>
<doc:descr>The name used for logging in, also the name
 displayed in the conversation threads.</doc:descr>
</doc:param>
<doc:param>
<doc:name>chat_room</doc:name>
<doc:type>string</doc:type>
<doc:descr>If a chat_room name is passed, then the user is
 automatically logged in at the chat room, otherwise, the
 user automatically starts in '_Home'. </doc:descr>
</doc:param>
</doc:term>

    <xsl:template match="request[command='@login']">
        <xsl:variable name="p_user_name" select="//param[@name='user_name']"/>
            <xsl:variable name="p_chat_room"
 select="//param[@name='chat_room']"/>
        <xsl:variable name="p_usersDoc">
            <xsl:copy-of select="state:document('users.xml')"/>
```

```
        </xsl:variable>
        <xsl:variable name="valid_user"
 select="$p_usersDoc//user[user_name=$p_user_name]"/>
        <xsl:choose>
            <xsl:when test="$valid_user">
                <xsl:call-template name="goRoom">
                    <xsl:with-param name="user_name" select="$p_user_name"/>
                    <xsl:with-param name="chat_room" select="$p_chat_room"/>
                    <xsl:with-param name="command" select="'login'"/>
                </xsl:call-template>
            </xsl:when>
            <xsl:otherwise>
                <xsl:variable name="new_user">
                    <xsl:call-template name="addNewUser">
                        <xsl:with-param name="user_name"
 select="$p_user_name"/>
                        <xsl:with-param name="chat_room"
 select="$p_chat_room"/>
                    </xsl:call-template>
                </xsl:variable>
                <response>
                    <command>newUser</command>
                    <status>OK</status>
                    <from>system</from>
                    <body><xsl:copy-of select="$new_user"/></body>
                </response>
            </xsl:otherwise>
        </xsl:choose>
    </xsl:template>

<doc:term>
<doc:title>@logout</doc:title>
<doc:type>Matched Template</doc:type>
<doc:body>@logout removes users from the system.</doc:body>
<doc:param>
<doc:name>user_name</doc:name>
<doc:type>string</doc:type>
<doc:descr>The name used for logging in, also the name
 displayed in the conversation threads.</doc:descr>
</doc:param>
</doc:term>

    <xsl:template match="request[command='@logout']">
        <xsl:variable name="p_user_name" select="//param[@name='user_name']"/>
            <xsl:variable name="p_chat_room"
 select="//param[@name='chat_room']"/>
        <xsl:variable name="p_usersDoc">
            <xsl:copy-of select="state:document('users.xml')"/>
        </xsl:variable>
        <xsl:variable name="valid_user"
 select="$p_usersDoc//user[user_name=$p_user_name]"/>
```

```
        <xsl:variable name="new_user_doc">
            <users>
                <xsl:for-each
 select="$p_usersDoc//user[user_name != $p_user_name]">
                    <xsl:copy-of select="."/>
                </xsl:for-each>
            </users>
        </xsl:variable>
        <xsl:variable name="persistUsers"
 select="state:persistDocument
('users.xml',$new_user_doc)"/>
        <xsl:call-template name="getResponseBlock">
            <xsl:with-param name="command" select="'logout'"/>
            <xsl:with-param name="status" select="'OK'"/>
            <xsl:with-param name="from" select="'system'"/>
            <xsl:with-param name="content" select="$valid_user"/>
        </xsl:call-template>
    </xsl:template>

    <xsl:template name="addNewUser">
        <xsl:param name="user_name"/>
        <xsl:param name="chat_room"/>
        <xsl:variable name="usersDoc">
            <xsl:copy-of select="state:document('users.xml')"/>
        </xsl:variable>
        <xsl:variable name="new_user">
        <user>
            <user_name><xsl:value-of select="$user_name"/></user_name>
            <chat_room><xsl:value-of select="$chat_room"/></chat_room>
        </user>
        </xsl:variable>
        <xsl:variable name="new_user_doc">
            <users>
                <xsl:copy-of select="$usersDoc//user"/>
                <xsl:copy-of select="$new_user"/>
            </users>
        </xsl:variable>
        <xsl:variable name="persist_doc"
 select="state:persistDocument
('users.xml',$new_user_doc)"/>
        <xsl:copy-of select="$new_user_doc"/>
    </xsl:template>

<doc:term>
<doc:title>@goRoom</doc:title>
<doc:type>Matched Template</doc:type>
<doc:body>@goRoom moves a user from one room to another,
 and initiates code to update the status displays in the
 client.</doc:body>
<doc:param>
<doc:name>user_name</doc:name>
```

```
<doc:type>string</doc:type>
<doc:descr>The name of the person to move. Note that if
 unspecified this defaults to the current user.</doc:descr>

</doc:param>
<doc:param>
<doc:name>chat_room</doc:name>
<doc:type>string</doc:type>
<doc:descr>The name of the room to move to.</doc:descr>
</doc:param>
</doc:term>

    <xsl:template match="request[command='@goRoom']">
        <xsl:call-template name="goRoom">
            <xsl:with-param name="user_name"
 select="//param[@name='user_name']"/>

            <xsl:with-param name="chat_room"
 select="//param[@name='chat_room']"/>
        </xsl:call-template>
    </xsl:template>

    <xsl:template name="goRoom">
        <xsl:param name="user_name"/>
        <xsl:param name="chat_room"/>
        <xsl:param name="command" select="'goRoom'"/>
        <xsl:variable name="usersDoc">
            <xsl:copy-of select="state:document('users.xml')"/>
        </xsl:variable>
        <xsl:variable name="changed_user">
        <user>
            <user_name><xsl:value-of select="$user_name"/></user_name>
            <chat_room><xsl:value-of select="$chat_room"/></chat_room>
        </user>
        </xsl:variable>
        <xsl:variable name="new_user_doc">
            <users>
                <xsl:copy-of
 select="$usersDoc//user[user_name != $user_name]"/>
                <xsl:copy-of select="$changed_user"/>
            </users>
        </xsl:variable>
        <xsl:variable name="persist_doc"
 select="state:persistDocument
('users.xml',$new_user_doc)"/>
        <xsl:call-template name="getResponseBlock">
        <xsl:with-param name="command" select="$command"/>
        <xsl:with-param name="content">
<xsl:copy-of select="$changed_user/user"/>
</xsl:with-param>
        </xsl:call-template>
    </xsl:template>
```

```
<doc:term>
<doc:title>@getUsers</doc:title>
<doc:type>Matched Template</doc:type>
<doc:body>@getUsers retrieves a list of all of the users
 that are currently in a specific chat room.</doc:body>
<doc:param>
<doc:name>chat_room</doc:name>
<doc:type>string</doc:type>
<doc:descr>The name of the room to query.</doc:descr>
</doc:param>
</doc:term>

    <xsl:template match="request[command='@getUsers']">
        <response>
            <command>getUsers</command>
            <status>OK</status>
            <from>system</from>
            <body>
                <xsl:call-template name="getUsers">
                    <xsl:with-param name="chat_room"
 select="params/param[@name='chat_room']"/>
                </xsl:call-template>
            </body>
        </response>
    </xsl:template>

    <xsl:template name="getUsers">
        <xsl:param name="chat_room"/>
        <xsl:variable name="usersDoc">
            <xsl:copy-of select="state:document('users.xml')"/>
        </xsl:variable>
        <users>
            <xsl:copy-of select="$usersDoc//user[chat_room=$chat_room]"/>
        </users>
    </xsl:template>
</xsl:stylesheet>
```

The server code maintains a number of different files, such as `chatrooms.xml`, which contains the chat-room identification information, `users.xml`, which contains the specific user data, and individual chat room records, which contain logs of every conversation (principally the "spoken" conversation within each chat room). These files are actually generated and maintained by the XSLT itself, using the `state:document()` and `state:persistDocument()` functions, with the documents carried internally by the XSLT in variables that can be accessed as if they were node elements themselves. For example,

```
<xsl:variable name="usersDoc">
    <xsl:copy-of select="state:document('users.xml')"/>
</xsl:variable>
<users>
```

```
            <xsl:copy-of select="$usersDoc//user[chat_room=$chat_room]"/>
        </users>
```

loads the contents of the file `users.xml` into a variable called `usersDoc`, via the `xsl:copy-of` tag. To get a specific set of users (those in the indicated chat room given by the variable `$chat_room`), you would then use the `$usersDoc` variable as if it were a node:

```
<xsl:copy-of select="
      $usersDoc//user[chat_room=$chat_room]"/>
```

TIP

This technique is quite powerful since it lets you effectively create multiple "working streams" in your XSLT filter. If the file or the source URLs are provided either as parameters or as part of the initial message, this also gives you a way to pull in resources indirectly. Rather than loading an XML document and passing it in as a parameter, you can just pass the URL (or even generate the URL internally, as is done several times in the chat room) and have the XSLT filter retrieve it.

The Chat Client

The chat client is a little more traditional Internet application compared to the server (as much as anything can be traditional after only three years), written in VBScript and using the XML-HTTP control (Listing 11.7). In a number of respects, it echoes the server: When a message is sent from the client, the server has a Message Map that locates the template associated with the message block and then returns a server object in response.

Because the call to the server is done asynchronously, the XML-HTTP control (contained in the variable `http`) needs to assign a handler to intercept the `onreadystatechange` event—in this case the function `processMessage()`, which, in turn, invokes `HandleSystemResponse()`.This function reads the result of the query, then attempts to match this result to a set of items in a select case switch, a client side Message Map.

In nearly all cases, the mapping on the client performs some additional visual interface processing. For example, when a query is made, the returned XML filters out the results using an inline XSLT data island, `displayCurrentConversations`. Since the result is applied only to the new lines that come in, the result of this transformation is inserted at the beginning of the `chatDisplay` field (rather than redrawing the entire field every time a new chat line arrives).

Listing 11.7: The Chat Client Is Written Primarily in Procedural Scripting Code but Illustrates the Same Message Map Capability That the Server Does. (*chatClient.asp*)

```
<html>
<head>
    <title>Simple-Chat</title>
</head>

<body>
<xml id="message_template">
```

```
<request>
    <chat_room/>
    <command/>
    <user_name/>
    <params/>
</request>
</xml>

<form>
User Name:<input type="text" id="userName"
 value="Anonymous" style="border:none;font
-size:10pt;color:green;font-family:Verdana;"/>
<div style="width:150px;position:absolute;left:420px;top:18px;">
Current Users:<br/>
<select id="users" size="8" style="width:150px;"></select>
</div>
<div style="position:absolute;left:420px;top:175px;width:150px;">
Available Rooms:<br/>
<select id="chatRoom" size="8" style="width:150px;"
onclick="sendMessage(document.all('userName'),this.value,'
@getUsers chat_room='+this.value)"
>
</select>
</div>
<div id="chatDisplay"
 style="width:400px;height:300px;position:relative;
overflow-y:auto;border:inset 3px gray;">
</div>
<input type="text" id="userText"
 style="width:400px;"/><input type="button" value="Send"
 onclick="sendMessage(chatRoom.value,userName.value,
userText.value)"/>
</form>
<xml id="displayCurrentConversations">
    <xsl:stylesheet
 xmlns:xsl="http://www.w3.org/1999/XSL/Transform"
 version="1.0">
        <xsl:template match="/">
            <xsl:apply-templates select="//action"/>
        </xsl:template>
        <xsl:template match="action">
            <div><span style="color:green;
font-weight:bold;"><xsl:value-of select="from"/>:
</span>
<span style="color:black;font-weight:normal;">
<xsl:value-of select="body"/>
</span></div>
        </xsl:template>
    </xsl:stylesheet>
</xml>
<div
style="width:300px;height:300px;position:absolute;
```

```
left:400px;top:300px;" id="returnObject">
</div>

<script language="VBscript">
dim http
dim rcptDoc
dim msgDoc
dim displayDoc
dim chatRoomState

function initialize()
    set http=createObject("MSXML2.XMLHTTP")
    set rcptDoc=createObject("MSXML2.DOMDocument")
    rcptDoc.async=true
    set msgDoc=createObject("MSXML2.DOMDocument")
    set displayDoc=createObject("MSXML2.DOMDocument")
    set chatRoomState=createObject("MSXML2.DOMDocument")
    msgDoc.async=true
    displayDoc.loadXML displayCurrentConversations.xmlDocument.xml
    chatRoomState.loadXML "<chat_rooms/>"
    sendMessage " "," ","@getRooms"
end function

function sendMessage(chatRoom,userName,userText)
    set msgDoc=message_template.XMLDocument.cloneNode(true)
    set pUserName=msgDoc.selectSingleNode("//user_name")
    pUserName.text=userName
    set pChatRoom=msgDoc.selectSingleNode("//chat_room")
    pchatRoom.text=chatRoom
    set pParams=msgDoc.selectSingleNode("//params")
    if left(userText,1)<>"@" then
        set pCommand=msgDoc.selectSingleNode("//command")
        pCommand.text="@speak"
        set pParam=pParams.appendChild(msgDoc.createElement("param"))
        pParam.setAttribute "name","text"
        pParam.text=userText
    else
        command=split(userText," ")(0)
        set pCommand=msgDoc.selectSingleNode("//command")
        pCommand.text=command
        if ubound(split(userText," "))>0 then
            paramString=split(userText," ")(1)
            params=split(paramString,";")
            set pParams=msgDoc.selectSingleNode("//params")
            for each param in params
                set pParam=pParams.appendChild(msgDoc.createElement("param"))
                paramName=split(param,"=")(0)
                paramValue=split(param,"=")(1)
                pParam.setAttribute "name",paramName
                pParam.text=paramValue
            next
        end if
    end if
```

```
    set pUser=pParams.selectSingleNode("param[@name='user_name']")
    if pUser is nothing then
        set pUser=pParams.appendChild(msgDoc.createElement("param"))
        pUser.setAttribute "name","user_name"
        pUser.text=userName
    end if
    set pChat=pParams.selectSingleNode("param[@name='chat_room']")
    if pChat is nothing then
        set pChat=pParams.appendChild(msgDoc.createElement("param"))
        pChat.setAttribute "name","chat_room"
        pChat.text=chatRoom
    end if
    if pCommand.text <> "@query" then
'        alert msgDoc.xml
    end if
    http.open "POST","chat.asp",true
    http.onreadystatechange=getRef("processMessage")
    http.send msgDoc
end function

function processMessage()
    if http.readystate<4 then exit function
    rcptDoc.loadXML http.responseText
    if left(http.responseText,6)=" <font" then
        chatDisplay.innerHTML=http.responseText
    else
        handleSystemResponse
    end if
end function

dim ct
ct=0
function queryServer()
'    exit function
    ct=ct+1
    chatRoomName=document.all("chatRoom").value
    user=document.all("userName").value
    set chatRoomNode=chatRoomState.selectSingleNode_
("//chat_room[@name='"+chatRoomName+"']")
    IDCounter=chatRoomNode.getAttribute("id")
    status=IDCounter
    sendMessage chatRoomName, user, "@query id="+cstr(IDCounter)
    setTimeout "queryServer",1000,"VBScript"
end function

function handleSystemResponse()
    set command=rcptDoc.selectSingleNode("//command")
    if command is nothing then
        status=http.responseText
        exit function
    end if
    select case command.text
        case "speak"
```

```
        case "getRooms"
            set crSelect=document.all("chatRoom")
            while not crSelect.options.length=0
                crSelect.options.remove 1
            wend
            for each chatRoomRec in rcptDoc.selectNodes("//chat_room")
                set opt=document.createElement("option")
                chatRoomName=chatRoomRec.selectSingleNode("title").text
                opt.value=chatRoomName
                opt.text=opt.value
                crSelect.options.add opt
                set _
 chatRoomNode=chatRoomState.selectSingleNode_
("//chat_room[@name='"+chatRoomName+"']")
                if chatRoomNode is nothing then
                    set _
 chatRoomNode=chatRoomState.documentElement.appendChild_
(chatRoomState.createElement("chat_room"))
                    chatRoomNode.setAttribute "name",chatRoomName
                end if
                chatRoomNode.setAttribute "id",clng(0)
            next
            if crSelect.options.length>0 then
                crSelect.value=crSelect.options(0).value
                sendMessage " "," ","@getUsers chat_room="+crSelect.value
            end if
        case "createRoom"
            set crSelect=document.all("chatRoom")
            set roomNode=rcptDoc.selectSingleNode("//title")
            set opt=document.createElement("option")
            chatRoomName=roomnode.text
            user=document.all("userName")
            opt.value=chatRoomName
            opt.text=opt.value
            crSelect.options.add opt
            crSelect.value=chatRoomNametext
            chatDisplay.insertAdjacentText_
 "afterBegin","*** Moving to room '"+roomNode.text+"' ***"
            sendMessage chatRoomName,user,"@query id=0"
            sendMessage chatRoomName,user,"@getRooms"
            sendMessage chatRoomName,user,"@getUsers chat_room="+chatRoomName
        case "goRoom"
            set crSelect=document.all("chatRoom")
            set roomNode=rcptDoc.selectSingleNode("//chat_room")
            set opt=document.createElement("option")
            opt.value=roomNode.text
            opt.text=opt.value
            crSelect.options.add opt
            crSelect.value=roomNode.text
            chatDisplay.insertAdjacentText _
 "afterBegin","*** Moving to room '"+roomNode.text+"' ***"

            sendMessage _
```

```
 roomNode.text,document.all("userName").value, _
"@query id=0"
            sendMessage _
 roomNode.text,document.all("userName").value, _
"@getUsers chat_room="+roomNode.text
    document.all("userName").value= _
rcptDoc.selectSingleNode("//user_name").text
            sendMessage chatRoomName,user,"@getUsers chat_room="+chatRoomName
        case "login","newUser"
            roomName=rcptDoc.selectSingleNode("//chat_room").text
            user=rcptDoc.selectSingleNode("//user_name").text
            chatDisplay.insertAdjacentText _ "afterBegin","***
"+user+ " has logged into "+roomName+_
" ***"
            document.all("userName").value=user
            document.all("chatRoom").value=roomName
            sendMessage roomName,user,"@query id=0"
            setTimeout "queryServer",1000,"VBScript"
            sendMessage _
 roomName,document.all("userName").value,"@getUsers _
 chat_room="+roomName
        case "logout"
            roomName=rcptDoc.selectSingleNode("//chat_room").text
            user=rcptDoc.selectSingleNode("//user_name").text
            chatDisplay.insertAdjacentText_
 "afterBegin","*** "+user+ " has logged out of "+ _
roomName+" ***"
            document.all("userName").value=user
            sendMessage roomName,user,"@getUsers chat_room="+roomName
            sendMessage roomName,user,"@getUsers chat_room="+roomName
        case "getUsers"
            set userSelect=document.all("users")
            while not userSelect.options.length=0
                userSelect.options.remove 0' opt
            wend
            for each userRec in rcptDoc.selectNodes("//user")
                set opt=document.createElement("option")
                opt.value=userRec.selectSingleNode("user_name").text
                opt.text=opt.value
                userSelect.options.add opt
            next
        case "message"
            alert http.responseText
        case "query"

            chatDisplay.insertAdjacentHTML _
  "afterBegin",rcptDoc.transformNode(displayDoc)
            chatRoomName=rcptDoc.selectSingleNode("//chat_room").text
            user=rcptDoc.selectSingleNode("//user_name").text
            currentID=rcptDoc.selectSingleNode("//@idcounter").text
            set _
 chatRoomNode=chatRoomState.selectSingleNode _
("//chat_room[@name='"+chatRoomName+"']")
```

```
            if chatRoomNode is nothing then
                set _
 chatRoomNode=chatRoomState.documentElement.appendChild _
(chatRoomState.createElement("chat_room"))
                chatRoomNode.setAttribute "name",chatRoomName
                chatRoomNode.setAttribute "id"
            else
                chatRoomNode.setAttribute "id",clng(currentID)
            end if
            sendMessage chatRoomName,user,"@getUsers chat_room="+chatRoomName
    end select
end function

function main()
    initialize
end function
main()
</script>

</body>
</html>
```

What Can You Do with a Chat Server?

A chat server by itself is an interesting novelty, although there are a number of different ways of handling the process of ferrying messages back and forth beyond the use of XML-HTTP and XSLT. The advantage to this approach, though, is that you can build a chat system without the need for proprietary servers or clients, downloaded ActiveX controls, or Java applets. Moreover, you don't need to establish a connection with the server, which is one of the problems of going through IRQ or similar processes; an XML chat room is basically stateless.

Beyond the ability to talk with your friends and neighbors, however, a chat room system like the one discussed here could easily form the core of a more collaborative environment. Messages could contain not just text or maintenance commands but state information for games (the position and owner of a moved piece in a chess game) or even additional code (sandboxed, of course) for expanding on the code base for the environment, making it extensible. Put another way, the same tools could let you upload a script for additional commands, which could be saved as part of an `xsl:include` node; this could then be incorporated into the XSLT filter in the next invocation of that filter, providing you with a mechanism for increasing your command structure over time. This feature, modeled off of online multi-user worlds (MUDs, or MOOs), lets you create ever more sophisticated environments over time.

The code shown here is fairly basic: It works, but there are a number of enhancements that could be made to it to extend its features.

RPCs and SOAP

The chat room example described in the previous section makes use of a number of features that are common to any messaging system:

- A message is represented as an XML envelope, typically with a set outer structure providing common hooks and a flexible inner structure holding the payload, or content.
- The message includes a command of some sort to the server and expects the server to know what to do with the command.
- There is a mechanism for error handling built into the message.
- Messages are agnostic as to their origin or destination—they embody the message, not the binary protocol (such as COM or CORBA), that have traditionally been used for such messaging systems.

The combination of flexibility and system independence has made XML-based messaging systems very attractive to a number of companies as a way of being able to request and process information about system components. One such mechanism, the Simple Object Access Protocol (SOAP) has been adopted by Microsoft as a way of handling RPCs.

The primary purpose of SOAP is to provide an envelope that can hold commands and parametric information to be processed by a specialized server called a SOAP server. Such a server would intercept these SOAP messages and then call the commands given on its behalf—in essence acting as a broker between the requesting client and the target machine.

The nature of that server is not terribly mysterious; the chat server, while not a SOAP server, per se, works on much the same principle: It looks at the command being passed and attempts to map it to a set of known commands, it calls those commands, then it encapsulates the results within a response message. If the command isn't recognized (or there are security issues that aren't satisfied), then the SOAP response XML is given an error-handling payload instead.

SOAP Structures

Because SOAP is encapsulated in XML, the expectation is that any SOAP message is sent via a `POST` or `M-POST` method. `M-POST`, short for mandatory post, is part of the HTTP 1.1 command set and forces the server to recognize the post and execute it at a higher priority than other post situations; you will likely almost never actually need it. Because they are `POST`ed, however, SOAP messages send HTTP headers in addition to the XML body of the `POST`. For example, suppose that you want to encode a `GetUsers` command much like the one in the previous section. To do so, you could send the following SOAP request message (Listing 11.8).

Listing 11.8: SOAP Request Message (*Listing11-8.txt*)

```
POST /ChatServer HTTP/1.1
Host: www.vbxml.com/chatServ
Content-Type: text/xml
Content-Length:252
SOAPMethodName: http://www.vbxml.com/chat#GetUsers
<SOAP:Envelope xmlns:SOAP="urn:schemas-xmlsoap-org:soap.v1">
    <SOAP:Body>
        <chat:GetUsers
           xmlns:chat="http://www.vbxml.com/chat">
              <chat_room>Programming</chat_room>
        </chat:GetUsers>
    </SOAP:Body>
</SOAP:Envelope>
```

The content header includes one element that may be unfamiliar, the `SOAP:MethodName:` header. This specifies a URI or a URL that uniquely identifies the specific function space, which, in turn, is used by the SOAP server to determine the specific domain to work on. For example, Microsoft Office will likely have a specific URN for handling SOAP calls to perform specific actions on Word, Excel, Outlook, and so forth. The link notation (`#GetUsers`, indicated by the hash mark, #), indicates the name of the method to call.

The SOAP envelope itself also contains a URN (`urn:schemas-xmlsoap-org:soap.v1`) for designating its namespace. This is again used by the SOAP processor (which will likely run as an IIS ISAPI filter, although it could also be a simple XSLT script similar to what was shown in the previous section).

The SOAP body then consists of the method call, which again defines the namespace. If this seems a little redundant, it's primarily because the XML parser will not likely see the HTTP header, but it will see the method declaration header. This method header (`<chat:GetUsers xmlns:chat="..">`), in turn, contains the payload, the message to be sent to the `GetUsers` command. In this case, the only payload is to pass the `<chat_room>` node, which tells the `GetUsers()` command to return the user nodes for people in the specified chat room.

When passed to the appropriate server, this message will be converted into a procedural call, and a result will be generated. In the case of the `GetUsers` command, this will be a list of XML `<user>` nodes in a `<users>` collection. This is then placed into a SOAP response structure (Listing 11.9).

Listing 11.9: SOAP Response Message (*Listing11-9.txt*)

```
HTTP/1.1 200 OK
Content-Type: text/xml
Content-Length:295
```

```
<SOAP:Envelope xmlns:SOAP="urn:schemas-xmlsoap-org:soap.v1">
    <SOAP:Body>
        <chat:GetUsers
           xmlns:chat="http://www.vbxml.com/chat">
            <return>
<users>
    <user>
        <user_name>Aleria</user_name>
        <chat_room>_Home</chat_room>
    </user>
    <user>
        <user_name>Akiko</user_name>
        <chat_room>_Home</chat_room>
    </user>
    <user>
        <user_name>Karen</user_name>
        <chat_room>_Home</chat_room>
    </user>
</users>
            </return>
        </chat:GetUsers>
    </SOAP:Body>
</SOAP:Envelope>
```

The SOAP response structure is nearly identical to the SOAP request structure, save that the former returns the result as a child of the `<result>` tag. This, of course, assumes that the query could be successfully completed. If the user had made a request for the (non-existent) `GetMyUsers`, then the SOAP server would have needed to indicate that an error occurred, and would do so with a SOAP error message (Listing 11.10).

Listing 11.10: SOAP Error Message (*Listing11-10.txt*)

```
<SOAP:Envelope xmlns:SOAP="urn:schemas-xmlsoap-org:soap.v1">
    <SOAP:Body>
        <faultcode>400</faultcode>
        <faultstring>
            SOAP Must Understand Error
        </faultstring>
        <runcode>1</runcode>
    </SOAP:Body>
</SOAP:Envelope>
```

Sometimes the error that's generated comes from within your application. For example, suppose that you attempted to do a `GetUsers` command and passed an undefined room name to the function. In this code, while the SOAP parser understands the message and its target function, the function doesn't itself understand the parameters. Hence, you could design your application to return a more detailed error message (Listing 11.11).

Listing 11.11: Extended SOAP Error Message (*Listing11-11.txt*)

```
<SOAP:Envelope xmlns:SOAP="urn:schemas-xmlsoap-org:soap.v1">
    <SOAP:Body>
        <faultcode>200</faultcode>
        <faultstring>
            SOAP Must Understand Error
        </faultstring>
        <runcode>1</runcode>
        <detail>
             chat_room 'myChatRoom' is not currently
 defined, and GetUsers cannot thus access it.
        </detail>
    </SOAP:Body>
</SOAP:Envelope>
```

SOAP and Datatypes

SOAP follows the XML standards closely, and so it is not surprising that the datatype mechanism that SOAP uses is the same one that XML uses—XML Schema Definition, or XSD. You can define an `xsd:` namespace for passing arguments as datatypes other than the default string type by setting the namespace to `http://www.w3.org/1999/XMLSchema-datatypes`. For example, suppose that you send a query to your `chat:` namespace to retrieve all messages that have been sent since a certain time through the `GetMessagesFromTime()` method. The request header may look something like Listing 11.12.

Listing 11.12: SOAP Request Message with a Data Object (*Listing11-12.txt*)

```
POST /ChatServer HTTP/1.1
Host: www.vbxml.com/chatServ
Content-Type: text/xml
Content-Length:252
SOAPMethodName:
   http://www.vbxml.com/chat#GetMessagesFromDate
<SOAP:Envelope xmlns:SOAP="urn:schemas-xmlsoap-org:soap.v1">
    <SOAP:Body>
        <chat:GetMessagesFromDate
            xmlns:chat="http://www.vbxml.com/chat"
            xmlns:xsd="W3C-Schemas-URI">
               <msg_date xsd:type="timeInstant">
2000-04-15T13:25:16.000</msg_date>
               <chat_room>Programming</chat_room>
        </chat:GetUsers>
    </SOAP:Body>
</SOAP:Envelope>
```

The `xsd:type="timeInstant"` attribute in the `msg_date` node indicates that the element should treat the string `2000-04-15T13:25:16.000` as a time instant.

NOTE Note that if the specific namespace already has an implicit XSD schema associated with it, then that schema will be used for determining datatypes, unless otherwise overridden by the SOAP type assignment.

Coming Clean with SOAP

SOAP is still very much an evolving technology, especially within Microsoft, though much of Microsoft's application development is currently planning on implementing SOAP hooks for the next generation of their tools. Microsoft Office, Exchange Server, SQL Server 2000, and the BizTalk server, as well as the next generation of Visual Basic and Visual InterDev, will likely support SOAP as an exchange protocol.

SOAP clearly offers a great benefit to users of Microsoft technology: By making SOAP-based RPC calls possible over HTTP, it makes it possible to create complex distributed networks that still work very much in a procedural model, and this is the focus of a new initiative by Microsoft called the Web Services model. In this model, Windows-based functionality will be made available to users from a server that hosts these Web services, and client applications can, in turn, call the server to request the results from a SOAP RPC call.

While SOAP is a very attractive paradigm and can be useful for a number of programming applications, it needs to be used with care. The primary problem with SOAP is the same one that traditional RPC calls have: The primary cost in time from an RPC call comes not from the time it takes to actually send the bytes of information so much as it does from establishing the connection in the first place.

Put another way, it is generally more efficient to have one connection pulling a fairly large amount of data in than it is for dozens of connections pulling much smaller chunks of data, since each transaction requires that a connection be established, the server queried, and the results encapsulated into XML. Moreover, connections are a relatively limited resource in most servers: While it may take a little longer to pull data from a single socket than if you had three or four sockets in parallel, a server has only so many sockets it can allocate, and tying up multiple sockets for RPC calls will likely end up causing a bottleneck in your service, making your performance suffer accordingly.

Another problem with SOAP has to do with industry politics: SOAP is far from the only RPC format available, with both Sun and IBM pushing heavily for different standards that are more advantageous to their own internal architectures. Thus, while intelligently designed XML applications may be vendor neutral, SOAP applications will probably be tied up very much with Microsoft's standards for some time to come.

Finally, SOAP forces developers to work with mechanisms that `POST` requests to the server, rather than using the more lightweight `GET` protocol. While more data can be sent in this manner (making it ideal for some types of applications, such as online editors), `POST` doesn't work as well from a resource-linking standpoint.

There is no question that SOAP (or some form of RPC) is a force for development for a number of years to come. It is likely, in fact, that an XML-RPC–type specification will become part of the XML corpus sometime within the next year, as Web applications eclipse database integration as the primary use of XML.

The Future of XML

I have spent the whole book waiting to write this section. Readers who are familiar with my articles and other publications know that, at heart, I am basically an essayist, someone who delights in analyzing the implications of what we do with what have. One of the things that attracted me to this field in the first place was that the implications of XML extended far beyond the humble beginning of the language. It started out as an alternative means of expressing HTML-like information, a somewhat slimmed-down version of SGML. It has, just in the last couple of years, become an obviously universal medium for data exchange of all sorts, not just for Web pages.

The use of XSLT pushes the boundaries farther, providing a sophisticated transformation engine that likewise started out as a way of applying visual styles to an XML document. This came about because of the fundamental nature of programming itself—almost all operations that take place within computer programming can be thought of as being mappings from one namespace to another. Moreover, the state machines that are characteristic of procedural programming can be replaced by stateless machines that are characteristic of declarative programming and that are also better for handling the disconnected nature of the Internet.

XML Schema provides a third piece of the puzzle, laying the foundation for describing objects as having rich datatypes, and describing the characteristics not just of simple scalar types but also object definitions themselves. This makes it possible to have on-demand object definitions while still working with the robustness of XML's manipulation capabilities, providing an intriguing (though largely unproven) model for intelligent distributed objects that don't require specific binary implementations to use.

The final piece, messaging systems, isn't so much a technology as it is an architecture—a way of designing applications. In a well-designed messaging system, the passing of data streams (either through RPCs or through a device/stream metaphor) places the focus on the movement of XML rather than through the operation of specific components. This validates the concept that XML is most powerful when it is moving—by passing messages (XML streams) back and forth in an anonymous fashion, you can build very sophisticated distributed applications.

Writing a book on technology always involves a certain amount of science fiction, of speculating where the API or operant code will be three, four, or six months down the road. With XML, this task is made even more complex and problematic since, in many ways, it is not just the tools that are changing but the way that we think about the tools that is most important. So now I'm doffing my technical writer's hat, donning my science fiction one, and looking at where the technology will be taking us now and in the future.

2001-01-01: Principal Standards Ratified

It's January 1, 2001, the real start of the next millennium. The primary XML standards (with one or two minor exceptions) have been ratified as recommendations by the W3C. The uncertainty about the way that people will work with data types has been worked out (although some last-minute lobbying by one or two large corporations pushed this decision out a couple of months as jockeying for favored primitive datatype definitions became intense). This is an important consideration as different database companies have implemented a number of SQL types in slightly different fashions, and having the XML standard use your type means that your XML data conversion engines go through the least amount of optimization.

The acceptance of the XML Schema specifications in mid-summer by all the major parties touches off a new round of brokering and arbitration as already-defined schemas for a number of common e-commerce, accounting, governmental, educational, and industry uses need to be modified slightly (or, in some cases, not so slightly). The schema specification is important in another way: It lets people define primitive objects that can then be incorporated into larger, more complex objects, such as when a name block, an address block, and a couple of general interest blocks all become part of a general profile object. While the debate about the specific components and how they would be utilized is far from resolved even six months after the fact, there is a growing consensus forming around the most popular of these object definitions.

XSLT is beginning to be taught in several winter curriculums at the college and community college levels. The use of XSLT is beginning to foment a bit of a revolution, and there is already a backlash among a number of C++ and Java programmers who deride this technology as being ungainly, complex, and otherwise unsuited for real work. The adherents to XSLT, on the other hand, have begun taking to the language with a near-religious fervor not seen since Java emerged from Oak several years before.

One consequence of the use of XSLT is the rise in companies that are beginning to offer Web stream services. In essence, a Webmaster can "subscribe" to a service to retrieve XML data, typically with a choice of XSLT filters that can be called upon from the service to format it to their output of choice. These services have a wide degree of breadth to them; for example, a couple of news gathering organizations offer filtered news services through a URL API, while stock markets likewise begin offering both filtered and unfiltered feeds.

First felt in Europe but increasingly a critical option in the United States is the rising prominence of the Wireless Application Protocol (WAP) and its directed markup language, WML (for Wireless Markup Language, of course). WAP targets devices that have much smaller viewports (or cards, to use the WAP parlance), either filtering XHTML-based Web sites so they better fit within the confined spaces that most handheld devices have or providing direct XML feeds that are specifically for portable devices.

Speaking of XHTML, the language has quickly replaced HTML as the preferred server-side markup language. The XHTML 1.1 specification, which more strongly supports the modularization of HTML into distinct parts, is close to ratification at this point, and a number of vendors are beginning to provide additional XHTML modules that handle such things as customized markup for mathematics (through MathML), chemistry (CML), and other specialized disciplines. One survey indicates that in universities XHTML and X*L variants are quickly being adopted by teaching assistants and students in a number of different fields, and at least some of the major HTML markup tools support an XHTML option, though this is by no means universal.

Business-to-business efforts are not going as quickly; the effort to define common schemas has slowed down efforts to provide a set of industry-wide standards, and much-earlier work in a number of these verticals has had to be revisited to handle some of the contentious arbitration going on. The key problem here comes in educating IT managers and developers that XML is a language that is remarkably flexible, and that the definition of schemas is not as significant as the development of transforms. On the flipside, most industry verticals have at least acknowledged the need for developing a set of XML schemas for that vertical, and the movement is now progressing into the more competitive arena of coalescing standards to one or a couple for any given object definition.

2004-01-01: Arbitration to Mediation

Things are moving quickly at this stage. Competition has weeded out those standards that weren't quite strong enough, resulting in a hyper-accelerated evolution of XML-based schemas. The arguments are highly political at this point and are taking place everywhere from government agencies and corporate board rooms to the United Nations. What no one can deny at this time is the importance of XML.

XSLT is beginning to make significant inroads in universities, corporations, government agencies, and research facilities, with people beginning to develop XSLT replacements for ASP or JSP systems. The second XSLT revision has begun in earnest, though it won't likely be completed for another year. This approach also looks at a way of representing XML in a more compact notation and starts dealing with the issues of context and topicality in information. The importance of associational links that do more than jump you from one Web page to another is beginning to become apparent, and questions about meaning begin to take on additional urgency.

The traditional shrink-wrapped software industry is disappearing at a fairly rapid clip in favor of Web services provided by companies handling everything from word processing and spreadsheets to the analysis of news stories, providing contractors for interim projects and managing your workflow. The monolithic Office application, while still present, is a dinosaur compared to the XML stream-based applications that are beginning to pop up.

One consequence of this is that you begin to see the emergence of subscription-based programming as a really viable alternative. For instance, you subscribe to a service to provide you with word processing or spreadsheets (hosted through an XML-based server sending XML messages back and forth to a client of intermediate intelligence), and you can effectively reference these from your browser. Of course, this same approach is also reducing the influence of the desktop system.

This makes it more likely that you'll start working with your "files" remotely, with the actual resources kept as XML or data resources on a distant server. One upshot of this is that the notion of a file system becomes inseparable from a URL—everything becomes a URL, and you cease thinking about the exact internal format used to store the data. This approach works especially well with WebDAV since you have much greater control over the editing and versioning capabilities than you would otherwise have.

This approach lies at the heart of the application service provider model, making XML (in all its myriad formats) a perfect vehicle for the development of such ASPs. At this stage, XML-based ASPs probably don't yet outnumber those written in Java or VB (or in Active Server Pages/Java Server Pages or the corresponding successors to these), but XML is becoming dominant in this area.

B2B and B2C XML-dominant solutions have become the norm, and many of them are replacing the scripted model with an XSLT-oriented one. Most major SQL databases now have XML interfaces to them, although not all of them give access to information in the same manner. You're also beginning to see the dominance of the XML database system, where the architecture is built pretty much exclusively to use XML technology; these are not necessarily as efficient as using SQL databases, but they are more powerful, and they better fit into the paradigm that XML offers.

You're also seeing the emergence of bridge languages—languages that combine the best of both procedural and declarative models of programming to help move developers from one to the other. RPC code has reached its zenith, with its emphasis on component-to-component architecture, but already there are signs that it is beginning to wane in favor of a purely declarative model. The principal advantage of a purely declarative model has to do with the ability of machines to be able to manipulate such a model with a minimal toolset: XSL can be managed with XML tools.

The XML generalist is beginning to be replaced by content specialists, with a Webmaster frequently being called to manage the streams, a graphic designer to handle selection (or creation) of component views, a content specialist for creating the content (or editing the content for publication), and an XML developer for creating the back-end components, defining

XML tags and otherwise handling that task. This mirrors the way that HTML expertise quickly split in the 1990s into specializations.

2007-01-01: The XML Web Coalesces

The world of declarative XML is beginning to make serious inroads into domains that have traditionally been considered highly procedural. The browser as most people defined it in the year 2000 has largely disappeared from the scene—so, apparently, has the operating system. In fact, the browser is still here, but it has encompassed the rest of the operating system—an approach that was beginning to be seen three years ago, but that was largely derided at the time because of the browser wars of the late 1990s.

Turning on your system largely involves flicking a switch, waiting for the half-gigabit wireless line to register itself with the local wireless service provider, and pulling in your resources from your central store. The thin client has never really appeared (too many requirements for too many different devices); instead, the fat server has come back into its own. The client is intelligent, containing more than enough speed to handle many of the systems that were formally the province of the operating system, which has continued to dwindle away like an appendix.

Many of the scripting solutions that were prominent in the late 1990s—Active Server Pages, Java Server Pages, PHP—have disappeared in all but legacy Web sites, although the notion of a Web site itself is becoming remarkably quaint; links have become far more transparent, so it is not uncommon for searches to be based more primarily on topicality to what was searched before than on explicit links. Moreover, the number of systems that bypass XHTML or WML entirely is on the rise, and XML, XSLT, and CSS filters are much more common than they were in years past. XML has also become the dominant paradigm not just for Web pages but for all documentation; indeed, the distinction between a Web page and a local file is now largely a relic of usage since even your local files are maintained on a server distinct from the devices you use to access them.

Voice-based systems are on the rise as well, primarily in automobiles. Most midsize and larger cars contain internal computer systems for accessing the Internet both by voice and through the console (luxury models and minivans also include such consoles in the passenger and back seats) in all but the remotest locations, and city planners are beginning to use the vehicle location and status information to help them design better traffic control systems. On the other hand, car theft is down dramatically; a car won't work without the proper access code (keys are beginning to become endangered species) in the computer, so you can't just remove the computer from the car, and the moment a car is reported stolen its position is automatically transmitted to police dispatchers.

B2B integration is largely complete at this point. Inventories can be managed now to within 12 hours for common items and 36 hours for specialty items. One upshot of this

XML integration is that custom orders become far more feasible. A customer can order an item over the Internet, specifying the customization required as (transparently as) an XML object definition. This definition goes into the manufacturing plant, where robot systems are emerging to read the specifications, which are transmitted, converted via XSLT into the requisite procedures, and sent on to the distribution channels. One upshot of this, however, is that the large mega-malls, dying in the latter half of the 1990s, are all but dead.

Also disappearing are stand-alone PCs, except as servers. Along with this, the development of software, in general, is beginning to enter a period of protracted decline. While procedural programming is still very much in evidence in the production of computer systems, the areas where they don't act with XML in some fashion are becoming harder to find. COM and CORBA are both largely dead, save in legacy systems; languages that can query components via asynchronous streams are the preferred way of dealing with component-to-component interactions.

The second XSLT specification has come and gone and is evolving nicely into a very rich programming language all its own, although old-time purists complain that it's becoming inefficient. Problems inherent in the XML Schema paradigm have been largely ironed out, and you are seeing the rise of concentrated XSLT repositories that can match two schemes and map one to the other (for a fee, of course).

There is a lively business in the production of XSL transformations, by the way, and whole virtual companies are born, build the automation code, and die within the space of six months. Indeed, the software company of today bears surprisingly little resemblance to the company of even four years ago. Specialized developers offer their services (either as producers of content or as producers of mediation—the code that hosts the content) through the Net, and a manager orchestrates most of the development remotely. There has been a rise in the number of accidents when programmers, working at their wearables, inadvertently walk in front of moving cars while attempting to coordinate code development, but all in all the model seems to work. One other facet of this is that the great silicon hubs are becoming more diffuse; people can work anytime, anywhere, which is beginning to have an impact on commuting (especially as older managers retire and are replaced by those to whom working remotely makes more sense).

2010-01-01: The Invisible Web

The "computer industry" is largely moribund. The concept of a desktop computer has disappeared, although most people have intelligent monitors for picking up wireless feeds from their local hub in much the same way that televisions were used a decade ago. For the most part, work is done not at the monitor but through intelligent notebooks, which are about the size of a clipboard, with either a single or a double pane of "paper" that can respond to signals transmitted from the hubs to arrange highly dense arrays of microscopic colored balls in particular patterns.

This paper is inexpensive and ubiquitous, although the primary problems it faces are not in the paper medium but in identifying the individual using it.

The solutions to this identification issue are still somewhat diverse, including everything from a piece of jewelry for the casual user to an identity tattoo for specialized Web users—a transmitter embedded into the skin that identifies that person to the surrounding wireless structure. With either solution, the transmitter broadcasts an XML identification code that the network retrieves, so that when the developer moves from one room to the next the piece of e-paper that they're using automatically shifts from one transmitter to the next transparently.

The large, bureaucratic accounting divisions that marked the 1980s and 1990s are, for the most part, gone, made transparent; paperwork passes invisibly through XML pipes, problems are logged and resolved via increasingly sophisticated business algorithms, and the number of people required for handling the exceptions has dropped from dozens to one or two (and they no longer have to come in to work to do their job).

One of the effects of moving programming from a procedural to a declarative model is that it has effectively meant that computer systems can write the code that runs it. If a computer needs a specific schema to handle an operation, it can query to get enough of the schema to provide the infrastructure for additional development. A consequence of this is that much of the computer-to-computer interaction is no longer written by software developers, but is inferred instead from the problem set at hand and built by the computers themselves.

XML places an emphasis on patterns rather than procedures, and the more sophisticated the pattern recognition becomes, the more readily systems can build patterns that are needed to solve problems. Moreover, the same recognition can be used to resolve another issue: legacy code. The human approach to software design is frequently very haphazard—if a problem exists in legacy code, it is often easier to build a workaround that just accretes additional layers of code that may often not have any other purpose than to tear the code down and rebuild it from scratch. A pattern recognition system, on the other hand, could resolve when there are patterns that have become completely or partially obsolete and restructure the code accordingly, in essence reducing the amount of legacy code to nearly nothing.

This introduces some worrisome dilemmas, however. Much of the infrastructure that existed in 2000 in most business sectors was oriented toward the moving and processing of information, either by a manager or by a developer. As corporations became more electronic, as the XML packets moving from one place to another through XSL switches became more pervasive, the role of the middle manager became increasingly tenuous. Similarly, sales personnel became less significant as transactions became more virtual, since the purpose of a salesperson is to broker products to consumers in need of those products. XML provided the basis for a number of companies that vended services and products through transparent brokerages, which means that the sales force has largely merged with the marketing force to promote products through the brokerages.

This points to where the growth sectors are in 2010: Marketing and advertising, entertainment, education, infotainment, publishing, and games now make up the bulk of the work that large software companies held in the late 20th century. Creation of content is mainly computer assisted, but people are still largely wary of programs that generate content in its entirety. Virtual communities have been rising for years, but, with a common infrastructure in place, people are far less limited by divergent hardware and standards. The same problem space can be displayed just as readily using a 3D-ML environment as with a 2D one, and by encoding to common object specifications and the use of digital signatures it becomes possible to create that rarity in the virtual space: completely unique items.

Note that the use of virtual space here needs to be understood as being more than a move to a 3D environment; while it sounded seductive, most 3D worlds never took off, in part because they imparted a sense of vertigo and disorientation to the fragile human senses. However, 3D is a useful tool, and by having transformations that can map abstract data in 3D terms, it is possible to see all sides (including the insides) of problems, as well as to map complex network relationships into multidimensional views.

There have also been reports of mathematicians and developers who are starting to regularly visualize problems in higher dimensional spaces directly, through specialized devices that can map the other dimensions into other senses, such as using tonal variations in sound. Mathematics is largely involved with the processes of transformation, and the encoding of mathematical markup into an XML format (MathML) has made it possible to perform symbolic mathematical transformations that act on complex networks, helping to build ever more sophisticated models of both physical and abstract phenomena.

Ironically, the market for programmers has largely dried up, save those who are manufacturing "content." It's easier to let databases create and optimize themselves, and the SQL-based relational database has largely disappeared from the scene because of its inflexibility in handling restructuring. Indeed, for most people, the "computer" itself has largely disappeared. You can rent space on an external server or even buy a pre-configured local server that automatically hooks into the wireless network, but the dedicated game machines and "the computer on every desktop" are largely gone.

The Web has also disappeared, or become so pervasive as to have become transparent. Because XML enables stronger models of relationship than procedural languages do, it's become far easier to see complex relationships that eluded mankind without these tools. Natural languages have not disappeared, but the barriers that a language raises to non-speakers of that language largely have gone by the wayside, again because XML is capable of capturing context from structure that makes it easier to place phrases and expressions from one language into another.

Consequences

The preceding timeline is speculation, of course, and probably on the liberal side, although it's worth keeping the perspective that the Internet itself did not exist a decade ago except as an obscure concept in the basements of a few universities and research labs. Regardless, however, the evolution of the XML language is pretty obvious, well in keeping with current developments.

Writing about the consequences of a technology is not a usual part of most computer books, but, especially in this case, the consequences of the widespread adoption of a declarative-model XML infrastructure will significantly alter the very fabric of our society, and not necessarily for the better.

One of the key points to consider here is that XML makes networks completely transparent. Currently, every network has a strong impedance factor: To connect one network to another, you need to spend a lot of energy to handle the conversion code (another form of transformation). Transparent networks, on the other hand, mean that data that you consume may come from any device anywhere on the planet (or off the planet since satellites sending back observational data will probably start encoding this information in XML). Similarly, any content that you produce may be used anywhere by anyone.

Traditionally, every increase in the level of transparency of a network has resulted in the creation of profit—whether financial or informational is largely irrelevant; money is simply another form of information that has the notion of uniqueness. Currency made it possible to transfer value in the first place, and standardized currency made it easier to trade across networks. The invention of the telegraph, the telephone, and the railway increased the power of the networks of information and distribution, respectively, while the radio and the television made large-scale broadcast networks feasible.

Disconnected PCs were largely toys, but by networking them you could start to better use precious resources (printers, for example) or to better allocate underutilized ones (disk space on various systems). The impedance costs between Mac and PC networks was initially fairly high, but once that bridge was negotiated multi-platform systems became feasible. The Internet provided a publishing model that anyone, anywhere could use, and the value of this network exploded as the number of nodes in it increased at an exponential rate.

XML is shaking out the inefficiencies of the current Internet, making possible the creation of large-scale distributed systems. The client platform is similarly becoming more anonymous through the use of XSLT to produce targeted output, and divergent networks are going to start integrating through the use of device/stream architectures and XML-based RPCs working over HTTP. The value of the network consequently explodes, especially since the tools for transforming data on the Web are similarly written in XML, making it possible to transform the transformations dynamically.

Looks perfect, but there are thorns hidden among the roses. One problem with this is that privacy and uniqueness become major issues. Personal information gets stored in semi-public data pools. It becomes possible to locate individuals practically anywhere on the planet, since to use the network they have to identify themselves. Moreover, it becomes much easier to correlate patterns and trends using XSLT-related tools on XML-based profiles, so that marketers can predict your tastes better than you can, so that employers can track your performance by dealing with performance metrics, and so that insurance companies can evaluate your food purchases and purchase history to determine whether you're a good candidate for medical insurance. ("Oops, Kurt here drinks too many lattes; he'll be in for a coronary in 15 years, no doubt about it—application denied.")

A second trend is that increasing the efficiencies of a network means that it takes fewer people to do the same job, and those people can work at more geographically diverse locations. Companies will become increasingly virtual, coming together for immediate projects and then dispersing. You are already seeing the rise of online employment boards and staffing solutions, and it is a small step from there to coordinating these people into virtual teams, something that's becoming more doable as the infrastructure becomes more pervasive for communication between team members. However, the rise of virtual corporations challenges tax laws, safety regulations, and governmental influence, which are likely to be much slower in developing their infrastructure to match what is happening in industry. While you can argue that this is actually a good thing, it does mean that the relationship the workforce has with business is undergoing a dramatic shift that is only just beginning to be felt.

The final problem has to do with the nature of open networks. XML is a pattern-oriented language, and it is much easier to develop self-replicating code that can pass through the pipes than it is with procedural code. This means that it is far easier to write a declarative virus than it is to write a procedural one. As a simple example, consider the following XSLT code:

```
<xsl:template select="somePatter">
   <xsl:call-template name="repeater"/>
</xsl:template>

<xsl:template name="repeater">
    <data/>

    <xsl:call-template name="repeater"/>
</xsl:template>
```

This creates the equivalent of an infinite loop but does so in a way that will effectively cause the parser's memory to overflow. If the code to do this could load and save these resources on the server, you could very quickly overflow the amount of available space on a hard drive.

I am deliberately not adding self-modifying code samples here, by the way, but you could very easily create an XSL document that creates an XSL document that is then applied to the initial document, and, well, what you've got then is a virus—one that could hide as fairly innocuous pieces of separate code until they come together; and they could do anything from launch a denial-of-service attack to corrupt massive data stores. The issues of protecting declarative structures from viruses has not yet been adequately explored, but it will be a large issue in the future.

Summary

Writing a book of this length is an experience that takes several months, a lot of patience, a certain amount of belt-tightening, and way too many hours writing sample code, editing samples, and staring at paragraphs that don't want to flow into anything else. In this case, I believe it was worth it.

XML seems simple on the surface—almost HTML-like: a text file with way too many brackets and an irregular way of formatting that has nowhere near the gee-whiz factor of a computer game or a graphics program or even a programming environment. This is deceptive.

XML has already had a profound effect on the ways that we program, communicate, and learn, and it's just getting started. It will likely replace much of the procedural code that is out there, will almost certainly change the way that we deal with data, and will make the Web a far richer place contextually. It will spell the end of the Desktop, will make it possible for geographically diverse components (and people) to communicate in a seamless manner, and will make it possible to view information through any number of glasses, without the requirement of system-limiting binary components. XML will let us start moving beyond the Object-Oriented Programming paradigm into a richer one where we are dealing with the relationships between objects, the network of interactions that make up systems.

That XML should come along when it did was no accident: We are waking up to the fact that we live in multiple, interconnected networks where the sum is far greater than the parts. Object-Oriented Programming concentrates on the parts and, as such, belongs very much in the same reductionist model as the ways we have tended to treat chemistry, biology, and physics: attempting to explain the whole on the basis of the actions of the parts. Ask any biologist how the brain works and most will tell you about ion transport and neural event firings and will point you to where, if you stimulate this region, you'll cause the arm to lift up and down. Ask them how the mind works, and they'll stare at you blankly—since the nature of the mind can no more be constructed from the nature of the constituent parts than a painting like the "Mona Lisa" can be inferred from the constitution of the paints.

XML opens up the possibility of holistic networks where information is moving, where the emergent behaviors are largely an expected part of the equation rather than a troublesome bug to be removed by diligent coding. Who knows what kind of consciousness will awaken in a planet-sized network? I, for one, am eager to find out.

INDEX

Note to Reader: In this index, **boldfaced** page numbers refer to primary discussions of the topic; *italics* page numbers refer to figures.

SYMBOLS & NUMBERS

A

B

C

D

E

F

G

H

I

J

K

L

M

N

O

P

Q

R

S

T

U

V

W

Z